C: The Complete Reference, Fourth Edition

About the Author

Herbert Schildt is the world's leading programming author. He is an authority on the C and C++ languages, a master Windows programmer, and an expert on Java. His programming books have sold more that 2.5 million copies worldwide and have been translated into all major foreign languages. He is the author of numerous bestsellers, including *C++: The Complete Reference, Teach Yourself C, Teach Yourself C++, C++ from the Ground Up, Windows 2000 Programming from the Ground Up,* and *Java: The Complete Reference*. Schildt holds a master's degree in computer science from the University of Illinois. He can be reached at his consulting office at (217) 586-4683.

C: The Complete Reference, Fourth Edition

Herbert Schildt

Osborne/**McGraw-Hill**

Berkeley   New York   St. Louis   San Francisco
Auckland   Bogotá   Hamburg   London   Madrid
Mexico City   Milan   Montreal   New Delhi   Panama City
Paris   São Paulo   Singapore   Sydney
Tokyo   Toronto

Osborne/**McGraw-Hill**
2600 Tenth Street
Berkeley, California 94710
U.S.A.

For information on translations or book distributors outside the U.S.A., or to arrange bulk purchase discounts for sales promotions, premiums, or fund-raisers, please contact Osborne/**McGraw-Hill** at the above address.

C: The Complete Reference, Fourth Edition

1234567890 AGM AGM 019876543210

ISBN 0-07-212124-6

Publisher
Brandon A. Nordin

Associate Publisher and Editor-in-Chief
Scott Rogers

Acquisitions Editor
Jane K. Brownlow

Project Editor
Madhu Prasher

Acquisitions Coordinator
Tara Davis

Technical Editor
Greg Guntle

Copy Editor
Judith Brown

Proofreader
Paul Tyler

Indexer
Sheryl Schildt

Computer Designers
Jani Beckwith and Elizabeth Jang

Illustrator
Michael Mueller

Series Design
Peter Hancik

This book was composed with Corel VENTURA ™ Publisher.

Contents

Part I

Foundational C

Part II
The C99 Standard

Part III

The C Standard Library

Part IV

Algorithms and Applications

Part VI

A C Interpreter

Preface

This is the fourth edition of *C: The Complete Reference.* In the years since the third edition was prepared, much has happened in the programming world. The Internet and the World Wide Web became an integral part of the computing landscape, Java was invented, and C++ was standardized. At the same time, a new standard for C, called C99, was created. Although C99 did not grab many headlines, it is still one of the most important computing events of the past five years. In the onrush of events, it is easy to focus only on the new, overlooking the sturdy foundation upon which the future is built. C is such a foundation. Much of the world's code runs on C. It is the language upon which C++ was built, and its syntax formed the basis for Java. However, if C were simply a starting point for other languages, it would be an interesting, but dead, language. Fortunately for us programmers, this is not the case. C is as vital today as when it was first invented. As you will see, the C99 standard contains new and innovative constructs that once again put C at the forefront of language development. Although C's progeny (C++ and Java) are certainly important, C has a staying power that no other computer language can claim.

The creation of the C99 standard was driven forward by some of computing's foremost language experts, including Rex Jaeschke, Jim Thomas, Tom MacDonald, and John Benito. As a member of the standardization committee, I watched the progress of the emerging standard, following the debates and arguments surrounding each new feature. The final stages of the process were marked by a daily exchange of ideas, conducted via e-mail, that involved participants from around the world. Although there were differences of opinion, there was unity of spirit. In the end, the C language emerged stronger than ever.

I must admit that when I wrote the first edition of *C: The Complete Reference*, I did not envision all of the changes and advancements that were to follow (although some, like the success of C++, were obvious from the start). However, the one thing that I knew then is the same thing that I know now: C is one of the finest programming languages that I have ever encountered. It is graceful, elegant, consistent, and (most importantly) powerful. Its continued success is a source of constant enjoyment for me.

A Book for All Programmers

This C reference is designed for all C programmers, regardless of their experience level. It does assume, however, that the reader has some knowledge of the basics and is able to create at least a simple C program. If you are just learning C, this book will make an excellent companion to any C tutorial and serve as a source of answers to your specific questions.

Because C++ (C's object-oriented enhancement) is built upon C, this book is also appropriate for C++ programmers wishing to have a detailed reference to the foundation upon which C++ is constructed.

Therefore, whether you are programming in C or C++, whether you are a newcomer to programming or a seasoned pro, you will find this book to be of value.

What's New in the Fourth Edition

For the most part, I have left the basic structure of this book unchanged from its three preceding editions. Most of the changes found in this edition reflect the features added by the new C99 standard. As a result, a new Part Two was created that details these features. In addition, Part Three, which covers the standard function library, has been updated and expanded to include the many new functions defined by C99. Of course, full coverage of the original C89 standard is still included. C89 is important since it is the version upon which C++ was built. It is also the version of C used by most programmers today. (In fact, at the time of this writing, no commonly available compiler supports all of the new features found in C99.)

In addition to the changes relating to C99, the entire book has been updated to reflect the current state of compilers, operating systems, and the computing environment in general.

What's Inside

This book covers in detail all aspects of the C language and its libraries. Its main emphasis is on ANSI/ISO Standard C. Both the C89 and the C99 standards are covered.

The book is divided into six parts, covering

- The foundational elements of C, which are those defined by C89
- The C99 enhancements
- The C libraries
- Common algorithms and applications
- The C programming environment
- The creation of a C interpreter

Part One provides a thorough discussion of the keywords, preprocessor directives, and features that define the C language. The emphasis in this part is on those features defined by C89, although new C99 features are mentioned in passing, where appropriate. Part Two describes in detail the features added by C99. There are two reasons for separating C89 from C99. First, most programmers today will be using C89. It is the version of C that programmers think of "as C," and it is the most widely used language in the world. C89 is also the version of C that forms the C subset of C++. Thus, the C89 version of C is an important part of programming today and into the foreseeable future. By clearly defining the dividing line between C89 and C99, you can easily know where one ends and the other begins. Second, many readers of this book will already be very familiar with C89. Putting the new C99 features into their own section makes it easy for those readers to quickly find the new material.

Part Three discusses the standard C library. This section describes all functions specified by both C89 and C99, with those functions added by C99 clearly flagged.

Part Four covers some of the more common and important algorithms and applications that all C programmers should have in their toolbox. It also includes a discussion of AI-based problem solving and Windows 2000 programming.

Part Five examines the C programming environment, including such things as efficiency, porting, and debugging.

Part Six illustrates the C language by creating an interpreter for it. This is easily the most exciting, challenging, and, at the same time, fun chapter in the book. If you are like most C programmers, exploring, enhancing, and otherwise tinkering with the C interpreter in Part Six will be irresistible! There is also no better way to understand the purity and elegance of the C language than by building an interpreter for it.

Source Code Free on the Web

The source code contained in this book is available free online at **www.osborne.com**.

HS
March 21, 2000
Mahomet, IL

For Further Study

C: The Complete Reference is just one of the many programming books written by Herbert Schildt. Here are some others that you will find of interest.

To learn about Windows programming, we recommend the following:

Windows 2000 Programming from the Ground Up

Windows 98 Programming from the Ground Up

Windows NT 4 Programming from the Ground Up

The Windows Programming Annotated Archives

If you want to learn more about the C language, the following titles will be of interest:

Teach Yourself C

C/C++ Annotated Archives

To learn more about C++, you will find these books especially helpful:

C++: The Complete Reference

Teach Yourself C++

C++ from the Ground Up

Expert C++

C/C++ Annotated Archives

If you are interested in Java, you will want to read

Java: The Complete Reference

When you need solid answers, fast, turn to Herbert Schildt, the recognized authority on programming.

The Complete Reference

Part I

Foundational C

This book divides its description of the C language into two parts. Part One discusses those features of C defined by the original, 1989 ANSI standard for C (commonly referred to as C89), along with those additions contained in Amendment 1, adopted in 1995. At the time of this writing, this is the version of C that is in widespread use and is the version of C that compilers are currently capable of compiling. It is also the version of C that forms the foundation upon which C++ was built, which is commonly referred to as the *C subset* of C++. Part Two describes the features added by the new C 1999 standard (C99). Part Two also details the few differences between C89 and C99. For the most part, the new 1999 standard incorporates the entire 1989 standard, adding features but not fundamentally changing the character of the language. Thus, C89 is both the foundation for C99 and the basis for C++.

In a book such as this *Complete Reference*, dividing the C language into two pieces—the C89 foundation and the C99-specific features—achieves three major benefits:

- The dividing line between the C89 and the C99 versions of C is clearly delineated. When maintaining legacy code for environments in which C99-compatible compilers are not available, an understanding of where C89 ends and C99 begins is important. It is a frustrating experience to plan a solution around a feature, only to find that the feature is not supported by the compiler!

- Readers already familiar with C89 can easily find the new features added by C99. Many readers—especially those who have an earlier edition of this book—already know C89. Covering those features of C99 in their own section makes it easier for the experienced programmer to quickly find information about C99 without having to "wade through" reams of information that he or she already knows. Of course, throughout Part One, any minor incompatibilities between C89 and C99 are noted and new features from C99 are mentioned where appropriate.

- By separately discussing the C89 standard, it is possible to clearly define the version of C that forms the C subset of C++. This is important if you want to be able to write C programs that can be compiled by C++ compilers. It is also important if you are planning to move on to C++, or work in both environments.

In the final analysis, understanding the difference between C89 and C99 is simply part of being a top-notch professional C programmer.

Part One is organized as follows. Chapter 1 provides an overview of C. Chapter 2 examines C's built-in data types, variables, operators, and expressions. Next, Chapter 3 presents program control statements. Chapter 4 discusses arrays and strings. Chapter 5 looks at pointers. Chapter 6 deals with functions, and Chapter 7 discusses structures, unions, and user-defined types. Chapter 8 examines console I/O. Chapter 9 covers file I/O, and Chapter 10 discusses the C preprocessor and comments.

Chapter 1

An Overview of C

The purpose of this chapter is to present an overview of the C programming language, its origins, its uses, and its underlying philosophy. This chapter is mainly for newcomers to C.

A Brief History of C

C was invented and first implemented by Dennis Ritchie on a DEC PDP-11 that used the Unix operating system. C is the result of a development process that started with an older language called BCPL. BCPL was developed by Martin Richards, and it influenced a language called B, which was invented by Ken Thompson. B led to the development of C in the 1970s.

For many years, the de facto standard for C was the version supplied with the Unix operating system. It was first described in *The C Programming Language* by Brian Kernighan and Dennis Ritchie (Englewood Cliffs, N.J.: Prentice-Hall, 1978). In the summer of 1983 a committee was established to create an ANSI (American National Standards Institute) standard that would define the C language. The standardization process took six years (much longer than anyone reasonably expected).

The ANSI C standard was finally adopted in December 1989, with the first copies becoming available in early 1990. The standard was also adopted by ISO (International Standards Organization), and the resulting standard was typically referred to as ANSI/ISO Standard C. In 1995, Amendment 1 to the C standard was adopted, which, among other things, added several new library functions. The 1989 standard for C, along with Amendment 1, became a *base document* for Standard C++, defining the *C subset* of C++. The version of C defined by the 1989 standard is commonly referred to as C89.

During the 1990s, the development of the C++ standard consumed most programmers' attention. However, work on C continued quietly along, with a new standard for C being developed. The end result was the 1999 standard for C, usually referred to as C99. In general, C99 retained nearly all of the features of C89. Thus, C is still C! The C99 standardization committee focused on two main areas: the addition of several numeric libraries and the development of some special-use, but highly innovative, new features, such as variable-length arrays and the **restrict** pointer qualifier. These innovations have once again put C at the forefront of computer language development.

As explained in the part opener, Part One of this book describes the foundation of C, which is the version defined by the 1989 standard. This is the version of C in widest use, it is currently accepted by all C compilers, and it forms the basis for C++. Thus, if you want to write C code that can be compiled by a legacy compiler, for example, you will want to restrict that code to the features described in Part One. Part Two will examine the features added by C99.

C Is a Middle-Level Language

C is often called a *middle-level* computer language. This does not mean that C is less powerful, harder to use, or less developed than a high-level language such as BASIC or Pascal, nor does it imply that C has the cumbersome nature of assembly language (and its associated troubles). Rather, C is thought of as a middle-level language because it combines the best elements of high-level languages with the control and flexibility of assembly language. Table 1-1 shows how C fits into the spectrum of computer languages.

As a middle-level language, C allows the manipulation of bits, bytes, and addresses—the basic elements with which the computer functions. Despite this fact, C code is also very portable. *Portability* means that it is easy to adapt software written for one type of computer or operating system to another type. For example, if you can easily convert a program written for DOS so that it runs under Windows 2000, that program is portable.

High level	Ada
	Modula-2
	Pascal
	COBOL
	FORTRAN
	BASIC
Middle level	Java
	C++
	C
	FORTH
	Macro-assembler
Low level	Assembler

Table 1-1.   *C's Place in the World of Programming Languages*

All high-level programming languages support the concept of data types. A *data type* defines a set of values that a variable can store along with a set of operations that can be performed on that variable. Common data types are integer, character, and floating-point. Although C has several built-in data types, it is not a strongly typed language, as are Pascal and Ada. C permits almost all type conversions. For example, you may freely intermix character and integer types in an expression.

Unlike most high-level languages, C specifies almost no run-time error checking. For example, no check is performed to ensure that array boundaries are not overrun. These types of checks are the responsibility of the programmer.

In the same vein, C does not demand strict type compatibility between a parameter and an argument. As you may know from your other programming experience, a high-level computer language will typically require that the type of an argument be (more or less) exactly the same type as the parameter that will receive the argument. Such is not the case for C. Instead, C allows an argument to be of any type so long as it can be reasonably converted into the type of the parameter. Further, C provides all of the automatic conversions to accomplish this.

C is special in that it allows the direct manipulation of bits, bytes, words, and pointers. This makes it well suited for system-level programming, where these operations are common.

Another important aspect of C is that it has only a small number of keywords, which are the commands that make up the C language. For example, C89 defined 32 keywords, and C99 adds only 5 more. High-level languages typically have many more keywords. As a comparison, consider that most versions of BASIC have well over 100 keywords!

C Is a Structured Language

In your previous programming experience, you may have heard the term *block-structured* applied to a computer language. Although the term block-structured language does not strictly apply to C, C is commonly referred to simply as a *structured* language. It has many similarities to other structured languages, such as ALGOL, Pascal, and Modula-2.

> **Note** *The reason that C is not, technically, a block-structured language is that block-structured languages permit procedures or functions to be declared inside other procedures or functions. However, since C does not allow the creation of functions within functions, it cannot formally be called block-structured.*

The distinguishing feature of a structured language is *compartmentalization* of code and data. This is the ability of a language to section off and hide from the rest of the program all information and instructions necessary to perform a specific task. One way that you achieve compartmentalization is by using subroutines that employ local (temporary) variables. By using local variables, you can write subroutines so that the events that occur within them cause no side effects in other parts of the program. This capability makes it very easy for your C programs to share sections of code. If you develop compartmentalized functions, you need to know only what a function does, not how it does it. Remember, excessive use of global variables (variables known throughout the entire program) may allow bugs to creep into a program by allowing unwanted side effects. (Anyone who has programmed in standard BASIC is well aware of this problem.)

A structured language offers a variety of programming possibilities. For example, structured languages typically support several loop constructs, such as **while**, **do-while**, and **for**. In a structured language, the use of **goto** is either prohibited or discouraged and is not the common form of program control (as is the case in standard BASIC and traditional FORTRAN, for example). A structured language allows you to place statements anywhere on a line and does not require a strict field concept (as some older FORTRANs do).

Here are some examples of structured and nonstructured languages:

Nonstructured	Structured
FORTRAN	Pascal
BASIC	Ada
COBOL	C++
	C
	Java
	Modula-2

Structured languages tend to be of more recent creation. In fact, a mark of an old computer language is that it is nonstructured. Today, few programmers would consider using a nonstructured language for serious, new programs.

New versions of many older languages have attempted to add structured elements. BASIC is an example. However, the shortcomings of these languages can never be fully mitigated because they were not designed along structured design principles from the beginning.

C's main structural component is the function—C's stand-alone subroutine. In C, functions are the building blocks in which all program activity occurs. They allow you to define and code individually the separate tasks in a program, thus allowing your programs to be modular. After you have created a function, you can rely on it to work properly in various situations without creating side effects in other parts of the program. Being able to create stand-alone functions is extremely important in larger projects where one programmer's code must not accidentally affect another's.

Another way to structure and compartmentalize code in C is through the use of blocks of code. A *code block* is a logically connected group of program statements that is treated as a unit. In C, you create a code block by placing a sequence of statements between opening and closing curly braces. In this example,

```
if (x < 10)   {
    printf("Too low, try again.\n");
    scanf("%d", &x);
}
```

the two statements after the **if** and between the curly braces are both executed if **x** is less than 10. These two statements together with the braces represent a code block. They are a logical unit: One of the statements cannot execute without the other executing also. Code blocks allow many algorithms to be implemented with clarity, elegance, and efficiency. Moreover, they help the programmer better conceptualize the true nature of the algorithm being implemented.

C Is a Programmer's Language

Surprisingly, not all computer programming languages are for programmers. Consider the classic examples of nonprogrammer languages, COBOL and BASIC. COBOL was designed not to better the programmer's lot, not to improve the reliability of the code produced, and not even to improve the speed with which code can be written. Rather, COBOL was designed, in part, to enable nonprogrammers to read and presumably (however unlikely) to understand the program. BASIC was created essentially to allow nonprogrammers to program a computer to solve relatively simple problems.

In contrast, C was created, influenced, and field-tested by working programmers. The end result is that C gives the programmer what the programmer wants: few restrictions, few complaints, block structure, stand-alone functions, and a compact set of keywords. By using C, you can nearly achieve the efficiency of assembly code combined with the structure of Pascal or Modula-2. It is no wonder that C has become the universal language of programmers around the world.

The fact that C can often be used in place of assembly language was a major factor in its initial success. Assembly language uses a symbolic representation of the actual binary code that the computer executes directly. Each assembly-language operation maps into a single task for the computer to perform. Although assembly language gives programmers the potential to accomplish tasks with maximum flexibility and efficiency, it is notoriously difficult to work with when developing and debugging a program. Furthermore, since assembly language is unstructured, the final program tends to be spaghetti code—a tangled mess of jumps, calls, and indexes. This lack of structure makes assembly-language programs difficult to read, enhance, and maintain. Perhaps more important, assembly-language routines are not portable between machines with different CPUs.

Initially, C was used for systems programming. A *systems program* forms a portion of the operating system of the computer or its support utilities, such as editors, compilers, linkers, and the like. As C grew in popularity, many programmers began to use it to program all tasks because of its portability and efficiency—and because they liked it! At the time of its creation, C was a much longed-for, dramatic improvement in programming languages. In the years that have since elapsed, C has proven that it is up to any task.

With the advent of C++, some programmers thought that C as a distinct language would cease to exist. Such is not the case. First, not all programs require the application of the object-oriented programming features provided by C++. For example, applications such as embedded systems are still typically programmed in C. Second, much of the world still runs on C code, and those programs will continue to be enhanced and maintained. Third, as the new C99 standard shows, C is still a venue in which leading-edge innovation is taking place. While it is undeniably true that C will always be remembered as forming the foundation for C++, it will also be known as one of the world's great programming languages on its own.

Compilers vs. Interpreters

It is important to understand that a computer language defines the nature of a program and not the way that the program will be executed. There are two general methods by which a program can be executed. It can be *compiled*, or it can be *interpreted*. Although programs written in any computer language can be compiled or interpreted, some languages are designed more for one form of execution than the other. For example, Java was designed to be interpreted, and C was designed to be compiled. However, in the case of C, it is important to understand that it was specifically optimized as a compiled language. Although C interpreters have been written and are available in some environments (especially as debugging aids or experimental platforms like the interpreter developed in Part Six of this book), C was developed with compilation in mind. Therefore, you will almost certainly be using a C compiler and not a C interpreter when developing your C programs. Since the difference between a compiler and interpreter may not be clear to all readers, the following brief description will clarify matters.

In its simplest form, an interpreter reads the source code of your program one line at a time, performing the specific instructions contained in that line. This is the way earlier versions of BASIC worked. In languages such as Java, a program's source code is first converted into an intermediary form that is then interpreted. In either case, a run-time interpreter is still required to be present to execute the program.

A compiler reads the entire program and converts it into *object code*, which is a translation of the program's source code into a form that the computer can execute directly. Object code is also referred to as *binary code* or *machine code*. Once the program is compiled, a line of source code is no longer meaningful in the execution of your program.

In general, an interpreted program runs slower than a compiled program. Remember, a compiler converts a program's source code into object code that a computer can execute directly. Therefore, compilation is a one-time cost, while interpretation incurs an overhead each time a program is run.

The Form of a C Program

Table 1-2 lists the 32 keywords defined by the C89 standard. These are also the C keywords that form the C subset of C++. Table 1-3 shows the keywords added by C99. The keywords, combined with the formal C syntax, form the C programming language.

In addition to the standard keywords, many compilers add nonstandard keywords that better exploit their operating environment. For example, several compilers include keywords to manage the memory organization of the 8086 family of processors, to support interlanguage programming, and to access interrupts. Here is a list of some commonly used extended keywords:

asm	_ds	huge	pascal
cdecl	_es	interrupt	_ss
_cs	far	near	

Your compiler may also support other extensions that help it take better advantage of its specific environment.

auto	double	int	struct
break	else	long	switch
case	enum	register	typedef
char	extern	return	union
const	float	short	unsigned
continue	for	signed	void
default	goto	sizeof	volatile
do	if	static	while

Table 1-2.   *Keywords Defined by C89*

_Bool	_Imaginary	restrict
_Complex	inline	

Table 1-3.   *Keywords Added by C99*

In C, uppercase and lowercase characters are different: **else** is a keyword; **ELSE** is not. You may not use a keyword for any purpose other than as a keyword in a C program—that is, you may not use it as a variable or function name.

All C programs consist of one or more functions. As a general rule, the only function that must be present is called **main( )**, which is the first function called when program execution begins. In well-written C code, **main( )** contains what is, in essence, an outline of what the program does. The outline is composed of function calls. Although **main( )** is not a keyword, treat it as if it were. For example, don't try to use **main** as the name of a variable because you will probably confuse the compiler.

The general form of a C program is illustrated in Figure 1-1, where **f1( )** through **fN( )** represent user-defined functions.

The Library and Linking

Technically speaking, you can create a useful, functional C program that consists solely of statements involving only the C keywords. However, this is quite rare because C does not provide keywords that perform such things as input/output (I/O) operations, high-level mathematical computations, or character handling. As a result, most programs include calls to various functions contained in C's *standard library*.

All C compilers come with a standard library of functions that perform most commonly needed tasks. Standard C specifies a minimal set of functions that will be supported by all compilers. However, your compiler will probably contain many other functions. For example, the standard library does not define any graphics functions, but your compiler will probably include some.

When you call a library function, the C compiler "remembers" its name. Later, the linker combines the code you wrote with the object code already found in the standard library. This process is called *linking*. Some compilers have their own linker, while others use the standard linker supplied by your operating system.

The functions in the library are in *relocatable* format. This means that the memory addresses for the various machine-code instructions have not been absolutely defined—only offset information has been kept. When your program links with the functions in the standard library, these memory offsets are used to create the actual addresses used. Several technical manuals and books explain this process in more

```
Global declarations

int main(parameter list)
{
  statement sequence
}

return-type f1(parameter list)
{
  statement sequence
}

return-type f2(parameter list)
{
  statement sequence
}
  .
  .
  .
return-type fN(parameter list)
{
  statement sequence
}
```

Figure 1-1.   *The general form of a C program*

detail. However, you do not need any further explanation of the actual relocation process to program in C.

Many of the functions that you will need as you write programs are in the standard library. They act as building blocks that you combine. If you write a function that you will use again and again, you can put it into a library, too.

Separate Compilation

Most short C programs are completely contained within one source file. However, as a program's length grows, so does its compile time (and long compile times make for short tempers). Thus, C allows a program to be spread across two or more files, and it lets you compile each file separately. Once you have compiled all files, they are linked, along with any library routines, to form the complete object code. The advantage of separate compilation is that if you change the code of one file, you do not need to recompile the entire program. On all but the most simple projects, this saves a substantial amount of time. Separate compilation also allows multiple programmers to more easily work together on a single project, and it provides a means of organizing the code for a large project. (Strategies for separate compilation are discussed in Part Five of this book.)

Compiling a C Program

Creating an executable form of your C program consists of these three steps:

1. Creating your program

2. Compiling your program

3. Linking your program with whatever functions are needed from the library

Today, most compilers supply integrated programming environments that include an editor. Most also include stand-alone compilers. For stand-alone versions, you must have a separate editor to create your program. In either case, be careful: Compilers only accept standard text files for input. For example, your compiler will not accept files created by certain word processors because they contain control codes and nonprinting characters.

The exact method you use to compile your program will depend upon what compiler you are using. Also, how linking is accomplished will vary between compilers and environments; for example, it may be included as part of the compiler or as a stand-alone application. Consult your compiler's documentation for details.

C's Memory Map

A compiled C program creates and uses four logically distinct regions of memory. The first region is the memory that actually holds the program's executable code. The next region is memory where global variables are stored. The remaining two regions are the stack and the heap. The *stack* is used for a great many things while your program executes. It holds the return addresses of function calls, arguments to functions, and local variables. It will also save the current state of the CPU. The *heap* is a region of free memory that your program can use via C's dynamic memory allocation functions.

Although the exact physical layout of each of the four regions of memory differs among CPU types and C implementations, the diagram in Figure 1-2 shows conceptually how your C programs appear in memory.

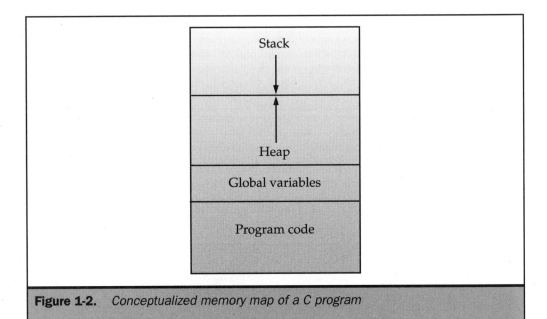

Figure 1-2.   *Conceptualized memory map of a C program*

C vs. C++

Before concluding this chapter, a few words about C++ are in order. Newcomers are sometimes confused about what C++ is and how it differs from C. In short, C++ is an object-oriented programming language that was built upon the foundation of C. In general terms, C is a subset of C++, or conversely, C++ is a superset of C.

In general, you can use a C++ compiler to compile a C program. In fact, today most compilers handle both C and C++ programs. Thus, most programmers will use a C++ compiler to compile their C code! However, since C++ was built upon the 1989 C standard, you must restrict your C code to the features defined by that standard (which are the features described in Part One of this book).

There is one thing that you must be careful about when using a C++ compiler to compile a C program: the file extension. By convention, C programs use the .C extension. C++ programs use .CPP. Don't accidentally give your C program a .CPP extension. Differences between the two languages might prevent a valid C program from being compiled *as if it were* a C++ program. By specifying the .C extension, you are telling the C++ compiler to perform a "C compile."

Note   *For a complete description of the C++ language, see* C++: The Complete Reference, *by Herbert Schildt (Berkeley, CA: Osborne/McGraw-Hill).*

Review of Terms

The terms that follow will be used frequently throughout the remainder of this reference. You should be completely familiar with them.

- *Source code* The text of a program that a user can read, commonly thought of as the program. The source code is input into the C compiler.

- *Object code* Translation of the source code of a program into machine code, which the computer can read and execute directly. Object code is the input to the linker.

- *Linker* A program that links separately compiled modules into one program. It also combines the functions in the Standard C library with the code that you wrote. The output of the linker is an executable program.

- *Library* The file containing the standard functions that your program can use. These functions include all I/O operations as well as other useful routines.

- *Compile time* The time during which your program is being compiled.

- *Run time* The time during which your program is executing.

The
Complete
Reference

Chapter 2

Expressions

This chapter examines the most fundamental element of the C language: the expression. Expressions in C are substantially more flexible and powerful than in many other computer languages. Expressions are formed from these atomic elements: data and operators. Data may be represented by variables, constants, or values returned by functions. C supports several different types of data. It also provides a wide variety of operators.

The Basic Data Types

C89 defines five foundational data types: character, integer, floating-point, double floating-point, and valueless. These are declared using **char**, **int**, **float**, **double**, and **void**, respectively. These types form the basis for several other types. The size and range of these data types may vary among processor types and compilers. However, in all cases an object of type **char** is 1 byte. The size of an **int** is usually the same as the word length of the execution environment of the program. For most 16-bit environments, such as DOS or Windows 3.1, an **int** is 16 bits. For most 32-bit environments, such as Windows 95/98/NT/2000, an **int** is 32 bits. However, you cannot make assumptions about the size of an integer if you want your programs to be portable to the widest range of environments. It is important to understand that C stipulates only the *minimal range* of each data type, not its size in bytes.

Note
*To the five basic data types defined by C89, C99 adds three more: **_Bool**, **_Complex**, and **_Imaginary**. They are described in Part Two.*

The exact format of floating-point values will depend upon how they are implemented. Variables of type **char** are generally used to hold values defined by the ASCII character set. Values outside that range may be handled differently by different compilers.

The range of **float** and **double** will depend upon the method used to represent the floating-point numbers. Standard C specifies that the minimum range for a floating-point value is 1E–37 to 1E+37. The minimum number of digits of precision for each floating-point type is shown in Table 2-1.

The type **void** either explicitly declares a function as returning no value or creates generic pointers. Both of these uses are discussed in subsequent chapters.

Modifying the Basic Types

Except type **void**, the basic data types may have various modifiers preceding them. A type modifier alters the meaning of the base type to more precisely fit a specific need. The list of modifiers is shown here:

signed
unsigned
long
short

The **int** base type can be modified by **signed**, **short**, **long**, and **unsigned**. The **char** type can be modified by **unsigned** and **signed**. You may also apply **long** to **double**. (C99 also allows **long** to modify **long**, thus creating **long long**. See Part Two for details.) Table 2-1 shows all valid data type combinations supported by C, along with their minimal ranges and typical bit widths. Remember, the table shows the *minimum range* that these types will have, not their typical range. For example, on computers that use two's complement arithmetic (which is nearly all), an integer will have a range of at least 32,767 to –32,768.

Type	Typical Size in Bits	Minimal Range
char	8	–127 to 127
unsigned char	8	0 to 255
signed char	8	–127 to 127
int	16 or 32	–32,767 to 32,767
unsigned int	16 or 32	0 to 65,535
signed int	16 or 32	Same as **int**
short int	16	–32,767 to 32,767
unsigned short int	16	0 to 65,535
signed short int	16	Same as **short int**
long int	32	–2,147,483,647 to 2,147,483,647
long long int	64	$-(2^{63} - 1)$ to $2^{63} - 1$ (Added by C99)
signed long int	32	Same as **long int**
unsigned long int	32	0 to 4,294,967,295
unsigned long long int	64	$2^{64} - 1$ (Added by C99)
float	32	1E–37 to 1E+37 with six digits of precision
double	64	1E–37 to 1E+37 with ten digits of precision
long double	80	1E–37 to 1E+37 with ten digits of precision

Table 2-1. *All Data Types Defined by the C Standard*

The use of **signed** on integers is allowed, but it is redundant because the default integer declaration assumes a signed number. The most important use of **signed** is to modify **char** in implementations in which **char** is unsigned by default.

Signed and unsigned integers differ in the way that the high-order bit of the integer is interpreted. If you specify a signed integer, the compiler generates code that assumes the high-order bit of an integer is to be used as a *sign flag*. If the sign flag is 0, the number is positive; if it is 1, the number is negative.

In general, negative numbers are represented using the *two's complement* approach, which reverses all bits in the number (except the sign flag), adds 1 to this number, and sets the sign flag to 1.

Signed integers are important for a great many algorithms, but they only have half the absolute magnitude of their unsigned relatives. For example, here is 32,767 in binary:

```
0 1 1 1 1 1 1 1   1 1 1 1 1 1 1 1
```

If the high-order bit were set to 1, the number would be interpreted as –1. However, if you declare this to be an **unsigned int**, the number becomes 65,535 when the high-order bit is set to 1.

When a type modifier is used by itself (that is, when it does not precede a basic type), then **int** is assumed. Thus, the following sets of type specifiers are equivalent:

Specifier	Same As
signed	signed int
unsigned	unsigned int
long	long int
short	short int

Although the **int** is implied, it is common practice today to specify the **int** anyway.

Identifier Names

In C, the names of variables, functions, labels, and various other user-defined items are called *identifiers*. The length of these identifiers can vary from one to several characters. The first character must be a letter or an underscore, and subsequent characters must be either letters, digits, or underscores. Here are some correct and incorrect identifier names:

Correct	Incorrect
count	1count
test23	hi!there
high_balance	high...balance

In C, identifiers may be of any length. However, not all characters will necessarily be significant. C defines two kinds of identifiers: external and internal. An external identifier will be involved in an external link process. These identifiers, called *external names*, include function names and global variable names that are shared between source files. If the identifier is not used in an external link process, then it is internal. This type of identifier is called an *internal name* and includes the names of local variables, for example. In C89, at least the first 6 characters of an external identifier and at least the first 31 characters of an internal identifier will be significant. C99 has increased these values. In C99, an external identifier has at least 31 significant characters, and an internal identifier has at least 63 significant characters. As a point of interest, in C++, at least the first 1,024 characters of an identifier are significant. These differences may be important if you are converting a program from C89 to C99, or from C to C++.

In an identifier, upper- and lowercase are treated as distinct. Hence, **count**, **Count**, and **COUNT** are three separate identifiers.

An identifier cannot be the same as a C keyword and should not have the same name as functions that are in the C library.

Variables

As you probably know, a *variable* is a named location in memory that is used to hold a value that can be modified by the program. All variables must be declared before they can be used. The general form of a declaration is

type variable_list;

Here, *type* must be a valid data type plus any modifiers, and *variable_list* may consist of one or more identifier names separated by commas. Here are some declarations:

```
int i, j, l;
short int si;
unsigned int ui;
double balance, profit, loss;
```

Remember, in C the name of a variable has nothing to do with its type.

Where Variables Are Declared

Variables can be declared in three places: inside functions, in the definition of function parameters, and outside of all functions. These positions correspond to local variables, formal parameters, and global variables, respectively.

Local Variables

Variables that are declared inside a function are called *local variables*. In some C literature, these variables are referred to as *automatic* variables. This book uses the more common term local variable. Local variables can be used only by statements that are inside the block in which the variables are declared. In other words, local variables are not known outside their own code block. Remember, a block of code begins with an opening curly brace and terminates with a closing curly brace.

Local variables exist only while the block of code in which they are declared is executing. That is, a local variable is created upon entry into its block and destroyed upon exit. Furthermore, a variable declared within one code block has no bearing on or relationship to another variable with the same name declared within a different code block.

The most common code block in which local variables are declared is the function. For example, consider the following two functions:

```
void func1(void)
{
  int x;

  x = 10;
}

void func2(void)
{
  int x;

  x = -199;
}
```

The integer variable **x** is declared twice, once in **func1( )** and once in **func2( )**. The **x** in **func1( )** has no bearing on or relationship to the **x** in **func2( )**. As explained, this is because each **x** is known only to the code within the block in which it is declared.

The C language contains the keyword **auto**, which you can use to declare local variables. However, since all nonglobal variables are, by default, assumed to be **auto**, this keyword is virtually never used. Hence, the examples in this book will not use it.

For reasons of convenience and tradition, most programmers declare all the variables used by a function immediately after the function's opening curly brace and before any other statements. However, you may declare local variables within any code block. The block defined by a function is simply a special case. For example:

```
void f(void)
{
  int t;

  scanf("%d%*c", &t);

  if(t==1) {
    char s[80];  /* this is created only upon
                    entry into this block */
    printf("Enter name:");
    gets(s);
    /* do something ... */
  }

  /* s not known here */
}
```

Here, the local variable **s** is created upon entry into the **if** code block and destroyed upon exit. Furthermore, **s** is known only within the **if** block and cannot be referenced elsewhere—even in other parts of the function that contains it.

Declaring variables within the block of code that uses them helps prevent unwanted side effects. Since the variable does not exist outside the block in which it is declared, it cannot be accidentally altered by other code.

When a variable declared within an inner block has the same name as a variable declared by an enclosing block, the variable in the inner block *hides* the variable in the outer block. Consider the following:

```
#include <stdio.h>

int main(void)
{
  int x;

  x = 10;

  if(x == 10) {
    int x; /* this x hides the outer x */

    x = 99;
    printf("Inner x: %d\n", x);
  }
```

```
    printf("Outer x: %d\n", x);

    return 0;
}
```

The program displays this output:

```
Inner x: 99
Outer x: 10
```

In this example, the **x** that is declared within the **if** block hides the outer **x**. Thus, the inner **x** and the outer **x** are two separate and distinct objects. Once that block ends, the outer **x** once again becomes visible.

In C89, you must declare all local variables at the start of a block, prior to any "action" statements. For example, the following function is in error if compiled by a C89-compatible compiler.

```
/* This function is in error if compiled as
   a C89 program.
*/
void f(void)
{
  int i;

  i = 10;

  int j;   /* this line will cause an error */

  j = 20;
}
```

However, in C99 (and in C++), this function is perfectly valid because you can declare local variables at any point within a block, prior to their first use.

Because local variables are created and destroyed with each entry and exit from the block in which they are declared, their content is lost once the block is left. This is especially important to remember when calling a function. When a function is called, its local variables are created, and upon its return they are destroyed. This means that local variables cannot retain their values between calls. (However, you can direct the compiler to retain their values by using the **static** modifier.)

Unless otherwise specified, local variables are stored on the stack. The fact that the stack is a dynamic and changing region of memory explains why local variables cannot, in general, hold their values between function calls.

You can initialize a local variable to some known value. This value will be assigned to the variable each time the block of code in which it is declared is entered. For example, the following program prints the number 10 ten times:

```c
#include <stdio.h>

void f(void);

int main(void)
{
  int i;

  for(i=0; i<10; i++)   f();

  return 0;
}

void f(void)
{
  int j = 10;

  printf("%d ", j);

  j++;   /* this line has no lasting effect */
}
```

Formal Parameters

If a function is to use arguments, it must declare variables that will accept the values of the arguments. These variables are called the *formal parameters* of the function. They behave like any other local variables inside the function. As shown in the following program fragment, their declarations occur after the function name and inside parentheses.

```c
/* Return 1 if c is part of string s; 0 otherwise */
int is_in(char *s, char c)
{
  while(*s)
    if(*s==c) return 1;
    else s++;

  return 0;
}
```

The function **is_in( )** has two parameters: **s** and **c**. This function returns 1 if the character specified in **c** is contained within the string **s**, 0 if it is not.

Even though the formal parameters receive the value of the arguments passed to the function, they otherwise act like "normal" local variables. For example, you can make assignments to a parameter or use one in any allowable expression. Keep in mind that, as local variables, they are also dynamic and are destroyed upon exit from the function.

Global Variables

Unlike local variables, *global variables* are known throughout the program and may be used by any piece of code. Also, they will hold their value throughout the program's execution. You create global variables by declaring them outside of any function. Any expression may access them, regardless of what block of code that expression is in.

In the following program, the variable **count** has been declared outside of all functions. Although its declaration occurs before the **main( )** function, you could have placed it anywhere before its first use as long as it was not in a function. However, it is usually best to declare global variables at the top of the program.

```
#include <stdio.h>
int count;   /* count is global  */

void func1(void);
void func2(void);

int main(void)
{
  count = 100;
  func1();

  return 0;
}

void func1(void)
{
  int temp;

  temp = count;
  func2();
  printf("count is %d", count); /* will print 100 */
}

void func2(void)
```

```
{
  int count;

  for(count=1; count<10; count++)
    putchar('.');
}
```

Look closely at this program. Notice that although neither **main( )** nor **func1( )** has declared the variable **count**, both may use it. **func2( )**, however, has declared a local variable called **count**. When **func2( )** refers to **count**, it refers to only its local variable, not the global one. If a global variable and a local variable have the same name, all references to that variable name inside the code block in which the local variable is declared will refer to that local variable and have no effect on the global variable.

Storage for global variables is in a fixed region of memory set aside for this purpose by the compiler. Global variables are helpful when many functions in your program use the same data. You should avoid using unnecessary global variables, however. They take up memory the entire time your program is executing, not just when they are needed. In addition, using a global where a local variable will do makes a function less general because it relies on something that must be defined outside itself. Finally, using a large number of global variables can lead to program errors because of unknown and unwanted side effects. A major problem in developing large programs is the accidental changing of a variable's value because it was used elsewhere in the program. This can happen in C if you use too many global variables in your programs.

The Four C Scopes

In the preceding discussion (and throughout the remainder of this book) the terms *local* and *global* are used to describe in a general way the difference between identifiers that are declared within a block and those declared outside all blocks. However, these two broad categories are more finely subdivided by C. Standard C defines four scopes that determine the visibility of an identifier. They are summarized here:

Scope	Meaning
File scope	Starts at the beginning of the file (also called a *translation unit*) and ends with the end of the file. It refers only to those identifiers that are declared outside of all functions. File scope identifiers are visible throughout the entire file. Variables that have file scope are global.

Scope	Meaning
Block scope	Begins with the opening { of a block and ends with its associated closing }. However, block scope also extends to function parameters in a function definition. That is, function parameters are included in a function's block scope. Variables with block scope are local to their block.
Function prototype scope	Identifiers declared in a function prototype; visible within the prototype.
Function scope	Begins with the opening { of a function and ends with its closing }. Function scope applies only to labels. A label is used as the target of a **goto** statement, and that label must be within the same function as the **goto**.

For the most part, this book will continue to use the more general categories of local and global. However, when a more finely grained distinction is required, one or more of the preceding scopes will be explicitly used.

Type Qualifiers

C defines type qualifiers that control how variables may be accessed or modified. C89 defines two of these qualifiers: **const** and **volatile**. (C99 adds a third, called **restrict**, which is described in Part Two.) The type qualifiers must precede the type names that they qualify.

const

Variables of type **const** may not be changed by your program. (A **const** variable can be given an initial value, however.) The compiler is free to place variables of this type into read-only memory (ROM). For example,

```
const int a=10;
```

creates an integer variable called **a** with an initial value of 10 that your program may not modify. However, you can use the variable **a** in other types of expressions. A **const** variable will receive its value either from an explicit initialization or by some hardware-dependent means.

The **const** qualifier can be used to prevent the object pointed to by an argument to a function from being modified by that function. That is, when a pointer is passed to a function, that function can modify the actual object pointed to by the pointer. However, if the pointer is specified as **const** in the parameter declaration, the function code won't be able to modify what it points to. For example, the **sp_to_dash( )** function in the following program prints a dash for each space in its string argument. That is, the string "this is a test" will be printed as "this-is-a-test". The use of **const** in the parameter declaration ensures that the code inside the function cannot modify the object pointed to by the parameter.

```c
#include <stdio.h>

void sp_to_dash(const char *str);

int main(void)
{
  sp_to_dash("this is a test");

  return 0;
}

void sp_to_dash(const char *str)
{
  while(*str) {
    if(*str== ' ') printf("%c", '-');
    else printf("%c", *str);
    str++;
  }
}
```

If you had written **sp_to_dash( )** in such a way that the string would be modified, it would not compile. For example, if you had coded **sp_to_dash( )** as follows, you would receive a compile-time error:

```c
/* This is wrong. */
void sp_to_dash(const char *str)
{
  while(*str) {
    if(*str==' ' ) *str = '-'; /* can't do this; str is const */
    printf("%c", *str);
    str++;
  }
}
```

Many functions in the standard library use **const** in their parameter declarations. For example, the **strlen( )** function has this prototype:

size_t strlen(const char *str);

Specifying *str* as **const** ensures that **strlen( )** will not modify the string pointed to by *str*. In general, when a standard library function has no need to modify an object pointed to by a calling argument, it is declared as **const**.

You can also use **const** to verify that your program does not modify a variable. Remember, a variable of type **const** can be modified by something outside your program. For example, a hardware device may set its value. However, by declaring a variable as **const**, you can prove that any changes to that variable occur because of external events.

volatile

The modifier **volatile** tells the compiler that a variable's value may be changed in ways not explicitly specified by the program. For example, a global variable's address may be passed to the operating system's clock routine and used to hold the system time. In this situation, the contents of the variable are altered without any explicit assignment statements in the program. This is important because most C compilers automatically optimize certain expressions by assuming that a variable's content is unchanging if it does not occur on the left side of an assignment statement; thus, it might not be reexamined each time it is referenced. Also, some compilers change the order of evaluation of an expression during the compilation process. The **volatile** modifier prevents these changes.

You can use **const** and **volatile** together. For example, if 0x30 is assumed to be the value of a port that is changed by external conditions only, the following declaration would prevent any possibility of accidental side effects:

```
const volatile char *port = (const volatile char *) 0x30;
```

Storage Class Specifiers

C supports four storage class specifiers:

> extern
> static
> register
> auto

These specifiers tell the compiler how to store the subsequent variable. The general form of a variable declaration that uses one is shown here:

> *storage_specifier type var_name;*

Notice that the storage specifier precedes the rest of the variable declaration.

Note   *Both C89 and C99 state that **typedef** is a storage class specifier for the purposes of syntactic convenience, but it is not a storage class specifier in the common meaning of the term. **typedef** is examined later in this book.*

extern

Before examining **extern**, a brief description of C linkage is in order. C defines three categories of linkage: external, internal, and none. In general, functions and global variables have external linkage. This means they are available to all files that constitute a program. File scope objects declared as **static** (described in the next section) have internal linkage. These are known only within the file in which they are declared. Local variables have no linkage and are therefore known only within their own block.

The principal use of **extern** is to specify that an object is declared with external linkage elsewhere in the program. To understand why this is important, it is necessary to understand the difference between a declaration and a definition. A *declaration* declares the name and type of an object. A *definition* causes storage to be allocated for the object. The same object may have many declarations, but there can be *only one* definition.

In most cases, variable declarations are also definitions. However, by preceding a variable name with the **extern** specifier, you can declare a variable without defining it. Thus, when you need to refer to a variable that is defined in another part of your program, you can declare that variable using **extern**.

Here is an example that uses **extern**. Notice that the global variables **first** and **last** are declared *after* **main( )**.

```
#include <stdio.h>

int main(void)
{
  extern int first, last; /* use global vars */

  printf("%d %d", first, last);

  return 0;
}

/* global definition of first and last */
int first = 10, last = 20;
```

This program outputs **10 20** because the global variables **first** and **last** used by the **printf( )** statement are initialized to these values. Because the **extern** declaration tells the compiler that **first** and **last** are declared elsewhere (in this case, later in the same file), the program can be compiled without error even though **first** and **last** are used prior to their definition.

It is important to understand that the **extern** variable declarations as shown in the preceding program are necessary only because **first** and **last** had not yet been declared prior to their use in **main( )**. Had their declarations occurred prior to **main( )**, there would have been no need for the **extern** statement. Remember, if the compiler finds a variable that has not been declared within the current block, the compiler checks whether it matches any of the variables declared within enclosing blocks. If it does not, the compiler then checks the global variables. If a match is found, the compiler assumes that is the variable being referenced. The **extern** specifier is needed when you want to use a variable that is declared later in the file.

As mentioned, **extern** allows you to declare a variable without defining it. However, if you give that variable an initialization, the **extern** declaration becomes a definition. This is important because, as stated earlier, an object can have multiple declarations, but only one definition.

An important use of **extern** relates to multiple-file programs. C allows a program to be spread across two or more files, compiled separately, and then linked together. When this is the case, there must be some way of telling all the files about the global variables required by the program. The best (and most portable) way to do this is to declare all of your global variables in one file and use **extern** declarations in the other, as in Figure 2-1.

In File 2, the global variable list was copied from File 1, and the **extern** specifier was added to the declarations. The **extern** specifier tells the compiler that the variable types and names that follow it have been defined elsewhere. In other words, **extern** lets the compiler know what the types and names are for these global variables without

```
File One                        File Two

int x, y;                       extern int x, y;

char ch;                        extern char ch;

int main(void)                  void func22(void)

{                               {

  /* ... */                       x = y / 10;

}                               }


void func1(void)                void func23(void)

{                               {

  x = 123;                        y = 10;

}                               }
```

Figure 2-1.   *Using global variables in separately compiled modules*

actually creating storage for them again. When the linker links the two modules, all references to the external variables are resolved.

One last point: In real-world, multiple-file programs, **extern** declarations are normally contained in a header file that is simply included with each source code file. This is both easier and less error prone than manually duplicating **extern** declarations in each file.

Note	*extern can also be applied to a function declaration, but doing so is redundant.*

static Variables

Variables declared as **static** are permanent variables within their own function or file. Unlike global variables, they are not known outside their function or file, but they maintain their values between calls. This feature makes them useful when you write generalized functions and function libraries that other programmers may use. The **static** modifier has different effects upon local variables and global variables.

static Local Variables

When you apply the **static** modifier to a local variable, the compiler creates permanent storage for it, much as it creates storage for a global variable. The key difference between a **static** local variable and a global variable is that the **static** local variable remains known only to the block in which it is declared. In simple terms, a **static** local variable is a local variable that retains its value between function calls.

static local variables are very important to the creation of stand-alone functions because several types of routines must preserve a value between calls. If **static** variables were not allowed, globals would have to be used, opening the door to possible side effects. An example of a function that benefits from a **static** local variable is a number-series generator that produces a new value based on the previous one. You could use a global variable to hold this value. However, each time the function is used in a program, you would have to declare that global variable and make sure it did not conflict with any other global variables already in place. The better solution is to declare the variable that holds the generated number to be **static**, as shown here:

```
int series(void)
{
  static int series_num;

  series_num = series_num+23;
  return series_num;
}
```

In this example, the variable **series_num** stays in existence between function calls, instead of coming and going the way a normal local variable would. This means that each call to **series( )** can produce a new member of the series based on the preceding number without declaring that variable globally.

You can give a **static** local variable an initialization value. This value is assigned only once, at program start-up—not each time the block of code is entered, as with normal local variables. For example, this version of **series( )** initializes **series_num** to 100:

```
int series(void)
{
  static int series_num = 100;

  series_num = series_num+23;
  return series_num;
}
```

As the function now stands, the series will always begin with the value 123. While this is acceptable for some applications, most series generators need to let the user specify the starting point. One way to give **series_num** a user-specified value is to make **series_num** a global variable and then let the user set its value. However, not defining **series_num** as global was the point of making it **static**. This leads to the second use of **static**.

static Global Variables

Applying the specifier **static** to a global variable instructs the compiler to create a global variable known only to the file in which it is declared. Thus, a static global variable has internal linkage (as described under the **extern** statement). This means that even though the variable is global, routines in other files have no knowledge of it and cannot alter its contents directly, keeping it free from side effects. For the few situations where a local **static** cannot do the job, you can create a small file that contains only the functions that need the global **static** variable, separately compile that file, and use it without fear of side effects.

To illustrate a global **static**, the series generator example from the previous section is recoded so that a seed value initializes the series through a call to a second function called **series_start( )**. The entire file containing **series( )**, **series_start( )**, and **series_num** is shown here:

```
/* This must all be in one file - preferably by itself. */

static int series_num;
void series_start(int seed);
int series(void);

int series(void)
{
```

```
   series_num = series_num+23;
   return series_num;
}

/* initialize series_num */
void series_start(int seed)
{
   series_num = seed;
}
```

Calling **series_start( )** with some known integer value initializes the series generator. After that, calls to **series( )** generate the next element in the series.

To review: The names of local **static** variables are known only to the block of code in which they are declared; the names of global **static** variables are known only to the file in which they reside. If you place the **series( )** and **series_start( )** functions in a library, you can use the functions but cannot reference the variable **series_num**, which is hidden from the rest of the code in your program. In fact, you can even declare and use another variable called **series_num** in your program (in another file, of course). In essence, the **static** modifier permits variables that are known only to the functions that need them, without unwanted side effects.

By using **static** variables, you can hide portions of your program from other portions. This can be a tremendous advantage when you are trying to manage a very large and complex program.

register Variables

The **register** storage specifier originally applied only to variables of type **int, char**, or pointer types. However, in Standard C, **register**'s definition has been broadened so that it can be applied to any type of variable.

Originally, the **register** specifier requested that the compiler keep the value of a variable in a register of the CPU rather than in memory, where normal variables are stored. This meant that operations on a **register** variable could occur much faster than on a normal variable because the **register** variable was actually held in the CPU and did not require a memory access to determine or modify its value.

Today, the definition of **register** has been greatly expanded, and it now may be applied to any type of variable. Both C89 and C99 simply state that "access to the object be as fast as possible." In practice, characters and integers are still stored in registers in the CPU. Larger objects, such as arrays, obviously cannot be stored in a register, but they may still receive preferential treatment by the compiler. Depending upon the implementation of the C compiler and its operating environment, **register** variables may be handled in any way deemed fit by the compiler's implementor. In fact, it is technically permissible for a compiler to ignore the **register** specifier altogether and treat variables modified by it as if they were "normal" variables, but this is seldom done in practice.

You can only apply the **register** specifier to local variables and to the formal parameters in a function. Global **register** variables are not allowed. Here is an example that uses **register** variables. This function computes the result of M^e for integers.

```
int int_pwr(register int m,  register int e)
{
  register int temp;

  temp = 1;

  for(; e; e--) temp = temp * m;
  return temp;
}
```

In this example, **e**, **m**, and **temp** are declared as **register** variables because they are all used within the loop. The fact that **register** variables are optimized for speed makes them ideal for control of or use in loops. Generally, **register** variables are used where they will do the most good, which is often in places where many references will be made to the same variable. This is important because you can declare any number of variables as being of type **register**, but not all will receive the same access speed optimization.

The number of **register** variables optimized for speed allowed within any one code block is determined by both the environment and the specific implementation of C. You don't have to worry about declaring too many **register** variables because the compiler automatically transforms **register** variables into nonregister variables when the limit is reached. (This ensures portability of code across a broad line of processors.)

Usually at least two **register** variables of type **char** or **int** can actually be held in the registers of the CPU. Because environments vary widely, consult your compiler's user manual to determine whether you can apply any other types of optimization options.

In C, you cannot obtain the address of a **register** variable by using the **&** operator (discussed later in this chapter). This makes sense because a **register** variable may be stored in a register of the CPU, which is not usually addressable.

Although the description of **register** has been broadened beyond its traditional meaning, in practice it still generally has a significant effect only with integer and character types. Thus, you should probably not count on substantial speed improvements for other variable types.

Variable Initializations

You can give variables a value as you declare them by placing an equal sign and a constant after the variable name. The general form of initialization is

type variable_name = constant;

Some examples are

```
char ch = 'a';
int first = 0;
double balance = 123.23;
```

Global and **static** local variables are initialized only at the start of the program. Local variables (excluding **static** local variables) are initialized each time the block in which they are declared is entered. Local variables that are not initialized have unknown values before the first assignment is made to them. Uninitialized global and **static** local variables are automatically set to zero.

Constants

Constants refer to fixed values that the program may not alter. Constants can be of any of the basic data types. The way each constant is represented depends upon its type. Constants are also called *literals*.

Character constants are enclosed between single quotes. For example, 'a' and '%' are both character constants. C defines both multibyte characters, which consist of one or more bytes, and wide characters (which are usually 16 bits long). Multibyte and wide characters are used primarily to represent languages that have large character sets. To specify a multibyte character, enclose the characters within single quotes, for example, 'xy'. To specify a wide character constant, precede the character with an L. For example:

```
wchar_t wc;
wc = L'A';
```

Here, **wc** is assigned the wide-character constant equivalent of A. The type of wide characters is **wchar_t,** which is defined in the **<stddef.h>** header file, and is not a built-in type.

Integer constants are specified as numbers without fractional components. For example, 10 and –100 are integer constants. Floating-point constants require the decimal point followed by the number's fractional component. For example, 11.123 is a floating-point constant. C also allows you to use scientific notation for floating-point numbers.

By default, the compiler fits a numeric constant into the smallest compatible data type that will hold it. Therefore, assuming 16-bit integers, 10 is **int** by default, but 103,000 is a **long int**. Even though the value 10 could fit into a character type, the compiler will not cross type boundaries. The only exception to the smallest type rule is floating-point constants, which are assumed to be **double**s.

For most programs you will write, the compiler defaults are adequate. However, you can specify precisely the type of numeric constant you want by using a suffix. For floating-point types, if you follow the number with an F, the number is treated as a **float**. If you follow it with an L, the number becomes a **long double**. For integer types, the U suffix stands for **unsigned** and the L for **long**. The type suffixes are not case dependent, and you can use lowercase, if you like. For example, both F and f specify a **float** constant. Here are some examples:

Data Type	Constant Examples
int	1 123 21000 –234
long int	35000L –34L
unsigned int	10000U 987u 40000U
float	123.23F 4.34e–3f
double	123.23 1.0 –0.9876324
long double	1001.2L

C99 also allows you to specify a **long long** integer constant by specifying the suffix LL (or ll).

Hexadecimal and Octal Constants

It is sometimes easier to use a number system based on 8 or 16 rather than 10. The number system based on 8 is called *octal* and uses the digits 0 through 7. In octal, the number 10 is the same as 8 in decimal. The base 16 number system is called *hexadecimal* and uses the digits 0 through 9 plus the letters A through F, which stand for 10, 11, 12, 13, 14, and 15, respectively. For example, the hexadecimal number 10 is 16 in decimal. Because these two number systems are used frequently, C allows you to specify integer constants in hexadecimal or octal instead of decimal. A hexadecimal constant must consist of a 0x followed by the constant in hexadecimal form. An octal constant begins with a 0. Here are some examples:

```
int hex = 0x80;   /* 128 in decimal */
int oct = 012;    /* 10 in decimal */
```

String Constants

C supports another type of constant: the string. A *string* is a set of characters enclosed in double quotes. For example, "this is a test" is a string. You have seen examples of strings in some of the **printf( )** statements in the sample programs. Although C allows you to define string constants, it does not formally have a string data type.

You must not confuse strings with characters. A single character constant is enclosed in single quotes, as in 'a'. However, "a" is a string containing only one letter.

Backslash Character Constants

Enclosing character constants in single quotes works for most printing characters. A few, however, such as the carriage return, can't be. For this reason, C includes the special *backslash character constants*, shown in Table 2-2, so that you may easily enter these special characters as constants. These are also referred to as *escape sequences*. You should use the backslash codes instead of their ASCII equivalents to help ensure portability.

For example, the following program outputs a new line and a tab and then prints the string **This is a test**.

```c
#include <stdio.h>

int main(void)
{
  printf("\n\tThis is a test.");

  return 0;
}
```

Code	Meaning
\b	Backspace
\f	Form feed
\n	New line
\r	Carriage return
\t	Horizontal tab
\"	Double quote
\'	Single quote
\\	Backslash
\v	Vertical tab
\a	Alert
\?	Question mark
\N	Octal constant (where N is an octal constant)
\xN	Hexadecimal constant (where N is a hexadecimal constant)

Table 2-2.   *Backslash Codes*

Operators

C is very rich in built-in operators. In fact, it places more significance on operators than do most other computer languages. There are four main classes of operators: *arithmetic*, *relational*, *logical*, and *bitwise*. In addition, there are some special operators, such as the assignment operator, for particular tasks.

The Assignment Operator

You can use the assignment operator within any valid expression. This is not the case with most computer languages (including Pascal, BASIC, and FORTRAN), which treat the assignment operator as a special case statement. The general form of the assignment operator is

variable_name = expression;

where an expression may be as simple as a single constant or as complex as you require. C uses a single equal sign to indicate assignment (unlike Pascal or Modula-2, which use the := construct). The *target*, or left part, of the assignment must be an object, such as a variable, that can receive a value.

Frequently in literature on C and in compiler error messages you will see these two terms: lvalue and rvalue. Simply put, an *lvalue* is an object. If that object can occur on the left side of an assignment statement, it is called a *modifiable lvalue*. Thus, for all practical purposes, a modifiable lvalue means "variable." The term *rvalue* refers to expressions on the right side of an assignment and simply means the value of an expression.

Type Conversion in Assignments

When variables of one type are mixed with variables of another type, a *type conversion* will occur. In an assignment statement, the type conversion rule is easy: The value of the right side (expression side) of the assignment is converted to the type of the left side (target variable), as illustrated here:

```
int x;
char ch;
float  f;

void func(void)
{
   ch = x;     /* line 1 */
   x = f;      /* line 2 */
   f = ch;     /* line 3 */
   f = x;      /* line 4 */
}
```

In line 1, the left high-order bits of the integer variable **x** are lopped off, leaving **ch** with the lower 8 bits. If **x** were between 255 and 0, **ch** and **x** would have identical values. Otherwise, the value of **ch** would reflect only the lower-order bits of **x**. In line 2, **x** will receive the nonfractional part of **f**. In line 3, **f** will convert the 8-bit integer value stored in **ch** to the same value in the floating-point format. This also happens in line 4, except that **f** will convert an integer value into floating-point format.

When converting from integers to characters and long integers to integers, the appropriate amount of high-order bits will be removed. In many 16-bit environments, this means that 8 bits will be lost when going from an integer to a character, and 16 bits will be lost when going from a long integer to an integer. For 32-bit environments, 24 bits will be lost when converting from an integer to a character, and 16 bits will be lost when converting from an integer to a short integer.

Table 2-3 summarizes several common assignment type conversions. Remember that the conversion of an **int** to a **float**, or a **float** to a **double**, and so on, does not add any precision or accuracy. These kinds of conversions only change the form in which

Target Type	Expression Type	Possible Info Loss
signed char	char	If value > 127, target is negative
char	short int	High-order 8 bits
char	int (16 bits)	High-order 8 bits
char	int (32 bits)	High-order 24 bits
char	long int	High-order 24 bits
short int	int (16 bits)	None
short int	int (32 bits)	High-order 16 bits
int (16 bits)	long int	High-order 16 bits
int (32 bits)	long int	None
long int (32 bits)	long long int (64 bits)	High-order 32 bits (applies to C99 only)
int	float	Fractional part and possibly more
float	double	Precision, result rounded
double	long double	Precision, result rounded

Table 2-3.   *Outcome of Common Type Conversions*

the value is represented. In addition, some compilers always treat a **char** variable as positive, no matter what value it has, when converting it to an **int** or **float**. Other compilers treat **char** variable values greater than 127 as negative numbers when converting. Generally speaking, you should use **char** variables for characters and use **int**s, **short int**s, or **signed char**s when needed to avoid possible portability problems.

To use Table 2-3 to make a conversion not shown, simply convert one type at a time until you finish. For example, to convert from **double** to **int**, first convert from **double** to **float** and then from **float** to **int**.

Multiple Assignments

You can assign many variables the same value by using multiple assignments in a single statement. For example, this program fragment assigns **x**, **y**, and **z** the value 0:

```
x = y = z = 0;
```

In professional programs, variables are frequently assigned common values using this method.

Compound Assignments

There is a variation on the assignment statement, called *compound assignment*, that simplifies the coding of a certain type of assignment operations. For example,

```
x = x+10;
```

can be written as

```
x += 10;
```

The operator += tells the compiler to assign to **x** the value of **x** plus 10.

Compound assignment operators exist for all the binary operators (those that require two operands). In general, statements like

var = var operator expression

can be rewritten as

var operator= expression

For another example,

```
x = x-100;
```

is the same as

```
x -= 100;
```

Because compound assignment is more compact than the corresponding = equivalent, compound assignment is also sometimes referred to as *shorthand assignment*. Compound assignment is widely used in professionally written C programs; you should be familiar with it.

Arithmetic Operators

Table 2-4 lists C's arithmetic operators. The operators +, –, *, and / work as they do in most other computer languages. You can apply them to almost any built-in data type. When you apply / to an integer or character, any remainder will be truncated. For example, 5/2 will equal 2 in integer division.

The modulus operator % also works in C as it does in other languages, yielding the remainder of an integer division. However, you cannot use it on floating-point types. The following code fragment illustrates %:

```
int x, y;

x = 5;
y = 2;

printf("%d ", x/y);    /* will display 2 */
printf("%d ", x%y);    /* will display 1, the remainder of
                          the integer division */

x = 1;
y = 2;

printf("%d %d", x/y, x%y); /*  will display 0 1 */
```

The last line prints a 0 and a 1 because 1/2 in integer division is 0 with a remainder of 1.

Operator	Action
–	Subtraction, also unary minus
+	Addition
*	Multiplication
/	Division
%	Modulus
––	Decrement
++	Increment

Table 2-4.   *Arithmetic Operators*

The unary minus multiplies its operand by –1. That is, any number preceded by a minus sign switches its sign.

The Increment and Decrement Operators

C includes two useful operators that simplify two common operations. These are the increment and decrement operators, **++** and **––**. The operator **++** adds 1 to its operand, and **––** subtracts 1. In other words:

```
x = x+1;
```

is the same as

```
++x;
```

and

```
x = x-1;
```

is the same as

```
x--;
```

Both the increment and decrement operators may either precede (prefix) or follow (postfix) the operand. For example,

```
x = x+1;
```

can be written

```
++x;
```

or

```
x++;
```

There is, however, a difference between the prefix and postfix forms when you use these operators in a larger expression. When an increment or decrement operator precedes its operand, the increment or decrement operation is performed before obtaining the value of the operand for use in the expression. If the operator follows its operand, the value of the operand is obtained before incrementing or decrementing it. For instance,

```
x = 10;
y = ++x;
```

sets **y** to 11. However, if you write the code as

```
x = 10;
y = x++;
```

y is set to 10. Either way, **x** is set to 11; the difference is in when it happens.

Most C compilers produce very fast, efficient object code for increment and decrement operations—code that is better than that generated by using the equivalent assignment statement. For this reason, you should use the increment and decrement operators when you can.

Here is the precedence of the arithmetic operators:

Highest	++ --
	- (unary minus)
	* / %
Lowest	+ -

Operators on the same level of precedence are evaluated by the compiler from left to right. Of course, you can use parentheses to alter the order of evaluation. C treats parentheses in the same way as virtually all other computer languages. Parentheses force an operation, or set of operations, to have a higher level of precedence.

Relational and Logical Operators

In the term relational operator, *relational* refers to the relationships that values can have with one another. In the term logical operator, *logical* refers to the ways these relationships can be connected. Because the relational and logical operators often work together, they are discussed together here.

The idea of true and false underlies the concepts of relational and logical operators. In C, true is any value other than zero. False is zero. Expressions that use relational or logical operators return 0 for false and 1 for true.

Note *Like C89, C99 defines true as nonzero and false as zero. However, C99 also defines the _Bool data type, which can hold the values 1 and 0. See Part Two for details.*

Table 2-5 shows the relational and logical operators. The truth table for the logical operators is shown here using 1's and 0's.

p	q	p && q	p ‖ q	!p
0	0	0	0	1
0	1	0	1	1
1	1	1	1	0
1	0	0	1	0

Both the relational and logical operators are lower in precedence than the arithmetic operators. That is, an expression like 10 > 1+12 is evaluated as if it were written 10 > (1+12). Of course, the result is false.

You can combine several operations into one expression, as shown here:

```
10>5 && !(10<9) || 3<=4
```

In this case, the result is true.

Although C does not contain an exclusive OR (XOR) logical operator, you can easily create a function that performs this task by using the other logical operators. The outcome of an XOR operation is true if and only if one operand (but not both) is true. The following program contains the function **xor( )**, which returns the outcome of an exclusive OR operation performed on its two arguments.

```
#include <stdio.h>
```

```
int xor(int a, int b);

int main(void)
{
  printf("%d", xor(1, 0));
  printf("%d", xor(1, 1));
  printf("%d", xor(0, 1));
  printf("%d", xor(0, 0));

  return 0;
}

/* Perform a logical XOR operation using the
   two arguments. */
int xor(int a, int b)
{
  return (a || b) && !(a && b);
}
```

Relational Operators	
Operator	**Action**
>	Greater than
>=	Greater than or equal
<	Less than
<=	Less than or equal
==	Equal
!=	Not equal
Logical Operators	
Operator	**Action**
&&	AND
||	OR
!	NOT

Table 2-5. *Relational and Logical Operators*

The following table shows the relative precedence of the relational and logical operators:

Highest	!
	> >= < <=
	== !=
	&&
Lowest	||

As with arithmetic expressions, you can use parentheses to alter the natural order of evaluation in a relational and/or logical expression. For example,

!0 && 0 || 0

is false. However, when you add parentheses to the same expression, as shown here, the result is true.

!(0 && 0) || 0

Remember, all relational and logical expressions produce a result of either 1 or 0. Therefore, the following program fragment is not only correct, but will print the number 1.

```
int x;

x = 100;
printf("%d", x>10);
```

Bitwise Operators

Unlike many other languages, C supports a full complement of bitwise operators. Since C was designed to take the place of assembly language for most programming tasks, it needed to be able to support many operations that can be done in assembler, including operations on bits. *Bitwise operation* refers to testing, setting, or shifting the actual bits in a byte or word, which correspond to the standard **char** and **int** data types and variants.

You cannot use bitwise operations on **float**, **double**, **long double**, **void**, or other more complex types. Table 2-6 lists the operators that apply to bitwise operations. These operations are applied to the individual bits of the operands.

The bitwise AND, OR, and NOT (one's complement) are governed by the same truth table as their logical equivalents, except that they work bit by bit. The exclusive OR has the truth table shown here:

p	q	p ^q
0	0	0
1	0	1
1	1	0
0	1	1

As the table indicates, the outcome of an XOR is true only if exactly one of the operands is true; otherwise, it is false.

Bitwise operations most often find application in device drivers—such as modem programs, disk file routines, and printer routines—because the bitwise operations can be used to mask off certain bits, such as parity. (The parity bit confirms that the rest of the bits in the byte are unchanged. It is often the high-order bit in each byte.)

Operator	Action
&	AND
|	OR
^	Exclusive OR (XOR)
~	One's complement (NOT)
>>	Shift right
<<	Shift left

Table 2-6.   *Bitwise Operators*

Think of the bitwise AND as a way to clear a bit. That is, any bit that is 0 in either operand causes the corresponding bit in the outcome to be set to 0. For example, the following function reads a character from the modem port and resets the parity bit to 0:

```
char get_char_from_modem(void)
{
  char ch;

  ch = read_modem(); /* get a character from the
                        modem port */
  return(ch & 127);
}
```

Parity is often indicated by the eighth bit, which is set to 0 by ANDing it with a byte that has bits 1 through 7 set to 1 and bit 8 set to 0. The expression **ch & 127** means to AND together the bits in **ch** with the bits that make up the number 127. The net result is that the eighth bit of **ch** is set to 0. In the following example, assume that **ch** had received the character A and had the parity bit set:

```
     Parity bit

        │
        ▼
     1 1 0 0 0 0 0 1     ch containing an "A" with parity set
     0 1 1 1 1 1 1 1     127 in binary
 &  ───────────────        do bitwise AND
     0 1 0 0 0 0 0 1     "A" without parity
```

The bitwise OR, as the reverse of AND, can be used to set a bit. Any bit that is set to 1 in either operand causes the corresponding bit in the outcome to be set to 1. For example, the following is 128 | 3:

```
     1 0 0 0 0 0 0 0     128 in binary
     0 0 0 0 0 0 1 1     3 in binary
 |  ───────────────     bitwise OR
     1 0 0 0 0 0 1 1     result
```

An exclusive OR, usually abbreviated XOR, will set a bit on, if and only if the bits being compared are different. For example, 127 ^120 is

```
     0 1 1 1 1 1 1 1     127 in binary
     0 1 1 1 1 0 0 0     120 in binary
 ^  ───────────────     bitwise XOR
     0 0 0 0 0 1 1 1     result
```

Remember, relational and logical operators always produce a result that is either true or false, whereas the similar bitwise operations may produce any arbitrary value in accordance with the specific operation. In other words, bitwise operations may produce values other than 0 or 1, while logical operators will always evaluate to 0 or 1.

The bit-shift operators, >> and <<, move all bits in a variable to the right or left as specified. The general form of the shift-right statement is

variable >> number of bit positions

The general form of the shift-left statement is

variable << number of bit positions

As bits are shifted off one end, zeroes are brought in the other end. (In the case of a signed, negative integer, a right shift will cause a 1 to be brought in so that the sign bit is preserved.) Remember, a shift is not a rotate. That is, the bits shifted off one end do not come back around to the other. The bits shifted off are lost.

Bit-shift operations can be very useful when you are decoding input from an external device, such as a D/A converter, and reading status information. The bitwise shift operators can also quickly multiply and divide integers. A shift right effectively divides a number by 2 and a shift left multiplies it by 2, as shown in Table 2-7. The following program illustrates the shift operators:

```
/* A bit shift example. */
#include <stdio.h>

int main(void)
{
  unsigned int i;
  int j;

  i = 1;

  /* left shifts */
  for(j=0; j<4; j++) {
    i = i << 1;  /* left shift i by 1, which
                    is same as a multiply by 2 */
    printf("Left shift %d: %d\n", j, i);
  }

  /* right shifts */
  for(j=0; j<4; j++) {
    i = i >> 1;  /* right shift i by 1, which
```

```
                        is same as a division by 2 */
      printf("Right shift %d: %d\n", j, i);
    }

    return 0;
}
```

The one's complement operator, ~, reverses the state of each bit in its operand. That is, all 1's are set to 0, and all 0's are set to 1.

The bitwise operators are often used in cipher routines. If you want to make a disk file appear unreadable, perform some bitwise manipulations on it. One of the simplest methods is to complement each byte by using the one's complement to reverse each bit in the byte, as is shown here:

Original byte	00101100
After 1st complement	11010011
After 2nd complement	00101100

Same

Notice that a sequence of two complements in a row always produces the original number. Hence, the first complement represents the coded version of that byte. The second complement decodes the byte to its original value.

unsigned char x;	x as each statement executes	value of x
x = 7;	00000111	7
x = x<<1;	00001110	14
x = x<<3;	01110000	112
x = x<<2;	11000000	192
x = x>>1;	01100000	96
x = x>>2;	00011000	24

Each left shift multiplies by 2. Notice that information has been lost after x<<2 because a bit was shifted off the end.

Each right shift divides by 2. Notice that subsequent divisions do not bring back any lost bits.

Table 2-7. *Multiplication and Division with Shift Operators*

You could use the **encode( )** function shown here to encode a character.

```
/* A simple cipher function. */
char encode(char ch)
{
  return(~ch); /* complement it */
}
```

Of course, a file encoded using **encode( )** would be very easy to crack!

The ? Operator

C contains a powerful and convenient operator that replaces certain statements of the if-then-else form. The ternary operator **?** takes the general form

   Exp1 ? Exp2 : Exp3;

where *Exp1*, *Exp2*, and *Exp3* are expressions. Notice the use and placement of the colon.

   The **?** operator works like this: *Exp1* is evaluated. If it is true, *Exp2* is evaluated and becomes the value of the expression. If *Exp1* is false, *Exp3* is evaluated, and its value becomes the value of the expression. For example, in

```
x = 10;

y = x>9 ? 100 : 200;
```

y is assigned the value 100. If **x** had been less than 9, **y** would have received the value 200. The same code written using the **if-else** statement is

```
x = 10;

if(x>9) y = 100;
else y = 200;
```

The **?** operator will be discussed more fully in Chapter 3 in relationship to the other conditional statements.

The & and * Pointer Operators

A *pointer* is the memory address of an object. A *pointer variable* is a variable that is specifically declared to hold a pointer to an object of its specified type. Pointers are one of C's most powerful features, and they are used for a wide variety of purposes. For example, they can provide a fast means of referencing array elements. They allow functions to modify their calling parameters. They support linked lists, binary trees, and other dynamic data structures. Chapter 5 is devoted exclusively to pointers. This chapter briefly covers the two operators that are used to manipulate pointers.

The first pointer operator is **&**, a unary operator that returns the memory address of its operand. (Remember, a unary operator requires only one operand.) For example,

```
m = &count;
```

places into **m** the memory address of the variable **count**. This address is the computer's internal location of the variable. It has nothing to do with the value of **count**. You can think of **&** as meaning "the address of." Therefore, the preceding assignment statement means "**m** receives the address of **count**."

To better understand this assignment, assume that the variable **count** is at memory location 2000. Also assume that **count** has a value of 100. Then, after the previous assignment, **m** will have the value 2000.

The second pointer operator is *****, which is the complement of **&**. The ***** is a unary operator that returns the value of the object located at the address that follows it. For example, if **m** contains the memory address of the variable **count**,

```
q = *m;
```

places the value of **count** into **q**. Now **q** has the value 100 because 100 is stored at location 2000, the memory address that was stored in **m**. Think of ***** as meaning "at address." In this case, you could read the statement as "**q** receives the value at address **m**."

Unfortunately, the multiplication symbol and the "at address" symbol are the same, and the symbol for the bitwise AND and the "address of" symbol are the same. These operators have no relationship to each other. Both **&** and ***** have a higher precedence than all other arithmetic operators except the unary minus, with which they share equal precedence.

Variables that will hold pointers must be declared as such, by putting ***** in front of the variable name. This indicates to the compiler that it will hold a pointer to that type of variable. For example, to declare **ch** as a pointer to a character, write

```
char *ch;
```

It is important to understand that **ch** is not a character but a pointer to a character—there is a big difference. The type of data that a pointer points to, in this case **char**, is called the *base type* of the pointer. The pointer variable itself is a variable that holds the address to an object of the base type. Thus, a character pointer (or any type of pointer) is of sufficient size to hold an address as defined by the architecture of the host computer. It is the base type that determines what that address contains.

You can mix both pointer and nonpointer variables in the same declaration statement. For example,

```
int x, *y, count;
```

declares **x** and **count** as integer types and **y** as a pointer to an integer type.

The following program uses * and **&** operators to put the value 10 into a variable called **target**. As expected, this program displays the value 10 on the screen.

```
#include <stdio.h>

int main(void)
{
  int target, source;
  int *m;

  source = 10;
  m = &source;
  target = *m;

  printf("%d", target);

  return 0;
}
```

The Compile-Time Operator sizeof

sizeof is a unary compile-time operator that returns the length, in bytes, of the variable or parenthesized type specifier that it precedes. For example, assuming that integers are 4 bytes and **double**s are 8 bytes, this fragment will display **8 4**.

```
double f;

printf("%d ", sizeof f);
printf("%d", sizeof(int));
```

Remember, to compute the size of a type, you must enclose the type name in parentheses. This is not necessary for variable names, although there is no harm done if you do so.

C defines (using **typedef**) a special type called **size_t**, which corresponds loosely to an unsigned integer. Technically, the value returned by **sizeof** is of type **size_t**. For all practical purposes, however, you can think of it (and use it) as if it were an unsigned integer value.

   sizeof primarily helps to generate portable code that depends upon the size of the built-in data types. For example, imagine a database program that needs to store six integer values per record. If you want to port the database program to a variety of computers, you must not assume the size of an integer, but must determine its actual length using **sizeof**. This being the case, you could use the following routine to write a record to a disk file:

```
/* Write 6 integers to a disk file. */
void put_rec(int rec[6], FILE *fp)
{
  int len;

  len = fwrite(rec, sizeof(int)*6, 1, fp);
  if(len != 1) printf("Write Error");
}
```

Coded as shown, **put_rec( )** compiles and runs correctly in any environment, including those that use 16- and 32-bit integers.

   One final point: **sizeof** is evaluated at compile time, and the value it produces is treated as a constant within your program.

The Comma Operator

The comma operator strings together several expressions. The left side of the comma operator is always evaluated as **void**. This means that the expression on the right side becomes the value of the total comma-separated expression. For example,

```
x = (y=3, y+1);
```

first assigns **y** the value 3 and then assigns **x** the value 4. The parentheses are necessary because the comma operator has a lower precedence than the assignment operator.

   Essentially, the comma causes a sequence of operations. When you use it on the right side of an assignment statement, the value assigned is the value of the last expression of the comma-separated list.

   The comma operator has somewhat the same meaning as the word "and" in English, as used in the phrase "do this and this and this."

The Dot (.) and Arrow (–>) Operators

In C, the . (dot) and the –> (arrow) operators access individual elements of structures and unions. *Structures* and *unions* are compound data types that may be referenced under a single name. (See Chapter 7 for a discussion of structures and unions.)

The dot operator is used when working with a structure or union directly. The arrow operator is used with a pointer to a structure or union. For example, given the fragment,

```
struct employee
{
  char name[80];
  int age;
  float wage;
} emp;

struct employee *p = &emp; /* address of emp into p */
```

you would write the following code to assign the value 123.23 to the **wage** member of structure variable **emp**:

```
emp.wage = 123.23;
```

However, the same assignment using a pointer to **emp** would be

```
p->wage = 123.23;
```

The [ ] and ( ) Operators

Parentheses are operators that increase the precedence of the operations inside them. Square brackets perform array indexing (arrays are discussed fully in Chapter 4). Given an array, the expression within square brackets provides an index into that array. For example,

```
#include <stdio.h>
char s[80];

int main(void)
{
  s[3] = 'X';
  printf("%c", s[3]);

  return 0;
}
```

first assigns the value 'X' to the fourth element (remember, all arrays begin at 0) of array **s**, and then prints that element.

Precedence Summary

Table 2-8 lists the precedence of all operators defined by C. Note that all operators, except the unary operators and **?**, associate from left to right. The unary operators (*, &, –) and **?** associate from right to left.

Expressions

Operators, constants, functions, and variables are the constituents of expressions. An *expression* in C is any valid combination of these elements. Because most expressions tend to follow the general rules of algebra, they are often taken for granted. However, a few aspects of expressions relate specifically to C.

Order of Evaluation

C does not specify the order in which the subexpressions of an expression are evaluated. This leaves the compiler free to rearrange an expression to produce more

Highest	( ) [ ] –> .
	! ~ ++ –– – (type) * & sizeof
	* / %
	+ –
	<< >>
	< <= > >=
	== !=
	&
	^
	|
	&&
	||
	?:
	= += –= *= /= etc.
Lowest	,

Table 2-8.   *Precedence of C Operators*

optimal code. However, it also means that your code should never rely upon the order in which subexpressions are evaluated. For example, the expression

```
x = f1() + f2();
```

does not ensure that **f1( )** will be called before **f2( )**.

Type Conversion in Expressions

When constants and variables of different types are mixed in an expression, they are all converted to the same type. The compiler converts all operands up to the type of the largest operand, which is called *type promotion*. First, all **char** and **short int** values are automatically elevated to **int**. This process is called *integral promotion*. (In C99, an integer promotion may also result in a conversion to **unsigned int**.) Once this step has been completed, all other conversions are done operation by operation, as described in the following type conversion algorithm:

IF an operand is a **long double**
THEN the second is converted to **long double**
ELSE IF an operand is a **double**
THEN the second is converted to **double**
ELSE IF an operand is a **float**
THEN the second is converted to **float**
ELSE IF an operand is an **unsigned long**
THEN the second is converted to **unsigned long**
ELSE IF an operand is **long**
THEN the second is converted to **long**
ELSE IF an operand is **unsigned int**
THEN the second is converted to **unsigned int**

There is one additional special case: If one operand is **long** and the other is **unsigned int**, and if the value of the **unsigned int** cannot be represented by a **long**, both operands are converted to **unsigned long**.

Note   *See Part Two for a description of the C99 integer promotion rules.*

Once these conversion rules have been applied, each pair of operands is of the same type, and the result of each operation is the same as the type of both operands.

For example, consider the type conversions that occur in Figure 2-2. First, the character **ch** is converted to an integer. Then the outcome of **ch/i** is converted to a **double** because **f*d** is **double**. The outcome of **f+i** is **float**, because **f** is a **float**. The final result is **double**.

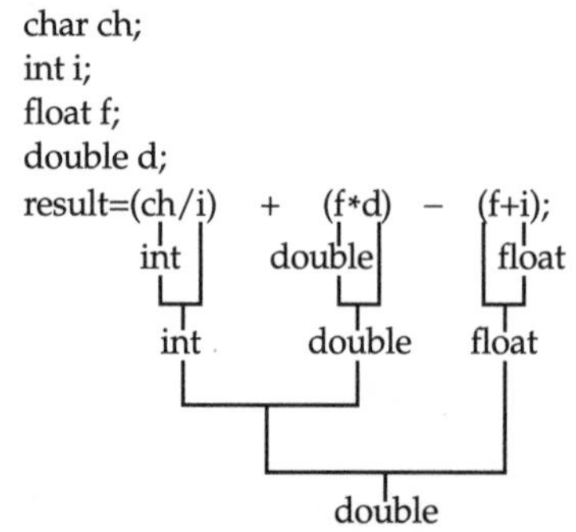

```
                    char ch;
                    int i;
                    float f;
                    double d;
                    result=(ch/i)   +   (f*d)   -   (f+i);
                            int       double       float

                             int     double    float


                                    double
```

Figure 2-2. *A type conversion example*

Casts

You can force an expression to be of a specific type by using a *cast*. The general form of a cast is

(type) expression

where *type* is a valid data type. For example, to cause the expression **x/2** to evaluate to type **float**, write

```
(float) x/2
```

Casts are technically operators. As an operator, a cast is unary and has the same precedence as any other unary operator.

Casts can be very useful. For example, suppose you want to use an integer for loop control, yet to perform computation on it requires a fractional part, as in the following program:

```
#include <stdio.h>

int main(void) /* print i and i/2 with fractions */
{
  int i;

  for(i=1; i<=100; ++i)
    printf("%d / 2 is: %f\n", i, (float) i /2);
```

```
    return 0;
}
```

Without the cast **(float)**, only an integer division would have been performed. The cast ensures that the fractional part of the answer is displayed.

Spacing and Parentheses

You can add tabs and spaces to expressions to make them easier to read. For example, the following two expressions are the same:

```
x=10/y~(127/x);

x = 10 / y ~(127/x);
```

Redundant or additional parentheses do not cause errors or slow down the execution of an expression. You should use parentheses to clarify the exact order of evaluation, both for yourself and for others. For example, which of the following two expressions is easier to read?

```
x = y/3-34*temp+127;

x = (y/3) - (34*temp) + 127;
```

The
Complete
Reference

Chapter 3

Statements

In the most general sense, a *statement* is a part of your program that can be executed. That is, a statement specifies an action. C categorizes statements into these groups:

- Selection
- Iteration
- Jump
- Label
- Expression
- Block

Included in the selection statements are **if** and **switch**. (The term *conditional statement* is often used in place of selection statement.) The iteration statements are **while, for,** and **do-while**. These are also commonly called *loop statements*. The jump statements are **break, continue, goto,** and **return**. The label statements include the **case** and **default** statements (discussed along with the **switch** statement) and the label statement itself (discussed with **goto**). Expression statements are statements composed of a valid expression. Block statements are simply blocks of code. (A block begins with a { and ends with a }.) Block statements are also referred to as *compound statements*.

Since many statements rely upon the outcome of some conditional test, let's begin by reviewing the concepts of true and false.

True and False in C

Many C statements rely upon a conditional expression that determines what course of action is to be taken. A conditional expression evaluates to either a true or false value. In C, true is any nonzero value, including negative numbers. A false value is 0. This approach to true and false allows a wide range of routines to be coded extremely efficiently.

Selection Statements

C supports two selection statements: **if** and **switch**. In addition, the **?** operator is an alternative to **if** in certain circumstances.

if

The general form of the **if** statement is

```
if (expression) statement;
else statement;
```

where a *statement* may consist of a single statement, a block of statements, or nothing (in the case of empty statements). The **else** clause is optional.

If *expression* evaluates to true (anything other than 0), the statement or block that forms the target of **if** is executed; otherwise, the statement or block that is the target of **else** will be executed, if it exists. Remember, only the code associated with **if** or the code associated with **else** executes, never both.

The conditional statement controlling **if** must produce a scalar result. A *scalar* is either an integer, character, pointer, or floating-point type. (In C99, **_Bool** is also a scalar type and may also be used in an **if** expression.) It is rare to use a floating-point number to control a conditional statement because this slows execution time considerably. It takes several instructions to perform a floating-point operation. It takes relatively few instructions to perform an integer or character operation.

The following program contains an example of **if**. The program plays a very simple version of the "guess the magic number" game. It prints the message ** **Right** ** when the player guesses the magic number. It generates the magic number using the standard random number generator **rand( )**, which returns an arbitrary number between 0 and **RAND_MAX** (which defines an integer value that is 32,767 or larger). The **rand( )** function requires the header **<stdlib.h>**.

```c
/* Magic number program #1. */
#include <stdio.h>
#include <stdlib.h>

int main(void)
{
  int magic; /* magic number */
  int guess; /* user's guess */

  magic = rand(); /* generate the magic number */

  printf("Guess the magic number: ");
  scanf("%d", &guess);

  if(guess == magic) printf("** Right **");

  return 0;
}
```

Taking the magic number program further, the next version illustrates the use of the **else** statement to print a message in response to the wrong number.

```c
/* Magic number program #2. */
#include <stdio.h>
#include <stdlib.h>
```

```
int main(void)
{
  int magic; /* magic number */
  int guess; /* user's guess */

  magic = rand(); /* generate the magic number */

  printf("Guess the magic number: ");
  scanf("%d", &guess);

  if(guess == magic) printf("** Right **");
  else printf("Wrong");

  return 0;
}
```

Nested ifs

A nested **if** is an **if** that is the target of another **if** or **else**. Nested **ifs** are very common in programming. In a nested **if**, an **else** statement always refers to the nearest **if** statement that is within the same block as the **else** and that is not already associated with an **else**. For example:

```
if(i)
{
  if(j) dosomething1();
  if(k) dosomething2(); /* this if */
  else  dosomething3(); /* is associated with this else */
}
else dosomething4(); /* associated with if(i) */
```

As noted, the final **else** is not associated with **if(j)** because it is not in the same block. Rather, the final **else** is associated with **if(i)**. Also, the inner **else** is associated with **if(k)**, which is the nearest **if**.

C89 specifies that at least 15 levels of nesting must be supported by the compiler. C99 raises this limit to 127. In practice, most compilers allow substantially more levels. However, nesting beyond a few levels is seldom necessary, and excessive nesting can quickly confuse the meaning of an algorithm.

You can use a nested **if** to further improve the magic number program by providing the player with feedback about a wrong guess.

```
/* Magic number program #3. */
#include <stdio.h>
#include <stdlib.h>

int main(void)
{
  int magic; /* magic number */
  int guess; /* user's guess */

  magic = rand(); /* get a random number */

  printf("Guess the magic number: ");
  scanf("%d", &guess);

  if (guess == magic) {
    printf("** Right **");
    printf(" %d is the magic number\n", magic);
  }
  else {
    printf("Wrong, ");
    if(guess > magic) printf("too high\n"); /* nested if */
    else printf("too low\n");
  }

  return 0;
}
```

The if-else-if Ladder

A common programming construct is the *if-else-if ladder,* sometimes called the *if-else-if staircase* because of its appearance. Its general form is

> if (*expression*) *statement;*
> else
>   if (*expression*) *statement;*
>   else
>   if (*expression*) *statement;*
>   .
>   .
>   .
>   else *statement;*

The conditions are evaluated from the top downward. As soon as a true condition is found, the statement associated with it is executed and the rest of the ladder is bypassed. If none of the conditions are true, the final **else** is executed. That is, if all other conditional tests fail, the last **else** statement is performed. If the final **else** is not present, no action takes place if all other conditions are false.

Although the indentation of the preceding if-else-if ladder is technically correct, it can lead to overly deep indentation. For this reason, the if-else-if ladder is usually indented like this:

if (*expression*)
  statement;
else if(*expression*)
  statement;
else if(*expression*)
  statement;
 .
 .
 .
else
  statement;

Using an if-else-if ladder, the magic number program becomes

```
/* Magic number program #4. */
#include <stdio.h>
#include <stdlib.h>

int main(void)
{
  int magic; /* magic number */
  int guess; /* user's guess */

  magic = rand(); /* generate the magic number */

  printf("Guess the magic number: ");
  scanf("%d", &guess);

  if(guess == magic) {
    printf("** Right ** ");
    printf("%d is the magic number", magic);
  }
  else if(guess > magic)
    printf("Wrong, too high");
```

```
    else printf("Wrong, too low");

    return 0;
}
```

The ? Alternative

You can use the **?** operator to replace **if-else** statements of the general form:

> if(*condition*) *var = expression*;
> else *var = expression*;

The **?** is called a *ternary operator* because it requires three operands. It takes the general form

> *Exp1 ? Exp2 : Exp3*

where *Exp1*, *Exp2*, and *Exp3* are expressions. Notice the use and placement of the colon.

The value of a **?** expression is determined as follows: *Exp1* is evaluated. If it is true, *Exp2* is evaluated and becomes the value of the entire **?** expression. If *Exp1* is false, then *Exp3* is evaluated and its value becomes the value of the expression. For example, consider

```
x = 10;
y = x>9 ? 100 : 200;
```

In this example, **y** is assigned the value 100. If **x** had been less than 9, **y** would have received the value 200. The same code written with the **if-else** statement would be

```
x = 10;
if(x>9) y = 100;
else y = 200;
```

The following program uses the **?** operator to square an integer value entered by the user. However, this program preserves the sign (10 squared is 100 and –10 squared is –100).

```
#include <stdio.h>

int main(void)
{
  int isqrd, i;
```

```
   printf("Enter a number: ");
   scanf("%d", &i);

   isqrd = i>0 ? i*i : -(i*i);

   printf("%d squared is %d", i, isqrd);

   return 0;
}
```

The use of the **?** operator to replace **if-else** statements is not restricted to assignments only. Remember, all functions (except those declared as **void**) return a value. Thus, you can use one or more function calls in a **?** expression. When the function's name is encountered, the function is executed so that its return value can be determined. Therefore, you can execute one or more function calls using the **?** operator by placing the calls in the expressions that form the **?**'s operands. Here is an example:

```
#include <stdio.h>

int f1(int n);
int f2(void);

int main(void)
{
  int t;

  printf("Enter a number: ");
  scanf("%d", &t);

  /* print proper message */
  t ? f1(t) + f2() : printf("zero entered.");
  printf("\n");

  return 0;
}

int f1(int n)
{
  printf("%d ", n);
  return 0;
}
```

```
int f2(void)
{
  printf("entered ");
  return 0;
}
```

The program first prompts the user for a value. Entering 0 causes the **printf( )** function to be called, which displays the message **zero entered**. If you enter any other number, both **f1( )** and **f2( )** execute. Note that the value of the **?** expression is discarded in this example. You don't need to assign it to anything.

One other point: It is permissible for a compiler to rearrange the order of evaluation of an expression in an attempt to optimize the object code. In the preceding example, this could cause the calls to the **f1( )** and **f2( )** functions in the **?** expression to execute in an unexpected sequence.

Using the **?** operator, you can rewrite the magic number program yet again.

```
/* Magic number program #5. */
#include <stdio.h>
#include <stdlib.h>

int main(void)
{
  int magic;
  int guess;

  magic = rand(); /* generate the magic number */

  printf("Guess the magic number: ");
  scanf("%d", &guess);

  if(guess == magic) {
    printf("** Right ** ");
    printf("%d is the magic number", magic);
  }
  else
    guess > magic ? printf("High") : printf("Low");

  return 0;
}
```

Here, the **?** operator displays the proper message based on the outcome of the test **guess > magic**.

The Conditional Expression

Sometimes newcomers to C are confused by the fact that you can use any valid expression to control the **if** or the **?** operator. That is, you are not restricted to expressions involving the relational and logical operators (as is the case in languages like BASIC or Pascal). The expression must simply evaluate to either a true or false (zero or nonzero) value. For example, the following program reads two integers from the keyboard and displays the quotient. It uses an **if** statement, controlled by the second number, to avoid a divide-by-zero error.

```
/* Divide the first number by the second. */

#include <stdio.h>

int main(void)
{
  int a, b;

  printf("Enter two numbers: ");
  scanf("%d%d", &a, &b);

  if(b) printf("%d\n", a/b);
  else printf("Cannot divide by zero.\n");

  return 0;
}
```

This approach works because if **b** is 0, the condition controlling the **if** is false, and the **else** executes. Otherwise, the condition is true (nonzero), and the division takes place.

One other point: Writing the **if** statement in the preceding example as shown here

```
if(b != 0) printf("%d\n", a/b);
```

is redundant, potentially inefficient, and is considered bad style. Since the value of **b** alone is sufficient to control the **if**, there is no need to test it against 0.

switch

C has a built-in multiple-branch selection statement, called **switch**, which successively tests the value of an expression against a list of integer or character constants. When a match is found, the statements associated with that constant are executed. The general form of the **switch** statement is

```
switch (expression) {
  case constant1:
    statement sequence
    break;
  case constant2:
    statement sequence
    break;
  case constant3:
    statement sequence
    break;
    .
    .
    .
  default
    statement sequence
}
```

The *expression* must evaluate to an integer type. Thus, you can use character or integer values, but floating-point expressions, for example, are not allowed. The value of *expression* is tested against the values, one after another, of the constants specified in the **case** statements. When a match is found, the statement sequence associated with that **case** is executed until the **break** statement or the end of the **switch** statement is reached. The **default** statement is executed if no matches are found. The **default** is optional, and if it is not present, no action takes place if all matches fail.

C89 specifies that a **switch** can have at least 257 **case** statements. C99 requires that at least 1,023 **case** statements be supported. In practice, you will usually want to limit the number of **case** statements to a smaller amount for efficiency. Although **case** is a label statement, it cannot exist by itself, outside of a **switch**.

The **break** statement is one of C's jump statements. You can use it in loops as well as in the **switch** statement (see the section "Iteration Statements"). When **break** is encountered in a **switch**, program execution "jumps" to the line of code following the **switch** statement.

There are three important things to know about the **switch** statement:

- The **switch** differs from the **if** in that **switch** can only test for equality, whereas **if** can evaluate any type of relational or logical expression.

- No two **case** constants in the same **switch** can have identical values. Of course, a **switch** statement enclosed by an outer **switch** may have **case** constants that are in common.

- If character constants are used in the **switch** statement, they are automatically converted to integers (as is specified by C's type conversion rules).

The **switch** statement is often used to process keyboard commands, such as menu selection. As shown here, the function **menu( )** displays a menu for a spelling-checker program and calls the proper procedures:

```
void menu(void)
{
  char ch;

  printf("1. Check Spelling\n");
  printf("2. Correct Spelling Errors\n");
  printf("3. Display Spelling Errors\n");
  printf("Strike Any Other Key to Skip\n");
  printf("       Enter your choice: ");

  ch = getchar(); /* read the selection from the keyboard */

  switch(ch) {
    case '1':
      check_spelling();
      break;
    case '2':
      correct_errors();
      break;
    case '3':
      display_errors();
      break;
    default :
      printf("No option selected");
  }
}
```

Technically, the **break** statements inside the **switch** statement are optional. They terminate the statement sequence associated with each constant. If the **break** statement is omitted, execution will continue on into the next **case**'s statements until either a **break** or the end of the **switch** is reached. For example, the following function uses the "drop through" nature of the **case**s to simplify the code for a device-driver input handler:

```
/* Process a value */
void inp_handler(int i)
{
  int flag;
```

```
    flag = -1;

    switch(i) {
      case 1:   /* These cases have common */
      case 2:   /* statement sequences. */
      case 3 :
        flag = 0;
        break;
      case 4:
        flag = 1;
      case 5:
        error(flag);
        break;
      default:
        process(i);
    }
}
```

This example illustrates two aspects of **switch**. First, you can have **case** statements that have no statement sequence associated with them. When this occurs, execution simply drops through to the next **case**. In this example, the first three **case**s all execute the same statements, which are

```
flag = 0;
break;
```

Second, execution of one statement sequence continues into the next **case** if no **break** statement is present. If **i** matches 4, **flag** is set to 1, and because there is no **break** statement at the end of that **case**, execution continues and the call to **error(flag)** is executed. If **i** had matched 5, **error(flag)** would have been called with a flag value of –1 (rather than 1).

The fact that **case**s can run together when no **break** is present prevents the unnecessary duplication of statements, resulting in more efficient code.

Nested switch Statements

You can have a **switch** as part of the statement sequence of an outer **switch**. Even if the **case** constants of the inner and outer **switch** contain common values, no conflicts arise. For example, the following code fragment is perfectly acceptable:

```
switch(x) {
  case 1:
```

```
    switch(y) {
      case 0: printf("Divide by zero error.\n");
              break;
      case 1: process(x, y);
              break;
    }
    break;
  case 2:
      .
      .
      .
```

Iteration Statements

In C, and all other modern programming languages, iteration statements (also called loops) allow a set of instructions to be repeatedly executed until a certain condition is reached. This condition may be predetermined (as in the **for** loop) or open ended (as in the **while** and **do-while** loops).

The for Loop

The general design of the **for** loop is reflected in some form or another in all procedural programming languages. However, in C, it provides unexpected flexibility and power.

The general form of the **for** statement is

for(*initialization; condition; increment*) *statement*;

The **for** loop allows many variations, but its most common form works like this: The *initialization* is an assignment statement that is used to set the loop control variable. The *condition* is a relational expression that determines when the loop exits. The *increment* defines how the loop control variable changes each time the loop is repeated. You must separate these three major sections by semicolons. The **for** loop continues to execute as long as the condition is true. Once the condition becomes false, program execution resumes on the statement following the **for**.

In the following program, a **for** loop is used to print the numbers 1 through 100 on the screen:

```
#include <stdio.h>

int main(void)
{
  int x;
```

```
    for(x=1; x <= 100; x++) printf("%d ", x);

    return 0;
}
```

In the loop, **x** is initially set to 1 and then compared with 100. Since **x** is less than 100, **printf( )** is called and the loop iterates. This causes **x** to be increased by 1 and again tested to see if it is still less than or equal to 100. If it is, **printf( )** is called. This process repeats until **x** is greater than 100, at which point the loop terminates. In this example, **x** is the loop control variable, which is changed and checked each time the loop repeats.

The following example is a **for** loop that iterates a block of statements:

```
for(x=100; x != 65; x -= 5) {
  z = x*x;
  printf("The square of %d, %d", x, z);
}
```

Both the squaring of **x** and the call to **printf( )** are executed until **x** equals 65. Note that the loop is *negative running*: **x** is initialized to 100, and 5 is subtracted from it each time the loop repeats.

In **for** loops, the conditional test is always performed at the top of the loop. This means that the code inside the loop may not be executed at all if the condition is false to begin with. For example, in

```
x = 10;
for(y=10; y != x; ++y) printf("%d", y);
printf("%d", y);  /* this is the only printf()
                     statement that will execute */
```

the loop will never execute because **x** and **y** are equal when the loop is entered. Because this causes the conditional expression to evaluate to false, neither the body of the loop nor the increment portion of the loop executes. Thus, **y** still has the value 10, and the only output produced by the fragment is the number 10 printed once on the screen.

for Loop Variations

The previous discussion described the most common form of the **for** loop. However, several variations of the **for** are allowed that increase its power, flexibility, and applicability to certain programming situations.

One of the most common variations uses the comma operator to allow two or more variables to control the loop. (Remember, the comma operator strings together a number of expressions in a "do this and this" fashion. See Chapter 2.) For example, the variables **x** and **y** control the following loop, and both are initialized inside the **for** statement:

```
for(x=0, y=0; x+y < 10; ++x) {
  y = getchar();
  y = y - '0'; /* subtract the ASCII code for 0 from y */
    .
    .
    .
}
```

Commas separate the two initialization statements. Each time the loop repeats, **x** is incremented and **y**'s value is set by keyboard input. Both **x** and **y** must be at the correct value for the loop to terminate. Even though **y**'s value is set by keyboard input, **y** must be initialized to 0 so that its value is defined before the first evaluation of the conditional expression. (If **y**'s value was not set, it could by chance contain the value 10, making the conditional test false and preventing the loop from executing.)

The **converge( )** function shown next demonstrates multiple loop control variables in action. The **converge( )** function copies the contents of one string into another by moving characters from both ends, converging in the middle.

```
/* Demonstrate multiple loop control variables. */
#include <stdio.h>
#include <string.h>

void converge(char *targ, char *src);

int main(void)
{
  char target[80] = "XXXXXXXXXXXXXXXXXXXXXXXXXXXXXX";

  converge(target, "This is a test of converge().");
  printf("Final string: %s\n", target);

  return 0;
}

/* This function copies one string into another.
   It copies characters to both the ends,
   converging at the middle. */
void converge(char *targ, char *src)
{
```

```
  int i, j;

  printf("%s\n", targ);
  for(i=0, j=strlen(src); i<=j; i++, j--) {
    targ[i] = src[i];
    targ[j] = src[j];
    printf("%s\n", targ);
  }
}
```

Here is the output produced by the program:

```
XXXXXXXXXXXXXXXXXXXXXXXXXXXXXX
TXXXXXXXXXXXXXXXXXXXXXXXXXXXXX
ThXXXXXXXXXXXXXXXXXXXXXXXXXXX.
ThiXXXXXXXXXXXXXXXXXXXXXXXX).
ThisXXXXXXXXXXXXXXXXXXXXXX().
This XXXXXXXXXXXXXXXXXXXXe().
This iXXXXXXXXXXXXXXXXXXge().
This isXXXXXXXXXXXXXXXXrge().
This is XXXXXXXXXXXXXXerge().
This is aXXXXXXXXXXXXverge().
This is a XXXXXXXXXXnverge().
This is a tXXXXXXXXonverge().
This is a teXXXXXXconverge().
This is a tesXXXX converge().
This is a testXXf converge().
This is a test of converge().
Final string: This is a test of converge().
```

In **converge( )**, the **for** loop uses two loop control variables, **i** and **j**, to index the string from opposite ends. As the loop iterates, **i** is increased and **j** is decreased. The loop stops when **i** is greater than **j**, thus ensuring that all characters are copied.

The conditional expression does not have to involve testing the loop control variable against some target value. In fact, the condition may be any relational or logical statement. This means that you can test for several possible terminating conditions. For example, you could use the following function to log a user onto a remote system. The user has three tries to enter the password. The loop terminates when the three tries are used up, or when the user enters the correct password.

```
void sign_on(void)
{
```

```
    char str[20];
    int x;

    for(x=0; x<3 && strcmp(str, "password"); ++x) {
      printf("Enter password please:");
      gets(str);
    }

    if(x == 3) return;
    /* else log user in ... */
}
```

This function uses **strcmp( )**, the standard library function that compares two strings and returns 0 if they match.

Remember, each of the three sections of the **for** loop may consist of any valid expression. The expressions need not actually have anything to do with what the sections are generally used for. With this in mind, consider the following example:

```
#include <stdio.h>

int sqrnum(int num);
int readnum(void);
int prompt(void);

int main(void)
{
  int t;

  for(prompt(); t=readnum(); prompt())
    sqrnum(t);

  return 0;
}

int prompt(void)
{
  printf("Enter a number: ");
  return 0;
}

int readnum(void)
```

```
{
  int t;

  scanf("%d", &t);
  return t;
}

int sqrnum(int num)
{
  printf("%d\n", num*num);
  return num*num;
}
```

Look closely at the **for** loop in **main( )**. Notice that each part of the **for** loop is composed of function calls that prompt the user and read a number entered from the keyboard. If the number entered is 0, the loop terminates because the conditional expression will be false. Otherwise, the number is squared. Thus, this **for** loop uses the initialization and increment portions in a nontraditional but completely valid manner.

Another interesting trait of the **for** loop is that pieces of the loop definition need not be there. In fact, there need not be an expression present for any of the sections—the expressions are optional. For example, this loop will run until the user enters **123**:

```
for(x=0; x != 123; ) scanf("%d", &x);
```

Notice that the increment portion of the **for** definition is blank. This means that each time the loop repeats, **x** is tested to see if it equals 123, but no further action takes place. If you type **123** at the keyboard, however, the loop condition becomes false and the loop terminates.

The initialization of the loop control variable can occur outside the **for** statement. This most frequently happens when the initial condition of the loop control variable must be computed by some complicated means, as in this example:

```
gets(s);  /* read a string into s */
if(*s) x = strlen(s); /* get the string's length */
else x = 10;

for( ; x < 10; ) {
  printf("%d", x);
  ++x;
}
```

The initialization section has been left blank, and **x** is initialized before the loop is entered.

The Infinite Loop

Although you can use any loop statement to create an infinite loop, **for** is traditionally used for this purpose. Since none of the three expressions that form the **for** loop are required, you can make an endless loop by leaving the conditional expression empty, as here:

```
for( ; ; ) printf("This loop will run forever.\n");
```

When the conditional expression is absent, it is assumed to be true. You may have an initialization and increment expression, but C programmers more commonly use the **for(;;)** construct to signify an infinite loop.

Actually, the **for(;;)** construct does not guarantee an infinite loop because a **break** statement, encountered anywhere inside the body of a loop, causes immediate termination. (**break** is discussed in detail later in this chapter.) Program control then resumes at the code following the loop, as shown here:

```
ch = '\0';

for( ; ; ) {
  ch = getchar(); /* get a character */
  if(ch == 'A') break; /* exit the loop */
}

printf("you typed an A");
```

This loop will run until the user types an **A** at the keyboard.

for Loops with No Bodies

A statement may be empty. This means that the body of the **for** loop (or any other loop) may also be empty. You can use this fact to simplify the coding of certain algorithms and to create time delay loops.

Removing spaces from an input stream is a common programming task. For example, a database program may allow a query such as "show all balances less than 400." The database needs to have each word fed to it separately, without leading spaces. That is, the database input processor recognizes "**show**" but not " **show**". The following loop shows one way to accomplish this. It advances past leading spaces in the string pointed to by **str**.

```
for( ; *str == ' '; str++) ;
```

As you can see, this loop has no body—and no need for one either.

Time delay loops are sometimes useful. The following code shows how to create one by using **for**:

```
for(t=0; t < SOME_VALUE; t++) ;
```

The only purpose of this loop is to eat up time. Be aware, however, that some compilers will optimize such a time delay loop out of existence, since (as far as the compiler is concerned) it has no effect! So, you might not always get the time delay you expect.

Declaring Variables Within a for Loop

In C99 and C++, but not C89, it is possible to declare a variable within the initialization portion of a **for** loop. A variable so declared has its scope limited to the block of code controlled by that statement. That is, a variable declared within a **for** loop will be local to that loop.

Here is an example that declares a variable within the initialization portion of a **for** loop:

```
/*
    Here, i is local to for loop; j is known outside loop.

    *** This example is invalid for C89. ***
*/
int j;
for(int i = 0; i<10; i++)
  j = i * i;

/* i = 10;  *** Error *** -- i not known here! */
```

Here, **i** is declared within the initialization portion of the **for** and is used to control the loop. Outside the loop, **i** is unknown.

Since a loop control variable is often needed only by that loop, the declaration of a variable in the initialization portion of the **for** is becoming common practice. Remember, however, that this is not supported by C89.

The while Loop

The second loop available in C is the **while** loop. Its general form is

while(*condition*) *statement*;

where *statement* is either an empty statement, a single statement, or a block of statements. The *condition* may be any expression, and true is any nonzero value. The loop iterates while the condition is true. When the condition becomes false, program control passes to the line of code immediately following the loop.

The following example shows a keyboard input routine that simply loops until the user types **A**:

```
char wait_for_char(void)
{
  char ch;

  ch = '\0';  /* initialize ch */
  while(ch != 'A') ch = getchar();
  return ch;
}
```

First, **ch** is initialized to null. As a local variable, its value is not known when **wait_for_char( )** is executed. The **while** loop then checks to see if **ch** is not equal to **A**. Because **ch** was initialized to null, the test is true and the loop begins. Each time you press a key, the condition is tested again. Once you enter an **A**, the condition becomes false because **ch** equals **A**, and the loop terminates.

Like **for** loops, **while** loops check the test condition at the top of the loop, which means that the body of the loop will not execute if the condition is false to begin with. This feature may eliminate the need to perform a separate conditional test before the loop. The **pad( )** function provides a good illustration of this. It adds spaces to the end of a string to fill the string to a predefined length. If the string is already at the desired length, no spaces are added.

```
#include <stdio.h>
#include <string.h>

void pad(char *s, int length);

int main(void)
{
  char str[80];

  strcpy(str, "this is a test");
  pad(str, 40);
  printf("%d", strlen(str));

  return 0;
```

```
}

/* Add spaces to the end of a string. */
void pad(char *s, int length)
{
  int l;

  l = strlen(s); /* find out how long it is */

  while(l < length) {
    s[l] = ' '; /* insert a space */
    l++;
  }
  s[l]= '\0'; /* strings need to be terminated in a null */
}
```

The two arguments of **pad( )** are **s**, a pointer to the string to lengthen, and **length**, the number of characters that **s** should have. If the length of string **s** is already equal to or greater than **length**, the code inside the **while** loop does not execute. If **s** is shorter than **length**, **pad( )** adds the required number of spaces. The **strlen( )** function, part of the standard library, returns the length of the string.

In cases in which any one of several separate conditions can terminate a **while** loop, often a single loop-control variable forms the conditional expression. The value of this variable is set at various points throughout the loop. In this example

```
void func1(void)
{
  int working;

  working = 1; /* i.e., true */

  while(working) {
    working = process1();
    if(working)
      working = process2();
    if(working)
      working = process3();
  }
}
```

any of the three routines may return false and cause the loop to exit.

There need not be any statements in the body of the **while** loop. For example,

```
while((ch=getchar()) != 'A') ;
```

will simply loop until the user types **A**. If you feel uncomfortable putting the assignment inside the **while** conditional expression, remember that the equal sign is just an operator that evaluates to the value of the right-hand operand.

The do-while Loop

Unlike **for** and **while** loops, which test the loop condition at the top of the loop, the **do-while** loop checks its condition at the bottom of the loop. This means that a **do-while** loop always executes at least once. The general form of the **do-while** loop is

do {
   statement;
} while(*condition*);

Although the curly braces are not necessary when only one statement is present, they are usually used to avoid confusion (to you, not the compiler) with the **while**. The **do-while** loop iterates until *condition* becomes false.

The following **do-while** loop will read numbers from the keyboard until it finds a number less than or equal to 100:

```
do {
  scanf("%d", &num);
} while(num > 100);
```

Perhaps the most common use of the **do-while** loop is in a menu selection function. When the user enters a valid response, it is returned as the value of the function. Invalid responses cause a reprompt. The following code shows an improved version of the spelling-checker menu shown earlier in this chapter:

```
void menu(void)
{
  char ch;

  printf("1. Check Spelling\n");
  printf("2. Correct Spelling Errors\n");
  printf("3. Display Spelling Errors\n");
  printf("     Enter your choice: ");
```

```
do {
  ch = getchar(); /* read the selection from
                      the keyboard */
  switch(ch) {
    case '1':
      check_spelling();
      break;
    case '2':
      correct_errors();
      break;
    case '3':
      display_errors();
      break;
  }
} while(ch!='1' && ch!='2' && ch!='3');
}
```

Here, the **do-while** loop is a good choice because you will always want a menu
function to execute at least once. After the options have been displayed, the program
will loop until a valid option is selected.

Jump Statements

C has four statements that perform an unconditional branch: **return**, **goto**, **break**, and
continue. Of these, you can use **return** and **goto** anywhere inside a function. You can
use the **break** and **continue** statements in conjunction with any of the loop statements.
As discussed earlier in this chapter, you can also use **break** with **switch**.

The return Statement

The **return** statement is used to return from a function. It is categorized as a jump
statement because it causes execution to return (jump back) to the point at which the
call to the function was made. A **return** may or may not have a value associated with it.
A **return** with a value can be used only in a function with a non-**void** return type. In
this case, the value associated with **return** becomes the return value of the function. A
return without a value is used to return from a **void** function.

Technically, in C89, a **return** statement in a non-**void** function does not have to
return a value. If no return value is specified, a garbage value is returned. However, in
C99, a **return** statement in a non-**void** function *must* return a value. (This is also true for
C++.) Of course, even for C89, if a function is declared as returning a value, it is good
practice to actually return one!

The general form of the **return** statement is

return *expression*;

The *expression* is present only if the function is declared as returning a value. In this case, the value of *expression* will become the return value of the function.

You can use as many **return** statements as you like within a function. However, the function will stop executing as soon as it encounters the first **return**. The } that ends a function also causes the function to return. It is the same as a **return** without any specified value. If this occurs within a non-**void** function, then the return value of the function is undefined.

A function declared as **void** cannot contain a **return** statement that specifies a value. Since a **void** function has no return value, it makes sense that no **return** statement within a **void** function can return a value.

See Chapter 6 for more information on **return**.

The goto Statement

Since C has a rich set of control structures and allows additional control using **break** and **continue**, there is little need for **goto**. Most programmers' chief concern about the **goto** is its tendency to render programs unreadable. Nevertheless, although the **goto** statement fell out of favor some years ago, it occasionally has it uses. While there are no programming situations that require **goto**, it is a convenience, which, if used wisely, can be a benefit in a narrow set of programming situations, such as jumping out of a set of deeply nested loops. The **goto** is not used in this book outside of this section.

The **goto** statement requires a label for operation. (A *label* is a valid identifier followed by a colon.) Furthermore, the label must be in the same function as the **goto** that uses it—you cannot jump between functions. The general form of the **goto** statement is

goto *label*;
.
.
.
label:

where *label* is any valid label either before or after **goto**. For example, you could create a loop from 1 to 100 using the **goto** and a label, as shown here:

```
x = 1;
loop1:
  x++;
  if(x <= 100) goto loop1;
```

The break Statement

The **break** statement has two uses. You can use it to terminate a **case** in the **switch** statement (covered in the section on **switch** earlier in this chapter). You can also use it to force immediate termination of a loop, bypassing the normal loop conditional test.

When the **break** statement is encountered inside a loop, the loop is immediately terminated, and program control resumes at the next statement following the loop. For example,

```
#include <stdio.h>

int main(void)
{
  int t;

  for(t=0; t < 100; t++) {
    printf("%d ", t);
    if(t == 10) break;
  }

  return 0;
}
```

prints the numbers 0 through 10 on the screen. Then the loop terminates because **break** causes immediate exit from the loop, overriding the conditional test **t<100**.

Programmers often use the **break** statement in loops in which a special condition can cause immediate termination. For example, here a keypress can stop the execution of the **look_up( )** function:

```
void look_up(char *name)
{
  do {
    /* look up names ... */
    if(kbhit()) break;
  } while(!found);
  /* process match */
}
```

The **kbhit( )** function returns 0 if you do not press a key. Otherwise, it returns a nonzero value. Because of the wide differences between computing environments, Standard C does not define **kbhit( )**, but you will almost certainly have it (or one with a slightly different name) supplied with your compiler.

A **break** causes an exit from only the innermost loop. For example,

```
for(t=0; t < 100; ++t) {
  count = 1;
  for(;;) {
    printf("%d ", count);
    count++;
    if(count == 10) break;
  }
}
```

prints the numbers 1 through 9 on the screen 100 times. Each time the compiler encounters **break**, control is passed back to the outer **for** loop.

A **break** used in a **switch** statement will affect only that **switch**. It does not affect any loop the **switch** happens to be in.

The exit( ) Function

Although **exit( )** is not a program control statement, a short digression that discusses it is in order at this time. Just as you can break out of a loop, you can break out of a program by using the standard library function **exit( )**. This function causes immediate termination of the entire program, forcing a return to the operating system. In effect, the **exit( )** function acts as if it were breaking out of the entire program.

The general form of the **exit( )** function is

void exit(int *return_code*);

The value of *return_code* is returned to the calling process, which is usually the operating system. Zero is commonly used as a return code to indicate normal program termination. Other arguments are used to indicate some sort of error. You can also use the macros **EXIT_SUCCESS** and **EXIT_FAILURE** for *return_code*. The **exit( )** function requires the header **<stdlib.h>**.

Programmers frequently use **exit( )** when a mandatory condition for program execution is not satisfied. For example, imagine a virtual-reality computer game that requires a special graphics adapter. The **main( )** function of this game might look like this,

```
#include <stdlib.h>

int main(void)
{
    if(!virtual_graphics()) exit(1);
    play();
```

```
   /* ... */
}
/* .... */
```

where **virtual_graphics( )** is some function that returns true if the virtual-reality
graphics adapter is present. If the adapter is not in the system, **virtual_graphics( )**
returns false and the program terminates.

As another example, this version of **menu( )** uses **exit( )** to quit the program and
return to the operating system:

```
void menu(void)
{
  char ch;

  printf("1. Check Spelling\n");
  printf("2. Correct Spelling Errors\n");
  printf("3. Display Spelling Errors\n");
  printf("4. Quit\n");
  printf("    Enter your choice: ");

  do {
    ch = getchar(); /* read the selection from
                        the keyboard */
      switch(ch) {
        case '1':
          check_spelling();
          break;
        case '2':
          correct_errors();
          break;
        case '3':
          display_errors();
          break;
        case '4':
          exit(0); /* return to OS */
      }
    } while(ch!='1' && ch!='2' && ch!='3');
}
```

The continue Statement

The **continue** statement works somewhat like the **break** statement. Instead of forcing
termination, however, **continue** forces the next iteration of the loop to take place,

skipping any code in between. For the **for** loop, **continue** causes the increment and then the conditional test portions of the loop to execute. For the **while** and **do-while** loops, program control passes to the conditional tests. For example, the following program counts the number of spaces contained in the string entered by the user:

```c
/* Count spaces */
#include <stdio.h>

int main(void)
{
  char s[80], *str;
  int space;

  printf("Enter a string: ");
  gets(s);
  str = s;

  for(space=0; *str; str++) {
    if(*str != ' ') continue;
    space++;
  }
  printf("%d spaces\n", space);

  return 0;
}
```

Each character is tested to see if it is a space. If it is not, the **continue** statement forces the **for** to iterate again. If the character is a space, **space** is incremented.

The following example shows how you can use **continue** to expedite the exit from a loop by forcing the conditional test to be performed sooner:

```c
void code(void)
{
  char done, ch;

  done = 0;
  while(!done) {
    ch = getchar();
    if(ch == '$') {
      done = 1;
      continue;
    }
```

FOUNDATIONAL C

```
    putchar(ch+1); /* shift the alphabet one position higher */
  }
}
```

This function codes a message by shifting all characters you type one letter higher. For example, an A becomes a B. The function will terminate when you type a $. After a $ has been input, no further output will occur because the conditional test, brought into effect by **continue**, will find **done** to be true and will cause the loop to exit.

Expression Statements

Chapter 2 covers expressions thoroughly. However, a few special points are mentioned here. Remember, an expression statement is simply a valid expression followed by a semicolon, as in

```
func();  /* a function call */
a = b+c; /* an assignment statement */
b+f();   /* a valid, but strange statement */
;        /* an empty statement */
```

The first expression statement executes a function call. The second is an assignment. The third expression, though strange, is still evaluated by the compiler because the function **f( )** may perform some necessary task. The final example shows that a statement can be empty (sometimes called a *null statement*).

Block Statements

Block statements are simply groups of related statements that are treated as a unit. The statements that make up a block are logically bound together. Block statements are also called *compound statements*. A block is begun with a { and terminated by its matching }. Programmers use block statements most commonly to create a multistatement target for some other statement, such as **if**. However, you may place a block statement anywhere you would put any other statement. For example, this is perfectly valid (although unusual) C code:

```
#include <stdio.h>

int main(void)
{
```

```
  int i;

  {  /* a free-standing block statement */
     i = 120;
     printf("%d", i);
  }

  return 0;
}
```

The Complete Reference

Chapter 4

Arrays and Strings

n *array* is a collection of variables of the same type that are referred to through a common name. A specific element in an array is accessed by an index. In C, all arrays consist of contiguous memory locations. The lowest address corresponds to the first element and the highest address to the last element. Arrays can have from one to several dimensions. The most common array is the *string*, which is simply an array of characters terminated by a null.

Arrays and pointers are closely related; a discussion of one usually refers to the other. This chapter focuses on arrays, while Chapter 5 looks closely at pointers. You should read both to understand fully these important constructs.

Single-Dimension Arrays

The general form for declaring a single-dimension array is

type var_name[*size*];

Like other variables, arrays must be explicitly declared so that the compiler can allocate space for them in memory. Here, *type* declares the base type of the array, which is the type of each element in the array, and *size* defines how many elements the array will hold. For example, to declare a 100-element array called **balance** of type **double**, use this statement:

```
double balance[100];
```

In C89, the size of an array must be specified using a constant expression. Thus, in C89, the size of an array is fixed at compile time. (C99 allows arrays whose sizes are determined at run time. They are briefly described later in this chapter and examined in detail in Part Two.)

An element is accessed by indexing the array name. This is done by placing the index of the element within square brackets after the name of the array. For example,

```
balance[3] = 12.23;
```

assigns element number 3 in **balance** the value 12.23.

In C, all arrays have 0 as the index of their first element. Therefore, when you write

```
char p[10];
```

you are declaring a character array that has 10 elements, **p[0]** through **p[9]**. For example, the following program loads an integer array with the numbers 0 through 99:

```
#include <stdio.h>

int main(void)
{
  int x[100]; /* this declares a 100-integer array */
  int t;

  /* load x with values 0 through 99 */
  for(t=0; t<100; ++t) x[t] = t;

  /* display contents of x */
  for(t=0; t<100; ++t) printf("%d ", x[t]);

  return 0;
}
```

The amount of storage required to hold an array is directly related to its type and size. For a single-dimension array, the total size in bytes is computed as shown here:

total bytes = sizeof(base type) × length of array

C has no bounds checking on arrays. You could overwrite either end of an array and write into some other variable's data or even into the program's code. As the programmer, it is your job to provide bounds checking where needed. For example, this code will compile without error, but it is incorrect because the **for** loop will cause the array **count** to be overrun.

```
int count[10], i;

/* this causes count to be overrun */
for(i=0; i<100; i++) count[i] = i;
```

Single-dimension arrays are essentially lists that are stored in contiguous memory locations in index order. For example, Figure 4-1 shows how array **a** appears in memory if it starts at memory location 1000 and is declared as shown here:

```
char a[7];
```

Generating a Pointer to an Array

You can generate a pointer to the first element of an array by simply specifying the array name, without any index. For example, given

```
int sample[10];
```

Element	a[0]	a[1]	a[2]	a[3]	a[4]	a[5]	a[6]
Address	1000	1001	1002	1003	1004	1005	1006

Figure 4-1.   *A seven-element character array beginning at location 1000*

you can generate a pointer to the first element by using the name **sample**. Thus, the following program fragment assigns **p** the address of the first element of **sample**:

```
int *p;
int sample[10];

p = sample;
```

You can also specify the address of the first element of an array by using the **&** operator. For example, **sample** and **&sample[0]** both produce the same results. However, in professionally written C code, you will almost never see **&sample[0]**.

Passing Single-Dimension Arrays to Functions

In C, you cannot pass an entire array as an argument to a function. You can, however, pass a pointer to an array by specifying the array's name without an index. For example, the following program fragment passes the address of **i** to **func1( )**:

```
int main(void)
{
  int i[10];

  func1(i);

  /* ... */
}
```

If a function receives a pointer to a single-dimension array, you can declare its formal parameter in one of three ways: as a pointer, as a sized array, or as an unsized array. For example, to receive **i**, a function called **func1( )** can be declared as

```
void func1(int *x) /* pointer */
{
```

```
   /* ... */
}
```

or

```
void func1(int x[10]) /* sized array */
{
   /* ... */
}
```

or finally as

```
void func1(int x[]) /* unsized array */
{
   /* ... */
}
```

All three declaration methods produce similar results because each tells the compiler that an integer pointer is going to be received. The first declaration actually uses a pointer. The second employs the standard array declaration. In the final version, a modified version of an array declaration simply specifies that an array of type **int** of some length is to be received. As you can see, the length of the array doesn't matter as far as the function is concerned because C performs no bounds checking. In fact, as far as the compiler is concerned,

```
void func1(int x[32])
{
   /* ... */
}
```

also works because the compiler generates code that instructs **func1( )** to receive a pointer—it does not actually create a 32-element array.

Strings

By far the most common use for the one-dimensional array is as a character string. In C, a *string* is a null-terminated character array. (A null is zero.) Thus, a string contains the characters that make up the string followed by a null. The null-terminated string is the only type of string defined by C.

C++ also defines a string class, called **string**, *which provides an object-oriented approach to string handling, but it is not supported by C.*

When declaring a character array that will hold a string, you need to declare it to be one character longer than the largest string that it will hold. For example, to declare an array **str** that can hold a 10-character string, you would write

```
char str[11];
```

Specifying 11 for the size makes room for the null at the end of the string.

When you use a quoted string constant in your program, you are also creating a null-terminated string. A *string constant* is a list of characters enclosed in double quotes. For example:

"hello there"

You do not need to add the null to the end of string constants manually—the compiler does this for you automatically.

C supports a wide range of functions that manipulate strings. The most common are listed here:

Name	Function
strcpy(*s1, s2*)	Copies *s2* into *s1*
strcat(*s1, s2*)	Concatenates *s2* onto the end of *s1*
strlen(*s1*)	Returns the length of *s1*
strcmp(*s1, s2*)	Returns 0 if *s1* and *s2* are the same; less than 0 if *s1<s2*; greater than 0 if *s1>s2*
strchr(*s1, ch*)	Returns a pointer to the first occurrence of *ch* in *s1*
strstr(*s1, s2*)	Returns a pointer to the first occurrence of *s2* in *s1*

These functions use the standard header **<string.h>**. The following program illustrates the use of these string functions:

```
#include <stdio.h>
#include <string.h>

int main(void)
{
  char s1[80], s2[80];

  gets(s1);
```

```
    gets(s2);

    printf("lengths: %d %d\n", strlen(s1), strlen(s2));

    if(!strcmp(s1, s2)) printf("The strings are equal\n");

    strcat(s1, s2);
    printf("%s\n", s1);

    strcpy(s1, "This is a test.\n");
    printf(s1);
    if(strchr("hello", 'e')) printf("e is in hello\n");
    if(strstr("hi there", "hi")) printf("found hi");

    return 0;
}
```

If you run this program and enter the strings "**hello**" and "**hello**", the output is

```
lengths: 5 5
The strings are equal
hellohello
This is a test.
e is in hello
found hi
```

Remember, **strcmp( )** returns false if the strings are equal. Be sure to use the logical **!** operator to reverse the condition, as just shown, if you are testing for equality.

Two-Dimensional Arrays

C supports multidimensional arrays. The simplest form of the multidimensional array is the two-dimensional array. A two-dimensional array is, essentially, an array of one-dimensional arrays. To declare a two-dimensional integer array **d** of size 10,20, you would write

```
int d[10][20];
```

Pay careful attention to the declaration. Some other computer languages use commas to separate the array dimensions; C places each dimension in its own set of brackets.

Similarly, to access point 1,2 of array **d**, you would use

```
d[1][2]
```

The following example loads a two-dimensional array with the numbers 1 through 12 and prints them row by row.

```c
#include <stdio.h>

int main(void)
{
  int t, i, num[3][4];

  for(t=0; t<3; ++t)
    for(i=0; i<4; ++i)
      num[t][i] = (t*4)+i+1;

  /* now print them out */
  for(t=0; t<3; ++t) {
    for(i=0; i<4; ++i)
      printf("%3d ", num[t][i]);
    printf("\n");
  }

  return 0;
}
```

In this example, **num[0][0]** has the value 1, **num[0][1]** the value 2, **num[0][2]** the value 3, and so on. The value of **num[2][3]** will be 12. You can visualize the **num** array as shown here:

num [t] [i]

	0	1	2	3
0	1	2	3	4
1	5	6	7	8
2	9	10	11	12

Two-dimensional arrays are stored in a row-column matrix, where the left index indicates the row and the right indicates the column. This means that the rightmost index changes faster than the leftmost when accessing the elements in the array in the order in which they are actually stored in memory. See Figure 4-2 for a graphic representation of a two-dimensional array in memory.

In the case of a two-dimensional array, the following formula yields the number of bytes of memory needed to hold it:

bytes = size of 1st index × size of 2nd index × sizeof(base type)

Therefore, assuming 4-byte integers, an integer array with dimensions 10,5 would have

$10 \times 5 \times 4$

or 200 bytes allocated.

When a two-dimensional array is used as an argument to a function, only a pointer to the first element is actually passed. However, the parameter receiving a two-dimensional array must define at least the size of the rightmost dimension. (You can specify the left dimension if you like, but it is not necessary.) The rightmost dimension is needed because the compiler needs to know the length of each row if it is to index the array correctly. For example, a function that receives a two-dimensional integer array with dimensions 10,10 can be declared like this:

```
void func1(int x[][10])
{
   /* ... */
}
```

The compiler needs to know the size of the right dimension in order to correctly execute expressions such as

```
x[2][4]
```

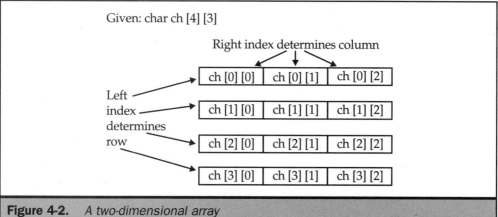

Figure 4-2.   *A two-dimensional array*

inside the function. If the length of a row is not known, the compiler cannot determine where the next row begins.

The following program uses a two-dimensional array to store the numeric grade for each student in a teacher's classes. The program assumes that the teacher has three classes and a maximum of 30 students per class. Notice the way the array **grade** is accessed by each of the functions.

```c
/* A simple student grades database. */
#include <stdio.h>
#include <ctype.h>
#include <stdlib.h>

#define CLASSES  3
#define GRADES   30

int grade[CLASSES][GRADES];

void enter_grades(void);
int get_grade(int num);
void disp_grades(int g[][GRADES]);

int main(void)
{
  char ch, str[80];

  for(;;) {
    do {
      printf("(E)nter grades\n");
      printf("(R)eport grades\n");
      printf("(Q)uit\n");
      gets(str);
      ch = toupper(*str);
    } while(ch!='E' && ch!='R' && ch!='Q');

    switch(ch) {
      case 'E':
        enter_grades();
        break;
      case 'R':
        disp_grades(grade);
        break;
```

```
      case 'Q':
        exit(0);
    }
  }

  return 0;
}

/* Enter the student's grades. */
void enter_grades(void)
{
  int t, i;

  for(t=0; t<CLASSES; t++) {
    printf("Class # %d:\n", t+1);
    for(i=0; i<GRADES; ++i)
      grade[t][i] = get_grade(i);
  }
}

/* Read a grade. */
int get_grade(int num)
{
  char s[80];

  printf("Enter grade for student # %d:\n", num+1);
  gets(s);
  return(atoi(s));
}

/* Display grades. */
void disp_grades(int g[][GRADES])
{
  int t, i;

  for(t=0; t<CLASSES; ++t) {
    printf("Class # %d:\n", t+1);
    for(i=0; i<GRADES; ++i)
      printf("Student #%d is %d\n", i+1, g[t][i]);
  }
}
```

Arrays of Strings

It is not uncommon in programming to use an array of strings. For example, the input processor to a database may verify user commands against an array of valid commands. To create an array of strings, use a two-dimensional character array. The size of the left dimension determines the number of strings, and the size of the right dimension specifies the maximum length of each string. The following declares an array of 30 strings, each with a maximum length of 79 characters:

```
char str_array[30][80];
```

It is easy to access an individual string: You simply specify only the left index. For example, the following statement calls **gets( )** with the third string in **str_array**.

```
gets(str_array[2]);
```

The preceding statement is functionally equivalent to

```
gets(&str_array[2][0]);
```

but the first of the two forms is much more common in professionally written C code.

To understand better how string arrays work, study the following short program, which uses a string array as the basis for a very simple text editor.

```
/* A very simple text editor. */
#include <stdio.h>

#define MAX 100
#define LEN 80

char text[MAX][LEN];

int main(void)
{
  register int t, i, j;

  printf("Enter an empty line to quit.\n");

  for(t=0; t<MAX; t++) {
    printf("%d: ", t);
    gets(text[t]);
```

```
    if(!*text[t]) break; /* quit on blank line */
  }

  for(i=0; i<t; i++) {
    for(j=0; text[i][j]; j++) putchar(text[i][j]);
    putchar('\n');
  }

  return 0;
}
```

This program inputs lines of text until a blank line is entered. Then it redisplays each line one character at a time.

Multidimensional Arrays

C allows arrays of more than two dimensions. The general form of a multidimensional array declaration is

type name[*Size1*][*Size2*][*Size3*]. . .[*SizeN*];

Arrays of more than three dimensions are not often used because of the amount of memory they require. For example, a four-dimensional character array with dimensions 10,6,9,4 requires

10 * 6 * 9 * 4

or 2,160 bytes. If the array held 2-byte integers, 4,320 bytes would be needed. If the array held **double**s (assuming 8 bytes per **double**), 17,280 bytes would be required. The storage required increases exponentially with the number of dimensions. For example, if a fifth dimension of size 10 was added to the preceding array, then 172,800 bytes would be required.

In multidimensional arrays, it takes the computer time to compute each index. This means that accessing an element in a multidimensional array can be slower than accessing an element in a single-dimension array.

When passing multidimensional arrays into functions, you must declare all but the leftmost dimension. For example, if you declare array **m** as

```
int m[4][3][6][5];
```

a function, **func1( )**, that receives **m**, would look like this:

```
void func1(int d[][3][6][5])
{
  /* ... */
}
```

Of course, you can include the first dimension if you like.

Indexing Pointers

Pointers and arrays are closely related. As you know, an array name without an index is a pointer to the first element in the array. For example, consider the following array:

```
char p[10];
```

The following statements are identical:

```
p
&p[0]
```

Put another way,

```
p == &p[0]
```

evaluates to true because the address of the first element of an array is the same as the address of the array.

As stated, an array name without an index generates a pointer. Conversely, a pointer can be indexed as if it were declared to be an array. For example, consider this program fragment:

```
int *p, i[10];
p = i;
p[5] = 100;   /* assign using index */
*(p+5) = 100; /* assign using pointer arithmetic */
```

Both assignment statements place the value 100 in the sixth element of **i**. The first statement indexes **p**; the second uses pointer arithmetic. Either way, the result is the same. (Chapter 5 discusses pointers and pointer arithmetic.)

This same concept also applies to arrays of two or more dimensions. For example, assuming that **a** is a 10-by-10 integer array, these two statements are equivalent:

```
a
&a[0][0]
```

Furthermore, the 0,4 element of **a** may be referenced two ways: either by array indexing, **a[0][4]**, or by the pointer, ***((int *)a+4)**. Similarly, element 1,2 is either **a[1][2]** or ***((int *)a+12)**. In general, for any two-dimensional array:

a[j][k] is equivalent to *((*base type* *)a+(j**row length*)+k)

The cast of the pointer to the array into a pointer of its base type is necessary in order for the pointer arithmetic to operate properly. Pointers are sometimes used to access arrays because pointer arithmetic is often faster than array indexing.

A two-dimensional array can be reduced to a pointer to an array of one-dimensional arrays. Therefore, using a separate pointer variable is one easy way to use pointers to access elements within a row of a two-dimensional array. The following function illustrates this technique. It will print the contents of the specified row for the global integer array **num**.

```
int num[10][10];

/* ... */

void  pr_row(int j)
{
  int *p, t;

  p = (int *) &num[j][0]; /* get address of first
                             element in row j */

  for(t=0; t<10; ++t) printf("%d ", *(p+t));
}
```

You can generalize this routine by making the calling arguments the row, the row length, and a pointer to the first array element, as shown here:

```
void pr_row(int j, int row_dimension, int *p)
{
  int t;
```

```
    p = p + (j * row_dimension);

    for(t=0; t<row_dimension; ++t)
      printf("%d ", *(p+t));
}

/* ... */

void f(void)
{
  int num[10][10];

  pr_row(0, 10, (int *) num); /* print first row */
}
```

Arrays of greater than two dimensions may be reduced in a similar way. For example, a three-dimensional array can be reduced to a pointer to a two-dimensional array, which can be reduced to a pointer to a single-dimension array. Generally, an *n*-dimensional array can be reduced to a pointer and an (*n*–1)-dimensional array. This new array can be reduced again with the same method. The process ends when a single-dimension array is produced.

Array Initialization

C allows the initialization of arrays at the time of their declaration. The general form of array initialization is similar to that of other variables, as shown here:

type_specifier array_name[size1]. . .[sizeN] = { value_list };

The *value_list* is a comma-separated list of constants whose type is compatible with *type_specifier*. The first constant is put in the first position of the array, the second constant in the second position, and so on. Note that a semicolon follows the }.

Note *C99 allows non-constant initializers to be used for local arrays, but C89 requires constant initializers to be used for all arrays.*

In the following example, a 10-element integer array is initialized with the numbers 1 through 10:

```
int i[10] = {1, 2, 3, 4, 5, 6, 7, 8, 9, 10};
```

This means that **i[0]** will have the value 1 and **i[9]** will have the value 10.

FOUNDATIONAL C

Character arrays that hold strings allow a shorthand initialization that takes the form:

char *array_name*[*size*] = "*string*";

For example, this code fragment initializes **str** to the phrase "I like C":

```
char str[9] = "I like C";
```

This is the same as writing

```
char str[9] = {'I', ' ', 'l', 'i', 'k', 'e',' ', 'C', '\0'};
```

Because strings end with a null, you must make sure that the array you declare is long enough to include the null. This is why **str** is nine characters long even though "I like C" is only eight. When you use the string constant, the compiler automatically supplies the null terminator.

Multidimensional arrays are initialized the same as single-dimension ones. For example, the following initializes **sqrs** with the numbers 1 through 10 and their squares.

```
int sqrs[10][2] = {
  1, 1,
  2, 4,
  3, 9,
  4, 16,
  5, 25,
  6, 36,
  7, 49,
  8, 64,
  9, 81,
  10, 100
};
```

When initializing a multidimensional array, you may add braces around the initializers for each dimension. This is called *subaggregate grouping*. For example, here is another way to write the preceding declaration:

```
int sqrs[10][2] = {
  {1, 1},
  {2, 4},
  {3, 9},
```

```
       {4, 16},
       {5, 25},
       {6, 36},
       {7, 49},
       {8, 64},
       {9, 81},
       {10, 100}
};
```

When using subaggregate grouping, if you don't supply enough initializers for a given group, the remaining members will be set to zero, automatically.

Unsized Array Initializations

Imagine that you are using array initialization to build a table of error messages, as shown here:

```
char e1[12] = "Read error\n";
char e2[13] = "Write error\n";
char e3[18] = "Cannot open file\n";
```

As you might guess, it is tedious to count the characters in each message manually to determine the correct array dimension. Fortunately, you can let the compiler automatically calculate the dimensions of the arrays. If, in an array initialization statement, the size of the array is not specified, the compiler automatically creates an array big enough to hold all the initializers present. This is called an *unsized array*. Using this approach, the message table becomes

```
char e1[] = "Read error\n";
char e2[] = "Write error\n";
char e3[] = "Cannot open file\n";
```

Given these initializations, this statement

```
printf("%s has length %d\n",  e2,  sizeof e2);
```

will print

```
Write error
 has length 13
```

Besides being less tedious, unsized array initialization allows you to change any of the messages without fear of using incorrect array dimensions.

Unsized array initializations are not restricted to one-dimensional arrays. For multidimensional arrays, you must specify all but the leftmost dimension. (The other dimensions are needed to allow the compiler to index the array properly.) In this way, you can build tables of varying lengths, and the compiler automatically allocates enough storage for them. For example, the declaration of **sqrs** as an unsized array is shown here:

```
int sqrs[][2] = {
   {1, 1},
   {2, 4},
   {3, 9},
   {4, 16},
   {5, 25},
   {6, 36},
   {7, 49},
   {8, 64},
   {9, 81},
   {10, 100}
};
```

The advantage of this declaration over the sized version is that you may lengthen or shorten the table without changing the array dimensions.

Variable-Length Arrays

As explained earlier, in C89 array dimensions must be declared using constant expressions. Thus, in C89 the size of an array is fixed at compile time. However, this is not the case for C99, which adds a powerful new feature to arrays: variable length. In C99, you can declare an array whose dimensions are specified by any valid expression, including those whose value is known only at run time. This is called a _variable-length array_. However, only local arrays (that is, those with block scope or prototype scope) can be of variable length. Here is an example of a variable-length array:

```
void f(int dim)
{
  char str[dim]; /* a variable-length character array */

  /* ... */
}
```

Here, the size of **str** is determined by the value passed to **f( )** in **dim**. Thus, each call to **f( )** can result in **str** being created with a different length.

One major reason for the addition of variable-length arrays to C99 is to support numeric processing. Of course, it is a feature that has widespread applicability. But remember, variable-length arrays are not supported by C89 (or by C++). We will look more closely at variable-length arrays in Part Two.

A Tic-Tac-Toe Example

The longer example that follows illustrates many of the ways that you can manipulate arrays with C. This section develops a simple tic-tac-toe program. Two-dimensional arrays are commonly used to simulate board game matrices.

The computer plays a very simple game. When it is the computer's turn, it uses **get_computer_move( )** to scan the matrix, looking for an unoccupied cell. When it finds one, it puts an **O** there. If it cannot find an empty location, it reports a draw game and exits. The **get_player_move( )** function asks you where you want to place an **X**. The upper-left corner is location 1,1; the lower-right corner is 3,3.

The matrix array is initialized to contain spaces. Each move made by the player or the computer changes a space into either an X or an O. This makes it easy to display the matrix on the screen.

Each time a move has been made, the program calls the **check( )** function. This function returns a space if there is no winner yet, an X if you have won, or an O if the computer has won. It scans the rows, the columns, and then the diagonals, looking for one that contains either all X's or all O's.

The **disp_matrix( )** function displays the current state of the game. Notice how initializing the matrix with spaces simplified this function.

The routines in this example all access the **matrix** array differently. Study them to make sure you understand each array operation.

```c
/* A simple Tic Tac Toe game. */
#include <stdio.h>
#include <stdlib.h>

char matrix[3][3];  /* the tic tac toe matrix */

char check(void);
void init_matrix(void);
void get_player_move(void);
void get_computer_move(void);
void disp_matrix(void);

int main(void)
```

```
{
  char done;

  printf("This is the game of Tic Tac Toe.\n");
  printf("You will be playing against the computer.\n");

  done = ' ';
  init_matrix();

  do {
    disp_matrix();
    get_player_move();
    done = check(); /* see if winner */
    if(done!= ' ') break; /* winner!*/
    get_computer_move();
    done = check(); /* see if winner */
  } while(done== ' ');

  if(done=='X') printf("You won!\n");
  else printf("I won!!!!\n");
  disp_matrix(); /* show final positions */

  return 0;
}

/* Initialize the matrix. */
void init_matrix(void)
{
  int i, j;

  for(i=0; i<3; i++)
    for(j=0; j<3; j++) matrix[i][j] = ' ';
}

/* Get a player's move. */
void get_player_move(void)
{
  int x, y;

  printf("Enter X,Y coordinates for your move: ");
  scanf("%d%*c%d", &x, &y);
```

```
    x--; y--;

  if(matrix[x][y]!= ' '){
    printf("Invalid move, try again.\n");
    get_player_move();
  }
  else matrix[x][y] = 'X';
}

/* Get a move from the computer. */
void get_computer_move(void)
{
  int i, j;
  for(i=0; i<3; i++){
    for(j=0; j<3; j++)
      if(matrix[i][j]==' ') break;
    if(matrix[i][j]==' ') break;
  }

  if(i*j==9)   {
    printf("draw\n");
    exit(0);
  }
  else
    matrix[i][j] = 'O';
}

/* Display the matrix on the screen. */
void disp_matrix(void)
{
  int t;

  for(t=0; t<3; t++) {
    printf(" %c | %c | %c ",matrix[t][0],
            matrix[t][1], matrix [t][2]);
    if(t!=2) printf("\n---|---|---\n");
  }
  printf("\n");
}

/* See if there is a winner. */
char check(void)
```

```
{
  int i;

  for(i=0; i<3; i++)  /* check rows */
    if(matrix[i][0]==matrix[i][1] &&
       matrix[i][0]==matrix[i][2]) return matrix[i][0];

  for(i=0; i<3; i++)  /* check columns */
    if(matrix[0][i]==matrix[1][i] &&
       matrix[0][i]==matrix[2][i]) return matrix[0][i];

  /* test diagonals */
  if(matrix[0][0]==matrix[1][1] &&
     matrix[1][1]==matrix[2][2])
       return matrix[0][0];

  if(matrix[0][2]==matrix[1][1] &&
     matrix[1][1]==matrix[2][0])
       return matrix[0][2];

  return ' ';
}
```

Chapter 5

Pointers

The correct understanding and use of pointers is crucial to successful C programming. There are several reasons for this: First, pointers provide the means by which functions can modify their calling arguments. Second, pointers support dynamic allocation. Third, pointers can improve the efficiency of certain routines. Finally, pointers provide support for dynamic data structures, such as binary trees and linked lists.

Pointers are one of the strongest but also one of the most dangerous features in C. For example, a pointer containing an invalid value can cause your program to crash. Perhaps worse, it is easy to use pointers incorrectly, causing bugs that are very difficult to find. Because of their importance and their potential for abuse, this chapter examines the subject of pointers in detail.

What Are Pointers?

A *pointer* is a variable that holds a memory address. This address is the location of another object (typically another variable) in memory. For example, if one variable contains the address of another variable, the first variable is said to *point to* the second. Figure 5-1 illustrates this situation.

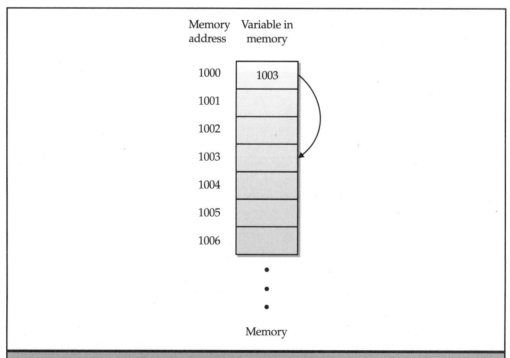

Figure 5-1.   *One variable points to another*

Pointer Variables

If a variable is going to be a pointer, it must be declared as such. A pointer declaration consists of a base type, an *****, and the variable name. The general form for declaring a pointer variable is

>   *type *name*;

where *type* is the base type of the pointer and may be any valid type. The name of the pointer variable is specified by *name.*

The base type of the pointer defines the type of object to which the pointer will point. Technically, any type of pointer can point anywhere in memory. However, all pointer operations are done relative to the pointer's base type. For example, when you declare a pointer to be of type **int ***, the compiler assumes that any address that it holds points to an integer—whether it actually does or not. (That is, an **int *** pointer always "thinks" that it points to an **int** object, no matter what that piece of memory actually contains.) Therefore, when you declare a pointer, you must make sure that its type is compatible with the type of object to which you want to point.

The Pointer Operators

The pointer operators were discussed in Chapter 2. We will review them here. There are two pointer operators: ***** and **&**. The **&** is a unary operator that returns the memory address of its operand. (Remember, a unary operator only requires one operand.) For example,

```
m = &count;
```

places into **m** the memory address of the variable **count**. This address is the computer's internal location of the variable. It has nothing to do with the value of **count**. You can think of **&** as returning "the address of." Therefore, the preceding assignment statement can be verbalized as "**m** receives the address of **count**."

To understand the above assignment better, assume that the variable **count** uses memory location 2000 to store its value. Also assume that **count** has a value of 100. Then, after the preceding assignment, **m** will have the value 2000.

The second pointer operator, *****, is the complement of **&**. It is a unary operator that returns the value located at the address that follows. For example, if **m** contains the memory address of the variable **count**,

```
q = *m;
```

places the value of **count** into **q**. Thus, **q** will have the value 100 because 100 is stored at location 2000, which is the memory address that was stored in **m**. You can think of ***** as "at address." In this case, the preceding statement can be verbalized as "**q** receives the value at address **m**."

Pointer Expressions

In general, expressions involving pointers conform to the same rules as other expressions. This section examines a few special aspects of pointer expressions, such as assignments, conversions, and arithmetic.

Pointer Assignments

You can use a pointer on the right-hand side of an assignment statement to assign its value to another pointer. When both pointers are the same type, the situation is straightforward. For example:

```
#include <stdio.h>

int main(void)
{
  int x = 99;
  int *p1, *p2;

  p1 = &x;
  p2 = p1;

  /* print the value of x twice */
  printf("Values at p1 and p2: %d %d\n", *p1, *p2);

  /* print the address of x twice */
  printf("Addresses pointed to by p1 and p2: %p %p", p1, p2);

  return 0;
}
```

After the assignment sequence

```
p1 = &x;
p2 = p1;
```

p1 and **p2** both point to **x**. Thus, both **p1** and **p2** refer to the same object. Sample output from the program, which confirms this, is shown here.

```
Values at p1 and p2: 99 99
Addresses pointed to by p1 and p2: 0063FDF0 0063FDF0
```

Notice that the addresses are displayed by using the **%p printf( )** format specifier, which causes **printf( )** to display an address in the format used by the host computer.

It is also possible to assign a pointer of one type to a pointer of another type. However, doing so involves a pointer conversion, which is the subject of the next section.

Pointer Conversions

One type of pointer can be converted into another type of pointer. There are two general categories of conversion: those that involve **void *** pointers, and those that don't. Each is examined here.

In C, it is permissible to assign a **void *** pointer to any other type of pointer. It is also permissible to assign any other type of pointer to a **void *** pointer. A **void *** pointer is called a *generic pointer*. The **void *** pointer is used to specify a pointer whose base type is unknown. The **void *** type allows a function to specify a parameter that is capable of receiving any type of pointer argument without reporting a type mismatch. It is also used to refer to raw memory (such as that returned by the **malloc( )** function described later in this chapter) when the semantics of that memory are not known. No explicit cast is required to convert to or from a **void *** pointer.

Except for **void ***, all other pointer conversions must be performed by using an explicit cast. However, the conversion of one type of pointer into another type may create undefined behavior. For example, consider the following program that attempts to assign the value of **x** to **y**, through the pointer **p**. This program compiles without error, but does not produce the desired result.

```c
#include <stdio.h>

int main(void)
{
  double x = 100.1, y;
  int   *p;

  /* The next statement causes p (which is an
     integer pointer) to point to a double. */
  p = (int *) &x;

  /* The next statement does not operate as expected. */
  y = *p; /* attempt to assign y the value x through p */

  /* The following statement won't output 100.1. */
  printf("The (incorrect) value of x is: %f", y);

  return 0;
}
```

Notice that an explicit cast is used when assigning the address of **x** (which is implicitly a **double *** pointer) to **p**, which is an **int *** pointer. While this cast is correct, it does not cause the program to act as intended (at least not in most environments). To understand the problem, assume 4-byte **int**s and 8-byte **double**s. Because **p** is declared as an integer pointer, only 4 bytes of information will be transferred to **y** by this assignment statement,

```
y = *p;
```

not the 8 bytes that make up a **double**. Thus, even though **p** is a valid pointer, the fact that it points to a **double** does not change the fact that operations on it expect **int** values. Thus, the use to which **p** is put is invalid.

The preceding example reinforces the rule stated earlier: Pointer operations are performed relative to the base type of the pointer. While it is technically permissible for a pointer to point to some other type of object, the pointer will still "think" that it is pointing to an object of its base type. Thus, pointer operations are governed by the type of the pointer, not the type of the object being pointed to.

One other pointer conversion is allowed: You can convert an integer into a pointer or a pointer into an integer. However, you must use an explicit cast, and the result of such a conversion is implementation defined and may result in undefined behavior. (A cast is not needed when converting zero, which is the null pointer.)

Note   *In C++, in all cases it is illegal to convert one type of pointer into another type of pointer without the use of an explicit type cast. This includes **void *** pointer conversions, too. For this reason, many C programmers cast all pointer conversions so that their code is also compatible with C++.*

Pointer Arithmetic

There are only two arithmetic operations that you can use on pointers: addition and subtraction. To understand what occurs in pointer arithmetic, let **p1** be an integer pointer with a current value of 2000. Also, assume **int**s are 2 bytes long. After the expression

```
p1++;
```

p1 contains 2002, not 2001. The reason for this is that each time **p1** is incremented, it will point to the next integer. The same is true of decrements. For example, assuming that **p1** has the value 2000, the expression

```
p1--;
```

causes **p1** to have the value 1998.

Generalizing from the preceding example, the following rules govern pointer arithmetic. Each time a pointer is incremented, it points to the memory location of the next element of its base type. Each time it is decremented, it points to the location of the previous element. When applied to **char** pointers, this will appear as "normal" arithmetic because a **char** object is always 1 byte long no matter what the environment. All other pointers will increase or decrease by the length of the data type they point to. This approach ensures that a pointer is always pointing to an appropriate element of its base type. Figure 5-2 illustrates this concept.

You are not limited to the increment and decrement operators. For example, you may add or subtract integers to or from pointers. The expression

```
p1 = p1 + 12;
```

makes **p1** point to the 12th element of **p1**'s type beyond the one it currently points to.

Besides addition and subtraction of a pointer and an integer, only one other arithmetic operation is allowed: You can subtract one pointer from another in order to find the number of objects of their base type that separate the two. All other arithmetic operations are prohibited. Specifically, you cannot multiply or divide pointers; you cannot add two pointers; you cannot apply the bitwise operators to them; and you cannot add or subtract type **float** or **double** to or from pointers.

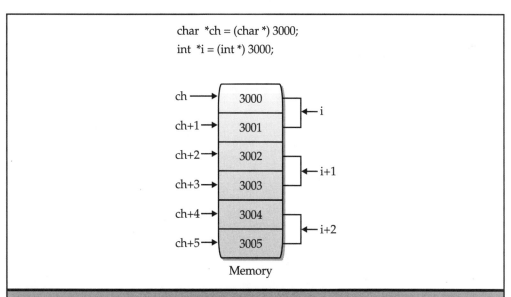

Figure 5-2.   *All pointer arithmetic is relative to its base type (assume 2-byte integers)*

Pointer Comparisons

You can compare two pointers in a relational expression. For instance, given two pointers **p** and **q**, the following statement is perfectly valid:

```
if(p < q) printf("p points to lower memory than q\n");
```

Generally, pointer comparisons are useful only when two pointers point to a common object, such as an array. As an example, a set of stack functions are developed that store and retrieve integer values. As most readers will know, a stack is a list that uses first-in, last-out accessing. It is often compared to a stack of plates on a table—the first one set down is the last one to be used. Stacks are used frequently in compilers, interpreters, spreadsheets, and other system-related software. To create a stack, you need two functions: **push( )** and **pop( )**. The **push( )** function places values on the stack, and **pop( )** takes them off. These routines are shown here with a simple **main( )** function to drive them. The program puts the values you enter into the stack. If you enter **0**, a value is popped from the stack. To stop the program, enter **–1**.

```c
#include <stdio.h>
#include <stdlib.h>

#define SIZE 50

void push(int i);
int pop(void);

int   *tos, *p1, stack[SIZE];

int main(void)
{
  int value;

  tos = stack; /* tos points to the top of stack */
  p1 = stack; /* initialize p1 */

  do {
    printf("Enter value: ");
    scanf("%d", &value);

    if(value != 0) push(value);
    else printf("value on top is %d\n", pop());
```

```
  } while(value != -1);

  return 0;
}

void push(int i)
{
  p1++;
  if(p1 == (tos+SIZE)) {
    printf("Stack Overflow.\n");
    exit(1);
  }
  *p1 = i;
}

int pop(void)
{
  if(p1 == tos) {
    printf("Stack Underflow.\n");
    exit(1);
  }
  p1--;
  return *(p1+1);
}
```

You can see that memory for the stack is provided by the array **stack**. The pointer **p1** is set to point to the first element in **stack**. The **p1** variable accesses the stack. The variable **tos** holds the memory address of the top of the stack. It is used to prevent stack overflows and underflows. Once the stack has been initialized, **push( )** and **pop( )** can be used. Both the **push( )** and **pop( )** functions perform a relational test on the pointer **p1** to detect limit errors. In **push( )**, **p1** is tested against the end of the stack by adding **SIZE** (the size of the stack) to **tos**. This prevents an overflow. In **pop( )**, **p1** is checked against **tos** to be sure that a stack underflow has not occurred.

In **pop( )**, the parentheses are necessary in the return statement. Without them, the statement would look like this,

```
return *p1+1;
```

which would return the value at location **p1** plus one, not the value of the location **p1+1**.

Pointers and Arrays

There is a close relationship between pointers and arrays. Consider this program fragment:

```
char str[80], *p1;
p1 = str;
```

Here, **p1** has been set to the address of the first array element in **str**. To access the fifth element in **str**, you could write

```
str[4]
```

or

```
*(p1+4)
```

Both statements will return the fifth element. Remember, arrays start at 0. To access the fifth element, you must use 4 to index **str**. You also add 4 to the pointer **p1** to access the fifth element because **p1** currently points to the first element of **str**. (Recall that an array name without an index returns the starting address of the array, which is the address of the first element.)

The preceding example can be generalized. In essence, C provides two methods of accessing array elements: pointer arithmetic and array indexing. Although the standard array-indexing notation is sometimes easier to understand, pointer arithmetic can be faster. Since speed is often a consideration in programming, C programmers often use pointers to access array elements.

These two versions of **putstr( )**—one with array indexing and one with pointers—illustrate how you can use pointers in place of array indexing. The **putstr( )** function writes a string to the standard output device one character at a time.

```
/* Index s as an array. */
void putstr(char *s)
{
  register int t;

  for(t=0; s[t]; ++t) putchar(s[t]);
}

/* Access s as a pointer. */
void putstr(char *s)
{
  while(*s) putchar(*s++);
}
```

Most professional C programmers would find the second version easier to read and understand. Depending upon the compiler, it might also be more efficient. In fact, the pointer version is the way routines of this sort are commonly written in C.

Arrays of Pointers

Pointers can be arrayed like any other data type. The declaration for an **int** pointer array of size 10 is

```
int *x[10];
```

To assign the address of an integer variable called **var** to the third element of the pointer array, write

```
x[2] = &var;
```

To find the value of **var**, write

```
*x[2]
```

If you want to pass an array of pointers into a function, you can use the same method that you use to pass other arrays: Simply call the function with the array name without any subscripts. For example, a function that can receive array **x** looks like this:

```
void display_array(int *q[])
{
  int t;

  for(t=0; t<10; t++)
    printf("%d ", *q[t]);
}
```

Remember, **q** is not a pointer to integers, but rather a pointer to an array of pointers to integers. Therefore you need to declare the parameter **q** as an array of integer pointers, as just shown. You cannot declare **q** simply as an integer pointer because that is not what it is.

Pointer arrays are often used to hold pointers to strings. For example, you can create a function that outputs an error message given its index, as shown here:

```
void syntax_error(int num)
{
  static char *err[] = {
```

```
      "Cannot Open File\n",
      "Read Error\n",
      "Write Error\n",
      "Media Failure\n"
   };

   printf("%s", err[num]);
}
```

The array **err** holds a pointer to each error string. This works because a string constant used in an expression (in this case, an initialization) produces a pointer to the string. The **printf( )** function is called with a character pointer that points to the error message whose index is passed to the function. For example, if **num** is passed a 2, the message **Write Error** is displayed.

As a point of interest, note that the command line argument **argv** is an array of character pointers. (See Chapter 6.)

Multiple Indirection

You can have a pointer point to another pointer that points to the target value. This situation is called *multiple indirection*, or *pointers to pointers*. Pointers to pointers can be confusing. Figure 5-3 helps clarify the concept of multiple indirection. As you can see, the value of a normal pointer is the address of the object that contains the desired value. In the case of a pointer to a pointer, the first pointer contains the address of the second pointer, which points to the object that contains the desired value.

Multiple indirection can be carried on to whatever extent desired, but more than a pointer to a pointer is rarely needed. In fact, excessive indirection is difficult to follow and prone to conceptual errors.

Note   *Do not confuse multiple indirection with high-level data structures, such as linked lists, that use pointers. These are two fundamentally different concepts.*

A variable that is a pointer to a pointer must be declared as such. You do this by placing an additional asterisk in front of the variable name. For example, the following declaration tells the compiler that **newbalance** is a pointer to a pointer of type **float**:

```
float **newbalance;
```

You should understand that **newbalance** is not a pointer to a floating-point number but rather a pointer to a **float** pointer.

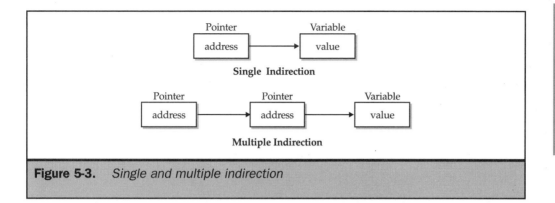

Figure 5-3.   *Single and multiple indirection*

To access the target value indirectly pointed to by a pointer to a pointer, you must apply the asterisk operator twice, as in this example:

```c
#include <stdio.h>

int main(void)
{
  int x, *p, **q;

  x = 10;
  p = &x;
  q = &p;

  printf("%d", **q); /* print the value of x */

  return 0;
}
```

Here, **p** is declared as a pointer to an integer and **q** as a pointer to a pointer to an integer. The call to **printf( )** prints the number **10** on the screen.

Initializing Pointers

After a nonstatic, local pointer is declared but before it has been assigned a value, it contains an unknown value. (Global and static local pointers are automatically initialized to null.) Should you try to use the pointer before giving it a valid value, you will probably crash your program—and possibly your computer's operating system as well—a very nasty type of error!

There is an important convention that most C programmers follow when working with pointers: A pointer that does not currently point to a valid memory location is given the value null (which is zero). Null is used because C guarantees that no object will exist at the null address. Thus, any pointer that is null implies that it points to nothing and should not be used.

One way to give a pointer a null value is to assign zero to it. For example, the following initializes **p** to null.

```
char *p = 0;
```

Additionally, many of C's headers, such as **<stdio.h>**, define the macro **NULL**, which is a null pointer constant. Therefore, you will often see a pointer assigned null using a statement such as this:

```
p = NULL;
```

However, just because a pointer has a null value, it is not necessarily "safe." The use of null to indicate unused pointers is simply a convention that programmers follow. It is not a rule enforced by the C language. For example, the following sequence, although incorrect, will still be compiled without error:

```
int *p = 0;
*p = 10; /* wrong! */
```

In this case, the assignment through **p** causes an assignment at 0, which will usually cause a program crash.

Because a null pointer is assumed to be unused, you can use the null pointer to make many of your pointer routines easier to code and more efficient. For example, you can use a null pointer to mark the end of a pointer array. A routine that accesses that array knows that it has reached the end when it encounters the null value. The **search( )** function shown in the following program illustrates this type of approach. Given a list of names, **search( )** determines whether a specified name is in that list.

```
#include <stdio.h>
#include <string.h>

int search(char *p[], char *name);

char *names[] = {
  "Herb",
  "Rex",
```

```
    "Dennis",
    "John",
    NULL}; /* null pointer constant ends the list */

int main(void)
{
  if(search(names, "Dennis") != -1)
    printf("Dennis is in list.\n");

  if(search(names, "Bill") == -1)
    printf("Bill not found.\n");

  return 0;
}

/* Look up a name. */
int search(char *p[], char *name)
{
  register int t;

  for(t=0; p[t]; ++t)
    if(!strcmp(p[t], name)) return t;

    return -1; /* not found */
}
```

The **search( )** function is passed two parameters. The first, **p**, is an array of **char ***
pointers that point to strings containing names. The second, **name**, is a pointer to a string
that points to the name being sought. The **search( )** function searches through the list of
pointers, seeking a string that matches the one pointed to by **name**. The **for** loop inside
search( ) runs until either a match is found or a null pointer is encountered. Assuming
the end of the array is marked with a null, the condition controlling the loop is false
when the end of the array is reached. That is, **p[t]** will be false when **p[t]** is null. In the
example, this occurs when the name Bill is tried, since it is not in the list of names.

C programmers commonly initialize **char *** pointers to point to string constants, as
the previous example shows. To understand why this works, consider the following
statement:

```
char *p = "hello world";
```

As you can see, **p** is a pointer, not an array. This raises a question: Where is the string
constant "hello world" being held? Since **p** is not an array, it can't be stored in **p**. Yet,

the string is obviously being stored somewhere. The answer to the question is found in the way C compilers handle string constants. The C compiler creates what is called a *string table*, which stores the string constants used by the program. Therefore, the preceding declaration statement places the address of "hello world", as stored in the string table, into the pointer **p**. Throughout a program, **p** can be used like any other string. For example, the following program is perfectly valid:

```c
#include <stdio.h>
#include <string.h>

char *p = "hello world";

int main(void)
{
  register int t;

  /* print the string forward and backwards */
  printf(p);
  for(t=strlen(p)-1; t>-1; t--) printf("%c", p[t]);

  return 0;
}
```

Pointers to Functions

A particularly confusing yet powerful feature of C is the *function pointer*. A function has a physical location in memory that can be assigned to a pointer. This address is the entry point of the function and it is the address used when the function is called. Once a pointer points to a function, the function can be called through that pointer. Function pointers also allow functions to be passed as arguments to other functions.

You obtain the address of a function by using the function's name without any parentheses or arguments. (This is similar to the way an array's address is obtained when only the array name, without indexes, is used.) To see how this is done, study the following program, which compares two strings entered by the user. Pay close attention to the declarations of **check( )** and the function pointer **p**, inside **main( )**.

```c
#include <stdio.h>
#include <string.h>

void check(char *a, char *b,
          int (*cmp)(const char *, const char *));
```

```
int main(void)
{
  char s1[80], s2[80];
  int (*p)(const char *, const char *); /* function pointer */

  p = strcmp; /* assign address of strcmp to p */

  printf("Enter two strings.\n");
  gets(s1);
  gets(s2);

  check(s1, s2, p); /* pass address of strcmp via p */

  return 0;
}

void check(char *a, char *b,
           int (*cmp)(const char *, const char *))
{
  printf("Testing for equality.\n");
  if(!(*cmp)(a, b)) printf("Equal");
  else printf("Not Equal");
}
```

Let's look closely at this program. First, examine the declaration for **p** in **main( )**. It is shown here:

```
int (*p)(const char *, const char *);
```

This declaration tells the compiler that **p** is a pointer to a function that has two **const char *** parameters, and returns an **int** result. The parentheses around **p** are necessary in order for the compiler to properly interpret this declaration. You must use a similar form when declaring other function pointers, although the return type and parameters of the function may differ.

Next, examine the **check( )** function. It declares three parameters: two character pointers, **a** and **b**, and one function pointer, **cmp**. Notice that the function pointer is declared using the same format as was **p** inside **main( )**. Thus, **cmp** is able to receive a pointer to a function that takes two **const char *** arguments and returns an **int** result. Like the declaration for **p**, the parentheses around the ***cmp** are necessary for the compiler to interpret this statement correctly.

When the program begins, it assigns **p** the address of **strcmp( )**, the standard string comparison function. Next, it prompts the user for two strings, and then it passes pointers to those strings along with **p** to **check( )**, which compares the strings for equality. Inside **check( )**, the expression

```
(*cmp)(a, b)
```

calls **strcmp( )**, which is pointed to by **cmp**, with the arguments **a** and **b**. The parentheses around ***cmp** are necessary. This is one way to call a function through a pointer. A second, simpler syntax, as shown here, can also be used.

```
cmp(a, b);
```

The reason that you will frequently see the first style is that it tips off anyone reading your code that a function is being called through a pointer (that is, that **cmp** is a function pointer, not the name of a function). Also, the first style was the form originally specified by C.

Note that you can call **check( )** by using **strcmp( )** directly, as shown here:

```
check(s1, s2, strcmp);
```

This eliminates the need for an additional pointer variable, in this case.

You may wonder why anyone would write a program like the one just shown. Obviously, nothing is gained, and significant confusion is introduced. However, at times it is advantageous to pass functions as parameters or to create an array of functions. For example, when an interpreter is written, the parser (the part that processes expressions) often calls various support functions, such as those that compute mathematical operations (sine, cosine, tangent, etc.), perform I/O, or access system resources. Instead of having a large **switch** statement with all of these functions listed in it, an array of function pointers can be created. In this approach, the proper function is selected by its index.

You can get a better idea of the value of function pointers by studying the expanded version of the previous example, shown next. In this version, **check( )** can be made to check for either alphabetical equality or numeric equality by simply calling it with a different comparison function. When checking for numeric equality, the string "0123" will compare equal to "123", even though the strings, themselves, differ.

```
#include <stdio.h>
#include <ctype.h>
#include <stdlib.h>
#include <string.h>

void check(char *a, char *b,
           int (*cmp)(const char *, const char *));
int compvalues(const char *a, const char *b);
```

```
int main(void)
{
  char s1[80], s2[80];

  printf("Enter two values or two strings.\n");
  gets(s1);
  gets(s2);

  if(isdigit(*s1)) {
    printf("Testing values for equality.\n");
    check(s1, s2, compvalues);
  }
  else {
    printf("Testing strings for equality.\n");
    check(s1, s2, strcmp);
  }

  return 0;
}

void check(char *a, char *b,
           int (*cmp)(const char *, const char *))
{
  if(!(*cmp)(a, b)) printf("Equal");
  else printf("Not Equal");
}

int compvalues(const char *a, const char *b)
{
  if(atoi(a)==atoi(b)) return 0;
  else return 1;
}
```

In this program, if you enter a string that begins with a digit, **compvalues( )** is passed to **check( )**. Otherwise, **strcmp( )** is used. Since **check( )** calls the function that it is passed, it can use a different comparison function in different cases. Two sample program runs are shown here:

```
Enter two values or two strings.
Test
Test
Testing strings for equality.
```

```
Equal

Enter two values or two strings.
0123
123
Testing values for equality.
Equal
```

As you can see, when comparing values, 0123 and 123 compare as equal.

C's Dynamic Allocation Functions

Pointers provide necessary support for C's dynamic allocation system. *Dynamic allocation* is the means by which a program can obtain memory while it is running. Global variables are allocated storage at compile time. Nonstatic, local variables use the stack. However, neither global nor local variables can be added during program execution. Yet there will be times when the storage needs of a program cannot be known ahead of time. For example, a program might want to use a dynamic data structure, such as a linked list or a binary tree. Such structures are inherently dynamic in nature, growing and shrinking as needed. To implement such a data structure requires that a program be able to allocate and free memory as needed.

Memory allocated by C's dynamic allocation functions is obtained from the *heap*. The heap is free memory that is not used by your program, the operating system, or any other program running in the computer. The size of the heap cannot usually be known in advance, but it typically contains a fairly large amount of free memory. (Most compilers supply library functions that allow you to obtain an estimate of the heap size at run time, but such functions are not defined by Standard C.) Although the size of the heap is often quite large, it is finite and can be exhausted.

The core of C's allocation system consists of the functions **malloc( )** and **free( )**. These functions work together using the free memory region to establish and maintain a list of available storage. The **malloc( )** function allocates memory, and the **free( )** function releases it. That is, each time a **malloc( )** memory request is made, a portion of the remaining free memory is allocated. Each time a **free( )** memory release call is made, memory is returned to the system. Any program that uses these functions must include the header <**stdlib.h**>.

The **malloc( )** function has this prototype:

```
void *malloc(size_t number_of_bytes);
```

Here, *number_of_bytes* is the number of bytes of memory you want to allocate. (The type **size_t** is defined in <**stdlib.h**> as some type of unsigned integer.) The **malloc( )** function returns a pointer of type **void ***, which means that you can assign it to any type of pointer. After a successful call, **malloc( )** returns a pointer to the first byte of the region of memory allocated from the heap. If there is not enough available memory to satisfy the **malloc( )** request, an allocation failure occurs and **malloc( )** returns a null.

The code fragment shown here allocates 1,000 bytes of contiguous memory:

```
char *p;
p = malloc(1000); /* get 1000 bytes */
```

After the assignment, **p** points to the first of 1,000 bytes of free memory.

In the preceding example, notice that no type cast is used to assign the return value of **malloc( )** to **p.** As explained, a **void *** pointer is automatically converted to the type of the pointer on the left side of an assignment. (However, this automatic conversion *does not* occur in C++, and an explicit type cast is needed.)

The next example allocates space for 50 integers. Notice the use of **sizeof** to ensure portability.

```
int *p;
p = malloc(50*sizeof(int));
```

Since the heap is not infinite, whenever you allocate memory, you must check the value returned by **malloc( )** to make sure that it is not null before using the pointer. Using a null pointer will almost certainly crash your program. The proper way to allocate memory and test for a valid pointer is illustrated in this code fragment:

```
p = malloc(100);
if(!p) {
  printf("Out of memory.\n");
  exit(1);
}
```

Of course, you can substitute some other sort of error handler in place of the call to **exit( ).** Just make sure that you do not use the pointer **p** if it is null.

The **free( )** function is the opposite of **malloc( )** in that it returns previously allocated memory to the system. Once the memory has been freed, it may be reused by a subsequent call to **malloc( ).** The function **free( )** has this prototype:

void free(void *p);

Here, *p* is a pointer to memory that was previously allocated using **malloc( ).** It is critical that you *never* call **free( )** with an invalid argument; this will damage the allocation system.

C's dynamic allocation subsystem is used in conjunction with pointers to support a variety of important programming constructs, such as linked lists and binary trees. Several examples of these are included in Part Four. Another important use of dynamic allocation is discussed next: dynamically allocated arrays.

Dynamically Allocated Arrays

Sometimes you will want to allocate memory using **malloc( )**, but operate on that memory as if it were an array, using array indexing. In essence, you may want to create a *dynamically allocated array*. Since any pointer can be indexed as if it were an array, this presents no trouble. For example, the following program shows how you can use a dynamically allocated array to hold a one-dimensional array—in this case, a string.

```c
/* Allocate space for a string dynamically, request user
   input, and then print the string backwards. */

#include <stdlib.h>
#include <stdio.h>
#include <string.h>

int main(void)
{
  char *s;
  register int t;

  s = malloc(80);

  if(!s) {
    printf("Memory request failed.\n");
    exit(1);
  }

  gets(s);
  for(t=strlen(s)-1; t>=0; t--) putchar(s[t]);
  free(s);

  return 0;
}
```

As the program shows, before its first use, **s** is tested to ensure that the allocation request succeeded and that a valid pointer was returned by **malloc( )**. This is absolutely necessary to prevent accidental use of a null pointer. Notice how the pointer **s** is used in the call to **gets( )** and then indexed as an array to print the string backwards.

You can also dynamically allocate multidimensional arrays. To do so, you must declare a pointer that specifies all but the leftmost array dimension. To see how this works, study the following example, which builds a table of the numbers 1 through 10 raised to their first, second, third, and fourth powers.

```c
#include <stdio.h>
#include <stdlib.h>

int pwr(int a, int b);

int main(void)
{
  /* Declare a pointer to an array that has 10
     ints in each row. */
  int (*p)[10];

  register int i, j;

  /* allocate memory to hold a 4 x 10 array */
  p = malloc(40*sizeof(int));

  if(!p) {
    printf("Memory request failed.\n");
    exit(1);
  }

  for(j=1; j<11; j++)
    for(i=1; i<5; i++) p[i-1][j-1] = pwr(j, i);

  for(j=1; j<11; j++) {
    for(i=1; i<5; i++) printf("%10d ", p[i-1][j-1]);
    printf("\n");
  }

  return 0;
}

/* Raise an integer to the specified power. */
pwr(int a, int b)
{
  register int  t=1;

  for(; b; b--) t = t*a;
  return t;
}
```

The output produced by this program is shown here.

1	1	1	1
2	4	8	16
3	9	27	81
4	16	64	256
5	25	125	625
6	36	216	1296
7	49	343	2401
8	64	512	4096
9	81	729	6561
10	100	1000	10000

In **main( )**, the pointer **p** is declared like this:

```
int (*p)[10];
```

The parentheses around ***p** are necessary. This declaration states that **p** is a pointer to an array of 10 integers. That is, its base type is a 10-**int** array. When **p** is incremented, it will point to the start of the next 10 integers; when decremented, **p** will point to the previous 10 integers. Thus, **p** is a pointer to a two-dimensional integer array that has 10 elements in each row. This means that **p** can be indexed as a two-dimensional array, as the program shows. The only difference is that the storage for the array is allocated manually using the **malloc( )** statement, rather than automatically using a normal array declaration statement.

One final point: As has been mentioned, in C++ you must cast all pointer conversions. Therefore, if you want to make the preceding program compatible with both C and C++, you must cast the pointer returned by **malloc( )**, as shown here:

```
p = (int (*)[10]) malloc(40*sizeof(int));
```

As explained earlier, many C programmers cast all pointer conversions for the sake of compatibility with C++.

restrict-Qualified Pointers

The C99 standard has added a new type qualifier that applies only to pointers: **restrict**. Pointers qualified by **restrict** are discussed in detail in Part Two, but a brief description is given here.

A pointer qualified by **restrict** is initially the only means by which the object it points to is accessed. Access to the object by another pointer can occur only if the second pointer is based on the first. Thus, access to the object is restricted to expressions based on the **restrict**-qualified pointer. Pointers qualified by **restrict** are primarily used as function parameters or to point to memory allocated via **malloc( )**. By qualifying a pointer with **restrict**, the compiler is better able to optimize certain types of routines. For example, if a function specifies two **restrict**-qualified pointer parameters, then the compiler can assume that the pointers point to different (that is, non-overlapping) objects. The **restrict** qualifier does not change the semantics of a program.

Problems with Pointers

Nothing will get you into more trouble than a wild pointer! Pointers are a mixed blessing. They give you tremendous power, but when a pointer is used incorrectly, or contains the wrong value, it can be a very difficult bug to find.

An erroneous pointer is difficult to find because the pointer, by itself, is not the problem. The trouble starts when you access an object through that pointer. In short, when you attempt to use a bad pointer, you are reading or writing to some unknown piece of memory. If you read from it, you will get a garbage value, which will probably cause your program to malfunction. If you write to it, you might be writing over other pieces of your code or data. In either case, the problem might not show up until later in the execution of your program and may lead you to look for the bug in the wrong place. There may be little or no evidence to suggest that the pointer is the original cause of the problem. Programmers lose sleep over this type of bug time and time again.

Because pointer errors are so troublesome, you should, of course, do your best never to generate one. To help you avoid them, a few of the more common errors are discussed here. The classic example of a pointer error is the *uninitialized pointer*. Consider this program:

```
/* This program is wrong. */
int main(void)
{
  int x, *p;

  x = 10;
  *p = x; /* error, p not initialized */

  return 0;
}
```

This program assigns the value 10 to some unknown memory location. Here is why. Since the pointer **p** has never been given a value, it contains an unknown value when the assignment ***p = x** takes place. This causes the value of **x** to be written to some unknown memory location. This type of problem often goes unnoticed when the program is small because the odds are in favor of **p** containing a "safe" address–one that is not in your code, data area, or operating system. However, as your program grows, the probability increases of **p** pointing to something vital. Eventually, your program stops working. In this simple example, most compilers will issue a warning message stating that you are attempting to use an uninitialized pointer, but the same type of error can occur in more roundabout ways that the compiler can't detect.

A second common error is caused by a simple misunderstanding of how to use a pointer. Consider the following:

```
/* This program is wrong. */
#include <stdio.h>

int main(void)
{
  int x, *p;

  x = 10;
  p = x;

  printf("%d", *p);

  return 0;
}
```

The call to **printf( )** does not print the value of **x**, which is 10, on the screen. It prints some unknown value because the assignment

```
p = x;
```

is wrong. That statement assigns the value 10 to the pointer **p**. However, **p** is supposed to contain an address, not a value. To correct the program, write

```
p = &x;
```

As with the earlier error, most compilers will issue at least a warning message when you attempt to assign **x** to **p**. But as before, this error can manifest itself in a more subtle fashion which the compiler can't detect.

Another error that sometimes occurs is caused by incorrect assumptions about the placement of variables in memory. In general, you cannot know where your data will be placed in memory, or whether it will be placed there the same way again, or whether different compilers will treat it in the same way. For these reasons, making any comparisons between pointers that do not point to a common object may yield unexpected results. For example,

```
char s[80], y[80];
char *p1, *p2;
```

```
p1 = s;
p2 = y;
if(p1 < p2) . . .
```

is generally an invalid concept. (In very unusual situations, you might use something like this to determine the relative position of the variables. But this would be rare.)

A related error results when you assume that two adjacent arrays may be indexed as one by simply incrementing a pointer across the array boundaries. For example:

```
int first[10], second[10];
int *p, t;

p = first;
for(t=0; t<20; ++t)  *p++ = t;
```

This is not a good way to initialize the arrays **first** and **second** with the numbers 0 through 19. Even though it may work on some compilers under certain circumstances, it assumes that both arrays will be placed back to back in memory with **first** first. This may not always be the case.

The next program illustrates a very dangerous type of bug. See if you can find it.

```
/* This program has a bug. */
#include <string.h>
#include <stdio.h>

int main(void)
{
  char *p1;
  char s[80];

  p1 = s;
  do {
    gets(s);  /* read a string */

    /* print the decimal equivalent of each
       character */
    while(*p1) printf(" %d", *p1++);

  } while(strcmp(s, "done"));

  return 0;
}
```

This program uses **p1** to print the ASCII values associated with the characters contained in **s**. The problem is that **p1** is assigned the address of **s** only once, outside the loop. The first time through the loop, **p1** points to the first character in **s**. However, the second time through, it continues where it left off because it is not reset to the start of **s**. This next character may be part of the second string, another variable, or a piece of the program! The proper way to write this program is

```
/* This program is now correct. */
#include <string.h>
#include <stdio.h>

int main(void)
{
  char *p1;
  char s[80];

  do {
    p1 = s; /* reset p1 to beginning of s */
    gets(s);  /* read a string */

    /* print the decimal equivalent of each
       character */
    while(*p1) printf(" %d", *p1++);

  } while(strcmp(s, "done"));

  return 0;
}
```

Here, each time the loop iterates, **p1** is set to the start of the string. In general, you should remember to reinitialize a pointer if it is to be reused.

The fact that handling pointers incorrectly can cause tricky bugs is no reason to avoid using them. Just be careful, and make sure that you know where each pointer is pointing before you use it.

The Complete Reference

Chapter 6

Functions

Functions are the building blocks of C and the place where all program activity occurs. This chapter examines their features, including function arguments, return values, prototypes, and recursion.

The General Form of a Function

The general form of a function is

ret-type function-name(parameter list)
{
  body of the function
}

The *ret-type* specifies the type of data that the function returns. A function may return any type of data except an array. The *parameter list* is a comma-separated list of variable names and their associated types. The parameters receive the values of the arguments when the function is called. A function can be without parameters, in which case the parameter list is empty. An empty parameter list can be explicitly specified as such by placing the keyword **void** inside the parentheses.

In variable declarations, you can declare several variables to be of the same type by using a comma-separated list of variable names. In contrast, all function parameters must be declared individually, each including both the type and name. That is, the parameter declaration list for a function takes this general form:

f(type varname1, type varname2, . . . , type varnameN)

For example, here are a correct and an incorrect function parameter declaration:

```
f(int i, int k, int j) /* correct */
f(int i, k, float j)   /* wrong, k must have its own type specifier */
```

Understanding the Scope of a Function

The scope rules of a language are the rules that govern whether a piece of code knows about or has access to another piece of code or data. The scopes defined by C were described in Chapter 2. Here we will look more closely at one specific scope: the one defined by a function.

Each function is a discrete block of code. Thus, a function defines a block scope. This means that a function's code is private to that function and cannot be accessed by any statement in any other function except through a call to that function. (For instance, you cannot use **goto** to jump into the middle of another function.) The code that constitutes the body of a function is hidden from the rest of the program, and unless it uses global variables, it can neither affect nor be affected by other parts of the program. Stated another way, the code and data defined within one function cannot interact with the code or data defined in another function because the two functions have different scopes.

Variables that are defined within a function are local variables. A local variable comes into existence when the function is entered and is destroyed upon exit. Thus, a local variable cannot hold its value between function calls. The only exception to this rule is when the variable is declared with the **static** storage class specifier. This causes the compiler to treat the variable as if it were a global variable for storage purposes, but limit its scope to the function. (See Chapter 2 for additional information on global and local variables.)

The formal parameters to a function also fall within the function's scope. This means that a parameter is known throughout the entire function. A parameter comes into existence when the function is called and is destroyed when the function is exited.

All functions have file scope. Thus, you cannot define a function within a function. This is why C is not technically a block-structured language.

Function Arguments

If a function is to accept arguments, it must declare the parameters that will receive the values of the arguments. As shown in the following function, the parameter declarations occur after the function name.

```
/* Return 1 if c is part of string s; 0 otherwise. */
int is_in(char *s,  char c)
{
  while(*s)
    if(*s==c) return 1;
    else s++;
  return 0;
}
```

The function **is_in( )** has two parameters: **s** and **c**. This function returns 1 if the character **c** is part of the string **s**; otherwise, it returns 0.

Even though parameters perform the special task of receiving the value of the arguments passed to the function, they behave like any other local variable. For example, you can make assignments to a function's formal parameters or use them in an expression.

Call by Value, Call by Reference

In a computer language there are two ways that arguments can be passed to a subroutine. The first is *call by value*. This method copies the *value of* an argument into the formal parameter of the subroutine. In this case, changes made to the parameter have no effect on the argument.

Call by reference is the second way of passing arguments to a subroutine. In this method, the *address* of an argument is copied into the parameter. Inside the subroutine, the address is used to access the actual argument used in the call. This means that changes made to the parameter affect the argument.

With few exceptions, C uses call by value to pass arguments. In general, this means that code within a function cannot alter the arguments used to call the function. Consider the following program:

```c
#include <stdio.h>

int sqr(int x);

int main(void)
{
  int t=10;

  printf("%d %d", sqr(t), t);

  return 0;
}

int sqr(int x)
{
  x = x*x;
  return(x);
}
```

In this example, the value of the argument to **sqr( )**, 10, is copied into the parameter **x**. When the assignment x = x*x takes place, only the local variable **x** is modified. The variable **t**, used to call **sqr( )**, still has the value 10. Hence, the output is **100 10**.

Remember that it is a copy of the value of the argument that is passed into a function. What occurs inside the function has no effect on the variable used in the call.

Creating a Call by Reference

Even though C uses call by value for passing parameters, you can create a call by reference by passing a pointer to an argument, instead of passing the argument itself. Since the address of the argument is passed to the function, code within the function can change the value of the argument outside the function.

Pointers are passed to functions just like any other argument. Of course, you need to declare the parameters as pointer types. For example, the function **swap( )**, which exchanges the values of the two integer variables pointed to by its arguments, shows how:

```c
void swap(int *x, int *y)
{
  int temp;

  temp = *x;  /* save the value at address x */
  *x = *y;    /* put y into x */
  *y = temp;  /* put x into y */
}
```

The **swap( )** function is able to exchange the values of the two variables pointed to by **x** and **y** because their addresses (not their values) are passed. Within the function, the contents of the variables are accessed using standard pointer operations, and their values are swapped.

Remember that **swap( )** (or any other function that uses pointer parameters) must be called with the *addresses of the arguments*. The following program shows the correct way to call **swap( )**:

```c
#include <stdio.h>
void swap(int *x, int *y);

int main(void)
{
  int i, j;

  i = 10;
  j = 20;

  printf("i and j before swapping: %d %d\n", i, j);

  swap(&i, &j); /* pass the addresses of i and j */

  printf("i and j after swapping: %d %d\n", i, j);

  return 0;
}

void swap(int *x, int *y)
{
  int temp;
```

```
    temp = *x;   /* save the value at address x */
    *x = *y;     /* put y into x */
    *y = temp;   /* put x into y */
}
```

The output from this program is shown here:

```
i and j before swapping: 10 20
i and j after swapping: 20 10
```

In the program, the variable **i** is assigned the value 10, and **j** is assigned the value 20. Then **swap( )** is called with the addresses of **i** and **j**. (The unary operator **&** is used to produce the address of the variables.) Therefore, the addresses of **i** and **j**, not their values, are passed into the function **swap( )**.

Note *C++ allows you to fully automate a call by reference through the use of reference parameters. Reference parameters are not supported by C.*

Calling Functions with Arrays

Arrays are covered in detail in Chapter 4. However, this section discusses passing arrays as arguments to functions because it is an exception to the normal call-by-value parameter passing.

When an array is used as a function argument, its address is passed to a function. This is an exception to the call-by-value parameter passing convention. In this case, the code inside the function is operating on, and potentially altering, the actual contents of the array used to call the function. For example, consider the function **print_upper( )**, which prints its string argument in uppercase:

```
#include <stdio.h>
#include <ctype.h>

void print_upper(char *string);

int main(void)
{
  char s[80];

  printf("Enter a string: ");
  gets(s);
  print_upper(s);
  printf("\ns is now uppercase: %s", s);
```

```
  return 0;
}

/* Print a string in uppercase. */
void print_upper(char *string)
{
  register int t;

  for(t=0; string[t]; ++t)  {
    string[t] = toupper(string[t]);
    putchar(string[t]);
  }
}
```

Here is sample output:

```
Enter a string: This is a test.
THIS IS A TEST.
s is now uppercase: THIS IS A TEST.
```

After the call to **print_upper( )**, the contents of array **s** in **main( )** are changed to
uppercase. If this is not what you want, you could write the program like this:

```
#include <stdio.h>
#include <ctype.h>

void print_upper(char *string);

int main(void)
{
  char s[80];

  printf("Enter a string: ");
  gets(s);
  print_upper(s);
  printf("\ns is unchanged: %s", s);

  return 0;
}

void print_upper(char *string)
```

```
{
  register int t;

  for(t=0; string[t]; ++t)
    putchar(toupper(string[t]));
}
```

Here is sample output from this version of the program:

```
Enter a string: This is a test.
THIS IS A TEST.
s is unchanged: This is a test.
```

In this case, the contents of array **s** remain unchanged because its values are not altered inside **print_upper( )**.

The standard library function **gets( )** is a classic example of passing arrays into functions. Although the **gets( )** in your standard library is more sophisticated, the following simpler version, called **xgets( )**, will give you an idea of how it works.

```
/* A simple version of the standard
   gets() library function. */
char *xgets(char *s)
{
  char ch, *p;
  int t;

  p = s;  /* gets() returns a pointer to s */

  for(t=0; t<80; ++t){
    ch = getchar();

    switch(ch) {
      case '\n':
        s[t] = '\0'; /* terminate the string */
        return p;
      case '\b':
        if(t>0) t--;
        break;
      default:
        s[t] = ch;
    }
```

```
    }
    s[79] = '\0';
    return p;
}
```

The **xgets( )** function must be called with a **char *** pointer. This, of course, can be the name of a character array, which by definition is a **char *** pointer. Upon entry, **xgets( )** establishes a **for** loop from 0 to 80. This prevents larger strings from being entered at the keyboard. If more than 80 characters are entered, the function returns. (The real **gets( )** function does not have this restriction.) Because C has no built-in bounds checking, you should make sure that any array used to call **xgets( )** can accept at least 80 characters. As you type characters on the keyboard, they are placed in the string. If you type a backspace, the counter **t** is reduced by 1, effectively removing the previous character from the array. When you press ENTER, a null is placed at the end of the string, signaling its termination. Because the array used to call **xgets( )** is modified, upon return it contains the characters that you type.

argc and argv—Arguments to main( )

Sometimes it is useful to pass information into a program when you run it. Generally, you pass information into the **main( )** function via command line arguments. A *command line argument* is the information that follows the program's name on the command line of the operating system. For example, when you compile a program, you might type something like the following after the command prompt,

    cc *program_name*

where *program_name* is a command line argument that specifies the name of the program you wish to compile.

Two special built-in arguments, **argc** and **argv**, are used to receive command line arguments. The **argc** parameter holds the number of arguments on the command line and is an integer. It is always at least 1 because the name of the program qualifies as the first argument. The **argv** parameter is a pointer to an array of character pointers. Each element in this array points to a command line argument. All command line arguments are strings—any numbers will have to be converted by the program into the proper binary format, manually.

Here is a simple example that uses a command line argument. It prints **Hello** and your name on the screen, if you specify your name as a command line argument.

```
#include <stdio.h>
#include <stdlib.h>
```

```
int main(int argc, char *argv[])
{
  if(argc!=2) {
    printf("You forgot to type your name.\n");
    exit(1);
  }
  printf("Hello %s", argv[1]);

  return 0;
}
```

If you called this program **name** and your name were Tom, you would type **name Tom** to run the program. The output from the program would be **Hello Tom**.

In many environments, each command line argument must be separated by a space or a tab. Commas, semicolons, and the like are not considered separators. For example,

```
run Spot, run
```

is made up of three strings, while

```
Herb,Rick,Fred
```

is a single string because commas are not generally legal separators.

Some environments allow you to enclose within double quotes a string containing spaces. This causes the entire string to be treated as a single argument. Check your operating system documentation for details on the definition of command line parameters for your system.

You must declare **argv** properly. The most common method is

```
char *argv[];
```

The empty brackets indicate that the array is of undetermined length. You can now access the individual arguments by indexing **argv**. For example, **argv[0]** points to the first string, which is always the program's name; **argv[1]** points to the first argument, and so on.

Another short example using command line arguments is the program called **countdown**, shown here. It counts down from a starting value (which is specified on the command line) and beeps when it reaches 0. Notice that the first argument containing the starting count is converted into an integer by the standard function **atoi( )**. If the string "display" is the second command line argument, the countdown will also be displayed on the screen.

```
/* Countdown program. */
#include <stdio.h>
#include <stdlib.h>
#include <ctype.h>
#include <string.h>

int main(int argc, char *argv[])
{
  int disp, count;

  if(argc<2) {
    printf("You must enter the length of the count\n");
    printf("on the command line. Try again.\n");
    exit(1);
  }

  if(argc==3 && !strcmp(argv[2], "display")) disp = 1;
  else disp = 0;

  for(count=atoi(argv[1]); count; --count)
    if(disp) printf("%d\n", count);

  putchar('\a');  /* this will ring the bell */
  printf("Done");

  return 0;
}
```

Notice that if no command line arguments have been specified, an error message is printed. A program with command line arguments often issues instructions if the user attempts to run the program without entering the proper information.

To access an individual character in one of the command line arguments, add a second index to **argv**. For example, the next program displays all of the arguments with which it was called, one character at a time:

```
#include <stdio.h>

int main(int argc, char *argv[])
{
  int t, i;

  for(t=0; t<argc; ++t) {
```

```
    i = 0;

    while(argv[t][i]) {
      putchar(argv[t][i]);
      ++i;
    }
    printf("\n");
  }

  return 0;
}
```

Remember, for **argv**, the first index accesses the string, and the second index accesses the individual characters of the string.

Usually, you use **argc** and **argv** to get initial commands into your program that are needed at start-up. For example, command line arguments often specify such things as a filename, an option, or an alternate behavior. Using command line arguments gives your program a professional appearance and facilitates its use in batch files.

The names **argc** and **argv** are traditional but arbitrary. You may name these two parameters to **main( )** anything you like. Also, some compilers may support additional arguments to **main( )**, so be sure to check your compiler's documentation.

When a program does not require command line parameters, it is common practice to explicitly declare **main( )** as having no parameters. This is accomplished by using the **void** keyword in its parameter list.

The return Statement

The mechanics of **return** are described in Chapter 3. As explained, it has two important uses. First, it causes an immediate exit from the function. That is, it causes program execution to return to the calling code. Second, it can be used to return a value. The following sections examine how the **return** statement is applied.

Returning from a Function

A function terminates execution and returns to the caller in two ways. The first occurs when the last statement in the function has executed, and, conceptually, the function's ending curly brace (}) is encountered. (Of course, the curly brace isn't actually present in the object code, but you can think of it in this way.) For example, the **pr_reverse( )** function in this program simply prints the string **I like C** backwards on the screen and then returns.

```
#include <string.h>
#include <stdio.h>

void pr_reverse(char *s);

int main(void)
{
  pr_reverse("I like C");

  return 0;
}

void pr_reverse(char *s)
{
  register int t;

  for(t=strlen(s)-1; t>=0; t--) putchar(s[t]);
}
```

Once the string has been displayed, there is nothing left for **pr_reverse( )** to do, so it returns to the place from which it was called.

Actually, not many functions use this default method of terminating their execution. Most functions rely on the **return** statement to stop execution either because a value must be returned or to make a function's code simpler and more efficient.

A function may contain several **return** statements. For example, the **find_substr( )** function in the following program returns the starting position of a substring within a string, or it returns –1 if no match is found. It uses two **return** statements to simplify the coding.

```
#include <stdio.h>

int find_substr(char *s1, char *s2);

int main(void)
{
  if(find_substr("C is fun", "is") != -1)
    printf("Substring is found.");

  return 0;
}

/* Return index of first match of s2 in s1. */
```

```
int find_substr(char *s1, char *s2)
{
  register int t;
  char *p, *p2;

  for(t=0; s1[t]; t++) {
    p = &s1[t];
    p2 = s2;

    while(*p2 && *p2==*p) {
      p++;
      p2++;
    }
    if(!*p2) return t; /* 1st return */
  }
   return -1; /* 2nd return */
}
```

Returning Values

All functions, except those of type **void**, return a value. This value is specified by the
return statement. In C89, if a non-**void** function executes a **return** statement that does
not include a value, then a garbage value is returned. This is, to say the least, bad
practice! In C99 (and C++), a non-**void** function *must* use a **return** statement that
returns a value. That is, in C99, if a function is specified as returning a value, any
return statement within it must have a value associated with it. However, if execution
reaches the end of a non-**void** function (that is, encounters the function's closing curly
brace), a garbage value is returned. Although this condition is not a syntax error, it is
still a fundamental flaw and should be avoided.

As long as a function is not declared as **void**, you can use it as an operand in an
expression. Therefore, each of the following expressions is valid:

```
x = power(y);
if(max(x,y) > 100) printf("greater");
for(ch=getchar(); isdigit(ch); ) ... ;
```

As a general rule, a function call cannot be on the left side of an assignment. A
statement such as

```
swap(x,y) = 100; /* incorrect statement */
```

is wrong. The C compiler will flag it as an error and will not compile a program that
contains it.

When you write programs, your functions will be of three types. The first type is simply computational. These functions are specifically designed to perform operations on their arguments and return a value based on that operation. A computational function is a "pure" function. Examples are the standard library functions **sqrt( )** and **sin( )**, which compute the square root and sine of their arguments.

The second type of function manipulates information and returns a value that simply indicates the success or failure of that manipulation. An example is the library function **fclose( )**, which closes a file. If the close operation is successful, the function returns 0; it returns **EOF** if an error occurs.

The last type of function has no explicit return value. In essence, the function is strictly procedural and produces no value. An example is **exit( )**, which terminates a program. All functions that do not return values should be declared as returning type **void**. By declaring a function as **void**, you keep it from being used in an expression, thus preventing accidental misuse.

Sometimes, functions that really don't produce an interesting result return something anyway. For example, **printf( )** returns the number of characters written. Yet, it is unusual to find a program that actually checks this. In other words, although all functions, except those of type **void**, return values, you don't have to use the return value for anything. A common question concerning function return values is, "Don't I have to assign this value to some variable since a value is being returned?" The answer is no. If there is no assignment specified, the return value is simply discarded. Consider the following program, which uses the function **mul( )**:

```c
#include <stdio.h>

int mul(int a, int b);

int main(void)
{
  int x, y, z;

  x = 10;   y = 20;
  z = mul(x, y);            /* 1 */
  printf("%d", mul(x,y));   /* 2 */
  mul(x, y);                /* 3 */

  return 0;
}

int mul(int a, int b)
{
  return a*b;
}
```

In line 1, the return value of **mul( )** is assigned to **z**. In line 2, the return value is not actually assigned, but it is used by the **printf( )** function. Finally, in line 3, the return value is lost because it is neither assigned to another variable nor used as part of an expression.

Returning Pointers

Although functions that return pointers are handled just like any other type of function, it is helpful to review some key concepts and look at an example. Pointers are neither integers nor unsigned integers. They are the memory addresses of a certain type of data. One reason for this distinction is that pointer arithmetic is relative to the base type. For example, if an integer pointer is incremented, it will contain a value that is four greater than its previous value (assuming 4-byte integers). In general, each time a pointer is incremented (or decremented), it points to the next (or previous) item of its type. Since the length of different data types may differ, the compiler must know what type of data the pointer is pointing to. For this reason, a function that returns a pointer must declare explicitly what type of pointer it is returning. For example, you should not use a return type of **int *** to return a **char *** pointer! In a few cases, a function will need to return a generic pointer. In this case, the function return type must be specified as **void ***.

To return a pointer, a function must be declared as having a pointer return type. For example, the following function returns a pointer to the first occurrence of the character **c** in string **s**: If no match is found, a pointer to the null terminator is returned.

```
/* Return pointer of first occurrence of c in s. */
char *match(char c, char *s)
{
  while(c!=*s && *s) s++;
  return(s);
}
```

Here is a short program that uses **match( )**:

```
#include <stdio.h>

char *match(char c, char *s);  /* prototype */

int main(void)
{
  char s[80], *p, ch;

  gets(s);
  ch = getchar();
  p = match(ch, s);
```

```
  if(*p)  /* there is a match */
    printf("%s ", p);
  else
    printf("No match found.");

  return 0;
}
```

This program reads a string and then a character. It then searches for an occurrence of the character in the string. If the character is in the string, **p** will point to that character, and the program prints the string from the point of match. When no match is found, **p** will be pointing to the null terminator, making ***p** false. In this case, the program prints **No match found**.

Functions of Type void

One of **void**'s uses is to explicitly declare functions that do not return values. This prevents their use in any expression and helps avert accidental misuse. For example, the function **print_vertical( )** prints its string argument vertically down the side of the screen. Since it returns no value, it is declared as **void**.

```
void print_vertical(char *str)
{
  while(*str)
    printf("%c\n", *str++);
}
```

Here is an example that uses **print_vertical( )**:

```
#include <stdio.h>

void print_vertical(char *str);  /* prototype */

int main(int argc, char *argv[])
{
  if(argc > 1) print_vertical(argv[1]);

  return 0;
}

void print_vertical(char *str)
{
```

```
  while(*str)
    printf("%c\n", *str++);
}
```

One last point: Early versions of C did not define the **void** keyword. Thus, in early C programs, functions that did not return values simply defaulted to type **int**, even though no value was returned.

What Does main( ) Return?

The **main( )** function returns an integer to the calling process, which is generally the operating system. Returning a value from **main( )** is the equivalent of calling **exit( )** with the same value. If **main( )** does not explicitly return a value, the value passed to the calling process is technically undefined. In practice, most C compilers automatically return 0, but do not rely on this if portability is a concern.

Recursion

In C, a function can call itself. In this case, the function is said to be *recursive*. Recursion is the process of defining something in terms of itself, and is sometimes called *circular definition*.

A simple example of a recursive function is **factr( )**, which computes the factorial of an integer. The factorial of a number **n** is the product of all the whole numbers between 1 and **n**. For example, 3 factorial is 1 x 2 x 3, or 6. Both **factr( )** and its iterative equivalent are shown here:

```
/* recursive */
int factr(int n) {
  int answer;

  if(n==1) return(1);
  answer = factr(n-1)*n; /* recursive call */
  return(answer);
}

/* non-recursive */
int fact(int n) {
  int t, answer;

  answer = 1;
```

```
    for(t=1; t<=n; t++)
        answer=answer*(t);

    return(answer);
}
```

The nonrecursive version of **fact( )** should be clear. It uses a loop that runs from 1 to **n** and progressively multiplies each number by the moving product.

The operation of the recursive **factr( )** is a little more complex. When **factr( )** is called with an argument of 1, the function returns 1. Otherwise, it returns the product of **factr(n-1)*n**. To evaluate this expression, **factr( )** is called with **n-1**. This happens until **n** equals 1 and the calls to the function begin returning.

Computing the factorial of 2, the first call to **factr( )** causes a second, recursive call with the argument of 1. This call returns 1, which is then multiplied by 2 (the original **n** value). The answer is then 2. Try working through the computation of 3 factorial on your own. (You might want to insert **printf( )** statements into **factr( )** to see the level of each call and what the intermediate answers are.)

When a function calls itself, a new set of local variables and parameters are allocated storage on the stack, and the function code is executed from the top with these new variables. A recursive call does not make a new copy of the function. Only the values being operated upon are new. As each recursive call returns, the old local variables and parameters are removed from the stack, and execution resumes immediately after the recursive call inside the function. Recursive functions could be said to "telescope" out and back.

Although recursion seems to offer the possibility of improved efficiency, such is seldom the case. Often, recursive routines do not significantly reduce code size or improve memory utilization. Also, the recursive versions of most routines may execute a bit slower than their iterative equivalents because of the overhead of the repeated function calls. In fact, many recursive calls to a function could cause a stack overrun. Because storage for function parameters and local variables is on the stack and each new call creates a new copy of these variables, the stack could be exhausted. A stack overrun is what usually causes a program to crash when a recursive function runs wild.

The main advantage to recursive functions is that you can use them to create clearer and simpler versions of several algorithms. For example, the quicksort algorithm (shown in Part Four) is difficult to implement in an iterative way. Also, some problems, especially ones related to artificial intelligence, lend themselves to recursive solutions. Finally, some people seem to think recursively more easily than iteratively.

When writing recursive functions, you must have a conditional statement, such as an **if**, somewhere to force the function to return without the recursive call being executed. If you don't, the function will never return once you call it. Omitting the conditional statement is a common error when writing recursive functions. Use

printf( ) liberally during program development so that you can watch what is going on and abort execution if you see a mistake.

Function Prototypes

In modern, properly written C programs, all functions must be declared before they are used. This is normally accomplished using a *function prototype*. Function prototypes were not part of the original C language, but were added by C89. Although prototypes are not technically required, their use is strongly encouraged. (Prototypes *are* required by C++, however.) In this book, all examples include full function prototypes. Prototypes enable the compiler to provide stronger type checking, somewhat like that provided by languages such as Pascal. When you use prototypes, the compiler can find and report any questionable type conversions between the arguments used to call a function and the type of its parameters. The compiler will also catch differences between the number of arguments used to call a function and the number of parameters in the function.

The general form of a function prototype is

type func_name(type parm_name1, type parm_name2,. . ., type parm_nameN);

The use of parameter names is optional. However, they enable the compiler to identify any type mismatches by name when an error occurs, so it is a good idea to include them.

The following program illustrates the value of function prototypes. It produces an error message because it contains an attempt to call **sqr_it( )** with an integer argument instead of the integer pointer required.

```
/* This program uses a function prototype to
   enforce strong type checking. */

void sqr_it(int *i); /* prototype */

int main(void)
{
  int x;

  x = 10;
  sqr_it(x);   /* type mismatch */

  return 0;
}
```

```
void sqr_it(int *i)
{
  *i = *i * *i;
}
```

A function's definition can also serve as its prototype if the definition occurs prior to the function's first use in the program. For example, this is a valid program:

```
#include <stdio.h>

/* This definition will also serve
   as a prototype within this program. */
void f(int a, int b)
{
  printf("%d ", a % b);
}

int main(void)
{
  f(10,3);

  return 0;
}
```

In this example, since **f( )** is defined prior to its use in **main( )**, no separate prototype is required. Although it is possible for a function's definition to serve as its prototype in small programs, it is seldom possible in large ones—especially when several files are used. The programs in this book include a separate prototype for each function because that is the way C code is normally written in practice.

The only function that does not require a prototype is **main( )** because it is the first function called when your program begins.

There is a small but important difference between how C and C++ handle the prototyping of a function that has no parameters. In C++, an empty parameter list is indicated in the prototype by the absence of any parameters. For example,

```
int f(); /* C++ prototype for a function with no parameters */
```

However, in C this statement means something different. Because of the need for compatibility with the original version of C, an empty parameter list simply says that *no parameter information* is given. As far as the compiler is concerned, the function could have several parameters or no parameters. (Such a statement is called an old-style function declaration and is described in the following section.)

In C, when a function has no parameters, its prototype uses **void** inside the parameter list. For example, here is **f( )**'s prototype as it would appear in a C program:

```
float f(void);
```

This tells the compiler that the function has no parameters, and any call to that function that has arguments is an error. In C++, the use of **void** inside an empty parameter list is still allowed, but redundant.

Function prototypes help you trap bugs before they occur. In addition, they help verify that your program is working correctly by not allowing functions to be called with mismatched arguments.

One last point: Since early versions of C did not support the full prototype syntax, prototypes are technically optional in C. This is necessary to support pre-prototype C code. If you are porting older C code to C++, you will need to add full function prototypes before the code will compile. Remember, although prototypes are optional in C, they are required by C++. This means that every function in a C++ program must be fully prototyped. Because of this, most C programmers also fully prototype their programs.

Old-Style Function Declarations

In the early days of C, prior to the creation of function prototypes, there was still a need to tell the compiler in advance about the return type of a function so that the proper code could be generated when the function was called. (Since sizes of different data types differ, the size of the return type needs to be known prior to a call to a function.) This was accomplished using a function declaration that did not contain any parameter information. The old-style approach is archaic by today's standards. However, it can still be found in older code. For this reason, it is important to understand how it works.

Using the old-style approach, the function's return type and name are declared near the start of your program, as illustrated here:

```
#include <stdio.h>

double div();  /* old-style function declaration */

int main(void)
{
  printf("%f", div(10.2, 20.0));

  return 0;
}
```

```
double div(double num, double denom)
{
  return num / denom;
}
```

The old-style function type declaration tells the compiler that **div( )** returns an object of type **double**. This allows the compiler to correctly generate code for calls to **div( )**. It does not, however, say anything about the parameters to **div( )**.

The old-style function declaration statement has the following general form:

type_specifier function_name( );

Notice that the parameter list is empty. Even if the function takes arguments, none are listed in its type declaration.

As stated, the old-style function declaration is outmoded and should not be used for new code. It is also incompatible with C++.

Standard Library Function Prototypes

Any standard library function used by your program must be prototyped. To accomplish this, you must include the appropriate *header* for each library function. All necessary headers are provided by the C compiler. In C, the library headers are (usually) files that use the **.h** extension. A header contains two main elements: any definitions used by the library functions and the prototypes for the library functions. For example, **<stdio.h>** is included in almost all programs in this book because it contains the prototype for **printf( )**. The headers for the standard library are described in Part Two.

Declaring Variable Length Parameter Lists

You can specify a function that has a variable number of parameters. The most common example is **printf( )**. To tell the compiler that an unknown number of arguments will be passed to a function, you must end the declaration of its parameters using three periods. For example, this prototype specifies that **func( )** will have at least two integer parameters and an unknown number (including 0) of parameters after that:

```
int func(int a, int b, ...);
```

This form of declaration is also used by a function's definition.

Any function that uses a variable number of parameters must have at least one actual parameter. For example, this is incorrect:

```
int func(...); /* illegal */
```

The "Implicit int" Rule

The original version of C included a feature that is sometimes described as the "implicit **int**" rule (also called the "default to **int**" rule). This rule states that in the absence of an explicit type specifier, the type **int** is assumed. This rule was included in the C89 standard, but has been eliminated by C99. (It is also not supported by C++.) Since the implicit **int** rule is now obsolete, this book does not use it. However, since it is still employed by many existing programs, a brief discussion is warranted.

The most common use of the implicit **int** rule was in the return type of functions. Years ago, many (probably most) C programmers took advantage of the rule when creating functions that returned an **int** result. Thus, years ago a function such as

```
int f(void) {
  /* ... */
  return 0;
}
```

would often have been written like this:

```
f(void) { /* return type int by default */
  /* ... */
  return 0;
}
```

In the first instance, the return type of **int** is explicitly specified. In the second, it is assumed by default.

The implicit **int** rule does not apply only to function return values (although that was its most common use). For example, for C89 and earlier, the following function is correct:

```
/* Here, the return type defaults to int, and so do
   the types of a and b. */
f(register a, register b) {
  register c; /* c defaults to int, too */

  c = a + b;
```

```
   printf("%d", c);

   return c;
}
```

Here, the return type of **f( )** defaults to **int**; so do the types of the parameters, **a** and **b**, and the local variable **c**.

Remember, the implicit **int** rule is not supported by C99 or C++. Thus, its use in C89-compatible programs is not recommended. It is best to explicitly specify every type used by your program.

Old-Style vs. Modern Function Parameter Declarations

Early versions of C used a different parameter declaration method than do modern versions of C, including both C89 and C99 (and C++). This early approach is sometimes called the *classic* form. This book uses a declaration approach called the *modern* form. Standard C supports both forms, but strongly recommends the modern form. (C++ supports only the modern parameter declaration method.) However, you should know the old-style form because many older C programs still use it.

The old-style function parameter declaration consists of two parts: a parameter list, which goes inside the parentheses that follow the function name, and the actual parameter declarations, which go between the closing parentheses and the function's opening curly brace. The general form of the old-style parameter definition is

type func_name(parm1, parm2, . . .parmN)
type parm1;
type parm2;
.
.
.
type parmN;
{
 function code
}

For example, this modern declaration

```
float f(int a, int b, char ch)
{
   /* ... */
}
```

will look like this in its old-style form:

```
float f(a, b, ch)
int a, b;
char ch;
{
   /* ... */
}
```

Notice that the old-style form allows the declaration of more than one parameter in a list after the type name.

 The old-style form of parameter declaration is designated as obsolete by Standard C and is not supported by C++.

The inline Keyword

C99 has added the keyword **inline**, which applies to functions. It is described fully in Part Two, but a brief description is given here. By preceding a function declaration with **inline**, you are telling the compiler to optimize calls to the function. Typically, this means that the function's code will be expanded in line, rather than called. However, **inline** is only a request to the compiler, and can be ignored.

Note *The **inline** specifier is also supported by C++.*

Chapter 7

Structures, Unions, Enumerations, and typedef

The C language gives you five ways to create a custom data type:

- The *structure*, which is a grouping of variables under one name and is called an *aggregate* data type. (The terms *compound* or *conglomerate* are also commonly used.)

- The *union*, which enables the same piece of memory to be defined as two or more different types of variables.

- The *bit-field*, which is a special type of structure or union element that allows easy access to individual bits.

- The *enumeration*, which is a list of named integer constants.

- The **typedef** keyword, which defines a new name for an existing type.

Each of these features is described in this chapter.

Structures

A structure is a collection of variables referenced under one name, providing a convenient means of keeping related information together. A *structure declaration* forms a template that can be used to create structure objects (that is, instances of a structure). The variables that make up the structure are called *members*. (Structure members are also commonly referred to as *elements* or *fields*.)

Usually, the members of a structure are logically related. For example, the name and address information in a mailing list would normally be represented in a structure. The following code fragment shows how to declare a structure that defines the name and address fields. The keyword **struct** tells the compiler that a structure is being declared.

```
struct addr
{
  char name[30];
  char street[40];
  char city[20];
  char state[3];
  unsigned long int zip;
};
```

Notice that the declaration is terminated by a semicolon. This is because a structure declaration is a statement. Also, the structure tag **addr** identifies this particular data structure and is its type specifier.

At this point, *no variable has actually been created*. Only the form of the data has been defined. When you declare a structure, you are defining an aggregate *type*, not a variable. Not until you declare a variable of that type does one actually exist. To declare a variable (that is, a physical object) of type **addr**, write

```
struct addr addr_info;
```

This declares a variable of type **addr** called **addr_info**. Thus, **addr** describes the form of a structure (its type), and **addr_info** is an instance (an object) of the structure.

When a structure variable (such as **addr_info**) is declared, the compiler automatically allocates sufficient memory to accommodate all of its members. Figure 7-1 shows how **addr_info** appears in memory, assuming 4-byte **long** integers.

You can also declare one or more objects when you declare a structure. For example,

```
struct addr {
  char name[30];
  char street[40];
  char city[20];
  char state[3];
  unsigned long int zip;
} addr_info, binfo, cinfo;
```

defines a structure type called **addr** and declares variables **addr_info**, **binfo**, and **cinfo** of that type. It is important to understand that each structure variable contains its own copies of the structure's members. For example, the **zip** field of **binfo** is separate and distinct from the **zip** field of **cinfo**. Changes to **zip** in **binfo** do not, for example, affect the **zip** in **cinfo**.

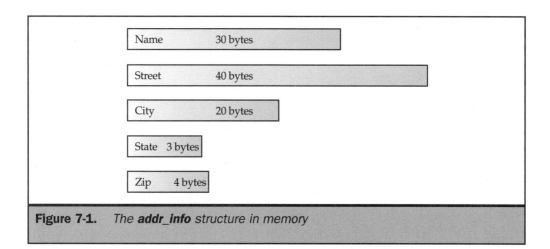

Figure 7-1.   *The **addr_info** structure in memory*

If you only need one structure variable, the structure tag is not needed. This means that

```
struct {
    char name[30];
    char street[40];
    char city[20];
    char state[3];
    unsigned long int zip;
} addr_info;
```

declares one variable named **addr_info** as defined by the structure preceding it.
The general form of a structure declaration is

```
struct tag {
    type member-name;
    type member-name;
    type member-name;
        .
        .
        .
} structure-variables;
```

where either *tag* or *structure-variables* may be omitted, but not both.

Accessing Structure Members

Individual members of a structure are accessed through the use of the **.** operator
(usually called the *dot operator*). For example, the following statement assigns the ZIP
code 12345 to the **zip** field of the structure variable **addr_info** declared earlier:

```
addr_info.zip = 12345;
```

The object name (in this case, **addr_info**) followed by a period and the member name
(in this case, **zip**) refers to that individual member. The general form for accessing a
member of a structure is

object-name.member-name

Therefore, to print the ZIP code on the screen, write

```
printf("%lu", addr_info.zip);
```

This prints the ZIP code contained in the **zip** member of the structure variable
addr_info.

In the same fashion, the character array **addr_info.name** can be used in a call to **gets( )**, as shown here:

```
gets(addr_info.name);
```

This passes a character pointer to the start of **name**.

Since **name** is a character array, you can access the individual characters of **addr_info.name** by indexing **name**. For example, you can print the contents of **addr_info.name** one character at a time by using the following code:

```
for(t=0; addr_info.name[t]; ++t)
  putchar(addr_info.name[t]);
```

Notice that it is **name** (not **addr_info**) that is indexed. Remember, **addr_info** is the name of an entire structure object; **name** is an element of that structure. Thus, if you want to index an element of a structure, you must put the subscript after the element's name.

Structure Assignments

The information contained in one structure can be assigned to another structure of the same type using a single assignment statement. You do not need to assign the value of each member separately. The following program illustrates structure assignments:

```
#include <stdio.h>

int main(void)
{
  struct {
    int a;
    int b;
  } x, y;

  x.a = 10;

  y = x;  /* assign one structure to another */

  printf("%d", y.a);

  return 0;
}
```

After the assignment, **y.a** will contain the value 10.

Arrays of Structures

Structures are often arrayed. To declare an array of structures, you must first define a structure and then declare an array variable of that type. For example, to declare a 100-element array of structures of type **addr** defined earlier, write

```
struct addr addr_list[100];
```

This creates 100 sets of variables that are organized as defined in the structure **addr**.

To access a specific structure, index the array name. For example, to print the ZIP code of structure 3, write

```
printf("%lu", addr_list[2].zip);
```

Like all array variables, arrays of structures begin indexing at 0.

To review: When you want to refer to a specific structure within an array of structures, index the structure array name. When you want to index a specific element of a structure, index the element. Thus, the following statement assigns 'X' to the first character of **name** in the third structure of **addr_list**.

```
addr_list[2].name[0] = 'X';
```

A Mailing List Example

To illustrate how structures and arrays of structures are used, this section develops a simple mailing list program that uses an array of structures to hold the address information. In this example, the stored information includes name, street, city, state, and ZIP code.

The address information is held in an array of **addr** structures, as shown here:

```
struct addr {
  char name[30];
  char street[40];
  char city[20];
  char state[3];
  unsigned long int zip;
} addr_list[MAX];
```

Notice that the **zip** field is an **unsigned long** integer. Frankly, it is more common to store postal codes using a character string because it accommodates postal codes that use letters as well as numbers (as used by Canada and other countries). However, this example stores the ZIP code in an integer as a means of illustrating a numeric structure element.

The first function needed for the program is **main( )**, shown here:

```c
int main(void)
{
  char choice;

  init_list(); /* initialize the structure array */

  for(;;) {
    choice = menu_select();
    switch(choice) {
      case 1: enter();
        break;
      case 2: delete();
        break;
      case 3: list();
        break;
      case 4: exit(0);
    }
  }

  return 0;
}
```

The function begins by initializing the structure array and then responds to menu selections.

The function **init_list( )** prepares the structure array for use by putting a null character into the first byte of the **name** field for each structure in the array. The program assumes that an array element is not in use if **name** is empty. The **init_list( )** function is shown here:

```c
/* Initialize the list. */
void init_list(void)
{
  register int t;

  for(t=0; t<MAX; ++t) addr_list[t].name[0] = '\0';
}
```

The **menu_select( )** function displays the menu and returns the user's selection.

```
/* Get a menu selection. */
int menu_select(void)
{
  char s[80];
  int c;

  printf("1. Enter a name\n");
  printf("2. Delete a name\n");
  printf("3. List the file\n");
  printf("4. Quit\n");

  do {
    printf("\nEnter your choice: ");
    gets(s);
    c = atoi(s);
  } while(c<0 || c>4);

  return c;
}
```

The **enter( )** function prompts the user for input and stores the information in the next free structure. If the array is full, the message **List Full** is displayed. **find_free( )** searches the structure array for an unused element.

```
/* Input addresses into the list. */
void enter(void)
{
  int slot;
  char s[80];

  slot = find_free();
  if(slot==-1) {
    printf("\nList Full");
    return;
  }

  printf("Enter name: ");
  gets(addr_list[slot].name);

  printf("Enter street: ");
  gets(addr_list[slot].street);
```

```
    printf("Enter city: ");
    gets(addr_list[slot].city);

    printf("Enter state: ");
    gets(addr_list[slot].state);

    printf("Enter zip: ");
    gets(s);
    addr_list[slot].zip = strtoul(s, '\0', 10);
}

/* Find an unused structure. */
int find_free(void)
{
    register int t;

    for(t=0; addr_list[t].name[0] && t<MAX; ++t) ;

    if(t==MAX) return -1; /* no slots free */
    return t;
}
```

Notice that **find_free( )** returns a –1 if every structure array variable is in use. This is a safe number because there cannot be a –1 element in an array.

The **delete( )** function asks the user to specify the index of the address that needs to be deleted. The function then puts a null character in the first character position of the **name** field.

```
/* Delete an address. */
void delete(void)
{
    register int slot;
    char s[80];

    printf("Enter record #: ");
    gets(s);
    slot = atoi(s);
    if(slot>=0 && slot < MAX)
        addr_list[slot].name[0] = '\0';
}
```

The final function needed by the program is **list( )**, which prints the entire mailing list on the screen. C does not define a standard function that sends output to the printer because of the wide variation among computing environments. However, all C compilers provide some means to accomplish this. You might want to add printing capability to the mailing list program on your own.

```c
/* Display the list on the screen. */
void list(void)
{
  register int t;

  for(t=0; t<MAX; ++t) {
    if(addr_list[t].name[0]) {
      printf("%s\n", addr_list[t].name);
      printf("%s\n", addr_list[t].street);
      printf("%s\n", addr_list[t].city);
      printf("%s\n", addr_list[t].state);
      printf("%lu\n\n", addr_list[t].zip);
    }
  }
  printf("\n\n");
}
```

The complete mailing list program is shown next. If you have any remaining doubts about structures, enter this program into your computer and study its execution, making changes and watching their effects.

```c
/* A simple mailing list example using an array of structures. */
#include <stdio.h>
#include <stdlib.h>

#define MAX 100

struct addr {
  char name[30];
  char street[40];
  char city[20];
  char state[3];
  unsigned long int zip;
} addr_list[MAX];
```

```
void init_list(void), enter(void);
void delete(void), list(void);
int menu_select(void), find_free(void);

int main(void)
{
  char choice;

  init_list(); /* initialize the structure array */
  for(;;) {
    choice = menu_select();
    switch(choice) {
      case 1: enter();
        break;
      case 2: delete();
        break;
      case 3: list();
        break;
      case 4: exit(0);
    }
  }

  return 0;
}

/* Initialize the list. */
void init_list(void)
{
  register int t;

  for(t=0; t<MAX; ++t) addr_list[t].name[0] = '\0';
}

/* Get a menu selection. */
int menu_select(void)
{
  char s[80];
  int c;

  printf("1. Enter a name\n");
  printf("2. Delete a name\n");
```

```
  printf("3. List the file\n");
  printf("4. Quit\n");
  do {
    printf("\nEnter your choice: ");
    gets(s);
    c = atoi(s);
  } while(c<0 || c>4);
  return c;
}

/* Input addresses into the list. */
void enter(void)
{
  int slot;
  char s[80];

  slot = find_free();

  if(slot==-1) {
    printf("\nList Full");
    return;
  }

  printf("Enter name: ");
  gets(addr_list[slot].name);

  printf("Enter street: ");
  gets(addr_list[slot].street);

  printf("Enter city: ");
  gets(addr_list[slot].city);

  printf("Enter state: ");
  gets(addr_list[slot].state);

  printf("Enter zip: ");
  gets(s);
  addr_list[slot].zip = strtoul(s, '\0', 10);
}
```

```
/* Find an unused structure. */
int find_free(void)
{
  register int t;

  for(t=0; addr_list[t].name[0] && t<MAX; ++t) ;

  if(t==MAX) return -1; /* no slots free */
  return t;
}

/* Delete an address. */
void delete(void)
{
  register int slot;
  char s[80];

  printf("enter record #: ");
  gets(s);
  slot = atoi(s);

  if(slot>=0 && slot < MAX)
    addr_list[slot].name[0] = '\0';
}

/* Display the list on the screen. */
void list(void)
{
  register int t;

  for(t=0; t<MAX; ++t) {
    if(addr_list[t].name[0]) {
      printf("%s\n", addr_list[t].name);
      printf("%s\n", addr_list[t].street);
      printf("%s\n", addr_list[t].city);
      printf("%s\n", addr_list[t].state);
      printf("%lu\n\n", addr_list[t].zip);
    }
  }
  printf("\n\n");
}
```

Passing Structures to Functions

This section discusses passing structures and their members to functions.

Passing Structure Members to Functions

When you pass a member of a structure to a function, you are passing the value of that member to the function. It is irrelevant that the value is obtained from a member of a structure. For example, consider this structure:

```
struct fred
{
  char x;
  int y;
  float z;
  char s[10];
} mike;
```

Here are examples of each member being passed to a function:

```
func(mike.x);    /* passes character value of x */
func2(mike.y);   /* passes integer value of y */
func3(mike.z);   /* passes float value of z */
func4(mike.s);   /* passes address of string s */
func(mike.s[2]); /* passes character value of s[2] */
```

In each case, it is the value of a specific element that is passed to the function. It does not matter that the element is part of a larger unit.

If you wish to pass the *address* of an individual structure member, put the **&** operator before the structure name. For example, to pass the address of the members of the structure **mike**, write

```
func(&mike.x);    /* passes address of character x */
func2(&mike.y);   /* passes address of integer y */
func3(&mike.z);   /* passes address of float z */
func4(mike.s);    /* passes address of string s */
func(&mike.s[2]); /* passes address of character s[2] */
```

Note that the **&** operator precedes the structure name, not the individual member name. Note also that **s** already signifies an address, so no **&** is required.

Passing Entire Structures to Functions

When a structure is used as an argument to a function, the entire structure is passed using the normal call-by-value method. Of course, this means that any changes made to the contents of the parameter inside the function do not affect the structure passed as the argument.

When using a structure as a parameter, remember that the type of the argument must match the type of the parameter. For example, in the following program both the argument **arg** and the parameter **parm** are declared as the same type of structure.

```c
#include <stdio.h>

/* Define a structure type. */
struct struct_type {
  int a, b;
  char ch;
} ;

void f1(struct struct_type parm);

int main(void)
{
  struct struct_type arg;

  arg.a = 1000;

  f1(arg);

  return 0;
}

void f1(struct struct_type parm)
{
  printf("%d", parm.a);
}
```

As this program illustrates, if you will be declaring parameters that are structures, you must make the declaration of the structure type global so that all parts of your program can use it. For example, had **struct_type** been declared inside **main( )**, it would not have been visible to **f1( )**.

As just stated, when passing structures, the type of the argument must match the type of the parameter. It is not sufficient for them simply to be physically similar; their type names must match. For example, the following version of the preceding program is incorrect and will not compile because the type name of the argument used to call **f1( )** differs from the type name of its parameter.

```c
/* This program is incorrect and will not compile. */
#include <stdio.h>

/* Define a structure type. */
struct struct_type {
  int a, b;
  char ch;
} ;

/* Define a structure similar to struct_type,
   but with a different name. */
struct struct_type2 {
  int a, b;
  char ch;
} ;

void f1(struct struct_type2 parm);

int main(void)
{
  struct struct_type arg;

  arg.a = 1000;

  f1(arg); /* type mismatch */

  return 0;
}

void f1(struct struct_type2 parm)
{
  printf("%d", parm.a);
}
```

Structure Pointers

C allows pointers to structures just as it allows pointers to any other type of object. However, there are some special aspects to structure pointers, which are described next.

Declaring a Structure Pointer

Like other pointers, structure pointers are declared by placing * in front of a structure variable's name. For example, assuming the previously defined structure **addr**, the following declares **addr_pointer** as a pointer to data of that type:

```
struct addr *addr_pointer;
```

Using Structure Pointers

There are two primary uses for structure pointers: to pass a structure to a function using call by reference and to create linked lists and other dynamic data structures that rely on dynamic allocation. This chapter covers the first use.

There is one major drawback to passing all but the simplest structures to functions: the overhead needed to push the structure onto the stack when the function call is executed. (Recall that arguments are passed to functions on the stack.) For simple structures with few members, this overhead is not too great. If the structure contains many members, however, or if some of its members are arrays, run-time performance may degrade to unacceptable levels. The solution to this problem is to pass a pointer to the structure.

When a pointer to a structure is passed to a function, only the address of the structure is pushed on the stack. This makes for very fast function calls. A second advantage, in some cases, is that passing a pointer makes it possible for the function to modify the contents of the structure used as the argument.

To find the address of a structure variable, place the **&** operator before the structure's name. For example, given the following fragment,

```
struct bal {
  float balance;
  char name[80];
} person;

struct bal *p;  /* declare a structure pointer */
```

this places the address of the structure **person** into the pointer **p**:

```
p = &person;
```

To access the members of a structure using a pointer to that structure, you must use the **–>** operator. For example, this references the **balance** field:

```
p->balance
```

The –>, usually called the *arrow operator*, consists of the minus sign followed by a greater than sign. The arrow is used in place of the dot operator when you are accessing a structure member through a pointer to the structure.

To see how a structure pointer can be used, examine this simple program, which displays the hours, minutes, and seconds using a software timer:

```c
/* Display a software timer. */
#include <stdio.h>

#define DELAY 128000

struct my_time {
  int hours;
  int minutes;
  int seconds;
} ;

void display(struct my_time *t);
void update(struct my_time *t);
void delay(void);

int main(void)
{
  struct my_time systime;

  systime.hours = 0;
  systime.minutes = 0;
  systime.seconds = 0;

  for(;;) {
    update(&systime);
    display(&systime);
  }

  return 0;
}

void update(struct my_time *t)
{
  t->seconds++;
  if(t->seconds==60) {
    t->seconds = 0;
```

```
    t->minutes++;
  }

  if(t->minutes==60) {
    t->minutes = 0;
    t->hours++;
  }

  if(t->hours==24) t->hours = 0;
  delay();
}

void display(struct my_time *t)
{
  printf("%02d:", t->hours);
  printf("%02d:", t->minutes);
  printf("%02d\n", t->seconds);
}

void delay(void)
{
  long int t;

  /* change this as needed */
  for(t=1; t<DELAY; ++t) ;
}
```

The timing of this program is adjusted by changing the definition of **DELAY**.

As you can see, a global structure called **my_time** is defined, but no variable is declared. Inside **main( )**, the structure **systime** is declared and initialized to 00:00:00. This means that **systime** is known directly only to the **main( )** function.

The functions **update( )** (which changes the time) and **display( )** (which prints the time) are passed the address of **systime**. In both functions, their arguments are declared as a pointer to a **my_time** structure.

Inside **update( )** and **display( )**, each member of **systime** is accessed via a pointer. Because **update( )** receives a pointer to the **systime** structure, it can update its value. For example, to set the hours back to 0 when 24:00:00 is reached, **update( )** contains this line of code:

```
if(t->hours==24) t->hours = 0;
```

This tells the compiler to take the address of **t** (which points to **systime** in **main( )**) and to reset **hours** to zero.

Remember, use the dot operator to access structure elements when operating on the structure itself. When you have a pointer to a structure, use the arrow operator.

Arrays and Structures Within Structures

A member of a structure can be either a simple variable, such as an **int** or **double**, or an aggregate type. In C, aggregate types are arrays and structures. You have already seen one type of aggregate element: the character arrays used in **addr**.

A member of a structure that is an array is treated as you might expect from the earlier examples. For example, consider this structure:

```
struct x {
  int a[10][10]; /* 10 x 10 array of ints */
  float b;
} y;
```

To reference integer 3,7 in **a** of structure **y**, write

```
y.a[3][7]
```

When a structure is a member of another structure, it is called a *nested structure*. For example, the structure **address** is nested inside **emp** in this example:

```
struct emp {
  struct addr address; /* nested structure */
  float wage;
} worker;
```

Here, structure **emp** has been defined as having two members. The first is a structure of type **addr**, which contains an employee's address. The other is **wage**, which holds the employee's wage. The following code fragment assigns 93456 to the **zip** element of **address**.

```
worker.address.zip = 93456;
```

As you can see, the members of each structure are referenced from outermost to innermost. The C89 standard specifies that structures can be nested to at least 15 levels. The C99 standard suggests that at least 63 levels of nesting be allowed.

Unions

A *union* is a memory location that is shared by two or more different types of variables. A union provides a way of interpreting the same bit pattern in two or more different ways. Declaring a **union** is similar to declaring a structure. Its general form is

> union *tag* {
>   *type member-name;*
>   *type member-name;*
>   *type member-name;*
>
>   .
>
>   .
>
>   .
>
> } *union-variables;*

For example:

```
union u_type {
  int i;
  char ch;
};
```

This declaration does not create any variables. You can declare a variable either by placing its name at the end of the declaration or by using a separate declaration statement. To declare a **union** variable called **cnvt** of type **u_type** using the definition just given, write

```
union u_type cnvt;
```

In **cnvt**, both integer **i** and character **ch** share the same memory location. Of course, **i** occupies 2 bytes (assuming 2-byte integers), and **ch** uses only 1. Figure 7-2 shows how **i** and **ch** share the same address. At any point in your program, you can refer to the data stored in a **cnvt** as either an integer or a character.

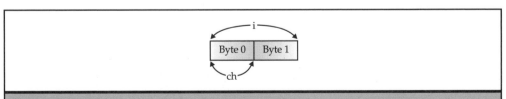

Figure 7-2.   *How **i** and **ch** utilize the union **cnvt** (assume 2-byte integers)*

When a **union** variable is declared, the compiler automatically allocates enough storage to hold the largest member of the **union**. For example, (assuming 2-byte integers) **cnvt** is 2 bytes long so that it can hold **i,** even though **ch** requires only 1 byte.

To access a member of a **union**, use the same syntax that you would use for structures: the dot and arrow operators. If you are operating on the **union** directly, use the dot operator. If the **union** is accessed through a pointer, use the arrow operator. For example, to assign the integer 10 to element **i** of **cnvt**, write

```
cnvt.i = 10;
```

In the next example, a pointer to **cnvt** is passed to a function:

```
void func1(union u_type *un)
{
  un->i = 10; /* assign 10 to cnvt through a pointer */
}
```

Unions are used frequently when specialized type conversions are needed because you can refer to the data held in the **union** in fundamentally different ways. For example, you might use a **union** to manipulate the bytes that constitute a **double** in order to alter its precision or to perform some unusual type of rounding.

To get an idea of the usefulness of a **union** when nonstandard type conversions are needed, consider the problem of writing a **short** integer to a disk file. The C standard library defines no function specifically designed to write a **short** integer to a file. Although you can write any type of data to a file using **fwrite( )**, using **fwrite( )** incurs excessive overhead for such a simple operation. However, using a **union**, you can easily create a function called **putw( )**, which writes the binary representation of a **short** integer to a file one byte at a time. (This example assumes that **short** integers are 2 bytes long.) To see how, first create a **union** consisting of one **short** integer and a 2-byte character array:

```
union pw {
  short int i;
  char ch[2];
};
```

Now, you can use **pw** to create the version of **putw( )** shown in the following program.

```
#include <stdio.h>
#include <stdlib.h>

union pw {
  short int i;
```

```
  char ch[2];
};

int putw(short int num, FILE *fp);

int main(void)
{
  FILE *fp;

  fp = fopen("test.tmp", "wb+");
  if(fp == NULL) {
    printf("Cannot open file.\n");
    exit(1);
  }

  putw(1025, fp);  /* write the value 1025 */
  fclose(fp);

  return 0;
}

int putw(short int num, FILE *fp)
{
  union pw word;

  word.i = num;

  putc(word.ch[0], fp); /* write first half */
  return putc(word.ch[1], fp); /* write second half */
}
```

Although **putw( )** is called with a **short** integer, it can still use the standard function
putc( ) to write each byte in the integer to a disk file one byte at a time.

Bit-Fields

Unlike some other computer languages, C has a built-in feature, called a *bit-field*, that
allows you to access a single bit. Bit-fields can be useful for a number of reasons, such as:

■ If storage is limited, you can store several Boolean (true/false) variables in
   one byte.

■ Certain devices transmit status information encoded into one or more bits within a byte.

■ Certain encryption routines need to access the bits within a byte.

Although these tasks can be performed using the bitwise operators, a bit-field can add more structure (and possibly efficiency) to your code.

A bit-field must be a member of a structure or union. It defines how long, in bits, the field is to be. The general form of a bit-field definition is

type name : *length*;

Here, *type* is the type of the bit-field, and *length* is the number of bits in the field. The type of a bit-field must be **int**, **signed**, or **unsigned**. (C99 also allows a bit-field to be of type **_Bool**.)

Bit-fields are frequently used when analyzing input from a hardware device. For example, the status port of a serial communications adapter might return a status byte organized like this:

Bit	Meaning When Set
0	Change in clear-to-send line
1	Change in data-set-ready
2	Trailing edge detected
3	Change in receive line
4	Clear-to-send
5	Data-set-ready
6	Telephone ringing
7	Received signal

You can represent the information in a status byte using the following bit-field:

```
struct status_type {
  unsigned delta_cts: 1;
  unsigned delta_dsr: 1;
  unsigned tr_edge:   1;
  unsigned delta_rec: 1;
  unsigned cts:       1;
  unsigned dsr:       1;
  unsigned ring:      1;
  unsigned rec_line:  1;
} status;
```

You might use statements like the ones shown here to enable a program to determine when it can send or receive data:

```
status = get_port_status();
if(status.cts) printf("clear to send");
if(status.dsr) printf("data ready");
```

To assign a value to a bit-field, simply use the form you would use for any other type of structure element. For example, this code fragment clears the **ring** field:

```
status.ring = 0;
```

As you can see from this example, each bit-field is accessed with the dot operator. However, if the structure is referenced through a pointer, you must use the –> operator.

You do not have to name each bit-field. This makes it easy to reach the bit you want, bypassing unused ones. For example, if you only care about the **cts** and **dsr** bits, you could declare the **status_type** structure like this:

```
struct status_type {
  unsigned :    4;
  unsigned cts: 1;
  unsigned dsr: 1;
} status;
```

Also, notice that the bits after **dsr** do not need to be specified if they are not used.

It is valid to mix normal structure members with bit-fields. For example,

```
struct emp {
  struct addr address;
  float pay;
  unsigned lay_off:    1; /* lay off or active */
  unsigned hourly:     1; /* hourly pay or wage */
  unsigned deductions: 3; /* IRS deductions */
};
```

defines an employee record that uses only 1 byte to hold three pieces of information: the employee's status, whether the employee is salaried, and the number of deductions. Without the bit-field, this information would take 3 bytes.

Bit-fields have certain restrictions. You cannot take the address of a bit-field. Bit-fields cannot be arrayed. You cannot know, from machine to machine, whether the fields will run from right to left or from left to right; this implies that any code using bit-fields may have some machine dependencies. Other restrictions may be imposed by various specific implementations.

Enumerations

An *enumeration* is a set of named integer constants. Enumerations are common in everyday life. For example, an enumeration of the coins used in the United States is

penny, nickel, dime, quarter, half-dollar, dollar

Enumerations are defined much like structures; the keyword **enum** signals the start of an enumeration type. The general form for enumerations is

enum *tag* { *enumeration list* } *variable_list*;

Here, both the tag and the variable list are optional. (But at least one must be present.) The following code fragment defines an enumeration called **coin**:

```
enum coin { penny, nickel, dime, quarter,
            half_dollar, dollar};
```

The enumeration tag name can be used to declare variables of its type. The following declares **money** to be a variable of type **coin**:

```
enum coin money;
```

Given these declarations, the following types of statements are perfectly valid:

```
money = dime;
if(money==quarter) printf("Money is a quarter.\n");
```

The key point to understand about an enumeration is that each of the symbols stands for an integer value. As such, they can be used anywhere that an integer can be used. Each symbol is given a value one greater than the symbol that precedes it. The value of the first enumeration symbol is 0. Therefore,

```
printf("%d %d", penny, dime);
```

displays **0 2** on the screen.

You can specify the value of one or more of the symbols by using an initializer. Do this by following the symbol with an equal sign and an integer value. Symbols that appear after an initializer are assigned values greater than the preceding value. For example, the following code assigns the value of 100 to **quarter**:

```
enum coin { penny, nickel, dime, quarter=100,
            half_dollar, dollar};
```

Now, the values of these symbols are

penny	0
nickel	1
dime	2
quarter	100
half_dollar	101
dollar	102

One common but erroneous assumption about enumerations is that the symbols can be input and output directly. This is not the case. For example, the following code fragment will not perform as desired:

```
/* this will not work */
money = dollar;
printf("%s", money);
```

Remember, **dollar** is simply a name for an integer; it is not a string. Thus, attempting to output **money** as a string is inherently invalid. For the same reason, you cannot use this code to achieve the desired results:

```
/* this code is wrong */
strcpy(money, "dime");
```

That is, a string that contains the name of a symbol is not automatically converted to that symbol.

Actually, creating code to input and output enumeration symbols is quite tedious (unless you are willing to settle for their integer values). For example, you need the following code to display, in words, the kind of coin that **money** contains:

```
switch(money) {
  case penny: printf("penny");
    break;
  case nickel: printf("nickel");
    break;
  case dime: printf("dime");
    break;
```

```
  case quarter: printf("quarter");
    break;
  case half_dollar: printf("half_dollar");
    break;
  case dollar: printf("dollar");
}
```

Sometimes, you can declare an array of strings and use the enumeration value as an index to translate that value into its corresponding string. For example, this code also outputs the proper string:

```
char name[][12]={
  "penny",
  "nickel",
  "dime",
  "quarter",
  "half_dollar",
  "dollar"
};
printf("%s", name[money]);
```

Of course, this only works if no symbol is initialized, because the string array must be indexed starting at 0 in strictly ascending order using increments of 1.

Since enumeration values must be converted manually to their human-readable string equivalents for I/O operations, they are most useful in routines that do not make such conversions. An enumeration is often used to define a compiler's symbol table, for example.

An Important Difference Between C and C++

There is an important difference between C and C++ related to the type names of structures, unions, and enumerations. To understand the difference, consider the following structure declaration:

```
struct MyStruct {
  int a;
  int b;
} ;
```

In C, the name **MyStruct** is called a *tag*. To declare an object of type **MyStruct**, you need to use a statement such as this:

```
struct MyStruct obj;
```

As you can see, the tag name **MyStruct** is preceded by the keyword **struct**. However, in C++, you can use this shorter form:

```
MyStruct obj; /* OK for C++, wrong for C */
```

Here, the keyword **struct** is not needed. In C++, once a structure has been declared, you can declare variables of its type using only its tag, without preceding it with the keyword **struct**. The reason for this difference is that in C, a structure's name does not define a complete type name. This is why C refers to this name as a tag. However, in C++, a structure's name is a complete type name and can be used by itself to define variables. Keep in mind, however, that it is still perfectly legal to use the C-style declaration in a C++ program.

The preceding discussion can be generalized to unions and enumerations. Thus, in C, you must precede a tag name with the keyword **struct**, **union**, or **enum** (whichever applies) when declaring objects. In C++, you don't need the keyword.

Since C++ accepts the C-style declarations, there is no trouble regarding this issue when porting from C to C++. However, if you are porting C++ code to C, you will need to make the appropriate changes.

Using sizeof to Ensure Portability

You have seen that structures and unions can be used to create variables of different sizes, and that the actual size of these variables might change from machine to machine. The **sizeof** operator computes the size of any variable or type and can help eliminate machine-dependent code from your programs. This operator is especially useful where structures or unions are concerned.

For the following discussion, assume an implementation that has the sizes for the data types shown here:

Type	Size in Bytes
char	1
int	4
double	8

Therefore, the following code will print the numbers **1**, **4**, and **8** on the screen:

```
char ch;
int i;
double f;

printf("%d", sizeof(ch));
printf("%d", sizeof(i));
printf("%d", sizeof(f));
```

The size of a structure is equal to *or greater than* the sum of the sizes of its members. For example:

```
struct s {
  char ch;
  int i;
  double f;
} s_var;
```

Here, **sizeof(s_var)** is at least 13 (8+4+1). However, the size of **s_var** might be greater because the compiler is allowed to pad a structure in order to achieve word or paragraph alignment. (A paragraph is 16 bytes.) Since the size of a structure may be greater than the sum of the sizes of its members, you should always use **sizeof** when you need to know the size of a structure. For example, if you want to dynamically allocate memory for an object of type **s**, you should use a statement sequence like the one shown here (rather than manually adding up the lengths of its members):

```
struct s *p;
p = malloc(sizeof(struct s));
```

Since **sizeof** is a compile-time operator, all the information necessary to compute the size of any variable is known at compile time. This is especially meaningful for **union**s, because the size of a **union** is always equal to the size of its largest member. For example, consider

```
union u {
  char ch;
  int i;
  double f;
} u_var;
```

Here, the **sizeof(u_var)** is 8. At run time, it does not matter what **u_var** is actually holding. All that matters is the size of its largest member, because any **union** must be as large as its largest element.

typedef

You can define new data type names by using the keyword **typedef**. You are not actually creating a new data type, but rather defining a new name for an existing type. This process can help make machine-dependent programs more portable. If you define your own type name for each machine-dependent data type used by your program, then only the **typedef** statements have to be changed when compiling for a new environment. **typedef** also can aid in self-documenting your code by allowing descriptive names for the standard data types. The general form of the **typedef** statement is

typedef *type newname*;

where *type* is any valid data type, and *newname* is the new name for this type. The new name you define is in addition to, not a replacement for, the existing type name. For example, you could create a new name for **float** by using

```
typedef float balance;
```

This statement tells the compiler to recognize **balance** as another name for **float**. Next, you could create a **float** variable using **balance**:

```
balance over_due;
```

Here, **over_due** is a floating-point variable of type **balance**, which is another word for **float**.

Now that **balance** has been defined, it can be used in another **typedef**. For example,

```
typedef balance overdraft;
```

tells the compiler to recognize **overdraft** as another name for **balance**, which is another name for **float**.

Using **typedef** can make your code easier to read and easier to port to a new machine. But you are not creating a new physical type.

The Complete Reference

Chapter 8

Console I/O

205

The C language does not define any keywords that perform I/O. Instead, input and output are accomplished through library functions. C's I/O system is an elegant piece of engineering that offers a flexible yet cohesive mechanism for transferring data between devices. C's I/O system is, however, quite large, and consists of several different functions. The header for the I/O functions is <**stdio.h**>.

There are both console and file I/O functions. Technically, there is little distinction between console I/O and file I/O. But conceptually they are in very different worlds. This chapter examines in detail the console I/O functions. The next chapter presents the file I/O system and describes how the two systems relate.

With one exception, this chapter covers only console I/O functions defined by Standard C. Standard C does not define any functions that perform various screen control operations (such as cursor positioning) or that display graphics, because these operations vary widely among machines. Nor does it define any functions that write to a window or dialog box under Windows. Instead, the console I/O functions perform only TTY-based output. However, most compilers include in their libraries screen control and graphics functions that apply to the specific environment in which the compiler is designed to run. And, of course, you can use C to write Windows programs. It is just that the C language does not define functions that perform these tasks directly.

This chapter refers to the console I/O functions as performing input from the keyboard and output to the screen. In actuality, these functions operate on standard input and standard output. Furthermore, standard input and standard output may be redirected to other devices. Thus, the "console functions" do not necessarily operate on the console. I/O redirection is covered in Chapter 9. In this chapter it is assumed that the standard input and standard output have not been redirected.

 In addition to I/O functions, C++ also includes I/O operators. These operators are, however, not supported by C.

Reading and Writing Characters

The simplest of the console I/O functions are **getchar( )**, which reads a character from the keyboard, and **putchar( )**, which writes a character to the screen. The **getchar( )** function waits until a key is pressed and then returns its value. The keypress is also automatically echoed to the screen. The **putchar( )** function writes a character to the screen at the current cursor position. The prototypes for **getchar( )** and **putchar( )** are shown here:

    int getchar(void);
    int putchar(int c);

As its prototype shows, the **getchar( )** function is declared as returning an integer. However, you can assign this value to a **char** variable, as is usually done, because the character is contained in the low-order byte. (The high-order byte is usually zero.) **getchar( )** returns **EOF** if an error occurs. (The **EOF** macro is defined in **<stdio.h>** and is often equal to –1.)

In the case of **putchar( )**, even though it is declared as taking an integer parameter, you will generally call it using a character argument. Only the low-order byte of its parameter is actually output to the screen. The **putchar( )** function returns the character written or **EOF** if an error occurs.

The following program illustrates **getchar( )** and **putchar( )**. It inputs characters from the keyboard and displays them in reverse case. That is, it prints uppercase as lowercase and lowercase as uppercase. To stop the program, enter a period.

```c
#include <stdio.h>
#include <ctype.h>

int main(void)
{
  char ch;

  printf("Enter some text (type a period to quit).\n");
  do {
    ch = getchar();

    if(islower(ch)) ch = toupper(ch);
    else ch = tolower(ch);

    putchar(ch);
  } while (ch != '.');

  return 0;
}
```

A Problem with getchar( )

There are some potential problems with **getchar( )**. For many compilers, **getchar( )** is implemented in such a way that it buffers input until ENTER is pressed. This is called *line-buffered* input; you have to press ENTER before any character is returned. Also, since **getchar( )** inputs only one character each time it is called, line buffering may leave one or more characters waiting in the input queue, which is annoying in interactive environments. Even though it is permissible for **getchar( )** to be implemented as an interactive function, it seldom is. Therefore, if the preceding program did not behave as you expected, you now know why.

Alternatives to getchar( )

Since **getchar( )** might not be implemented by your compiler in such a way that it is useful in an interactive environment, you might want to use a different function to read characters from the keyboard. Standard C does not define any function that is guaranteed to provide interactive input, but virtually all C compilers do. Although these functions are not defined by Standard C, they are commonly used because **getchar( )** does not fill the needs of most programmers.

Two of the most common alternative functions, **getch( )** and **getche( )**, have these prototypes:

```
int getch(void);
int getche(void);
```

For most compilers, the prototypes for these functions are found in the header file **<conio.h>**. For some compilers, these functions have a leading underscore. For example, in Microsoft's Visual C++, they are called **_getch( )** and **_getche( )**.

The **getch( )** function waits for a keypress after which it returns immediately. It does not echo the character to the screen. The **getche( )** function is the same as **getch( )**, but the key is echoed. You will frequently see **getche( )** or **getch( )** used instead of **getchar( )** when a character needs to be read from the keyboard in an interactive program. For example, the previous program is shown here using **getch( )** instead of **getchar( )**:

```c
#include <stdio.h>
#include <conio.h>
#include <ctype.h>

int main(void)
{
  char ch;

  printf("Enter some text (type a period to quit).\n");
  do {
    ch = getch();

    if(islower(ch)) ch = toupper(ch);
    else ch = tolower(ch);

    putchar(ch);
  } while (ch != '.');
```

FOUNDATIONAL C

```
      return 0;
   }
```

When you run this version of the program, each time you press a key, it is immediately transmitted to the program and displayed in reverse case. Input is no longer line buffered. Although the code in this book will not make further use of **getch( )** or **getche( )**, they may be useful in the programs that you write.

At the time of this writing, when using Microsoft's Visual C++ compiler, _getche( ) and _getch( ) are not compatible with the standard C input functions, such as scanf( ) or gets( ). Instead, you must use special versions of the standard functions, such as cscanf( ) or cgets( ). You will need to examine the Visual C++ documentation for details.

Reading and Writing Strings

The next step up in console I/O, in terms of complexity and power, are the functions **gets( )** and **puts( )**. They enable you to read and write strings of characters.

The **gets( )** function reads a string of characters entered at the keyboard and stores them at the address pointed to by its argument. You can type characters at the keyboard until you strike a carriage return. The carriage return does not become part of the string; instead, a null terminator is placed at the end, and **gets( )** returns. In fact, you cannot use **gets( )** to return a carriage return (although **getchar( )** can do so). You can correct typing mistakes by using the backspace key before pressing ENTER. The prototype for **gets( )** is

    char *gets(char *str);

where *str* is a pointer to a character array that receives the characters entered by the user. **gets( )** also returns *str*. The following program reads a string into the array **str** and prints its length:

```
#include <stdio.h>
#include <string.h>

int main(void)
{
  char str[80];

  gets(str);
  printf("Length is %d", strlen(str));

  return 0;
}
```

You need to be careful when using **gets( )** because it performs no boundary checks on the array that is receiving input. Thus, it is possible for the user to enter more characters than the array can hold. While **gets( )** is fine for sample programs and simple utilities that only you will use, you will want to avoid its use in commercial code. One alternative is the **fgets( )** function described in the next chapter, which allows you to prevent an array overrun.

The **puts( )** function writes its string argument to the screen followed by a newline. Its prototype is

int puts(const char *str);

puts( ) recognizes the same backslash escape sequences as **printf( )**, such as \t for tab. A call to **puts( )** requires far less overhead than the same call to **printf( )** because **puts( )** can only output a string of characters—it cannot output numbers or do format conversions. Therefore, **puts( )** takes up less space and runs faster than **printf( )**. For this reason, the **puts( )** function is often used when no format conversions are required.

The **puts( )** function returns a nonnegative value if successful or **EOF** if an error occurs. However, when writing to the console, you can usually assume that no error will occur, so the return value of **puts( )** is seldom monitored. The following statement displays **hello**:

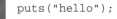

```
puts("hello");
```

Table 8-1 summarizes the basic console I/O functions.

Function	Operation
getchar( )	Reads a character from the keyboard; usually waits for carriage return.
getche( )	Reads a character with echo; does not wait for carriage return; not defined by Standard C, but a common extension.
getch( )	Reads a character without echo; does not wait for carriage return; not defined by Standard C, but a common extension.
putchar( )	Writes a character to the screen.
gets( )	Reads a string from the keyboard.
puts( )	Writes a string to the screen.

Table 8-1. *The Basic I/O Functions*

The following program—a simple computerized dictionary—demonstrates several basic console I/O functions. It prompts the user to enter a word and then checks to see if the word matches one in its built-in database. If a match is found, the program prints the word's meaning. Pay special attention to the indirection used in this program. If you have any trouble understanding it, remember that the **dic** array is an array of pointers to strings. Notice that the list must be terminated by two nulls.

```c
/* A simple dictionary. */
#include <stdio.h>
#include <string.h>
#include <ctype.h>

/* list of words and meanings */
char  *dic[][40] = {
  "atlas", "A volume of maps.",
  "car", "A motorized vehicle.",
  "telephone", "A communication device.",
  "airplane", "A flying machine.",
  "", ""   /* null terminate the list */
};

int main(void)
{
  char word[80], ch;
  char **p;

  do {
    puts("\nEnter word: ");
    scanf("%s", word);

    p = (char **)dic;

    /* find matching word and print its meaning */
    do {
      if(!strcmp(*p, word)) {
        puts("Meaning:");
        puts(*(p+1));
        break;
      }
      if(!strcmp(*p, word)) break;
      p = p + 2;  /* advance through the list */
    } while(*p);
```

```
        if(!*p) puts("Word not in dictionary.");
        printf("Another? (y/n): ");
        scanf(" %c%*c", &ch);
    } while(toupper(ch) != 'N');

    return 0;
}
```

Formatted Console I/O

The functions **printf( )** and **scanf( )** perform formatted output and input—that is, they can read and write data in various formats that are under your control. The **printf( )** function writes data to the console. The **scanf( )** function, its complement, reads data from the keyboard. Both functions can operate on any of the built-in data types, plus null-terminated character strings.

printf( )

The prototype for **printf( )** is

int printf(const char *control_string, ...);

The **printf( )** function returns the number of characters written or a negative value if an error occurs.

The *control_string* consists of two types of items. The first type is composed of characters that will be printed on the screen. The second type contains format specifiers that define the way the subsequent arguments are displayed. A format specifier begins with a percent sign and is followed by the format code. There must be exactly the same number of arguments as there are format specifiers, and the format specifiers and the arguments are matched in order from left to right. For example, this **printf( )** call

```
printf("I like %c %s", 'C', "very much!");
```

displays

```
I like C very much!
```

Here, the **%c** matches the character 'C', and the **%s** matches the string "very much".

The **printf( )** function accepts a wide variety of format specifiers, as shown in Table 8-2.

Code	Format
%a	Hexadecimal output in the form 0x*h.hhhh*p+*d* (C99 only).
%A	Hexadecimal output in the form 0X*h.hhhh*P+*d* (C99 only).
%c	Character.
%d	Signed decimal integers.
%i	Signed decimal integers.
%e	Scientific notation (lowercase e).
%E	Scientific notation (uppercase E).
%f	Decimal floating point.
%g	Uses %e or %f, whichever is shorter.
%G	Uses %E or %F, whichever is shorter.
%o	Unsigned octal.
%s	String of characters.
%u	Unsigned decimal integers.
%x	Unsigned hexadecimal (lowercase letters).
%X	Unsigned hexadecimal (uppercase letters).
%p	Displays a pointer.
%n	The associated argument must be a pointer to an integer. This specifier causes the number of characters written (up to the point at which the **%n** is encountered) to be stored in that integer.
%%	Prints a % sign.

Table 8-2.   *printf( ) Format Specifiers*

Printing Characters

To print an individual character, use **%c**. This causes the matching argument to be output, unmodified, to the screen.

To print a string, use **%s**.

Printing Numbers

You can use either **%d** or **%i** to display a signed integer in decimal format. These format specifiers are equivalent; both are supported for historical reasons, of which one is the desire to maintain an equivalence relationship with the **scanf( )** format specifiers.

To output an unsigned integer, use **%u**.

The **%f** format specifier displays numbers in floating point. The matching argument must be of type **double**.

The **%e** and **%E** specifiers tell **printf( )** to display a **double** argument in scientific notation. Numbers represented in scientific notation take this general form:

x.dddddE+/–yy

If you want to display the letter E in uppercase, use the **%E** format; otherwise, use **%e**. You can tell **printf( )** to use either **%f** or **%e** by using the **%g** or **%G** format specifiers. This causes **printf( )** to select the format specifier that produces the shortest output. Where applicable, use **%G** if you want E shown in uppercase; otherwise, use **%g**. The following program demonstrates the effect of the **%g** format specifier:

```
#include <stdio.h>

int main(void)
{
  double f;

  for(f=1.0; f<1.0e+10; f=f*10)
    printf("%g ", f);

  return 0;
}
```

It produces the following output:

```
1 10 100 1000 10000 100000 1e+006 1e+007 1e+008 1e+009
```

You can display unsigned integers in octal or hexadecimal format using **%o** and **%x**, respectively. Since the hexadecimal number system uses the letters A through F to represent the numbers 10 through 15, you can display these letters in either upper- or lowercase. For uppercase, use the **%X** format specifier; for lowercase, use **%x**, as shown here:

```
#include <stdio.h>

int main(void)
```

```
{
  unsigned num;

  for(num=0; num < 16; num++) {
    printf("%o ", num);
    printf("%x ", num);
    printf("%X\n", num);
  }

  return 0;
}
```

The output is shown here:

```
0 0 0
1 1 1
2 2 2
3 3 3
4 4 4
5 5 5
6 6 6
7 7 7
10 8 8
11 9 9
12 a A
13 b B
14 c C
15 d D
16 e E
17 f F
```

Displaying an Address

If you want to display an address, use **%p**. This format specifier causes **printf( )** to display a machine address in a format compatible with the type of addressing used by the computer. The next program displays the address of **sample**:

```
#include <stdio.h>

int sample;

int main(void)
```

```
{
   printf("%p", &sample);

   return 0;
}
```

The %n Specifier

The **%n** format specifier is different from the others. Instead of telling **printf( )** to display something, it causes **printf( )** to load the integer variable pointed to by its corresponding argument with a value equal to the number of characters that have been output. In other words, the value that corresponds to the **%n** format specifier must be a pointer to a variable. After the call to **printf( )** has returned, this variable will hold the number of characters output, up to the point at which the **%n** was encountered. Examine the next program to understand this somewhat unusual format code:

```
#include <stdio.h>

int main(void)
{
   int count;

   printf("this%n is a test\n", &count);
   printf("%d", count);

   return 0;
}
```

This program displays **this is a test** followed by the number **4**. The **%n** format specifier is used primarily to enable your program to perform dynamic formatting.

Format Modifiers

Many format specifiers can take modifiers that alter their meaning slightly. For example, you can specify a minimum field width, the number of decimal places, and left justification. The format modifier goes between the percent sign and the format code. These modifiers are discussed next.

The Minimum Field Width Specifier

An integer placed between the % sign and the format code acts as a *minimum field width specifier*. This pads the output with spaces to ensure that it reaches a certain minimum length. If the string or number is longer than that minimum, it will still be printed in full. The default padding is done with spaces. If you wish to pad with 0's, place a 0 before the field width specifier. For example, **%05d** will pad a number of less than five digits with 0's so that its total length is five. The following program demonstrates the minimum field width specifier:

```
#include <stdio.h>

int main(void)
{
  double item;

  item = 10.12304;

  printf("%f\n", item);
  printf("%10f\n", item);
  printf("%012f\n", item);

  return 0;
}
```

This program produces the following output:

```
10.123040
 10.123040
00010.123040
```

The minimum field width modifier is most commonly used to produce tables in which the columns line up. For example, the next program produces a table of squares and cubes for the numbers between 1 and 19:

```
#include <stdio.h>

int main(void)
{
  int i;

  /* display a table of squares and cubes */
  for(i=1; i<20; i++)
    printf("%8d %8d %8d\n", i, i*i, i*i*i);

  return 0;
}
```

A sample of its output is shown here:

```
 1         1         1
 2         4         8
 3         9        27
 4        16        64
 5        25       125
 6        36       216
 7        49       343
 8        64       512
 9        81       729
10       100      1000
11       121      1331
12       144      1728
13       169      2197
14       196      2744
15       225      3375
16       256      4096
17       289      4913
18       324      5832
19       361      6859
```

The Precision Specifier

The *precision specifier* follows the minimum field width specifier (if there is one). It consists of a period followed by an integer. Its exact meaning depends upon the type of data to which it is applied.

When you apply the precision specifier to floating-point data using the **%f**, **%e**, or **%E** specifiers, it determines the number of decimal places displayed. For example, **%10.4f** displays a number at least 10 characters wide with four decimal places.

When the precision specifier is applied to **%g** or **%G**, it specifies the number of significant digits.

Applied to strings, the precision specifier specifies the maximum field length. For example, **%5.7s** displays a string at least five and not exceeding seven characters long. If the string is longer than the maximum field width, the end characters will be truncated.

When applied to integer types, the precision specifier determines the minimum number of digits that will appear for each number. Leading zeroes are added to achieve the required number of digits.

The following program illustrates the precision specifier:

```c
#include <stdio.h>

int main(void)
{
```

```
    printf("%.4f\n", 123.1234567);
    printf("%3.8d\n", 1000);
    printf("%10.15s\n", "This is a simple test.");

    return 0;
}
```

It produces the following output:

```
123.1235
00001000
This is a simpl
```

Justifying Output

By default, all output is right justified. That is, if the field width is larger than the data printed, the data will be placed on the right edge of the field. You can force output to be left justified by placing a minus sign directly after the %. For example, **%–10.2f** left-justifies a floating-point number with two decimal places in a 10-character field.

The following program illustrates left justification:

```
#include <stdio.h>

int main(void)
{
    printf(".......................\n");
    printf("right-justified: %8d\n", 100);
    printf(" left-justified: %-8d\n", 100);

    return 0;
}
```

The output is shown here:

```
.......................
right-justified:      100
 left-justified: 100
```

Handling Other Data Types

There are format modifiers that allow **printf( )** to display **short** and **long** integers. These modifiers can be applied to the **d**, **i**, **o**, **u**, and **x** type specifiers. The **l** (*ell*) modifier tells **printf( )** that a **long** data type follows. For example, **%ld** means that a **long int** is to be displayed. The **h** modifier instructs **printf( )** to display a **short** integer. For instance, **%hu** indicates that the data is of type **short unsigned int**.

The **l** and **h** modifiers can also be applied to the **n** specifier, to indicate that the corresponding argument is a pointer to a long or short integer, respectively.

If you are using a compiler that supports the wide-character features added by the 1995 Amendment 1, you can use the **l** modifier with the **c** format to indicate a wide character. You can also use the **l** modifier with the **s** format to indicate a wide-character string.

The **L** modifier may prefix the floating-point specifiers **e**, **f**, and **g** and indicates that a **long double** follows.

C99 adds two new format modifiers: **hh** and **ll**. The **hh** modifier can be applied to **d**, **i**, **o**, **u**, **x**, or **n**. It specifies that the corresponding argument is a **signed** or **unsigned char** value or, in the case of **n**, a pointer to a **signed char** variable. The **ll** modifier also can be applied to **d**, **i**, **o**, **u**, **x**, or **n**. It specifies that the corresponding argument is a **signed** or **unsigned long long int** value or, in the case of **n**, a pointer to a **long long int**. C99 also allows the **l** to be applied to the floating-point specifiers **a**, **e**, **f**, and **g**, but it has no effect.

Note	*C99 includes some additional **printf( )** type modifiers, which are described in Part Two.*

The * and # Modifiers

The **printf( )** function supports two additional modifiers to some of its format specifiers: * and #.

Preceding **g**, **G**, **f**, **E**, or **e** specifiers with a # ensures that there will be a decimal point even if there are no decimal digits. If you precede the **x** or **X** format specifier with a #, the hexadecimal number will be printed with a **0x** prefix. Preceding the **o** specifier with # causes the number to be printed with a leading zero. You cannot apply # to any other format specifiers. (In C99, the # can also be applied to the **%a** conversion, which ensures that a decimal point will be displayed.)

Instead of constants, the minimum field width and precision specifiers can be provided by arguments to **printf( )**. To accomplish this, use an * as a placeholder. When the format string is scanned, **printf( )** will match the * to an argument in the order in which they occur. For example, in Figure 8-1, the minimum field width is 10, the precision is 4, and the value to be displayed is **123.3**.

The following program illustrates both # and *:

```c
#include <stdio.h>

int main(void)
{
  printf("%x %#x\n", 10, 10);
  printf("%*.*f", 10, 4, 1234.34);

  return 0;
}
```

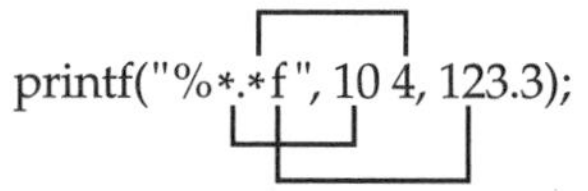

$$printf("\%*.*f", 10\ 4, 123.3);$$

Figure 8-1.   *How the * is matched to its value*

scanf( )

scanf( ) is the general-purpose console input routine. It can read all the built-in data types and automatically convert numbers into the proper internal format. It is much like the reverse of **printf( )**. The prototype for **scanf( )** is

```
int scanf(const char *control_string, ...);
```

The **scanf( )** function returns the number of data items successfully assigned a value. If an error occurs, **scanf( )** returns **EOF**. The *control_string* determines how values are read into the variables pointed to in the argument list.

The control string consists of three classifications of characters:

- Format specifiers
- White-space characters
- Non-white-space characters

Let's take a look at each of these now.

Format Specifiers

The input format specifiers are preceded by a % sign and tell **scanf( )** what type of data is to be read next. These codes are listed in Table 8-3. The format specifiers are matched, in order from left to right, with the arguments in the argument list. Let's look at some examples.

Inputting Numbers

To read an integer, use either the **%d** or **%i** specifier. To read a floating-point number represented in either standard or scientific notation, use **%e**, **%f**, or **%g**. (C99 also includes **%a**, which reads a floating-point number.)

You can use **scanf( )** to read integers in either octal or hexadecimal form by using the **%o** and **%x** format commands, respectively. The **%x** can be in either upper- or lowercase. Either way, you can enter the letters A through F in either case

Code	Meaning
%a	Reads a floating-point value (C99 only).
%c	Reads a single character.
%d	Reads a decimal integer.
%i	Reads an integer in either decimal, octal, or hexadecimal format.
%e	Reads a floating-point number.
%f	Reads a floating-point number.
%g	Reads a floating-point number.
%o	Reads an octal number.
%s	Reads a string.
%x	Reads a hexadecimal number.
%p	Reads a pointer.
%n	Receives an integer value equal to the number of characters read so far.
%u	Reads an unsigned decimal integer.
%[ ]	Scans for a set of characters.
%%	Reads a percent sign.

Table 8-3. *scanf( ) Format Specifiers*

when entering hexadecimal numbers. The following program reads an octal and hexadecimal number:

```
#include <stdio.h>

int main(void)
{
  int i, j;

  scanf("%o%x", &i, &j);
  printf("%o %x", i, j);

  return 0;
}
```

The **scanf( )** function stops reading a number when the first non-numeric character is encountered.

Inputting Unsigned Integers

To input an unsigned integer, use the **%u** format specifier. For example,

```
unsigned num;
scanf("%u", &num);
```

reads an unsigned number and puts its value into **num**.

Reading Individual Characters Using scanf( )

As explained earlier in this chapter, you can read individual characters using **getchar( )** or a derivative function. You can also use **scanf( )** for this purpose if you use the **%c** format specifier. However, like most implementations of **getchar( )**, **scanf( )** will generally line-buffer input when the **%c** specifier is used. This makes it somewhat troublesome in an interactive environment.

Although spaces, tabs, and newlines are used as field separators when reading other types of data, when reading a single character, white-space characters are read like any other character. For example, with an input stream of "**x y**," this code fragment

```
scanf("%c%c%c", &a, &b, &c);
```

returns with the character **x** in **a**, a space in **b**, and the character **y** in **c**.

Reading Strings

The **scanf( )** function can be used to read a string from the input stream using the **%s** format specifier. Using **%s** causes **scanf( )** to read characters until it encounters a white-space character. The characters that are read are put into the character array pointed to by the corresponding argument, and the result is null terminated. As it applies to **scanf( )**, a white-space character is either a space, a newline, a tab, a vertical tab, or a formfeed. Unlike **gets( )**, which reads a string until ENTER is pressed, **scanf( )** reads a string until the first white space is entered. This means that you cannot use **scanf( )** to read a string like "this is a test" because the first space terminates the reading process. To see the effect of the **%s** specifier, try this program using the string "hello there":

```
#include <stdio.h>

int main(void)
```

```
{
  char str[80];

  printf("Enter a string: ");
  scanf("%s", str);
  printf("Here's your string: %s", str);

  return 0;
}
```

The program responds with only the "hello" portion of the string.

Inputting an Address

To input a memory address, use the **%p** format specifier. This specifier causes **scanf( )** to read an address in the format defined by the architecture of the CPU. For example, this program inputs an address and then displays what is at that memory address:

```
#include <stdio.h>

int main(void)
{
  char *p;

  printf("Enter an address: ");
  scanf("%p", &p);
  printf("Value at location %p is %c\n", p, *p);

  return 0;
}
```

The %n Specifier

The **%n** specifier instructs **scanf( )** to store the number of characters read from the input stream (up to the point at which the **%n** was encountered) in the integer variable pointed to by the corresponding argument.

Using a Scanset

The **scanf( )** function supports a general-purpose format specifier called a scanset. A *scanset* defines a set of characters. When **scanf( )** processes a scanset, it will input characters as long as those characters are part of the set defined by the scanset. The characters read will be assigned to the character array that is pointed to by the scanset's corresponding argument. You define a scanset by putting the characters to scan for inside square brackets. The beginning square bracket must be prefixed by a percent sign. For example, the following scanset tells **scanf( )** to read only the characters X, Y, and Z:

```
%[XYZ]
```

When you use a scanset, **scanf( )** continues to read characters, putting them into the corresponding character array until it encounters a character that is not in the scanset. Upon return from **scanf( )**, this array will contain a null-terminated string that consists of the characters that have been read. To see how this works, try this program:

```
#include <stdio.h>

int main(void)
{
  int i;
  char str[80], str2[80];

  scanf("%d%[abcdefg]%s", &i, str, str2);
  printf("%d %s %s", i, str, str2);

  return 0;
}
```

Enter **123abcdtye** followed by ENTER. The program will then display **123 abcd tye**. Because the "t" is not part of the scanset, **scanf( )** stops reading characters into **str** when it encounters the "t." The remaining characters are put into **str2**.

You can specify an inverted set if the first character in the set is a ^. The ^ instructs **scanf( )** to accept any character that is *not* defined by the scanset.

In most implementations you can specify a range using a hyphen. For example, this tells **scanf( )** to accept the characters A through Z:

```
%[A-Z]
```

One important point to remember is that the scanset is case sensitive. If you want to scan for both upper- and lowercase letters, you must specify them individually.

Discarding Unwanted White Space

A white-space character in the control string causes **scanf( )** to skip over one or more leading white-space characters in the input stream. A white-space character is either a space, a tab, vertical tab, formfeed, or a newline. In essence, one white-space character in the control string causes **scanf( )** to read, but not store, any number (including zero) of white-space characters up to the first non-white-space character.

Non-White-Space Characters in the Control String

A non-white-space character in the control string causes **scanf( )** to read and discard matching characters in the input stream. For example, **"%d,%d"** causes **scanf( )** to read an integer, read and discard a comma, and then read another integer. If the specified character is not found, **scanf( )** terminates. If you want to read and discard a percent sign, use %% in the control string.

You Must Pass scanf( ) Addresses

All the variables used to receive values through **scanf( )** must be passed by their addresses. This means that all arguments must be pointers. Recall that this is how C creates a call by reference, which allows a function to alter the contents of an argument. For example, to read an integer into the variable **count**, you would use the following **scanf( )** call:

```
scanf("%d", &count);
```

Strings will be read into character arrays, and the array name, without any index, is the address of the first element of the array. So, to read a string into the character array **str**, you would use

```
scanf("%s", str);
```

In this case, **str** is already a pointer and need not be preceded by the **&** operator.

Format Modifiers

As with **printf( )**, **scanf( )** allows a number of its format specifiers to be modified. The format specifiers can include a maximum field length modifier. This is an integer, placed between the % and the format specifier, that limits the number of characters read for that field. For example, to read no more than 20 characters into **str**, write

```
scanf("%20s", str);
```

If the input stream is greater than 20 characters, a subsequent call to input begins where this call leaves off. For example, if you enter

ABCDEFGHIJKLMNOPQRSTUVWXYZ

as the response to the **scanf( )** call in this example, only the first 20 characters, or up to the T, are placed into **str** because of the maximum field width specifier. This means that the remaining characters, UVWXYZ, have not yet been used. If another **scanf( )** call is made, such as

```
scanf("%s", str);
```

the letters UVWXYZ are placed into **str**. Input for a field may terminate before the maximum field length is reached if a white space is encountered. In this case, **scanf( )** moves on to the next field.

To read a long integer, put an **l** (*ell*) in front of the format specifier. To read a short integer, put an **h** in front of the format specifier. These modifiers can be used with the **d, i, o, u, x,** and **n** format codes.

By default, the **f, e,** and **g** specifiers tell **scanf( )** to assign data to a **float**. If you put an **l** (*ell*) in front of one of these specifiers, **scanf( )** assigns the data to a **double**. Using an **L** tells **scanf( )** that the variable receiving the data is a **long double**.

The **l** modifier can also be used with the **c** and **s** format codes as long as your compiler implements the wide-character features added to C by the 1995 Amendment 1. Preceding **c** with an **l** indicates a pointer to an object of type **wchar_t**. Preceding **s** with an **l** indicates a pointer to a **wchar_t** array. The **l** can also be used to modify a scanset for use with wide characters.

C99 adds the **ll** and **hh** modifiers. The **hh** modifier can be applied to **d, i, o, u, x,** or **n**. It specifies that the corresponding argument is a pointer to a **signed** or **unsigned char** value. The **ll** modifier also can be applied to **d, i, o, u, x,** or **n**. It specifies that the corresponding argument is a pointer to a **signed** or **unsigned long long int** value.

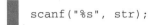 *C99 includes some additional **scanf( )** type modifiers, which are described in Part Two.*

Suppressing Input

You can tell **scanf( )** to read a field but not assign it to any variable by preceding that field's format code with an *. For example, given

```
scanf("%d%*c%d", &x, &y);
```

you could enter the coordinate pair **10,10**. The comma would be correctly read, but not assigned to anything. Assignment suppression is especially useful when you need to process only a part of what is being entered.

Chapter 9

File I/O

This chapter describes the C file system. As explained in Chapter 8, the C I/O system is implemented through library functions, not through keywords. This makes the I/O system extremely powerful and flexible. For example, when operating on files, data can be transferred either in its internal binary representation, or in its human-readable text format. This makes it easy to create files to fit any need.

C vs. C++ File I/O

Because C forms the foundation for C++, there is sometimes confusion over how C's file system relates to C++. First, C++ supports the entire C file system. Thus, if you will be porting older C code to C++, you will not have to change all of your I/O routines right away. Second, C++ defines its own, object-oriented I/O system, which includes both I/O functions and I/O operators. The C++ I/O system completely duplicates the functionality of the C I/O system and renders the C file system redundant. In general, if you are writing C++ programs, you will usually want to use the C++ I/O system, but you are free to use the C file system if you like.

Standard C vs. Unix File I/O

C was originally implemented for the Unix operating system. As such, early versions of C (and many still today) support a set of I/O functions that are compatible with Unix. This set of I/O functions is sometimes referred to as the *Unix-like I/O system*, or the *unbuffered I/O system*. However, when C was standardized, the Unix-like functions were not incorporated into the standard, largely because they are redundant. Also, the Unix-like system may not be relevant to certain environments that could otherwise support C.

This chapter discusses only those I/O functions that are defined by Standard C. In previous editions of this work, the Unix-like file system was given a small amount of coverage. In the time that has elapsed since the previous edition, use of the standard I/O functions has steadily risen and use of the Unix-like functions has steadily decreased. Today, most programmers use the standard functions because they are portable to all environments (and to C++). Programmers wanting to use the Unix-like functions should consult their compiler's documentation.

Streams and Files

Before beginning our discussion of the C file system it is necessary to know the difference between the terms *streams* and *files*. The C I/O system supplies a consistent interface to the programmer independent of the actual device being accessed. That is, the C I/O system provides a level of abstraction between the programmer and the device. This abstraction is called a *stream*, and the actual device is called a *file*. It is important to understand how streams and files interact.

Streams

The C file system is designed to work with a wide variety of devices, including terminals, disk drives, and tape drives. Even though each device is very different, the buffered file system transforms each into a logical device called a stream. All streams behave similarly. Because streams are largely device independent, the same function that can write to a disk file can also write to another type of device, such as the console. There are two types of streams: text and binary.

Text Streams

A *text stream* is a sequence of characters. Standard C states that a text stream is organized into lines terminated by a newline character. However, the newline character is optional on the last line. In a text stream, certain character translations may occur as required by the host environment. For example, a newline may be converted to a carriage return/linefeed pair. Therefore, there may not be a one-to-one relationship between the characters that are written (or read) and those stored on the external device. Also, because of possible translations, the number of characters written (or read) may not be the same as the number that is stored on the external device.

Binary Streams

A *binary stream* is a sequence of bytes that has a one-to-one correspondence to the bytes in the external device—that is, no character translations occur. Also, the number of bytes written (or read) is the same as the number on the external device. However, an implementation-defined number of null bytes may be appended to a binary stream. These null bytes might be used to pad the information so that it fills a sector on a disk, for example.

Files

In C, a *file* may be anything from a disk file to a terminal or printer. You associate a stream with a specific file by performing an *open* operation. Once a file is open, information can be exchanged between it and your program.

Not all files have the same capabilities. For example, a disk file can support random access, while some printers cannot. This brings up an important point about the C I/O system: All streams are the same, but all files are not.

If the file can support *position requests*, opening that file also initializes the *file position indicator* to the start of the file. As each character is read from or written to the file, the position indicator is incremented, ensuring progression through the file.

You disassociate a file from a specific stream with a *close* operation. If you close a file opened for output, the contents, if any, of its associated stream are written to the external device. This process, generally referred to as *flushing* the stream, guarantees that no information is accidentally left in the disk buffer. All files are closed automatically when your program terminates normally, either by **main( )** returning to the operating system or by a call to **exit( )**. Files are not closed when a program terminates abnormally, such as when it crashes or when it calls **abort( )**.

Each stream that is associated with a file has a file control structure of type **FILE**. Never modify this file control block.

If you are new to programming, the separation of streams and files may seem unnecessary or contrived. Just remember that its main purpose is to provide a consistent interface. You need only think in terms of streams and use only one file system to accomplish all I/O operations. The I/O system automatically converts the raw input or output from each device into an easily managed stream.

File System Basics

The C file system is composed of several interrelated functions. The most common of these are shown in Table 9-1. They require the header **<stdio.h>**.

The header **<stdio.h>** provides the prototypes for the I/O functions and defines these three types: **size_t**, **fpos_t**, and **FILE**. The **size_t** type is some variety of unsigned integer, as is **fpos_t**. The **FILE** type is discussed in the next section.

Also defined in **<stdio.h>** are several macros. The ones relevant to this chapter are **NULL**, **EOF**, **FOPEN_MAX**, **SEEK_SET**, **SEEK_CUR**, and **SEEK_END**. The **NULL** macro defines a null pointer. The **EOF** macro, often defined as -1, is the value returned when an input function tries to read past the end of the file. **FOPEN_MAX** defines an integer value that determines the number of files that may be open at any one time. The other macros are used with **fseek( )**, which is the function that performs random access on a file.

The File Pointer

The file pointer is the common thread that unites the C I/O system. A *file pointer* is a pointer to a structure of type **FILE**. It points to information that defines various things about the file, including its name, status, and the current position of the file. In essence, the file pointer identifies a specific file and is used by the associated stream to direct the operation of the I/O functions. In order to read or write files, your program needs to use file pointers. To obtain a file pointer variable, use a statement like this:

```
FILE *fp;
```

Opening a File

The **fopen( )** function opens a stream for use and links a file with that stream. Then it returns the file pointer associated with that file. Most often (and for the rest of this discussion), the file is a disk file. The **fopen( )** function has this prototype,

FILE *fopen(const char *filename, const char *mode);

Name	Function
fopen( )	Opens a file
fclose( )	Closes a file
putc( )	Writes a character to a file
fputc( )	Same as **putc( )**
getc( )	Reads a character from a file
fgetc( )	Same as **getc( )**
fgets( )	Reads a string from a file
fputs( )	Writes a string to a file
fseek( )	Seeks to a specified byte in a file
ftell( )	Returns the current file position
fprintf( )	Is to a file what **printf( )** is to the console
fscanf( )	Is to a file what **scanf( )** is to the console
feof( )	Returns true if end-of-file is reached
ferror( )	Returns true if an error has occurred
rewind( )	Resets the file position indicator to the beginning of the file
remove( )	Erases a file
fflush( )	Flushes a file

Table 9-1. *Commonly Used C File-System Functions*

where *filename* is a pointer to a string of characters that make up a valid filename and may include a path specification. The string pointed to by *mode* determines how the file will be opened. Table 9-2 shows the legal values for *mode*. Strings like "r+b" may also be represented as "rb+".

As stated, the **fopen( )** function returns a file pointer. Your program should never alter the value of this pointer. If an error occurs when it is trying to open the file, **fopen( )** returns a null pointer.

The following code uses **fopen( )** to open a file named TEST for output.

```
FILE *fp;
fp = fopen("test", "w");
```

Mode	Meaning
r	Open a text file for reading
w	Create a text file for writing
a	Append to a text file
rb	Open a binary file for reading
wb	Create a binary file for writing
ab	Append to a binary file
r+	Open a text file for read/write
w+	Create a text file for read/write
a+	Append or create a text file for read/write
r+b	Open a binary file for read/write
w+b	Create a binary file for read/write
a+b	Append or create a binary file for read/write

Table 9-2. *Legal Values for Mode*

Although the preceding code is technically correct, you will usually see it written like this:

```
FILE *fp;

if ((fp = fopen("test","w"))==NULL) {
  printf("Cannot open file.\n");
  exit(1);
}
```

This method will detect any error in opening a file, such as a write-protected or a full disk, before your program attempts to write to it. In general, you will always want to confirm that **fopen( )** succeeded before attempting any other operations on the file.

Although most of the file modes are self-explanatory, a few comments are in order. If, when opening a file for read-only operations, the file does not exist, **fopen( )** will fail. When opening a file using append mode, if the file does not exist, it will be created. Further, when a file is opened for append, all new data written to the file will be written to the end of the file. The original contents will remain unchanged. If, when a file is opened for writing, the file does not exist, it will be created. If it does exist, the contents of the original file will be destroyed, and a new file will be created. The difference between modes **r+** and **w+** is that **r+** will not create a file if it does not exist; however, **w+** will. Further, if the file already exists, opening it with **w+** destroys its contents; opening it with **r+** does not.

As Table 9-2 shows, a file can be opened in either text or binary mode. In most implementations, in text mode, carriage return/linefeed sequences are translated to newline characters on input. On output, the reverse occurs: Newlines are translated to carriage return/linefeeds. No such translations occur on binary files.

The number of files that may be open at any one time is specified by **FOPEN_MAX**. This value will be at least 8, but you must check your compiler manual for its exact value.

Closing a File

The **fclose( )** function closes a stream that was opened by a call to **fopen( )**. It writes any data still remaining in the disk buffer to the file and does a formal operating-system-level close on the file. Failure to close a stream invites all kinds of trouble, including lost data, destroyed files, and possible intermittent errors in your program. **fclose( )** also frees the file control block associated with the stream, making it available for reuse. Since there is a limit to the number of files you can have open at any one time, you may have to close one file before opening another.

The **fclose( )** function has this prototype,

int fclose(FILE *fp);

where *fp* is the file pointer returned by the call to **fopen( )**. A return value of zero signifies a successful close operation. The function returns **EOF** if an error occurs. You can use the standard function **ferror( )** (discussed shortly) to determine the precise cause of the problem. Generally, **fclose( )** will fail only when a disk has been prematurely removed from the drive or there is no more space on the disk.

Writing a Character

The C I/O system defines two equivalent functions that output a character: **putc( )** and **fputc( )**. (Actually, **putc( )** is usually implemented as a macro.) The two identical functions exist simply to preserve compatibility with older versions of C. This book uses **putc( )**, but you can use **fputc( )** if you like.

The **putc( )** function writes characters to a file that was previously opened for writing using the **fopen( )** function. The prototype of this function is

int putc(int *ch*, FILE *fp);

where *fp* is the file pointer returned by **fopen( )**, and *ch* is the character to be output. The file pointer tells **putc( )** which file to write to. Although *ch* is defined as an **int,** only the low-order byte is written.

If a **putc( )** operation is successful, it returns the character written. Otherwise, it returns **EOF**.

Reading a Character

There are also two equivalent functions that input a character: **getc( )** and **fgetc( )**. Both are defined to preserve compatibility with older versions of C. This book uses **getc( )** (which is usually implemented as a macro), but you can use **fgetc( )** if you like.

The **getc( )** function reads characters from a file opened in read mode by **fopen( )**. The prototype of **getc( )** is

int getc(FILE *fp);

where *fp* is a file pointer of type **FILE** returned by **fopen( )**. **getc( )** returns an integer, but the character is contained in the low-order byte. Unless an error occurs, the high-order byte (or bytes) is zero.

The **getc( )** function returns an **EOF** when the end of the file has been reached. Therefore, to read to the end of a text file, you could use the following code:

```
do {
  ch = getc(fp);
} while(ch!=EOF);
```

However, **getc( )** also returns **EOF** if an error occurs. You can use **ferror( )** to determine precisely what has occurred.

Using fopen( ), getc( ), putc( ), and fclose( )

The functions **fopen( )**, **getc( )**, **putc( )**, and **fclose( )** constitute the minimal set of file routines. The following program, KTOD, is a simple example that uses **putc( )**, **fopen( )**, and **fclose( )**. It reads characters from the keyboard and writes them to a disk file until the user types a dollar sign. The filename is specified from the command line. For example, if you call this program KTOD, typing **KTOD TEST** allows you to enter lines of text into the file called TEST.

```
/* KTOD: A key to disk program. */
#include <stdio.h>
#include <stdlib.h>

int main(int argc, char *argv[])
{
  FILE *fp;
  char ch;

  if(argc!=2) {
    printf("You forgot to enter the filename.\n");
```

```
    exit(1);
  }

  if((fp=fopen(argv[1], "w"))==NULL) {
    printf("Cannot open file.\n");
    exit(1);
  }

  do {
    ch = getchar();
    putc(ch, fp);
  } while (ch != '$');

  fclose(fp);

  return 0;
}
```

The complementary program DTOS reads any text file and displays the contents on the screen.

```
/* DTOS: A program that reads files and displays them
         on the screen. */
#include <stdio.h>
#include <stdlib.h>

int main(int argc, char *argv[])
{
  FILE *fp;
  char ch;

  if(argc!=2) {
    printf("You forgot to enter the filename.\n");
    exit(1);
  }

  if((fp=fopen(argv[1], "r"))==NULL) {
    printf("Cannot open file.\n");
    exit(1);
  }
```

```
  ch = getc(fp);    /* read one character */

  while (ch!=EOF) {
    putchar(ch);   /* print on screen */
    ch = getc(fp);
  }

  fclose(fp);

  return 0;
}
```

To try these two programs, first use KTOD to create a text file. Then read its contents using DTOS.

Using feof( )

As just described, **getc( )** returns **EOF** when the end of the file has been encountered. However, testing the value returned by **getc( )** may not be the best way to determine when you have arrived at the end of a file. First, the C file system can operate on both text and binary files. When a file is opened for binary input, an integer value that will test equal to **EOF** may be read. This would cause the input routine to indicate an end-of-file condition even though the physical end of the file had not been reached. Second, **getc( )** returns **EOF** when it fails and when it reaches the end of the file. Using only the return value of **getc( )**, it is impossible to know which occurred. To solve these problems, C includes the function **feof( )**, which determines when the end of the file has been encountered. The **feof( )** function has this prototype:

int feof(FILE *fp);

feof( ) returns true if the end of the file has been reached; otherwise, it returns zero. Therefore, the following routine reads a binary file until the end of the file is encountered:

```
while(!feof(fp)) ch = getc(fp);
```

Of course, you can apply this method to text files as well as binary files.

The following program, which copies text or binary files, contains an example of **feof( )**. The files are opened in binary mode, and **feof( )** checks for the end of the file.

```
/* Copy a file. */
#include <stdio.h>
```

```
#include <stdlib.h>

int main(int argc, char *argv[])
{
  FILE *in, *out;
  char ch;

  if(argc!=3) {
    printf("You forgot to enter a filename.\n");
    exit(1);
  }

  if((in=fopen(argv[1], "rb"))==NULL) {
    printf("Cannot open source file.\n");
    exit(1);
  }
  if((out=fopen(argv[2], "wb")) == NULL) {
    printf("Cannot open destination file.\n");
    exit(1);
  }

  /* This code actually copies the file. */
  while(!feof(in)) {
    ch = getc(in);
    if(!feof(in)) putc(ch, out);
  }

  fclose(in);
  fclose(out);

  return 0;
}
```

Working with Strings: fputs( ) and fgets( )

In addition to **getc( )** and **putc( )**, C supports the related functions **fgets( )** and **fputs( )**, which read and write character strings from and to a disk file. These functions work just like **putc( )** and **getc( )**, but instead of reading or writing a single character, they read or write strings. They have the following prototypes:

int fputs(const char *str, FILE *fp);
char *fgets(char *str, int length, FILE *fp);

The **fputs( )** function writes the string pointed to by *str* to the specified stream. It returns **EOF** if an error occurs.

The **fgets( )** function reads a string from the specified stream until either a newline character is read or *length*–1 characters have been read. If a newline is read, it will be part of the string (unlike the **gets( )** function). The resultant string will be null terminated. The function returns *str* if successful and a null pointer if an error occurs.

The following program demonstrates **fputs( )**. It reads strings from the keyboard and writes them to the file called TEST. To terminate the program, enter a blank line. Since **gets( )** does not store the newline character, one is added before each string is written to the file so that the file can be read more easily.

```c
#include <stdio.h>
#include <stdlib.h>
#include <string.h>

int main(void)
{
  char str[80];
  FILE *fp;

  if((fp = fopen("TEST", "w"))==NULL) {
    printf("Cannot open file.\n");
    exit(1);
  }

  do {
    printf("Enter a string (CR to quit):\n");
    gets(str);
    strcat(str, "\n");  /* add a newline */
    fputs(str, fp);
  } while(*str!='\n');

  return 0;
}
```

rewind( )

The **rewind( )** function resets the file position indicator to the beginning of the file specified as its argument. That is, it "rewinds" the file. Its prototype is

void rewind(FILE *fp);

where *fp* is a valid file pointer.

To see an example of **rewind( )**, you can modify the program from the previous section so that it displays the contents of the file just created. To accomplish this, the program rewinds the file after input is complete and then uses **fgets( )** to read back the file. Notice that the file must now be opened in read/write mode using "w+" for the mode parameter.

```c
#include <stdio.h>
#include <stdlib.h>
#include <string.h>

int main(void)
{
  char str[80];
  FILE *fp;

  if((fp = fopen("TEST", "w+"))==NULL) {
    printf("Cannot open file.\n");
    exit(1);
  }

  do {
    printf("Enter a string (CR to quit):\n");
    gets(str);
    strcat(str, "\n");  /* add a newline */
    fputs(str, fp);
  } while(*str!='\n');

  /* now, read and display the file */
  rewind(fp);  /* reset file position indicator to
                  start of the file. */
  while(!feof(fp)) {
    fgets(str, 79, fp);
    printf(str);
  }

  return 0;
}
```

ferror( )

The **ferror( )** function determines whether a file operation has produced an error. The **ferror( )** function has this prototype,

int ferror(FILE *fp);

where *fp* is a valid file pointer. It returns true if an error has occurred during the last file operation; otherwise, it returns false. Because each file operation sets the error condition, **ferror( )** should be called immediately after each file operation; otherwise, an error may be lost.

The following program illustrates **ferror( )** by removing tabs from a file and substituting the appropriate number of spaces. The tab size is defined by **TAB_SIZE**. Notice how **ferror( )** is called after each file operation. To use the program, specify the names of the input and output files on the command line.

```c
/* The program substitutes spaces for tabs
   in a text file and supplies error checking. */

#include <stdio.h>
#include <stdlib.h>

#define TAB_SIZE 8
#define IN 0
#define OUT 1

void err(int e);

int main(int argc, char *argv[])
{
  FILE *in, *out;
  int tab, i;
  char ch;

  if(argc!=3) {
    printf("usage: detab <in> <out>\n");
    exit(1);
  }

  if((in = fopen(argv[1], "rb"))==NULL) {
    printf("Cannot open %s.\n", argv[1]);
    exit(1);
  }

  if((out = fopen(argv[2], "wb"))==NULL) {
    printf("Cannot open %s.\n", argv[1]);
    exit(1);
  }
```

```
    tab = 0;
    do {
      ch = getc(in);
      if(ferror(in)) err(IN);

      /* if tab found, output appropriate number of spaces */
      if(ch=='\t') {
        for(i=tab; i<8; i++) {
          putc(' ', out);
          if(ferror(out)) err(OUT);
        }
        tab = 0;
      }
      else {
        putc(ch, out);
        if(ferror(out)) err(OUT);
        tab++;
        if(tab==TAB_SIZE) tab = 0;
        if(ch=='\n' || ch=='\r') tab = 0;
      }
    } while(!feof(in));
    fclose(in);
    fclose(out);

    return 0;
}

void err(int e)
{
  if(e==IN) printf("Error on input.\n");
  else printf("Error on output.\n");
  exit(1);
}
```

Erasing Files

The **remove( )** function erases the specified file. Its prototype is

int remove(const char *filename);

It returns zero if successful. Otherwise, it returns a nonzero value.

The following program erases the file specified on the command line. However, it first gives you a chance to change your mind. A utility like this might be useful for new computer users.

```
/* Double check before erasing. */
#include <stdio.h>
#include <stdlib.h>
#include <ctype.h>

int main(int argc, char *argv[])
{
  char str[80];

  if(argc!=2) {
    printf("usage: xerase <filename>\n");
    exit(1);
  }

  printf("Erase %s? (Y/N): ", argv[1]);
  gets(str);

  if(toupper(*str)=='Y')
    if(remove(argv[1])) {
      printf("Cannot erase file.\n");
      exit(1);
    }
  return 0;
}
```

Flushing a Stream

If you wish to flush the contents of an output stream, use the **fflush( )** function, whose prototype is shown here:

int fflush(FILE *fp);

This function writes the contents of any buffered data to the file associated with fp. If you call **fflush( )** with fp being null, all files opened for output are flushed.

The **fflush( )** function returns zero if successful; otherwise, it returns **EOF**.

fread( ) and fwrite( )

To read and write data types that are longer than 1 byte, the C file system provides two functions: **fread( )** and **fwrite( )**. These functions allow the reading and writing of blocks of any type of data. Their prototypes are

size_t fread(void *buffer*, size_t *num_bytes*, size_t *count*, FILE *fp*);
size_t fwrite(const void *buffer*, size_t *num_bytes*, size_t *count*, FILE *fp*);

For **fread( )**, *buffer* is a pointer to a region of memory that will receive the data from the file. For **fwrite( )**, *buffer* is a pointer to the information that will be written to the file. The value of *count* determines how many items are read or written, with each item being *num_bytes* bytes in length. (Remember, the type **size_t** is defined as some kind of unsigned integer.) Finally, *fp* is a file pointer to a previously opened stream.

The **fread( )** function returns the number of items read. This value may be less than *count* if the end of the file is reached or an error occurs. The **fwrite( )** function returns the number of items written. This value will equal *count* unless an error occurs.

Using fread( ) and fwrite( )

As long as the file has been opened for binary data, **fread( )** and **fwrite( )** can read and write any type of information. For example, the following program writes and then reads back a **double**, an **int**, and a **long** to and from a disk file. Notice how it uses **sizeof** to determine the length of each data type.

```c
/* Write some non-character data to a disk file
   and read it back. */
#include <stdio.h>
#include <stdlib.h>

int main(void)
{
  FILE *fp;
  double d = 12.23;
  int i = 101;
  long l = 123023L;

  if((fp=fopen("test", "wb+"))==NULL) {
    printf("Cannot open file.\n");
    exit(1);
  }
```

```
fwrite(&d, sizeof(double), 1, fp);
fwrite(&i, sizeof(int), 1, fp);
fwrite(&l, sizeof(long), 1, fp);

rewind(fp);

fread(&d, sizeof(double), 1, fp);
fread(&i, sizeof(int), 1, fp);
fread(&l, sizeof(long), 1, fp);

printf("%f %d %ld", d, i, l);

fclose(fp);

return 0;
}
```

As this program illustrates, the buffer can be (and often is) simply the memory used to hold a variable. In this simple program, the return values of **fread( )** and **fwrite( )** are ignored. In the real world, however, you should check their return values for errors.

One of the most useful applications of **fread( )** and **fwrite( )** involves reading and writing user-defined data types, especially structures. For example, given this structure,

```
struct struct_type {
  float balance;
  char name[80];
} cust;
```

the following statement writes the contents of **cust** to the file pointed to by **fp**:

```
fwrite(&cust, sizeof(struct struct_type), 1, fp);
```

A Mailing List Example

To illustrate just how easy it is to write large amounts of data using **fread( )** and **fwrite( )**, we will rework the mailing list program first shown in Chapter 7. The enhanced version will be capable of storing the addresses in a file. As before, addresses will be stored in an array of structures of this type:

```
struct addr {
  char name[30];
  char street[40];
  char city[20];
  char state[3];
  unsigned long int zip;
} addr_list[MAX];
```

The value of **MAX** determines how many addresses the list can hold.

When the program executes, the **name** field of each structure is initialized with a null. By convention, the program assumes that a structure is unused if the name is of zero length.

The **save( )** and **load( )** functions, shown next, are used to save and load the mailing list database. Note how little code is contained in each function because of the power of **fread( )** and **fwrite( )**. Notice also how these functions check the return values of **fread( )** and **fwrite( )** for errors.

```
/* Save the list. */
void save(void)
{
  FILE  *fp;
  register int i;

  if((fp=fopen("maillist", "wb"))==NULL) {
    printf("Cannot open file.\n");
    return;
  }

  for(i=0; i<MAX; i++)
    if(*addr_list[i].name)
      if(fwrite(&addr_list[i],
          sizeof(struct addr), 1, fp)!=1)
            printf("File write error.\n");

  fclose(fp);
}

/* Load the file. */
void load(void)
{
  FILE  *fp;
  register int i;
```

```
   if((fp=fopen("maillist", "rb"))==NULL) {
     printf("Cannot open file.\n");
     return;
   }

   init_list();
   for(i=0; i<MAX; i++)
     if(fread(&addr_list[i],
         sizeof(struct addr), 1, fp)!=1) {
           if(feof(fp)) break;
           printf("File read error.\n");
     }

   fclose(fp);
}
```

Both functions confirm a successful file operation by checking the return value of **fread( )** or **fwrite( )**. Also, **load( )** must explicitly check for the end of the file via **feof( )** because **fread( )** returns the same value whether the end of the file has been reached or an error has occurred.

The entire mailing list program is shown next. You may wish to use this as a core for further enhancements, such as the ability to search for addresses.

```c
/* A simple mailing list example using an array of structures. */
#include <stdio.h>
#include <stdlib.h>

#define MAX 100

struct addr {
  char name[30];
  char street[40];
  char city[20];
  char state[3];
  unsigned long int zip;
} addr_list[MAX];

void init_list(void), enter(void);
void delete(void), list(void);
void load(void), save(void);
int menu_select(void), find_free(void);
```

```
int main(void)
{
  char choice;

  init_list(); /* initialize the structure array */
  for(;;) {
    choice = menu_select();
    switch(choice) {
      case 1: enter();
        break;
      case 2: delete();
        break;
      case 3: list();
        break;
      case 4: save();
        break;
      case 5: load();
        break;
      case 6: exit(0);
    }
  }

  return 0;
}

/* Initialize the list. */
void init_list(void)
{
  register int t;

  for(t=0; t<MAX; ++t) addr_list[t].name[0] = '\0';
}

/* Get a menu selection. */
int menu_select(void)
{
  char s[80];
  int c;

  printf("1. Enter a name\n");
  printf("2. Delete a name\n");
```

```
   printf("3. List the file\n");
   printf("4. Save the file\n");
   printf("5. Load the file\n");
   printf("6. Quit\n");
   do {
     printf("\nEnter your choice: ");
     gets(s);
     c = atoi(s);
   } while(c<0 || c>6);
   return c;
}

/* Input addresses into the list. */
void enter(void)
{
   int slot;
   char s[80];

   slot = find_free();

   if(slot==-1) {
     printf("\nList Full");
     return;
   }

   printf("Enter name: ");
   gets(addr_list[slot].name);

   printf("Enter street: ");
   gets(addr_list[slot].street);

   printf("Enter city: ");
   gets(addr_list[slot].city);

   printf("Enter state: ");
   gets(addr_list[slot].state);

   printf("Enter zip: ");
   gets(s);
   addr_list[slot].zip = strtoul(s, '\0', 10);
}

/* Find an unused structure. */
```

FOUNDATIONAL C

```
int find_free(void)
{
  register int t;

  for(t=0; addr_list[t].name[0] && t<MAX; ++t) ;

  if(t==MAX) return -1; /* no slots free */
  return t;
}

/* Delete an address. */
void delete(void)
{
  register int slot;
  char s[80];

  printf("enter record #: ");
  gets(s);
  slot = atoi(s);

  if(slot>=0 && slot < MAX)
    addr_list[slot].name[0] = '\0';
}

/* Display the list on the screen. */
void list(void)
{
  register int t;

  for(t=0; t<MAX; ++t) {
    if(addr_list[t].name[0]) {
      printf("%s\n", addr_list[t].name);
      printf("%s\n", addr_list[t].street);
      printf("%s\n", addr_list[t].city);
      printf("%s\n", addr_list[t].state);
      printf("%lu\n\n", addr_list[t].zip);
    }
  }
  printf("\n\n");
}

/* Save the list. */
```

```
void save(void)
{
  FILE  *fp;
  register int i;

  if((fp=fopen("maillist", "wb"))==NULL) {
    printf("Cannot open file.\n");
    return;
  }

  for(i=0; i<MAX; i++)
    if(*addr_list[i].name)
      if(fwrite(&addr_list[i],
          sizeof(struct addr), 1, fp)!=1)
            printf("File write error.\n");

  fclose(fp);
}

/* Load the file. */
void load(void)
{
  FILE  *fp;
  register int i;

  if((fp=fopen("maillist", "rb"))==NULL) {
    printf("Cannot open file.\n");
    return;
  }

  init_list();
  for(i=0; i<MAX; i++)
    if(fread(&addr_list[i],
        sizeof(struct addr), 1, fp)!=1) {
          if(feof(fp)) break;
          printf("File read error.\n");
    }

  fclose(fp);
}
```

fseek( ) and Random-Access I/O

You can perform random read and write operations using the C I/O system with the help of **fseek( )**, which sets the file position indicator. Its prototype is shown here:

int fseek(FILE *fp, long int *numbytes*, int *origin*);

Here, *fp* is a file pointer returned by a call to **fopen( )**, *numbytes* is the number of bytes from *origin*, which will become the new current position, and *origin* is one of the following macros:

Origin	Macro Name
Beginning of file	SEEK_SET
Current position	SEEK_CUR
End of file	SEEK_END

Therefore, to seek *numbytes* from the start of the file, *origin* should be **SEEK_SET**. To seek from the current position, use **SEEK_CUR**, and to seek from the end of the file, use **SEEK_END**. The **fseek( )** function returns zero when successful and a nonzero value if an error occurs.

The following program illustrates **fseek( )**. It seeks to and displays the specified byte in the specified file. Specify the filename and then the byte to seek to on the command line.

```c
#include <stdio.h>
#include <stdlib.h>

int main(int argc, char *argv[])
{
  FILE *fp;

  if(argc!=3) {
    printf("Usage: SEEK filename byte\n");
    exit(1);
  }

  if((fp = fopen(argv[1], "rb"))==NULL) {
    printf("Cannot open file.\n");
    exit(1);
  }
```

```
    if(fseek(fp, atol(argv[2]), SEEK_SET)) {
      printf("Seek error.\n");
      exit(1);
    }

    printf("Byte at %ld is %c.\n", atol(argv[2]), getc(fp));
    fclose(fp);

    return 0;
}
```

You can use **fseek( )** to seek in multiples of any type of data by simply multiplying the size of the data by the number of the item you want to reach. For example, assume a mailing list that consists of structures of type **addr** (as shown earlier). To seek to the tenth address in the file that holds the addresses, use this statement:

```
    fseek(fp, 9*sizeof(struct addr), SEEK_SET);
```

You can determine the current location of a file using **ftell( )**. Its prototype is

long int ftell(FILE *fp);

It returns the location of the current position of the file associated with *fp*. If a failure occurs, it returns −1.

In general, you will want to use random access only on binary files. The reason for this is simple. Because text files may have character translations performed on them, there may not be a direct correspondence between what is in the file and the byte that it would appear you want to seek to. The only time you should use **fseek( )** with a text file is when seeking to a position previously determined by **ftell( )**, using **SEEK_SET** as the origin.

Remember one important point: Even a file that contains only text can be opened as a binary file, if you like. There is no inherent restriction about random access on files containing text. The restriction applies only to files opened *as* text files.

fprintf( ) and fscanf( )

In addition to the basic I/O functions already discussed, the C I/O system includes **fprintf( )** and **fscanf( )**. These functions behave exactly like **printf( )** and **scanf( )** except that they operate with files. The prototypes of **fprintf( )** and **fscanf( )** are

int fprintf(FILE *fp, const char *control_string,. . .);
int fscanf(FILE *fp, const char *control_string,. . .);

where *fp* is a file pointer returned by a call to **fopen( )**. **fprintf( )** and **fscanf( )** direct their I/O operations to the file pointed to by *fp*.

As an example, the following program reads a string and an integer from the keyboard and writes them to a disk file called TEST. The program then reads the file and displays the information on the screen. After running this program, examine the TEST file. As you will see, it contains human-readable text.

```c
/* fscanf() - fprintf() example */
#include <stdio.h>
#include <io.h>
#include <stdlib.h>

int main(void)
{
  FILE *fp;
  char s[80];
  int t;

  if((fp=fopen("test", "w")) == NULL) {
    printf("Cannot open file.\n");
    exit(1);
  }

  printf("Enter a string and a number: ");
  fscanf(stdin, "%s%d", s, &t); /* read from keyboard */

  fprintf(fp, "%s %d", s, t); /* write to file */
  fclose(fp);

  if((fp=fopen("test","r")) == NULL) {
    printf("Cannot open file.\n");
    exit(1);
  }

  fscanf(fp, "%s%d", s, &t); /* read from file */
  fprintf(stdout, "%s %d", s, t); /* print on screen */

  return 0;
}
```

A word of warning: Although **fprintf( )** and **fscanf( )** often are the easiest way to write and read assorted data to disk files, they are not always the most efficient. Because formatted ASCII data is being written as it would appear on the screen (instead of in binary), extra overhead is incurred with each call. So, if speed or file size is a concern, you should probably use **fread( )** and **fwrite( )**.

The Standard Streams

As it relates to the C file system, when a program starts execution, three streams are opened automatically. They are **stdin** (standard input), **stdout** (standard output), and **stderr** (standard error). Normally, these streams refer to the console, but they can be redirected by the operating system to some other device in environments that support redirectable I/O. (Redirectable I/O is supported by Windows, DOS, Unix, and OS/2, for example.)

Because the standard streams are file pointers, they may be used by the C I/O system to perform I/O operations on the console. For example, **putchar( )** could be defined like this:

```
int putchar(char c)
{
  return putc(c, stdout);
}
```

In general, **stdin** is used to read from the console, and **stdout** and **stderr** are used to write to the console.

You can use **stdin**, **stdout**, and **stderr** as file pointers in any function that uses a variable of type **FILE ***. For example, you could use **fgets( )** to input a string from the console using a call like this:

```
char str[255];
fgets(str, 80, stdin);
```

In fact, using **fgets( )** in this manner can be quite useful. As mentioned earlier in this book, when using **gets( )**, it is possible to overrun the array that is being used to receive the characters entered by the user because **gets( )** provides no bounds checking. When used with **stdin**, the **fgets( )** function offers a useful alternative because it can limit the number of characters read and thus prevent array overruns. The only trouble is that **fgets( )** does not remove the newline character and **gets( )** does, so you will have to manually remove it, as shown in the following program:

```
#include <stdio.h>
#include <string.h>
```

FOUNDATIONAL C

```
int main(void)
{
  char str[80];
  int i;

  printf("Enter a string: ");
  fgets(str, 10, stdin);

  /* remove newline, if present */
  i = strlen(str)-1;
  if(str[i]=='\n') str[i] = '\0';

  printf("This is your string: %s", str);

  return 0;
}
```

Keep in mind that **stdin, stdout**, and **stderr** are not variables in the normal sense and can not be assigned a value using **fopen( )**. Also, just as these file pointers are created automatically at the start of your program, they are closed automatically at the end; you should not try to close them.

The Console I/O Connection

C makes little distinction between console I/O and file I/O. The console I/O functions described in Chapter 8 actually direct their I/O operations to either **stdin** or **stdout**. In essence, the console I/O functions are simply special versions of their parallel file functions. The reason they exist is as a convenience to you, the programmer.

As described in the previous section, you can perform console I/O using any of C's file system functions. However, what might surprise you is that you can perform disk file I/O using console I/O functions, such as **printf( )**! This is because all of the console I/O functions described in Chapter 8 operate on **stdin** and **stdout**. In environments that allow redirection of I/O, this means that **stdin** and **stdout** could refer to a device other than the keyboard and screen. For example, consider this program:

```
#include <stdio.h>

int main(void)
{
  char str[80];
```

```
    printf("Enter a string: ");
    gets(str);
    printf(str);

    return 0;
}
```

Assume that this program is called TEST. If you execute TEST normally, it displays its prompt on the screen, reads a string from the keyboard, and displays that string on the screen. However, in an environment that supports I/O redirection, either **stdin**, **stdout**, or both could be redirected to a file. For example, in a DOS or Windows environment, executing TEST like this,

```
TEST > OUTPUT
```

causes the output of TEST to be written to a file called OUTPUT. Executing TEST like this,

```
TEST < INPUT > OUTPUT
```

directs **stdin** to the file called INPUT and sends output to the file called OUTPUT.

When a C program terminates, any redirected streams are reset to their default status.

Using freopen( ) to Redirect the Standard Streams

You can redirect the standard streams by using the **freopen( )** function. This function associates an existing stream with a new file. Thus, you can use it to associate a standard stream with a new file. Its prototype is

FILE *freopen(const char *filename, const char *mode, FILE *stream);

where filename is a pointer to the filename you want associated with the stream pointed to by stream. The file is opened using the value of mode, which may have the same values as those used with **fopen( )**. **freopen( )** returns stream if successful or **NULL** on failure.

The following program uses **freopen( )** to redirect **stdout** to a file called OUTPUT:

```c
#include <stdio.h>

int main(void)
{
  char str[80];

  freopen("OUTPUT", "w", stdout);

  printf("Enter a string: ");
  gets(str);
  printf(str);

  return 0;
}
```

In general, redirecting the standard streams by using **freopen( )** is useful in special situations, such as debugging. However, performing disk I/O using redirected **stdin** and **stdout** is not as efficient as using functions like **fread( )** or **fwrite( )**.

Chapter 10

The Preprocessor
and Comments

Y ou can include various instructions to the compiler in the source code of a C program. These are called *preprocessor directives*, and they expand the scope of the programming environment. This chapter also examines comments.

The Preprocessor

The preprocessor directives are shown here:

#define	#endif	#ifdef	#line
#elif	#error	#ifndef	#pragma
#else	#if	#include	#undef

As you can see, all preprocessor directives begin with a # sign. In addition, each preprocessing directive must be on its own line. For example, this will not work:

```
#include <stdio.h>  #include <stdlib.h>
```

#define

The **#define** directive defines an identifier and a character sequence (a set of characters) that will be substituted for the identifier each time it is encountered in the source file. The identifier is referred to as a *macro name* and the replacement process as *macro replacement*. The general form of the directive is

#define *macro-name char-sequence*

Notice that there is no semicolon in this statement. There may be any number of spaces between the identifier and the character sequence, but once the character sequence begins, it is terminated only by a newline.

For example, if you wish to use the word **LEFT** for the value 1 and the word **RIGHT** for the value 0, you could declare these two **#define** directives:

```
#define LEFT 1
#define RIGHT 0
```

This causes the compiler to substitute a 1 or a 0 each time **LEFT** or **RIGHT** is encountered in your source file. For example, the following prints **0 1 2** on the screen:

```
printf("%d %d %d", RIGHT, LEFT, LEFT+1);
```

Once a macro name has been defined, it may be used as part of the definition of other macro names. For example, this code defines the values of **ONE**, **TWO**, and **THREE**:

```
#define ONE     1
#define TWO     ONE+ONE
#define THREE   ONE+TWO
```

Macro substitution is simply the replacement of an identifier by the character sequence associated with it. Therefore, if you wish to define a standard error message, you might write something like this:

```
#define E_MS "standard error on input\n"
/* ... */
printf(E_MS);
```

The compiler will substitute the string "standard error on input\n" when the identifier **E_MS** is encountered. To the compiler, the **printf( )** statement will actually appear to be

```
printf("standard error on input\n");
```

No text substitutions occur if the identifier is within a quoted string. For example,

```
#define XYZ this is a test

printf("XYZ");
```

does not print **this is a test**, but rather **XYZ**.

If the character is longer than one line, you may continue it on the next by placing a backslash at the end of the line, as shown here:

```
#define LONG_STRING "this is a very long \
string that is used as an example"
```

C programmers often use uppercase letters for defined identifiers. This convention helps anyone reading the program know at a glance that a macro replacement will take place. Also, it is usually best to put all **#define**s at the start of the file or in a separate header file rather than sprinkling them throughout the program.

Macros are most frequently used to define names for "magic numbers" that occur in a program. For example, you may have a program that defines an array and has several routines that access that array. Instead of "hard-coding" the array's size with a constant, you can define the size using a **#define** statement and then use that macro name whenever the array size is needed. In this way, if you need to change the size of the array, you will need to change only the **#define** statement and then recompile your program. For example:

```
#define MAX_SIZE 100
/* ... */
float balance[MAX_SIZE];
/* ... */
for(i=0; i<MAX_SIZE; i++) printf("%f", balance[i]);
/* ... */
for(i=0; i<MAX_SIZE; i++) x =+ balance[i];
```

Since **MAX_SIZE** defines the size of the array **balance**, if the size of **balance** needs to be changed in the future, you need change only the definition of **MAX_SIZE**. All subsequent references to it will be automatically updated when you recompile your program.

Defining Function-like Macros

The **#define** directive has another powerful feature: The macro name can have arguments. Each time the macro name is encountered, the arguments used in its definition are replaced by the actual arguments found in the program. This form of a macro is called a *function-like macro*. For example:

```
#include <stdio.h>

#define ABS(a)   (a) < 0 ? -(a) : (a)

int main(void)
{
  printf("abs of -1 and 1: %d %d", ABS(-1), ABS(1));

  return 0;
}
```

When this program is compiled, **a** in the macro definition will be substituted with the values –1 and 1. The parentheses that enclose **a** ensure proper substitution in all cases. For example, if the parentheses around **a** were removed, this expression

```
ABS(10-20)
```

would be converted to

```
10-20 < 0 ? -10-20 : 10-20
```

after macro replacement and would yield the wrong result.

The use of a function-like macro in place of real functions has one major benefit: It increases the execution speed of the code because there is no function call overhead. However, if the size of the function-like macro is very large, this increased speed may be paid for with an increase in the size of the program because of duplicated code.

One other point: Although parameterized macros are a valuable feature, C99 (and C++) has a better way of creating in-line code, which uses the **inline** keyword.

Note *In C99, you can create a macro with a variable number of arguments. This is described in Part Two of this book.*

#error

The **#error** directive forces the compiler to stop compilation. It is used primarily for debugging. The general form of the **#error** directive is

#error *error-message*

The *error-message* is not between double quotes. When the **#error** directive is encountered, the error message is displayed, possibly along with other information defined by the compiler.

#include

The **#include** directive tells the compiler to read another source file in addition to the one that contains the **#include** directive. The name of the source file must be enclosed between double quotes or angle brackets. For example,

```
#include "stdio.h"
#include <stdio.h>
```

both cause the compiler to read and compile the header for the I/O system library functions.

Include files can have **#include** directives in them. This is referred to as *nested includes*. The number of levels of nesting allowed varies between compilers. However, C89 stipulates that at least 8 nested inclusions will be available. C99 specifies that at least 15 levels of nesting be supported.

Whether the filename is enclosed by quotes or by angle brackets determines how the search for the specified file is conducted. If the filename is enclosed in angle brackets, the file is searched for in a manner defined by the creator of the compiler. Often, this means searching some special directory set aside for include files. If the filename is enclosed in quotes, the file is looked for in another implementation-defined manner. For many compilers, this means searching the current working directory. If the file is not found, the search is repeated as if the filename had been enclosed in angle brackets.

Typically, most programmers use angle brackets to include standard header files. The use of quotes is generally reserved for including files specifically related to the program at hand. However, there is no hard and fast rule that demands this usage.

In addition to files, a C program uses the **#include** directive to include a *header*. C defines a set of standard headers that provide the information necessary for the various C libraries. A header is a standard identifier that might map to a filename, but need not. Thus, a header is simply an abstraction that guarantees that the appropriate information is included. As a practical matter, however, C headers are nearly always files.

Conditional Compilation Directives

There are several directives that allow you to selectively compile portions of your program's source code. This process is called *conditional compilation* and is used widely by commercial software houses that provide and maintain many customized versions of one program.

#if, #else, #elif, and #endif

Perhaps the most commonly used conditional compilation directives are **#if**, **#else**, **#elif**, and **#endif**. These directives allow you to conditionally include portions of code based upon the outcome of a constant expression.

The general form of **#if** is

#if *constant-expression*
    statement sequence
#endif

If the constant expression following **#if** is true, the code that is between it and **#endif** is compiled. Otherwise, the intervening code is skipped. The **#endif** directive marks the end of an **#if** block. For example:

```
/* Simple #if example. */
#include <stdio.h>

#define MAX 100
```

FOUNDATIONAL C

```
int main(void)
{
#if MAX>99
  printf("Compiled for array greater than 99.\n");
#endif

  return 0;
}
```

This program displays the message on the screen because **MAX** is greater than 99. This example illustrates an important point. The expression that follows the **#if** is evaluated at compile time. Therefore, it must contain only previously defined identifiers and constants—no variables may be used.

The **#else** directive works much like the **else** that is part of the C language: It establishes an alternative if **#if** fails. The previous example can be expanded as shown here:

```
/* Simple #if/#else example. */
#include <stdio.h>

#define MAX 10

int main(void)
{
#if MAX>99
  printf("Compiled for array greater than 99.\n");
#else
  printf("Compiled for small array.\n");
#endif

  return 0;
}
```

In this case, **MAX** is defined to be less than 99, so the **#if** portion of the code is not compiled. The **#else** alternative is compiled, however, and the message **Compiled for small array** is displayed.

Notice that **#else** is used to mark both the end of the **#if** block and the beginning of the **#else** block. This is necessary because there can only be one **#endif** associated with any **#if**.

The **#elif** directive means "else if" and establishes an if-else-if chain for multiple compilation options. **#elif** is followed by a constant expression. If the expression is true, that block of code is compiled and no other **#elif** expressions are tested. Otherwise, the next block in the series is checked. The general form for **#elif** is

#if *expression*
  statement sequence
#elif *expression 1*
  statement sequence
#elif *expression 2*
  statement sequence
#elif *expression 3*
  statement sequence
#elif *expression 4*
  .
  .
  .
#elif *expression N*
  statement sequence
#endif

For example, the following fragment uses the value of **ACTIVE_COUNTRY** to define the currency sign:

```
#define US 0
#define ENGLAND 1
#define FRANCE 2

#define ACTIVE_COUNTRY US

#if ACTIVE_COUNTRY == US
  char currency[] = "dollar";
#elif ACTIVE_COUNTRY == ENGLAND
  char currency[] = "pound";
#else
  char currency[] = "franc";
#endif
```

C89 states that **#if**s and **#elif**s may be nested at least 8 levels. C99 states that at least 63 levels of nesting be allowed. When nested, each **#endif**, **#else**, or **#elif** associates with the nearest **#if** or **#elif**. For example, the following is perfectly valid:

```
#if MAX>100
  #if SERIAL_VERSION
    int port=198;
```

```
#elif
   int port=200;
  #endif
#else
  char out_buffer[100];
#endif
```

#ifdef and #ifndef

Another method of conditional compilation uses the directives **#ifdef** and **#ifndef**, which mean "if defined" and "if not defined," respectively. The general form of **#ifdef** is

> #ifdef *macro-name*
>   *statement sequence*
> #endif

If *macro-name* has been previously defined in a **#define** statement, the block of code will be compiled.

The general form of **#ifndef** is

> #ifndef *macro-name*
>   *statement sequence*
> #endif

If *macro-name* is currently undefined by a **#define** statement, the block of code is compiled.

Both **#ifdef** and **#ifndef** may use an **#else** or **#elif** statement.

For example,

```
#include <stdio.h>

#define TED 10

int main(void)
{
#ifdef TED
  printf("Hi Ted\n");
#else
  printf("Hi anyone\n");
#endif
#ifndef RALPH
```

```
    printf("RALPH not defined\n");
#endif

    return 0;
}
```

will print **Hi Ted** and **RALPH not defined**. However, if **TED** were not defined, **Hi anyone** would be displayed, followed by **RALPH not defined**.

You may nest **#ifdef**s and **#ifndef**s to at least 8 levels in C89. C99 specifies that at least 63 levels of nesting be supported.

#undef

The **#undef** directive removes a previously defined definition of the macro name that follows it—that is, it "undefines" a macro. The general form for **#undef** is

#undef *macro-name*

For example:

```
#define LEN 100
#define WIDTH 100

char array[LEN][WIDTH];

#undef LEN
#undef WIDTH
/* at this point both LEN and WIDTH are undefined */
```

Both **LEN** and **WIDTH** are defined until the **#undef** statements are encountered.

#undef is used principally to allow macro names to be localized to only those sections of code that need them.

Using defined

In addition to **#ifdef**, there is a second way to determine whether a macro name is defined. You can use the **#if** directive in conjunction with the **defined** compile-time operator. The **defined** operator has this general form:

defined *macro-name*

If *macro-name* is currently defined, the expression is true; otherwise, it is false. For example, to determine whether the macro **MYFILE** is defined, you can use either of these two preprocessing commands:

```
#if defined MYFILE
```

or

```
#ifdef MYFILE
```

You can also precede **defined** with the ! to reverse the condition. For example, the following fragment is compiled only if **DEBUG** is not defined:

```
#if !defined DEBUG
  printf("Final version!\n");
#endif
```

One reason for using **defined** is that it allows the existence of a macro name to be determined by a **#elif** statement.

#line

The **#line** directive changes the contents of _ _**LINE**_ _ and _ _**FILE**_ _ , which are predefined identifiers in the compiler. The _ _**LINE**_ _ identifier contains the line number of the currently compiled line of code. The _ _**FILE**_ _ identifier is a string that contains the name of the source file being compiled. The general form for **#line** is

    #line *number "filename"*

where *number* is any positive integer and becomes the new value of _ _**LINE**_ _ , and the optional *filename* is any valid file identifier, which becomes the new value of _ _**FILE**_ _. **#line** is primarily used for debugging and special applications.

For example, the following code specifies that the line count will begin with 100, and the **printf( )** statement displays the number 102 because it is the third line in the program after the **#line 100** statement.

```
#include <stdio.h>

#line 100                 /* reset the line counter */
int main(void)            /* line 100 */
{                         /* line 101 */
```

```
    printf("%d\n", _ _LINE_ _); /* line 102 */

    return 0;
}
```

#pragma

#pragma is an implementation-defined directive that allows various instructions to be given to the compiler. For example, a compiler may have an option that supports program execution tracing. A trace option would then be specified by a **#pragma** statement. You must check the compiler's documentation for details and options.

Note *C99 has added an alternative to #pragma: the _Pragma operator. It is described in Part Two of this book.*

The # and ## Preprocessor Operators

There are two preprocessor operators: # and ##. These operators are used with the **#define** statement.

The # operator, which is generally called the *stringize* operator, turns the argument it precedes into a quoted string. For example, consider this program:

```
#include <stdio.h>

#define mkstr(s)  # s

int main(void)
{
  printf(mkstr(I like C));

  return 0;
}
```

The preprocessor turns the line

```
printf(mkstr(I like C));
```

into

```
printf("I like C");
```

The ## operator, called the *pasting* operator, concatenates two tokens. For example:

```
#include <stdio.h>

#define concat(a, b)   a ## b

int main(void)
{
  int xy = 10;

  printf("%d", concat(x, y));

  return 0;
}
```

The preprocessor transforms

```
printf("%d", concat(x, y));
```

into

```
printf("%d", xy);
```

If these operators seem strange to you, keep in mind that they are not needed or used in most programs. They exist primarily to allow the preprocessor to handle some special cases.

Predefined Macro Names

C specifies five built-in predefined macro names. They are

```
_ _LINE_ _
_ _FILE_ _
_ _DATE_ _
_ _TIME_ _
_ _STDC_ _
```

Each will be described here, in turn.

The _ _**LINE**_ _ and _ _**FILE**_ _ macros were described in the discussion of **#line**. Briefly, they contain the current line number and filename of the program when it is being compiled.

The _ _**DATE**_ _ macro contains a string of the form *month/day/year* that is the date of the translation of the source file into object code.

The _ _**TIME**_ _ macro contains the time at which the program was compiled. The time is represented in a string having the form *hour:minute:second*.

If _ _**STDC**_ _ is defined as 1, then the compiler conforms to Standard C. C99 also defines these two macros:

_ _STDC_HOSTED_ _

_ _STDC_VERSION_ _

_ _**STDC_HOSTED**_ _ is 1 for environments in which an operating system is present and 0 otherwise. _ _**STDC_VERSION**_ _ will be at least 199901 and will be increased with each new version of C. (Other macros may also be defined by C99 and are described in Part Two.)

Comments

C89 defines only one style of comment, which begins with the character pair /* and ends with */. There must be no spaces between the asterisk and the slash. The compiler ignores any text between the beginning and ending comment symbols. For example, this program prints only **hello** on the screen:

```c
#include <stdio.h>

int main(void)
{
  printf("hello");
  /* printf("there"); */

  return 0;
}
```

This style of comment is commonly called a *multiline comment* because the text of the comment may extend over two or more lines. For example:

```c
/* this is a
multiline
comment */
```

Comments may be placed anywhere in a program, as long as they do not appear in the middle of a keyword or identifier. That is, this comment is valid,

```
x = 10+ /* add the numbers */5;
```

while

```
swi/*this will not work*/tch(c) { ...
```

is incorrect because a keyword cannot contain a comment. However, you should not generally place comments in the middle of expressions because it obscures their meaning.

Multiline comments may not be nested. That is, one comment may not contain another comment. For example, this code fragment causes a compile-time error:

```
/* this is an outer comment
  x = y/a;
  /* this is an inner comment - and causes an error */
*/
```

Single-Line Comments

C99 (and C++) supports two types of comments. The first is the /* */, or multiline comment just described. The second is the single-line comment. Single-line comments begin with // and end at the end of the line. For example,

```
// this is a single-line comment
```

Single-line comments are especially useful when short, line-by-line descriptions are needed. Although they are not technically supported by C89, many C compilers accept them.

A single-line comment can be nested within a multiline comment. For example, the following comment is valid.

```
/* this is a // test of nested comments. */
```

You should include comments whenever they are needed to explain the operation of the code. All but the most obvious functions should have a comment at the top that states what the function does, how it is called, and what it returns.

The
Complete
Reference

Part II

The C99 Standard

Computer languages are not static; they evolve, reacting to changes in methodologies, applications, generally accepted practices, and hardware. C is no exception. In the case of C, two evolutionary paths were set in motion. The first is the continuing development of the C language. The second is C++, for which C provided the starting point. While most of the focus of the past several years has been on C++, the refinement of C has continued unabated. For example, reacting to the internationalization of the computing environment, the original C89 standard was amended in 1995 to include various wide-character and multibyte functions. Once the 1995 amendment was complete, work began on updating the language, in general. The end result is, of course, C99.

In the course of creating the 1999 standard, each element of the C language was thoroughly reexamined, usage patterns were analyzed, and future demands were anticipated. As expected, C's relationship to C++ provided a backdrop for the entire process. The resulting C99 standard is a testimonial to the strengths of the original. Very few of the key elements of C were altered. For the most part, the changes consist of a small number of carefully selected additions to the language and the inclusion of several new library functions. Thus C is still C!

Part One of this book described those features of C that were defined by the C89 standard. Here we will examine those features added by C99 and the few differences between C99 and C89.

The
Complete
Reference

Chapter 11

C99

Perhaps the greatest cause for concern that accompanies the release of a new language standard is the issue of compatibility with its predecessor. Does the new specification render old programs obsolete? Have important constructs been altered? Do I have to change the way that I write code? The answers to these types of questions often determine the degree to which the new standard is accepted and, in the longer term, the viability of the language itself. Fortunately, the creation of C99 was a controlled, even-handed process that reflects the fact that several experienced pilots were at the controls. Put simply: If you liked C the way it was, you will like the version of C defined by C99. What many programmers think of as the world's most elegant programming language, still is!

In this chapter we will examine the changes and additions made to C by the 1999 standard. Many of these changes were mentioned in passing in Part One. Here they are examined in closer detail. Keep in mind, however, that as of this writing, there are no widely used compilers that support many of C99's new features. Thus, you may need to wait a while before you can "test drive" such exciting new constructs as variable-length arrays, restricted pointers, and the **long long** data type.

C89 vs. C99: An Overview

There are three general categories of changes between C89 and C99:

- Features added to C89
- Features removed from C89
- Features that have been changed or enhanced

Many of the differences between C89 and C99 are quite small and clarify nuances of the language. This book will concentrate on the larger changes that affect the way programs are written.

Features Added

Perhaps the most important features added by C99 are the new keywords:

```
inline
restrict
_Bool
_Complex
_Imaginary
```

Other major additions include

- Variable-length arrays
- Support for complex arithmetic
- The **long long int** data type

- The // comment
- The ability to intersperse code and data
- Additions to the preprocessor
- Variable declarations inside the **for** statement
- Compound literals
- Flexible array structure members
- Designated initializers
- Changes to the **printf( )** and **scanf( )** family of functions
- The _ _ **func** _ _ predefined identifier
- New libraries and headers

Most of the features added by C99 are innovations created by the standardization committee, of which many were based on language extensions offered by a variety of C implementations. In a few cases, however, features were borrowed from C++. The **inline** keyword and // style comments are examples. It is important to understand that C99 does not add C++-style classes, inheritance, or member functions. The consensus of the committee was to keep C as C.

Features Removed

The single most important feature removed by C99 is the "implicit **int**" rule. In C89, in many cases when no explicit type specifier is present, the type **int** is assumed. This is not allowed by C99. Also removed is implicit function declaration. In C89, if a function was not declared before it is used, an implicit declaration is assumed. This is not supported by C99. Both of these changes may require existing code to be rewritten if compatibility with C99 is desired.

Features Changed

C99 incorporates several changes to existing features. For the most part, these changes expand features or clarify their meaning. In a few cases, the changes restrict or narrow the applicability of a feature. Many such changes are small, but a few are quite important, including:

- Increased translation limits
- Extended integer types
- Expanded integer type promotion rules
- Tightening of the **return** statement

As it affects existing programs, the change to **return** has the most significant effect because it might require that code be rewritten slightly.

Throughout the remainder of this chapter we will examine the major differences between C89 and C99.

restrict-Qualified Pointers

One of the most important innovations in C99 is the **restrict** type qualifier. This qualifier applies only to pointers. A pointer qualified by **restrict** is initially the only means by which the object it points to can be accessed. Access to the object by another pointer can occur only if the second pointer is based on the first. Thus, access to the object is restricted to expressions based on the **restrict**-qualified pointer. Pointers qualified by **restrict** are primarily used as function parameters, or to point to memory allocated via **malloc( )**. The **restrict** qualifier does not change the semantics of a program.

By qualifying a pointer with **restrict**, the compiler is better able to optimize certain types of routines by making the assumption that the **restrict**-qualified pointer is the sole means of access to the object. For example, if a function specifies two **restrict**-qualified pointer parameters, the compiler can assume that the pointers point to different (that is, non-overlapping) objects. For example, consider what has become the classic example of **restrict**: the **memcpy( )** function. In C89, it is prototyped as shown here:

    void *memcpy(void *str1, const void *str2, size_t size);

The description for **memcpy( )** states that if the objects pointed to by str1 and str2 overlap, the behavior is undefined. Thus, **memcpy( )** is guaranteed to work for only non-overlapping objects.

In C99, **restrict** can be used to explicitly state in **memcpy( )**'s prototype what C89 must explain with words. Here is the C99 prototype for **memcpy( )**:

    void *memcpy(void * restrict str1, const void * restrict str2, size_t size);

By qualifying str1 and str2 with **restrict**, the prototype explicitly asserts that they point to non-overlapping objects.

Because of the potential benefits that result from using **restrict**, C99 has added it to the prototypes for many of the library functions originally defined by C89.

inline

C99 adds the keyword **inline**, which applies to functions. By preceding a function declaration with **inline**, you are telling the compiler to optimize calls to the function. Typically, this means that the function's code will be expanded in line, rather than called. However, **inline** is only a request to the compiler, and can be ignored. Specifically, C99 states that using **inline** "suggests that calls to the function be as fast as possible." The **inline** specifier is also supported by C++, and the C99 syntax for **inline** is compatible with C++.

To create an in-line function, precede its definition with the **inline** keyword. For example, in this program, calls to the function **max( )** are optimized:

```c
#include <stdio.h>

inline int max(int a, int b)
{
  return a > b ? a : b;
}

int main(void)
{
  int x=5, y=10;

  printf("Max of %d and %d is: %d\n", x, y, max(x, y));

  return 0;
}
```

For a typical implementation of **inline**, the preceding program is equivalent to this one:

```c
#include <stdio.h>

int main(void)
{
  int x=5, y=10;

  printf("Max of %d and %d is: %d\n", x, y, (x>y ? x : y));

  return 0;
}
```

The reason that **inline** functions are important is that they help you create more efficient code while maintaining a structured, function-based approach. As you probably know, each time a function is called, a significant amount of overhead is generated by the calling and return mechanism. Typically, arguments are pushed onto the stack and various registers are saved when a function is called, and then restored when the function returns. The trouble is that these instructions take time. However, when a function is expanded in line, none of those operations occur. Although expanding function calls in line can produce faster run times, it can also result in larger code size because of duplicated code. For this reason, it is best to **inline** only very small functions. Further, it is also a good idea to **inline** only those functions that will have significant impact on the performance of your program.

Remember: Although **inline** typically causes a function's code to be expanded in line, the compiler can ignore this request or use some other means to optimize calls to the function.

New Built-in Data Types

C99 adds several new built-in data types. Each is examined here.

_Bool

C99 adds the **_Bool** data type, which is capable of storing the values 1 and 0 (true and false). **_Bool** is an integer type. As many readers know, C++ defines the keyword **bool**, which is different from **_Bool**. Thus, C99 and C++ are incompatible on this point. Also, C++ defines the built-in Boolean constants **true** and **false**, but C99 does not. However, C99 adds the header **<stdbool.h>**, which defines the macros **bool**, **true**, and **false**. Thus, code that is compatible with C/C++ can be easily created.

The reason that **_Bool** rather than **bool** is specified as a keyword is that many existing C programs have already defined their own custom versions of **bool**. By defining the Boolean type as **_Bool**, C99 avoids breaking this preexisting code. However, for new programs, it is best to include **<stdbool.h>** and then use the **bool** macro.

_Complex and _Imaginary

C99 adds support for complex arithmetic, which includes the keywords **_Complex** and **_Imaginary**, additional headers, and several new library functions. However, no implementation is required to implement imaginary types, and freestanding implementations (those without operating systems) do not have to support complex types. Complex arithmetic was added to C99 to provide better support for numerical programming.

The following complex types are defined:

    float _Complex
    float _Imaginary
    double _Complex
    double _Imaginary
    long double _Complex
    long double _Imaginary

The reason that **_Complex** and **_Imaginary**, rather than **complex** and **imaginary**, are specified as keywords is that many existing C programs have already defined their own custom complex data types using the names **complex** and **imaginary**. By defining the keywords **_Complex** and **_Imaginary**, C99 avoids breaking this preexisting code.

The header **<complex.h>** defines (among other things) the macros **complex** and **imaginary**, which expand to **_Complex** and **_Imaginary**. Thus, for new programs, it is best to include **<complex.h>** and then use the **complex** and **imaginary** macros.

The long long Integer Types

C99 adds the **long long int** and **unsigned long long int** data types. A **long long int** has a range of at least $-(2^{63}-1)$ to $2^{63}-1$. An **unsigned long long int** has a minimal range of 0 to $2^{64}-1$. The **long long** types allow 64-bit integers to be supported as a built-in type.

Array Enhancements

C99 has added two important features to arrays: variable length and the ability to include type qualifiers in their declarations.

Variable-Length Arrays

In C89 array dimensions must be declared using integer constant expressions, and the size of an array is fixed at compile time. C99 changes this for certain circumstances. In C99, you can declare an array whose dimensions are specified by any valid integer expression, including those whose value is known only at run time. This is called a *variable-length array* (VLA). However, only local arrays (that is, those with block scope or prototype scope) can be of variable length. Here is an example of a variable-length array:

```
void f(int dim1, int dim2)
{
  int matrix[dim1][dim2]; /* a variable-length, 2-D array */

  /* ... */
}
```

Here, the size of **matrix** is determined by the values passed to **f( )** in **dim1** and **dim2**. Thus, each call to **f( )** can result in **matrix** being created with different dimensions.

It is important to understand that variable-length arrays do not change their dimensions during their lifetime. (That is, they are not dynamic arrays.) Rather, a variable-length array can be created with a different size each time its declaration is encountered.

You can specify a variable-length array of an unspecified size by using * as the size.

The inclusion of variable-length arrays causes a small change in the **sizeof** operator. In general, **sizeof** is a compile-time operator. That is, it is normally translated into an integer constant whose value is equal to the size of the type or object when a program is compiled. However, when it is applied to a variable-length array, **sizeof** is evaluated at run time. This change is necessary because the size of a variable-length array cannot be known until run time.

One of the major reasons for the addition of variable-length arrays to C99 is to support numeric processing. Of course, it is a feature that has widespread applicability. But remember, variable-length arrays are not supported by C89 (or by C++).

Use of Type Qualifiers in an Array Declaration

In C99 you can use the keyword **static** inside the brackets of an array declaration when that declaration is for a function parameter. It tells the compiler that the array pointed to by the parameter will always contain at least the specified number of elements. Here is an example:

```
int f(char str[static 80])
{
  // here, str is always a pointer to an 80-element array
  // ...
}
```

In this example, **str** is guaranteed to point to the start of an array of **char**s that contains at least 80 elements.

You can also use the keywords **restrict**, **volatile**, and **const** inside the brackets, but only for function parameters. Using **restrict** specifies that the pointer is the sole initial means of access to the object. Using **const** states that the same array is always pointed to (that is, the pointer always points to the same object). The use of **volatile** is allowed, but meaningless.

Single-Line Comments

C99 adds the single-line comment to C. This type of comment begins with **//** and runs to the end of the line. For example:

```
// This is a comment
int i; // this is another comment
```

Single-line comments are also supported by C++. They are convenient when only brief, single-line remarks are needed. Many programmers use C's traditional multiline comments for longer descriptions, reserving single-line comments for "play-by-play" explanations.

Interspersed Code and Declarations

In C89, within a block, all declarations must precede the first code statement. This rule does not apply for C99. For example:

```
#include <stdio.h>

int main(void)
{
```

```
    int i;

    i = 10;

    int j; // wrong for C89; OK for C99 and C++

    j = i;

    printf("%d %d", i, j);

    return 0;
}
```

Here, the statement

```
    i = 10;
```

comes between the declaration of **i** and the declaration of **j**. This is not allowed by C89. It *is* allowed by C99 (and by C++). The ability to intersperse declarations and code is widely used in C++. Adding this feature to C makes it easier to write code that will be used in both environments.

Preprocessor Changes

C99 makes a number of small changes to the preprocessor.

Variable Argument Lists

Perhaps the most important change to the preprocessor is the ability to create macros that take a variable number of arguments. This is indicated by an ellipsis (...) in the definition of the macro. The built-in preprocessing identifier _ _**VA_ARGS**_ _ determines where the arguments will be substituted. For example, given this definition

```
    #define MyMax(...) max(__VA_ARGS__)
```

this statement

```
    MyMax(a, b);
```

is transformed into

```
    max(a, b);
```

There can be other arguments prior to the variable ones. For example, given

```
#define compare(compfunc, ...) compfunc(__VA_ARGS__)
```

this statement

```
compare(strcmp, "one", "two");
```

is transformed into

```
strcmp("one", "two");
```

As the example shows, _ _**VA_ARGS**_ _ is replaced by all of the remaining arguments.

The _Pragma Operator

C99 includes another way to specify a pragma in a program: the **_Pragma** operator. It has this general form:

_Pragma (*"directive"*)

Here, *directive* is the pragma being invoked. The addition of the **_Pragma** operator allows pragmas to participate in macro replacement.

Built-in Pragmas

C99 defines the following built-in pragmas:

Pragma	Meaning
STDC FP_CONTRACT ON/OFF/DEFAULT	When on, floating-point expressions are treated as indivisible units that are handled by hardware-based methods. The default state is implementation defined.
STDC FENV_ACCESS ON/OFF/DEFAULT	Tells the compiler that the floating-point environment might be accessed. The default state is implementation defined.
STDC CX_LIMITED_RANGE ON/OFF/DEFAULT	When on, tells the compiler that certain formulas involving complex values are safe. The default state is off.

You should refer to your compiler's documentation for details concerning these pragmas.

Additional Built-in Macros

C99 adds the following macros to those already supported by C89:

_ _STDC_HOSTED_ _	1 if an operating system is present.
_ _STDC_VERSION_ _	199901L or greater. Represents version of C.
_ _STDC_IEC_559_ _	1 if IEC 60559 floating-point arithmetic is supported.
_ _STDC_IEC_599_COMPLEX_ _	1 if IEC 60559 complex arithmetic is supported.
_ _STDC_ISO_10646_ _	A value of the form *yyyymmL* that states the year and month of the ISO/IEC 10646 specification supported by the compiler.

Declaring Variables Within a for Loop

C99 enhances the **for** loop by allowing one or more variables to be declared within the initialization portion of the loop. A variable declared in this way has its scope limited to the block of code controlled by that statement. That is, a variable declared within a **for** loop will be local to that loop. This feature has been included in C because often the variable that controls a **for** loop is needed only by that loop. By localizing this variable to the loop, unwanted side effects can be avoided.

Here is an example that declares a variable within the initialization portion of a **for** loop:

```
#include <stdio.h>

int main(void)
{
  // declare i within for
  for(int i=0; i < 10; i++)
    printf("%d ", i);

  return 0;
}
```

Here, **i** is declared within the **for** loop, rather than prior to it.

As mentioned, a variable declared within a **for** is local to that loop. Consider the following program. Notice that the variable **i** is declared twice: at the start of **main( )** and inside the **for** loop.

```
#include <stdio.h>

int main(void)
{
  int i = -99;

  // declare i within for
  for(int i=0; i < 10; i++)
    printf("%d ", i);

  printf("\n");

  printf("Value of i is: %d", i); // displays -99

  return 0;
}
```

This program displays the following:

```
0 1 2 3 4 5 6 7 8 9
Value of i is: -99
```

As the output shows, once the **for** loop ends, the scope of the **i** declared within that loop ends. Thus, the final **printf( )** statement displays **–99**, the value of the **i** declared at the start of **main( )**.

The ability to declare a loop-control variable inside the **for** has been available in C++ for quite some time, and is widely used. It is expected that most C programmers will do the same.

Compound Literals

C99 allows you to define *compound literals*, which are array, structure, or union expressions designating objects of the given type. A compound literal is created by specifying a parenthesized type name, which is then followed by an initialization list, which must be enclosed between curly braces. When the type name is an array, its size must not be specified. The object created is unnamed.

Here is an example of a compound literal:

```
double *fp = (double[]) {1.0, 2.0, 3.0};
```

This creates a pointer to **double**, called **fp**, which points to the first of a three-element array of **double** values.

A compound literal created at file scope exists throughout the lifetime of the program. A compound literal created within a block is a local object that is destroyed when the block is left.

Flexible Array Structure Members

C99 allows you to specify an unsized array as the last member of a structure. (The structure must have at least one other member prior to the flexible array member.) This is referred to as a *flexible array member*. It allows a structure to contain an array of variable size. The size of such a structure returned by **sizeof** does not include memory for the flexible array.

Typically, memory to hold a structure containing a flexible array member is allocated dynamically, using **malloc( )**. Extra memory must be allocated beyond the size of the structure to accommodate the desired size of the flexible array. For example, given

```
struct mystruct {
  int a;
  int b;
  float fa[]; // flexible array
};
```

the following statement allocates room for a 10-element array:

```
struct mystruct *p;
p = (struct mystruct *) malloc(sizeof(struct mystruct) + 10 *
    sizeof(float));
```

Since **sizeof(struct mystruct)** yields a value that does not include any memory for **fa**, room for the 10-element array of **float**s is added by the expression

```
10 * sizeof(float)
```

when **malloc( )** is called.

Designated Initializers

A new feature of C99 that will be especially helpful to those programmers working with sparse arrays is *designated initializers*. Designators take two forms: one for arrays and one for structures and unions. For arrays, this form is used,

[*index*] = *val*

where *index* specifies the element being initialized to the value *val*. For example:

```
int a[10] = { [0] = 100, [3] = 200 };
```

Here, only elements 0 and 3 are initialized.

For structure or union members, this form is used:

. *member-name*

Using a designator with a structure allows an easy means of initializing only selected members of a structure. For example:

```
struct mystruct {
   int a;
   int b;
   int c;
} ob = { .c = 30, .a = 10 };
```

Here, **b** is uninitialized.

Using designators also allows you to initialize a structure without knowing the order of its members. This is useful for predefined structures, such as **div_t**, or for structures defined by some third party.

Additions to the printf( ) and scanf( ) Family of Functions

C99 adds to the **printf( )** and **scanf( )** family of functions the ability to handle the **long long int** and **unsigned long long int** data types. The format modifier for **long long** is ll. For example, the following fragment shows how to output a **long long int** and an **unsigned long long int**:

```
long long int val;
unsigned long long int u_val;
printf("%lld %llu", val, val2);
```

The ll can be applied to the **d, i, o, u,** and **x** format specifiers for both **printf( )** and **scanf( )**.

C99 adds the **hh** modifier, which is used to specify a **char** argument when using the **d, i, o, u,** or **x** format specifiers.

Both the ll and **hh** specifiers can also be applied to the **n** specifier.

The format specifiers **a** and **A**, which were added to **printf( )**, cause a floating-point value to be output in a hexadecimal format. The format of the value is

[–]0x*h.hhhh*p+d

When **A** is used, the x and the p are uppercase. The format specifiers **a** and **A** were also added to **scanf( )**, and read a floating-point value.

In a call to **printf( )**, C99 allows the l modifier to be added to the %f specifier (as in, %lf), but it has no effect. In C89, %lf is undefined for **printf( )**.

New Libraries in C99

C99 adds several new libraries and headers. They are shown here:

Header	Purpose
<complex.h>	Supports complex arithmetic.
<fenv.h>	Gives access to the floating-point status flags and other aspects of the floating-point environment.
<inttypes.h>	Defines a standard, portable set of integer type names. Also supports functions that handle greatest-width integers.
<iso646.h>	Added in 1995 by Amendment 1. Defines macros that correspond to various operators, such as && and ^.
<stdbool.h>	Supports Boolean data types. Defines the macros **bool**, **true**, and **false**, which helps with C++ compatibility.
<stdint.h>	Defines a standard, portable set of integer type names. This header is included by **<inttypes.h>**.
<tgmath.h>	Defines type-generic floating-point macros.
<wchar.h>	Added in 1995 by Amendment 1. Supports multibyte and wide-character functions.
<wctype.h>	Added in 1995 by Amendment 1. Supports multibyte and wide-character classification functions.

The contents of these headers and the functions they support are covered in Part Three.

The _ _func_ _ Predefined Identifier

C99 defines _ _**func**_ _, which specifies the name (as a string literal) of the function in which _ _**func**_ _ occurs. For example:

```
void StrUpper(char *str)
{
```

```
static int i = 0;

i++;
printf("%s has been called %d time(s).\n", __func__, i);

while(*str) {
  *str = toupper(*str);
  str++;
}
}
```

When called the first time, **StrUpper( )** will display this output:

```
StrUpper has been called 1 time(s).
```

Increased Translation Limits

The term "translation limits" refers to the minimum number of various elements that a C compiler must be able to handle. These include such things as the length of identifiers, levels of nesting, number of **case** statements, and number of members allowed in a structure or union. C99 has increased several of these limits beyond the already generous ones specified by C89. Here are some examples:

Limit	C89	C99
Nesting levels of blocks	15	127
Nesting levels of conditional inclusion	8	63
Significant characters in an internal identifier	31	63
Significant characters in an external identifier	6	31
Members of a structure or union	127	1023
Arguments in a function call	31	127

Implicit int No Longer Supported

Several years ago, C++ dropped the implicit **int** rule, and with the advent of C99, C follows suit. In C89, the implicit **int** rule states that in the absence of an explicit type specifier, the type **int** is assumed. The most common use of the implicit **int** rule was in the return type of functions. In the past, C programmers often omitted the **int** when declaring functions that returned an **int** value. For example, in the early days of C, **main( )** was often written like this:

```
main()
{
  /* ... */
}
```

In this approach, the return type was simply allowed to default to **int**. In C99 (and in C++) this default no longer occurs, and the **int** must be explicitly specified, as it is for all of the programs in this book.

Here is another example. In the past a function such as

```
int isEven(int val)
{
  return !(val%2);
}
```

would often have been written like this:

```
/* use integer default */
isEven(int val)
{
  return !(val%2);
}
```

In the first instance, the return type of **int** is explicitly specified. In the second, it is assumed by default.

The implicit **int** rule does not apply only to function return values (although that was its most common use). For example, for C89 and earlier, the **isEven( )** function could also be written like this:

```
isEven(const val)
{
  return !(val%2);
}
```

Here, the parameter **val** also defaults to **int**—in this case, **const int**. Again, this default to **int** is not supported by C99.

*Technically, a C99-compatible compiler can accept code containing implied **int**s after reporting a warning error. This allows old code to be compiled. However, there is no requirement that a C99-compatible compiler accept such code.*

Implicit Function Declarations Have Been Removed

In C89, if a function is called without a prior explicit declaration, then an implicit declaration of that function is created. This implicit declaration has the following form:

extern int *name*( );

Implicit function declarations are no longer supported by C99.

Technically, a C99-compatible compiler can accept code containing implied function declarations after reporting a warning error. This allows old code to be compiled. However, there is no requirement that a C99-compatible compiler accept such code.

Restrictions on return

In C89, a function that has a non-**void** return type (that is, a function that supposedly returns a value) could use a **return** statement that did not include a value. Although this creates undefined behavior, it was not technically illegal. In C99, a non-**void** function *must* use a **return** statement that returns a value. That is, in C99, if a function is specified as returning a value, any **return** statement within it must have a value associated with it. Thus, the following function is technically valid for C89, but invalid for C99:

```
int f(void)
{
  /* ... */
  return ; // in C99, this statement must return a value
}
```

Extended Integer Types

C99 defines several extended integer types in **<stdint.h>**. Extended types include exact-width, minimum-width, maximum-width, and fastest integer types. Here is a sampling:

Extended Type	Meaning
int16_t	An integer consisting of exactly 16 bits
int_least16_t	An integer consisting of at least 16 bits
int_fast32_t	Fastest integer type that has at least 32 bits
intmax_t	Largest integer type
uintmax_t	Largest unsigned integer type

The extended types make it easier for you to write portable code. They are described in greater detail in Part Three.

Changes to the Integer Promotion Rules

C99 enhances the integer promotion rules. In C89, a value of type **char**, **short int**, or an **int** bit-field can be used in place of an **int** or **unsigned int** in an expression. If the promoted value can be held in an **int**, the promotion is made to **int**; otherwise, the original value is promoted to **unsigned int**.

In C99, each of the integer types is assigned a *rank*. For example, the rank of **long long int** is greater than **int**, which is greater than **char**, and so on. In an expression, any integer type that has a rank less than **int** or **unsigned int** can be used in place of an **int** or **unsigned int**.

THE C99 STANDARD

The Complete Reference

Part III

The C Standard Library

Part Three of this book examines the C standard library. Chapter 12 discusses linking, libraries, and headers. Chapters 13 through 20 describe the functions in the standard library, with each chapter concentrating on a specific function subsystem.

This book describes the standard functions defined by both C89 and C99. C99 includes all functions specified by C89. Thus, if you have a C99-compatible compiler, you will be able to use all of the functions described in Part Three. If you are using a C89-compatible compiler, the C99 functions will not be available. Also, Standard C++ includes the functions defined by C89, but not those specified by C99. Throughout Part Three, the functions added by C99 are so indicated.

When exploring the standard library, remember this: Most compiler implementors take great pride in the completeness of their library. Your compiler's library will probably contain many additional functions beyond those described here. For example, the C standard library does not define any screen-handling or graphics functions because of differences between environments, but your compiler very likely includes such functions. Therefore, it is always a good idea to browse through your compiler's documentation.

Chapter 12

Linking, Libraries, and Headers

When a C compiler is written, there are actually two parts to the job. First, the compiler itself must be created. The compiler translates source code into object code. Second, the standard library must be implemented. Somewhat surprisingly, the compiler is relatively easy to develop. Often, it is the library functions that take the most time and effort. One reason for this is that many functions (such as the I/O system) must interface with the operating system for which the compiler is being written. In addition, the C standard library defines a large and diverse set of functions. Indeed, it is the richness and flexibility of the standard library that sets C apart from many other languages.

While subsequent chapters describe the C library functions, this chapter covers several foundational concepts that relate to their use, including the link process, libraries, and headers.

The Linker

The linker has two functions. The first, as the name implies, is to combine (link) various pieces of object code. The second is to resolve the addresses of call and load instructions found in the object files that it is combining. To understand its operation, let's look more closely at the process of separate compilation.

Separate Compilation

Separate compilation is the feature that allows a program to be broken down into two or more files, compiled separately, and then linked to form the finished executable program. The output of the compiler is an object file, and the output of the linker is an executable file. The linker physically combines the files specified in the link list into one program file and resolves external references. An *external reference* is created any time the code in one file refers to code in another file. This may be through either a function call or a reference to a global variable. For example, when the two files shown here are linked, File 2's reference to **count** (which is declared in File 1) must be resolved. The linker tells the code in File 2 where **count** will be found.

File 1	File 2

```
  int count;                    #include <stdio.h>
  void display(void);           extern int count;

  int main(void)                void display(void)
  {                             {
    count = 10;                     printf("%d", count);
    display();                  }

    return 0;
  }
```

In a similar fashion, the linker tells File 1 where the function **display( )** is located so that it can be called.

When the compiler generates the object code for **display( )**, it substitutes a placeholder for the address of **count** because the compiler has no way of knowing where **count** is. The same sort of thing occurs when **main( )** is compiled. The address of **display( )** is unknown, so a placeholder is used. When these two files are linked together, these placeholders are replaced with the addresses of the items. Whether these addresses are absolute or relocatable depends upon your environment.

Relocatable vs. Absolute Code

For most modern environments, the output of a linker is *relocatable code*. This is object code that can run in any available memory region large enough to hold it. In a relocatable object file, the address of each call or load instruction is not fixed, but is relative. Thus, the addresses in relocatable code are offsets from the beginning of the program. When the program is loaded into memory for execution, the loader converts the relative addresses into physical addresses that correspond to the memory into which the program is loaded.

For some environments, such as dedicated controllers in which the same address space is used for all programs, the output of the linker actually contains the physical addresses. When this is the case, the output of the linker is *absolute code*.

Linking with Overlays

Although no longer commonplace, C compilers for some environments supply an overlay linker in addition to a standard linker. An *overlay linker* works like a regular linker but can also create overlays. An *overlay* is a piece of object code that is stored in a disk file and loaded and executed only when needed. The place in memory into which an overlay is loaded is called the *overlay region*. Overlays allow you to create and run programs that would be larger than available memory, because only the parts of the program that are currently in use are in memory.

To understand how overlays work, imagine that you have a program consisting of seven object files called F1 through F7. Assume also that there is insufficient free memory to run the program if the object files are all linked together in the normal way—you can only link the first five files before running out of memory. To remedy this situation, instruct the linker to create overlays consisting of files F5, F6, and F7. Each time a function in one of these files is invoked, the *overlay manager* (provided by the linker) finds the proper file and places it into the overlay region, allowing execution to proceed. The code in files F1 through F4 remains resident at all times. Figure 12-1 illustrates this situation.

As you might guess, the principal advantage of overlays is that they enable you to write very large programs. The main disadvantage—and the reason that overlays are usually a last resort—is that the loading process takes time and has a significant impact on the overall speed of execution. For this reason, you should group related functions

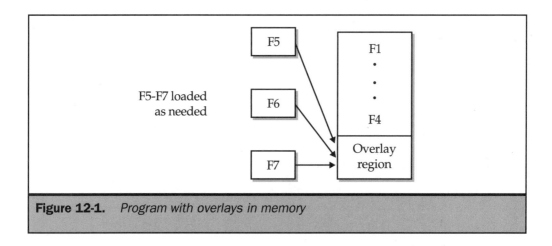

Figure 12-1.   *Program with overlays in memory*

together if you have to use overlays, so that the number of overlay loads is minimized. For example, if the application is a mailing list, it makes sense to place all sorting routines in one overlay, printing routines in another, and so on.

As mentioned, overlays are not often used in today's modern computing environments.

Linking with DLLs

Windows provides another form of linking, called *dynamic linking*. Dynamic linking is the process by which the object code for a function remains in a separate file on disk until a program that uses it is executed. When the program is executed, the dynamically linked functions required by the program are also loaded. Dynamically linked functions reside in a special type of library called a *Dynamic Link Library*, or DLL, for short.

The main advantage to using dynamically linked libraries is that the size of executable programs is dramatically reduced because each program does not have to store redundant copies of the library functions that it uses. Also, when DLL functions are updated, programs that use them will automatically obtain their benefits.

Although the C standard library is not contained in a dynamic link library, many other types of functions are. For example, when you program for Windows, the entire set of API (Application Program Interface) functions are stored in DLLs. Fortunately, relative to your C program, it does not usually matter whether a library function is stored in a DLL or in a regular library file.

The C Standard Library

The ANSI/ISO standard for C defines both the content and form of the C standard library. That is, the C standard specifies a set of functions that all standard compilers must support. However, a compiler is free to supply additional functions not specified by the standard. (And, indeed, most compilers do.) For example, it is common for a compiler to have graphics functions, mouse-handler routines, and the like, even though none of these is defined by Standard C. As long as you will not be porting your programs to a new environment, you can use these nonstandard functions without any negative consequences. However, if your code must be portable, the use of these functions must be restricted. From a practical point of view, virtually all nontrivial C programs will make use of nonstandard functions, so you should not necessarily shy away from their use just because they are not part of the standard function library.

Library Files vs. Object Files

Although libraries are similar to object files, they have one important difference. When you link object files, the entire contents of each object file becomes part of the finished executable file. This happens whether the code is actually used or not. This is not the case with library files.

A library is a collection of functions. Unlike an object file, a library file stores each function individually. When your program uses a function contained in a library, the linker looks up that function and adds its code to your program. In this way, only functions that you actually use in your program—not the contents of the entire library—are added to the executable file. Because functions are selectively added to your program when a library is used, the C standard functions are contained in libraries rather than object files.

Headers

Each function defined in the C standard library has a header associated with it. The headers that relate to the functions that you use in your programs are included using **#include**. The headers perform two important jobs. First, many functions in the standard library work with their own specific data types, to which your program must have access. These data types are defined in the header related to each function. One of the most common examples is the file system header **<stdio.h>**, which provides the type **FILE** that is necessary for disk file operations.

The second reason to include headers is to obtain the prototypes for the standard library functions. Function prototypes allow stronger type checking to be performed by the compiler. Although prototypes are technically optional, they are for all practical purposes necessary. Also, they are required by C++. All programs in this book include full prototyping.

Table 12-1 shows the standard headers defined by C89. Table 12-2 shows the headers added by C99.

Standard C reserves identifier names beginning with an underscore and followed by either a second underscore or a capital letter for use in headers.

As explained in Part One, headers are usually files, but they are not necessarily files. It is permissible for a compiler to predefine the contents of a header internally. However, for all practical purposes, the Standard C headers are contained in files that correspond to their names.

The remaining chapters in Part Three, which describe each function in the standard library, will indicate which of these headers are necessary for each function.

Header	Purpose
<assert.h>	Defines the **assert( )** macro
<ctype.h>	Character handling
<errno.h>	Error reporting
<float.h>	Defines implementation-dependent floating-point limits
<limits.h>	Defines various implementation-dependent limits
<locale.h>	Supports localization
<math.h>	Various definitions used by the math library
<setjmp.h>	Supports nonlocal jumps
<signal.h>	Supports signal handling
<stdarg.h>	Supports variable argument lists
<stddef.h>	Defines some commonly used constants
<stdio.h>	Supports the I/O system
<stdlib.h>	Miscellaneous declarations
<string.h>	Supports string functions
<time.h>	Supports system time functions

Table 12-1. *Headers Defined by C89*

Header	Purpose
<complex.h>	Supports complex arithmetic.
<fenv.h>	Gives access to the floating-point status flags and other aspects of the floating-point environment.
<inttypes.h>	Defines a standard, portable set of integer type names. Also supports functions that handle greatest-width integers.
<iso646.h>	Added in 1995 by Amendment 1. Defines macros that correspond to various operators, such as **&&** and **^**.
<stdbool.h>	Supports Boolean data types. Defines the macro **bool**, which helps with C++ compatibility.
<stdint.h>	Defines a standard, portable set of integer type names. This file is included by **<inttypes.h>**.
<tgmath.h>	Defines type-generic floating-point macros.
<wchar.h>	Added in 1995 by Amendment 1. Supports multibyte and wide-character functions.
<wctype.h>	Added in 1995 by Amendment 1. Supports multibyte and wide-character classification functions.

Table 12-2.   *Headers Added by C99*

Macros in Headers

Many of the C standard functions can be implemented either as actual functions or as function-like macros defined in a header. For example, **abs( )**, which returns the absolute value of its integer argument, could be defined as a macro, as shown here:

```
#define abs(i) (i)<0 ? -(i) : (i)
```

Whether a standard function is defined as a macro or as a regular C function is usually of no consequence. However, in rare situations where a macro is unacceptable—for example, where code size is to be minimized or where an argument must not be evaluated more than once—you will have to create a real function and substitute it for the macro. Sometimes the C library itself also has a real function that you can use to replace a macro.

To force the compiler to use the real function, you need to prevent the compiler from substituting the macro when the function name is encountered. Although there are several ways to do this, by far the best is simply to undefine the macro name using **#undef**. For example, to force the compiler to substitute the real **abs( )** function for the previously defined macro, you would insert this line of code near the beginning of your program:

```
#undef abs
```

Then, since **abs** is no longer defined as a macro, the function version is used.

Redefinition of Library Functions

Although linkers may vary slightly between implementations, they all operate in essentially the same way. For example, if your program consists of three files called F1, F2, and F3, the linker command line looks something like this,

LINK F1 F2 F3 LIBC

where LIBC is the name of the standard library.

 Some linkers automatically use the standard library and do not require that it be specified explicitly. Also, integrated programming environments often include the appropriate library files automatically.

As the link process begins, usually the linker first attempts to resolve all external references by using only the files F1, F2, and F3. Once this is done, the library is searched if unresolved external references still exist.

Because most linkers proceed in the order just described, you can redefine a function that is contained in the standard library. For instance, you could create your own version of **fwrite( )** that handled file output in some special way. In this case, when you link a program that includes your redefined version of **fwrite( )**, that implementation is found first and used to resolve all references to it. Therefore, by the time the library is scanned, there are no unresolved references to the **fwrite( )** function, and it is not loaded from the library.

You must be very careful when you redefine library functions because you could be creating unexpected side effects. Another part of your program might use the library function that you are redefining. In this case, the other part will be expecting the library function but will get your redefined function instead. For example, if you redefine **fwrite( )** for use in one part of a program and another part of your program uses **fwrite( )**, expecting it to be the standard library function, then (to say the least) unexpected behavior may result. It is a better idea simply to use a different name for your function than to redefine a library function.

Chapter 13

I/O Functions

This chapter describes the Standard C I/O functions. It includes the functions defined by C89 and those added by C99. The header associated with the I/O functions is **<stdio.h>**. This header defines several macros and types used by the file system. The most important type is **FILE**, which is used to declare a file pointer. Two other frequently used types are **size_t** and **fpos_t**. The **size_t** type, which is some form of unsigned integer, is the type of the result returned by **sizeof**. The **fpos_t** type defines an object that can uniquely specify each location within a file. The most commonly used macro defined by the header is **EOF**, which is the value that indicates end-of-file. Other data types and macros defined in **<stdio.h>** are described in conjunction with the functions to which they relate.

Many of the I/O functions set the built-in global integer variable **errno** when an error occurs. Your program can check this variable to obtain more information about the error. The values that **errno** may have are implementation dependent.

C99 adds the **restrict** qualifier to certain parameters of several functions originally defined by C89. When this is the case, the function will be shown using its C89 prototype (which is also the prototype used by C++), but the **restrict**-qualified parameters will be pointed out in the function's description.

For an overview of the I/O system, see Chapters 8 and 9 in Part One.

Note

*This chapter describes the character-based I/O functions. These are the functions that were originally defined for Standard C and are, by far, the most widely used. In 1995 several wide-character (**wchar_t**) functions were added, and they are briefly described in Chapter 19.*

clearerr

```
#include <stdio.h>
void clearerr(FILE *stream);
```

The **clearerr( )** function resets (that is, sets to zero) the error flag associated with the stream pointed to by *stream*. The end-of-file indicator is also reset.

The error flags for each stream are initially set to zero by a successful call to **fopen( )**. File errors can occur for a wide variety of reasons, many of which are system dependent. The exact nature of the error can be determined by calling **perror( )**, which displays a message describing the error (see **perror**).

Example

This program copies one file to another. If an error is encountered, a message is printed and the error is cleared.

```c
/* Copy one file to another. */
#include <stdio.h>
#include <stdlib.h>

int main(int argc, char *argv[])
{
  FILE *in, *out;
  char ch;

  if(argc!=3) {
    printf("You forgot to enter a filename.\n");
    exit(1);
  }

  if((in=fopen(argv[1], "rb")) == NULL) {
    printf("Cannot open input file.\n");
    exit(1);
  }
  if((out=fopen(argv[2], "wb")) == NULL) {
    printf("Cannot open output file.\n");
    exit(1);
  }

  while(!feof(in)) {
    ch = getc(in);
    if(ferror(in)) {
      printf("Read Error");
      clearerr(in);
      break;
    } else {
      if(!feof(in)) putc(ch, out);
      if(ferror(out)) {
        printf("Write Error");
        clearerr(out);
        break;
      }
    }
  }
  fclose(in);
  fclose(out);

  return 0;
}
```

Related Functions

feof( ), **ferror( )**, and **perror( )**

fclose

```
#include <stdio.h>
int fclose(FILE *stream);
```

The **fclose( )** function closes the file associated with *stream* and flushes its buffer. After a call to **fclose( )**, *stream* is no longer connected with the file, and any automatically allocated buffers are deallocated.

If **fclose( )** is successful, zero is returned; otherwise **EOF** is returned. Trying to close a file that has already been closed is an error. Removing the storage media before closing a file will also generate an error, as will lack of sufficient free disk space.

Example

The following code opens and closes a file:

```
#include <stdio.h>
#include <stdlib.h>

int main(void)
{
  FILE *fp;

  if((fp=fopen("test", "rb"))==NULL) {
    printf("Cannot open file.\n");
    exit(1);
  }

  if(fclose(fp)) printf("File close error.\n");

  return 0;
}
```

Related Functions

fopen( ), **freopen( )**, and **fflush( )**

feof

```
#include <stdio.h>
int feof(FILE *stream);
```

The **feof( )** function determines whether the end of the file associated with *stream* has been reached. A nonzero value is returned if the file position indicator is at the end of the file; zero is returned otherwise.

Once the end of the file has been reached, subsequent read operations will return **EOF** until either **rewind( )** is called or the file position indicator is moved using **fseek( )**.

The **feof( )** function is particularly useful when working with binary files because the end-of-file marker is also a valid binary integer. Explicit calls must be made to **feof( )** rather than simply testing the return value of **getc( )**, for example, to determine when the end of a binary file has been reached.

Example

This code fragment shows one way to read to the end of a file:

```
/*
    Assume that fp has been opened for read operations.
*/
while(!feof(fp)) getc(fp);
```

Related Functions

clearerr( ), **ferror( )**, **perror( )**, **putc( )**, and **getc( )**

ferror

```
#include <stdio.h>
int ferror(FILE *stream);
```

The **ferror( )** function checks for a file error on the given *stream*. A return value of zero indicates that no error has occurred, while a nonzero value means an error.

To determine the exact nature of the error, use the **perror( )** function.

Example

The following code fragment aborts program execution if a file error occurs:

```
/*
  Assume that fp points to a stream opened for write
  operations.
*/

while(!done) {
  putc(info, fp);
  if(ferror(fp)) {
    printf("File Error\n");
    exit(1);
  }
}
```

Related Functions

clearerr( ), **feof( )**, and **perror( )**

fflush

```
#include <stdio.h>
int fflush(FILE *stream);
```

If *stream* is associated with a file opened for writing, a call to **fflush( )** causes the contents of the output buffer to be physically written to the file. The file remains open.

A return value of zero indicates success; **EOF** indicates that a write error has occurred.

All buffers are automatically flushed upon normal termination of the program or when they are full. Also, closing a file flushes its buffer.

Example

The following code fragment flushes the buffer after each write operation:

```
/*
  Assume that fp is associated with an output file.
*/
```

```
for(i=0; i<MAX; i++) {
  fwrite(buf, sizeof(some_type), 1, fp);
  fflush(fp);
}
```

Related Functions

fclose( ), fopen( ), fread( ), fwrite( ), getc( ), and putc( )

fgetc

```
#include <stdio.h>
int fgetc(FILE *stream);
```

The **fgetc( )** function returns the next character from the specified input stream and increments the file position indicator. The character is read as an **unsigned char** that is converted to an integer.

If the end of the file is reached, **fgetc( )** returns **EOF**. However, since **EOF** is a valid integer value, when working with binary files you must use **feof( )** to check for the end of the file. If **fgetc( )** encounters an error, **EOF** is also returned. If working with binary files, you must use **ferror( )** to check for file errors.

Example

The following program reads and displays the contents of a text file:

```
#include <stdio.h>
#include <stdlib.h>

int main(int argc, char *argv[])
{
  FILE *fp;
  char ch;

  if((fp=fopen(argv[1],"r"))==NULL) {
    printf("Cannot open file.\n");
    exit(1);
  }

  while((ch=fgetc(fp)) != EOF) {
```

```
      printf("%c", ch);
    }
    fclose(fp);

    return 0;
}
```

Related Functions

fputc( ), **getc( )**, **putc( )**, and **fopen( )**

---

fgetpos

```
#include <stdio.h>
int fgetpos(FILE *stream, fpos_t *position);
```

For the specified stream, the **fgetpos( )** function stores the current value of the file position indicator in the object pointed to by *position*. The object pointed to by *position* must be of type **fpos_t**. The value stored there is useful only in a subsequent call to **fsetpos( )**.

In C99, both *stream* and *position* are qualified by **restrict**.

If an error occurs, **fgetpos( )** returns nonzero; otherwise it returns zero.

Example

The following fragment stores the current file location in **file_loc**:

```
FILE *fp;
fpos_t file_loc;
    .
    .
    .
fgetpos(fp, &file_loc);
```

Related Functions

fsetpos( ), **fseek( )**, and **ftell( )**

fgets

```
#include <stdio.h>
char *fgets(char *str, int num, FILE *stream);
```

The **fgets( )** function reads up to *num–1* characters from *stream* and stores them in the character array pointed to by *str*. Characters are read until either a newline or an **EOF** is received or until the specified limit is reached. After the characters have been read, a null is stored in the array immediately after the last character read. A newline character will be retained and will be part of the array pointed to by *str*.

In C99, *str* and *stream* are qualified by **restrict**.

If successful, **fgets( )** returns *str*; a null pointer is returned upon failure. If a read error occurs, the contents of the array pointed to by *str* are indeterminate. Because a null pointer will be returned when either an error has occurred or when the end of the file is reached, you should use **feof( )** or **ferror( )** to determine what has actually happened.

Example

This program uses **fgets( )** to display the contents of the text file whose name is specified as the first command line argument:

```
#include <stdio.h>
#include <stdlib.h>

int main(int argc, char *argv[])
{
  FILE *fp;
  char str[128];

  if((fp=fopen(argv[1], "r"))==NULL) {
    printf("Cannot open file.\n");
    exit(1);
  }

  while(!feof(fp)) {
    if(fgets(str, 126, fp)) printf("%s", str);
  }

  fclose(fp);

  return 0;
}
```

Related Functions

fputs( ), fgetc( ), gets( ), and **puts( )**

fopen

```
#include <stdio.h>
FILE *fopen(const char *fname, const char *mode);
```

The **fopen( )** function opens a file whose name is pointed to by *fname* and returns the stream that is associated with it. The type of operations that will be allowed on the file are defined by the value of *mode*. The legal values for *mode* are shown in Table 13-1. The filename must be a string of characters constituting a valid filename as defined by the operating system and may include a path specification if the environment supports it.

In C99, *fname* and *mode* are qualified by **restrict**.

If **fopen( )** is successful in opening the specified file, a **FILE** pointer is returned. If the file cannot be opened, a null pointer is returned.

Mode	Meaning
"r"	Open text file for reading
"w"	Create a text file for writing
"a"	Append to text file
"rb"	Open binary file for reading
"wb"	Create binary file for writing
"ab"	Append to a binary file
"r+"	Open text file for read/write
"w+"	Create text file for read/write
"a+"	Open text file for read/write
"rb+" or "r+b"	Open binary file for read/write
"wb+" or "w+b"	Create binary file for read/write
"ab+" or "a+b"	Open binary file for read/write

Table 13-1.   *Legal Values for the* mode *Parameter of* ***fopen( )***

As the table shows, a file can be opened in either text or binary mode. In text mode, some character translations may occur. For example, newlines may be converted into carriage return/linefeed sequences. No such translations occur on binary files.

The correct method of opening a file is illustrated by this code fragment:

```
FILE *fp;

if ((fp = fopen("test", "w"))==NULL) {
  printf("Cannot open file.\n");
  exit(1);
}
```

This method detects any error in opening a file, such as a write-protected or a full disk, before attempting to write to it.

If you use **fopen( )** to open a file for output, any preexisting file by that name will be erased and a new file started. If no file by that name exists, one will be created. Opening a file for read operations requires that the file exists. If it does not exist, an error will be returned. If you want to add to the end of the file, you must use mode "a". If the file does not exist, it will be created.

When accessing a file opened for read/write operations, you cannot follow an output operation with an input operation without first calling either **fflush( )**, **fseek( )**, **fsetpos( )**, or **rewind( )**. Also, you cannot follow an input operation with an output operation without first calling one of the previously mentioned functions, except when the end of the file is reached during input. That is, output can directly follow input at the end of the file.

Up to **FOPEN_MAX** files can be open at any one time. **FOPEN_MAX** is defined in **<stdio.h>**.

Example

This fragment opens a file called TEST for binary read/write operations:

```
FILE *fp;

if((fp=fopen("test", "rb+"))==NULL) {
  printf("Cannot open file.\n");
  exit(1);
}
```

Related Functions

fclose( ), **fread( )**, **fwrite( )**, **putc( )**, and **getc( )**

fprintf

```
#include <stdio.h>
int fprintf(FILE *stream, const char *format, ...);
```

The **fprintf( )** function outputs the values of the arguments that make up the argument list as specified in the *format* string to the stream pointed to by *stream*. The return value is the number of characters actually printed. If an error occurs, a negative number is returned.

In C99, *stream* and *format* are qualified by **restrict**.

The operations of the format control string and commands are identical to those in **printf( )**; see **printf** for a complete description.

Example

This program creates a file called TEST and writes **this is a test 10 20.01** into the file using **fprintf( )** to format the data:

```
#include <stdio.h>
#include <stdlib.h>

int main(void)
{
  FILE *fp;

  if((fp=fopen("test", "wb"))==NULL) {
    printf("Cannot open file.\n");
    exit(1);
  }

  fprintf(fp, "this is a test %d %f", 10, 20.01);
  fclose(fp);

  return 0;
}
```

Related Functions

printf( ) and **fscanf( )**

fputc

```
#include <stdio.h>
int fputc(int ch, FILE *stream);
```

The **fputc( )** function writes the character *ch* to the specified stream at the current file position and then advances the file position indicator. Even though *ch* is declared to be an **int** for historical reasons, it is converted by **fputc( )** into an **unsigned char**. Because a character argument is elevated to an integer at the time of the call, you will generally see character values used as arguments. If an integer were used, the high-order byte(s) would simply be discarded.

The value returned by **fputc( )** is the value of the character written. If an error occurs, **EOF** is returned. For files opened for binary operations, an **EOF** may be a valid character, and the function **ferror( )** will need to be used to determine whether an error has actually occurred.

Example

This function writes the contents of a string to the specified stream:

```
void write_string(char *str, FILE *fp)
{
   while(*str) if(!ferror(fp)) fputc(*str++, fp);
}
```

Related Functions

fgetc( ), **fopen( )**, **fprintf( )**, **fread( )**, and **fwrite( )**

fputs

```
#include <stdio.h>
int fputs(const char *str, FILE *stream);
```

The **fputs( )** function writes the contents of the string pointed to by *str* to the specified stream. The null terminator is not written.

In C99, *str* and *stream* are qualified by **restrict**.

The **fputs( )** function returns nonnegative on success and **EOF** on failure.

If the stream is opened in text mode, certain character translations may take place. This means that there may not be a one-to-one mapping of the string onto the file.

However, if the stream is opened in binary mode, no character translations will occur, and a one-to-one mapping between the string and the file will exist.

Example

This code fragment writes the string **this is a test** to the stream pointed to by **fp**:

```
fputs("this is a test", fp);
```

Related Functions

fgets( ), **gets( )**, **puts( )**, **fprintf( )**, and **fscanf( )**

fread

```
#include <stdio.h>
size_t fread(void *buf, size_t size, size_t count, FILE *stream);
```

The **fread( )** function reads *count* number of objects, each object being *size* bytes in length, from the stream pointed to by *stream* and stores them in the array pointed to by *buf*. The file position indicator is advanced by the number of characters read.

In C99, *buf* and *stream* are qualified by **restrict**.

The **fread( )** function returns the number of items actually read. If fewer items are read than are requested in the call, either an error has occurred or the end of the file has been reached. You must use **feof( )** or **ferror( )** to determine what has taken place.

If the stream is opened for text operations, certain character translations, such as carriage return/linefeed sequences being transformed into newlines, may occur.

Example

The following program writes five floating-point numbers from the **bal** array to a disk file called TEST and then reads them back:

```
#include <stdio.h>
#include <stdlib.h>

int main(void)
{
  FILE *fp;
  float bal[5] = { 1.1F, 2.2F, 3.3F, 4.4F, 5.5F };
  int i;

  /* write the values */
```

```
  if((fp=fopen("test", "wb"))==NULL) {
    printf("Cannot open file.\n");
    exit(1);
  }

  if(fwrite(bal, sizeof(float), 5, fp) != 5)
    printf("File read error.");
  fclose(fp);

  /* read the values */
  if((fp=fopen("test", "rb"))==NULL) {
    printf("Cannot open file.\n");
    exit(1);
  }

  if(fread(bal, sizeof(float), 5, fp) != 5) {
    if(feof(fp)) printf("Premature end of file.");
    else printf("File read error.");
  }
  fclose(fp);

  for(i=0; i<5; i++)
    printf("%f ", bal[i]);

  return 0;
}
```

Related Functions

fwrite( ), **fopen( )**, **fscanf( )**, **fgetc( )**, and **getc( )**

freopen

```
#include <stdio.h>
FILE *freopen(const char *fname, const char *mode, FILE *stream);
```

The **freopen( )** function associates an existing stream with a different file. The end-of-file and error flags are cleared in the process. The new file's name is pointed to by *fname*, the access mode is pointed to by *mode*, and the stream to be reassigned is pointed to by *stream*. The *mode* parameter uses the same format as **fopen( )**; a complete discussion is found in the **fopen( )** description.

In C99, *fname*, *mode*, and *stream* are qualified by **restrict**.

When called, **freopen( )** first tries to close a file that may currently be associated with *stream*. However, if the attempt to close the file fails, the **freopen( )** function still continues to open the other file.

The **freopen( )** function returns a pointer to *stream* on success and a null pointer otherwise.

The main use of **freopen( )** is to redirect the system-defined files **stdin**, **stdout**, and **stderr** to some other file.

Example

The program shown here uses **freopen( )** to redirect the stream **stdout** to the file called OUT. Because **printf( )** writes to **stdout**, the first message is displayed on the screen and the second is written to the disk file.

```
#include <stdio.h>
#include <stdlib.h>

int main(void)
{
  FILE *fp;

  printf("This will display on the screen.\n");

  if((fp=freopen("OUT", "w" ,stdout))==NULL) {
    printf("Cannot open file.\n");
    exit(1);
  }

  printf("This will be written to the file OUT.");

  fclose(fp);

  return 0;
}
```

Related Functions

fopen( ) and **fclose( )**

fscanf

```
#include <stdio.h>
int fscanf(FILE *stream, const char *format, ...);
```

The **fscanf( )** function works exactly like the **scanf( )** function except that it reads the information from the stream specified by *stream* instead of **stdin**. See **scanf** for details.

In C99, *stream* and *format* are qualified by **restrict**.

The **fscanf( )** function returns the number of arguments actually assigned values. This number does not include skipped fields. A return value of **EOF** means that a failure occurred before the first assignment was made.

Example

This code fragment reads a string and a **float** from the stream **fp**:

```
char str[80];
float f;

fscanf(fp, "%s%f", str, &f);
```

Related Functions

scanf( ) and fprintf( )

fseek

```
#include <stdio.h>
int fseek(FILE *stream, long int offset, int origin);
```

The **fseek( )** function sets the file position indicator associated with *stream* according to the values of *offset* and *origin*. Its purpose is to support random access I/O operations. The *offset* is the number of bytes from *origin* to seek to. The values for *origin* must be one of these macros (defined in **<stdio.h>**):

Name	Meaning
SEEK_SET	Seek from start of file
SEEK_CUR	Seek from current location
SEEK_END	Seek from end of file

A return value of zero means that **fseek( )** succeeded. A nonzero value indicates failure.

In general, **fseek( )** should be used only with binary files. If used on a text file, *origin* must be **SEEK_SET** and *offset* must be a value obtained by calling **ftell( )** on the same file, or zero (to set the file position indicator to the start of the file).

The **fseek( )** function clears the end-of-file flag associated with the specified stream. Furthermore, it nullifies any prior **ungetc( )** on the same stream (see **ungetc**).

Example

The following function seeks to the specified structure of type **addr**. Notice the use of **sizeof** to obtain the size of the structure.

```
struct addr {
  char name[40];
  char street[40];
  char city[40];
  char state[3];
  char zip[10];
} info;

void find(long int client_num)
{
  FILE *fp;

  if((fp=fopen("mail", "rb")) == NULL) {
    printf("Cannot open file.\n");
    exit(1);
  }

  /* find the proper structure */
  fseek(fp, client_num*sizeof(struct addr), SEEK_SET);

  /* read the data into memory */
  fread(&info, sizeof(struct addr), 1, fp);

  fclose(fp);
}
```

Related Functions

ftell( ), rewind( ), fopen( ), fgetpos( ), and fsetpos( )

fsetpos

```
#include <stdio.h>
int fsetpos(FILE *stream, const fpos_t *position);
```

The **fsetpos( )** function moves the file position indicator to the location specified by the object pointed to by *position*. This value must have been previously obtained through a call to **fgetpos( )**. After **fsetpos( )** is executed, the end-of-file indicator is reset. Also, any previous call to **ungetc( )** is nullified.

If **fsetpos( )** fails, it returns nonzero. If it is successful, it returns zero.

Example

This code fragment resets the current file position indicator to the value stored in **file_loc**:

```
fsetpos(fp, &file_loc);
```

Related Functions

fgetpos( ), **fseek( )**, and **ftell( )**

ftell

```
#include <stdio.h>
long int ftell(FILE *stream);
```

The **ftell( )** function returns the current value of the file position indicator for the specified stream. In the case of binary streams, the value is the number of bytes the indicator is from the beginning of the file. For text streams, the return value may not be meaningful except as an argument to **fseek( )** because of possible character translations, such as carriage return/linefeeds being substituted for newlines, which affect the apparent size of the file.

The **ftell( )** function returns –1 when an error occurs.

Example

This code fragment obtains the current value of the file position indicator for the stream pointed to by **fp**:

```
long int i;

if((i=ftell(fp)) == -1L)
  printf("A file error has occurred.\n");
```

Related Functions

fseek( ) and fgetpos( )

fwrite

```
#include <stdio.h>
size_t fwrite(const void *buf, size_t size, size_t count,
              FILE *stream);
```

The **fwrite( )** function writes *count* number of objects, each object being *size* bytes in length, to the stream pointed to by *stream* from the character array pointed to by *buf*. The file position indicator is advanced by the number of characters written.

In C99, *buf* and *stream* are qualified by **restrict**.

The **fwrite( )** function returns the number of items actually written, which, if the function is successful, will equal the number requested. If fewer items are written than are requested, an error has occurred.

Example

This program writes a **float** to the file TEST. Notice that **sizeof** is used both to determine the number of bytes in a **float** and to ensure portability.

```
#include <stdio.h>
#include <stdlib.h>

int main(void)
{
  FILE *fp;
  float f=12.23;

  if((fp=fopen("test", "wb"))==NULL) {
    printf("Cannot open file.\n");
    exit(1);
  }

  fwrite(&f, sizeof(float), 1, fp);

  fclose(fp);

  return 0;
}
```

Related Functions

fread( ), **fscanf( )**, **getc( )**, and **fgetc( )**

getc

```
#include <stdio.h>
int getc(FILE *stream);
```

The **getc( )** function returns the next character from the specified input stream and increments the file position indicator. The character is read as an **unsigned char** that is converted to an integer.

If the end of the file is reached, **getc( )** returns **EOF**. However, since **EOF** is a valid integer value, when working with binary files you must use **feof( )** to check for the end-of-file condition. If **getc( )** encounters an error, **EOF** is also returned. If working with binary files, you must use **ferror( )** to check for file errors.

The functions **getc( )** and **fgetc( )** are identical except that in most implementations **getc( )** is defined as a macro.

Example

The following program reads and displays the contents of a text file:

```
#include <stdio.h>
#include <stdlib.h>

int main(int argc, char *argv[])
{
  FILE *fp;
  char ch;

  if((fp=fopen(argv[1], "r"))==NULL) {
    printf("Cannot open file.\n");
    exit(1);
  }

  while((ch=getc(fp))!=EOF) {
    printf("%c", ch);
  }

  fclose(fp);
```

```
    return 0;
}
```

Related Functions

fputc( ), **fgetc( )**, **putc( )**, and **fopen( )**

---

getchar

```
#include <stdio.h>
int getchar(void);
```

The **getchar( )** function returns the next character from **stdin**. The character is read as an **unsigned char** that is converted to an integer.

If the end of the file is reached, **getchar( )** returns **EOF**. If **getchar( )** encounters an error, **EOF** is also returned.

The **getchar( )** function is often implemented as a macro.

Example

This program reads characters from **stdin** into the array **s** until the user presses ENTER. Then, the string is displayed.

```
#include <stdio.h>

int main(void)
{
  char s[256], *p;

  p = s;

  while((*p++ = getchar())!= '\n') ;
  *p = '\0'; /* add null terminator */
  printf(s);

  return 0;
}
```

Related Functions

fputc( ), **fgetc( )**, **putc( )**, and **fopen( )**

gets

```
#include <stdio.h>
char *gets(char *str);
```

The **gets( )** function reads characters from **stdin** and places them into the character array pointed to by *str*. Characters are read until a newline or an **EOF** is received. The newline character is not made part of the string; instead, it is translated into a null to terminate the string.

If successful, **gets( )** returns *str*; a null pointer is returned upon failure. If a read error occurs, the contents of the array pointed to by *str* are indeterminate. Because a null pointer will be returned when either an error has occurred or when the end of the file is reached, you should use **feof( )** or **ferror( )** to determine what has actually happened.

There is no way to limit the number of characters that **gets( )** will read, which means that the array pointed to by *str* could be overrun. Thus, this function is inherently dangerous. Its use should be limited to sample programs (such as those in this book) or utilities for your own use. It should not be used for production code.

Example

This program uses **gets( )** to read a filename:

```c
#include <stdio.h>
#include <stdlib.h>

int main(void)
{
  FILE *fp;
  char fname[128];

  printf("Enter filename: ");
  gets(fname);

  if((fp=fopen(fname, "r"))==NULL) {
    printf("Cannot open file.\n");
```

THE C STANDARD LIBRARY

```
      exit(1);
   }

   fclose(fp);

   return 0;
}
```

Related Functions

fputs( ), fgetc( ), fgets( ), and puts( )

perror

```
#include <stdio.h>
void perror(const char *str);
```

The **perror( )** function maps the value of the global variable **errno** onto a string and writes that string to **stderr**. If the value of *str* is not null, the string is written first, followed by a colon and then the implementation-defined error message.

Example

This fragment reports any I/O error that may have occurred on the stream associated with **fp**:

```
if(ferror(fp)) perror("File error ");
```

printf

```
#include <stdio.h>
int printf(const char *format, ...);
```

The **printf( )** function writes to **stdout** the arguments that make up the argument list as specified by the string pointed to by *format*.

In C99, *format* is qualified with restrict.

The string pointed to by *format* consists of two types of items. The first type is made up of characters that will be printed on the screen. The second type contains format specifiers that define the way the arguments are displayed. A format specifier begins with a percent sign and is followed by the format code. There must be exactly the same number of arguments as there are format specifiers, and the format specifiers and the arguments are matched in order. For example, the following **printf( )** call displays "**Hi c 10 there!**"

```
printf("Hi %c %d %s", 'c', 10, "there!");
```

If there are insufficient arguments to match the format specifiers, the output is undefined. If there are more arguments than format specifiers, the remaining arguments are discarded. The format specifiers are shown in Table 13-2.

The **printf( )** function returns the number of characters actually printed. A negative return value indicates that an error has taken place.

The format codes can accept modifiers that specify the field width, precision, and left justification. An integer placed between the % sign and the format code acts as a *minimum field-width specifier*. This pads the output with spaces or zeros to ensure that it is at least a certain minimum length. If the string or number is greater than that minimum, it will be printed in full, even if it overruns the minimum. The default padding is done with spaces. If you want to pad with zeros, place a zero before the field-width specifier. For example, **%05d** will pad a number of less than five digits with zeros so that its total length is five.

The exact meaning of the *precision modifier* depends on the format code being modified. To add a precision modifier, place a decimal point followed by the precision after the field-width specifier. For **a**, **A**, **e**, **E**, **f**, and **F** formats, the precision modifier determines the number of decimal places printed. For example, **%10.4f** will display a number at least 10 characters wide with four decimal places. When the precision modifier is applied to the **g** or **G** format code, it determines the maximum number of significant digits displayed. When applied to integers, the precision modifier specifies the minimum number of digits that will be displayed. Leading zeros are added, if necessary.

When the precision modifier is applied to strings, the number following the period specifies the maximum field length. For example, **%5.7s** will display a string that will be at least five characters long and will not exceed seven characters. If the string is longer than the maximum field width, the characters will be truncated off the end.

By default, all output is *right justified*: If the field width is larger than the data printed, the data will be placed on the right edge of the field. You can force the information to be left justified by putting a minus sign directly after the %. For example, **%–10.2f** will left-justify a floating point number with two decimal places in a 10-character field.

There are two format modifiers that allow **printf( )** to display short and long integers. These modifiers can be applied to the **d**, **i**, **o**, **u**, **x**, and **X** type specifiers. The l modifier tells **printf( )** that a long data type follows. For example, **%ld** means that a **long int** is to be displayed. The **h** modifier tells **printf( )** to display a short integer. Therefore, **%hu** indicates that the data is of type **short unsigned int**.

Code	Format
%a	Hexadecimal output in the form 0x*h.hhhh*p+*d* (C99 only).
%A	Hexadecimal output in the form 0X*h.hhhh*P+*d* (C99 only).
%c	Character.
%d	Signed decimal integers.
%i	Signed decimal integers.
%e	Scientific notation (lowercase e).
%E	Scientific notation (uppercase E).
%f	Decimal floating point.
%F	Decimal floating point (C99 only; produces uppercase INF, INFINITY, or NAN when applied to infinity or a value that is not a number. The **%f** specifier produces lowercase equivalents.)
%g	Uses **%e** or **%f**, whichever is shorter.
%G	Uses **%E** or **%F**, whichever is shorter.
%o	Unsigned octal.
%s	String of characters.
%u	Unsigned decimal integers.
%x	Unsigned hexadecimal (lowercase letters).
%X	Unsigned hexadecimal (uppercase letters).
%p	Displays a pointer.
%n	The associated argument must be a pointer to an integer. This specifier causes the number of characters written (up to the point at which the **%n** is encountered) to be stored in that integer.
%%	Prints a percent sign.

Table 13-2. *The **printf( )** Format Specifiers*

If you are using a modern compiler that supports the wide-character features added in 1995, you can use the l modifier with the **c** specifier to indicate a wide character. You can also use the l modifier with the **s** format command to indicate a wide-character string.

An **L** modifier can prefix the floating-point commands of **a**, **A**, **e**, **E**, **f**, **F**, **g**, and **G** and indicates that a **long double** follows.

The **n** command causes the number of characters that have been written at the time the **n** is encountered to be placed in an integer variable whose pointer is specified in the argument list. For example, this code fragment displays the number **14** after the line "**this is a test**":

```
int i;

printf("This is a test%n", &i);
printf("%d", i);
```

You can apply the l modifier to the **n** specifier to indicate that the corresponding argument points to a long integer. You can specify the **h** modifier to indicate that the corresponding argument points to a short integer.

The **#** has a special meaning when used with some **printf( )** format codes. Preceding **a**, **A**, **g**, **G**, **f**, **e**, or **E** with a **#** ensures that the decimal point will be present, even if there are no decimal digits. If you precede the **x** or **X** format code with a **#**, the hexadecimal number will be printed with a **0x** prefix. If you precede the **o** format with a **#**, the octal value will be printed with a **0** prefix. The **#** cannot be applied to any other format specifiers.

The minimum field-width and precision specifiers may be provided by arguments to **printf( )** instead of by constants. To accomplish this, use an ***** as a placeholder. When the format string is scanned, **printf( )** will match each ***** to an argument in the order in which they occur.

Format Modifiers for printf( ) Added by C99

C99 adds several format modifiers to **printf( )**: **hh**, **ll**, **j**, **z**, and **t**. The **hh** modifier can be applied to **d**, **i**, **o**, **u**, **x**, **X**, or **n**. It specifies that the corresponding argument is a **signed** or **unsigned char** value or, in the case of **n**, a pointer to a **signed char** variable. The **ll** modifier also can be applied to **d**, **i**, **o**, **u**, **x**, **X**, or **n**. It specifies that the corresponding argument is a **signed** or **unsigned long long int** value or, in the case of **n**, a pointer to a **long long int**. C99 also allows the l to be applied to the floating-point specifiers **a**, **A**, **e**, **E**, **f**, **F**, **g**, and **G**, but it has no effect.

The **j** format modifier, which applies to **d**, **i**, **o**, **u**, **x**, **X**, or **n**, specifies that the matching argument is of type **intmax_t** or **uintmax_t**. These types are declared in **<stdint.h>** and specify greatest-width integers.

The **z** format modifier, which applies to **d**, **i**, **o**, **u**, **x**, **X**, or **n**, specifies that the matching argument is of type **size_t**. This type is declared in **<stddef.h>** and specifies the result of **sizeof**.

The **t** format modifier, which applies to **d**, **i**, **o**, **u**, **x**, **X**, or **n**, specifies that the matching argument is of type **ptrdiff_t**. This type is declared in **<stddef.h>** and specifies the difference between two pointers.

THE C STANDARD LIBRARY

Example

This program displays the output shown in its comments:

```
#include <stdio.h>

int main(void)
{
  /* This prints "this is a test" left justified
     in 20 character field.
  */
  printf("%-20s", "this is a test");

  /* This prints a float with 3 decimal places in a 10
     character field. The output will be "    12.235".
  */
  printf("%10.3f", 12.234657);

  return 0;
}
```

Related Functions

scanf( ) and fprintf( )

putc

```
#include <stdio.h>
int putc(int ch, FILE *stream);
```

The **putc( )** function writes the character contained in the least significant byte of *ch* to the output stream pointed to by *stream*. Because character arguments are elevated to integer at the time of the call, you can use character values as arguments to **putc( )**. **putc( )** is often implemented as a macro.

The **putc( )** function returns the character written if successful or **EOF** if an error occurs. If the output stream has been opened in binary mode, **EOF** is a valid value for *ch*. This means that you may need to use **ferror( )** to determine whether an error has occurred.

Example

The following loop writes the characters in string **str** to the stream specified by **fp**. The null terminator is not written.

```
for(; *str; str++) putc(*str, fp);
```

Related Functions

fgetc( ), **fputc( )**, **getchar( )**, and **putchar( )**

putchar

```
#include <stdio.h>
int putchar(int ch);
```

The **putchar( )** function writes the character contained in the least significant byte of *ch* to **stdout**. It is functionally equivalent to **putc(ch, stdout)**. Because character arguments are elevated to integer at the time of the call, you can use character values as arguments to **putchar( )**.

The **putchar( )** function returns the character written if successful or **EOF** if an error occurs.

Example

The following loop writes to **stdout** the characters in string **str**. The null terminator is not written.

```
for(; *str; str++) putchar(*str);
```

Related Function

putc( )

puts

```
#include <stdio.h>
int puts(const char *str);
```

THE C STANDARD LIBRARY

The **puts( )** function writes the string pointed to by *str* to the standard output device. The null terminator is translated to a newline.

The **puts( )** function returns a nonnegative value if successful and an **EOF** upon failure.

Example

The following code writes the string **this is an example** to **stdout**:

```
#include <stdio.h>
#include <string.h>

int main(void)
{
  char str[80];

  strcpy(str, "this is an example");

  puts(str);

  return 0;
}
```

Related Functions

putc( ), **gets( )**, and **printf( )**

remove

```
#include <stdio.h>
int remove(const char *fname);
```

The **remove( )** function erases the file specified by *fname*. It returns zero if the file was successfully deleted and nonzero if an error occurred.

Example

This program removes the file whose name is specified on the command line:

```
#include <stdio.h>

int main(int argc, char *argv[])
```

```
{
  if(remove(argv[1])) printf("Remove Error");

  return 0;
}
```

Related Function

rename( )

rename

```
#include <stdio.h>
int rename(const char *oldfname, const char *newfname);
```

The **rename( )** function changes the name of the file specified by *oldfname* to *newfname*. The *newfname* must not match any existing directory entry.

The **rename( )** function returns zero if successful and nonzero if an error has occurred.

Example

This program renames the file specified as the first command line argument to that specified by the second command line argument. Assuming the program is called CHANGE, a command line consisting of

CHANGE THIS THAT

will change the name of a file called THIS to THAT.

```
#include <stdio.h>

int main(int argc, char *argv[])
{
  if(rename(argv[1], argv[2]) != 0) printf("Rename Error");

  return 0;
}
```

Related Function

remove( )

rewind

```
#include <stdio.h>
void rewind(FILE *stream);
```

The **rewind( )** function moves the file position indicator to the start of the specified stream. It also clears the end-of-file and error flags associated with *stream.*

Example

This function twice reads the stream pointed to by **fp**, displaying the file each time:

```
void re_read(FILE *fp)
{
  /* read once */
  while(!feof(fp)) putchar(getc(fp));

  rewind(fp);

  /* read twice */
  while(!feof(fp)) putchar(getc(fp));
}
```

Related Function

fseek( )

scanf

```
#include <stdio.h>
int scanf(const char *format, ...);
```

The **scanf( )** function is a general-purpose input routine that reads the stream **stdin** and stores the information in the variables pointed to in its argument list. It can read all the built-in data types and automatically converts them into the proper internal format.
In C99, *format* is qualified with **restrict**.
The control string pointed to by *format* consists of three classifications of characters:

Format specifiers
White-space characters
Non-white-space characters

The input format specifiers begin with a **%** sign and tell **scanf( )** what type of data is to be read next. The format specifiers are listed in Table 13-3. For example, **%s** reads a string, while **%d** reads an integer. The format string is read left to right, and the format specifiers are matched, in order, with the arguments that make up the argument list.

To read a long integer, put an **l** (*ell*) in front of the format specifier. To read a short integer, put an **h** in front of the format specifier. These modifiers can be used with the **d, i, o, u**, and **x** format codes.

Code	Meaning
%a	Read a floating-point value (C99 only)
%A	Same as **%a** (C99 only)
%c	Read a single character
%d	Read a decimal integer
%i	Read an integer in either decimal, octal, or hexadecimal format
%e	Read a floating-point number
%E	Same as **%e**
%f	Read a floating-point number
%F	Same as **%f** (C99 only)
%g	Read a floating-point number
%G	Same as **%g**
%o	Read an octal number
%s	Read a string
%x	Read a hexadecimal number
%X	Same as **%x**
%p	Read a pointer
%n	Receive an integer value equal to the number of characters read so far
%u	Read an unsigned decimal integer
%[ ]	Scan for a set of characters
%%	Read a percent sign

Table 13-3.   *The scanf( ) Format Specifiers*

By default, the **a**, **f**, **e**, and **g** tell **scanf( )** to assign data to a **float**. If you put an l (*ell*) in front of one of these specifiers, **scanf( )** assigns the data to a **double**. Using an L tells **scanf( )** that the variable receiving the data is a **long double**.

If you are using a modern compiler that supports wide-character features added in 1995, you can use the l modifier with the **c** format code to indicate a pointer to a wide character of type **whcar_t**. You can also use the l modifier with the **s** format code to indicate a pointer to a wide-character string. The l may also be used to modify a scanset to indicate wide characters.

A white-space character in the format string causes **scanf( )** to skip over one or more white-space characters in the input stream. A white-space character is either a space, a tab character, or a newline. In essence, one white-space character in the control string will cause **scanf( )** to read, but not store, any number (including zero) of white-space characters up to the first non-white-space character.

A non-white-space character in the format string causes **scanf( )** to read and discard a matching character. For example, **%d,%d** causes **scanf( )** to first read an integer, then read and discard a comma, and finally, read another integer. If the specified character is not found, **scanf( )** will terminate.

All the variables used to receive values through **scanf( )** must be passed by their addresses. This means that all arguments must be pointers to the variables used as arguments.

In the input stream, items must be separated by spaces, tabs, or newlines. Punctuation such as commas, semicolons, and the like do not count as separators. This means that

```
scanf("%d%d", &r, &c);
```

will accept an input of **10 20** but fail with **10,20**.

An * placed after the % and before the format code will read data of the specified type but suppress its assignment. Thus, the following command,

```
scanf("%d%*c%d", &x, &y);
```

given the input **10/20**, will put the value 10 into **x**, discard the divide sign, and give **y** the value 20.

The format commands can specify a maximum field-length modifier. This is an integer number placed between the % and the format code that limits the number of characters read for any field. For example, if you wish to read no more than 20 characters into **address**, you would write

```
scanf("%20s", address);
```

If the input stream were greater than 20 characters, a subsequent call to input would begin where this call left off. Input for a field may terminate before the maximum field length is reached if a white space is encountered. In this case, **scanf( )** moves on to the next field.

Although spaces, tabs, and newlines are used as field separators, when reading a single character, these are read like any other character. For example, given an input stream of **x y**,

```
scanf("%c%c%c", &a, &b, &c);
```

will return with the character x in **a**, a space in **b**, and the character y in **c**.

Beware: Besides format commands, other characters in the control string—including spaces, tabs, and newlines—will be used to match and discard characters from the input stream. Any character that matches is discarded. For example, given the input stream **10t20**,

```
scanf("%dt%d", &x, &y);
```

will store 10 in **x** and 20 in **y**. The **t** is discarded because of the **t** in the control string.

Another feature of **scanf( )** is called a *scanset*. A scanset defines a set of characters that will be read by **scanf( )** and assigned to the corresponding character array. A scanset is defined by putting the characters you want to scan for inside square brackets. The beginning square bracket must be prefixed by a percent sign. For example, this scanset tells **scanf( )** to read only the characters A, B, and C:

```
%[ABC]
```

When a scanset is used, **scanf( )** continues to read characters and put them into the corresponding character array until a character that is not in the scanset is encountered. The corresponding variable must be a pointer to a character array. Upon return from **scanf( )**, the array will contain a null-terminated string made up of the characters read.

You can specify an inverted set if the first character in the set is a ^. When the ^ is present, it instructs **scanf( )** to accept any character that *is not* defined by the scanset.

For many implementations, you can specify a range using a hyphen. For example, this tells **scanf( )** to accept the characters A through Z:

```
%[A-Z]
```

One important point to remember is that the scanset is case sensitive. Therefore, if you want to scan for both upper- and lowercase letters, they must be specified individually.

The **scanf( )** function returns a number equal to the number of fields that were successfully assigned values. This number will not include fields that were read but not assigned because the * modifier was used to suppress the assignment. **EOF** is returned if an error occurs before the first field is assigned.

Format Modifiers for scanf( ) Added by C99

C99 adds several format modifiers to **scanf( )**: **hh**, **ll**, **j**, **z**, and **t**. The **hh** modifier can be applied to **d**, **i**, **o**, **u**, **x**, or **n**. It specifies that the corresponding argument is a pointer to a **signed** or **unsigned char** value. The **ll** modifier also can be applied to **d**, **i**, **o**, **u**, **x**, or **n**. It specifies that the corresponding argument is a pointer to a **signed** or **unsigned long long int** value.

The **j** format modifier, which applies to **d**, **i**, **o**, **u**, **x**, or **n**, specifies that the matching argument is a pointer to an object of type **intmax_t** or **uintmax_t**. These types are declared in **<stdint.h>** and specify greatest-width integers.

The **z** format modifier, which applies to **d**, **i**, **o**, **u**, **x**, or **n**, specifies that the matching argument is a pointer to an object of type **size_t**. This type is declared in **<stddef.h>** and specifies the result of **sizeof**.

The **t** format modifier, which applies to **d**, **i**, **o**, **u**, **x**, or **n**, specifies that the matching argument is a pointer to an object of type **ptrdiff_t**. This type is declared in **<stddef.h>** and specifies the difference between two pointers.

Example

The operation of these **scanf( )** statements is explained in their comments:

```
#include <stdio.h>

int main(void)
{
  char str[80], str2[80];
  int i;

  /* read a string and an integer */
  scanf("%s%d", str, &i);

  /* read up to 79 chars into str */
  scanf("%79s", str);

  /* skip the integer between the two strings */
  scanf("%s%*d%s", str, str2);

  return 0;
}
```

Related Functions

printf( ) and **fscanf( )**

setbuf

```
#include <stdio.h>
void setbuf(FILE *stream, char *buf);
```

The **setbuf( )** function specifies the buffer that *stream* will use or, if called with *buf* set to null, turns off buffering. If a programmer-defined buffer is to be specified, it must be **BUFSIZ** characters long. **BUFSIZ** is defined in **<stdio.h>.**

In C99, *stream* and *buf* are qualified by **restrict**.

Example

The following fragment associates a programmer-defined buffer with the stream pointed to by **fp**:

```
char buffer[BUFSIZ];
.
.
.
setbuf(fp, buffer);
```

Related Functions

fopen( ), fclose( ), and **setvbuf( )**

setvbuf

```
#include <stdio.h>
int setvbuf(FILE *stream, char *buf, int mode, size_t size);
```

The **setvbuf( )** function allows the programmer to specify a buffer, its size, and its mode for the specified stream. The character array pointed to by *buf* is used as the buffer for I/O operations on *stream*. The size of the buffer is set by *size*, and *mode* determines how buffering will be handled. If *buf* is null, **setvbuf( )** will allocate its own buffer.

In C99, *stream* and *buf* are qualified by **restrict**.

The legal values of *mode* are **_IOFBF**, **_IONBF**, and **_IOLBF**. These are defined in **<stdio.h>**. When *mode* is set to **_IOFBF**, full buffering will take place. If *mode* is **_IOLBF**, the stream will be line buffered. For output streams, this means that the buffer will be flushed each time a newline character is written. The buffer is also flushed when full. For input streams, input is buffered until a newline is read. If mode is **_IONBF**, no buffering takes place.

The **setvbuf( )** function returns zero on success, nonzero on failure.

Example

This code fragment sets the stream **fp** to line-buffered mode with a buffer size of 128:

```
#include <stdio.h>
char buffer[128];
.
.
.
setvbuf(fp, buffer, _IOLBF, 128);
```

Related Function

setbuf( )

snprintf

```
#include <stdio.h>
int snprintf(char * restrict buf, size_t num,
            const char * restrict format, ...)
```

The **snprintf( )** function was added by C99.

The **snprintf( )** function is identical to **sprintf( )** except that a maximum of *num*–1 characters will be stored into the array pointed to by *buf*. On completion, this array is null terminated. Thus, **snprintf( )** allows you to prevent *buf* from being overrun.

Related Functions

printf( ), sprintf( ), and fsprintf( )

sprintf

```
#include <stdio.h>
int sprintf(char *buf, const char *format, ...);
```

The **sprintf( )** function is identical to **printf( )** except that the output is put into the array pointed to by *buf* instead of being written to the **stdout**. The array pointed to by *buf* is null terminated. See **printf** for details.

In C99, *buf* and *format* are qualified by **restrict**.

The return value is equal to the number of characters actually placed into the array.

It is important to understand that **sprintf( )** provides no bounds checking on the array pointed to by *buf*. This means that the array will be overrun if the output generated by **sprintf( )** is greater than the array can hold. See **snprintf** for an alternative.

Example

After this code fragment executes, **str** holds **one 2 3**:

```
char str[80];

sprintf(str,"%s %d %c", "one", 2, '3');
```

Related Functions

printf( ) and **fsprintf( )**

sscanf

```
#include <stdio.h>
int sscanf(const char *buf, const char *format, ...);
```

The **sscanf( )** function is identical to **scanf( )** except that data is read from the array pointed to by *buf* rather than **stdin**. See **scanf** for details.

In C99, *buf* and *format* are qualified by **restrict**.

The return value is equal to the number of variables that were actually assigned values. This number does not include fields that were skipped through the use of the * format command modifier. A value of zero means that no fields were assigned, and **EOF** indicates that an error occurred prior to the first assignment.

Example

This program prints the message **hello 1** on the screen:

```c
#include <stdio.h>

int main(void)
{
  char str[80];
  int i;

  sscanf("hello 1 2 3 4 5", "%s%d", str, &i);
  printf("%s %d", str, i);

  return 0;
}
```

Related Functions

scanf( ) and **fscanf( )**

tmpfile

```c
#include <stdio.h>
FILE *tmpfile(void);
```

The **tmpfile( )** function opens a temporary binary file for read/write operations and returns a pointer to the stream. The function automatically uses a unique filename to avoid conflicts with existing files.

The **tmpfile( )** function returns a null pointer on failure; otherwise it returns a pointer to the stream.

The temporary file created by **tmpfile( )** is automatically removed when the file is closed or when the program terminates.

You can open **TMP_MAX** temporary files (up to the limit set by **FOPEN_MAX**).

Example

The following fragment creates a temporary working file:

```c
FILE *temp;
```

```
if((temp=tmpfile())==NULL) {
  printf("Cannot open temporary work file.\n");
  exit(1);
}
```

Related Function

tmpnam( )

tmpnam

```
#include <stdio.h>
char *tmpnam(char *name);
```

The **tmpnam( )** function generates a unique filename and stores it in the array pointed to by *name*. This array must be at least **L_tmpnam** characters long. (**L_tmpnam** is defined in **<stdio.h>**.) The main purpose of **tmpnam( )** is to generate a temporary filename that is different from any other file in the current disk directory.

The function can be called up to **TMP_MAX** times. **TMP_MAX** is defined in **<stdio.h>**, and it will be at least 25. Each time **tmpnam( )** is called, it will generate a new temporary filename.

A pointer to *name* is returned on success; otherwise a null pointer is returned. If *name* is null, the temporary filename is held in a static array owned by **tmpnam( )**, and a pointer to this array is returned. This array will be overwritten by a subsequent call.

Example

This program displays three unique temporary filenames:

```
#include <stdio.h>

int main(void)
{
  char name[40];
  int i;

  for(i=0; i<3; i++) {
    tmpnam(name);
    printf("%s ", name);
  }
```

```
    return 0;
  }
```

Related Function

tmpfile( )

ungetc

```
#include <stdio.h>
int ungetc(int ch, FILE *stream);
```

The **ungetc( )** function returns the character specified by the low-order byte of *ch* to the input stream *stream*. This character will then be obtained by the next read operation on *stream*. A call to **fflush( )**, **fseek( )**, or **rewind( )** undoes an **ungetc( )** operation and discards the character.

A one-character pushback is guaranteed; however, some implementations will accept more.

You may not unget an **EOF**.

A call to **ungetc( )** clears the end-of-file flag associated with the specified stream. The value of the file position indicator for a text stream is undefined until all pushed-back characters are read, in which case it will be the same as it was prior to the first **ungetc( )** call. For binary streams, each **ungetc( )** call decrements the file position indicator.

The return value is equal to *ch* on success and **EOF** on failure.

Example

This function reads words from the input stream pointed to by **fp**. The terminating character is returned to the stream for later use. For example, given the input **count/10**, the first call to **read_word( )** returns **count** and puts the "/" back into the input stream.

```
void read_word(FILE *fp, char *token)
{
  while(isalpha(*token=getc(fp))) token++;
  ungetc(*token, fp);
}
```

Related Function

getc( )

vprintf, vfprintf, vsprintf, and vsnprintf

```
#include <stdarg.h>
#include <stdio.h>
int vprintf(char *format, va_list arg_ptr);
int vfprintf(FILE *stream, const char *format,
            va_list arg_ptr);
int vsprintf(char *buf, const char *format,
            va_list arg_ptr);
int vsnprintf(char * restrict buf, size_t num,
              const char * restrict format,  va_list arg_ptr);
```

The functions **vprintf( )**, **vfprintf( )**, **vsprintf( )**, and **vsnprintf( )** are functionally equivalent to **printf( )**, **fprintf( )**, **sprintf( )**, and **snprintf( )**, respectively, except that the argument list has been replaced by a pointer to a list of arguments. This pointer must be of type **va_list**, which is defined in the header **<stdarg.h>**.

In C99, *buf* and *format* are qualified by **restrict**. The **vsnprintf( )** function was added by C99.

Example

This code fragment shows how to set up a call to **vprintf( )**. The call to **va_start( )** creates a variable-length argument pointer to the start of the argument list. This pointer must be used in the call to **vprintf( )**. The call to **va_end( )** clears the variable-length argument pointer.

```
#include <stdio.h>
#include <stdarg.h>

void print_message(char *format, ...);

int main(void)
{
  print_message("Cannot open file %s.", "test");

  return 0;
}

void print_message(char *format, ...)
{
  va_list ptr; /* get an arg ptr */

  /* initialize ptr to point to the first argument after the
```

```
      format string
   */
   va_start(ptr, format);

   /* print out message */
   vprintf(format, ptr);

   va_end(ptr);
}
```

Related Functions

vscanf( ), **vfscanf( )**, **vsscanf( )**, **va_arg( )**, **va_start( )**, and **va_end( )**

vscanf, vfscanf, and vsscanf

```
#include <stdarg.h>
#include <stdio.h>
int vscanf(char * restrict format, va_list arg_ptr);
int vfscanf(FILE * restrict stream, const char * restrict format,
         va_list arg_ptr);
int vsscanf(char * restrict buf, const char * restrict format,
         va_list arg_ptr);
```

These functions were added by C99.

The functions **vscanf( )**, **vfscanf( )**, and **vsscanf( )** are functionally equivalent to **scanf( )**, **fscanf( )**, and **sscanf( )**, respectively, except that the argument list has been replaced by a pointer to a list of arguments. This pointer must be of type **va_list**, which is defined in the header **<stdarg.h>**.

Related Functions

vprintf( ), **vfprintf( )**, **vsprintf( )**, **va_arg( )**, **va_start( )**, and **va_end( )**

Chapter 14

String and Character Functions

The standard function library has a rich and varied set of string- and character-handling functions. The string functions operate on null-terminated arrays of characters and require the header **<string.h>**. The character functions use the header **<ctype.h>**.

Because C has no bounds checking on array operations, it is the programmer's responsibility to prevent an array overflow. Neglecting to do so may cause your program to crash.

In C, a *printable character* is one that can be displayed on a terminal. In ASCII environments, these are the characters between a space (0x20) and tilde (0xFE). *Control characters* have values between 0 and 0x1F, and DEL (0x7F) in ASCII environments.

For historical reasons, the arguments to the character functions are integers, but only the low-order byte is used; the character functions automatically convert their arguments to **unsigned char**. Of course, you are free to call these functions with character arguments because characters are automatically elevated to integers at the time of the call.

The header **<string.h>** defines the **size_t** type, which is the result of the **sizeof** operator and is some form of unsigned integer.

This chapter describes only those functions that operate on characters of type **char**. These are the functions originally defined by Standard C, and they are, by far, the most widely used and supported. Wide-character functions that operate on characters of type **wchar_t** are discussed in Chapter 19.

C99 adds the **restrict** qualifier to certain parameters of several functions originally defined by C89. When this is the case, the function will be shown using its C89 prototype (which is also the prototype used by C++), but the **restrict**-qualified parameters will be pointed out in the function's description.

isalnum

```
#include <ctype.h>
int isalnum(int ch);
```

The **isalnum( )** function returns nonzero if its argument is either a letter of the alphabet or a digit. If the character is not alphanumeric, zero is returned.

Example

This program checks each character read from **stdin** and reports all alphanumeric characters:

```
#include <ctype.h>
#include <stdio.h>
```

```
int main(void)
{
  char ch;

  for(;;) {
    ch = getc(stdin);
    if(ch == '.') break;
    if(isalnum(ch)) printf("%c is alphanumeric\n", ch);
  }

  return 0;
}
```

Related Functions

isalpha( ), **iscntrl( )**, **isdigit( )**, **isgraph( )**, **isprint( )**, **ispunct( )**, and **isspace( )**

isalpha

```
#include <ctype.h>
int isalpha(int ch);
```

The **isalpha( )** function returns nonzero if *ch* is a letter of the alphabet; otherwise zero is returned. What constitutes a letter of the alphabet may vary from language to language. For English, these are the upper- and lowercase letters A through Z.

Example

This program checks each character read from **stdin** and reports all letters:

```
#include <ctype.h>
#include <stdio.h>

int main(void)
{
  char ch;

  for(;;) {
  ch = getchar();
  if(ch == '.') break;
```

```
    if(isalpha(ch)) printf("%c is a letter\n", ch);
  }

  return 0;
}
```

Related Functions

isalnum( ), iscntrl( ), isdigit( ), isgraph( ), isprint( ), ispunct( ), and isspace( )

---

isblank

```
#include <ctype.h>
int isblank(int ch);
```

The **isblank( )** function was added by C99.

The **isblank( )** function returns nonzero if *ch* is a character for which **isspace( )** returns true *and* is used to separate words. Thus, for English, the blank characters are space and horizontal tab.

Example

This program checks each character read from **stdin** and reports the number of characters that separate words:

```
#include <ctype.h>
#include <stdio.h>

int main(void)
{
  char ch;

  for(;;) {
  ch = getchar();
  if(ch == '.') break;
  if(isblank(ch)) printf("%c is a word separator\n", ch);
  }

  return 0;
}
```

Related Functions

isalnum( ), isalpha( ), iscntrl( ), isdigit( ), isgraph( ), ispunct( ), and isspace( )

iscntrl

```
#include <ctype.h>
int iscntrl(int ch);
```

The **iscntrl( )** function returns nonzero if *ch* is a control character, which in ASCII environments is a value between zero and 0x1F, or equal to 0x7F (DEL). Otherwise zero is returned.

Example

This program checks each character read from **stdin** and reports all control characters:

```
#include <ctype.h>
#include <stdio.h>

int main(void)
{
  char ch;

  for(;;) {
   ch = getchar( );
   if(ch == '.') break;
   if(iscntrl(ch)) printf("%c is a control char\n", ch);
  }

  return 0;
}
```

Related Functions

isalnum( ), isalpha( ), isdigit( ), isgraph( ), isprint( ), ispunct( ), and isspace( )

THE C STANDARD LIBRARY

isdigit

```
#include <ctype.h>
int isdigit(int ch);
```

The **isdigit( )** function returns nonzero if *ch* is a digit, that is, 0 through 9. Otherwise zero is returned.

Example

This program checks each character read from **stdin** and reports all digits:

```
#include <ctype.h>
#include <stdio.h>

int main(void)
{
  char ch;

  for(;;) {
    ch = getchar();
    if(ch == '.') break;
    if(isdigit(ch)) printf("%c is a digit\n", ch);
  }

  return 0;
}
```

Related Functions

isalnum( ), isalpha( ), iscntrl( ), isgraph( ), isprint( ), ispunct( ), and isspace( )

isgraph

```
#include <ctype.h>
int isgraph(int ch);
```

The **isgraph( )** function returns nonzero if *ch* is any printable character other than a space; otherwise zero is returned. For ASCII environments, printable characters are in the range 0x21 through 0x7E.

Example

This program checks each character read from **stdin** and reports all printable characters:

```c
#include <ctype.h>
#include <stdio.h>

int main(void)
{
  char ch;

  for(;;) {
    ch = getchar();
    if(isgraph(ch)) printf("%c is printable\n", ch);
    if(ch == '.') break;
  }

  return 0;
}
```

Related Functions

isalnum( ), **isalpha( )**, **iscntrl( )**, **isdigit( )**, **isprint( )**, **ispunct( )**, and **isspace( )**

islower

```c
#include <ctype.h>
int islower(int ch);
```

The **islower( )** function returns nonzero if *ch* is a lowercase letter; otherwise zero is returned.

Example

This program checks each character read from **stdin** and reports all lowercase letters:

```c
#include <ctype.h>
#include <stdio.h>

int main(void)
{
```

```
  char ch;

  for(;;) {
    ch = getchar();
    if(ch == '.') break;
    if(islower(ch)) printf("%c is lowercase\n", ch);
  }

  return 0;
}
```

Related Function

isupper( )

isprint

```
#include <ctype.h>
int isprint(int ch);
```

The **isprint( )** function returns nonzero if *ch* is a printable character, including a space; otherwise zero is returned. In ASCII environments, printable characters are in the range 0x20 through 0x7E.

Example

This program checks each character read from **stdin** and reports all printable characters:

```
#include <ctype.h>
#include <stdio.h>

int main(void)
{
  char ch;

  for(;;) {
    ch = getchar();
    if(isprint(ch)) printf("%c is printable\n",ch);
    if(ch == '.') break;
  }
```

```
      return 0;
    }
```

Related Functions

isalnum( ), isalpha( ), iscntrl( ), isdigit( ), isgraph( ), ispunct( ), and isspace( )

---

ispunct

```
#include <ctype.h>
int ispunct(int ch);
```

The **ispunct( )** function returns nonzero if *ch* is a punctuation character; otherwise zero is returned. The term "punctuation," as defined by this function, includes all printing characters that are neither alphanumeric nor a space.

Example

This program checks each character read from **stdin** and reports all punctuation:

```
#include <ctype.h>
#include <stdio.h>

int main(void)
{
  char ch;

  for(;;) {
    ch = getchar();
    if(ispunct(ch)) printf("%c is punctuation\n", ch);
    if(ch == '.') break;
  }

  return 0;
}
```

Related Functions

isalnum( ), isalpha( ), iscntrl( ), isdigit( ), isgraph( ), and isspace( )

isspace

```
#include <ctype.h>
int isspace(int ch);
```

The **isspace( )** function returns nonzero if *ch* is a white-space character, including space, horizontal tab, vertical tab, formfeed, carriage return, or newline character; otherwise zero is returned.

Example

This program checks each character read from **stdin** and reports all white-space characters:

```
#include <ctype.h>
#include <stdio.h>

int main(void)
{
  char ch;

  for(;;) {
  ch = getchar();
  if(isspace(ch)) printf("%c is white space\n", ch);
  if(ch == '.') break;
  }

  return 0;
}
```

Related Functions

isalnum( ), **isalpha( )**, **isblank( )**, **iscntrl( )**, **isdigit( )**, **isgraph( )**, and **ispunct( )**

isupper

```
#include <ctype.h>
int isupper(int ch);
```

The **isupper( )** function returns nonzero if *ch* is an uppercase letter; otherwise zero is returned.

Example

This program checks each character read from **stdin** and reports all uppercase letters:

```c
#include <ctype.h>
#include <stdio.h>

int main(void)
{
  char ch;

  for(;;) {
    ch = getchar();
    if(ch == '.') break;
    if(isupper(ch)) printf("%c is uppercase\n", ch);
  }

  return 0;
}
```

Related Function

islower( )

isxdigit

```c
#include <ctype.h>
int isxdigit(int ch);
```

The **isxdigit( )** function returns nonzero if *ch* is a hexadecimal digit; otherwise zero is returned. A hexadecimal digit will be in one of these ranges: A–F, a–f, or 0–9.

Example

This program checks each character read from **stdin** and reports all hexadecimal digits:

```c
#include <ctype.h>
#include <stdio.h>

int main(void)
{
```

```
  char ch;

  for(;;) {
    ch = getchar();
    if(ch == '.') break;
    if(isxdigit(ch)) printf("%c is hexadecimal digit\n", ch);
  }

  return 0;
}
```

Related Functions

isalnum( ), **isalpha( )**, **iscntrl( )**, **isdigit( )**, **isgraph( )**, **ispunct( )**, and **isspace( )**

memchr

```
#include <string.h>
void *memchr(const void *buffer, int ch, size_t count);
```

The **memchr( )** function searches the array pointed to by *buffer* for the first occurrence of *ch* in the first *count* characters.

The **memchr( )** function returns a pointer to the first occurrence of *ch* in *buffer*, or it returns a null pointer if *ch* is not found.

Example

This program prints **is a test** on the screen:

```
#include <stdio.h>
#include <string.h>

int main(void)
{
  char *p;

  p = memchr("this is a test", ' ', 14);
  printf(p);

  return 0;
}
```

Related Functions

memcpy( ) and isspace( )

---

memcmp

```
#include <string.h>
int memcmp(const void *buf1, const void *buf2,  size_t count);
```

The **memcmp( )** function compares the first *count* characters of the arrays pointed to by *buf1* and *buf2*.

The **memcmp( )** function returns an integer that is interpreted as indicated here:

Value	Meaning
Less than zero	*buf1* is less than *buf2*
Zero	*buf1* is equal to *buf2*
Greater than zero	*buf1* is greater than *buf2*

Example

This program shows the outcome of a comparison of its two command line arguments:

```
#include <stdio.h>
#include <string.h>
#include <stdlib.h>

int main(int argc, char *argv[])
{
  int outcome, len, l1, l2;

  if(argc!=3) {
    printf("Incorrect number of arguments.");
    exit(1);
  }

  /* find the length of shortest string */
  l1 = strlen(argv[1]);
  l2 = strlen(argv[2]);
  len = l1 < l2 ? l1:l2;
```

```
outcome = memcmp(argv[1], argv[2], len);
if(!outcome) printf("Equal");
else if(outcome<0) printf("First less than second.");
else printf("First greater than second.");

return 0;
}
```

Related Functions

memchr( ), memcpy( ), and strcmp( )

memcpy

```
#include <string.h>
void *memcpy(void *to, const void *from, size_t count);
```

The **memcpy( )** function copies *count* characters from the array pointed to by *from* into the array pointed to by *to*. If the arrays overlap, the behavior of **memcopy( )** is undefined. In C99, *to* and *from* are qualified by **restrict**.

The **memcpy( )** function returns a pointer to *to*.

Example

This program copies the contents of **buf1** into **buf2** and displays the result:

```
#include <stdio.h>
#include <string.h>

#define SIZE 80

int main(void)
{
  char buf1[SIZE], buf2[SIZE];

  strcpy(buf1, "When, in the course of...");
  memcpy(buf2, buf1, SIZE);
  printf(buf2);

  return 0;
}
```

Related Function

memmove( )

memmove

```
#include <string.h>
void *memmove(void *to, const void *from, size_t count);
```

The **memmove( )** function copies *count* characters from the array pointed to by *from* into the array pointed to by *to*. If the arrays overlap, the copy will take place correctly, placing the correct contents into *to* but leaving *from* modified.

The **memmove( )** function returns a pointer to *to*.

Example

This program shifts the contents of **str** down 10 places and displays the result:

```
#include <stdio.h>
#include <string.h>

#define SIZE 80

int main(void)
{
  char str[SIZE], *p;

  strcpy(str, "When, in the course of...");
  p = str + 10;

  memmove(str, p, SIZE);
  printf("result after shift: %s", str);

  return 0;
}
```

Related Function

memcpy( )

memset

```
#include <string.h>
void *memset(void *buf, int ch, size_t count);
```

The **memset( )** function copies the low-order byte of *ch* into the first *count* characters of the array pointed to by *buf*. It returns *buf*.

The most common use of **memset( )** is to initialize a region of memory to some known value.

Example

This fragment initializes to null the first 100 bytes of the array pointed to by **buf**. Then it sets the first 10 bytes to **X** and displays the string **XXXXXXXXXX**.

```
memset(buf, '\0', 100);
memset(buf, 'X', 10);
printf(buf);
```

Related Functions

memcmp( ), memcpy( ), and memmove( )

strcat

```
#include <string.h>
char *strcat(char *str1, const char *str2);
```

The **strcat( )** function concatenates a copy of *str2* to *str1* and terminates *str1* with a null. The null terminator originally ending *str1* is overwritten by the first character of *str2*. The string *str2* is untouched by the operation. If the arrays overlap, the behavior of **strcat( )** is undefined.

In C99, *str1* and *str2* are qualified by **restrict**.

The **strcat( )** function returns *str1*.

Remember, no bounds checking takes place, so it is the programmer's responsibility to ensure that *str1* is large enough to hold both its original contents and those of *str2*.

Example

This program appends the first string read from **stdin** to the second. For example, assuming the user enters **hello** and **there**, the program prints **therehello**.

```
#include <stdio.h>
#include <string.h>

int main(void)
{
  char s1[80], s2[80];

  gets(s1);
  gets(s2);

  strcat(s2, s1);
  printf(s2);

  return 0;
}
```

Related Functions

strchr( ), **strcmp( )**, and **strcpy( )**

strchr

```
#include <string.h>
char *strchr(const char *str, int ch);
```

The **strchr( )** function returns a pointer to the first occurrence of the low-order byte of *ch* in the string pointed to by *str*. If no match is found, a null pointer is returned.

Example

This program prints the string **is a test**:

```
#include <stdio.h>
#include <string.h>
```

```
int main(void)
{
  char *p;

  p = strchr("this is a test", ' ');
  printf(p);

  return 0;
}
```

Related Functions

strpbrk( ), **strspn( )**, **strstr( )**, and **strtok( )**

strcmp

```
#include <string.h>
int strcmp(const char *str1, const char *str2);
```

The **strcmp( )** function lexicographically compares two strings and returns an integer based on the outcome as shown here:

Value	Meaning
Less than zero	*str1* is less than *str2*
Zero	*str1* is equal to *str2*
Greater than zero	*str1* is greater than *str2*

Example

You can use the following function as a password-verification routine. It returns zero on failure and 1 on success.

```
int password(void)
{
  char s[80];

  printf("Enter password: ");
  gets(s);
```

```
   if(strcmp(s, "pass")) {
     printf("Invalid Password\n");
     return 0;
   }
   return 1;
}
```

Related Functions

strchr( ), strcpy( ), and strncmp( )

strcoll

```
#include <string.h>
int strcoll(const char *str1, const char *str2);
```

The **strcoll( )** function compares the string pointed to by *str1* with the one pointed to by *str2*. The comparison is performed in accordance with the locale specified using the **setlocale( )** function. (See **setlocale( )** for details.)

The **strcoll( )** function returns an integer that is interpreted as indicated here:

Value	Meaning
Less than zero	*str1* is less than *str2*
Zero	*str1* is equal to *str2*
Greater than zero	*str1* is greater than *str2*

Example

This code fragment prints **Equal** on the screen:

```
if(strcoll("hi", "hi")) printf("Equal");
```

Related Functions

memcmp( ) and strcmp( )

strcpy

```
#include <string.h>
char *strcpy(char *str1, const char *str2);
```

The **strcpy( )** function copies the contents of *str2* into *str1*. *str2* must be a pointer to a null-terminated string. The **strcpy( )** function returns a pointer to *str1*.

In C99, *str1* and *str2* are qualified by **restrict**.

If *str1* and *str2* overlap, the behavior of **strcpy( )** is undefined.

Example

The following code fragment copies **hello** into string **str**:

```
char str[80];
strcpy(str, "hello");
```

Related Functions

memcpy( ), **strchr( )**, **strcmp( )**, and **strncmp( )**

strcspn

```
#include <string.h>
size_t strcspn(const char *str1, const char *str2);
```

The **strcspn( )** function returns the length of the initial substring of the string pointed to by *str1* that is made up of only those characters not contained in the string pointed to by *str2*. Stated differently, **strcspn( )** returns the index of the first character in the string pointed to by *str1* that matches any of the characters in the string pointed to by *str2*.

Example

The following program prints the number **8**:

```
#include <string.h>
#include <stdio.h>

int main(void)
{
  int len;
```

```
   len = strcspn("this is a test", "ab");
   printf("%d", len);

   return 0;
}
```

Related Functions

strrchr( ), **strpbrk( )**, **strstr( )**, and **strtok( )**

strerror

```
#include <string.h>
char *strerror(int errnum);
```

The **strerror( )** function returns a pointer to an implementation-defined string associated with the value of *errnum*. Under no circumstances should you modify the string.

Example

This code fragment prints an implementation-defined error message on the screen:

```
printf(strerror(10));
```

THE C STANDARD LIBRARY

strlen

```
#include <string.h>
size_t strlen(const char *str);
```

The **strlen( )** function returns the length of the null-terminated string pointed to by *str*. The null terminator is not counted.

Example

The following code fragment prints **5** on the screen:

```
printf("%d", strlen("hello"));
```

Related Functions

memcpy( ), **strchr( )**, **strcmp( )**, and **strncmp( )**

strncat

```
#include <string.h>
char *strncat(char *str1, const char *str2,  size_t count);
```

The **strncat( )** function concatenates not more than *count* characters of the string pointed to by *str2* to the string pointed to by *str1* and terminates *str1* with a null. The null terminator originally ending *str1* is overwritten by the first character of *str2*. The string *str2* is untouched by the operation. If the strings overlap, the behavior is undefined.

In C99, *str1* and *str2* are qualified by **restrict**.

The **strncat( )** function returns *str1*.

Remember that no bounds checking takes place, so it is the programmer's responsibility to ensure that *str1* is large enough to hold both its original contents and also those of *str2*.

Example

This program appends the first string read from **stdin** to the second and prevents an array overflow from occurring to **s1**. For example, assuming the user enters **hello** and **there**, the program prints **therehello**.

```
#include <stdio.h>
#include <string.h>

int main(void)
{
  char s1[80], s2[80];
  unsigned int len;

  gets(s1);
  gets(s2);

  /* compute how many chars will actually fit */
  len = 79-strlen(s2);
```

```
    strncat(s2, s1, len);
    printf(s2);

    return 0;
}
```

Related Functions

strcat( ), strnchr( ), strncmp( ), and strncpy( )

strncmp

```
#include <string.h>
int strncmp(const char *str1, const char *str2, size_t count);
```

The **strncmp( )** function lexicographically compares not more than *count* characters from the two null-terminated strings and returns an integer based on the outcome, as shown here:

Value	Meaning
Less than zero	*str1* is less than *str2*
Zero	*str1* is equal to *str2*
Greater than zero	*str1* is greater than *str2*

If there are less than *count* characters in either string, the comparison ends when the first null is encountered.

Example

The following function compares the first eight characters of two command line arguments and reports if they are equal:

```
#include <stdio.h>
#include <string.h>
#include <stdlib.h>

int main(int argc, char *argv[])
```

THE C STANDARD LIBRARY

```
{
  if(argc!=3) {
    printf("Incorrect number of arguments.");
    exit(1);
  }

  if(!strncmp(argv[1], argv[2], 8))
    printf("The strings are the same.\n");

  return 0;
}
```

Related Functions

strcmp( ), strnchr( ), and strncpy( )

strncpy

```
#include <string.h>
char *strncpy(char *str1, const char *str2, size_t count);
```

The **strncpy( )** function copies up to *count* characters from the string pointed to by *str2* into the array pointed to by *str1*. *str2* must be a pointer to a null-terminated string.

In C99, *str1* and *str2* are qualified by **restrict**.

If *str1* and *str2* overlap, the behavior of **strncpy( )** is undefined.

If the string pointed to by *str2* has less than *count* characters, nulls will be appended to the end of *str1* until *count* characters have been copied.

Alternatively, if the string pointed to by *str2* is longer than *count* characters, the resultant array pointed to by *str1* will not be null terminated.

The **strncpy( )** function returns a pointer to *str1*.

Example

The following code fragment copies at most 79 characters of **str1** into **str2**, thus ensuring that no array boundary overflow occurs.

```
char str1[128], str2[80];

gets(str1);
strncpy(str2, str1, 79);
```

Related Functions

memcpy( ), **strchr( )**, **strncat( )**, and **strncmp( )**

strpbrk

```
#include <string.h>
char *strpbrk(const char *str1, const char *str2);
```

The **strpbrk( )** function returns a pointer to the first character in the string pointed to by *str1* that matches any character in the string pointed to by *str2*. The null terminators are not included. If there are no matches, a null pointer is returned.

Example

This program prints the message **s is a test** on the screen:

```
#include <stdio.h>
#include <string.h>

int main(void)
{
  char *p;

  p = strpbrk("this is a test", " absj");
  printf(p);

  return 0;
}
```

Related Functions

strspn( ), **strrchr( )**, **strstr( )**, and **strtok( )**

strrchr

```
#include <string.h>
char *strrchr(const char *str, int ch);
```

The **strrchr( )** function returns a pointer to the last occurrence of the low-order byte of *ch* in the string pointed to by *str*. If no match is found, a null pointer is returned.

Example

This program prints the string **is a test**:

```
#include <string.h>
#include <stdio.h>

int main(void)
{
  char *p;

  p = strrchr("this is a test", 'i');
  printf(p);

  return 0;
}
```

Related Functions

strpbrk( ), **strspn( )**, **strstr( )**, and **strtok( )**

strspn

```
#include <string.h>
size_t strspn(const char *str1, const char *str2);
```

The **strspn( )** function returns the length of the initial substring of the string pointed to by *str1* that is made up of only those characters contained in the string pointed to by *str2*. Stated differently, **strspn( )** returns the index of the first character in the string pointed to by *str1* that does not match any of the characters in the string pointed to by *str2*.

Example

This program prints **8**:

```
#include <string.h>
#include <stdio.h>
```

```
int main(void)
{
  int len;

  len = strspn("this is a test", "siht ");
  printf("%d", len);

  return 0;
}
```

Related Functions

strpbrk( ), **strrchr( )**, **strstr( )**, and **strtok( )**

strstr

```
#include <string.h>
char *strstr(const char *str1, const char *str2);
```

The **strstr( )** function returns a pointer to the first occurrence in the string pointed to by *str1* of the string pointed to by *str2*. It returns a null pointer if no match is found.

move pointer to first occurrence in str1 that matches str2.

Example

This program displays the message **is is a test**:

```
#include <string.h>
#include <stdio.h>

int main(void)
{
  char *p;

  p = strstr("this is a test", "is");
  printf(p);        ↑

  return 0;
}
```

Related Functions

strchr( ), strcspn( ), strpbrk( ), strspn( ), strtok( ), and strrchr( )

strtok

```
#include <string.h>
char *strtok(char *str1, const char *str2);
```

The **strtok( )** function returns a pointer to the next token in the string pointed to by *str1*. The characters making up the string pointed to by *str2* are the delimiters that determine the token. A null pointer is returned when there is no token to return.

In C99, *str1* and *str2* are qualified by **restrict**.

To tokenize a string, the first call to **strtok( )** must have *str1* point to the string being tokenized. Subsequent calls must use a null pointer for *str1*. In this way the entire string can be reduced to its tokens.

It is possible to use a different set of delimiters for each call to **strtok( )**.

Example

This program tokenizes the string "The summer soldier, the sunshine patriot," with spaces and commas being the delimiters. The output is

The | summer | soldier | the | sunshine | patriot

```
#include <stdio.h>
#include <string.h>

int main(void)
{
  char *p;

  p = strtok("The summer soldier, the sunshine patriot", " ");
  printf(p);
  do {
    p = strtok('\0', ", ");
    if(p) printf("|%s", p);
  } while(p);

  return 0;
}
```

Related Functions

strchr( ), **strcspn( )**, **strpbrk( )**, **strrchr( )**, and **strspn( )**

strxfrm

```
#include <string.h>
size_t strxfrm(char *str1, const char *str2, size_t count);
```

The **strxfrm( )** function transforms the string pointed to by *str2* so that it can be used by the **strcmp( )** function and puts the result into the string pointed to by *str1*. After the transformation, the outcome of a **strcmp( )** using *str1* and a **strcoll( )** using the original string pointed to by *str2* will be the same. Not more than *count* characters are written to the array pointed to by *str1*.

In C99, *str1* and *str2* are qualified by **restrict**.

The **strxfrm( )** function returns the length of the transformed string.

Example

The following line transforms the first 10 characters of the string pointed to by **s2** and puts the result in the string pointed to by **s1**.

```
strxfrm(s1, s2, 10);
```

Related Function

strcoll( )

tolower

```
#include <ctype.h>
int tolower(int ch);
```

The **tolower( )** function returns the lowercase equivalent of *ch* if *ch* is a letter; otherwise *ch* is returned unchanged.

Example

This code fragment displays **q**:

```
putchar(tolower('Q'));
```

Related Function

toupper( )

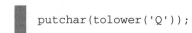 # toupper

```
#include <ctype.h>
int toupper(int ch);
```

The **toupper( )** function returns the uppercase equivalent of *ch* if *ch* is a letter; otherwise *ch* is returned unchanged.

Example

This code displays **A**:

```
putchar(toupper('a'));
```

Related Function

tolower( )

Chapter 15

Mathematical Functions

C99 has greatly increased the size of the C mathematical library. The C89 standard defined just 22 mathematical functions. C99 has more than tripled this number. Expanding the usability of C for numeric processing was one of the primary goals of the C99 committee. It is safe to say that they succeeded!

All the math functions require the header **<math.h>**. In addition to declaring the math functions, this header defines one or more macros. For C89, the only macro defined by **<math.h>** is HUGE_VAL, which is a **double** value indicating that an overflow has occurred. C99 defines several more, including

HUGE_VALF	A **float** version of **HUGE_VAL**
HUGE_VALL	A **long double** version of **HUGE_VAL**
INFINITY	A value representing infinity
math_errhandling	Contains either **MATH_ERRNO** and/or **MATH_ERREXCEPT**
MATH_ERRNO	**errno** used to report errors
MATH_ERREXCEPT	Floating-point exception raised to report errors
NAN	Not a number

C99 defines several function-like macros that classify a value. They are shown here.

int fpclassify(*fpval*)	Returns **FP_INFINITE**, **FP_NAN**, **FP_NORMAL**, **FP_SUBNORMAL**, or **FP_ZERO**, depending upon the value in *fpval*. These macros are defined by **<math.h>**.
int isfinite(*fpval*)	Returns nonzero if *fpval* is finite.
int isinf(*fpval*)	Returns nonzero if *fpval* is infinite.
int isnan(*fpval*)	Returns nonzero if *fpval* is not a number.
int isnormal(*fpval*)	Returns nonzero if *fpval* is a normal value.
int signbit(*fpval*)	Returns nonzero if *fpval* is negative (that is, its sign bit is set).

C99 defines the following comparison macros. For each, *a* and *b* must be floating-point types.

int isgreater(*a, b*)	Returns nonzero if *a* is greater than *b*.
int isgreaterequal(*a, b*)	Returns nonzero if *a* is greater than or equal to *b*.
int isless(*a, b*)	Returns nonzero if *a* is less than *b*.

int islessequal(*a*, *b*)   Returns nonzero if *a* is less than or equal to *b*.

int islessgreater(*a*, *b*)   Returns nonzero if *a* is greater than or less than *b*.

int isunordered(*a*, *b*)   Returns 1 if *a* and *b* are unordered relative to each
                                 other; zero is returned if *a* and *b* are ordered.

The reason for these macros is that they gracefully handle values that are not numbers, without causing a floating-point exception.

The macros **EDOM** and **ERANGE** are also used by the math functions. These macros are defined in the header **<errno.h>**.

C89 and C99 handle errors somewhat differently. For C89, if an argument to a math function is not in the domain for which it is defined, an implementation-defined value is returned, and the built-in global integer variable **errno** is set equal to **EDOM**. For C99, a domain error also causes an implementation-defined value to be returned. However, the value of **math_errhandling** determines what other actions take place. If **math_errhandling** contains **MATH_ERRNO**, then the built-in global integer variable **errno** is set equal to **EDOM**. If **math_errhandling** contains **MATH_ERREXCEPT**, a floating-point exception is raised.

For C89, if a function produces a result that is too large to be represented, an overflow occurs. This causes the function to return **HUGE_VAL**, and **errno** is set to **ERANGE**, indicating a range error. If an underflow happens, the function returns zero and sets **errno** to **ERANGE**. For C99, an overflow error also causes the function to return **HUGE_VAL**, and an underflow also causes the function to return zero. Then, if **math_errhandling** contains **MATH_ERRNO**, **errno** is set to **ERANGE**, indicating a range error. If **math_errhandling** contains **MATH_ERREXCEPT**, a floating-point exception is raised.

In C89, the mathematical functions are specified as operating on values of type **double**, and returning **double** values. C99 added **float** and **long double** versions of these functions, which use the **f** and **l** suffixes, respectively. For example, C89 defines **sin( )** as shown here:

    double sin(double *arg*);

C99 keeps **sin( )** and adds **sinf( )** and **sinl( )**, shown next.

    float sinf(float *arg*);

    long double sinl(long double *arg*);

The operation of all three functions is the same except for the data upon which they operate. The addition of the **f** and **l** math functions allows you to use the version that precisely fits the data upon which you are operating.

Since C99 has added so many new functions, it will be helpful to list those functions that are supported by C89. They are shown here:

acos	cos	fmod	modf	tan
asin	cosh	frexp	pow	tanh
atan	exp	ldexp	sin	
atan2	fabs	log	sinh	
ceil	floor	log10	sqrt	

Furthermore, as just explained, only the **double** version of these functions is supported by C89.

One last point: Throughout, all angles are in radians.

acos

```
#include <math.h>
float acosf(float arg);
double acos(double arg);
long double acosl(long double arg);
```

acosf( ) and **acosl( )** were added by C99.

The **acos( )** family of functions returns the arc cosine of *arg*. The argument must be in the range −1 to 1; otherwise a domain error will occur.

Example

This program prints the arc cosines of the values −1 through 1, in increments of one tenth:

```
#include <math.h>
#include <stdio.h>

int main(void)
{
  double val = -1.0;

  do {
```

```
    printf("Arc cosine of %f is %f.\n", val, acos(val));
    val += 0.1;
  } while(val<=1.0);

  return 0;
}
```

Related Functions

asin( ), **atan( )**, **atan2( )**, **sin( )**, **cos( )**, **tan( )**, **sinh( )**, **cosh( )**, and **tanh( )**

acosh

```
#include <math.h>
float acoshf(float arg);
double acosh(double arg);
long double acoshl(long double arg);
```

acosh( ), **acoshf( )**, and **acoshl( )** were added by C99.

The **acosh( )** family of functions returns the arc hyperbolic cosine of *arg*. The argument must be zero or greater; otherwise a domain error will occur.

Related Functions

asinh( ), **atanh( )**, **sinh( )**, **cosh( )**, and **tanh( )**

asin

```
#include <math.h>
float asinf(float arg);
double asin(double arg);
long double asinl(long double arg);
```

asinf( ) and **asinl( )** were added by C99.

The **asin( )** family of functions returns the arc sine of *arg*. The argument must be in the range −1 to 1; otherwise a domain error will occur.

Example

This program prints the arc sines of the values –1 through 1, in increments of one tenth:

```
#include <math.h>
#include <stdio.h>

int main(void)
{
  double val = -1.0;

  do {
    printf("Arc sine of %f is %f.\n", val, asin(val));
    val += 0.1;
  } while(val<=1.0);

  return 0;
}
```

Related Functions

acos( ), atan( ), atan2( ), sin( ), cos( ), tan( ), sinh( ), cosh( ), and tanh( )

---

asinh

```
#include <math.h>
float asinhf(float arg);
double asinh(double arg);
long double asinhl(long double arg);
```

asinh( ), asinhf( ), and asinhl( ) were added by C99.
The asinh( ) family of functions returns the arc hyperbolic sine of *arg*.

Related Functions

acosh( ), atanh( ), sinh( ), cosh( ), and tanh( )

---

atan

```
#include <math.h>
float atanf(float arg);
```

```
double atan(double arg);
long double atanl(long double arg);
```

atanf( ) and **atanl( )** were added by C99.

The **atan( )** family of functions returns the arc tangent of *arg*.

Example

This program prints the arc tangents of the values –1 through 1, in increments of one tenth:

```
#include <math.h>
#include <stdio.h>

int main(void)
{
  double val = -1.0;

  do {
    printf("Arc tangent of %f is %f.\n", val, atan(val));
    val += 0.1;
  } while(val<=1.0);

  return 0;
}
```

Related Functions

asin( ), **acos( )**, **atan2( )**, **tan( )**, **cos( )**, **sin( )**, **sinh( )**, **cosh( )**, and **tanh( )**

atanh

```
#include <math.h>
float atanhf(float arg);
double atanh(double arg);
long double atanhl(long double arg);
```

atanh( ), **atanhf( )**, and **atanhl( )** were added by C99.

The **atanh( )** family of functions returns the arc hyperbolic tangent of *arg*. This argument must be in the range –1 to 1; otherwise a domain error will occur. If *arg* equals 1 or –1, a range error is possible.

Related Functions

acosh( ), asinh( ), sinh( ), cosh( ), and tanh( )

atan2

```
#include <math.h>
float atan2f(float a, float b);
double atan2(double a, double b);
long double atan2l(long double a, long double b);
```

atan2f( ) and atan2l( ) were added by C99.

The atan2( ) family of functions returns the arc tangent of *a/b*. The functions use the signs of its arguments to compute the quadrant of the return value.

Example

This program prints the arc tangents of *y*, from –1 through 1, in increments of one tenth:

```
#include <math.h>
#include <stdio.h>

int main(void)
{
  double val = -1.0;

  do {
    printf("Atan2 of %f is %f.\n", val, atan2(val,1.0));
    val += 0.1;
  } while(val<=1.0);

  return 0;
}
```

Related Functions

asin( ), acos( ), atan( ), tan( ), cos( ), sin( ), sinh( ), cosh( ), and tanh( )

cbrt

```
#include <math.h>
float cbrtf(float num);
double cbrt(double num);
long double cbrtl(long double num);
```

cbrt( ), **cbrtf( )**, and **cbrtl( )** were added by C99.
The **cbrt( )** family of functions returns the cube root of *num*.

Example

This code fragment prints **2** on the screen:

```
printf("%f", cbrt(8));
```

Related Function

sqrt( )

ceil

```
#include <math.h>
float ceilf(float num);
double ceil(double num);
long double ceill(long double num);
```

ceilf( ) and **ceill( )** were added by C99.
The **ceil( )** family of functions returns the smallest integer (represented as a floating-point value) not less than *num*. For example, given 1.02, **ceil( )** would return 2.0. Given –1.02, **ceil( )** would return –1.

Example

This code fragment prints **10** on the screen:

```
printf("%f", ceil(9.9));
```

THE C STANDARD LIBRARY

Related Functions

floor( ) and **fmod( )**

copysign

```
#include <math.h>
float copysignf(float val, float signval);
double copysign(double val, double signval);
long double copysignl(long double val, long double signval);
```

copysign( ), copysignf( ), and **copysignl( )** were added by C99.

The **copysign( )** family of functions gives *val* the same sign as the value passed in *signval*, and return the result. Thus, the value returned has a magnitude equal to *val*, but with the same sign as that of *signval*.

Related Function

fabs( )

cos

```
#include <math.h>
float cosf(float arg);
double cos(double arg);
long double cosl(long double arg);
```

cosf( ) and **cosl( )** were added by C99.

The **cos( )** family of functions returns the cosine of *arg*. The value of *arg* must be in radians.

Example

This program prints the cosines of the values –1 through 1, in increments of one tenth:

```
#include <math.h>
#include <stdio.h>
```

```
int main(void)
{
  double val = -1.0;

  do {
    printf("Cosine of %f is %f.\n", val, cos(val));
    val += 0.1;
  } while(val<=1.0);

  return 0;
}
```

Related Functions

asin( ), **acos( )**, **atan2( )**, **atan( )**, **tan( )**, **sin( )**, **sinh( )**, **cos( )**, and **tanh( )**

cosh

```
#include <math.h>
float coshf(float arg);
double cosh(double arg);
long double coshl(long double arg);
```

coshf( ) and **coshl( )** were added by C99.
The **cosh( )** family of functions returns the hyperbolic cosine of *arg*.

Example

The following program prints the hyperbolic cosines of the values –1 through 1, in increments of one tenth:

```
#include <math.h>
#include <stdio.h>

int main(void)
{
  double val = -1.0;

  do {
```

```
    printf("Hyperbolic cosine of %f is %f.\n", val, cosh(val));
    val += 0.1;
  } while(val<=1.0);

  return 0;
}
```

Related Functions

asin( ), **acos( )**, **atan2( )**, **atan( )**, **tan( )**, **sin( )**, and **tanh( )**

erf

```
#include <math.h>
float erff(float arg);
double erf(double arg);
long double erfl(long double arg);
```

erf( ), **erff( )**, and **erfl( )** were added by C99.
The **erf( )** family of functions returns the error function of *arg*.

Related Function

erfc( )

erfc

```
#include <math.h>
float erfcf(float arg);
double erfc(double arg);
long double erfcl(long double arg);
```

erfc( ), **erfcf( )**, and **erfcl( )** were added by C99.
The **erfc( )** family of functions returns the complementary error function of *arg*.

Related Function

erf( )

exp

```
#include <math.h>
float expf(float arg);
double exp(double arg);
long double expl(long double arg);
```

expf( ) and **expl( )** were added by C99.
The **exp( )** family of functions returns the natural logarithm *e* raised to the *arg* power.

Example

This fragment displays the value of **e** (rounded to 2.718282):

```
printf("Value of e to the first: %f.", exp(1.0));
```

Related Functions

exp2( ) and **log( )**

THE C STANDARD
LIBRARY

exp2

```
#include <math.h>
float exp2f(float arg);
double exp2(double arg);
long double exp2l(long double arg);
```

exp2( ), **exp2f( )**, and **exp2l( )** were added by C99.
The **exp2( )** family of functions returns 2 raised to the *arg* power.

Related Functions

exp( ) and **log( )**

expm1

```
#include <math.h>
float expm1f(float arg);
```

```
double expm1(double arg);
long double expm1l(long double arg);
```

expm1( ), **expm1f( )**, and **expm1l( )** were added by C99.

The **expm1( )** family of functions returns the natural logarithm *e* raised to the *arg* power, minus 1. That is, it returns $e^{arg} - 1$.

Related Functions

exp( ) and **log( )**

fabs

```
#include <math.h>
float fabsf(float num);
double fabs(double num);
long double fabsl(long double num);
```

fabsf( ) and **fabsl( )** were added by C99.

The **fabs( )** family of functions returns the absolute value of *num*.

Example

This program prints **1.0 1.0** on the screen:

```
#include <math.h>
#include <stdio.h>

int main(void)
{
  printf("%1.1f %1.1f", fabs(1.0), fabs(-1.0));

  return 0;
}
```

Related Function

abs( )

fdim

```
#include <math.h>
float fdimf(float a, float b);
double fdim(double a, double b);
long double fdiml(long double a, long double b);
```

fdim( ), **fdimf( )**, and **fdiml( )** were defined by C99.

The **fdim( )** family of functions returns zero if a is less than or equal to b. Otherwise, the result of $a - b$ is returned.

Related Functions

remainder( ) and **remquo( )**

floor

```
#include <math.h>
float floorf(float num);
double floor(double num);
long double floorl(long double num);
```

floorf( ) and **floorl( )** were added by C99.

The **floor( )** family of functions returns the largest integer (represented as a floating-point value) not greater than *num*. For example, given 1.02, **floor( )** would return 1.0. Given –1.02, **floor( )** would return –2.0.

Example

This code fragment prints **10** on the screen:

```
printf("%f", floor(10.9));
```

Related Functions

ceil( ) and **fmod( )**

fma

```
#include <math.h>
float fmaf(float a, float b, float c);
double fma(double a, double b, double c);
long double fmal(long double a, long double b, long double c);
```

fma( ), **fmaf( )**, and **fmal( )** were defined by C99.
The **fma( )** family of functions returns the value of $a * b + c$. Rounding takes place only once, after the entire operation has been completed.

Related Functions

round( ), **lround( )**, and **llround( )**

fmax

```
#include <math.h>
float fmaxf(float a, float b);
double fmax(double a, double b);
long double fmaxl(long double a, long double b);
```

fmax( ), **fmaxf( )**, and **fmaxl( )** were defined by C99.
The **fmax( )** family of functions returns the greater of a and b.

Related Function

fmin( )

fmin

```
#include <math.h>
float fminf(float a, float b);
double fmin(double a, double b);
long double fminl(long double a, long double b);
```

fmin( ), **fminf( )**, and **fminl( )** were defined by C99.
The **fmin( )** family of functions returns the lesser of a and b.

Related Function

fmax( )

fmod

```
#include <math.h>
float fmodf(float a, float b);
double fmod(double a, double b);
long double fmodl(long double a, long double b);
```

fmodf( ) and **fmodl( )** were added by C99.
The **fmod( )** family of functions returns the remainder of *a/b*.

Example

The following program prints **1.0** on the screen, which is the remainder of 10/3:

```
#include <math.h>
#include <stdio.h>

int main(void)
{
  printf("%1.1f", fmod(10.0, 3.0));

  return 0;
}
```

Related Functions

ceil( ), floor( ), and fabs( )

frexp

```
#include <math.h>
float frexpf(float num, int *exp);
double frexp(double num, int *exp);
long double frexpl(long double num, int *exp);
```

frexpf( ) and **frexpl( )** were added by C99.

The **frexp( )** family of functions decomposes the number *num* into a mantissa in the range 0.5 to less than 1, and an integer exponent such that *num* = *mantissa* * 2^{exp}. The mantissa is returned by the function, and the exponent is stored at the variable pointed to by *exp*.

Example

This code fragment prints **0.625** for the mantissa and **4** for the exponent:

```
int e;
double f;

f = frexp(10.0, &e);
printf("%f %d", f, e);
```

Related Function

ldexp( )

hypot

```
#include <math.h>
float hypotf(float side1, float side2);
double hypot(double side1, double side2);
long double hypotl(long double side1, long double side2);
```

hypot( ), **hypotf( )**, and **hypotl( )** were added by C99.

The **hypot( )** family of functions returns the length of the hypotenuse given the lengths of the two opposing sides. That is, the functions return the square root of the sum of the squares of *side1* and *side2*.

Related Function

sqrt( )

ilogb

```
#include <math.h>
int ilogbf(float num);
```

```
int ilogb(double num);
int ilogbl(long double num);
```

ilogb( ), ilogbf( ), and ilogbl( ) were added by C99.

The ilogb( ) family of functions returns the exponent of *num*. This value is returned as an **int** value.

Related Function

logb( )

ldexp

```
#include <math.h>
float ldexpf(float num, int exp);
double ldexp(double num, int exp);
long double ldexpl(long double num, int exp);
```

ldexpf( ) and ldexpl( ) were added by C99.

The **ldexp( )** family of functions returns the value of $num * 2^{exp}$.

Example

This program displays the number **4:**

```
#include <math.h>
#include <stdio.h>

int main(void)
{
  printf("%f", ldexp(1,2));

  return 0;
}
```

Related Functions

frexp( ) and modf( )

lgamma

```
#include <math.h>
float lgammaf(float arg);
double lgamma(double arg);
long double lgammal(long double arg);
```

lgamma( ), **lgammaf( )**, and **lgammal( )** were added by C99.

The **lgamma( )** family of functions computes the absolute value of the gamma of *arg* and returns its natural logarithm.

Related Function

tgamma( )

llrint

```
#include <math.h>
long long int llrintf(float arg);
long long int llrint(double arg);
long long int llrintl(long double arg);
```

llrint( ), **llrintf( )**, and **llrintl( )** were added by C99.

The **llrint( )** family of functions returns the value of *arg* rounded to the nearest **long long** integer.

Related Functions

lrint( ) and rint( )

llround

```
#include <math.h>
long long int llroundf(float arg);
long long int llround(double arg);
long long int llroundl(long double arg);
```

llround( ), **llroundf( )**, and **llroundl( )** were added by C99.

The **llround( )** family of functions returns the value of *arg* rounded to the nearest **long long** integer. Values precisely between two values, such as 3.5, are rounded up.

Related Functions

lround( ) and **round( )**

log

```
#include <math.h>
float logf(float num);
double log(double num);
long double logl(long double num);
```

logf( ) and **logl( )** were added by C99.

The **log( )** family of functions returns the natural logarithm for *num*. A domain error occurs if *num* is negative. If *num* is zero, a range error is possible.

Example

The following program prints the natural logarithms for the numbers 1 through 10:

```
#include <math.h>
#include <stdio.h>

int main(void)
{
  double val = 1.0;

  do {
    printf("%f %f\n", val, log(val));
    val++;
  } while (val<11.0);

  return 0;
}
```

Related Functions

log10( ) and **log2( )**

log1p

```
#include <math.h>
float log1pf(float num);
double log1p(double num);
long double log1pl(long double num);
```

log1p( ), log1pf( ), and **log1pl( )** were added by C99.

The **log1p( )** family of functions returns the natural logarithm for *num*+1. A domain error occurs if *num* is negative. If *num* is –1, a range error is possible.

Related Function

log( )

log10

```
#include <math.h>
float log10f(float num);
double log10(double num);
long double log10l(long double num);
```

log10f( ) and **log10l( )** were added by C99.

The **log10( )** family of functions returns the base 10 logarithm for *num*. A domain error occurs if *num* is negative. If *num* is zero, a range error is possible.

Example

This program prints the base 10 logarithms for the numbers 1 through 10:

```
#include <math.h>
#include <stdio.h>

int main(void)
{
  double val = 1.0;

  do {
    printf("%f %f\n", val, log10(val));
    val++;
```

```
    } while (val<11.0);

    return 0;
}
```

Related Functions

log( ) and log2( )

log2

```
#include <math.h>
float log2f(float num);
double log2(double num);
long double log2l(long double num);
```

log2( ), **log2f( )**, and **log2l( )** were added by C99.

The **log2( )** family of functions returns the base 2 logarithm for *num*. A domain error occurs if *num* is negative. If *num* is zero, a range error is possible.

Related Functions

log( ) and log10( )

logb

```
#include <math.h>
float logbf(float num);
double logb(double num);
long double logbl(long double num);
```

logb( ), **logbf( )**, and **logbl( )** were added by C99.

The **logb( )** family of functions returns the exponent of *num*. This value is returned as a floating-point integer value. A domain error is possible when *num* is zero.

Related Function

ilogb( )

lrint

```
#include <math.h>
long int lrintf(float arg);
long int lrint(double arg);
long int lrintl(long double arg);
```

lrint( ), **lrintf( )**, and **lrintl( )** were added by C99.

The **lrint( )** family of functions returns the value of *arg* rounded to the nearest **long** integer.

Related Functions

llrint( ) and **rint( )**

lround

```
#include <math.h>
long int lroundf(float arg);
long int lround(double arg);
long int lroundl(long double arg);
```

lround( ), **lroundf( )**, and **lroundl( )** were added by C99.

The **lround( )** family of functions returns the value of *arg* rounded to the nearest **long** integer. Values precisely between two values, such as 3.5, are rounded up.

Related Functions

llround( ) and **round( )**

modf

```
#include <math.h>
float modff(float num, float *i);
double modf(double num, double *i);
long double modfl(long double num, long double *i);
```

modff( ) and **modfl( )** were added by C99.

The **modf( )** family of functions decomposes *num* into its integer and fractional parts. The functions return the fractional portion and place the integer part in the variable pointed to by *i*.

Example

This code fragment displays **10** and **0.123**:

```
double i;
double f;

f = modf(10.123, &i);
printf("%f %f",i , f);
```

Related Functions

frexp( ) and **ldexp( )**

nan

```
#include <math.h>
float nanf(const char *content);
double nan(const char *content);
long double nanl(const char *content);
```

nan( ), **nanf( )**, and **nanl( )** were defined by C99.

The **nan( )** family of functions returns a value that is not a number and that contains the string pointed to by *content*.

Related Function

isnan( )

nearbyint

```
#include <math.h>
float nearbyintf(float arg);
double nearbyint(double arg);
long double nearbyintl(long double arg);
```

nearbyint( ), **nearbyintf( )**, and **nearbyintl( )** were added by C99.

The **nearbyint( )** family of functions returns the value of *arg* rounded to the nearest integer. However, the number is returned as a floating-point value.

Related Functions

rint( ) and **round( )**

nextafter

```
#include <math.h>
float nextafterf(float from, float towards);
double nextafter(double from, double towards);
long double nextafterl(long double from, long double towards);
```

nextafter( ), **nextafterf( )**, and **nextafterl( )** were defined by C99.

The **nextafter( )** family of functions returns the next value after *from* that is closer to *towards*.

Related Function

nexttoward( )

nexttoward

```
#include <math.h>
float nexttowardf(float from, long double towards);
double nexttoward(double from, long double towards);
long double nexttowardl(long double from, long double towards);
```

nexttoward( ), **nexttowardf( )**, and **nexttowardl( )** were defined by C99.

The **nexttoward( )** family of functions returns the next value after *from* that is closer to *towards*. They are the same as the **nextafter( )** family except that *towards* is a **long double** for all three functions.

Related Function

nextafter( )

pow

```
#include <math.h>
float powf(float base, float exp);
double pow(double base, double exp);
long double powl(long double base, long double exp);
```

powf( ) and **powl( )** were added by C99.

The **pow( )** family of functions returns *base* raised to the *exp* power (*base^exp*). A domain error may occur if *base* is zero and *exp* is less than or equal to zero. It will also happen if *base* is negative and *exp* is not an integer. A range error is possible.

Example

The following program prints the first ten powers of 10:

```
#include <math.h>
#include <stdio.h>

int main(void)
{
  double x = 10.0, y = 0.0;

  do {
    printf("%f\n", pow(x, y));
    y++;
  } while(y<11.0);

  return 0;
}
```

Related Functions

exp( ), **log( )**, and **sqrt( )**

remainder

```
#include <math.h>
float remainderf(float a, float b);
```

```
double remainder(double a, double b);
long double remainderl(long double a, long double b);
```

remainder( ), **remainderf( )**, and **remainderl( )** were added by C99.
The **remainder( )** family of functions returns the remainder of *a/b*.

Related Function

remquo( )

remquo

```
#include <math.h>
float remquof(float a, float b, int *quo);
double remquo(double a, double b, int *quo);
long double remquol(long double a, long double b, int *quo);
```

remquo( ), **remquof( )**, and **remquol( )** were added by C99.
The **remquo( )** family of functions returns the remainder of a/b. On return, the
integer pointed to by *quo* will contain the quotient.

Related Function

remainder( )

rint

```
#include <math.h>
float rintf(float arg);
double rint(double arg);
long double rintl(long double arg);
```

rint( ), **rintf( )**, and **rintl( )** were added by C99.
The **rint( )** family of functions returns the value of *arg* rounded to the nearest
integer. However, the number is returned as a floating-point value. It is possible that a
floating-point exception will be raised.

Related Functions

nearbyint( ) and round( )

round

```
#include <math.h>
float roundf(float arg);
double round(double arg);
long double roundl(long double arg);
```

round( ), **roundf( )**, and **roundl( )** were added by C99.

The **round( )** family of functions returns the value of *arg* rounded to the nearest integer. However, the number is returned as a floating-point value. Values precisely between two values, such as 3.5, are rounded up.

Related Function

lround( ) and llround( )

scalbln

```
#include <math.h>
float scalblnf(float val, long int exp);
double scalbln(double val, long int exp);
long double scalblnl(long double val, long int exp);
```

scalbln( ), **scalblnf( )**, and **scalblnl( )** were added by C99.

The **scalbln( )** family of functions returns the product of *val* and **FLT_RADIX** raised to the *exp* power, that is,

$$val * FLT\_RADIX^{exp}$$

The macro **FLT_RADIX** is defined in **<float.h>**, and its value is the radix of exponent representation.

Related Function

scalbn( )

scalbn

```
#include <math.h>
float scalbnf(float val, int exp);
double scalbn(double val, int exp);
long double scalbnl(long double val, int exp);
```

scalbn( ), **scalbnf( )**, and **scalbnl( )** were added by C99.

The **scalbn( )** family of functions returns the product of *val* and **FLT_RADIX** raised to the *exp* power, that is,

$$val * FLT\_RADIX^{exp}$$

The macro **FLT_RADIX** is defined in **<float.h>**, and its value is the radix of exponent representation.

Related Function

scalbln( )

sin

```
#include <math.h>
float sinf(float arg);
double sin(double arg);
long double sinl(long double arg);
```

sinf( ) and **sinl( )** were added by C99.

The **sin( )** family of functions returns the sine of *arg*. The value of *arg* must be in radians.

Example

This program prints the sines of the values –1 through 1, in increments of one tenth:

```
#include <math.h>
#include <stdio.h>

int main(void)
{
  double val = -1.0;

  do {
```

```
      printf("Sine of %f is %f.\n", val, sin(val));
      val += 0.1;
   } while(val<=1.0);

   return 0;
}
```

Related Functions

asin( ), **acos( )**, **atan2( )**, **atan( )**, **tan( )**, **cos( )**, **sinh( )**, **cosh( )**, and **tanh( )**

sinh

```
#include <math.h>
float sinhf(float arg);
double sinh(double arg);
long double sinhl(long double arg);
```

sinhf( ) and **sinhl( )** were added by C99.
The **sinh( )** family of functions returns the hyperbolic sine of *arg*.

Example

This program prints the hyperbolic sines of the values –1 through 1, in increments of one tenth:

```
#include <math.h>
#include <stdio.h>

int main(void)
{
  double val = -1.0;

  do {
    printf("Hyperbolic sine of %f is %f.\n", val, sinh(val));
    val += 0.1;
  } while(val<=1.0);

  return 0;
}
```

Related Functions

asin( ), **acos( )**, **atan2( )**, **atan( )**, **tan( )**, **cos( )**, **tanh( )**, **cosh( )**, and **sin( )**

sqrt

```
#include <math.h>
float sqrtf(float num);
double sqrt(double num);
long double sqrtl(long double num);
```

sqrtf( ) and **sqrtl( )** were added by C99.

The **sqrt( )** family of functions returns the square root of *num*. If they are called with a negative argument, a domain error will occur.

Example

This code fragment prints **4** on the screen:

```
printf("%f", sqrt(16.0));
```

Related Functions

exp( ), **log( )**, and **pow( )**

tan

```
#include <math.h>
float tanf(float arg);
double tan(double arg);
long double tanl(long double arg);
```

tanf( ) and **tanl( )** were added by C99.

The **tan( )** family of functions returns the tangent of *arg*. The value of *arg* must be in radians.

Example

This program prints the tangent of the values –1 through 1, in increments of one tenth:

```
#include <math.h>
#include <stdio.h>

int main(void)
{
  double val = -1.0;

  do {
    printf("Tangent of %f is %f.\n", val, tan(val));
    val += 0.1;
  } while(val<=1.0);

  return 0;
}
```

Related Functions

acos( ), asin( ), atan( ), atan2( ), cos( ), sin( ), sinh( ), cosh( ), and tanh( )

tanh

```
#include <math.h>
float tanhf(float arg);
double tanh(double arg);
long double tanhl(long double arg);
```

tanhf( ) and tanhl( ) were added by C99.
The tanh( ) family of functions returns the hyperbolic tangent of *arg*.

Example

This program prints the hyperbolic tangent of the values –1 through 1, in increments of
one tenth:

```
#include <math.h>
#include <stdio.h>

int main(void)
{
  double val = -1.0;
```

```
do {
  printf("Hyperbolic tangent of %f is %f.\n", val, tanh(val));
  val += 0.1;
} while(val<=1.0);

return 0;
}
```

Related Functions

acos( ), **asin( )**, **atan( )**, **atan2( )**, **cos( )**, **sin( )**, **cosh( )**, **sinh( )**, and **tan( )**

tgamma

```
#include <math.h>
float tgammaf(float arg);
double tgamma(double arg);
long double tgammal(long double arg);
```

tgamma( ), **tgammaf( )**, and **tgammal( )** were added by C99.
The **tgamma( )** family of functions returns the gamma function of *arg*.

Related Function

lgamma( )

trunc

```
#include <math.h>
float truncf(float arg);
double trunc(double arg);
long double truncl(long double arg);
```

trunc( ), **truncf( )**, and **truncl( )** were added by C99.
The **trunc( )** family of functions returns the truncated value of *arg*.

Related Function

nearbyint( )

Chapter 16

Time, Date, and
Localization Functions

The standard function library defines several functions that deal with the date and time. It also defines functions that handle the geopolitical information associated with a program. These functions are described here.

The time and date functions require the header **<time.h>**. This header defines three time-related types: **clock_t**, **time_t**, and **tm**. The types **clock_t** and **time_t** are capable of representing the system time and date as some sort of integer. This is called the *calendar time*. The structure type **tm** holds the date and time broken down into its elements. The **tm** structure contains the following members:

```
int tm_sec;   /* seconds, 0-60 */
int tm_min;   /* minutes, 0-59 */
int tm_hour;  /* hours, 0-23 */
int tm_mday;  /* day of the month, 1-31 */
int tm_mon;   /* months since Jan, 0-11 */
int tm_year;  /* years from 1900 */
int tm_wday;  /* days since Sunday, 0-6 */
int tm_yday;  /* days since Jan 1, 0-365 */
int tm_isdst  /* Daylight Saving Time indicator */
```

The value of **tm_isdst** will be positive if daylight saving time is in effect, zero if it is not in effect, and negative if there is no information available. This form of the time and date is called the *broken-down time*.

In addition, **<time.h>** defines the macro **CLOCKS_PER_SEC**, which is the number of system clock ticks per second.

The geopolitical environmental functions require the header **<locale.h>**. It defines the structure **lconv**, which is described under the function **localeconv( )**.

asctime

```
#include <time.h>
char *asctime(const struct tm *ptr);
```

The **asctime( )** function returns a pointer to a string that contains the information stored in the structure pointed to by *ptr* converted into the following form:

day month date hours:minutes:seconds year\n\0

For example:

```
Fri Apr 15 12:05:34 2005
```

The structure pointed to by *ptr* is usually obtained from either **localtime( )** or **gmtime( )**.

The buffer used by **asctime( )** to hold the formatted output string is a statically allocated character array and is overwritten each time the function is called. If you wish to save the contents of the string, you must copy it elsewhere.

Example

This program displays the local time defined by the system:

```
#include <time.h>
#include <stdio.h>

int main(void)
{
  struct tm *ptr;
  time_t lt;

  lt = time(NULL);
  ptr = localtime(&lt);
  printf(asctime(ptr));

  return 0;
}
```

Related Functions

localtime( ), **gmtime( )**, **time( )**, and **ctime( )**

clock

```
#include <time.h>
clock_t clock(void);
```

The **clock( )** function returns a value that approximates the amount of time the calling program has been running. To transform this value into seconds, divide it by **CLOCKS_PER_SEC**. A value of –1 is returned if the time is not available.

Example

The following function displays the current execution time, in seconds, for the program calling it:

```
void elapsed_time(void)
{
  printf("Elapsed time: %u secs.\n", clock()/CLOCKS_PER_SEC);
}
```

Related Functions

time( ), **asctime( )**, and **ctime( )**

ctime

```
#include <time.h>
char *ctime(const time_t *time);
```

The **ctime( )** function returns a pointer to a string of the form

day month year hours:minutes:seconds year\n\0

given a pointer to the calendar time. The calendar time is often obtained through a call to **time( )**.

The buffer used by **ctime( )** to hold the formatted output string is a statically allocated character array and is overwritten each time the function is called. If you wish to save the contents of the string, it is necessary to copy it elsewhere.

Example

This program displays the local time defined by the system:

```
#include <time.h>
#include <stdio.h>

int main(void)
{
  time_t lt;

  lt = time(NULL);
```

```
printf(ctime(&lt));

return 0;
}
```

Related Functions

localtime( ), gmtime( ), time( ), and **asctime( )**

difftime

```
#include <time.h>
double difftime(time_t time2, time_t time1);
```

The **difftime( )** function returns the difference, in seconds, between *time1* and *time2*—that is, *time2 – time1*.

Example

This program times the number of seconds that it takes for the empty **for** loop to go from 0 to 5,000,000:

```
#include <time.h>
#include <stdio.h>

int main(void)
{
  time_t start,end;
  volatile long unsigned t;

  start = time(NULL);
  for(t=0; t<5000000; t++) ;
  end = time(NULL);
  printf("Loop used %f seconds.\n", difftime(end, start));

  return 0;
}
```

Related Functions

localtime( ), gmtime( ), time( ), and **asctime( )**

gmtime

```
#include <time.h>
struct tm *gmtime(const time_t *time);
```

The **gmtime( )** function returns a pointer to the broken-down form of *time* in the form of a **tm** structure. The time is represented in Coordinated Universal Time (UTC), which is essentially Greenwich mean time. The *time* pointer is usually obtained through a call to **time( )**. If the system does not support Coordinated Universal Time, **NULL** is returned.

The structure used by **gmtime( )** to hold the broken-down time is statically allocated and is overwritten each time the function is called. If you wish to save the contents of the structure, you must copy it elsewhere.

Example

This program prints both the local time and the UTC of the system:

```
#include <time.h>
#include <stdio.h>

/* Print local and UTC time. */
int main(void)
{
  struct tm *local, *gm;
  time_t t;

  t = time(NULL);
  local = localtime(&t);
  printf("Local time and date: %s\n", asctime(local));
  gm = gmtime(&t);
  printf("Coordinated Universal Time and date: %s", asctime(gm));

  return 0;
}
```

Related Functions

localtime( ), time( ), and asctime( )

localeconv

```
#include <locale.h>
struct lconv *localeconv(void);
```

The **localeconv( )** function returns a pointer to a structure of type **lconv**, which contains a variety of geopolitical environmental information relating to the way numbers are formatted. The **lconv** structure contains the following members:

```
char *decimal_point;       /* Decimal point character
                              for nonmonetary values. */
char *thousands_sep;       /* Thousands separator
                              for nonmonetary values. */
char *grouping;            /* Specifies grouping for
                              nonmonetary values. */
char *int_curr_symbol;     /* International currency symbol. */
char *currency_symbol;     /* Local currency symbol. */
char *mon_decimal_point;   /* Decimal point character for
                              monetary values. */
char *mon_thousands_sep;   /* Thousands separator for
                              monetary values. */
char *mon_grouping;        /* Specifies grouping for
                              monetary values. */
char *positive_sign;       /* Positive value indicator for
                              monetary values. */
char *negative_sign;       /* Negative value indicator for
                              monetary values. */
char int_frac_digits;      /* Number of digits displayed to the
                              right of the decimal point for
                              monetary values displayed using
                              international format. */
char frac_digits;          /* Number of digits displayed to the
                              right of the decimal point for
                              monetary values displayed using
                              local format. */
char p_cs_precedes;        /* 1 if currency symbol precedes
                              positive value, 0 if currency
                              symbol follows value. */
char p_sep_by_space;       /* 1 if currency symbol is
                              separated from value by a space,
                              0 otherwise. In C99, contains a
                              value that indicates separation. */
```

THE C STANDARD
LIBRARY

```
    char n_cs_precedes;         /* 1 if currency symbol precedes
                                   a negative value, 0 if currency
                                   symbol follows value. */
    char n_sep_by_space;        /* 1 if currency symbol is
                                   separated from a negative
                                   value by a space, 0 if
                                   currency symbol follows value.
                                   In C99, contains a value that
                                   indicates separation. */
    char p_sign_posn;           /* Indicates position of
                                   positive value symbol. */
    char n_sign_posn;           /* Indicates position of
                                   negative value symbol. */

    /* The following members were added by C99. */
    char _p_cs_precedes;        /* 1 if currency symbol precedes
                                   positive value, 0 if currency
                                   symbol follows value. Applies to
                                   internationally formatted values. */
    char _p_sep_by_space;       /* Indicates the separation between the
                                   currency symbol, sign, and a positive value.
                                   Applies to internationally formatted values. */
    char _n_cs_precedes;        /* 1 if currency symbol precedes
                                   a negative value, 0 if currency
                                   symbol follows value. Applies to
                                   internationally formatted values. */
    char _n_sep_by_space;       /* Indicates the separation between the
                                   currency symbol, sign, and a negative value.
                                   Applies to internationally formatted values. */
    char _p_sign_posn;          /* Indicates position of
                                   positive value symbol. Applies to
                                   internationally formatted values. */
    char _n_sign_posn;          /* Indicates position of
                                   negative value symbol. Applies to
                                   internationally formatted values. */
```

The **localeconv( )** function returns a pointer to the **lconv** structure. You must not alter the contents of this structure. Refer to your compiler's documentation for implementation-specific information relating to the **lconv** structure.

Example

The following program displays the decimal point character used by the current locale:

```
#include <stdio.h>
#include <locale.h>

int main(void)
{
  struct lconv lc;

  lc = *localeconv();

  printf("Decimal symbol is: %s\n", lc.decimal_point);

  return 0;
}
```

Related Function

setlocale( )

localtime

```
#include <time.h>
struct tm *localtime(const time_t *time);
```

The **localtime( )** function returns a pointer to the broken-down form of *time* in the form of a **tm** structure. The time is represented in local time. The *time* pointer is usually obtained through a call to **time( )**.

The structure used by **localtime( )** to hold the broken-down time is statically allocated and is overwritten each time the function is called. If you wish to save the contents of the structure, you must copy it elsewhere.

Example

This program prints both the local time and the Coordinated Universal Time (UTC) of the system:

```c
#include <time.h>
#include <stdio.h>

/* Print local and UTC time. */
int main(void)
{
  struct tm *local;
  time_t t;

  t = time(NULL);
  local = localtime(&t);
  printf("Local time and date: %s\n", asctime(local));
  local = gmtime(&t);
  printf("UTC time and date: %s\n", asctime(local));

  return 0;
}
```

Related Functions

gmtime( ), **time( )**, and **asctime( )**

mktime

```c
#include <time.h>
time_t mktime(struct tm *time);
```

The **mktime( )** function returns the calendar-time equivalent of the broken-down time found in the structure pointed to by *time*. The elements **tm_wday** and **tm_yday** are set by the function, so they need not be defined at the time of the call.

If **mktime( )** cannot represent the information as a valid calendar time, –1 is returned.

Example

This program tells you the day of the week for January 3, 2005:

```
#include <time.h>
#include <stdio.h>

int main(void)
{
  struct tm t;
  time_t t_of_day;

  t.tm_year = 2005-1900;
  t.tm_mon = 0;
  t.tm_mday = 3;
  t.tm_hour = 0;   /* hour, min, sec don't matter */
  t.tm_min = 0;    /* as long as they don't cause a */
  t.tm_sec = 1;    /* new day to occur */
  t.tm_isdst = 0;

  t_of_day = mktime(&t);
  printf(ctime(&t_of_day));

  return 0;
}
```

Related Functions

time( ), **gmtime( )**, **asctime( )**, and **ctime( )**

setlocale

```
#include <locale.h>
char *setlocale(int type, const char *locale);
```

The **setlocale( )** function allows certain parameters that are sensitive to the geopolitical environment of a program's execution to be queried or set. If *locale* is null, **setlocale( )** returns a pointer to the current localization string. Otherwise, **setlocale( )** attempts to use the string specified by *locale* to set the locale parameters as specified by *type*. To specify the standard C locale, use the string "C". To specify the native environment, use the null string "". Refer to your compiler's documentation for the localization strings that it supports.

At the time of the call, *type* must be one of the following macros (defined in **<locale.h>**):

LC_ALL
LC_COLLATE

LC_CTYPE
LC_MONETARY
LC_NUMERIC
LC_TIME

LC_ALL refers to all localization categories. **LC_COLLATE** affects the operation of the **strcoll( )** function. **LC_CTYPE** alters the way the character functions work. **LC_MONETARY** determines the monetary format. **LC_NUMERIC** changes the decimal-point character for formatted input/output functions. Finally, **LC_TIME** determines the behavior of the **strftime( )** function.

The **setlocale( )** function returns a pointer to a string associated with the *type* parameter.

Example

This program displays the current locale setting:

```
#include <locale.h>
#include <stdio.h>

int main(void)
{
  printf(setlocale(LC_ALL, ""));

  return 0;
}
```

Related Functions

localeconv( ), **time( )**, **strcoll( )**, and **strftime( )**

strftime

```
#include <time.h>
size_t strftime(char *str, size_t maxsize,  const char *fmt,
                const struct tm *time);
```

The **strftime( )** function stores time and date information, along with other information, into the string pointed to by *str* according to the format commands found in the string pointed to by *fmt* and using the broken-down time pointed to by *time*. A maximum of *maxsize* characters will be placed into *str*.

In C99, *str*, *fmt*, and *time* are qualified by **restrict**.

The **strftime( )** function works a little like **sprintf( )** in that it recognizes a set of format commands that begin with the percent sign (%), and it stores its formatted output into a string. The format commands are used to specify the exact way various time and date information is represented in *str*. Any other characters found in the format string are placed into *str* unchanged. The time and date displayed are in local time. The format commands are shown in the table below. Notice that many of the commands are case sensitive.

The **strftime( )** function returns the number of characters stored in the string pointed to by *str* or zero if an error occurs.

Command	Replaced By
%a	Abbreviated weekday name
%A	Full weekday name
%b	Abbreviated month name
%B	Full month name
%c	Standard date and time string
%C	Last two digits of year
%d	Day of month as a decimal (1–31)
%D	month/day/year (added by C99)
%e	Day of month as a decimal (1–31) in a two-character field (added by C99)
%F	year-month-day (added by C99)
%g	Last two digits of year using a week-based year (added by C99)
%G	The year using a week-based year (added by C99)
%h	Abbreviated month name (added by C99)
%H	Hour (0–23)
%I	Hour (1–12)
%j	Day of year as a decimal (1–366)
%m	Month as decimal (1–12)
%M	Minute as decimal (0–59)
%n	A newline (added by C99)
%p	Locale's equivalent of AM or PM
%r	12-hour time (added by C99)
%R	hh:mm (added by C99)

Command	Replaced By
%S	Second as decimal (0–60)
%t	Horizontal tab (added by C99)
%T	hh:mm:ss (added by C99)
%u	Day of week; Monday is first day of week (0–53) (added by C99)
%U	Week of year, Sunday being first day (0–53)
%V	Week of year using a week-based year (added by C99)
%w	Weekday as a decimal (0–6, Sunday being 0)
%W	Week of year, Monday being first day (0–53)
%x	Standard date string
%X	Standard time string
%y	Year in decimal without century (0–99)
%Y	Year including century as decimal
%z	Offset from UTC (added by C99)
%Z	Time zone name
%%	The percent sign

C99 allows certain of the **strftime( )** format commands to be modified by **E** or **O**. The **E** can modify **c, C, x, X, y, Y, d, e**, and **H**. The **O** can modify **I, m, M, S, u, U, V, w, W**, and **y**. These modifiers cause an alternative representation of the time and/or date to be displayed. Consult your compiler's documentation for details.

A week-based year is used by the **%g, %G**, and **%V** format commands. With this representation, Monday is the first day of the week, and the first week of a year must include January 4.

Example

Assuming that **ltime** points to a structure that contains 10:00:00 AM, the following program prints **It is now 10 AM**:

```
#include <time.h>
#include <stdio.h>

int main(void)
{
```

```
    struct tm *ptr;
    time_t lt;
    char str[80];

    lt = time(NULL);
    ptr = localtime(&lt);

    strftime(str, 100, "It is now %H %p.", ptr);
    printf(str);

    return 0;
}
```

Related Functions

time( ), localtime( ), and gmtime( )

time

```
#include <time.h>
time_t time(time_t *time);
```

The **time( )** function returns the current calendar time of the system. If the system has no time, –1 is returned.

The **time( )** function can be called either with a null pointer or with a pointer to a variable of type **time_t**. If the latter is used, the variable will also be assigned the calendar time.

Example

This program displays the local time defined by the system:

```
#include <time.h>
#include <stdio.h>

int main(void)
{
  struct tm *ptr;
  time_t lt;
```

```
    lt = time(NULL);
    ptr = localtime(&lt);
    printf(asctime(ptr));

    return 0;
}
```

Related Functions

localtime( ), gmtime( ), strftime( ), and ctime( )

Chapter 17

Dynamic Allocation Functions

his chapter describes C's dynamic allocation functions. At their core are **malloc( )** and **free( )**. Each time **malloc( )** is called, a portion of the remaining free memory is allocated. Each time **free( )** is called, memory is returned to the system. The region of free memory from which memory is allocated is called the *heap*. The prototypes for the dynamic allocation functions are in **<stdlib.h>**.

Note   *An overview of dynamic allocation is found in Chapter 5.*

Standard C defines four dynamic allocation functions that all compilers will supply: **calloc( )**, **malloc( )**, **free( )**, and **realloc( )**. However, your compiler will almost certainly contain several nonstandard variants on these functions to accommodate various options and environmental differences. For example, special allocation functions are supplied by compilers that produce code for the segmented memory model of the 8086. You will want to refer to your compiler's documentation for details and descriptions of additional allocation functions.

calloc

```
#include <stdlib.h>
void *calloc(size_t num, size_t size);
```

The **calloc( )** function allocates memory the size of which is equal to *num * size*. That is, **calloc( )** allocates sufficient memory for an array of *num* objects of size *size*. All bits in the allocated memory are initially set to zero.

The **calloc( )** function returns a pointer to the first byte of the allocated region. If there is not enough memory to satisfy the request, a null pointer is returned. It is always important to verify that the return value is not null before attempting to use it.

Example

This function returns a pointer to a dynamically allocated array of 100 **float**s:

```
#include <stdlib.h>
#include <stdio.h>

float *get_mem(void)
{
  float *p;

  p = calloc(100, sizeof(float));
  if(!p) {
```

```
      printf("Allocation Error\n");
      exit(1);
    }
    return p;
}
```

Related Functions

free( ), malloc( ), and realloc( )

free

```
#include <stdlib.h>
void free(void *ptr);
```

The **free( )** function returns the memory pointed to by *ptr* to the heap. This makes the memory available for future allocation.

It is imperative that **free( )** only be called with a pointer that was previously allocated using one of the dynamic allocation system's functions. Using an invalid pointer in the call most likely will destroy the memory management mechanism and possibly cause a system crash. If you pass a null pointer, **free( )** performs no operation.

Example

This program allocates room for the strings entered by the user and then frees the memory:

```
#include <stdlib.h>
#include <stdio.h>

int main(void)
{
  char *str[100];
  int i;

  for(i=0; i<100; i++) {
    if((str[i] = malloc(128))==NULL) {
      printf("Allocation Error\n");
      exit(1);
    }
```

```
      gets(str[i]);
   }

   /* now free the memory */
   for(i=0; i<100; i++) free(str[i]);

   return 0;
}
```

Related Functions

calloc( ), malloc( ), and realloc( )

malloc

```
#include <stdlib.h>
void *malloc(size_t size);
```

The **malloc( )** function returns a pointer to the first byte of a region of memory of size *size* that has been allocated from the heap. If there is insufficient memory in the heap to satisfy the request, **malloc( )** returns a null pointer. It is always important to verify that the return value is not null before attempting to use it. Attempting to use a null pointer will usually result in a system crash.

Example

This function allocates sufficient memory to hold structures of type **addr**:

```
struct addr {
  char name[40];
  char street[40];
  char city[40];
  char state[3];
  char zip[10];
};

struct addr *get_struct(void)
{
  struct addr *p;

  if((p = malloc(sizeof(struct addr)))==NULL) {
```

```
      printf("Allocation Error\n");
      exit(1);
   }
   return p;
}
```

Related Functions

free( ), realloc( ), and calloc( )

realloc

```
#include <stdlib.h>
void *realloc(void *ptr, size_t size);
```

The precise operation of **realloc( )** differs slightly between C89 and C99, although the net effect is the same. For C89, **realloc( )** changes the size of the previously allocated memory pointed to by *ptr* to that specified by *size*. The value of *size* can be greater or less than the original. A pointer to the memory block is returned because it may be necessary for **realloc( )** to move the block in order to change its size. If this occurs, the contents of the old block (up to *size* bytes) are copied into the new block.

For C99, the block of memory pointed to by *ptr* is freed, and a new block is allocated. The new block contains the same contents as the original block (up to the length passed in *size*). A pointer to the new block is returned. It is permissible, however, for the new block and the old block to begin at the same address. That is, the pointer returned by **realloc( )** might be the same as the one passed in *ptr*.

If *ptr* is null, **realloc( )** simply allocates *size* bytes of memory and returns a pointer to it. If *size* is zero, the memory pointed to by *ptr* is freed.

If there is not enough free memory in the heap to allocate *size* bytes, a null pointer is returned, and the original block is left unchanged.

Example

This program first allocates 17 characters, copies the string "This is 16 chars" into them, and then uses **realloc( )** to increase the size to 18 in order to place a period at the end.

```
#include <stdlib.h>
#include <stdio.h>
#include <string.h>
```

```
int main(void)
{
  char *p;

  p = malloc(17);
  if(!p) {
    printf("Allocation Error\n");
    exit(1);
  }

  strcpy(p, "This is 16 chars");

  p = realloc(p, 18);
  if(!p) {
    printf("Allocation Error\n");
    exit(1);
  }

  strcat(p, ".");

  printf(p);

  free(p);

  return 0;
}
```

Related Functions

free( ), **malloc( )**, and **calloc( )**

Chapter 18

Utility Functions

The standard function library defines several utility functions. They include various conversions, variable-length argument processing, sorting and searching, and random number generation. Many of the functions covered here require the use of the header **<stdlib.h>**. In this header are declared the types **div_t** and **ldiv_t**, which are the types of the values returned by **div( )** and **ldiv( )**, respectively. C99 adds the **lldiv_t** type and the **lldiv( )** function. Also declared are the types **size_t** and **wchar_t**. The following macros are also defined:

Macro	Meaning
MB_CUR_MAX	Maximum length (in bytes) of a multibyte character
NULL	A null pointer
RAND_MAX	The maximum value that can be returned by the **rand( )** function
EXIT_FAILURE	The value returned to the calling process if program termination is unsuccessful
EXIT_SUCCESS	The value returned to the calling process if program termination is successful

If a function requires a header other than **<stdlib.h>**, that function description will discuss it.

abort

```
#include <stdlib.h>
void abort(void);
```

The **abort( )** function causes immediate abnormal termination of a program. Generally, no files are flushed. In environments that support it, **abort( )** will return an implementation-defined value to the calling process (usually the operating system) indicating failure.

Example

In this program, the program terminates if the user enters an **A**:

```
#include <stdlib.h>
#include <stdio.h>
```

```
int main(void)
{
  for(;;)
    if(getchar()=='A') abort();

  return 0;
}
```

Related Functions

exit( ) and atexit( )

abs

```
#include <stdlib.h>
int abs(int num);
```

The **abs( )** function returns the absolute value of *num*.

Example

This function converts a user-entered number into its absolute value:

```
int get_abs(void)
{
  char num[80];

  gets(num);
  return abs(atoi(num));
}
```

Related Function

fabs( )

assert

```
#include <assert.h>
void assert(int exp);
```

The **assert( )** macro, defined in its header **<assert.h>**, writes error information to **stderr** and then aborts program execution if the expression *exp* evaluates to zero. Otherwise, **assert( )** does nothing. Although the exact output is implementation defined, many compilers use a message similar to this:

Assertion failed: *<expression>*, file *<file>*, line *<linenum>*

For C99, the message will also include the name of the function that contained **assert( )**.

The **assert( )** macro is generally used to help verify that a program is operating correctly, with the expression being devised in such a way that it evaluates to true only when no errors have taken place.

It is not necessary to remove the **assert( )** statements from the source code once a program is debugged because if the macro **NDEBUG** is defined (as anything), the **assert( )** macros will be ignored.

Example

This code fragment tests whether the data read from a serial port is an ASCII character (that is, it does not use the seventh bit):

```
/* ... */
ch = read_port();
assert(!(ch & 128)); /* check bit 7 */
```

Related Function

abort( )

atexit

```
#include <stdlib.h>
int atexit(void (*func)(void));
```

The **atexit( )** function causes the function pointed to by *func* to be called upon normal program termination. The **atexit( )** function returns zero if the function is successfully registered as a termination function and nonzero otherwise.

At least 32 termination functions can be registered, and they will be called in the reverse order of their registration.

Example

This program prints **Hello There** on the screen when it terminates:

```
#include <stdlib.h>
#include <stdio.h>

void done(void);

int main(void)
{
  if(atexit(done)) printf("Error in atexit().");

  return 0;
}

void done(void)
{
  printf("Hello There");
}
```

Related Functions

exit( ) and **abort( )**

atof

```
#include <stdlib.h>
double atof(const char *str);
```

The **atof( )** function converts the string pointed to by *str* into a **double** value. The string must contain a valid floating-point number. If this is not the case, the returned value is undefined.

The number can be terminated by any character that cannot be part of a valid floating-point number. This includes white space, punctuation (other than periods), and characters other than E or e. This means that if **atof( )** is called with "100.00HELLO", the value 100.00 will be returned.

Example

This program reads two floating-point numbers and displays their sum:

```
#include <stdlib.h>
#include <stdio.h>
```

```
int main(void)
{
  char num1[80], num2[80];

  printf("Enter first: ");
  gets(num1);
  printf("Enter second: ");
  gets(num2);
  printf("The sum is: %lf.", atof(num1) + atof(num2));

  return 0;
}
```

Related Functions

atoi( ) and atol( )

atoi

```
#include <stdlib.h>
int atoi(const char *str);
```

The **atoi( )** function converts the string pointed to by *str* into an **int** value. The string must contain a valid integer number. If this is not the case, the returned value is undefined.

The number can be terminated by any character that cannot be part of an integer number. This includes white space, punctuation, and characters. This means that if **atoi( )** is called with "123.23", the integer value 123 will be returned, and the ".23" is ignored.

Example

The following program reads two integers and displays their sum:

```
#include <stdlib.h>
#include <stdio.h>

int main(void)
{
  char num1[80], num2[80];
```

```
   printf("Enter first: ");
   gets(num1);
   printf("Enter second: ");
   gets(num2);
   printf("The sum is: %d.", atoi(num1)+atoi(num2));

   return 0;
}
```

Related Functions

atof( ) and atol( )

atol

```
#include <stdlib.h>
long int atol(const char *str);
```

The **atol( )** function converts the string pointed to by *str* into a **long int** value. The string must contain a valid integer number. If this is not the case, the returned value is undefined.

The number can be terminated by any character that cannot be part of an integer number. This includes white space, punctuation, and characters. This means that if **atol( )** is called with "123.23", the long integer value 123L will be returned, and the ".23" is ignored.

Example

This program reads two long integers and displays their sum:

```
#include <stdlib.h>
#include <stdio.h>

int main(void)
{
  char num1[80], num2[80];

  printf("Enter first: ");
  gets(num1);
  printf("Enter second: ");
```

```
    gets(num2);
    printf("The sum is: %ld.", atol(num1)+atol(num2));

    return 0;
}
```

Related Functions

atof( ), atoi( ), and atoll( )

atoll

```
#include <stdlib.h>
long long int atoll(const char *str);
```

atoll( ) was added by C99.

The atoll( ) function converts the string pointed to by *str* into a **long long int** value. It is otherwise similar to **atol( )**.

Related Functions

atof( ), atoi( ), and atol( )

bsearch

```
#include <stdlib.h>
void *bsearch(const void *key, const void *buf,
              size_t num, size_t size,
              int (*compare)(const void *, const void *));
```

The **bsearch( )** function performs a binary search on the sorted array pointed to by *buf* and returns a pointer to the first member that matches the key pointed to by *key*. The number of elements in the array is specified by *num*, and the size (in bytes) of each element is described by *size*.

The function pointed to by *compare* is used to compare an element of the array with the key. The form of the *compare* function must be as follows:

int *func_name*(const void **arg1*, const void **arg2*);

It must return values as described in the following table:

Comparison	Value Returned
arg1 is less than *arg2*	Less than zero
arg1 is equal to *arg2*	Zero
arg1 is greater than *arg2*	Greater than zero

The array must be sorted in ascending order with the lowest address containing the lowest element. If the array does not contain the key, a null pointer is returned.

Example

The following program reads a character entered at the keyboard and determines whether it belongs to the alphabet:

```
#include <stdlib.h>
#include <ctype.h>
#include <stdio.h>

char *alpha = "abcdefghijklmnopqrstuvwxyz";

int comp(const void *ch, const void *s);

int main(void)
{
  char ch;
  char *p;

  printf("Enter a character: ");
  ch = getchar();
  ch = tolower(ch);
  p = (char *) bsearch(&ch, alpha, 26, 1, comp);
  if(p) printf(" %c is in alphabet\n", *p);
  else printf("is not in alphabet\n");

  return 0;
}

/* Compare two characters. */
int comp(const void *ch, const void *s)
{
```

```
    return *(char *)ch - *(char *)s;
}
```

Related Function

qsort( )

div

```
#include <stdlib.h>
div_t div(int numerator, int denominator);
```

The **div( )** function returns the quotient and the remainder of the operation *numerator/denominator* in a structure of type **div_t**.

The structure type **div_t** has these two fields:

```
int quot; /* quotient */
int rem;  /* remainder */
```

Example

This program displays the quotient and remainder of 10/3:

```
#include <stdlib.h>
#include <stdio.h>

int main(void)
{
  div_t n;

  n = div(10, 3);

  printf("Quotient and remainder: %d %d.\n", n.quot, n.rem);

  return 0;
}
```

Related Functions

ldiv( ) and lldiv( )

exit

```
#include <stdlib.h>
void exit(int exit_code);
```

The **exit( )** function causes immediate, normal termination of a program. This means that termination functions registered by **atexit( )** are called, and any open files are flushed and closed.

The value of *exit_code* is passed to the calling process—usually the operating system—if the environment supports it. By convention, if the value of *exit_code* is zero, or **EXIT_SUCCESS**, normal program termination is assumed. A nonzero value, or **EXIT_FAILURE**, is used to indicate an implementation-defined error.

Example

This function performs menu selection for a mailing list program. If **Q** is selected, the program is terminated.

```
int menu(void)
{
  char choice;

  do {
    printf("Enter names (E)\n");
    printf("Delete name (D)\n");
    printf("Print (P)\n");
    printf("Quit (Q)\n");
    choice = getchar();
  } while(!strchr("EDPQ", toupper(choice)));

  if(choice=='Q') exit(0);

  return choice;
}
```

Related Functions

atexit( ), abort( ) and _Exit( )

_Exit

```
#include <stdlib.h>
void _Exit(int exit_code);
```

_Exit( ) was added by C99.

The **_Exit( )** function is similar to **exit( )** except for the following:

- No calls to termination functions registered by **atexit( )** are made.

- No calls to signal handlers registered by **signal( )** are made.

- Open files are not necessarily flushed or closed.

Related Functions

atexit( ), abort( ) and exit( )

getenv

```
#include <stdlib.h>
char *getenv(const char *name);
```

The **getenv( )** function returns a pointer to environmental information associated with the string pointed to by *name* in the implementation-defined environmental information table. The string must not be changed by your code.

The environment of a program may include such things as path names and devices online. The exact nature of this data is implementation defined. You will need to refer to your compiler's documentation for details.

If a call is made to **getenv( )** with an argument that does not match any of the environment data, a null pointer is returned.

Example

Assuming that a specific compiler maintains environmental information about the devices connected to the system, the following fragment returns a pointer to the list of devices:

```
char *p
/* ... (/
p = getevn("DEVICES");
```

Related Function

system( )

---

labs

```
#include <stdlib.h>
long int labs(long int num);
```

The **labs( )** function returns the absolute value of *num*.

Example

This function converts the number entered at the keyboard into its absolute value:

```
long int get_labs()
{
  char num[80];

  gets(num);

  return labs(atol(num));
}
```

Related Functions

abs( ) and **llabs( )**

---

llabs

```
#include <stdlib.h>
long long int llabs(long long int num);
```

llabs( ) was added by C99.

The **llabs( )** function returns the absolute value of *num*. It is similar to **labs( )** except that it operates on values of type **long long int**.

Related Functions

abs( ) and labs( )

ldiv

```
#include <stdlib.h>
ldiv_t ldiv(long int numerator, long int denominator);
```

The **ldiv( )** function returns the quotient and remainder of the operation *numerator/denominator* in an **ldiv_t** structure.

The structure type **ldiv_t** has these two fields:

```
long int quot; /* quotient */
long int rem;  /* remainder */
```

Example

This program displays the quotient and remainder of 10/3:

```
#include <stdlib.h>
#include <stdio.h>

int main(void)
{
  ldiv_t n;

  n = ldiv(10L, 3L);

  printf("Quotient and remainder: %ld %ld.\n", n.quot, n.rem);

  return 0;
}
```

Related Functions

div( ) and lldiv( )

lldiv

```
#include <stdlib.h>
lldiv_t lldiv(long long int numerator, long long int denominator);
```

lldiv( ) was added by C99.

The **lldiv( )** function returns the quotient and remainder of the operation *numerator/denominator* in an **lldiv_t** structure. It is similar to **ldiv( )** except that it operates on **long long** integers.

The structure type **lldiv_t** has these two fields:

```
long long int quot; /* quotient */
long long int rem;  /* remainder */
```

Related Functions

div( ) and **ldiv( )**

longjmp

```
#include <setjmp.h>
void longjmp(jmp_buf envbuf, int status);
```

The **longjmp( )** function causes program execution to resume at the point of the last call to **setjmp( )**. Thus, **longjmp( )** and **setjmp( )** provide a means of jumping between functions. Notice that the header **<setjmp.h>** is required.

The **longjmp( )** function operates by resetting the stack to the state as described in *envbuf*, which must have been set by a prior call to **setjmp( )**. This causes program execution to resume at the statement following the **setjmp( )** invocation. That is, the computer is "tricked" into thinking that it never left the function that called **setjmp( )**. (As a somewhat graphic explanation, the **longjmp( )** function "warps" across time and (memory) space to a previous point in your program without having to perform the normal function return process.)

The buffer *envbuf* is of type **jmp_buf**, which is defined in the header **<setjmp.h>**. Again, the buffer must have been set through a call to **setjmp( )** prior to calling **longjmp( )**.

The value of *status* becomes the return value of **setjmp( )** and is used to determine where the long jump came from. The only value that is not allowed is zero. Zero is returned by **setjmp( )** when it is actually called directly by your program, not indirectly through the execution of **longjmp( )**.

By far the most common use of **longjmp( )** is to return from a deeply nested set of routines when an error occurs.

Example

This program prints **1 2 3**:

```
#include <setjmp.h>
#include <stdio.h>

jmp_buf ebuf;
void f2(void);

int main(void)
{
  int i;

  printf("1 ");
  i = setjmp(ebuf);
  if(i == 0) {
    f2();
    printf("This will not be printed.");
  }
  printf("%d", i);

  return 0;
}

void f2(void)
{
  printf("2 ");
  longjmp(ebuf, 3);
}
```

Related Function

setjmp( )

mblen

```
#include <stdlib.h>
int mblen(const char *str, size_t size);
```

The **mblen( )** function returns the length (in bytes) of a multibyte character pointed to by *str*. Only the first *size* number of characters are examined. It returns –1 on error.

If *str* is null, then **mblen( )** returns nonzero if multibyte characters have state-dependent encodings. If they do not, zero is returned.

Example

This statement displays the length of the multibyte character pointed to by **mb**:

```
printf("%d", mblen(mb, 2));
```

Related Functions

mbtowc( ) and **wctomb( )**

mbstowcs

```
#include <stdlib.h>
size_t mbstowcs(wchar_t *out, const char *in, size_t size);
```

The **mbstowcs( )** function converts the multibyte string pointed to by *in* into a wide-character string and puts that result in the array pointed to by *out*. Only *size* number of bytes will be stored in *out*.

In C99, *out* and *in* are qualified by **restrict**.

The **mbstowcs( )** function returns the number of multibyte characters that are converted. If an error occurs, the function returns –1.

Example

This statement converts the first four characters in the multibyte string pointed to by **mb** and puts the result in **str**:

```
mbstowcs(str, mb, 4);
```

Related Functions

wcstombs( ) and **mbtowc( )**

---

mbtowc

```
#include <stdlib.h>
int mbtowc(wchar_t *out, const char *in, size_t size);
```

The **mbtowc( )** function converts the multibyte character in the array pointed to by *in* into its wide-character equivalent and puts that result in the object pointed to by *out*. Only *size* number of characters will be examined.

In C99, *out* and *in* are qualified by **restrict**.

This function returns the number of bytes that are put into *out*. If an error occurs, –1 is returned. If *in* is null, then **mbtowc( )** returns nonzero if multibyte characters have state-dependent encodings. If they do not, zero is returned.

Example

This statement converts the multibyte character in **mbstr** into its equivalent wide character and puts the result in the array pointed to by **widenorm**. (Only the first 2 bytes of **mbstr** are examined.)

```
mbtowc(widenorm, mbstr, 2);
```

Related Functions

mblen( ) and **wctomb( )**

---

qsort

```
#include <stdlib.h>
void qsort(void *buf, size_t num, size_t size,
           int (*compare) (const void *, const void *));
```

The **qsort( )** function sorts the array pointed to by *buf* using a Quicksort (developed by C. A. R. Hoare). Quicksort is generally considered the best general-purpose sorting algorithm. The number of elements in the array is specified by *num*, and the size (in bytes) of each element is described by *size*.

The function pointed to by *compare* is used to compare two elements of the array. The form of the *compare* function must be as follows:

int *func_name*(const void *arg1, const void *arg2);

It must return values as described here:

Comparison	Value Returned
arg1 is less than *arg2*	Less than zero
arg1 is equal to *arg2*	Zero
arg1 is greater than *arg2*	Greater than zero

The array is sorted into ascending order with the lowest address containing the lowest element.

Example

This program sorts a list of integers and displays the result:

```
#include <stdlib.h>
#include <stdio.h>

int num[10] = {
  1, 3, 6, 5, 8, 7, 9, 6, 2, 0
};

int comp(const void *, const void *);

int main(void)
{
  int i;

  printf("Original array: ");
  for(i=0; i<10; i++) printf("%d ", num[i]);

  qsort(num, 10, sizeof(int), comp);

  printf("Sorted array: ");
  for(i=0; i<10; i++) printf("%d ", num[i]);

  return 0;
```

```
}

/* compare the integers */
int comp(const void *i, const void *j)
{
  return *(int *)i - *(int *)j;
}
```

Related Function

bsearch( )

raise

```
#include <signal.h>
int raise(int signal);
```

The **raise( )** function sends the specified by *signal* to the executing program. It returns zero if successful; otherwise it returns nonzero. It uses the header **<signal.h>**.

The following signals are defined by Standard C. Of course, your compiler is free to provide additional signals.

Macro	Meaning
SIGABRT	Termination error
SIGFPE	Floating-point error
SIGILL	Bad instruction
SIGINT	User pressed CTRL-C
SIGSEGV	Illegal memory access
SIGTERM	Terminate program

Related Function

signal( )

rand

```
#include <stdlib.h>
int rand(void);
```

The **rand( )** function generates a sequence of pseudorandom numbers. Each time it is called, an integer between zero and **RAND_MAX** is returned. **RAND_MAX** will be at least 32,767.

Example

The following program displays 10 pseudorandom numbers:

```
#include <stdlib.h>
#include <stdio.h>

int main(void)
{
  int i;

  for(i=0; i<10; i++)
    printf("%d ", rand());

  return 0;
}
```

Related Function

srand( )

setjmp

```
#include <setjmp.h>
int setjmp(jmp_buf envbuf);
```

The **setjmp( )** macro saves the contents of the system stack in the buffer *envbuf* for later use by **longjmp( )**. It uses the header **<setjmp.h>**.

THE C STANDARD LIBRARY

The **setjmp( )** macro returns zero upon invocation. However, **longjmp( )** passes an argument to **setjmp( )**, and it is this value (always nonzero) that will appear to be the value of **setjmp( )** after a call to **longjmp( )** has occurred.

See **longjmp** for additional information.

Related Function

longjmp( )

signal

```
#include <signal.h>
void (*signal(int signal, void (*func)(int))) (int);
```

The **signal( )** function registers the function pointed to by *func* as a handler for the signal specified by *signal*. That is, the function pointed to by *func* will be called when *signal* is received by your program. The header **<signal.h>** is required.

The value of *func* can be the address of a signal handler function or one of the following macros, defined in **<signal.h>**:

Macro	Meaning
SIG_DFL	Use default signal handling.
SIG_IGN	Ignore the signal.

If a function address is used, the specified handler will be executed when its signal is received. Check your compiler's documentation for additional details.

On success, **signal( )** returns the address of the previously defined function for the specified signal. On error, **SIG_ERR** (defined in **<signal.h>**) is returned.

Related Function

raise( )

srand

```
#include <stdlib.h>
void srand(unsigned int seed);
```

The **srand( )** function sets a starting point for the sequence generated by **rand( )**. (The **rand( )** function returns pseudorandom numbers.)

srand( ) is often used to allow multiple program runs to use different sequences of pseudorandom numbers by specifying different starting points. Conversely, you can also use **srand( )** to generate the same pseudorandom sequence over and over again by calling it with the same seed before starting the sequence.

Example

This program uses the system time to randomly initialize the **rand( )** function by using **srand( )**:

```
#include <stdio.h>
#include <stdlib.h>
#include <time.h>

/* Seed rand() with the system time
   and display the first 10 numbers.
*/
int main(void)
{
  int i, stime;
  long ltime;

  /* get the current calendar time */
  ltime = time(NULL);
  stime = (unsigned) ltime/2;
  srand(stime);

  for(i=0; i<10; i++) printf("%d ", rand());

  return 0;
}
```

Related Function

rand( )

strtod

```
#include <stdlib.h>
double strtod(const char *start, char **end);
```

The **strtod( )** function converts the string representation of a number stored in the string pointed to by *start* into a **double** and returns the result.

In C99, *start* and *end* are qualified by **restrict**.

The **strtod( )** function works as follows. First, any white space in the string pointed to by *start* is stripped. Next, each character that makes up the number is read. Any character that cannot be part of a floating-point number will cause this process to stop. This includes white space, punctuation (other than periods), and characters other than E or e. Finally, *end* is set to point to the remainder, if any, of the original string. This means that if **strtod( )** is called with " 100.00 Pliers", the value 100.00 will be returned, and *end* will point to the space that precedes "Pliers".

If overflow occurs, either **HUGE_VAL** or **–HUGE_VAL** (indicating positive or negative overflow) is returned, and the global variable **errno** is set to **ERANGE**, indicating a range error. If underflow occurs, the function returns zero, and the global variable **errno** is set to **ERANGE**. If *start* does not point to a number, no conversion takes place and zero is returned.

Example

This program reads floating-point numbers from a character array:

```c
#include <stdlib.h>
#include <ctype.h>
#include <stdio.h>

int main(void)
{
  char *end, *start = "100.00 pliers 200.00 hammers";

  end = start;
  while(*start) {
    printf("%f, ", strtod(start, &end));
    printf("Remainder: %s\n" ,end);
    start = end;
    /* move past the non-digits */
    while(!isdigit(*start) && *start) start++;
  }

  return 0;
}
```

The output is

```
100.000000, Remainder: pliers 200.00 hammers
200.000000, Remainder: hammers
```

Related Functions

atof( ), strtold( ), and strtof( )

strtof

```
#include <stdlib.h>
long double strtof(const char * restrict start,
                 char restrict ** restrict end);
```

strtof( ) was added by C99.

The **strtof( )** function is similar to **strtod( )** except that it returns a **float** value. If overflow occurs, then either **HUGE_VALF** or **–HUGE_VALF** is returned, and the global variable **errno** is set to **ERANGE**, indicating a range error. If *start* does not point to a number, no conversion takes place and zero is returned.

Related Functions

atof( ), strtod( ), and strtold( )

strtol

```
#include <stdlib.h>
long int strtol(const char *start, char **end, int radix);
```

The **strtol( )** function converts the string representation of a number stored in the string pointed to by *start* into a **long int** and returns the result. The base of the number is determined by *radix*. If *radix* is zero, the base is determined by the rules that govern constant specification. If *radix* is other than zero, it must be in the range 2 through 36.

In C99, *start* and *end* are qualified by **restrict**.

The **strtol( )** function works as follows. First, any white space in the string pointed to by *start* is stripped. Next, each character that makes up the number is read. Any character that cannot be part of a long integer number will cause this process to stop. This includes white space, punctuation, and characters. Finally, *end* is set to point to the remainder, if any, of the original string. This means that if **strtol( )** is called with " 100 Pliers", the value 100L will be returned, and *end* will point to the space that precedes "Pliers".

If the result cannot be represented by a **long int**, **LONG_MAX** or **LONG_MIN** is returned, and the global **errno** is set to **ERANGE**, indicating a range error. If *start* does not point to a number, no conversion takes place and zero is returned.

Example

This function reads base 10 numbers from standard input and returns their **long** equivalent:

```
long int read_long(void)
{
  char start[80], *end;

  printf("Enter a number: ");
  gets(start);
  return strtol(start, &end, 10);
}
```

Related Functions

atol( ) and **strtoll( )**

strtold

```
#include <stdlib.h>
long double strtold(const char * restrict start,
                    char restrict ** restrict end);
```

strtold( ) was added by C99.

The **strtold( )** function is similar to **strtod( )** except that it returns a **long double** value. If overflow occurs, then either **HUGE_VALL** or **–HUGE_VALL** is returned, and the global variable **errno** is set to **ERANGE**, indicating a range error. If *start* does not point to a number, no conversion takes place and zero is returned.

Related Functions

atof( ), strtod( ), and **strtof( )**

strtoll

```
#include <stdlib.h>
long long int strtoll(const char * restrict start,
                      char ** restrict end, int radix);
```

strtoll( ) was added by C99.

The **strtoll( )** function is similar to **strtol( )** except that it returns a **long long int**. If the result cannot be represented by a long integer, **LLONG_MAX** or **LLONG_MIN** is returned, and the global **errno** is set to **ERANGE**, indicating a range error. If *start* does not point to a number, no conversion takes place and zero is returned.

Related Functions

atol( ) and **strtol( )**

strtoul

```
#include <stdlib.h>
unsigned long int strtoul(const char *start, char **end,
                          int radix);
```

The **strtoul( )** function converts the string representation of a number stored in the string pointed to by *start* into an **unsigned long int** and returns the result. The base of the number is determined by *radix*. If *radix* is zero, the base is determined by the rules that govern constant specification. If the radix is specified, it must be in the range 2 through 36.

In C99, *start* and *end* are qualified by **restrict**.

The **strtoul( )** function works as follows. First, any white space in the string pointed to by *start* is stripped. Next, each character that makes up the number is read. Any character that cannot be part of an unsigned integer number will cause this process to stop. This includes white space, punctuation, and characters. Finally, *end* is set to point to the remainder, if any, of the original string. This means that if **strtoul( )** is called with " 100 Pliers", the value 100L will be returned, and *end* will point to the space that precedes "Pliers".

If the result cannot be represented as an unsigned long integer, **ULONG_MAX** is returned and the global variable **errno** is set to **ERANGE**, indicating a range error. If *start* does not point to a number, no conversion takes place and zero is returned.

Example

This function reads unsigned base 16 (hexadecimal) numbers from standard input and returns their unsigned long equivalent:

```
unsigned long int read_unsigned_long(void)
{
  char start[80], *end;

  printf("Enter a hex number: ");
  gets(start);
  return strtoul(start, &end, 16);
}
```

Related Functions

strtol( ) and strtoull( )

strtoull

```
#include <stdlib.h>
unsigned long long int strtoull(const char *restrict start, char
                              **restrict end, int radix);
```

strtoull( ) was added by C99.

The **strtoull( )** function is similar to **strtoul( )** except that it returns an **unsigned long long int**. If the result cannot be represented as an unsigned long integer, **ULLONG_MAX** is returned and the global variable **errno** is set to **ERANGE**. If *start* does not point to a number, no conversion takes place and zero is returned.

Related Functions

strtol( ) and strtoul( )

system

```
#include <stdlib.h>
int system(const char *str);
```

The **system( )** function passes the string pointed to by *str* as a command to the command processor of the operating system.

If **system( )** is called with a null pointer, it will return nonzero if a command processor is present; otherwise, it will return zero. (C code executed in unhosted environments will not have access to a command processor.) The return value of **system( )** is implementation defined, but typically, zero is returned if the command was successfully executed, and a nonzero return value indicates an error.

Example

Using the Windows operating system, this program displays the contents of the current working directory:

```
#include <stdlib.h>

int main(void)
{
  return system("dir");
}
```

Related Function

exit( )

va_arg, va_copy, va_start, and va_end

```
#include <stdarg.h>
type va_arg(va_list argptr, type);
void va_copy(va_list target, va_list source);
void va_end(va_list argptr);
void va_start(va_list argptr, last_parm);
```

va_copy( ) was added by C99.

The **va_arg( )**, **va_start( )**, and **va_end( )** macros work together to allow a variable number of arguments to be passed to a function. The most common example of a function that takes a variable number of arguments is **printf( )**. The type **va_list** is defined by **<stdarg.h>**.

The general procedure for creating a function that can take a variable number of arguments is as follows. The function must have at least one known parameter, but may have more, prior to the variable parameter list. The rightmost known parameter is called the *last_parm*. The name of *last_parm* is used as the second parameter in a call to **va_start( )**. Before any of the variable-length parameters can be accessed, the argument pointer *argptr* must be initialized through a call to **va_start( )**. After that, parameters are returned via calls to **va_arg( )**, with *type* being the type of the next parameter. Finally, once all the parameters have been read, and prior to returning from the function, a call to **va_end( )** must be made to ensure that the stack is properly restored. If **va_end( )** is not called, a program crash is very likely.

The **va_copy( )** macro copies the argument list in *source* to *target*.

Example

This program uses **sum_series( )** to return the sum of a series of numbers. The first argument contains a count of the number of arguments to follow. In this example, the program sums the first five elements of the series:

$$\frac{1}{2} + \frac{1}{4} + \frac{1}{8} + \frac{1}{16} + \ldots \frac{1}{2^N}$$

The output displayed is **0.968750**.

```
#include <stdio.h>
#include <stdarg.h>

double sum_series(int num, ...);

/* Variable length argument example - sum a series. */
int main(void)
{
  double d;

  d = sum_series(5, 0.5, 0.25, 0.125, 0.0625, 0.03125);

  printf("Sum of series is %f.\n", d);
```

```
    return 0;
}

double sum_series(int num, ...)
{
    double sum=0.0, t;
    va_list argptr;

    /* initialize argptr */
    va_start(argptr, num);

    /* sum the series */
    for( ; num; num--) {
        t = va_arg(argptr, double); /* get next argument */
        sum += t;
    }

    /* do orderly shutdown */
    va_end(argptr);
    return sum;
}
```

Related Function

vprintf( )

wcstombs

```
#include <stdlib.h>
size_t wcstombs(char *out, const wchar_t *in, size_t size);
```

The **wcstombs( )** function converts the wide-character array pointed to by *in* into its multibyte equivalent and puts the result in the array pointed to by *out*. Only the first *size* bytes of *in* are converted. Conversion stops before that if the null terminator is encountered.

In C99, *out* and *in* are qualified by **restrict**.

If successful, **wcstombs( )** returns the number of bytes written. On failure, –1 is returned.

Related Functions

wctomb( ) and mbstowcs( )

wctomb

```
#include <stdlib.h>
int wctomb(char *out,  wchar_t in);
```

The **wctomb( )** function converts the wide character in *in* into its multibyte equivalent and puts the result in the object pointed to by *out*. The array pointed to by *out* must be at least **MB_CUR_MAX** characters long.

If successful, **wctomb( )** returns the number of bytes contained in the multibyte character. On failure, –1 is returned.

If *out* is null, **wctomb( )** returns nonzero if the multibyte character has state-dependent encodings; it returns zero otherwise.

Related Functions

wcstombs( ) and mbtowc( )

Chapter 19

Wide-Character Functions

In 1995 a number of wide-character functions were added to C89. These functions were also incorporated into C99. The wide-character functions operate on characters of type **wchar_t**, which are 16 bits. For the most part these functions parallel their **char** equivalents. For example, the function **iswspace( )** is the wide-character version of **isspace( )**. In general, the wide-character functions use the same names as their **char** equivalents, except that a "w" is added.

The wide-character functions use two headers: **<wchar.h>** and **<wctype.h>**. The header **<wctype.h>** defines the types **wint_t**, **wctrans_t**, and **wctype_t**. Many of the wide-character functions receive a wide character as a parameter. The type of this parameter is **wint_t**. It is capable of holding a wide character. The use of the **wint_t** type in the wide-character functions parallels the use of **int** in the **char**-based functions. The types **wctrans_t** and **wctype_t** are the types of objects used to represent a character mapping (character translation) and the classification of a character, respectively. Also defined is the wide-character EOF mark, which is defined as **WEOF**.

In addition to defining **win_t**, the header **<wchar.h>** defines the types **wchar_t**, **size_t**, and **mbstate_t**. The **wchar_t** type creates a wide-character object, and **size_t** is the type of value returned by **sizeof**. The **mbstate_t** type describes an object that holds the state of a multibyte to wide-character conversion. The **<wchar.h>** header also defines the macros **NULL**, **WEOF**, **WCHAR_MAX**, and **WCHAR_MIN**. The last two define the maximum and minimum value that can be held in an object of type **wchar_t**.

Since most of the wide-character functions simply parallel their **char** equivalents and are not frequently used by most C programmers, only a brief description of these functions is provided.

Wide-Character Classification Functions

The header **<wctype.h>** provides the prototypes for the wide-character functions that support character classification. These functions categorize wide characters as to their type or convert the case of a character. Table 19-1 lists these functions along with their **char** equivalents, which are described in Chapter 14.

Function	char Equivalent
int iswalnum(wint_t *ch*)	isalnum( )
int iswalpha(wint_t *ch*)	isalpha( )
int iswblank(wint_t *ch*)	isblank( ) (added by C99)

Table 19-1. *Wide-Character Classification Functions and Their **char** Equivalents*

Function	char Equivalent
int iswcntrl(wint_t *ch*)	iscntrl( )
int iswdigit(wint_t *ch*)	isdigit( )
int iswgraph(wint_t *ch*)	isgraph( )
int iswlower(wint_t *ch*)	islower( )
int iswprint(wint_t *ch*)	isprint( )
int iswpunct(wint_t *c*)	ispunct( )
int iswspace(wint_t *ch*)	isspace( )
int iswupper(wint_t *ch*)	isupper( )
int iswxdigit(wint_t *ch*)	isxdigit( )
wint_t towlower(wint_t *ch*)	tolower( )
wint_t towupper(wint_t *ch*)	toupper( )

Table 19-1.   *Wide-Character Classification Functions and Their **char** Equivalents (continued)*

In addition to the functions shown in Table 19-1, **<wctype.h>** defines the following functions, which provide an open-ended means of classifying characters.

wctype_t wctype(const char *attr*);

int iswctype(wint_t *ch*, wctype_t *attr_ob*);

The function **wctype( )** returns a value that can be passed to the *attr_ob* parameter to **iswctype( )**. The string pointed to by *attr* specifies a property that a character must have. This value can then be used to determine whether *ch* is a character that has that property. If it has the property, **iswctype( )** returns nonzero. Otherwise, it returns zero. The following property strings are defined for all execution environments:

alnum	digit	print	upper
alpha	graph	punct	xdigit
cntrl	lower	space	

For C99, the string "blank" is also defined.

The following fragment demonstrates the **wctype( )** and **iswctype( )** functions:

```
wctype_t x;

x = wctype("space");

if(iswctype(L' ', x))
  printf("Is a space.\n");
```

This displays "Is a space."

The functions **wctrans( )** and **towctrans( )** are also defined in **<wctype.h>**. They are shown here:

wctrans_t wctrans(const char *mapping);

wint_t towctrans(wint_t ch, wctrans_t mapping_ob);

The function **wctrans( )** returns a value that can be passed as the mapping_ob parameter to **towctrans( )**. The string pointed to by mapping specifies a mapping of one character to another. This value can then be used by **iswctrans( )** to map ch. The mapped value is returned. The following mapping strings are supported in all execution environments:

    tolower   toupper

The following sequence demonstrates **wctrans( )** and **towctrans( )**:

```
wctrans_t x;

x = wctrans("tolower");

wchar_t ch = towctrans(L'W', x);
printf("%c", (char) ch);
```

This displays a lowercase w.

Wide-Character I/O Functions

Several of the I/O functions described in Chapter 13 have wide-character implementations. These functions are shown in Table 19-2. The wide-character I/O functions use the header **<wchar.h>**. Notice that **swprintf( )** and **vswprintf( )** require an additional parameter not needed by their **char** equivalents.

In addition to those shown in the table, the following wide-character I/O function has been added:

int fwide(FILE *stream*, int *how*);

Function	char Equivalent
win_t fgetwc(FILE *stream*)	fgetc( )
wchar_t *fgetws(wchar_t *str*, int *num*, FILE *stream*)	fgets( ) In C99, *str* and *stream* are qualified by **restrict**.
wint_t fputwc(wchar_t *ch*, FILE *stream*)	fputc( )
int fputws(const wchar_t *str*, FILE *stream*)	fputs( ) In C99, *str* and *stream* are qualified by **restrict**.
int fwprintf(FILE *stream*, const wchar_t *fmt*, ...)	fprintf( ) In C99, *stream* and *fmt* are qualified by **restrict**.
int fwscanf(FILE *stream*, const wchar_t *fmt*, ...)	fscanf( ) In C99, *stream* and *fmt* are qualified by **restrict**.
wint_t getwc(FILE *stream*)	getc( )
wint_t getwchar(void)	getchar( )
wint_t putwc(wchar_t *ch*, FILE *stream*)	putc( )
wint_t putwchar(wchar_t *ch*)	putchar( )
int swprintf(wchar_t *str*, size_t *num*, const wchar_t *fmt*, ...)	sprintf( ) Note the addition of the parameter *num*, which limits the number of characters written to *str*. In C99, *str* and *fmt* are qualified by **restrict**.
int swscanf(const wchar_t *str*, const wchar_t *fmt*, ...)	sscanf( ) In C99, *str* and *fmt* are qualified by **restrict**.

Table 19-2. *Wide-Character I/O Functions and Their **char** Equivalents*

THE C STANDARD LIBRARY

Function	char Equivalent
wint_t ungetwc(wint_t *ch*, FILE *stream*)	ungetc( )
int vfwprintf(FILE *stream*, const wchar_t *fmt*, va_list *arg*)	vfprintf( ) In C99, *str* and *fmt* are qualified by **restrict**.

int vfwscanf(FILE * restrict *stream*,
            const wchar_t * restrict *fmt*,
            va_list *arg*);
	vfscanf( ) (added by C99)

int vswprintf(wchar_t *str*, size_t *num*, const wchar_t *fmt*, va_list *arg*)	vsprintf( ) Note the addition of the parameter *num*, which limits the number of characters written to *str*. In C99, *str* and *fmt* are qualified by **restrict**.

int vswscanf(const wchar_t * restrict *str*,
            const wchar_t * restrict *fmt*,
            va_list *arg*);
	vsscanf( ) (added by C99)

int vwprintf(const wchar_t *fmt*, va_list *arg*)	vprintf( ) In C99, *str* and *fmt* are qualified by **restrict**.
int vwscanf(const wchar_t * restrict *fmt*, va_list *arg*);	vscanf( ) (added by C99),
int wprintf(const wchar_t *fmt*, ...)	printf( ) In C99, *fmt* is qualified by **restrict**.
int wscanf(const wchar_t *fmt*, ...)	scanf( ) In C99, *fmt* is qualified by **restrict**.

Table 19-2. *Wide-Character I/O Functions and Their **char** Equivalents* (continued)

If *how* is positive, **fwide( )** makes *stream* a wide-character stream. If *how* is negative, **fwide( )** makes *stream* into a **char** stream. If *how* is zero, *stream* is unaffected. If the stream has already been oriented to either wide or normal characters, it will not be changed. The function returns positive if the stream uses wide characters, negative if the stream uses **char**s, and zero if the stream has not yet been oriented. A stream's orientation is also determined by its first use.

Wide-Character String Functions

There are wide-character versions of the string manipulation functions described in Chapter 14. These are shown in Table 19-3. They use the header **<wchar.h>**. Note that **wcstok( )** requires an additional parameter not used by its **char** equivalent.

Function	char Equivalent
wchar_t *wcscat(wchar_t *str1, const wchar_t *str2)	strcat( ) In C99, str1 and str2 are qualified by **restrict**.
wchar_t *wcschr(const wchar_t *str, wchar_t ch)	strchr( )
int wcscmp(const wchar_t *str1, const wchar_t *str2)	strcmp( )
int wcscoll(const wchar_t *str1, const wchar_t *str2)	strcoll( )
size_t wcscspn(const wchar_t *str1, const wchar_t *str2)	strcspn( )
wchar_t *wcscpy(wchar_t *str1, const wchar_t *str2)	strcpy( ) In C99, str1 and str2 are qualified by **restrict**.
size_t wcslen(const wchar_t *str)	strlen( )

wchar_t *wcsncpy(wchar_t *str1,
    const wchar_t str2,
    size_t num)
	strncpy( )
	In C99, str1 and str2 are qualified by **restrict**.

wchar_t *wcsncat(wchar_t *str1,
    const wchar_t str2,
    size_t num)
	strncat( )
	In C99, str1 and str2 are qualified by **restrict**.

int wcsncmp(const wchar_t *str1,
    const wchar_t *str2,
    size_t num)
	strncmp( )

Table 19-3. *Wide-Character String Functions and Their **char** Equivalents*

Function	char Equivalent
wchar_t *wcspbrk(const wchar_t *str1, const wchar_t *str2)	strpbrk( )
wchar_t *wcsrchr(const wchar_t *str, wchar_t ch)	strrchr( )
size_t wcsspn(const wchar_t *str1, const wchar_t *str2)	strspn( )
wchar_t *wcstok(wchar_t *str1, const wchar_t *str2, wchar_t **endptr)	strtok( ) Here, endptr is a pointer that holds information necessary to continue the tokenizing process. In C99, str1, str2, and endptr are qualified by **restrict**.
wchar_t *wcsstr(const wchar_t *str1, const wchar_t *str2)	strstr( )
size_t wcsxfrm(wchar_t *str1, const wchar_t *str2, size_t num)	strxfrm( ) In C99, str1 and str2 are qualified by **restrict**.

Table 19-3.   *Wide-Character String Functions and Their **char** Equivalents* (continued)

Wide-Character String Conversion Functions

The functions shown in Table 19-4 provide wide-character versions of the standard numeric and time conversion functions. These functions use the header **<wchar.h>**.

Function	char Equivalent
size_t wcsftime(wchar_t *str, size_t max, const wchar_t *fmt, const struct tm *ptr)	strftime( ) In C99 str, fmt, and ptr are qualified by **restrict**.
double wcstod(const wchar_t *start, wchar_t **end);	strtod( ) In C99 start and end are qualified by **restrict**.

Table 19-4.   *Wide-Character Conversion Functions and Their **char** Equivalents*

float wcstof(const wchar_t * restrict *start*, wchar_t ** restrict *end*);	strtof( ) (added by C99)
long double wcstold(const wchar_t * restrict *start*, wchar_t ** restrict *end*);	strtold( ) (added by C99)
long int wcstol(const wchar_t **start*, wchar_t ***end*, int *radix*)	strtol( ) In C99 *start* and *end* are qualified by **restrict**.
long long int wcstoll(const wchar_t * restrict *start*, wchar_t ** restrict *end*, int *radix*)	strtoll( ) (added by C99)
unsigned long int wcstoul(const wchar_t * restrict *start*, wchar_t ** restrict *end*, int *radix*)	strtoul( ) In C99 *start* and *end* are qualified by **restrict**.
unsigned long long int wcstoull(const wchar_t **start*, wchar_t ***end*, int *radix*)	strtoull( ) (added by C99)

Table 19-4.   *Wide-Character Conversion Functions and Their **char** Equivalents (continued)*

Wide-Character Array Functions

The standard character array–manipulation functions, such as **memcpy( )**, also have wide-character equivalents. They are shown in Table 19-5. These functions use the header **<wchar.h>**.

Function	**char Equivalent**
wchar_t *wmemchr(const wchar_t **str*, wchar_t *ch*, size_t *num*)	memchr( )
int wmemcmp(const wchar_t **str1*, const wchar_t **str2*, size_t *num*)	memcmp( )

Table 19-5.   *Wide-Character Array Functions and Their **char** Equivalents*

Function	char Equivalent

wchar_t *wmemcpy(wchar_t *str1,
          const wchar_t *str2,
          size_t num)
	memcpy( )
	In C99 str1 and str2 are
	qualified by **restrict**.

wchar_t *wmemmove(wchar_t *str1,
          const wchar_t *str2,
          size_t num)
	memmove( )

wchar_t *wmemset(wchar_t *str, wchar_t ch, size_t num)	memset( )

Table 19-5.   *Wide-Character Array Functions and Their **char** Equivalents* (continued)

Multibyte/Wide-Character Conversion Functions

The standard function library supplies various functions that support conversions between multibyte and wide characters. These functions are shown in Table 19-6. They use the header **<wchar.h>**. Many of these functions are *restartable* versions of the normal multibyte functions. The restartable version utilizes the state information passed to it in a parameter of type **mbstate_t**. If this parameter is null, the function will provide its own **mbstate_t** object.

Function	Description
win_t btowc(int ch)	Converts ch into its wide-character equivalent and returns the result. Returns **WEOF** on error or if ch is not a one-byte, multibyte character.

Table 19-6.   *Wide-Character/Multibyte Conversion Functions*

Function	Description
size_t mbrlen(const char *str, size_t *num*, mbstate_t *state*)	Restartable version of **mblen( )** as described by *state*. Returns a positive value that indicates the length of the next multibyte character. Zero is returned if the next character is null. A negative value is returned if an error occurs. In C99, *str* and *state* are qualified by **restrict**.
size_t mbrtowc(wchar_t *out*, const char *in*, size_t *num*, mbstate_t *state*)	Restartable version of **mbtowc( )** as described by *state*. Returns a positive value that indicates the length of the next multibyte character. Zero is returned if the next character is null. A value of –1 is returned if an error occurs and the macro **EILSEQ** is assigned to **errno**. If the conversion is incomplete, –2 is returned. In C99, *out*, *in*, and *state* are qualified by **restrict**.
int mbsinit(const mbstate_t *state*)	Returns true if *state* represents an initial conversion state.
size_t mbsrtowcs(wchar_t *out*, const char **in*, size_t *num*, mbstate_t *state*)	Restartable version of **mbstowcs( )** as described by *state*. Also, **mbsrtowcs( )** differs from **mbstowcs( )** in that *in* is an indirect pointer to the source array. If an error occurs, the macro **EILSEQ** is assigned to **errno**. In C99, *out*, *in*, and *state* are qualified by **restrict**.
size_t wcrtomb(char *out*, wchar_t *ch*, mbstate_t *state*)	Restartable version of **wctomb( )** as described by *state*. If an error occurs, the macro **EILSEQ** is assigned to **errno**. In C99, *out* and *state* are qualified by **restrict**.

Table 19-6. *Wide-Character/Multibyte Conversion Functions* (continued)

Function	Description

size_t wcsrtombs(char *out,
        const wchar_t **in,
        size_t num,
        mbstate_t *state)
	Restartable version of **wcstombs( )** as described by *state*. Also, **wcsrtombs( )** differs from **wcstombs( )** in that *in* is an indirect pointer to the source array. If an error occurs, the macro **EILSEQ** is assigned to **errno**.
	In C99, *out*, *in*, and *state* are qualified by **restrict**.

int wctob(wint_t *ch*)	Converts *ch* into its one-byte, multibyte equivalent. It returns **EOF** on failure.

Table 19-6. *Wide-Character/Multibyte Conversion Functions* (continued)

The
Complete
Reference

Chapter 20

Library Features Added by C99

T he C99 standard increased the size of the C library two ways. First, it added functions to headers previously defined by C89. For example, significant additions were made to the mathematics library supported by the **<math.h>** header. These additional functions were covered in the preceding chapters. Second, new categories of functions, ranging from support for complex arithmetic to type-generic macros, were created, along with new headers to support them. These new library elements are described in this chapter.

The Complex Library

C99 adds complex arithmetic capabilities to C. The complex library is supported by the **<complex.h>** header. The following macros are defined:

Macro	Expands To
complex	_Complex
imaginary	_Imaginary
_Complex_I	(const float _Complex) *i*
_Imaginary_I	(const float _Imaginary) *i*
I	_Imaginary_I (or _Complex_I if imaginary types are not supported)

Here, *i* represents the imaginary value, which is the square root of –1. Support for imaginary types is optional.

   _Complex and **_Imaginary**, rather than **complex** and **imaginary**, were specified as keywords by C99 because many existing C89 programs had already defined their own custom complex data types using the names **complex** and **imaginary**. By using the keywords **_Complex** and **_Imaginary**, C99 avoids breaking preexisting code. For new programs, however, it is best to include **<complex.h>** and then use the **complex** and **imaginary** macros.

Note *C++ defines the **complex** class, which, of course, provides a different way of performing complex math.*

   The complex math functions are shown in Table 20-1. Notice that **float complex**, **double complex**, and **long double complex** versions of each function are defined. The **float complex** version uses the suffix **f**, and the **long double complex** version uses the suffix **l**. Also, angles are in radians.

Function	Description

float cabsf(float complex *arg*);
double cabs(double complex *arg*);
long double cabsl(long double complex *arg*);
	Returns the complex absolute value of *arg*

float complex cacosf(float complex *arg*);
double complex cacos(double complex *arg*);
long double complex cacosl(long double complex *arg*);
	Returns the complex arc cosine of *arg*

float complex cacoshf(float complex *arg*);
double complex cacosh(double complex *arg*);
long double complex cacoshl(long double complex *arg*);
	Returns the complex arc hyperbolic cosine of *arg*

float cargf(float complex *arg*);
double carg(double complex *arg*);
long double cargl(long double complex *arg*);
	Returns the phase angle of *arg*

float complex casinf(float complex *arg*);
double complex casin(double complex *arg*);
long double complex casinl(long double complex *arg*);
	Returns the complex arc sine of *arg*

float complex casinhf(float complex *arg*);
double complex casinh(double complex *arg*);
long double complex casinhl(long double complex *arg*);
	Returns the complex arc hyperbolic sine of *arg*

float complex catanf(float complex *arg*);
double complex catan(double complex *arg*);
long double complex catanl(long double complex *arg*);
	Returns the complex arc tangent of *arg*

float complex catanhf(float complex *arg*);
double complex catanh(double complex *arg*);
long double complex catanhl(long double complex *arg*);
	Returns the complex arc hyperbolic tangent of *arg*

Table 20-1. *The Complex Math Functions*

Function

float complex ccosf(float complex *arg*);
double complex ccos(double complex *arg*);
long double complex ccosl(long double complex *arg*);

float complex ccoshf(float complex *arg*);
double complex ccosh(double complex *arg*);
long double complex ccoshl(long double complex *arg*);

float complex cexpf(float complex *arg*);
double complex cexp(double complex *arg*);
long double complex cexpl(long double complex *arg*);

float complex cimagf(float complex *arg*);
double complex cimag(double complex *arg*);
long double complex cimagl(long double complex *arg*);

float complex clogf(float complex *arg*);
double complex clog(double complex *arg*);
long double complex clogl(long double complex *arg*);

float complex conjf(float complex *arg*);
double complex conj(double complex *arg*);
long double complex conjl(long double complex *arg*);

float complex cpowf(float complex *a*,
            long double complex *b*);
double complex cpow(double complex *a*,
            double complex *b*);
long double complex cpowl(long double complex *a*,
            long double complex *b*);

Description

Returns the complex cosine of *arg*

Returns the complex hyperbolic cosine of *arg*

Returns the complex value e^{arg}, where e is the natural logarithm base

Returns the imaginary part of *arg*

Returns the complex natural logarithm of *arg*

Returns the complex conjugate of *arg*

Returns the complex value of a^b

Table 20-1. *The Complex Math Functions (continued)*

Function	Description

float complex cprojf(float complex *arg*);
double complex cproj(double complex *arg*);
long double complex cprojl(long double complex *arg*);
	Returns the projection of *arg* onto the Riemann sphere

float crealf(float complex *arg*);
double creal(double complex *arg*);
long double creall(long double complex *arg*);
	Returns the real part of *arg*

float complex csinf(float complex *arg*);
double complex csin(double complex *arg*);
long double complex csinl(long double complex *arg*);
	Returns the complex sine of *arg*

float complex csinhf(float complex *arg*);
double complex csinh(double complex *arg*);
long double complex csinhl(long double complex *arg*);
	Returns the complex hyperbolic sine of *arg*

float complex csqrtf(float complex *arg*);
double complex csqrt(double complex *arg*);
long double complex csqrtl(long double complex *arg*);
	Returns the complex square root of *arg*

float complex ctanf(float complex *arg*);
double complex ctan(double complex *arg*);
long double complex ctanl(long double complex *arg*);
	Returns the complex tangent of *arg*

float complex ctanhf(float complex *arg*);
double complex ctanh(double complex *arg*);
long double complex ctanhl(long double complex *arg*);
	Returns the complex hyperbolic tangent of *arg*

Table 20-1.   *The Complex Math Functions (continued)*

The Floating-Point Environment Library

In the header **<fenv.h>**, C99 declares functions that access the floating-point environment. These functions are shown in Table 20-2. The **<fenv.h>** header also defines the types **fenv_t** and **fexcept_t**, which represent the floating-point environment and the floating-point status flags, respectively. The macro **FE_DFL_ENV** specifies a pointer to the default floating-point environment defined at the start of program execution.

The following floating-point exception macros are defined:

FE_DIVBYZERO	FE_INEXACT	FW_INVALID
FE_OVERFLOW	FE_UNDERFLOW	FE_ALL_EXCEPT

Any combination of these macros can be stored in an **int** object by ORing them together.

The following rounding-direction macros are defined:

FE_DOWNWARD   FE_TONEAREST   FE_TOWARDZERO   FE_UPWARD

These macros indicate the method that is used to round values.

In order for the floating-point environment flags to be tested, the pragma **FENV_ACCESS** must be set to the on position. Whether floating-point flag access is on or off by default is implementation-defined.

The <stdint.h> Header

The C99 header **<stdint.h>** does not declare any functions, but it does define a large number of integer types and macros. The integer types are used to declare integers of known sizes, or integers that manifest a specified trait.

Macros of the form **intN_t** specify an integer with N bits. For example, **int16_t** specifies a 16-bit signed integer. Macros of the form **uintN_t** specify an unsigned integer with N bits. For example, **uint32_t** specifies a 32-bit unsigned integer. Macros with the values 8, 16, 32, and 64 for N will be available in all environments that offer integers in these widths.

Macros of the form **int_leastN_t** specify an integer with at least N bits. Macros of the form **uint_leastN_t** specify an unsigned integer with at least N bits. Macros with the values 8, 16, 32, and 64 for N will be available in all environments. For example, **int_least16_t** is a valid type.

Macros of the form **int_fastN_t** specify the fastest integer type that has at least N bits. Macros of the form **uint_fastN_t** specify the fastest unsigned integer type that has at least N bits. Macros with the values 8, 16, 32, and 64 for N will be available in all environments. For example, **int_fast32_t** is valid in all settings.

Function	Description
void feclearexcept(int *ex*);	Clears the exceptions specified by *ex*.
void fegetexceptflag(fexcept_t *fptr*, int *ex*);	The state of the floating-point exception flags specified by *ex* are stored in the variable pointed to by *fptr*.
void feraiseexcept(int *ex*);	Raises the exceptions specified by *ex*.
void fesetexceptflag(const fexcept_t *fptr*, int *ex*);	Sets the floating-point status flags specified by *ex* to the state of the flags in the object pointed to by *fptr*.
int fetestexcept(int *ex*);	Bitwise ORs the exceptions specified in *ex* with the current floating-point status flags and returns the result.
int fegetround(void);	Returns a value that indicates the current rounding direction.
int fesetround(int *direction*);	Sets the current rounding direction to that specified by *direction*. A return value of zero indicates success.
void fegetenv(fenv_t *envptr*);	The object pointed to by *envptr* receives the floating-point environment.
int feholdexcept(fenv_t *envptr*);	Causes nonstop floating-point exception handling to be used. It also stores the floating-point environment in the variable pointed to by *envptr* and clears the status flags. It returns zero if successful.
void fesetenv(const fenv_t *envptr*);	Sets the floating-point environment to that pointed to by *envptr*, but does not raise floating-point exceptions. This object must have been obtained by calling either **fegetenv( )** or **feholdexcept( )**.
void feupdateenv(const fenv_t *envptr*);	Sets the floating-point environment to that pointed to by *envptr*. It first saves any current exceptions and then raises these exceptions after the environment pointed to by *envptr* has been set. The object pointed to by *envptr* must have been obtained by calling either **fegetenv( )** or **feholdexcept( )**.

Table 20-2.   *Floating-Point Environment Functions*

The type **intmax_t** specifies a maximum-sized signed integer, and the type **uintmax_t** specifies a maximum-sized unsigned integer.

Also defined are the **intptr_t** and **uintptr_t** types. These can be used to create integers that can hold pointers. These types are optional.

<stdint.h> defines several functionlike macros that expand into constants of a specified integer type. These macros have the following general forms,

INT*N*_C(*value*)

UINT*N*_C(*value*)

where *N* is the bit-width of the desired type. Each macro creates a constant that has at least *N* bits containing the specified value.

Also defined are the macros

INTMAX_C(*value*)

UINTMAX_C(*value*)

These create maximum-width constants of the specified value.

Integer Format Conversion Functions

C99 adds a few specialized integer format conversion functions that allow you to convert to and from greatest-width integers. The header that supports these functions is **<inttypes.h>**, which includes **<stdint.h>**. The **<inttypes.h>** header defines one type: the structure **imaxdiv_t**, which holds the value returned by the **imaxdiv( )** function. The integer conversion functions are shown in Table 20-3.

<inttypes.h> also defines many macros that can be used in calls to the **printf( )** and **scanf( )** family of functions, to specify various integer conversions. The **printf( )** macros begin with **PRI**, and the **scanf( )** macros begin with **SCN**. These prefixes are then followed by a conversion specifier, such as **d** or **u,** and then a type name, such as *N*, **MAX**, **PTR**, **FAST***N*, or **LEAST***N*, where *N* specifies the number of bits. Consult your compiler's documentation for a precise list of conversion macros supported.

Type-Generic Math Macros

As described in Chapter 15, C99 defines three versions for most mathematical functions: one for **float**, one for **double**, and one for **long double** parameters. For example, C99 defines these functions for the sine operation:

double sin(double *arg*);

float sinf(float *arg*);

long double sinl(long double *arg*);

Function	Description
intmax_t imaxabs(intmax_t *arg*);	Returns the absolute value of *arg*.
imaxdiv_t imaxdiv(intmax_t *numerator*, intmax_t *denominator*);	Returns an **imaxdiv_t** structure that contains the outcome of *numerator / denominator*. The quotient is in the **quot** field, and the remainder is in the **rem** field. Both **quot** and **rem** are of type **intmax_t**.
intmax_t strtoimax(const char * restrict *start*, char ** restrict *end*, int *base*);	The greatest-width integer version of **strtol**( ).
uintmax_t strtoumax(const char * restrict *start*, char ** restrict *end*, int *base*);	The greatest-width integer version of **strtoul**( ).
intmax_t wcstoimax(const char * restrict *start*, char ** restrict *end*, int *base*);	The greatest-width integer version of **wcstol**( ).
uintmax_t wcstoumax(const char * restrict *start*, char ** restrict *end*, int *base*);	The greatest-width integer version of **wcstoul**( ).

Table 20-3. *Greatest-Width Integer Conversion Functions*

The operation of all three functions is the same, except for the data upon which they operate. In all cases, the **double** version is the original function defined by C89. The **float** and **long double** versions were added by C99. As explained in Chapter 15, the **float** versions use the **f** suffix, and **long double** versions use the l suffix. By providing three different functions, C99 enables you to call the one that most precisely fits the circumstances. As described earlier in this chapter, the complex math functions also provide three versions of each function, for the same reason.

As useful as the three versions of the math and complex functions are, they are not particularly convenient. First, you have to remember to specify the proper suffix for the data you are passing. This is both tedious and error prone. Second, if you change the type of data being passed to one of these functions during project development, you will need to remember to change the suffix as well—again, tedious and error prone. To address these (and other) issues, C99 defines a set of *type-generic macros* that can be used in place of the math or complex functions. These macros automatically translate into the proper function based upon the type of the argument. The type-generic macros are defined in **<tgmath.h>**, which automatically includes **<math.h>** and **<complex.h>**.

The type-generic macros use the same names as the **double** version of the math or complex functions to which they translate. (These are also the same names defined by C89.) Thus, the type-generic macro for **sin( )**, **sinf( )**, and **sinl( )** is **sin( )**. The type-generic macro for **csin( )**, **csinf( )**, and **csinl( )** is also **sin( )**. As explained, the proper function is called based upon the argument. For example, given

```
long double ldbl;
float complex fcmplx;
```

then,

```
cos(ldbl)
```

translates into

```
cosl(ldbl)
```

and

```
cos(fcmplx)
```

translates into

```
ccosf(fcmplx)
```

As these examples illustrate, the use of type-generic macros offers the programmer convenience without loss of performance, precision, or portability.

The <stdbool.h> Header

C99 adds the header **<stdbool.h>**, which supports the **_Bool** data type. Although it does not define any functions, it does define these four macros:

Macro	Expands To
bool	_Bool
true	1
false	0
_ _bool_true_false_are_defined	1

The reason that C99 specified **_Bool** rather than **bool** as a keyword is that many existing C programs had already defined their own custom versions of **bool**. By defining the Boolean type as **_Bool**, C99 avoids breaking this preexisting code. The same reasoning goes for **true** and **false**. However, for new programs, it is best to include **<stdbool.h>** and then use the **bool**, **true**, and **false** macros. One advantage of doing so is that it allows you to create code that is compatible with C++.

The Complete Reference

Part IV

Algorithms and Applications

The purpose of Part Four is to show how C can be applied to a wide range of programming tasks. In the process, many useful algorithms and applications that illustrate several aspects of the C language are presented. Many examples contained in Part Four can be used as starting points for your own C projects.

The Complete Reference

Chapter 21

Sorting and Searching

In the world of computers, sorting and searching are two of the most fundamental and extensively analyzed tasks. Sorting and searching routines are used in almost all database programs as well as in compilers, interpreters, and operating systems. This chapter introduces the basics of sorting and searching. As you will see, they illustrate several important C programming techniques. Since the point of sorting data is generally to make searching that data easier and faster, sorting is discussed first.

Sorting

Sorting is the process of arranging a set of similar information into an increasing or decreasing order. Sorting is one of the most intellectually pleasing categories of algorithms because the process is so well defined. Sorting algorithms have also been extensively analyzed and are well understood. Unfortunately, because sorting is so well understood, it is sometimes taken for granted. When data needs to be sorted, many programmers simply use the standard **qsort( )** function provided by the C standard library. However, different approaches to sorting have different characteristics. Although some sorts may be better than others on average, no sort is perfect for all situations. Therefore, a useful addition to any programmer's toolbox is a wide variety of sorts.

Before starting, it will be useful to explain briefly why **qsort( )** is not the answer to all sorting tasks. First, you cannot apply a generalized function like **qsort( )** to every situation. For example, it will only sort arrays in memory. It can't sort data stored in a linked list, for example. Second, **qsort( )** is parameterized so that it can operate on a wide variety of data, but this causes it to run more slowly than would an equivalent sort that operates on only one type of data. Finally, as you will see, although the quicksort algorithm used by **qsort( )** is very effective in the general case, it may not be the best sort for specialized situations.

There are two general categories of sorting algorithms: algorithms that sort random-access objects, such as arrays or random-access disk files, and algorithms that sort sequential objects, such as disk or tape files, or linked lists. This chapter is concerned only with the first category, because it is most relevant to the average programmer.

Most often when information is sorted, only a portion of the information is used as the sort key. The *key* is that part of the data that determines which item comes before another. Thus, the key is used in comparisons, but when an exchange is made, the entire data structure is swapped. For example, in a mailing list the postal code might be used as the key, but the entire address is sorted. For the sake of simplicity, the next few examples will sort character arrays, in which the key and the data are the same. Later, you will see how to adapt these methods to sort any type of data structure.

Classes of Sorting Algorithms

There are three general methods for sorting arrays:

- Exchange

■ Selection

■ Insertion

To understand these three methods, imagine a deck of cards. To sort the cards by using *exchange*, spread them on a table, face up, and then exchange out-of-order cards until the deck is ordered. Using *selection*, spread the cards on the table, select the card of lowest value, take it out of the deck, and hold it in your hand. Then, from the remaining cards on the table, select the lowest card and place it behind the one already in your hand. This process continues until all the cards are in your hand. The cards in your hand will be sorted when you finish the process. To sort the cards by using *insertion*, hold all the cards in your hand. Place one card at a time on the table, always inserting it in the correct position. The deck will be sorted when you have no cards in your hand.

Judging Sorting Algorithms

There are many different sorting algorithms. They all have some merit, but the general criteria for judging a sorting algorithm are

■ How fast can it sort information in an average case?

■ How fast are its best and worst cases?

■ Does it exhibit natural or unnatural behavior?

■ Does it rearrange elements with equal keys?

Look closely at these criteria now. Clearly, how fast a particular algorithm sorts is of great concern. The speed with which an array can be sorted is directly related to the number of comparisons and the number of exchanges that take place, with exchanges taking more time. A *comparison* occurs when one array element is compared to another; an *exchange* happens when two elements are swapped. The run times of some sort routines increase exponentially, while others increase logarithmically relative to the number of items being sorted.

The best- and worst-case run times are important if you expect to encounter one of these situations frequently. Often a sort has a good average case but a terrible worst case.

A sort is said to exhibit *natural* behavior if it works least when the list is already in order, works harder as the list becomes less ordered, and works hardest when a list is in inverse order. How hard a sort works is based on the number of comparisons and exchanges that it makes.

To understand why rearranging elements with equal keys may be important, imagine a database such as a mailing list, which is sorted on a main key and a subkey. The main sort key is the postal code, and within postal codes, the last name is the subkey. When a new address is added to the list and the list is re-sorted, you do not want the subkeys (that is, the last names within postal codes) to be rearranged. To guarantee that this doesn't happen, a sort must not exchange keys of equal value.

The discussion that follows first examines the representative sorts from each category and then analyzes the efficiency of each. Later, you'll see improved sorting methods.

The Bubble Sort

The most well-known (and infamous) sort is the *bubble sort*. Its popularity is derived from its catchy name and its simplicity. However, for general-purpose sorting, it is one of the worst sorts ever conceived.

The bubble sort is an exchange sort. It involves the repeated comparison and, if necessary, the exchange of adjacent elements. The elements are like bubbles in a tank of water—each seeks its own level. A simple form of the bubble sort is shown here:

```
/* The Bubble Sort. */
void bubble(char *items, int count)
{
  register int a, b;
  register char t;

  for(a=1; a < count; ++a)
    for(b=count-1; b >= a; --b) {
      if(items[b-1] > items[b]) {
        /* exchange elements */
        t = items[b-1];
        items[b-1] = items[b];
        items[b] = t;
      }
    }
}
```

Here, **items** is a pointer to the character array to be sorted, and **count** is the number of elements in the array. The bubble sort is driven by two loops. Given that there are **count** elements in the array, the outer loop causes the array to be scanned **count**–1 times. This ensures that, in the worst case, every element is in its proper position when the function terminates. The inner loop actually performs the comparisons and exchanges. (A slightly improved version of the bubble sort terminates if no exchanges occur, but this adds another comparison in each pass through the inner loop.)

You can use this version of the bubble sort to sort a character array into ascending order. For example, the following short program sorts a string entered by the user:

```
/* Sort Driver */

#include <string.h>
#include <stdio.h>
#include <stdlib.h>

void bubble(char *items, int count);

int main(void)
{
  char s[255];

  printf("Enter a string:");
  gets(s);
  bubble(s, strlen(s));
  printf("The sorted string is: %s.\n", s);

  return 0;
}
```

To see how the bubble sort works, assume that the array to be sorted is **dcab**. Each pass is shown here:

Initial	d c a b
Pass 1	a d c b
Pass 2	a b d c
Pass 3	a b c d

In analyzing any sort, it is useful to have an idea about how many comparisons and exchanges will be performed for the best, average, and worst case. Because compiler optimizations, differences in processors, and implementation details can affect the characteristics of the executable code, we won't worry about precise values for these quantities. Instead, we will concentrate on the general efficiency of each algorithm.

With the bubble sort, the number of comparisons is always the same because the two **for** loops repeat the specified number of times whether the list is initially ordered or not. This means that the bubble sort always performs

$$1/2(n^2-n)$$

comparisons, where n is the number of elements to be sorted. This formula is derived from the fact that the outer loop executes $n-1$ times and the inner loop executes an average of $n/2$ times. Multiplied together, these numbers result in the preceding formula.

Notice the n^2 term in the preceding formula. The bubble sort is said to be an *n-squared* algorithm because its execution time is proportional to the square of the number of elements that it is sorting. Frankly, an *n*-squared algorithm is ineffective when applied to a large number of elements because execution time grows exponentially relative to the number of elements being sorted. Figure 21-1 shows how execution time increases relative to the size of the array.

For the bubble sort, the number of exchanges is zero for the best case—an already sorted list. However, the number of exchanges for the average- and worst-case exchanges are also on the order of *n*-squared.

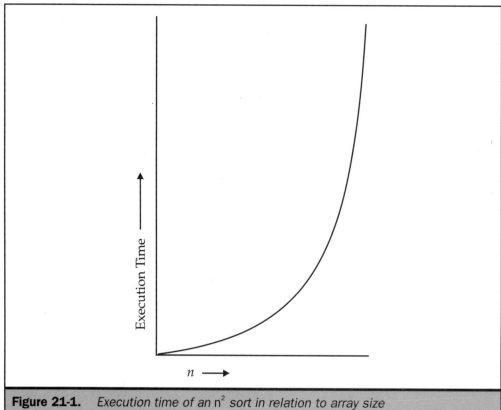

Figure 21-1.   *Execution time of an n² sort in relation to array size*

You can make slight improvements to the bubble sort in an attempt to speed it up. For example, the bubble sort has one peculiarity: An out-of-order element at the large end (such as "a" in the **dcab** example) goes to its proper position in one pass, but a misplaced element in the small end (such as "d") rises very slowly to its proper place. This suggests an improvement to the bubble sort. Instead of always reading the array in the same direction, alternate passes could reverse direction. In this way, greatly out-of-place elements travel quickly to their correct position. This version of the bubble sort is called the *shaker sort*, because it imparts the effect of a shaking motion to the array. The code that follows shows how a shaker sort can be implemented.

```c
/* The Shaker Sort. */
void shaker(char *items, int count)
{
  register int a;
  int exchange;
  char t;

  do {
    exchange = 0;
    for(a=count-1; a > 0; --a) {
      if(items[a-1] > items[a]) {
        t = items[a-1];
        items[a-1] = items[a];
        items[a] = t;
        exchange = 1;
      }
    }

    for(a=1; a < count; ++a) {
      if(items[a-1] > items[a]) {
        t = items[a-1];
        items[a-1] = items[a];
        items[a] = t;
        exchange = 1;
      }
    }
  } while(exchange); /* sort until no exchanges take place */
}
```

Although the shaker sort improves the bubble sort, it still executes on the order of an *n*-squared algorithm. This is because the number of comparisons has not been changed and the number of exchanges has been reduced by only a relatively small constant. The shaker sort is better than the bubble sort, but better sorts exist.

Sorting by Selection

A *selection sort* selects the element with the lowest value and exchanges it with the first element. Then, from the remaining *n*–1 elements, the element with the smallest key is found and exchanged with the second element, and so forth. The exchanges continue to the last two elements. For example, if the selection method were used on the array **dcab**, each pass would look like this:

Initial	d c a b
Pass 1	a c d b
Pass 2	a b d c
Pass 3	a b c d

The code that follows shows the basic selection sort.

```
/* The Selection Sort. */
void select(char *items, int count)
{
  register int a, b, c;
  int exchange;
  char t;

  for(a=0; a < count-1; ++a) {
    exchange = 0;
    c = a;
    t = items[a];
    for(b=a+1; b < count; ++b) {
      if(items[b] < t) {
        c = b;
        t = items[b];
        exchange = 1;
      }
    }
    if(exchange) {
      items[c] = items[a];
      items[a] = t;
    }
  }
}
```

Unfortunately, as with the bubble sort, the outer loop executes $n-1$ times and the inner loop averages $n/2$ times. As a result, the selection sort requires

$$1/2(n^2-n)$$

comparisons. Thus, this is an n-squared algorithm, which makes it too slow for sorting a large number of items. Although the number of comparisons for both the bubble sort and the selection sort is the same, the number of exchanges in the average case is far less for the selection sort.

Sorting by Insertion

The *insertion sort* is the third and last of the simple sorting algorithms. It initially sorts the first two members of the array. Next, the algorithm inserts the third member into its sorted position in relation to the first two members. Then it inserts the fourth element into the list of three elements. The process continues until all elements have been sorted. For example, given the array **dcab**, each pass of the insertion sort is shown here:

Initial	d c a b
Pass 1	c d a b
Pass 2	a c d b
Pass 3	a b c d

The code for a version of the insertion sort is shown next.

```
/* The Insertion Sort. */
void insert(char *items, int count)
{

  register int a, b;
  char t;

  for(a=1; a < count; ++a) {
    t = items[a];
    for(b=a-1; (b >= 0) && (t < items[b]); b--)
      items[b+1] = items[b];
    items[b+1] = t;
  }
}
```

Unlike the bubble and selection sorts, the number of comparisons that occur during an insertion sort depends upon how the list is initially ordered. If the list is in order, the number of comparisons is $n-1$; otherwise, its performance is on the order of n-squared.

In general, for worst cases the insertion sort is as bad as the bubble sort and selection sort, and for average cases it is only slightly better. However, the insertion sort does have two advantages. First, it behaves naturally. That is, it works the least when the array is already sorted and the hardest when the array is sorted in inverse order. This makes the insertion sort excellent for lists that are almost in order. The second advantage is that it leaves the order of equal keys the same. This means that if a list is sorted by two keys, it remains sorted for both keys after an insertion sort.

Even though the number of comparisons may be fairly low for certain sets of data, the array must be shifted over each time an element is placed in its proper location. As a result, the number of moves can be significant.

Improved Sorts

All of the algorithms in the preceding sections have the fatal flaw of executing in n-squared time. For large amounts of data, this makes the sorts very slow. In fact, at some point, the sorts would be too slow to use. Unfortunately, horror stories of "the sort that took three days" are often real. When a sort takes too long, it is usually the fault of the underlying algorithm. However, the first response is often "let's hand optimize," perhaps by using assembly language. Although manual optimization does sometimes speed up a routine by a constant factor, if the underlying algorithm is inefficient, the sort will be slow no matter how optimal the coding. Remember: When a routine is running relative to n^2, increasing the speed of the code or the computer only causes a small improvement because the rate at which the run time is increasing is exponential. (In essence, the n^2 curve in Figure 21-1 is shifted to the right slightly, but is otherwise unchanged.) The rule of thumb is that if the underlying algorithm is too slow, no amount of hand optimizations will make it fast enough. The solution is to use a better sorting algorithm.

Two excellent sorts are described here. The first is the *Shell sort*. The second, the *quicksort*, is usually considered the best sorting routine. Both of these improved sorts are substantially better in their general performance than any of the simple sorts shown earlier.

The Shell Sort

The Shell sort is named after its inventor, D. L. Shell. However, the name probably stuck because its method of operation is often described in terms of seashells piled upon one another. The general sorting method is derived from the insertion sort and is based on diminishing increments. Consider the diagram in Figure 21-2. First, all elements that are three positions apart are sorted. Then, all elements that are two positions apart are sorted. Finally, all elements adjacent to each other are sorted.

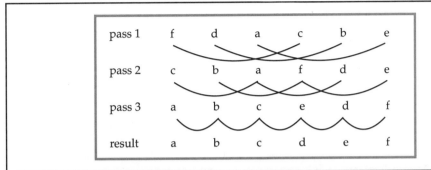

Figure 21-2. *The Shell sort*

It is not easy to see that this method yields good results, or in fact that it even sorts the array. But it does. Each sorting pass involves relatively few elements, or elements that are already in reasonable order; so the Shell sort is efficient, and each pass increases order.

The exact sequence for the increments can be changed. The only rule is that the last increment must be 1. For example, the sequence

9, 5, 3, 2, 1

works well and is used in the Shell sort shown here. Avoid sequences that are powers of 2—for mathematically complex reasons, they reduce the efficiency of the sorting algorithm (but the sort still works).

```
/* The Shell Sort. */
void shell(char *items, int count)
{

  register int i, j, gap, k;
  char x, a[5];

  a[0]=9; a[1]=5; a[2]=3; a[3]=2; a[4]=1;

  for(k=0; k < 5; k++) {
    gap = a[k];
    for(i=gap; i < count; ++i) {
      x = items[i];
      for(j=i-gap; (x < items[j]) && (j >= 0); j=j-gap)
```

```
        items[j+gap] = items[j];
      items[j+gap] = x;
    }
  }
}
```

You may have noticed that the inner **for** loop has two test conditions. The comparison **x<items[j]** is obviously necessary for the sorting process. The test **j>=0** keeps the sort from overrunning the boundary of the array **items**. These extra checks will degrade the performance of the Shell sort to some extent.

Slightly different versions of the sort employ special array elements called *sentinels*, which are not actually part of the array to be sorted. Sentinels hold special termination values that indicate the least and greatest possible element. In this way, the bounds checks are unnecessary. However, using sentinels requires a specific knowledge of the data, which limits the generality of the sort function.

The Shell sort presents some very difficult mathematical problems that are far beyond the scope of this discussion. Take it on faith that execution time is proportional to

$$n^{1.2}$$

for sorting n elements. This is a significant improvement over the n-squared sorts. To understand how great the improvement is, see Figure 21-3, which graphs both an n^2 and an $n^{1.2}$ sort. However, before getting too excited about the Shell sort, you should know that the quicksort is even better.

The Quicksort

The quicksort, invented and named by C. A. R. Hoare, is superior to all others in this book, and it is generally considered the best general-purpose sorting algorithm currently available. It is based on the exchange sort—surprising in light of the terrible performance of the bubble sort!

The quicksort is built on the idea of partitions. The general procedure is to select a value, called the *comparand*, and then to partition the array into two sections. All elements greater than or equal to the partition value are put on one side, and those less than the value are put on the other. This process is then repeated for each remaining section until the array is sorted. For example, given the array **fedacb** and using the value **d** as the comparand, the first pass of the quicksort would rearrange the array as follows:

Initial	f e d a c b
Pass1	b c a d e f

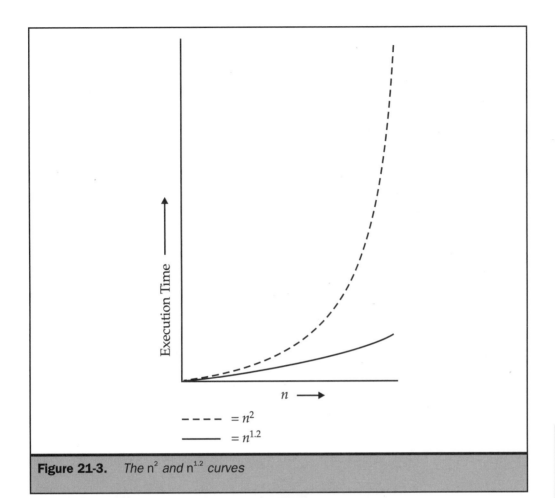

Figure 21-3. *The n² and n¹·² curves*

This process is then repeated for each section—that is, **bca** and **def**. As you can see, the process is essentially recursive in nature, and, indeed, the cleanest implementation of quicksort is as a recursive function.

You can select the comparand value in two ways. You can either choose it at random, or you can select it by averaging a small set of values taken from the array. For optimal sorting, you should select a value that is precisely in the middle of the range of values. However, this is not easy to do for most sets of data. In the worst case, the value chosen is at one extremity. Even in this case, however, quicksort still performs correctly. The following version of quicksort selects the middle element of the array as the comparand:

```
/* Quicksort setup function. */
void quick(char *items, int count)
{
  qs(items, 0, count-1);
}

/* The Quicksort. */
void qs(char *items, int left, int right)
{
  register int i, j;
  char x, y;

  i = left; j = right;
  x = items[(left+right)/2];

  do {
    while((items[i] < x) && (i < right)) i++;
    while((x < items[j]) && (j > left)) j--;

    if(i <= j) {
      y = items[i];
      items[i] = items[j];
      items[j] = y;
      i++; j--;
    }
  } while(i <= j);

  if(left < j) qs(items, left, j);
  if(i < right) qs(items, i, right);
}
```

In this version, the function **quick( )** sets up a call to the main sorting function **qs( )**. This enables the same common interface of **items** and **count** to be maintained, but it is not essential because **qs( )** could have been called directly by using three arguments.

Deriving the number of comparisons and exchanges that quicksort performs requires mathematics beyond the scope of this book. However, the average number of comparisons is

$n \log n$

and the average number of exchanges is approximately

$n/6 \log n$

These numbers are significantly lower than those provided by any of the previous sorts.

You should be aware of one particularly problematic aspect of quicksort. If the comparand value for each partition is the largest value, quicksort degenerates into "slowsort" with an n-squared run time. Therefore, be careful when you choose a method of defining the value of the comparand. The method is frequently determined by the data that you are sorting. For example, in very large mailing lists, in which the sorting is often by postal code, the selection is simple because the postal codes are fairly evenly distributed—and a simple algebraic function can determine a suitable comparand. However, in other databases, a random selection is often a better choice. A common and fairly effective method is to sample three elements from a partition and take the middle value.

Choosing a Sort

Every programmer should have a wide selection of sorts from which to choose. Although quicksort is the optimal sort for the average case, it will not be the best sort in all cases. For example, when only very small lists are sorted (with, say, less than 100 items), the overhead created by quicksort's recursive calls may offset the benefits of its superior algorithm. In rare cases like this, one of the simpler sorts—perhaps even the bubble sort—may be quicker. Also, if you know that a list is already nearly ordered or if you don't want like keys to be exchanged, then one of the other sorts may out-perform quicksort. The point is that just because quicksort is the best general-purpose sorting algorithm does not mean that you cannot do better with another approach in special situations.

Sorting Other Data Structures

Until now, we have been sorting only arrays of characters. Obviously, arrays of any of the built-in data types can be sorted by simply changing the data types of the parameters and variables to the sort function. Generally, however, compound data types, such as strings, or groupings of information, such as structures, need to be sorted. Most sorting involves a key and information linked to that key. To change the algorithms to accommodate a key, you need to alter the comparison section, the exchange section, or both. The algorithm itself remains unchanged.

Because quicksort is one of the best general-purpose routines available at this time, it is used in the following examples. However, the same techniques apply to any of the sorts described earlier.

ALGORITHMS AND
APPLICATIONS

Sorting Strings

Sorting strings is a common programming task. By far, strings are easiest to sort when they are contained in a string table. A *string table* is simply an array of strings. And an array of strings is a two-dimensional character array in which the number of strings in the table is determined by the size of the left dimension and the maximum length of each string is determined by the size of the right dimension. (Refer to Chapter 4 for information about arrays of strings.) The string version of quicksort that follows accepts an array of strings in which each string is up to ten characters long. (You can change this length if you want.) This version sorts the strings in dictionary order.

```
/* A Quicksort for strings. */
void quick_string(char items[][10], int count)
{
  qs_string(items, 0, count-1);
}

void qs_string(char items[][10], int left, int right)
{
  register int i, j;
  char *x;
  char temp[10];

  i = left; j = right;
  x = items[(left+right)/2];

  do {
    while((strcmp(items[i],x) < 0) && (i < right)) i++;
    while((strcmp(items[j],x) > 0) && (j > left)) j--;
    if(i <= j) {
      strcpy(temp, items[i]);
      strcpy(items[i], items[j]);
      strcpy(items[j], temp);
      i++; j--;
    }
  } while(i <= j);

  if(left < j) qs_string(items, left, j);
  if(i < right) qs_string(items, i, right);
}
```

Notice that the comparison step has been changed to use the function **strcmp( )**. The function returns a negative number if the first string is lexicographically less than the second, zero if the strings are equal, and a positive number if the first string is lexicographically greater than the second. Also notice that when two strings must be swapped, three calls to **strcpy( )** are required.

Be aware that **strcmp( )** slows down the sort for two reasons. First, it involves a function call, which always takes time. Second, **strcmp( )** itself performs several comparisons to determine the relationship of the two strings. In the first case, if speed is absolutely critical, place the code for **strcmp( )** in line inside the routine by duplicating the **strcmp( )** code. In the second case, there is no way to avoid comparing the strings since, by definition, this is what the task involves. The same line of reasoning also applies to the **strcpy( )** function. The use of **strcpy( )** to exchange two strings involves a function call and a character-by-character exchange of the two strings—both of which add time. The overhead of the function call could be eliminated through the use of in-line code. However, the fact that exchanging two strings means exchanging their individual characters (one by one) cannot be altered.

Here is a simple **main( )** function that demonstrates **quick_string( )**:

```
#include <stdio.h>
#include <string.h>

void quick_string(char items[][10], int count);
void qs_string(char items[][10], int left, int right);

char str[][10] = { "one",
                   "two",
                   "three",
                   "four"
                 };

int main(void)
{
  int i;

  quick_string(str, 4);

  for(i=0; i<4; i++) printf("%s ", str[i]);

  return 0;
}
```

Sorting Structures

Most application programs that require a sort probably need to have a collection of data sorted. For example, mailing lists, inventory databases, and employee records all contain collections of data. As you know, in C programs collections of data are typically stored in structures. Although a structure will generally contain several members, it will usually be sorted on the basis of only one member, which is used as the sort key. Aside from the selection of the key, the techniques used to sort other types of data also apply to sorting structures.

To see an example of sorting structures, let's use a structure, called **address**, that is capable of holding a mailing address. Such a structure could be used by a mailing list program. The **address** structure is shown here:

```
struct address {
  char name[40];
  char street[40];
  char city[20];
  char state[3];
  char zip[11];
};
```

Since it is reasonable to arrange a mailing list as an array of structures, assume for this example that the sort routine will sort an array of structures of type **address**. Such a routine is shown here. It sorts the addresses by postal code.

```
/* A Quicksort for structures of type address. */
void quick_struct(struct address items[], int count)
{
  qs_struct(items,0,count-1);
}

void qs_struct(struct address items[], int left, int right)
{

  register int i, j;
  char *x;
  struct address temp;

  i = left; j = right;
  x = items[(left+right)/2].zip;

  do {
    while((strcmp(items[i].zip,x) < 0) && (i < right)) i++;
    while((strcmp(items[j].zip,x) > 0) && (j > left)) j--;
    if(i <= j) {
      temp = items[i];
      items[i] = items[j];
      items[j] = temp;
```

```
      i++; j--;
    }
  } while(i <= j);

  if(left < j) qs_struct(items, left, j);
  if(i < right) qs_struct(items, i, right);
}
```

Sorting Random-Access Disk Files

There are two types of disk files: *sequential* and *random access*. If either type of disk file is small enough, it may be read into memory, and the array-sorting routines presented earlier will be able to sort it. However, many disk files are too large to be sorted easily in memory and require special techniques. Most database applications use random-access disk files. This section shows one way random-access disk files may be sorted.

Random-access disk files have two major advantages over sequential disk files. First, they are easy to maintain. You can update information without having to copy the entire list. Second, they can be treated as a very large array on disk, which greatly simplifies sorting.

Treating a random-access file as an array means that you can use the quicksort with just a few modifications. Instead of indexing an array, the disk version of the quicksort must use **fseek( )** to seek to the appropriate records on the disk.

In reality, each sorting situation differs in relation to the exact data structure that is sorted and the key that is used. However, you can learn the general idea of sorting random-access disk files by using a short program to sort structures of type **address**—the mailing list structure defined earlier. The sample program that follows first creates a disk file that contains unsorted addresses. It then sorts the file. The number of addresses to sort is specified by **NUM_ELEMENTS** (which is 4 for this program). However, for a real-world application, a record count would have to be maintained dynamically. You should experiment with this program on your own, trying different types of structures, containing different types of data.

```
/* Disk sort for structures of type address. */
#include <stdio.h>
#include <stdlib.h>
#include <string.h>

#define NUM_ELEMENTS 4   /* This is an arbitrary number
                            that should be determined
                            dynamically for each list. */
```

```
struct address {
  char name[30];
  char street[40];
  char city[20];
  char state[3];
  char zip[11];
} ainfo;

struct address addrs[NUM_ELEMENTS] = {
  "A. Alexander", "101 1st St", "Olney", "Ga", "55555",
  "B. Bertrand", "22 2nd Ave", "Oakland", "Pa", "34232",
  "C. Carlisle", "33 3rd Blvd", "Ava", "Or", "92000",
  "D. Dodger", "4 Fourth Dr", "Fresno", "Mi", "45678"
};

void quick_disk(FILE *fp, int count);
void qs_disk(FILE *fp, int left, int right);
void swap_all_fields(FILE *fp, long i, long j);
char *get_zip(FILE *fp, long rec);

int main(void)
{
  FILE *fp;

  /* first, create a file to sort */
  if((fp=fopen("mlist", "wb"))==NULL) {
    printf("Cannot open file for write.\n");
    exit(1);
  }
  printf("Writing unsorted data to disk.\n");
  fwrite(addrs, sizeof(addrs), 1, fp);
  fclose(fp);

  /* now, sort the file */
  if((fp=fopen("mlist", "rb+"))==NULL) {
    printf("Cannot open file for read/write.\n");
    exit(1);
  }

  printf("Sorting disk file.\n");
  quick_disk(fp, NUM_ELEMENTS);
  fclose(fp);
```

```
  printf("List sorted.\n");

  return 0;
}

/* A Quicksort for files. */
void quick_disk(FILE *fp, int count)
{
  qs_disk(fp, 0, count-1);
}

void qs_disk(FILE *fp, int left, int right)
{
  long int i, j;
  char x[100];

  i = left; j = right;

  strcpy(x, get_zip(fp, (long)(i+j)/2)); /* get the middle zip */

  do {
    while((strcmp(get_zip(fp,i),x) < 0) && (i < right)) i++;
    while((strcmp(get_zip(fp,j),x) > 0) && (j > left)) j--;

    if(i <= j) {
      swap_all_fields(fp, i, j);
      i++; j--;
    }
  } while(i <= j);

  if(left < j) qs_disk(fp, left, (int) j);
  if(i < right) qs_disk(fp, (int) i, right);
}

void swap_all_fields(FILE *fp, long i, long j)
{
  char a[sizeof(ainfo)], b[sizeof(ainfo)];

  /* first read in record i and j */
  fseek(fp, sizeof(ainfo)*i, SEEK_SET);
  fread(a, sizeof(ainfo), 1, fp);
```

```
    fseek(fp, sizeof(ainfo)*j, SEEK_SET);
    fread(b, sizeof(ainfo), 1, fp);

    /* then write them back in opposite slots */
    fseek(fp, sizeof(ainfo)*j, SEEK_SET);
    fwrite(a, sizeof(ainfo), 1, fp);
    fseek(fp, sizeof(ainfo)*i, SEEK_SET);
    fwrite(b, sizeof(ainfo), 1, fp);
}

/* Return a pointer to the zip code */
char *get_zip(FILE *fp, long rec)
{
  struct address *p;

  p = &ainfo;

  fseek(fp, rec*sizeof(ainfo), SEEK_SET);
  fread(p, sizeof(ainfo), 1, fp);

  return ainfo.zip;
}
```

As you can see, two support functions had to be written to sort the address records. In the comparison section of the sort, the function **get_zip( )** is used to return a pointer to the **zip** field of the comparand and the record being checked. The function **swap_all_fields( )** performs the actual data exchange. The order of the reads and writes has a great impact on the speed of this sort. When an exchange occurs, the code, as it is shown, forces a seek to record **i**, then to **j**. While the head of the disk drive is still positioned at **j**, **i**'s data is written. This means that the head does not need to move a great distance. Had the code been written with **i**'s data written first, an extra seek would have been necessary.

Searching

Databases of information exist so that, from time to time, a user can locate a record by entering its key. There is one method of finding information in an unsorted array and another for a sorted array. C compilers supply the standard **bsearch( )** function as part of the standard library. However, as with sorting, general-purpose routines are sometimes too inefficient for use in demanding situations because of the extra overhead created by their generalization. Also, **bsearch( )** cannot be applied to unsorted data.

Searching Methods

Finding information in an unsorted array requires a sequential search starting at the first element and stopping either when a match is found or at the end of the array. This method must be used on unsorted data but can be applied to sorted data as well. However, if the data has been sorted, you can use a binary search, which helps you locate the data more quickly.

The Sequential Search

The sequential search is simple to code. The following function searches a character array of known length until a match of the specified key is found.

```
int sequential_search(char *items, int count, char key)
{
  register int t;

  for(t=0; t < count; ++t)
    if(key == items[t]) return t;
  return -1; /* no match */
}
```

Here, **items** is a pointer to the array that contains the information. This function returns the index number of the matching entry if there is one; otherwise, it returns –1.

It is easy to see that a sequential search will, on the average, test $n/2$ elements. In the best case it tests only one element, and in the worst case it tests n elements. If the information is stored on disk, the search time can be lengthy. But if the data is unsorted, you can only search sequentially.

The Binary Search

If the data to be searched is sorted, you can use a vastly superior method to find a match. It is the *binary search*, which uses the divide-and-conquer approach. To employ this method, test the middle element. If it is larger than the key, test the middle element of the first half; otherwise, test the middle element of the second half. Repeat this procedure until a match is found or there are no more elements to test.

For example, to find the number 4 given the array

1 2 3 4 5 6 7 8 9

a binary search first tests the middle, which is 5. Since this is greater than 4, the search continues with the first half, or

1 2 3 4 5

The middle element is now 3. This is less than 4, so the first half is discarded. The search continues with

4 5

This time the match is found.

In a binary search, the number of comparisons in the worst case is

$\log_2 n$

In the average case, the number is somewhat lower, and in the best case the number of comparisons is one.

A binary search function for character arrays follows. You can make this search for any arbitrary data structure by changing the comparison portion of the routine.

```c
/* The Binary search. */
int binary_search(char *items, int count, char key)
{
  int low, high, mid;

  low = 0; high = count-1;
  while(low <= high) {
    mid = (low+high)/2;
    if(key < items[mid]) high = mid-1;
    else if(key > items[mid]) low = mid+1;
    else return mid; /* found */
  }
  return -1;
}
```

Chapter 22

Queues, Stacks, Linked Lists, and Trees

Programs consist of two things: algorithms and data structures. A good program is an effective blend of both. The choice and implementation of a data structure are as important as the routines that manipulate it. How information is organized and accessed is usually determined by the nature of the programming problem. Thus, it is important for you to have on hand the right techniques for a variety of situations.

How closely a data type is bound to its machine representation has an inverse correlation to its abstraction. That is, as data types become more abstract, the way the programmer thinks of them bears a decreasing resemblance to the way they are actually represented in memory. Simple types, such as **char** and **int**, are tightly bound to their machine representation. For example, the machine representation of an integer value closely approximates the programmer's concept of that value. As data types become more complicated, they are conceptually less similar to their machine equivalents. For example, floating-point values are more abstract than are integers. The actual representation of a **float** inside the machine is little like the average programmer's conception of a floating-point number. Even more abstract is the structure, which is an aggregate data type.

The next level of abstraction transcends the mere physical aspects of the data by adding the mechanism by which that data may be accessed—that is, *stored* and *retrieved*. In essence, the physical data is linked with a *data engine*, which controls the way information can be accessed by your program. It is these data engines that are the subject of this chapter.

There are four basic types of data engines:

- A queue
- A stack
- A linked list
- A binary tree

Each of these methods provides a solution to a class of problems. These methods are essentially devices that perform a specific storage-and-retrieval operation on the information that they are given, based on the requests that they receive. They all store an item and retrieve an item, where an item is one informational unit. The rest of this chapter shows you how to build these data engines using the C language. In the process, several common C programming techniques are illustrated, including dynamic allocation and pointer manipulation.

Queues

A *queue* is simply a linear list of information that is accessed in *first-in, first-out* order, which is sometimes called FIFO. That is, the first item placed on the queue is the first item retrieved, the second item put in is the second item retrieved, and so on. This is the only means of storage and retrieval in a queue; random access of any specific item is not allowed.

Queues are very common in real life. For example, lines at a bank or a fast-food restaurant are queues. To visualize how a queue works, consider two functions: **qstore( )** and **qretrieve( )**. The **qstore( )** function places an item onto the end of the queue, and **qretrieve( )** removes the first item from the queue and returns its value. Table 22-1 shows the effect of a series of these operations.

Keep in mind that a retrieval operation removes an item from the queue and destroys it if it is not stored elsewhere. Therefore, a queue will be empty after all items have been removed.

Queues are used in many programming situations. One of the most common is in simulations. Queues are also used by the task scheduler of an operating system and for I/O buffering.

To see an example of a queue in action, we will use a simple appointment-scheduler program. This program allows you to enter a number of appointments; then, as each appointment is met, it is taken off the list. For the sake of simplicity, each appointment description will be limited to 255 characters, and the number of appointments is arbitrarily limited to 100.

First, the functions **qstore( )** and **qretrieve( )** shown here are needed for the simple scheduling program. They will store pointers to the strings that describe the appointments.

Action	Contents of Queue
qstore(A)	A
qstore(B)	A B
qstore(C)	A B C
qretrieve( ) returns A	B C
qstore(D)	B C D
qretrieve( ) returns B	C D
qretrieve( ) returns C	D

Table 22-1.   *A Queue in Action*

```
#define MAX 100

char *p[MAX];
int spos = 0;
int rpos = 0;

/* Store an appointment. */
void qstore(char *q)
{
  if(spos==MAX) {
    printf("List Full\n");
    return;
  }
  p[spos] = q;
  spos++;
}

/* Retrieve an appointment. */
char *qretrieve()
{
  if(rpos==spos) {
    printf("No more appointments.\n");
    return '\0';
  }
  rpos++;
  return p[rpos-1];
}
```

Notice that these functions require two global variables: **spos** (which holds the index of the next free storage location) and **rpos** (which holds the index of the next item to retrieve). You can use these functions to maintain a queue of other data types by simply changing the base type of the array that they operate on.

The function **qstore( )** places pointers to new appointments on the end of the list and checks to see if the list is full. The function **qretrieve( )** takes appointments off the queue while there are events to perform. With each new appointment scheduled, **spos** is incremented, and with each appointment completed, **rpos** is incremented. In essence, **rpos** chases **spos** through the queue. Figure 22-1 shows how this may appear in memory as the program executes. If **rpos** and **spos** are equal, there are no events left in the schedule. Even though the information stored in the queue is not actually destroyed by **qretrieve( )**, it is effectively destroyed because it can never be accessed again.

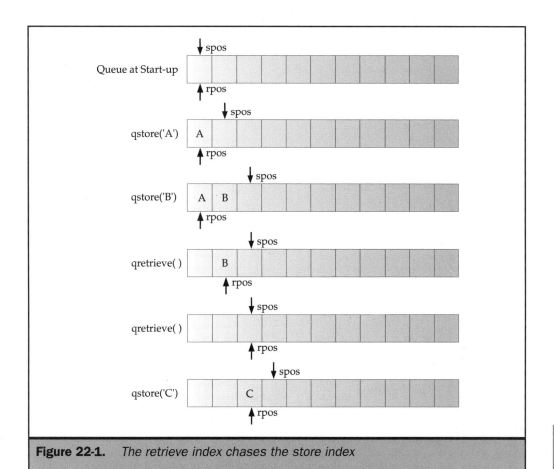

Figure 22-1. *The retrieve index chases the store index*

The entire program for this simple appointment scheduler is listed here. You may want to enhance this program for your own use.

```
/* Mini Appointment-Scheduler */

#include <string.h>
#include <stdlib.h>
#include <stdio.h>
#include <ctype.h>

#define MAX 100

char *p[MAX], *qretrieve(void);
int spos = 0;
int rpos = 0;
```

```
void enter(void), qstore(char *q), review(void), delete_ap(void);

int main(void)
{
  char s[80];
  register int t;

  for(t=0; t < MAX; ++t) p[t] = NULL; /* init array to nulls */

  for(;;) {
    printf("Enter, List, Remove, Quit: ");
    gets(s);
    *s = toupper(*s);

    switch(*s) {
      case 'E':
        enter();
        break;
      case 'L':
        review();
        break;
      case 'R':
        delete_ap();
        break;
      case 'Q':
        exit(0);
    }
  }
  return 0;
}

/* Enter appointments in queue. */
void enter(void)
{
  char s[256], *p;

  do {
    printf("Enter appointment %d: ", spos+1);
    gets(s);
    if(*s==0) break; /* no entry */
    p = (char *) malloc(strlen(s)+1);
    if(!p) {
      printf("Out of memory.\n");
```

```
      return;
    }
    strcpy(p, s);
    if(*s) qstore(p);
  } while(*s);
}

/* See what's in the queue. */
void review(void)
{
  register int t;

  for(t=rpos; t < spos; ++t)
    printf("%d. %s\n", t+1, p[t]);
}

/* Delete an appointment from the queue. */
void delete_ap(void)
{
  char *p;

  if((p=qretrieve())==NULL) return;
  printf("%s\n", p);
}

/* Store an appointment. */
void qstore(char *q)
{
  if(spos==MAX) {
    printf("List Full\n");
    return;
  }
  p[spos] = q;
  spos++;
}

/* Retrieve an appointment. */
char *qretrieve(void)
{
  if(rpos==spos) {
    printf("No more appointments.\n");
    return NULL;
  }
```

```
   rpos++;
   return p[rpos-1];
}
```

The Circular Queue

In studying the preceding appointment-scheduler program, an improvement may have occurred to you. Instead of having the program stop when the limit of the array used to store the queue is reached, you could have both the store index (**spos**) and the retrieve index (**rpos**) loop back to the start of the array. In this way, any number of items could be placed on the queue, so long as items were also being taken off. This implementation of a queue is called a *circular queue* because it uses its storage array as if it were a circle instead of a linear list.

To create a circular queue for use in the scheduler program, you need to change the functions **qstore( )** and **qretrieve( )** as shown here:

```
void qstore(char *q)
{
  /* The queue is full if either spos is one less than rpos
     or if spos is at the end of the queue array and rpos
     is at the beginning.
  */
  if(spos+1==rpos || (spos+1==MAX && !rpos)) {
    printf("List Full\n");
    return;
  }

  p[spos] = q;
  spos++;
  if(spos==MAX) spos = 0; /* loop back */
}

char *qretrieve(void)
{
  if(rpos==MAX) rpos = 0; /* loop back */
  if(rpos==spos) {
    printf("No events to retrieve.\n");
    return NULL;
  }
  rpos++;
  return p[rpos-1];
}
```

In this version, the queue is full when the store index is one less than the retrieve index; otherwise, there is room in the queue for another event. The queue is empty when **rpos** equals **spos**.

Perhaps the most common use of a circular queue is in operating systems, where a circular queue holds the information read from and written to disk files or the console. Circular queues are also used in real-time application programs, which must continue to process information while buffering I/O requests. Many word processors do this when they reformat a paragraph or justify a line. What is being typed is not displayed until the other process is complete. To accomplish this, the application program needs to check for keyboard entry during execution of the other process. If a key has been typed, it is quickly placed in the queue, and the other process continues. Once the process is complete, the characters are retrieved from the queue.

To get a feel for this use of a circular queue, consider a simple program that contains two processes. The first process in the program prints the numbers 1 to 32,000 on the screen. The second process places characters into a circular queue as they are typed, without echoing them to the screen, until you press ENTER. The characters you type are not displayed because the first process is given priority over the screen. Once you have pressed ENTER, the characters in the queue are retrieved and printed.

For the program to function as described, it must use two functions not defined by Standard C: **_kbhit( )** and **_getch( )**. The **_kbhit( )** function returns true if a key has been pressed; otherwise, it returns false. The **_getch( )** function reads a keystroke but does not echo the character to the screen. Standard C does not define functions that check keyboard status or read keyboard characters without echoing them to the display because these functions are highly operating-system dependent. Nonetheless, most compilers supply routines to do these things. The short program shown here works with the Microsoft compiler:

```c
/* A circular queue example using a keyboard buffer. */
#include <stdio.h>
#include <conio.h>
#include <stdlib.h>

#define MAX 80

char buf[MAX+1];
int spos = 0;
int rpos = 0;

void qstore(char q);
char qretrieve(void);

int main(void)
{
```

```
    register char ch;
    int t;

    buf[80] = '\0';

    /* Input characters until a carriage return is typed. */
    for(ch=' ',t=0; t<32000 && ch!='\r'; ++t) {
      if(_kbhit()) {
        ch = _getch();
        qstore(ch);
      }
      printf("%d ", t);
      if(ch == '\r') {
        /* Display and empty the key buffer. */
        printf("\n");
        while((ch=qretrieve()) != '\0') printf("%c", ch);
        printf("\n");
      }
    }
    return 0;
}

/* Store characters in the queue. */
void qstore(char q)
{
  if(spos+1==rpos || (spos+1==MAX && !rpos)) {
    printf("List Full\n");
    return;
  }
  buf[spos] = q;
  spos++;
  if(spos==MAX) spos = 0; /* loop back */
}

/* Retrieve a character. */
char qretrieve(void)
{
  if(rpos==MAX) rpos = 0; /* loop back */
  if(rpos==spos) return '\0';

  rpos++;
  return buf[rpos-1];
}
```

Stacks

A *stack* is the opposite of a queue because it uses *last-in, first-out* accessing, which is sometimes called LIFO. To visualize a stack, just imagine a stack of plates. The first plate on the table is the last to be used, and the last plate placed on the stack is the first to be used. Stacks are used frequently in system software, including compilers and interpreters.

When working with stacks, the two basic operations—store and retrieve—are traditionally called *push* and *pop*, respectively. Therefore, to implement a stack you need two functions: **push( )**, which places a value on the stack, and **pop( )**, which retrieves a value from the stack. You also need a region of memory to use as the stack. You can use an array for this purpose or allocate a region of memory using C's dynamic allocation functions. As with the queue, the retrieval function takes a value off the list and destroys it if it is not stored elsewhere. The general forms of **push( )** and **pop( )** that use an integer array follow. You can maintain stacks of other data types by changing the base type of the array on which **push( )** and **pop( )** operate.

```c
int stack[MAX];
int tos=0;   /* top of stack */

/* Put an element on the stack. */
void push(int i)
{

  if(tos >= MAX) {
    printf("Stack Full\n");
    return;
  }
  stack[tos] = i;
  tos++;
}

/* Retrieve the top element from the stack. */
int pop(void)
{
  tos--;
  if(tos < 0) {
    printf("Stack Underflow\n");
    return 0;
  }
  return stack[tos];
}
```

ALGORITHMS AND
APPLICATIONS

The variable **tos** is the index of the top of the stack. When implementing these functions, you must remember to prevent overflow and underflow. In these routines, an empty stack is signaled by **tos** being zero and a full stack by **tos** being greater than the last storage location. To see how a stack works, see Table 22-2.

An excellent example of stack usage is a four-function calculator. Most calculators today accept a standard form of an expression called *infix notation*, which takes the general form *operand-operator-operand.* For example, to add 200 to 100, enter **100**, then press the plus (+) key, then **200**, and press the equals (=) key. In contrast, many early calculators (and some still made today) use *postfix notation*, in which both operands are entered first, and then the operator is entered. For example, to add 200 to 100 by using postfix notation, you enter **100**, then **200**, and then press the plus key. In this method, as operands are entered, they are placed on a stack. Each time an operator is entered, two operands are removed from the stack, and the result is pushed back on the stack. One advantage of the postfix form is that long, complex expressions can be easily entered by the user.

The following example demonstrates a stack by implementing a postfix calculator for integer expressions. To begin, the **push( )** and **pop( )** functions must be modified, as shown here. They also will use dynamically allocated memory (instead of a fixed-size array) for the stack. Although the use of dynamically allocated memory is not necessary for this simple example, it illustrates how dynamically allocated memory can be used to support a stack.

Action	Contents of Stack
push(A)	A
push(B)	B A
push(C)	C B A
pop( ) retrieves **C**	B A
push(F)	F B A
pop( ) retrieves **F**	B A
pop( ) retrieves **B**	A
pop( ) retrieves **A**	*empty*

Table 22-2.   *A Stack in Action*

```
int *p;    /* will point to a region of free memory */
int *tos; /* points to top of stack */
int *bos; /* points to bottom of stack */

/* Store an element on the stack. */
void push(int i)
{
  if(p > bos) {
    printf("Stack Full\n");
    return;
  }
  *p = i;
  p++;
}

/* Retrieve the top element from the stack. */
int pop(void)
{
  p--;
  if(p < tos) {
    printf("Stack Underflow\n");
    return 0;
  }
  return *p;
}
```

Before these functions can be used, a region of free memory must be allocated with **malloc( )**, the address of the beginning of that region assigned to **tos**, and the address of the end assigned to **bos**.

The entire postfix-based calculator program is shown here:

```
/* A simple four-function calculator. */

#include <stdio.h>
#include <stdlib.h>

#define MAX 100

int *p;    /* will point to a region of free memory */
int *tos; /* points to top of stack */
int *bos; /* points to bottom of stack */
```

```c
void push(int i);
int pop(void);

int main(void)
{
  int a, b;
  char s[80];

  p = (int *) malloc(MAX*sizeof(int)); /* get stack memory */
  if(!p) {
    printf("Allocation Failure\n");
    exit(1);
  }
  tos = p;
  bos = p + MAX-1;

  printf("Four Function Calculator\n");
  printf("Enter 'q' to quit\n");

  do {
    printf(": ");
    gets(s);
    switch(*s) {
      case '+':
        a = pop();
        b = pop();
        printf("%d\n", a+b);
        push(a+b);
        break;
      case '-':
        a = pop();
        b = pop();
        printf("%d\n", b-a);
        push(b-a);
        break;
      case '*':
        a = pop();
        b = pop();
        printf("%d\n", b*a);
        push(b*a);
        break;
      case '/':
        a = pop();
```

```
          b = pop();
          if(a==0) {
            printf("Divide by 0.\n");
            break;
          }
          printf("%d\n", b/a);
          push(b/a);
          break;
        case '.': /* show contents of top of stack */
          a = pop();
          push(a);
          printf("Current value on top of stack: %d\n", a);
          break;
        default:
          push(atoi(s));
    }
  } while(*s != 'q');

  return 0;
}

/* Put an element on the stack. */
void push(int i)
{
  if(p > bos) {
    printf("Stack Full\n");
    return;
  }
  *p = i;
  p++;
}

/* Retrieve the top element from the stack. */
int pop(void)
{
  p--;
  if(p < tos) {
    printf("Stack Underflow\n");
    return 0;
  }
  return *p;
}
```

Linked Lists

Queues and stacks share two traits: They both have strict rules for accessing the data stored in them, and the retrieval operations are, by nature, consumptive. In other words, accessing an item in a stack or queue requires its removal, and unless the item is stored elsewhere, it is destroyed. Also, stacks and queues both use a contiguous region of memory. Unlike a stack or a queue, a *linked list* can be accessed in a flexible fashion, because each piece of information carries with it a link to the next data item in the chain. In addition, a linked list retrieval operation does not remove and destroy an item from the list. In fact, you need to add a specific deletion operation to do this.

Linked lists can be either singly linked or doubly linked. A singly linked list contains a link to the next data item. A doubly linked list contains links to both the next and the previous element in the list. You will use one or the other of these linked list types, depending upon your application.

Singly Linked Lists

A singly linked list requires that each item of information contain a link to the next element in the list. Each data item usually consists of a structure that includes information fields and a link pointer. Conceptually, a singly linked list looks like the one shown in Figure 22-2.

Basically, there are two ways to build a singly linked list. The first is simply to put each new item on the end of the list. The other is to insert items into specific places in the list—in ascending sorted order, for example. How you build the list determines the way the storage function is coded. Let's start with the simpler case of creating a linked list by adding items on the end.

The items stored in a linked list generally consist of structures because each item must carry with it a link to the next item in the list as well as the data itself. Therefore, we will need to define a structure that will be used in the examples that follow. Since mailing lists are commonly stored in a linked list, an address structure makes a good choice. The data structure for each element in the mailing list is defined here:

```
struct address {
  char name[40];
  char street[40];
  char city[20];
  char state[3];
  char zip[11];
  struct address *next; /* link to next address */
} info;
```

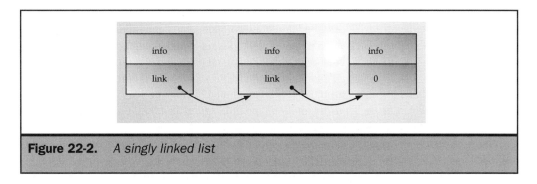

Figure 22-2. *A singly linked list*

The **slstore( )** function, shown next, builds a singly linked list by placing each new element on the end. It must be passed a pointer to a structure of type **address** that contains the new entry, and a pointer to the last element in the list. If the list is empty, the pointer to the last element in the list must be null.

```
void slstore(struct address *i,
             struct address **last)
{
  if(!*last) *last = i; /* first item in list */
  else (*last)->next = i;
  i->next = NULL;
  *last = i;
}
```

Although you can sort the list created with the function **slstore( )** as a separate operation, it is easier to sort the list while building it by inserting each new item in the proper sequence of the chain. Also, if the list is already sorted, it would be advantageous to keep it sorted by inserting new items in their proper location. You do this by sequentially scanning the list until the proper location is found, inserting the new entry at that point, and rearranging the links as necessary.

Three possible situations can occur when you insert an item in a singly linked list. First, it may become the new first item; second, it can go between two other items; or third, it can become the last element. Figure 22-3 diagrams how the links are changed for each case.

Keep in mind that if you change the first item in the list, you must update the entry point to the list elsewhere in your program. To avoid this overhead, you can use a *sentinel* as a first item. In this case, choose a special value that will always be first in the list to keep the entry point to the list from changing. This method has the disadvantage of using one extra storage location to hold the sentinel, but this is usually not an important factor.

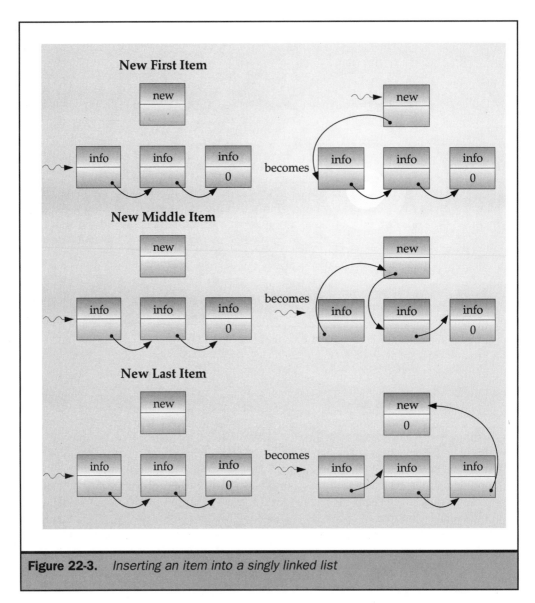

New First Item

New Middle Item

New Last Item

Figure 22-3. *Inserting an item into a singly linked list*

The function shown next, **sls_store( )**, will insert **address** structures into the mailing list in ascending order based on the **name** field. The function must be passed a pointer to the pointer to the first element and the last element in the list along with a pointer to the information to be stored. Since the first or last element in the list could change, **sls_store( )** automatically updates the pointers to the beginning and end of the list if necessary. The first time your program calls **sls_store( )**, **first** and **last** must point to null.

```
/* Store in sorted order. */
void sls_store(struct address *i, /* new element to store */
               struct address **start, /* start of list */
               struct address **last) /* end of list */
{
  struct address *old, *p;

  p = *start;

  if(!*last) { /* first element in list */
    i->next = NULL;
    *last = i;
    *start = i;
    return;
  }

  old = NULL;
  while(p) {
    if(strcmp(p->name, i->name)<0) {
      old = p;
      p = p->next;
    }
    else {
      if(old) { /* goes in middle */
        old->next = i;
        i->next = p;
        return;
      }
      i->next = p; /* new first element */
      *start = i;
      return;
    }
  }
  (*last)->next = i; /* put on end */
  i->next = NULL;
  *last = i;
}
```

It is quite easy to step through a linked list: Begin at the top of the list, and then follow the links. Usually this code is so short that it is simply placed inside another routine such as a search, delete, or display function. For example, the routine shown here displays all of the names in a mailing list:

```
void display(struct address *start)
{
  while(start) {
    printf("%s\n", start->name);
    start = start->next;
  }
}
```

When **display( )** is called, **start** must be a pointer to the first structure in the list. After that, the **next** field points to the next item. The process stops when **next** is null.

Retrieving items from the list is as simple as following a chain. A search routine based on the **name** field could be written like this:

```
struct address *search(struct address *start, char *n)
{
  while(start) {
    if(!strcmp(n, start->name)) return start;
    start = start->next;
  }
  return NULL;  /* no match */
}
```

Because **search( )** returns a pointer to the list item that matches the search name, it must be declared as returning a structure pointer of type **address**. If there is no match, null is returned.

Deleting an item from a singly linked list is straightforward. As with insertion, there are three cases: deleting the first item, deleting an item in the middle, and deleting the last item. Figure 22-4 shows each of these operations.

The function that follows deletes a given item from a list of structures of type **address**:

```
void sldelete(
      struct address *p, /* previous item */
      struct address *i, /* item to delete */
      struct address **start, /* start of list */
      struct address **last) /* end of list */
{
  if(p) p->next = i->next;
  else *start = i->next;

  if(i==*last && p) *last = p;
}
```

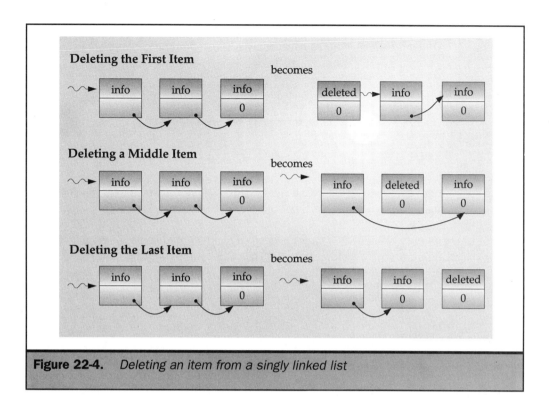

Figure 22-4.   *Deleting an item from a singly linked list*

sldelete( ) must be sent pointers to the deleted item, the item before it in the chain, and the first and last items in the list. If the first item is to be removed, the previous pointer must be null. The function automatically updates **start** and **last** when the item one of them points to is deleted.

Singly linked lists have one major drawback that prevents their extensive use: The list cannot be read in reverse order. For this reason, doubly linked lists are usually used.

Doubly Linked Lists

Doubly linked lists consist of data plus links to the next item as well as the preceding item. Figure 22-5 shows how these links are arranged.

Having two links instead of just one has several advantages. Perhaps the most important is that the list can be read in either direction. This simplifies list management, making insertions and deletions easier. It also allows a user to scan the list in either direction. Another advantage is meaningful only in the case of some type of failure. Since the entire list can be read using either forward links or backward links, should one of the links become invalid, the list could be reconstructed by using the other.

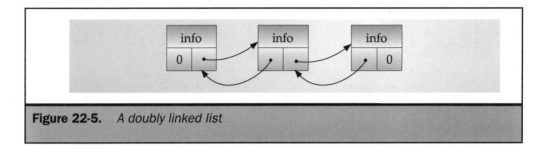

Figure 22-5.   *A doubly linked list*

A new element can be inserted into a doubly linked list in three ways: insert a new first element, insert in the middle, and insert a new last element. These operations are illustrated in Figure 22-6.

Building a doubly linked list is similar to building a singly linked list except that two links are maintained. Therefore, the structure must have room for both links. Using the mailing list example again, you can modify the structure **address** as shown here to accommodate both links:

```
struct address {
  char name[40];
  char street[40];
  char city[20];
  char state[3];
  char zip[11];
  struct address *next;
  struct address *prior;
} info;
```

Using **address** as the basic data item, the following function, **dlstore( )**, builds a doubly linked list:

```
void dlstore(struct address *i, struct address **last)
{

  if(!*last) *last = i; /* is first item in list */
  else (*last)->next = i;
  i->next = NULL;
  i->prior = *last;
  *last = i;
}
```

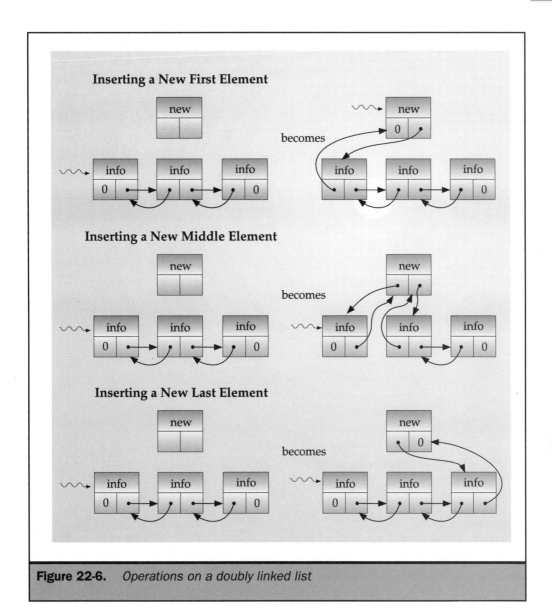

Figure 22-6.   *Operations on a doubly linked list*

The function **dlstore( )** puts each new entry on the end of the list. You must call it with a pointer to the data to be stored as well as a pointer to the end of the list, which must be null on the first call.

Like singly linked lists, a doubly linked list can be built by a function that stores each element in a specific location in the list instead of always placing each new item on the end. The function shown here, **dls_store( )**, creates a list that is sorted in ascending order:

```c
/* Create a doubly linked list in sorted order. */
void dls_store(
  struct address *i,    /* new element */
  struct address **start, /* first element in list */
  struct address **last /* last element in list */
)
{
  struct address *old, *p;

  if(*last==NULL) { /* first element in list */
    i->next = NULL;
    i->prior = NULL;
    *last = i;
    *start = i;
    return;
   }

  p = *start; /* start at top of list */

  old = NULL;
  while(p) {
    if(strcmp(p->name, i->name)<0){
      old = p;
      p = p->next;
    }
    else {
      if(p->prior) {
        p->prior->next = i;
        i->next = p;
        i->prior = p->prior;
        p->prior = i;
        return;
      }
      i->next = p; /* new first element */
      i->prior = NULL;
      p->prior = i;
      *start = i;
```

```
     return;
   }
 }
 old->next = i; /* put on end */
 i->next = NULL;
 i->prior = old;
 *last = i;
}
```

Because the first or last element in the list can change, the **dls_store( )** function automatically updates pointers to the beginning and ending elements of the list through the **start** and **last** parameters. You must call the function with a pointer to the data to be stored and a pointer to the pointers to the first and last items in the list. When called the first time, the objects pointed to by **first** and **last** must be null.

As in singly linked lists, retrieving a specific data item in a doubly linked list is simply the process of following the links until the proper element is found.

There are three cases to consider when deleting an element from a doubly linked list: deleting the first item, deleting an item from the middle, and deleting the last item. Figure 22-7 shows how the links are rearranged. The function **dldelete( )**, shown here, deletes an item from a doubly linked list:

```
void dldelete(
  struct address *i, /* item to delete */
  struct address **start,  /* first item */
  struct address **last) /* last item */
{
  if(i->prior) i->prior->next = i->next;
  else { /* new first item */
    *start = i->next;
    if(start) start->prior = NULL;
  }

  if(i->next) i->next->prior = i->prior;
  else    /* deleting last element */
    *last = i->prior;
}
```

Because the first or last element in the list could be deleted, the **dldelete( )** function automatically updates pointers to the beginning and ending elements of the list through the **start** and **last** parameters. You must call the function with a pointer to the data to be deleted and a pointer to the pointers to the first and last items in the list.

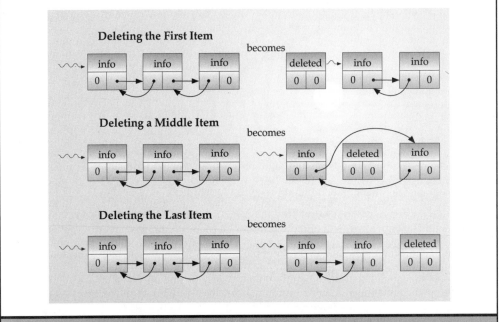

Figure 22-7.   *Deletion in a doubly linked list*

A Mailing List Example

To finish the discussion of doubly linked lists, this section presents a simple but
complete mailing list program. The entire list is kept in memory while in use.
However, it can be stored in a disk file and loaded for later use.

```c
/* A simple mailing list program that illustrates the
   use and maintenance of doubly linked lists.
*/
#include <stdio.h>
#include <stdlib.h>
#include <string.h>

struct address {
  char name[30];
  char street[40];
  char city[20];
  char state[3];
  char zip[11];
  struct address *next;  /* pointer to next entry */
```

```
    struct address *prior;  /* pointer to previous record */
};

struct address *start;  /* pointer to first entry in list */
struct address *last;  /* pointer to last entry */
struct address *find(char *);

void enter(void), search(void), save(void);
void load(void), list(void);
void mldelete(struct address **, struct address **);
void dls_store(struct address *i, struct address **start,
               struct address **last);
void inputs(char *, char *, int), display(struct address *);
int menu_select(void);

int main(void)
{
  start = last = NULL;  /* initialize start and end pointers */

  for(;;) {
    switch(menu_select()) {
      case 1: enter(); /* enter an address */
        break;
      case 2: mldelete(&start, &last); /* remove an address */
        break;
      case 3: list(); /* display the list */
        break;
      case 4: search(); /* find an address */
        break;
      case 5: save();  /* save list to disk */
        break;
      case 6: load();  /* read from disk */
        break;
      case 7: exit(0);
    }
  }
  return 0;
}

/* Select an operation. */
int menu_select(void)
{
```

```
    char s[80];
    int c;

    printf("1. Enter a name\n");
    printf("2. Delete a name\n");
    printf("3. List the file\n");
    printf("4. Search\n");
    printf("5. Save the file\n");
    printf("6. Load the file\n");
    printf("7. Quit\n");
    do {
      printf("\nEnter your choice: ");
      gets(s);
      c = atoi(s);
    } while(c<0 || c>7);
    return c;
}

/* Enter names and addresses. */
void enter(void)
{
  struct address *info;

  for(;;) {
    info = (struct address *)malloc(sizeof(struct address));
    if(!info) {
      printf("\nout of memory");
      return;
    }

    inputs("Enter name: ", info->name, 30);
    if(!info->name[0]) break;  /* stop entering */
    inputs("Enter street: ", info->street, 40);
    inputs("Enter city: ", info->city, 20);
    inputs("Enter state: ", info->state, 3);
    inputs("Enter zip: ", info->zip, 10);

    dls_store(info, &start, &last);
  } /* entry loop */
}

/* This function will input a string up to
```

```
    the length in count and will prevent
    the string from being overrun. It will also
    display a prompting message. */
void inputs(char *prompt, char *s, int count)
{
  char p[255];

  do {
    printf(prompt);
    fgets(p, 254, stdin);
    if(strlen(p) > count) printf("\nToo Long\n");
  } while(strlen(p) > count);

  p[strlen(p)-1] = 0; /* remove newline character */
  strcpy(s, p);
}

/* Create a doubly linked list in sorted order. */
void dls_store(
  struct address *i,   /* new element */
  struct address **start, /* first element in list */
  struct address **last /* last element in list */
)
{
  struct address *old, *p;

  if(*last==NULL) {  /* first element in list */
    i->next = NULL;
    i->prior = NULL;
    *last = i;
    *start = i;
    return;
  }
  p = *start; /* start at top of list */

  old = NULL;
  while(p) {
    if(strcmp(p->name, i->name)<0){
      old = p;
      p = p->next;
    }
    else {
```

ALGORITHMS AND
APPLICATIONS

```
      if(p->prior) {
        p->prior->next = i;
        i->next = p;
        i->prior = p->prior;
        p->prior = i;
        return;
      }
      i->next = p; /* new first element */
      i->prior = NULL;
      p->prior = i;
      *start = i;
      return;
    }
  }
  old->next = i; /* put on end */
  i->next = NULL;
  i->prior = old;
  *last = i;
}

/* Remove an element from the list. */
void mldelete(struct address **start, struct address **last)
{
  struct address *info;
  char s[80];

  inputs("Enter name: ", s, 30);
  info = find(s);
  if(info) {
    if(*start==info) {
      *start=info->next;
      if(*start) (*start)->prior = NULL;
      else *last = NULL;
    }
    else {
      info->prior->next = info->next;
      if(info!=*last)
          info->next->prior = info->prior;
      else
        *last = info->prior;
    }
    free(info);  /* return memory to system */
```

```
  }
}

/* Find an address. */
struct address *find( char *name)
{
  struct address *info;

  info = start;
  while(info) {
    if(!strcmp(name, info->name)) return info;
    info = info->next;  /* get next address */
  }
  printf("Name not found.\n");
  return NULL;  /* not found */
}

/* Display the entire list. */
void list(void)
{
  struct address *info;

  info = start;
  while(info) {
    display(info);
    info = info->next;  /* get next address */
  }
  printf("\n\n");
}

/* This function actually prints the fields in each address. */
void display(struct address *info)
{
    printf("%s\n", info->name);
    printf("%s\n", info->street);
    printf("%s\n", info->city);
    printf("%s\n", info->state);
    printf("%s\n", info->zip);
    printf("\n\n");
}

/* Look for a name in the list. */
```

```
void search(void)
{
  char name[40];
  struct address *info;

  printf("Enter name to find: ");
  gets(name);
  info = find(name);
  if(!info) printf("Not Found\n");
  else display(info);
}

/* Save the file to disk. */
void save(void)
{
  struct address *info;

  FILE *fp;

  fp = fopen("mlist", "wb");
  if(!fp) {
    printf("Cannot open file.\n");
    exit(1);
  }
  printf("\nSaving File\n");

  info = start;
  while(info) {
    fwrite(info, sizeof(struct address), 1, fp);
    info = info->next;  /* get next address */
  }
  fclose(fp);
}

/* Load the address file. */
void load()
{
  struct address *info;
  FILE *fp;

  fp = fopen("mlist", "rb");
  if(!fp) {
```

```
      printf("Cannot open file.\n");
      exit(1);
  }

  /* free any previously allocated memory */
  while(start) {
    info = start->next;
    free(info);
    start = info;
  }

  /* reset top and bottom pointers */
  start = last = NULL;

  printf("\nLoading File\n");
  while(!feof(fp)) {
    info = (struct address *) malloc(sizeof(struct address));
    if(!info) {
      printf("Out of Memory");
      return;
    }
    if(1 != fread(info, sizeof(struct address), 1, fp)) break;
    dls_store(info, &start, &last);
  }
  fclose(fp);
}
```

Binary Trees

The final data structure to be examined is the *binary tree*. Although there can be many different types of trees, binary trees are special because, when sorted, they lend themselves to rapid searches, insertions, and deletions. Each item in a tree consists of information along with a link to the left member and a link to the right member. Figure 22-8 shows a small tree.

Special terminology is needed when discussing trees. Computer scientists are not known for their grammar, and terminology for trees is a classic case of a confused metaphor. The *root* is the first item in the tree. Each data item is called a *node* of the tree, and any piece of the tree is called a *subtree*. A node that has no subtrees attached to it is called a *terminal node* or *leaf*. The *height* of the tree is equal to the number of layers deep that its roots grow. When working with trees, you can think of them existing in memory looking the way they do on paper. But remember: A tree is only a way to logically organize data in memory, and memory is linear.

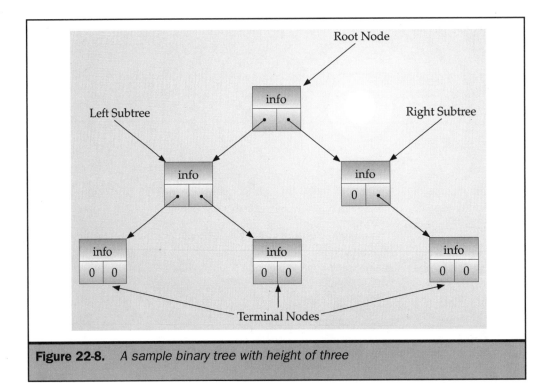

Figure 22-8. *A sample binary tree with height of three*

In a sense, the binary tree is a special form of linked list. Items can be inserted, deleted, and accessed in any order. Also, the retrieval operation is nondestructive. Although trees are easy to visualize, they present some difficult programming problems. This discussion only scratches the surface.

Most functions that use trees are recursive because the tree itself is a recursive data structure. That is, each subtree is itself a tree. Therefore, the routines that this discussion develops will be recursive. Remember, nonrecursive versions of these functions exist, but their code is much harder to understand.

How a tree is ordered depends on how it is going to be accessed. The process of accessing each node in a tree is called a *tree traversal*. Consider the following tree:

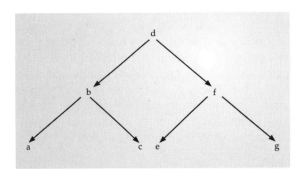

There are three ways to traverse a tree: *inorder*, *preorder*, and *postorder*. Using inorder, you visit the left subtree, the root, and then the right subtree. In preorder, you visit the root, the left subtree, and then the right subtree. With postorder, you visit the left subtree, the right subtree, and then the root. Using each method, the order of access for the tree shown is

inorder	a b c d e f g
preorder	d b a c f e g
postorder	a c b e g f d

Although a tree need not be sorted, most uses require this. Of course, what constitutes a sorted tree depends on how you will be traversing the tree. The rest of this chapter assumes inorder. Therefore, a sorted binary tree is one where the subtree on the left contains nodes that are less than or equal to the root, and those on the right are greater than the root.

The following function, **stree( )**, builds a sorted binary tree:

```c
struct tree {
  char info;
  struct tree *left;
  struct tree *right;
};

struct tree *stree(
  struct tree *root,
  struct tree *r,
  char info)
{
  if(!r) {
    r = (struct tree *) malloc(sizeof(struct tree));
    if(!r) {
      printf("Out of Memory\n");
      exit(0);
    }
    r->left = NULL;
    r->right = NULL;
    r->info = info;
    if(!root) return r; /* first entry */
    if(info < root->info) root->left = r;
    else root->right = r;
    return r;
```

```
   }
   if(info < r->info)
      stree(r,r->left,info);
   else
      stree(r,r->right,info);

   return root;
}
```

The preceding algorithm simply follows the links through the tree going left or right based on the **info** field until it finds the correct location for the new entry. To use this function, you need a global variable that points to the root of the tree. This pointer must initially be set to null. The first call to **stree( )** will return a pointer to the root of the tree, and it must be assigned to the root pointer. Subsequent calls will continue to return a pointer to the root. Assuming the name of this global root pointer is **rt**, here is how to call **stree( )**:

```
/* call stree() */
rt = stree(rt, rt, info);
```

The function **stree( )** is a recursive algorithm, as are most tree routines. The same routine would be several times longer if you employed iterative methods. The function must be called with the following arguments (proceeding left to right): a pointer to the root of the entire tree, a pointer to the root of the next subtree to search, and the information to be stored. The first time the function is called, the first two parameters are both pointers to the root of the entire tree. For the sake of clarity, only a character is used as the information stored in the tree. However, you could substitute any other data type.

To traverse inorder the tree built by using **stree( )**, and to print the **info** field of each node, you could use the **inorder( )** function shown here:

```
void inorder(struct tree *root)
{
   if(!root) return;

   inorder(root->left);
   if(root->info) printf("%c ", root->info);
   inorder(root->right);
}
```

This recursive function returns when a terminal node (a null pointer) is encountered.

The functions for traversing the tree in preorder and postorder are shown in the following listing:

```
void preorder(struct tree *root)
{
  if(!root) return;

  if(root->info) printf("%c ", root->info);
  preorder(root->left);
  preorder(root->right);
}

void postorder(struct tree *root)
{
  if(!root) return;

  postorder(root->left);
  postorder(root->right);
  if(root->info) printf("%c ", root->info);
}
```

Now consider a short but interesting program that builds a sorted binary tree and then prints that tree inorder, sideways on your screen. The program requires only a small modification to the function **inorder( )** to print the tree. Because the tree is printed sideways on the screen, the right subtree must be printed before the left subtree for the tree to look correct. (This is technically the opposite of an inorder traversal.) This new function is called **print_tree( )** and is shown here:

```
void print_tree(struct tree *r, int l)
{
  int i;

  if(r == NULL) return;

  print_tree(r->right, l+1);
  for(i=0; i<l; ++i) printf(" ");
  printf("%c\n", r->info);
  print_tree(r->left, l+1);
}
```

The entire tree-printing program follows. Try entering various trees to see how each one is built.

```c
/* This program displays a binary tree. */

#include <stdlib.h>
#include <stdio.h>

struct tree {
  char info;
  struct tree *left;
  struct tree *right;
};

struct tree *root; /* first node in tree */
struct tree *stree(struct tree *root,
                   struct tree *r, char info);
void print_tree(struct tree *root, int l);

int main(void)
{
  char s[80];

  root = NULL;  /* initialize the root */

  do {
    printf("Enter a letter: ");
    gets(s);
    root = stree(root, root, *s);
  } while(*s);

  print_tree(root, 0);

  return 0;
}

struct tree *stree(
  struct tree *root,
  struct tree *r,
  char info)
{

  if(!r) {
    r = (struct tree *) malloc(sizeof(struct tree));
```

```
      if(!r) {
        printf("Out of Memory\n");
        exit(0);
      }
      r->left = NULL;
      r->right = NULL;
      r->info = info;
      if(!root) return r; /* first entry */
      if(info < root->info) root->left = r;
      else root->right = r;
      return r;
    }

    if(info < r->info)
      stree(r, r->left, info);
    else
      stree(r, r->right, info);

    return root;
  }

void print_tree(struct tree *r, int l)
{
  int i;

  if(!r) return;

  print_tree(r->right, l+1);
  for(i=0; i<l; ++i) printf(" ");
  printf("%c\n", r->info);
  print_tree(r->left, l+1);
}
```

This program is actually sorting the information that you give it. It is essentially a variation of the insertion sort that you saw in the previous chapter. In the average case, its performance can be quite good.

If you have run the tree-printing program, you have probably noticed that some trees are *balanced*—that is, each subtree is the same or nearly the same height as any other—and that others are very far out of balance. In fact, if you entered the tree **abcd**, it would have looked like this:

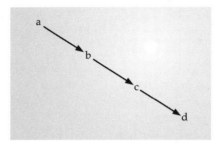

There would have been no left subtrees. This is called a *degenerate tree* because it has degenerated into a linear list. In general, if the data you are using as input to build a binary tree is fairly random, the tree produced approximates a balanced tree. However, if the information is already sorted, a degenerate tree results. (It is possible to readjust the tree with each insertion to keep the tree in balance, but this process is fairly complicated and beyond the scope of this chapter.)

Search functions are easy to implement for binary trees. The following function returns a pointer to the node in the tree that matches the key; otherwise, it returns a null.

```c
struct tree *search_tree(struct tree *root, char key)
{
  if(!root) return root;   /* empty tree */
  while(root->info != key) {
    if(key<root->info) root = root->left;
    else root = root->right;
    if(root == NULL) break;
  }
  return root;
}
```

Unfortunately, deleting a node from a tree is not as simple as searching a tree. The deleted node may be either the root, a left node, or a right node. Also, the node may have from zero to two subtrees attached to it. The process of rearranging the pointers lends itself to a recursive algorithm, which is shown here:

```c
struct tree *dtree(struct tree *root, char key)
{
  struct tree *p,*p2;

  if(!root) return root; /* not found */

  if(root->info == key) { /* delete root */
    /* this means an empty tree */
```

```
    if(root->left == root->right){
      free(root);
      return NULL;
    }
    /* or if one subtree is null */
    else if(root->left == NULL) {
      p = root->right;
      free(root);
      return p;
    }
    else if(root->right == NULL) {
      p = root->left;
      free(root);
      return p;
    }
    /* or both subtrees present */
    else {
      p2 = root->right;
      p = root->right;
      while(p->left) p = p->left;
      p->left = root->left;
      free(root);
      return p2;
    }
  }
  if(root->info < key) root->right = dtree(root->right, key);
  else root->left = dtree(root->left, key);
  return root;
}
```

Remember to update the pointer to the root in the rest of your program code because the node deleted could be the root of the tree. The best way to accomplish this is to assign the return value from **dtree( )** to the variable in your program that points to the root, using a call similar to the following:

```
root = dtree(root,  key);
```

Binary trees offer tremendous power, flexibility, and efficiency. Because a balanced binary tree performs, as a worst case, $\log_2 n$ comparisons when searching, it is far better than a linked list, which must rely on a sequential search.

Chapter 23

Sparse Arrays

One of the more intriguing programming problems is the implementation of a sparse array. A *sparse array* is one in which not all the elements of the array are actually in use, present, or needed. Sparse arrays are valuable when both of the following conditions are met: The size of the array required by an application is quite large (possibly exceeding available memory), and not all array locations will be used. Thus, a sparse array is typically a thinly populated, large array. As you will see, there are several ways in which sparse arrays can be implemented. Before we begin, let's examine the problem that sparse arrays are designed to solve.

Understanding the Need for Sparse Arrays

To understand the need for sparse arrays, consider the following two points:

- When you declare a normal C array, all of the memory required by the array is allocated when that array comes into existence.

- Large arrays—especially multidimensional arrays—can consume vast quantities of memory.

The fact that memory for an array is allocated when the array is created means that the largest array that you can declare within your program is limited (in part) by the amount of available memory. If you need an array larger than will fit within the physical confines of your computer, you must use some other mechanism to support the array. (For example, a fully populated large array typically uses some form of virtual memory.) Even if the large array will fit in memory, declaring it may not always be a good idea because the memory consumed by the large array is not available to the rest of your program or to other processes running within the system. This may degrade the overall performance of your program or the computer itself. In situations in which not all array locations will actually be used, allocating memory for a large array is especially wasteful of system resources.

To solve the problems caused by large, thinly populated arrays, several sparse array techniques have been invented. All sparse array techniques share one thing in common: they allocate memory for elements of the array only as needed. Therefore, the advantage of a sparse array is that it requires memory only for elements actually in use. This leaves the rest of memory free for other uses. It also allows extremely large arrays—larger than would normally be allowed by the system—to be employed.

There are numerous examples of applications that require sparse-array processing. Many apply to matrix operations, or to scientific and engineering problems that are easily understood only by experts in those fields. However, one very familiar application typically uses a sparse array: a spreadsheet program. Even though the matrix of the average spreadsheet is very large, only a portion of the matrix is actually in use at any one time. Spreadsheets use the matrix to hold formulas, values, and strings associated with each location. Using a sparse array, storage for each element is allocated from the pool of free memory as it is needed. Because only a small portion of the array elements are actually in use, the array (that is, the spreadsheet) may appear very large while requiring memory only for those cells actually in use.

Two terms will be used repeatedly in this chapter: *logical array* and *physical array*. The logical array is the array that you think of as existing in the system. For example, if a spreadsheet matrix has dimensions of 1,000 by 1,000, then the logical array that supports that matrix also has dimensions of 1,000 by 1,000—even though this array does not physically exist within the computer. The physical array is the array that actually exists inside the computer. Thus, if only 100 elements of a spreadsheet matrix are in use, the physical array requires memory for only these 100 elements. The sparse-array techniques developed in this chapter provide the link between the logical and physical arrays.

This chapter examines four distinct techniques for creating a sparse array: the linked list, the binary tree, a pointer array, and hashing. Although no spreadsheet program is actually developed, all examples relate to a spreadsheet matrix that is organized as shown in Figure 23-1. In the figure, the X is located in cell B2.

The Linked-List Sparse Array

When you implement a sparse array by using a linked list, the first thing you must do is create a structure that holds the following items:

- The data that is being stored
- Its logical position in the array
- Links to the previous and next element

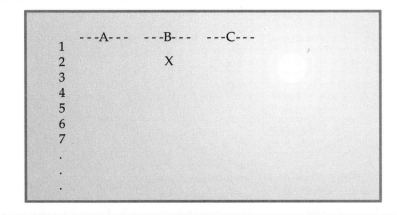

Figure 23-1.   *Organization of a simple spreadsheet*

Each new structure is placed in the list with the elements inserted in sorted order based on the array index. The array is accessed by following the links.

For example, you can use the following structure as the basis of a sparse array in a spreadsheet program:

```
struct cell {
  char cell_name[9];  /* cell name e.g., A1, B34 */
  char  formula[128]; /* info e.g., 10/B2 */
  struct cell *next;  /* pointer to next entry */
  struct cell *prior; /* pointer to previous record */
} ;
```

The field **cell_name** holds a string that contains a cell name such as A1, B34, or Z19. The string **formula** holds the formula (data) that is assigned to each spreadsheet location.

An entire spreadsheet program would be far too large to use as an example. Instead this chapter examines the key functions that support the linked-list sparse array. Remember, there are many ways to implement a spreadsheet program. The data structure and routines here are just examples of sparse-array techniques.

The following global variables point to the beginning and end of the linked-list array:

```
struct cell *start = NULL; /* first element in list */
struct cell *last = NULL;  /* last element in list */
```

When you enter a formula into a cell in most spreadsheets, you are, in effect, creating a new element in the sparse array. If the spreadsheet uses a linked list, that new cell is inserted into it via a function similar to **dls_store( )**, which was developed in Chapter 22. Remember that the list is sorted according to the cell name; that is, A12 precedes A13, and so on.

```
/* Store cells in sorted order. */
void dls_store(struct cell *i, /* pointer to new cell to insert */
            struct cell **start,
            struct cell **last)
{
  struct cell *old, *p;

  if(!*last) { /* first element in list */
    i->next = NULL;
    i->prior = NULL;
    *last = i;
```

```
      *start = i;
      return;
  }

  p = *start; /* start at top of list */

  old = NULL;
  while(p) {
    if(strcmp(p->cell_name, i->cell_name) < 0){
      old = p;
      p = p->next;
    }
    else {
      if(p->prior) { /* is a middle element */
        p->prior->next = i;
        i->next = p;
        i->prior = p->prior;
        p->prior = i;
        return;
      }
      i->next = p; /* new first element */
      i->prior = NULL;
      p->prior = i;
      *start = i;
      return;
    }
  }
  old->next = i; /* put on end */
  i->next = NULL;
  i->prior = old;
  *last = i;
  return;
}
```

ALGORITHMS AND
APPLICATIONS

Here, the parameter **i** is a pointer to the new cell to insert. The **start** and **last** parameters are pointers to pointers that point to the beginning and end of the list, respectively.

The **deletecell( )** function, which follows, removes from the list the cell whose name is an argument to the function.

```
void deletecell(char *cell_name,
            struct cell **start,
            struct cell **last)
```

```
{
  struct cell *info;

  info = find(cell_name, *start);
  if(info) {
    if(*start==info) {
      *start = info->next;
      if(*start) (*start)->prior = NULL;
      else *last = NULL;
    }
    else {
      if(info->prior) info->prior->next = info->next;
      if(info != *last)
          info->next->prior = info->prior;
      else
        *last = info->prior;
    }
    free(info); /* return memory to system */
  }
}
```

The final function that you need in order to support a linked-list sparse array is **find( )**, which locates any specific cell. The function requires a linear search to locate each item; and, as you saw in Chapter 21, the average number of comparisons in a linear search is $n/2$, where n is the number of elements in the list. Here is **find( )**:

```
struct cell *find(char *cell_name, struct cell *start)
{
  struct cell *info;

  info = start;
  while(info) {
    if(!strcmp(cell_name, info->cell_name)) return info;
    info = info->next; /* get next cell */
  }
  printf("Cell not found.\n");
  return NULL; /* not found */
}
```

Analysis of the Linked-List Approach

The principal advantage of the linked-list approach to sparse arrays is that it makes efficient use of memory—memory is used only for those elements in the array that actually contain information. It is also simple to implement. However, it has one major drawback: It must use a linear search to access cells in the list. Also, the store routine uses a linear search to find the proper place to insert a new cell into the list. You can solve these problems by using a binary tree to support the sparse array, as shown next.

The Binary-Tree Approach to Sparse Arrays

In essence, the binary tree is simply a modified doubly linked list. Its major advantage over a list is that it can be searched quickly, which means that insertions and lookups are very fast. In applications where you want a linked-list structure but need fast search times, the binary tree is perfect.

To use a binary tree to support the spreadsheet example, you must change the structure **cell** as shown in the code that follows:

```c
struct cell {
  char cell_name[9];   /* cell name e.g., A1, B34 */
  char  formula[128]; /* info e.g., 10/B2 */
  struct cell *left;   /* pointer to left subtree */
  struct cell *right; /* pointer to right subtree */
} list_entry;
```

You can modify the **stree( )** function from Chapter 22 so that it builds a tree based on the cell name. Notice that the following assumes that the parameter **n** is a pointer to a new entry in the tree.

```c
struct cell *stree(
        struct cell *root,
        struct cell *r,
        struct cell *n)
{
  if(!r) {     /* first node in subtree */
    n->left = NULL;
    n->right = NULL;
    if(!root) return n;  /* first entry in tree */
    if(strcmp(n->cell_name, root->cell_name) < 0)
      root->left = n;
    else
      root->right = n;
    return n;
  }

  if(strcmp(r->cell_name, n->cell_name) <= 0)
```

```
      stree(r, r->right, n);
   else
      stree(r, r->left, n);

   return root;
}
```

The **stree( )** function must be called with a pointer to the root node for the first two parameters and a pointer to the new cell for the third. It returns a pointer to the root.

To delete a cell from the spreadsheet, modify the **dtree( )** function, as shown here, to accept the name of the cell as a key:

```
struct cell *dtree(
        struct cell *root,
        char *key)
{
   struct cell *p, *p2;

   if(!root) return root; /* item not found */

   if(!strcmp(root->cell_name, key)) { /* delete root */
     /* this means an empty tree */
     if(root->left == root->right){
       free(root);
       return NULL;
     }
     /* or if one subtree is null */
     else if(root->left == NULL) {
       p = root->right;
       free(root);
       return p;
     }
     else if(root->right == NULL) {
       p = root->left;
       free(root);
       return p;
     }
     /* or both subtrees present */
     else {
```

```
        p2 = root->right;
        p = root->right;
        while(p->left) p = p->left;
        p->left = root->left;
        free(root);
        return p2;
    }
  }
  if(strcmp(root->cell_name, key)<=0)
    root->right = dtree(root->right, key);
  else root->left = dtree(root->left, key);
  return root;
}
```

Finally, you can use a modified version of the **search( )** function to quickly locate any cell in the spreadsheet if you specify its cell name.

```
struct cell *search_tree(
        struct cell *root,
        char *key)
{
  if(!root) return root;   /* empty tree */
  while(strcmp(root->cell_name, key)) {
    if(strcmp(root->cell_name, key) <= 0)
      root = root->right;
    else root = root->left;
    if(root == NULL) break;
  }
  return root;
}
```

Analysis of the Binary-Tree Approach

A binary tree results in much faster insert and search times than a linked list. Remember, a sequential search requires, on average, $n/2$ comparisons, where n is the number of elements in the list. A binary search, in contrast, requires only $\log_2 n$ comparisons (assuming a balanced tree). Also, the binary tree is as memory-efficient as a doubly linked list. However, in some situations, there is a better alternative than the binary tree.

The Pointer-Array Approach to Sparse Arrays

Suppose your spreadsheet has the dimensions 26 by 100 (A1 through Z100), or a total of 2,600 elements. In theory, you could use the following array of structures to hold the spreadsheet entries:

```
struct cell {
  char cell_name[9];
  char  formula[128];
} list_entry[2600];    /* 2,600 cells */
```

However, 2,600 multiplied by 137 (the raw size of the structure) amounts to 356,200 bytes of memory. This is a lot of memory to waste on an array that is not fully populated. However, you could create an *array of pointers* to structures of type **cell**. This array of pointers would require a significantly smaller amount of permanent storage than the actual array. Each time an array location is assigned data, memory would be allocated for that data and the appropriate pointer in the pointer array would be set to point to that data. This scheme offers superior performance over the linked-list and binary-tree methods. The declaration that creates such an array of pointers is

```
struct cell {
  char cell_name[9];
  char formula[128];
} list_entry;

struct cell *sheet[2600]; /* array of 2,600 pointers */
```

You can use this smaller array to hold pointers to the information that is actually entered by the spreadsheet user. As each entry is made, a pointer to the information about the cell is stored in the proper location in the array. Figure 23-2 shows how this might appear in memory, with the pointer array providing support for the sparse array.

Before the pointer array can be used, each element must be initialized to null, which indicates that there is no entry in that location. The function that does this is

```
void init_sheet(void)
{
  register int t;

  for(t=0; t < 2600; ++t) sheet[t] = NULL;
}
```

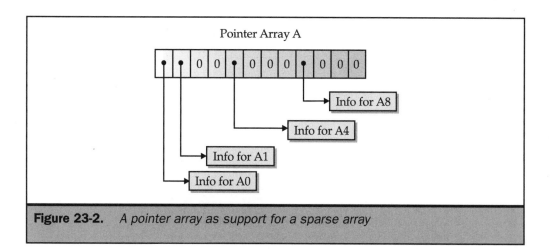

Pointer Array A

Info for A8

Info for A4

Info for A1

Info for A0

Figure 23-2.   *A pointer array as support for a sparse array*

When the user enters a formula for a cell, the cell location (which is defined by its name) is used to produce an index for the pointer array **sheet**. The index is derived from the cell name by converting the name into a number, as shown in the following listing:

```
void store(struct cell *i)
{
  int loc;
  char *p;

  /* compute index given cell name */
  loc = *(i->cell_name) - 'A'; /* column */
  p = &(i->cell_name[1]);
  loc += (atoi(p)-1) * 26; /* number of rows * row width + column */

  if(loc >= 2600) {
    printf("Cell out of bounds.\n");
    return;
  }
  sheet[loc] = i; /* place pointer in the array */
}
```

When computing the index, **store( )** assumes that all cell names start with a capital letter and are followed by an integer—for example, B34, C19, and so on. Therefore, using the formula shown in **store( )**, the cell name A1 produces an index of 0, B1 produces an index of 1, A2 produces an index of 26, and so on. Because each cell name is unique, each index is also unique, and the pointer to each entry is stored in the proper array element. If you compare this procedure to the linked-list or binary-tree version, you will see how much shorter and simpler it is.

The **deletecell( )** function also becomes very short. Called with the name of the cell to remove, it simply zeroes the pointer to the element and returns the memory to the system.

```c
void deletecell(struct cell *i)
{
  int loc;
  char *p;

  /* compute index given cell name */
  loc = *(i->cell_name) - 'A'; /* column */
  p = &(i->cell_name[1]);
  loc += (atoi(p)-1) * 26; /* number of rows * row width + column */

  if(loc >= 2600) {
    printf("Cell out of bounds.\n");
    return;
  }
  if(!sheet[loc]) return; /* don't free a null pointer */

  free(sheet[loc]);  /* return memory to system */
  sheet[loc] = NULL;
}
```

Once again, this code is much faster and simpler than the linked-list version.

The process of locating a cell given its name is simple because the name itself directly produces the array index. Therefore, the function **find( )** becomes

```c
struct cell *find(char *cell_name)
{
  int loc;
  char *p;

  /* compute index given name */
  loc = *(cell_name) - 'A'; /* column */
  p = &(cell_name[1]);
  loc += (atoi(p)-1) * 26; /* number of rows * row width + column */
```

```
  if(loc>=2600 || !sheet[loc]) { /* no entry in that cell */
    printf("Cell not found.\n");
    return NULL;   /* not found */
  }
  else return sheet[loc];
}
```

Analysis of the Pointer-Array Approach

The pointer-array method of sparse-array handling provides much faster access to array elements than either the linked-list or binary-tree method. Unless the array is very large, the memory used by the pointer array is not usually a significant drain on the free memory of the system. However, the pointer array itself uses some memory for every location—whether the pointers are pointing to actual information or not. This may be a limitation for certain applications, but it is not a problem in general.

Hashing

Hashing is the process of extracting the index of an array element directly from the information that is stored there. The index generated is called the *hash*. Traditionally, hashing has been applied to disk files as a means of decreasing access time. However, you can use the same general methods to implement sparse arrays. The preceding pointer-array example used a special form of hashing called *direct indexing*, where each key maps onto one and only one array location. In other words, each hashed index is unique. (The pointer-array method does not require a direct indexing hash—this was just an obvious approach given the spreadsheet problem.) In actual practice, such direct hashing schemes are few, and a more flexible method is required. This section shows how hashing can be generalized to allow greater power and flexibility.

The spreadsheet example makes clear that even in the most rigorous environments, not every cell in the sheet will be used. Suppose that for virtually all cases, no more than 10 percent of the potential locations are occupied by actual entries. Therefore, if the spreadsheet has dimensions 26 by 100 (2,600 locations), only about 260 are actually used at any one time. This implies that the largest array necessary to hold all the entries will normally consist of only 260 elements. But how do the logical array locations get mapped onto and accessed from this smaller physical array? And what happens when this array is full? The following discussion describes one possible solution.

When data for a cell is entered by the user of the spreadsheet (which is the logical array), the cell location, defined by its name, is used to produce an index (a hash) into the smaller physical array. As it relates to hashing, the physical array is also called the *primary array*. The index is derived from the cell name, which is converted into a number, as in the pointer-array example. However, this number is then divided by 10 to produce an initial entry point into the primary array. (Remember, in this example the size of the physical array is only 10 percent of the logical array.) If the location referenced by this index is free, the logical index and the value are stored there. However, since 10 logical locations actually map onto one physical location, hash collisions can occur. When this happens, a linked list, sometimes called the *collision list*, is used to hold the entry. A separate collision list is associated with each entry in the primary array. Of course, these lists are zero length until a collision occurs, as depicted in Figure 23-3.

Suppose you want to find an element in the physical array, given its logical array index. First, transform the logical index into its hash value, and check the physical array at the index generated by the hash to see if the logical index stored there matches the one that you are searching for. If it does, return the information. Otherwise, follow the collision list until either the proper index is found or the end of the chain is reached.

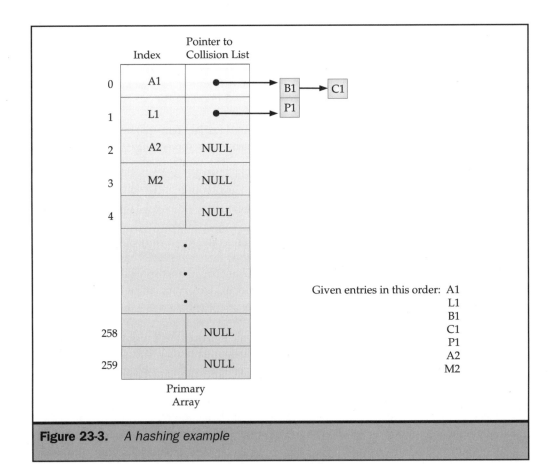

Figure 23-3.   *A hashing example*

The hashing example uses an array of structures, called **primary**, shown here:

```
#define MAX 260

struct htype {
  int index;    /* logical index */
  int val;      /* actual value of the array element */
  struct htype *next; /* pointer to next value with same hash */
} primary[MAX];
```

Before this array can be used, it must be initialized. The following function initializes the **index** field to –1 (a value that, by definition, cannot be generated) to indicate an empty element. A **NULL** in the **next** field indicates an empty hash chain.

```
/* Initialize the hash array. */
void init(void)
{
  register int i;

  for (i=0; i<MAX; i++) {
    primary[i].index = -1;
    primary[i].next = NULL;  /* null chain */
    primary[i].val = 0;
  }
}
```

The **store( )** procedure converts a cell name into a hashed index into the **primary** array. If the location directly pointed to by the hashed value is occupied, the procedure automatically adds the entry to the collision list using a modified version of **slstore( )** developed in the preceding chapter. The logical index must be stored because it will be needed when that element is accessed again. These functions are shown here:

```
/* Compute hash and store value. */
void store(char *cell_name, int v)
{
  int h, loc;
  struct htype *p;

  /* produce the hash value */
  loc = *cell_name - 'A'; /* column */
  loc += (atoi(&cell_name[1])-1) * 26; /* rows * width + columns */
  h = loc/10; /* hash */
```

```
/* Store in the location unless full or
   store there if logical indexes agree - i.e., update.
*/
if(primary[h].index==-1 || primary[h].index==loc) {
  primary[h].index = loc;
  primary[h].val = v;
  return;
}

/* otherwise, create or add to collision list */
p = (struct htype *) malloc(sizeof(struct htype));
if(!p) {
  printf("Out of Memory\n");
  return;
}
p->index = loc;
p->val = v;
slstore(p, &primary[h]);
}

/* Add elements to the collision list. */
void slstore(struct htype *i,
             struct htype *start)
{
  struct htype *old, *p;

  old = start;
  /* find end of list */
  while(start) {
    old = start;
    start = start->next;
  }
  /* link in new entry */
  old->next = i;
  i->next = NULL;
}
```

Before finding the value of an element, your program must first compute the hash and then check to see if the logical index stored in the physical array matches the index of the logical array that is requested. If it does, that value is returned; otherwise, the collision chain is searched. The **find( )** function, which performs these tasks, is shown here:

```
/* Compute hash and return value. */
int find(char *cell_name)
{
  int h, loc;
  struct htype *p;

  /* produce the hash value */
  loc = *cell_name - 'A'; /* column */
  loc += (atoi(&cell_name[1])-1) * 26; /* rows * width + column */
  h = loc/10;

  /* return the value if found */
  if(primary[h].index == loc) return(primary[h].val);
  else { /* look in collision list */
    p = primary[h].next;
    while(p) {
      if(p->index == loc) return p->val;
      p = p->next;
    }
    printf("Not in Array\n");
    return -1;
  }
}
```

Creating a deletion function is left to you as an exercise. (*Hint*: Just reverse the insertion process.)

Keep in mind that the preceding hashing algorithm is very simple. Generally, you would use a more complex method to provide a more even distribution of indexes in the primary array, thus avoiding long hash chains. However, the basic principle is the same.

Analysis of Hashing

In its best case (quite rare), each physical index created by the hash is unique, and access times approximate that of direct indexing. This means that no collision lists are created, and all lookups are essentially direct accesses. However, this will seldom be the case because it requires that the logical indexes be evenly distributed throughout the physical index space. In a worst case (also rare), a hashed scheme degenerates into a linked list. This can happen when the hashed values of the logical indexes are all the same. In the average (and the most likely) case, the hash method can access any specific element in the time it takes to use a direct index plus some constant that is proportional to the average length of the hash chains. The most critical factor in using hashing to support a sparse array is to make sure that the hashing algorithm spreads the physical index evenly so that long collision lists are avoided.

Choosing an Approach

You must consider speed and the efficient use of memory when deciding whether to use a linked list, a binary tree, a pointer array, or a hashing approach to implement a sparse array. Further, you must consider whether your sparse array will most likely be thinly populated or thickly populated.

When the logical array is very sparse, the most memory-efficient approaches are the linked lists and binary trees, because only array elements that are actually in use have memory allocated to them. The links themselves require very little additional memory and generally have a negligible effect. The pointer-array design requires that the entire pointer array exist, even if some of its elements are not used. Not only must the entire pointer array be in memory, but enough memory must be left over for the application to use. This could be a serious problem for certain applications, whereas it may not be a problem at all for others. Usually you can calculate the approximate amount of free memory and determine whether it is sufficient for your program. The hashing method lies somewhere between the pointer-array and the linked-list/binary-tree approaches. Although it requires that all of the primary array exist even if it is not all used, it will still be smaller than a pointer array.

When the logical array is fairly full, the situation changes substantially. In this case, the pointer array and hashing become more appealing. Further, the time it takes to find an element in the pointer array is constant no matter how full the logical array is. While not constant, the search time for the hashing approach is bounded by some low value. However, for the linked list and binary tree, average search time increases as the array becomes more heavily populated. You will want to keep this in mind if consistent access times are important.

Chapter 24

Expression Parsing and Evaluation

How do you write a program that will take as input a string containing a numeric expression, such as (10 − 5) * 3, and compute the proper answer? If there is still a "high priesthood" among programmers, it must be those few who know how to do this. Many otherwise accomplished programmers are mystified by the way a high-level language converts algebraic expressions into instructions that a computer can execute. This procedure is called *expression parsing*, and it is the backbone of all language compilers and interpreters, spreadsheets, and anything else that needs to convert numeric expressions into a form that the computer can use.

Although mysterious, expression parsing is actually quite straightforward and is, in many ways, easier than several other programming tasks. The reason for this is that the problem is well defined and works according to the strict rules of algebra. This chapter will develop what is commonly referred to as a *recursive-descent parser* and all the necessary support routines that enable you to evaluate numeric expressions. Once you have mastered the operation of the parser, you can easily enhance and modify it to suit your needs.

The C interpreter presented in Part Six of this book uses an enhanced form of the parser developed here. If you will be exploring the C interpreter, you will find the material in this chapter especially useful.

Expressions

Although expressions can be made up of all types of information, this chapter deals only with numeric expressions. For our purposes, *numeric expressions* are composed of the following items:

- Numbers
- The operators +, −, /, *, ^, %, =
- Parentheses
- Variables

The operator ^ indicates exponentiation, as in BASIC, and = is the assignment operator. These items can be combined in expressions according to the rules of algebra. Here are some examples:

```
10 − 8
(100 − 5) * 14/6
a + b − c
10^5
a = 10 − b
```

Assume this precedence for each operator:

highest	unary + and −
	^
	* / %
	+ −
lowest	=

Operators of equal precedence evaluate from left to right.

In the examples in this chapter, all variables are single letters (in other words, 26 variables, **A** through **Z**, are available). The variables are not case sensitive (**a** and **A** are treated as the same variable). Each numeric value is a **double**, although you could easily write the routines to handle other types of values. Finally, to keep the logic clear and easy to understand, only a minimal amount of error checking is included.

In case you have not thought much about the process of expression parsing, try to evaluate this sample expression:

$10 - 2 * 3$

You know that this expression is equal to the value 4. Although you could easily create a program that would compute that *specific* expression, the question is how to create a program that gives the correct answer for any *arbitrary* expression. At first you might think of a routine something like this:

```
a = get first operand
while(operands present) {
        op = get operator
        b = get second operand
        a = a op b
}
```

This routine gets the first operand, the operator, and the second operand to perform the first operation and then gets the next operator and operand—if any—to perform the next operation, and so on.

However, if you use this approach, the expression $10 - 2 * 3$ evaluates to 24 (that is, 8 * 3) instead of 4 because this procedure neglects the precedence of the operators. You cannot just take the operands and operators in order from left to right because the rules of algebra dictate that multiplication must be done before subtraction. Some beginners think that this problem can be easily overcome, and sometimes—in very restricted cases—it can. But the problem only gets worse when you add parentheses, exponentiation, variables, function calls, and the like.

Although there are a few ways to write a routine that evaluates expressions, the one developed here is most easily written by a person. It is also the most common. (Some of the other methods used to write parsers employ complex tables that must be generated by another computer program. These are sometimes called *table-driven parsers*.) The method used here is called a *recursive-descent parser*, and in the course of this chapter, you will see how it got its name.

Dissecting an Expression

Before you can develop a parser to evaluate expressions, you need to be able to break an expression into its components. For example, the expression

A * B – (W + 10)

contains the components A, *, B, –, (, W, +, 10, and). Each component represents an indivisible unit of the expression. In general, you need a function that returns each item in the expression individually. This function must also be able to skip over spaces and tabs and detect the end of the expression.

Each component of an expression is called a *token*. Therefore, the function that returns the next token in the expression is often called **get_token( )**. **get_token( )** requires a global character pointer to the string that holds the expression. In the version of **get_token( )** shown here, **prog** is the global character pointer. **prog** is global because it must maintain its value between calls to **get_token( )** and allow other functions to use it. Besides returning a token, you need to know what type of token is being returned. For the parser developed in this chapter, you need only three types: **VARIABLE**, **NUMBER**, and **DELIMITER**. (**DELIMITER** is used for both operators and parentheses.) Here is **get_token( )** along with its necessary globals, **#define**s, and support function:

```
#define DELIMITER 1
#define VARIABLE  2
#define NUMBER    3

extern char *prog;  /* points to the expression to be analyzed */
char token[80];
char tok_type;

/* Return the next token. */
void get_token(void)
{
  register char *temp;
```

```
  tok_type = 0;
  temp = token;
  *temp = '\0';

  if(!*prog) return; /* at end of expression */
  while(isspace(*prog)) ++prog;   /* skip over white space */

  if(strchr("+-*/%^=()", *prog)){
    tok_type = DELIMITER;
    /* advance to next char */
    *temp++ = *prog++;
  }
  else if(isalpha(*prog)) {
    while(!isdelim(*prog)) *temp++ = *prog++;
    tok_type = VARIABLE;
  }
  else if(isdigit(*prog)) {
    while(!isdelim(*prog)) *temp++ = *prog++;
    tok_type = NUMBER;
  }

  *temp = '\0';
}

/* Return true if c is a delimiter. */
int isdelim(char c)
{
  if(strchr(" +-/*%^=()", c) || c==9 || c=='\r' || c==0)
    return 1;
  return 0;
}
```

Look closely at the preceding functions. After the first few initializations, **get_token( )** checks to see if the null terminating the expression has been found. If it has, the end of the expression has been reached. If there are still more tokens to retrieve from the expression, **get_token( )** first skips over any leading spaces. Once the spaces have been skipped, **prog** is pointing to either a number, a variable, an operator, or—if trailing spaces end the expression—a null. If the next character is an operator, it is returned as a string in the global variable **token**, and **DELIMITER** is placed in **tok_type**. If the next character is a letter instead, it is assumed to be one of the variables. It is returned as a string in **token**, and **tok_type** is assigned the value **VARIABLE**. If the next character is a digit, the entire number is read and placed in the string **token**, and its type is

NUMBER. Finally, if the next character is none of the preceding, it is assumed that the end of the expression has been reached. In this case, **token** is null, which signals the end of the expression.

As stated earlier, to keep the code in this function clean, a certain amount of error checking has been omitted, and some assumptions have been made. For example, any unrecognized character can end an expression. Also, in this version, variables can be of any length, but only the first letter is significant. You can add more error checking and other details as your specific application dictates. You can easily modify or enhance **get_token( )** to enable character strings, other types of numbers, or whatever, to be returned one token at a time from an input string.

To understand better how **get_token( )** works, study what it returns for each token and type in the following expression:

A + 100 – (B * C) /2

Token	Token Type
A	VARIABLE
+	DELIMITER
100	NUMBER
–	DELIMITER
(	DELIMITER
B	VARIABLE
*	DELIMITER
C	VARIABLE
)	DELIMITER
/	DELIMITER
2	NUMBER
null	Null

Remember that **token** always holds a null-terminated string, even if it contains only a single character.

Expression Parsing

There are a number of ways to parse and evaluate an expression. When working with a recursive-descent parser, think of expressions as *recursive data structures*—that is, expressions that are defined in terms of themselves. If, for the moment, expressions can only use +, –, *, /, and parentheses, all expressions can be defined with the following rules:

expression -> term [+ term] [– term]
term -> factor [* factor] [/ factor]
factor -> variable, number, or (expression)

The square brackets designate an optional element, and -> means "produces." In fact, the rules are usually called the *production rules* of an expression. Therefore, you could say: "Term produces factor times factor or factor divided by factor" for the definition of *term*. Notice that the precedence of the operators is implicit in the way an expression is defined.

Let's look at an example. The expression

10 + 5 * B

has two terms: 10 and 5 * B. The second term contains two factors: 5 and B. These factors consist of one number and one variable.

On the other hand, the expression

14 * (7 – C)

has two factors: 14 and (7 – C). The factors consist of one number and one parenthesized expression. The parenthesized expression contains two terms: one number and one variable.

This process forms the basis for a *recursive-descent parser*, which is essentially a set of mutually recursive functions that work in a chainlike fashion. At each appropriate step, the parser performs the specified operations in the algebraically correct sequence. To see how this process works, parse the input expression that follows, using the preceding production rules, and perform the arithmetic operations at the appropriate time.

9/3 – (100 + 56)

If you parsed the expression correctly, you followed these steps:

1. Get the first term, 9/3.
2. Get each factor and divide the integers. The resulting value is 3.
3. Get the second term, (100 + 56). At this point, start recursively analyzing the second subexpression.
4. Get each term and add. The resulting value is 156.
5. Return from the recursive call and subtract 156 from 3. The answer is –153.

If you are a little confused at this point, don't feel bad. Expression parsing is a fairly complex concept that takes some getting used to. There are two basic things to remember about this recursive view of expressions. First, the precedence of the operators is implicit in the way the production rules are defined. Second, this method of parsing and evaluating expressions is very similar to the way humans evaluate mathematical expressions.

A Simple Expression Parser

The remainder of this chapter develops two parsers. The first will parse and evaluate only constant expressions—that is, expressions with no variables. This example shows the parser in its simplest form. The second parser will include the 26 variables **A** through **Z**.

Here is the entire version of the simple recursive-descent parser for floating-point expressions:

```c
/* This module contains a simple expression parser
   that does not recognize variables.
*/

#include <stdlib.h>
#include <ctype.h>
#include <stdio.h>
#include <string.h>

#define DELIMITER 1
#define VARIABLE  2
#define NUMBER    3

extern char *prog;   /* holds expression to be analyzed */
char token[80];
char tok_type;

void eval_exp(double *answer), eval_exp2(double *answer);
void eval_exp3(double *answer), eval_exp4(double *answer);
void eval_exp5(double *answer), eval_exp6(double *answer);
void atom(double *answer);
void get_token(void), putback(void);
void serror(int error);
int isdelim(char c);

/* Parser entry point. */
void eval_exp(double *answer)
{
```

```
  get_token();
  if(!*token) {
    serror(2);
    return;
  }
  eval_exp2(answer);

  if(*token) serror(0); /* last token must be null */
}

/* Add or subtract two terms. */
void eval_exp2(double *answer)
{
  register char  op;
  double temp;

  eval_exp3(answer);
  while((op = *token) == '+' || op == '-') {
    get_token();
    eval_exp3(&temp);
    switch(op) {
      case '-':
        *answer = *answer - temp;
        break;
      case '+':
        *answer = *answer + temp;
        break;
    }
  }
}

/* Multiply or divide two factors. */
void eval_exp3(double *answer)
{
  register char op;
  double temp;

  eval_exp4(answer);
  while((op = *token) == '*' || op == '/' || op == '%') {
    get_token();
    eval_exp4(&temp);
    switch(op) {
```

```
      case '*':
        *answer = *answer * temp;
        break;
      case '/':
        if(temp == 0.0) {
          serror(3); /* division by zero */
          *answer = 0.0;
        } else *answer = *answer / temp;
        break;
      case '%':
        *answer = (int) *answer % (int) temp;
        break;
    }
  }
}

/* Process an exponent */
void eval_exp4(double *answer)
{
  double temp, ex;
  register int t;

  eval_exp5(answer);

  if(*token == '^') {
    get_token();
    eval_exp4(&temp);
    ex = *answer;
    if(temp==0.0) {
      *answer = 1.0;
      return;
    }
    for(t=temp-1; t>0; --t) *answer = (*answer) * (double)ex;
  }
}

/* Evaluate a unary + or -. */
void eval_exp5(double *answer)
{
  register char  op;

  op = 0;
```

```
  if((tok_type == DELIMITER) && *token=='+' || *token == '-') {
    op = *token;
    get_token();
  }
  eval_exp6(answer);
  if(op == '-') *answer = -(*answer);
}

/* Process a parenthesized expression. */
void eval_exp6(double *answer)
{
  if((*token == '(')) {
    get_token();
    eval_exp2(answer);
    if(*token != ')')
      serror(1);
    get_token();
  }
  else
    atom(answer);
}

/* Get the value of a number. */
void atom(double *answer)
{
  if(tok_type == NUMBER) {
    *answer = atof(token);
    get_token();
    return;
  }
  serror(0);  /* otherwise syntax error in expression */
}

/* Return a token to the input stream. */
void putback(void)
{
  char *t;

  t = token;
  for(; *t; t++) prog--;
}
```

```c
/* Display a syntax error. */
void serror(int error)
{
  static char *e[]= {
      "Syntax Error",
      "Unbalanced Parentheses",
      "No Expression Present",
      "Division by Zero"
  };
  printf("%s\n", e[error]);
}

/* Return the next token. */
void get_token(void)
{
  register char *temp;

  tok_type = 0;
  temp = token;
  *temp = '\0';

  if(!*prog) return; /* at end of expression */
  while(isspace(*prog)) ++prog; /* skip over white space */

  if(strchr("+-*/%^=()", *prog)){
    tok_type = DELIMITER;
    /* advance to next char */
    *temp++ = *prog++;
  }
  else if(isalpha(*prog)) {
    while(!isdelim(*prog)) *temp++ = *prog++;
    tok_type = VARIABLE;
  }
  else if(isdigit(*prog)) {
    while(!isdelim(*prog)) *temp++ = *prog++;
    tok_type = NUMBER;
  }

  *temp = '\0';
}

/* Return true if c is a delimiter. */
```

```
int isdelim(char c)
{

  if(strchr(" +-/*%^=()", c) || c==9 || c=='\r' || c==0)
    return 1;
  return 0;
}
```

The parser as it is shown can handle the following operators: +, –, *, /, %. In addition, it can handle integer exponentiation (^) and the unary minus. The parser can also deal with parentheses correctly. Notice that it has six levels as well as the **atom( )** function, which returns the value of a number. As discussed, the two globals **token** and **tok_type** return, respectively, the next token and its type from the expression string. The pointer **prog** points to the string that holds the expression.

The simple **main( )** function that follows demonstrates the use of the parser:

```
/* Parser demo program. */
#include <stdlib.h>
#include <ctype.h>
#include <stdio.h>
#include <string.h>

char *prog;
void eval_exp(double *answer);

int main(void)
{
  double answer;
  char *p;

  p = (char *) malloc(100);
  if(!p) {
    printf("Allocation failure.\n");
    exit(1);
  }

  /* Process expressions until a blank line
     is entered.
  */
  do {
    prog = p;
```

ALGORITHMS AND APPLICATIONS

```
      printf("Enter expression: ");
      gets(prog);
      if(!*prog) break;
      eval_exp(&answer);
      printf("Answer is: %.2f\n", answer);
    } while(*p);

    return 0;
}
```

To understand exactly how the parser evaluates an expression, work through the following expression. (Assume that **prog** points to the start of the expression.)

10 – 3 * 2

When **eval_exp( )**, the entry point into the parser, is called, it gets the first token. If the token is null, the function prints the message **No Expression Present** and returns. However, in this case, the token contains the number **10**. Since the token is not null, **eval_exp2( )** is called. As a result, **eval_exp2( )** calls **eval_exp3( )**, and **eval_exp3( )** calls **eval_exp4( )**, which in turn calls **eval_exp5( )**. Then **eval_exp5( )** checks whether the token is a unary plus or minus, which in this case, it is not, so **eval_exp6( )** is called. At this point **eval_exp6( )** recursively calls either **eval_exp2( )** (in the case of a parenthesized expression) or **atom( )** to find the value of a number. Since the token is not a left parentheses, **atom( )** is executed, and ***answer** is assigned the value 10. Next, another token is retrieved, and the functions begin to return up the chain. The token is now the operator –, and the functions return up to **eval_exp2( )**.

What happens next is very important. Because the token is –, it is saved in **op**. The parser then gets the next token, which is 3, and the descent down the chain begins again. As before, **atom( )** is entered. The value 3 is returned in ***answer**, and the token * is read. This causes a return back up the chain to **eval_exp3( )**, where the final token 2 is read. At this point, the first arithmetic operation occurs—the multiplication of 2 and 3. The result is returned to **eval_exp2( )**, and the subtraction is performed. The subtraction yields the answer 4. Although this process may seem complicated at first, working through some other examples on your own will clarify the parser's operation.

This parser would be suitable for use by a desktop calculator, as illustrated by the previous program. It also could be used in a limited database. Before it could be used in a computer language or in a sophisticated calculator, however, it would need the ability to handle variables. This is the subject of the next section.

Adding Variables to the Parser

All programming languages, many calculators, and spreadsheets use variables to store values for later use. The simple parser in the preceding section needs to be expanded to include variables before it can store values. To include variables, you need to add several things to the parser. First, of course, are the variables themselves. As stated earlier, the parser recognizes only the variables **A** through **Z** (although you could expand that capability if you wanted to). Each variable uses one array location in a 26-element array of **double**s. Therefore, add the following to the parser:

```
double vars[26] = { /* 26 user variables,  A-Z */
  0.0, 0.0, 0.0, 0.0, 0.0, 0.0, 0.0, 0.0, 0.0, 0.0,
  0.0, 0.0, 0.0, 0.0, 0.0, 0.0, 0.0, 0.0, 0.0, 0.0,
  0.0, 0.0, 0.0, 0.0, 0.0, 0.0
};
```

As you can see, the variables are initialized to zero as a courtesy to the user.

You also need a routine to look up the value of a given variable. Because the variables are named **A** through **Z**, they can easily be used to index the array **vars** by subtracting the ASCII value for **A** from the variable name. The function **find_var( )** is shown here:

```
/* Return the value of a variable. */
double find_var(char *s)
{
  if(!isalpha(*s)){
    serror(1);
    return 0;
  }
  return vars[toupper(*token)-'A'];
}
```

As this function is written, it will actually accept long variable names, but only the first letter is significant. You can modify this to fit your needs.

You must also modify the **atom( )** function to handle both numbers and variables. The new version is shown here:

```
/* Get the value of a number or a variable. */
void atom(double *answer)
```

```
{
  switch(tok_type) {
    case VARIABLE:
      *answer = find_var(token);
      get_token();
      return;
    case NUMBER:
      *answer = atof(token);
      get_token();
      return;
    default:
      serror(0);
  }
}
```

Technically, these additions are all that is needed for the parser to use variables correctly; however, there is no way for these variables to be assigned a value. Often this is done outside the parser, but you can treat the equal sign as an assignment operator and make it part of the parser. There are various ways to do this. One method is to add **eval_exp1( )** to the parser, as shown here:

```
/* Process an assignment. */
void eval_exp1(double *result)
{
  int slot, ttok_type;
  char temp_token[80];

  if(tok_type == VARIABLE) {
    /* save old token */
    strcpy(temp_token, token);
    ttok_type = tok_type;

    /* compute the index of the variable */
    slot = toupper(*token) - 'A';

    get_token();
    if(*token != '=') {
      putback(); /* return current token */
      /* restore old token - not assignment */
      strcpy(token, temp_token);
      tok_type = ttok_type;
```

```
    }
    else {
      get_token(); /* get next part of exp */
      eval_exp2(result);
      vars[slot] = *result;
      return;
    }
  }

  eval_exp2(result);
}
```

As you can see, the function needs to look ahead to determine whether an assignment is actually being made. This is because a variable name always precedes an assignment, but a variable name alone does not guarantee that an assignment expression follows. That is, the parser will accept A = 100 as an assignment, but it is also smart enough to know that A/10 is not. To accomplish this, **eval_exp1( )** reads the next token from the input stream. If it is not an equal sign, the token is returned to the input stream for later use by calling **putback( )**, shown here:

```
/* Return a token to the input stream. */
void putback(void)
{
  char *t;

  t = token;
  for(; *t; t++) prog--;
}
```

Here is the entire enhanced parser:

```
/* This module contains the recursive descent
   parser that recognizes variables.
*/

#include <stdlib.h>
#include <ctype.h>
#include <stdio.h>
#include <string.h>

#define DELIMITER 1
```

```
#define VARIABLE  2
#define NUMBER     3

extern char *prog; /* points to the expression to be analyzed */
char token[80];
char tok_type;

double vars[26] = { /* 26 user variables,  A-Z */
 0.0, 0.0, 0.0, 0.0, 0.0, 0.0, 0.0, 0.0, 0.0, 0.0,
 0.0, 0.0, 0.0, 0.0, 0.0, 0.0, 0.0, 0.0, 0.0, 0.0,
 0.0, 0.0, 0.0, 0.0, 0.0, 0.0
};

void eval_exp(double *answer), eval_exp2(double *answer);
void eval_exp1(double *result);
void eval_exp3(double *answer), eval_exp4(double *answer);
void eval_exp5(double *answer), eval_exp6(double *answer);
void atom(double *answer);
void get_token(void), putback(void);
void serror(int error);
double find_var(char *s);
int isdelim(char c);

/* Parser entry point. */
void eval_exp(double *answer)
{
  get_token();
  if(!*token) {
    serror(2);
    return;
  }
  eval_exp1(answer);
  if(*token) serror(0); /* last token must be null */
}

/* Process an assignment. */
void eval_exp1(double *answer)
{
  int slot;
  char ttok_type;
  char temp_token[80];
```

```
  if(tok_type == VARIABLE) {
    /* save old token */
    strcpy(temp_token, token);
    ttok_type = tok_type;
    /* compute the index of the variable */
    slot = toupper(*token) - 'A';

    get_token();
    if(*token != '=') {
      putback(); /* return current token */
      /* restore old token - not assignment */
      strcpy(token, temp_token);
      tok_type = ttok_type;
    }
    else {
      get_token(); /* get next part of exp */
      eval_exp2(answer);
      vars[slot] = *answer;
      return;
    }
  }
  eval_exp2(answer);
}

/* Add or subtract two terms. */
void eval_exp2(double *answer)
{
  register char op;
  double temp;

  eval_exp3(answer);
  while((op = *token) == '+' || op == '-') {
    get_token();
    eval_exp3(&temp);
    switch(op) {
      case '-':
        *answer = *answer - temp;
        break;
      case '+':
        *answer = *answer + temp;
        break;
    }
```

```
    }
}

/* Multiply or divide two factors. */
void eval_exp3(double *answer)
{
  register char op;
  double temp;

  eval_exp4(answer);
  while((op = *token) == '*' || op == '/' || op == '%') {
    get_token();
    eval_exp4(&temp);
    switch(op) {
      case '*':
        *answer = *answer * temp;
        break;
      case '/':
        if(temp == 0.0) {
          serror(3); /* division by zero */
          *answer = 0.0;
        } else *answer = *answer / temp;
        break;
      case '%':
        *answer = (int) *answer % (int) temp;
        break;
    }
  }
}

/* Process an exponent */
void eval_exp4(double *answer)
{
  double temp, ex;
  register int t;

  eval_exp5(answer);
  if(*token == '^') {
    get_token();
    eval_exp4(&temp);
    ex = *answer;
    if(temp==0.0) {
```

```
      *answer = 1.0;
      return;
    }
    for(t=temp-1; t>0; --t) *answer = (*answer) * (double)ex;
  }
}

/* Evaluate a unary + or -. */
void eval_exp5(double *answer)
{
  register char  op;

  op = 0;
  if((tok_type == DELIMITER) && *token=='+' || *token == '-') {
    op = *token;
    get_token();
  }
  eval_exp6(answer);
  if(op == '-') *answer = -(*answer);
}

/* Process a parenthesized expression. */
void eval_exp6(double *answer)
{
  if((*token == '(')) {
    get_token();
    eval_exp2(answer);
    if(*token != ')')
      serror(1);
    get_token();
  }
  else atom(answer);
}

/* Get the value of a number or a variable. */
void atom(double *answer)
{
  switch(tok_type) {
    case VARIABLE:
      *answer = find_var(token);
      get_token();
      return;
```

```
      case NUMBER:
        *answer = atof(token);
        get_token();
        return;
      default:
        serror(0);
    }
}

/* Return a token to the input stream. */
void putback(void)
{
  char *t;

  t = token;
  for(; *t; t++) prog--;
}

/* Display a syntax error. */
void serror(int error)
{
  static char *e[]= {
      "Syntax Error",
      "Unbalanced Parentheses",
      "No Expression Present",
      "Division by Zero"
  };
  printf("%s\n", e[error]);
}

/* Return the next token. */
void get_token(void)
{
  register char *temp;

  tok_type = 0;
  temp = token;
  *temp = '\0';

  if(!*prog) return; /* at end of expression */

  while(isspace(*prog)) ++prog; /* skip over white space */
```

```
  if(strchr("+-*/%^=()", *prog)){
    tok_type = DELIMITER;
    /* advance to next char */
    *temp++ = *prog++;
  }
  else if(isalpha(*prog)) {
    while(!isdelim(*prog)) *temp++ = *prog++;
    tok_type = VARIABLE;
  }
  else if(isdigit(*prog)) {
    while(!isdelim(*prog)) *temp++ = *prog++;
    tok_type = NUMBER;
  }

  *temp = '\0';
}

/* Return true if c is a delimiter. */
int isdelim(char c)
{
  if(strchr(" +-/*%^=()", c) || c==9 || c=='\r' || c==0)
    return 1;
  return 0;
}

/* Return the value of a variable. */
double find_var(char *s)
{
  if(!isalpha(*s)){
    serror(1);
    return 0.0;
  }
  return vars[toupper(*token)-'A'];
}
```

You can still use the same **main( )** function that you used for the simple parser. With the enhanced parser, you can now enter expressions like

A = 10/4
A – B
C = A * (F – 21)

ALGORITHMS AND
APPLICATIONS

Syntax Checking in a Recursive-Descent Parser

In expression parsing, a syntax error is simply a situation in which the input expression does not conform to the strict rules required by the parser. Most of the time, this is caused by human error—usually typing mistakes. For example, the following expressions are not valid for the parsers in this chapter:

```
10 ** 8
(10 – 5) * 9)
/8
```

The first contains two operators in a row, the second has unbalanced parentheses, and the last has a division sign at the start of an expression. None of these conditions is allowed by the parsers in this chapter. Because syntax errors can cause the parser to give erroneous results, you need to guard against them.

As you studied the code of the parsers, you probably noticed the **serror( )** function, which is called under certain situations. This function is used to report errors. Unlike many other parsers, the recursive-descent method makes syntax checking easy because, for the most part, it occurs in **atom( )**, **find_var( )**, or **eval_exp6( )**, where parentheses are checked. The only problem with the syntax checking as it now stands is that the entire parser is not aborted on syntax error. This can lead to multiple error messages.

The best way to implement the **serror( )** function is to have it execute some sort of reset. For example, all modern compilers come with a pair of companion functions called **setjmp( )** and **longjmp( )**. These two functions allow a program to branch to a *different* function. Therefore, **serror( )** could execute a **longjmp( )** to some safe point in your program outside the parser.

If you leave the code the way it is, multiple syntax-error messages may be issued. This can be an annoyance in some situations, but it can be a blessing in others because multiple errors may be caught. Generally, however, you will want to enhance the parser's syntax checking before using it in commercial programs.

The Complete Reference

Chapter 25

AI-Based Problem Solving

The field of artificial intelligence (AI) comprises several different and exciting aspects, but fundamental to most AI applications is problem solving. Essentially, there are two types of problems. The first type can be solved through the use of some sort of deterministic procedure that is guaranteed success—in other words, a *computation*. The methods used to solve these types of problems are often easily translated into an algorithm that a computer can execute. However, few real-world problems lend themselves to computational solutions. In fact, many problems are noncomputational. These problems are solved by *searching for a solution*—the method of problem solving with which AI is concerned.

One of the goals of AI is the creation of a *general problem solver*. A general problem solver is a program that can produce solutions to all sorts of different problems about which it has no specific designed-in knowledge. This chapter shows why the goal is as tantalizing as it is difficult to realize.

In early AI research, developing good search methods was a primary objective. There are two reasons for this: necessity and desire. One of the most difficult obstacles when applying AI techniques to real-world problems is the sheer magnitude and complexity of most situations. Solving these problems requires good search techniques. In addition, researchers believed then as they do now that searching is central to problem solving, which is a crucial ingredient of intelligence.

Representation and Terminology

Imagine that you have lost your car keys. You know that they are somewhere in your house, which looks like this:

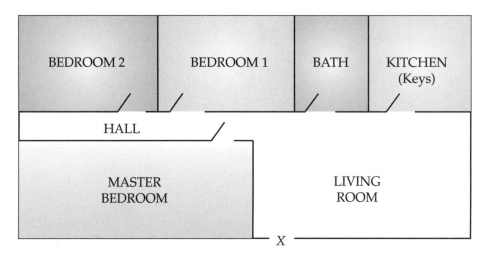

You are standing at the front door (where the X is). As you begin your search, you check the living room. Then you go down the hall to the first bedroom, through the hall to the second bedroom, back to the hall, and to the master bedroom. Not having found your keys, you backtrack further by going back through the living room. You find your keys in the kitchen. This situation is easily represented by a graph, as shown in Figure 25-1.

The fact that search problems can be represented by a graph is important because a graph provides a means to visualize the way the different search techniques work. (Also, being able to represent problems by graphs allows AI researchers to apply various theorems from graph theory. However, these theorems are beyond the scope of this book.) With this in mind, study the following definitions:

Node	A discrete point
Terminal node	A node that ends a path
Search space	The set of all nodes
Goal	The node that is the object of the search
Heuristics	Information about whether any specific node is a better next choice than another
Solution path	A directed graph of the nodes visited en route to a solution

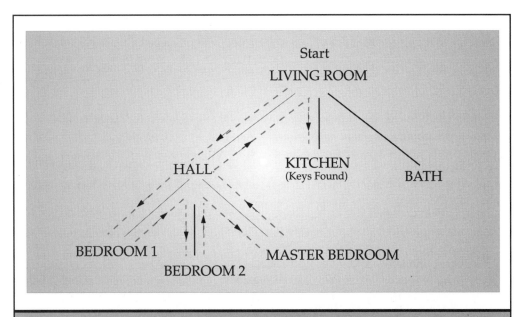

Figure 25-1.   *The solution path to find the missing keys*

In the example of the lost keys, each room in the house is a node; the entire house is the search space; the goal, as it turns out, is the kitchen; and the solution path is shown in Figure 25-1. The bedrooms, kitchen, and the bath are terminal nodes because they lead nowhere. This example doesn't use heuristics, but you will see some later in this chapter.

Combinatorial Explosions

At this point, you may think that searching for a solution is easy—you start at the beginning and work your way to the conclusion. In the extremely simple case of the lost keys, this is not a bad method. But for most problems that you would use a computer to solve, the situation is much different. In general, you use a computer to solve problems where the number of nodes in the search space is very large, and as the search space grows, so does the number of different possible paths to the goal. The trouble is that each node added to the search space adds more than one path. That is, the number of potential pathways to the goal increases faster as each node is added.

For instance, consider the number of ways three objects—A, B, and C—can be arranged on a table. The six possible permutations are

A	B	C
A	C	B
B	C	A
B	A	C
C	B	A
C	A	B

You can quickly prove to yourself that these six are the only ways that A, B, and C can be arranged. However, you can derive the same number by using a theorem from the branch of mathematics called *combinatorics*—the study of the way things can be combined. According to the theorem, the number of ways that N objects can be arranged is equal to $N!$ (N factorial). The factorial of a number is the product of all whole numbers equal to or less than itself down to 1. Therefore, 3! is 3 x 2 x 1, or 6. If you had four objects to arrange, there would be 4!, or 24, permutations. With five objects, the number is 120, and with six it is 720. With 1,000 objects, the number of possible permutations is huge!

The graph in Figure 25-2 gives you a visual feel for what AI researchers commonly refer to as a *combinatoric explosion*. Once there are more than a handful of possibilities, it very quickly becomes difficult to examine (indeed, even to enumerate) all the arrangements. In other words, each additional node in the search space increases the number of possible solutions by a number far greater than one. Hence, at some point

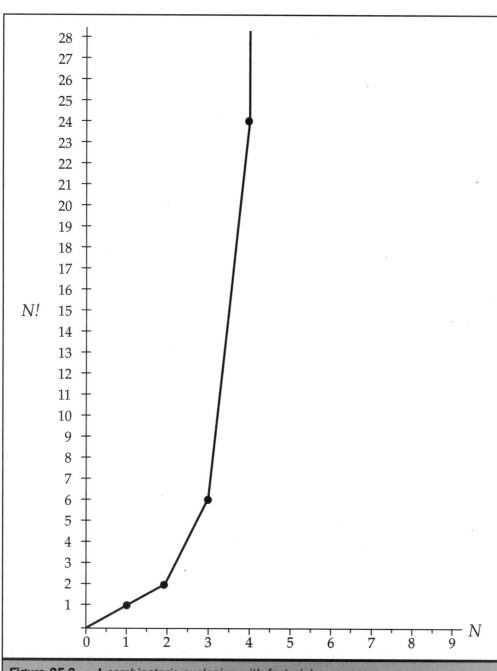

Figure 25-2.   *A combinatoric explosion with factorials*

there are too many possibilities to work with. Because the number of possibilities grows so quickly, only the simplest problems lend themselves to exhaustive searches. An *exhaustive search* is one that examines all nodes—think of it as a "brute-force" technique. Brute force always works, but is not often practical because it consumes far too much time, too many computing resources, or both. For this reason, researchers have developed other search techniques.

Search Techniques

There are several ways to search for a solution. The four most fundamental are

- Depth-first
- Breadth-first
- Hill-climbing
- Least-cost

This chapter examines each of these searches.

Evaluating a Search

Evaluating the performance of a search technique can be very complicated. In fact, the evaluation of searches forms a large part of AI. However, for our purposes there are two important measurements:

- How quickly the search finds a solution
- How good the solution is

There are several types of problems for which all that matters is that a solution, any solution, be found with the minimum effort. For these problems, the first measurement is especially important. However, in other situations, the solution must be good, perhaps even optimal.

The speed of a search is determined both by the length of the solution path and by the number of nodes actually traversed in the process of finding the solution. Remember that backtracking from dead ends is essentially wasted effort, so you want a search that seldom backtracks.

You should understand that there is a difference between finding an optimal solution and finding a good solution. Finding an optimal solution can imply an exhaustive search because sometimes this is the only way to know that the best solution has been found. Finding a good solution, in contrast, means finding a solution that is within a set of constraints—it does not matter if a better solution exists.

As you will see, the search techniques described in this chapter all work better in certain situations than in others. So, it is difficult to say whether one search method is *always* superior to another. But some search techniques have a greater probability of being better for the average case. In addition, the way a problem is defined can sometimes help you choose an appropriate search method.

Let us now consider a problem that we will use various searches to solve. Imagine that you are a travel agent and a rather quarrelsome customer wants you to book a flight from New York to Los Angeles with XYZ Airlines. You try to tell the customer that XYZ does not have a direct flight from New York to Los Angeles, but the customer insists that XYZ is the only airline that he will fly. XYZ's scheduled flights are as follows:

Flight	Distance
New York to Chicago	1,000 miles
Chicago to Denver	1,000 miles
New York to Toronto	800 miles
New York to Denver	1,900 miles
Toronto to Calgary	1,500 miles
Toronto to Los Angeles	1,800 miles
Toronto to Chicago	500 miles
Denver to Urbana	1,000 miles
Denver to Houston	1,500 miles
Houston to Los Angeles	1,500 miles
Denver to Los Angeles	1,000 miles

You quickly see that there is a way to fly from New York to Los Angeles by using XYZ if you book connecting flights, and you book the fellow his flights.

Your task is to write C programs that do the same thing even better.

A Graphic Representation

The flight information in XYZ's schedule can be translated into the directed graph shown in Figure 25-3. A *directed graph* is simply a graph in which the lines connecting

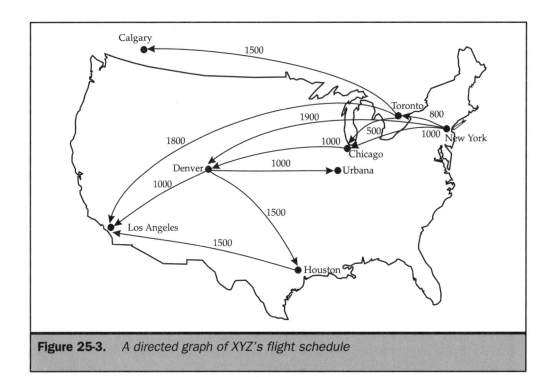

Figure 25-3.   *A directed graph of XYZ's flight schedule*

each node include an arrow to indicate the direction of motion. In a directed graph, you cannot travel in the direction against the arrow.

To make things easier to understand, this graph is redrawn as the tree in Figure 25-4. Refer to this version for the rest of this chapter. The goal, Los Angeles, is circled. Also notice that various cities appear more than once to simplify the construction of the graph.

Now you are ready to develop the various search programs that will find paths from New York to Los Angeles.

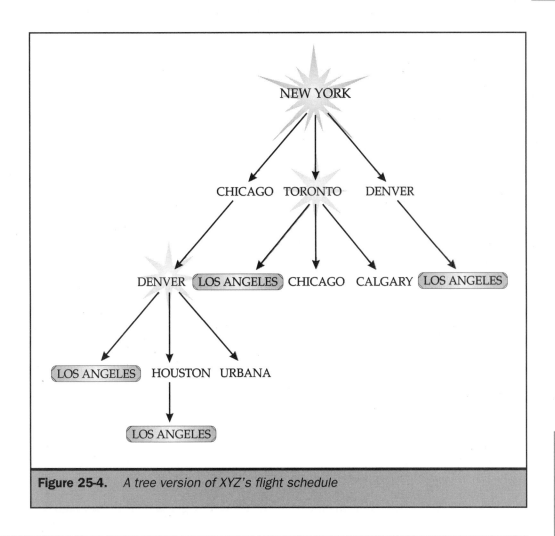

Figure 25-4.   *A tree version of XYZ's flight schedule*

The Depth-First Search

The *depth-first search* explores each possible path to its conclusion before another
path is tried. To understand exactly how this works, consider the tree that follows.
F is the goal.

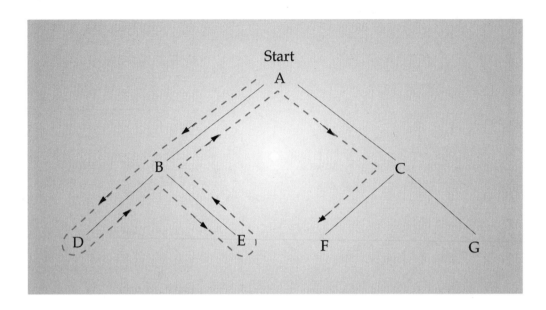

A depth-first search traverses the graph in the following order: ABDBEBACF. If you are familiar with trees, you recognize this type of search as a variation of an inorder tree traversal. That is, the path goes left until a terminal node is reached or the goal is found. If a terminal node is reached, the path backs up one level, goes right, and then left until either the goal or a terminal node is encountered. This procedure is repeated until the goal is found or the last node in the search space has been examined.

As you can see, a depth-first search is certain to find the goal because in the worst case it degenerates into an exhaustive search. In this example, an exhaustive search would result if G were the goal.

Writing a C program to find a route from New York to Los Angeles requires a database that contains the information about XYZ's flights. Each entry in the database must contain the departure and destination cities, the distance between them, and a flag that aids in backtracking (as you will see shortly). The following structure holds such information:

```
#define MAX 100

/* structure of the flight database */
struct FL {
  char from[20];
  char to[20];
  int distance;
```

```
    char skip;  /* used in backtracking */
};

struct FL flight[MAX];  /* array of db structures */

int f_pos = 0;     /* number of entries in flight db */
int find_pos = 0; /* index for searching flight db */
```

Individual entries are placed into the database using the function **assert_flight( )**, and **setup( )** initializes all the flight information. The global **f_pos** holds the index of the last item in the database. These routines are shown here:

```
void setup(void)
{
  assert_flight("New York", "Chicago", 1000);
  assert_flight("Chicago", "Denver", 1000);
  assert_flight("New York", "Toronto", 800);
  assert_flight("New York", "Denver", 1900);
  assert_flight("Toronto", "Calgary", 1500);
  assert_flight("Toronto", "Los Angeles", 1800);
  assert_flight("Toronto", "Chicago", 500);
  assert_flight("Denver", "Urbana", 1000);
  assert_flight("Denver", "Houston", 1500);
  assert_flight("Houston", "Los Angeles", 1500);
  assert_flight("Denver", "Los Angeles", 1000);
}

/* Put facts into the database. */
void assert_flight(char *from, char *to, int dist)
{
  if(f_pos < MAX) {
    strcpy(flight[f_pos].from, from);
    strcpy(flight[f_pos].to, to);
    flight[f_pos].distance = dist;
    flight[f_pos].skip = 0;
    f_pos++;
  }
  else printf("Flight database full.\n");
}
```

In keeping with the spirit of AI, think of the database as containing facts. The program to be developed will use these facts to arrive at a solution. For this reason, many AI researchers refer to the "database" as a "knowledge base." This chapter uses the two terms interchangeably.

Before you can write the actual code to find a route between New York and Los Angeles, you need several support functions. First, you need a routine that determines whether there is a flight between the two cities. This function is called **match( )**, and it returns zero if no such flight exists or returns the distance between the two cities if there is a flight. This function is shown here:

```c
/* If flight between from and to, then return
   the distance of flight; otherwise, return 0. */
int match(char *from, char *to)
{
  register int t;

  for(t=f_pos-1; t > -1; t--)
    if(!strcmp(flight[t].from, from) &&
       !strcmp(flight[t].to, to)) return flight[t].distance;

  return 0;  /* not found */
}
```

Another necessary routine is **find( )**. Given a city, **find( )** searches the database for any connection. If a connection is found, the name of the destination city and its distance are returned; otherwise, zero is returned. The **find( )** routine follows:

```c
/* Given from, find anywhere. */
int find(char *from, char *anywhere)
{
  find_pos = 0;
  while(find_pos < f_pos) {
    if(!strcmp(flight[find_pos].from, from) &&
       !flight[find_pos].skip) {
        strcpy(anywhere, flight[find_pos].to);
        flight[find_pos].skip = 1; /* make active */
        return flight[find_pos].distance;
    }
    find_pos++;
  }
  return 0;
}
```

As you can see, cities that have the **skip** field set to 1 are not valid connections. Also, if a connection is found, its **skip** field is marked as active—this controls backtracking from dead ends.

Backtracking is a crucial ingredient in many AI techniques. Backtracking is accomplished through the use of recursive routines and a backtrack stack. Almost all backtracking situations are stacklike in operation—that is, they are first-in, last-out. As a path is explored, nodes are pushed onto the stack as they are encountered. At each dead end, the last node is popped off the stack and a new path, from that point, is tried. This process continues until either the goal is reached or all paths have been exhausted. The functions **push( )** and **pop( )**, which manage the backtrack stack, follow. They use the globals **tos** and **bt_stack** to hold the top-of-stack pointer and the stack array, respectively.

```
/* Stack Routines */
void push(char *from, char *to, int dist)
{
  if(tos < MAX) {
    strcpy(bt_stack[tos].from, from);
    strcpy(bt_stack[tos].to, to);
    bt_stack[tos].dist = dist;
    tos++;
  }
  else printf("Stack full.\n");
}

void pop(char *from, char *to, int *dist)
{
  if(tos > 0) {
    tos--;
    strcpy(from, bt_stack[tos].from);
    strcpy(to, bt_stack[tos].to);
    *dist = bt_stack[tos].dist;
  }
  else printf("Stack underflow.\n");
}
```

Now that the required support routines have been developed, consider the code that follows. It defines the **isflight( )** function—the key routine in finding a route between New York and Los Angeles.

```
/* Determine if there is a route between from and to. */
void isflight(char *from, char *to)
{
  int d, dist;
  char anywhere[20];

  /* see if at destination */
  if(d=match(from, to)) {
    push(from, to, d);
    return;
  }

  /* try another connection */
  if(dist=find(from, anywhere)) {
    push(from, to, dist);
    isflight(anywhere, to);
  }
  else if(tos > 0) {
    /* backtrack */
    pop(from, to, &dist);
    isflight(from, to);
  }
}
```

The routine works as follows: First, the database is checked by **match( )** to see if there is a flight between **from** and **to**. If there is, the goal has been reached—the connection is pushed onto the stack and the function returns. Otherwise, **find( )** checks if there is a connection between **from** and any place else. If there is, this connection is pushed onto the stack and **isflight( )** is called recursively. Otherwise, backtracking takes place. The previous node is removed from the stack and **isflight( )** is called recursively. This process continues until the goal is found. The **skip** field is necessary to backtracking to prevent the same connections from being tried over and over again.

Therefore, if called with Denver and Houston, the first **if** would succeed and **isflight( )** would terminate. Say, however, that **isflight( )** is called with Chicago and Houston. In this case, the first **if** would fail because there is no direct flight connecting these two cities. Then, the second **if** is tried by attempting to find a connection between the origin city and any other city. In this case, Chicago connects with Denver; therefore, **isflight( )** is called recursively with Denver and Houston. Once again, the first condition is tested. A connection is found this time. Finally, the recursive calls unravel and **isflight( )** terminates. Verify in your mind that, as **isflight( )** is presented here, it performs a depth-first search of the knowledge base.

It is important to understand that **isflight( )** does not actually *return* the solution—it *generate*s it. Upon exit from **isflight( )**, the backtrack stack contains the route between

Chicago and Houston—that is, the solution. In fact, the success or failure of **isflight( )** is determined by the state of the stack. An empty stack indicates failure; otherwise, the stack holds a solution. Thus, you need one more function to complete the entire program. The function is called **route( )**, and it prints the path as well as the total distance. The **route( )** function is shown here:

```
/* Show the route and total distance. */
void route(char *to)
{
  int dist, t;

  dist = 0;
  t = 0;
  while(t < tos) {
    printf("%s to ", bt_stack[t].from);
    dist += bt_stack[t].dist;
    t++;
  }
  printf("%s\n", to);
  printf("Distance is %d.\n", dist);
}
```

The entire depth-first search program follows.

```
/* Depth-first search. */
#include <stdio.h>
#include <string.h>

 #define MAX 100

/* structure of the flight database */
struct FL {
  char from[20];
  char to[20];
  int distance;
  char skip; /* used in backtracking */
};

struct FL flight[MAX]; /* array of db structures */

int f_pos = 0;    /* number of entries in flight db */
int find_pos = 0; /* index for searching flight db */
```

ALGORITHMS AND
APPLICATIONS

```
int tos = 0;        /* top of stack */
struct stack {
  char from[20];
  char to[20];
  int dist;
} ;
struct stack bt_stack[MAX]; /* backtrack stack */

void setup(void), route(char *to);
void assert_flight(char *from, char *to, int dist);
void push(char *from, char *to, int dist);
void pop(char *from, char *to, int *dist);
void isflight(char *from, char *to);
int find(char *from, char *anywhere);
int match(char *from, char *to);

int main(void)
{
  char from[20], to[20];

  setup();

  printf("From? ");
  gets(from);
  printf("To? ");
  gets(to);

  isflight(from,to);
  route(to);

  return 0;
}

/* Initialize the flight database. */
void setup(void)
{
  assert_flight("New York", "Chicago", 1000);
  assert_flight("Chicago", "Denver", 1000);
  assert_flight("New York", "Toronto", 800);
  assert_flight("New York", "Denver", 1900);
  assert_flight("Toronto", "Calgary", 1500);
  assert_flight("Toronto", "Los Angeles", 1800);
```

```
    assert_flight("Toronto", "Chicago", 500);
    assert_flight("Denver", "Urbana", 1000);
    assert_flight("Denver", "Houston", 1500);
    assert_flight("Houston", "Los Angeles", 1500);
    assert_flight("Denver", "Los Angeles", 1000);
}

/* Put facts into the database. */
void assert_flight(char *from, char *to, int dist)
{

  if(f_pos < MAX) {
    strcpy(flight[f_pos].from, from);
    strcpy(flight[f_pos].to, to);
    flight[f_pos].distance = dist;
    flight[f_pos].skip = 0;
    f_pos++;
  }
  else printf("Flight database full.\n");
}

/* Show the route and total distance. */
void route(char *to)

{
  int dist, t;

  dist = 0;
  t = 0;
  while(t < tos) {
    printf("%s to ", bt_stack[t].from);
    dist += bt_stack[t].dist;
    t++;
  }
  printf("%s\n", to);
  printf("Distance is %d.\n", dist);
}

/* If flight between from and to, then return
   the distance of flight; otherwise, return 0. */
int match(char *from, char *to)
{
```

```c
  register int t;

  for(t=f_pos-1; t > -1; t--)
    if(!strcmp(flight[t].from, from) &&
      !strcmp(flight[t].to, to)) return flight[t].distance;

  return 0; /* not found */
}

/* Given from, find anywhere. */
int find(char *from, char *anywhere)
{
  find_pos = 0;
  while(find_pos < f_pos) {
    if(!strcmp(flight[find_pos].from,from) &&
      !flight[find_pos].skip) {
        strcpy(anywhere,flight[find_pos].to);
        flight[find_pos].skip = 1; /* make active */
        return flight[find_pos].distance;
      }
    find_pos++;
  }
  return 0;
}

/* Determine if there is a route between from and to. */
void isflight(char *from, char *to)
{
  int d, dist;
  char anywhere[20];

  /* see if at destination */
  if(d=match(from, to)) {
    push(from, to, d);
    return;
  }
  /* try another connection */
  if(dist=find(from, anywhere)) {
    push(from, to, dist);
    isflight(anywhere, to);
  }
  else if(tos > 0) {
```

```
      /* backtrack */
      pop(from, to, &dist);
      isflight(from, to);
   }
}

/* Stack Routines */
void push(char *from, char *to, int dist)
{
  if(tos < MAX) {
    strcpy(bt_stack[tos].from,from);
    strcpy(bt_stack[tos].to,to);
    bt_stack[tos].dist = dist;
    tos++;
  }
  else printf("Stack full.\n");
}

void pop(char *from, char *to, int *dist)
{
  if(tos > 0) {
    tos--;
    strcpy(from,bt_stack[tos].from);
    strcpy(to,bt_stack[tos].to);
    *dist = bt_stack[tos].dist;
  }
  else printf("Stack underflow.\n");
}
```

Notice that **main( )** prompts you for both the city of origin and the city of
destination. This means that you can use the program to find routes between any two
cities. However, the rest of this chapter assumes that New York is the origin and Los
Angeles is the destination.

When run with New York as the origin and Los Angeles as the destination, the
solution is

```
New York to Chicago to Denver to Los Angeles
Distance is 3000.
```

Figure 25-5 shows the path of the search.

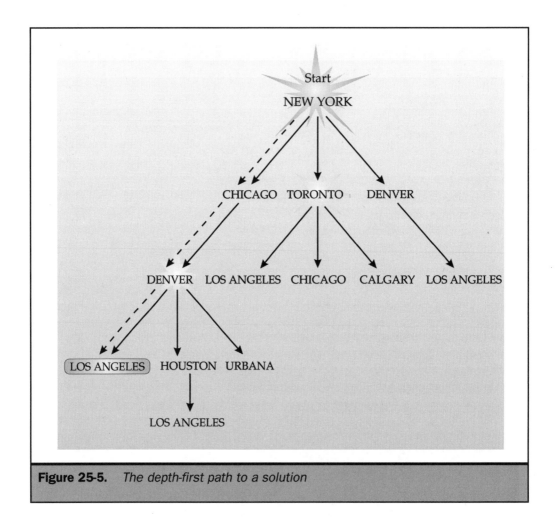

Figure 25-5.   *The depth-first path to a solution*

If you refer to Figure 25-5, you see that this is indeed the first solution that would be found by a depth-first search. It is not the optimal solution—which is New York to Toronto to Los Angeles with a distance of 2,600 miles—but it is not bad.

Analysis of the Depth-First Search

The depth-first approach found a fairly good solution. Also, relative to this specific problem, depth-first searching found a solution on its first try with no backtracking—this is very good. But it would have had to traverse nearly all the nodes to arrive at the optimal solution—this is not so good.

Note that the performance of depth-first searches can be quite poor when a particularly long branch with no solution at the end is explored. In this case, a depth-first search wastes considerable time not only exploring this chain, but also backtracking to the goal.

The Breadth-First Search

The opposite of the depth-first search is the *breadth-first search*. In this method, each node on the same level is checked before the search proceeds to the next deeper level. This traversal method is shown here with C as the goal:

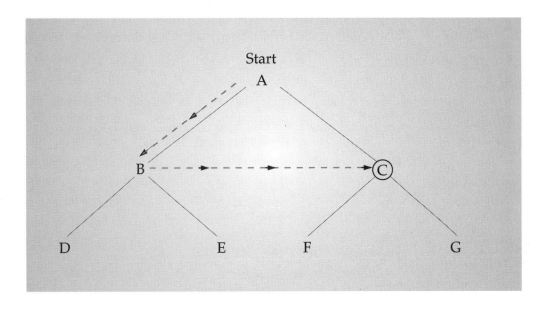

To make the route-seeking program perform a breadth-first search, you only need to alter the procedure **isflight( )**, as shown here:

```
void isflight(char *from, char *to)
{
  int d, dist;
  char anywhere[20];

  while(dist=find(from, anywhere)) {
    /* breadth-first modification */
    if(d=match(anywhere, to)) {
      push(from, to, dist);
      push(anywhere, to, d);
```

```
      return;
    }
  }
}
/* try any connection */
if(dist=find(from, anywhere)) {
  push(from, to, dist);
  isflight(anywhere, to);
}
else if(tos>0) {
  pop(from, to, &dist);
  isflight(from, to);
}
}
```

As you can see, only the first condition has been altered. Now all connecting cities to the departure city are checked to see if they connect with the destination city.

Substitute this version of **isflight( )** in the program and run it. The solution is

```
New York to Toronto to Los Angeles
Distance is 2600.
```

The solution is optimal. Figure 25-6 shows the breadth-first path to the solution.

Analysis of the Breadth-First Search

In this example, the breadth-first search performed very well by finding the first solution without backtracking. As it turned out, this was also the optimal solution. In fact, the first three solutions that would be found are the best three routes there are. However, remember that this result does not generalize to other situations because the path depends upon the physical organization of the information as it is stored in the computer. The example does illustrate, however, how radically different depth-first and breadth-first searches are.

A disadvantage to breadth-first searching becomes apparent when the goal is several layers deep. In this case, a breadth-first search expends substantial effort to find the goal. In general, you choose between depth-first and breadth-first searching by making an educated guess about the most likely position of the goal.

Adding Heuristics

You have probably guessed by now that both the depth-first and breadth-first search routines are blind. They are methods of looking for a solution that rely solely upon

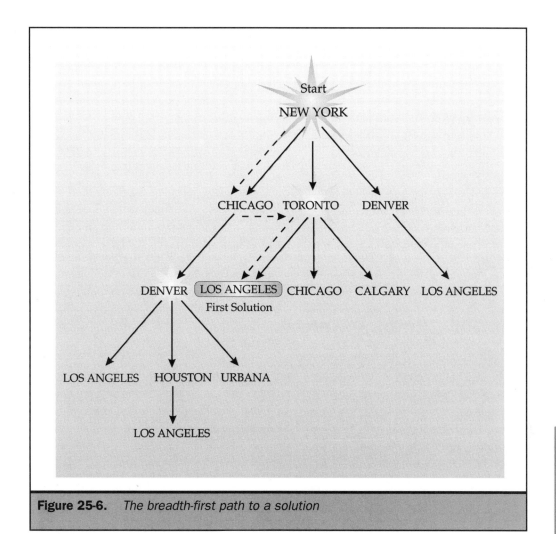

Figure 25-6.   *The breadth-first path to a solution*

moving from one goal to the other without any educated guesswork on the part of the computer. This may be fine for certain controlled situations where you know that one method is better than the other. However, a generalized AI program needs a search procedure that is on the average superior to either of these two techniques. The only way to achieve such a search is to add heuristic capabilities.

Heuristics are simply rules that qualify the possibility that a search is proceeding in the correct direction. For example, imagine that you are lost in the woods and need a drink of water. The woods are so thick that you cannot see far ahead, and the trees are too big to climb and get a look around. However, you know that rivers, streams, and ponds are most likely in valleys; that animals frequently make paths to their watering places; that when you are near water it is possible to "smell" it; and that you can hear running water. So, you begin by moving downhill because water is unlikely to be uphill. Next you come across a deer trail that also runs downhill. Knowing that this may lead to water, you follow it. You begin to hear a slight rushing off to your left. Knowing that this may be water, you cautiously move in that direction. As you move, you begin to detect the increased humidity in the air; you can smell the water. Finally, you find a stream and have your drink. As you can see, heuristic information, although neither precise nor guaranteed, increases the chances that a search method will find a goal quickly, optimally, or both. In short, it increases the odds in favor of a quick success.

You may think that heuristic information could easily be included in programs designed for specific applications, but that it would be impossible to create generalized heuristic searches. This is not the case. Most often, heuristic search methods are based on maximizing or minimizing some aspect of the problem. In fact, the two heuristic approaches that we will look at use opposite heuristics and yield different results. Both of these searches will be built upon the depth-first search routines.

The Hill-Climbing Search

In the problem of scheduling a flight from New York to Los Angeles, there are two possible constraints that a passenger may want to minimize. The first is the number of connections that have to be made. The second is the length of the route. Remember, the shortest route does not necessarily imply the fewest connections. A search algorithm that attempts to find as a first solution a route that minimizes the number of connections uses the heuristic that the longer the length of the flight, the greater the likelihood that it takes the traveler closer to the destination; therefore, the number of connections is minimized.

In the language of AI, this is called *hill climbing*. The hill-climbing algorithm chooses as its next step the node that appears to place it closest to the goal (that is, farthest away from the current position). It derives its name from the analogy of a hiker being lost in the dark, halfway up a mountain. Assuming that the hiker's camp is at the top of the mountain, even in the dark the hiker knows that each step that goes up is a step in the right direction.

Working only with the information contained in the flight-scheduling knowledge base, here is how to incorporate the hill-climbing heuristic into the routing program: Choose the connecting flight that is as far away as possible from the current position in the hope that it will be closer to the destination. To do this, modify the **find( )** routine as shown here:

```
/* Given from, find the farthest away "anywhere". */
int find(char *from, char *anywhere)
{
```

```
    int pos, dist;

  pos=dist = 0;
  find_pos = 0;

  while(find_pos < f_pos) {
    if(!strcmp(flight[find_pos].from, from) &&
       !flight[find_pos].skip) {
         if(flight[find_pos].distance>dist) {
         pos = find_pos;
         dist = flight[find_pos].distance;
      }
    }
    find_pos++;
  }
  if(pos) {
    strcpy(anywhere, flight[pos].to);
    flight[pos].skip = 1;
    return flight[pos].distance;
  }
  return 0;
}
```

The **find( )** routine now searches the entire database, looking for the connection that is farthest away from the departure city.

The entire hill-climbing program follows.

```
/* Hill-climbing */
#include <stdio.h>
#include <string.h>

 #define MAX 100

/* structure of the flight database */
struct FL {
  char from[20];
  char to[20];
  int distance;
  char skip; /* used for backtracking */
};

struct FL flight[MAX];  /* array of db structures */
```

```c
int f_pos = 0;     /* number of entries in flight db */
int find_pos = 0; /* index for searching flight db */

int tos = 0;       /* top of stack */
struct stack {
  char from[20];
  char to[20];
  int dist;
} ;

struct stack bt_stack[MAX]; /* backtrack stack */

void setup(void), route(char *to);
void assert_flight(char *from, char *to, int dist);
void push(char *from, char *to, int dist);
void pop(char *from, char *to, int *dist);
void isflight(char *from, char *to);
int find(char *from, char *anywhere);
int match(char *from, char *to);

int main(void)
{
  char from[20], to[20];

  setup();

  printf("From? ");
  gets(from);
  printf("To? ");
  gets(to);

  isflight(from,to);
  route(to);

  return 0;
}

/* Initialize the flight database. */
void setup(void)
{
  assert_flight("New York", "Chicago", 1000);
  assert_flight("Chicago", "Denver", 1000);
  assert_flight("New York", "Toronto", 800);
```

```
  assert_flight("New York", "Denver", 1900);
  assert_flight("Toronto", "Calgary", 1500);
  assert_flight("Toronto", "Los Angeles", 1800);
  assert_flight("Toronto", "Chicago", 500);
  assert_flight("Denver", "Urbana", 1000);
  assert_flight("Denver", "Houston", 1500);
  assert_flight("Houston", "Los Angeles", 1500);
  assert_flight("Denver", "Los Angeles", 1000);
}

/* Put facts into the database. */
void assert_flight(char *from, char *to, int dist)
{

  if(f_pos < MAX) {
    strcpy(flight[f_pos].from, from);
    strcpy(flight[f_pos].to, to);
    flight[f_pos].distance = dist;
    flight[f_pos].skip = 0;
    f_pos++;
  }
  else printf("Flight database full.\n");
}

/* Show the route and the total distance. */
void route(char *to)
{
  int dist, t;

  dist = 0;
  t = 0;
  while(t < tos) {
    printf("%s to ", bt_stack[t].from);
    dist += bt_stack[t].dist;
    t++;
  }
  printf("%s\n", to);
  printf("Distance is %d.\n", dist);
}

/* If flight between from and to, then return
   the distance of flight; otherwise, return 0. */
int match(char *from, char *to)
```

```
{
  register int t;

  for(t=f_pos-1; t > -1; t--)
    if(!strcmp(flight[t].from, from) &&
      !strcmp(flight[t].to, to)) return flight[t].distance;

  return 0;  /* not found */
}

/* Given from, find the farthest away "anywhere". */
int find(char *from, char *anywhere)
{
  int pos, dist;

  pos=dist = 0;
  find_pos = 0;

  while(find_pos < f_pos) {
    if(!strcmp(flight[find_pos].from, from) &&
      !flight[find_pos].skip) {
        if(flight[find_pos].distance>dist) {
          pos = find_pos;
          dist = flight[find_pos].distance;
        }
    }
    find_pos++;
  }
  if(pos) {
    strcpy(anywhere, flight[pos].to);
    flight[pos].skip = 1;
    return flight[pos].distance;
  }
  return 0;
}

/* Determine if there is a route between from and to. */
void isflight(char *from, char *to)
{
  int d, dist;
  char anywhere[20];

  if(d=match(from, to)) {
```

```
    /* is goal */
    push(from, to, d);
    return;
  }

  /* find any connection */
  if(dist=find(from, anywhere)) {
    push(from, to, dist);
    isflight(anywhere, to);
  }
  else if(tos > 0) {
    pop(from, to, &dist);
    isflight(from, to);
  }
}

/* Stack Routines */
void push(char *from, char *to, int dist)
{
  if(tos < MAX) {
    strcpy(bt_stack[tos].from, from);
    strcpy(bt_stack[tos].to, to);
    bt_stack[tos].dist = dist;
    tos++;
  }
  else printf("Stack full.\n");
}

void pop(char *from, char *to, int *dist)
{
  if(tos > 0) {
    tos--;
    strcpy(from, bt_stack[tos].from);
    strcpy(to, bt_stack[tos].to);
    *dist = bt_stack[tos].dist;
  }
  else printf("Stack underflow.\n");
}
```

When the program is run, the solution is

```
New York to Denver to Los Angeles
Distance is 2900.
```

This is quite good! The route contains the minimal number of stops on the way (only one), and it is very close to the shortest route. Furthermore, the program arrives at the solution with no time or effort wasted through extensive backtracking.

However, if the Denver to Los Angeles connection did not exist, the solution would not be quite so good. It would be New York to Denver to Houston to Los Angeles—a distance of 4,900 miles! This solution climbs a "false peak." As you can easily see, the route to Houston does not take us closer to the goal of Los Angeles. Figure 25-7 shows the first solution as well as the path to the false peak.

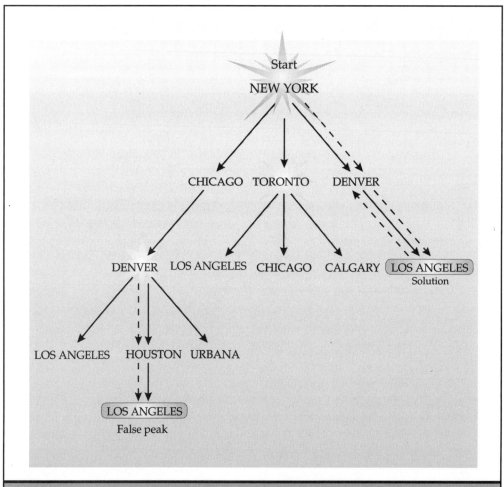

Figure 25-7.   *The hill-climbing path to a solution and to a false peak*

Analysis of Hill Climbing

Hill climbing provides fairly good solutions in many circumstances because it tends to reduce the number of nodes that need to be visited before a solution is reached. However, it can suffer from three maladies. First, there is the problem of false peaks, as you saw in the second solution in the example. In this case, extensive backtracking must be used to find the solution. The second problem relates to plateaus—a situation in which all next steps look equally good (or bad). In this case, hill climbing is no better than depth-first searching. The final problem is that of a ridge. In this case, hill climbing performs poorly because the algorithm causes the ridge to be crossed several times as backtracking occurs.

In spite of these potential troubles, hill climbing generally leads to a closer-to-optimal solution more quickly than any of the nonheuristic methods.

The Least-Cost Search

The opposite of a hill-climbing search is a *least-cost search*. This strategy is similar to standing in the middle of a street on a big hill while wearing roller skates. You have the definite feeling that it's a lot easier to go down than up! In other words, a least-cost search takes the path of least resistance.

Applying a least-cost search to the flight-scheduling problem implies that the shortest connecting flight is taken in all cases so that the route found has a good chance of covering the shortest distance. Unlike hill climbing, which minimized the number of connections, a least-cost search minimizes the number of miles.

To use a least-cost search, you must again alter **find( )**, as shown here:

```
/* Find closest "anywhere". */
int find(char *from, char *anywhere)
{
  int pos, dist;

  pos = 0;
  dist = 32000;   /* larger than the longest route */
  find_pos = 0;

  while(find_pos < f_pos) {
    if(!strcmp(flight[find_pos].from, from) &&
      !flight[find_pos].skip) {
        if(flight[find_pos].distance<dist) {
        pos = find_pos;
        dist = flight[find_pos].distance;
      }
```

```
      }
      find_pos++;
    }
    if(pos) {
      strcpy(anywhere, flight[pos].to);
      flight[pos].skip = 1;
      return flight[pos].distance;
    }
    return 0;
}
```

Using this version of **find( )**, the solution is

```
New York to Toronto to Los Angeles
Distance is 2600.
```

As you can see, this search found the shortest route. Figure 25-8 shows the least-cost path to the goal.

Analysis of the Least-Cost Search

The least-cost search and hill climbing have the same advantages and disadvantages, but in reverse. There can be false valleys, lowlands, and gorges, but a least-cost search usually works fairly well. However, don't assume that just because the least-cost search performed better than hill climbing in this problem that it is better in general. All that can be said is that on average it will outperform a blind search.

Choosing a Search Technique

As you have seen, the heuristic techniques tend, on the average, to work better than blind searching. However, it is not always possible to use a heuristic search because there may not be enough information to qualify the likelihood of the next node being on a path to the goal. Therefore, the rules for choosing a search method are separated into two categories: one for problems that can utilize a heuristic search and one for those that cannot.

If you cannot apply heuristics to a problem, depth-first searching is usually the best approach. The only exception to this is when you know something that indicates that a breadth-first search will be better.

The choice between hill climbing and a least-cost search is really one of deciding what constraint you are trying to minimize or maximize. In general, hill climbing produces a solution with the least nodes visited, but a least-cost search finds a path that requires the least effort.

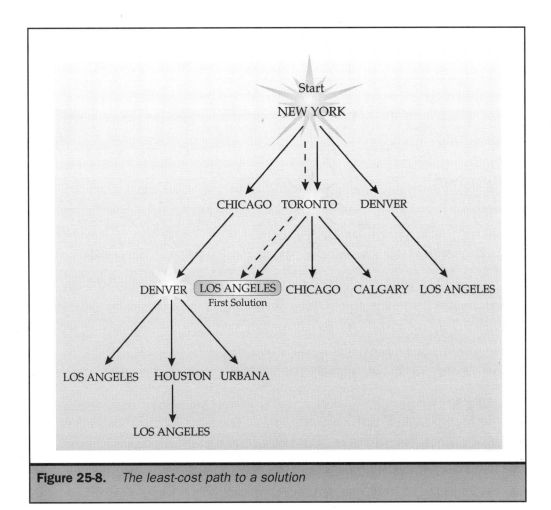

Figure 25-8. *The least-cost path to a solution*

If you are seeking a near-optimal solution but cannot apply an exhaustive search for the reasons already stated, an effective method is to apply each of the four searches, and then use the best solution. Since the searches all work in substantially different ways, one should produce better results than the others.

Finding Multiple Solutions

Sometimes it is valuable to find several solutions to the same problem. This is not the same as finding all solutions (an exhaustive search), however. For instance, think about designing your dream house. You want to sketch several different floor plans to help you decide upon the best design, but you don't need sketches of *all possible houses*. In essence, multiple solutions can help you see many different ways to approach a solution before implementing one.

There are several ways to generate multiple solutions, but only two are examined here. The first is path removal, and the second is node removal. As their names imply, generating multiple solutions without redundancy requires that already found solutions be removed from the system. Remember that neither of these methods attempts (nor can even be used) to find all solutions. Finding all solutions is a different problem that is usually not attempted because it implies an exhaustive search.

Path Removal

The *path-removal* method of generating multiple solutions removes all nodes that form a current solution from the database and then attempts to find another solution. In essence, path removal prunes limbs from the tree.

To find multiple solutions by using path removal, you need to alter **main( )** in the depth-first search, as shown here:

```
int main(void)
{
  char from[20], to[20];

  setup();

  printf("From? ");
  gets(from);
  printf("To? ");
  gets(to);
  do {
    isflight(from, to);
    route(to);
    tos = 0;  /* reset the backtrack stack */
  } while(getchar() != 'q');

  return 0;
}
```

Any connection that is part of a solution will have its **skip** field marked. Consequently, such a connection can no longer be found by **find( )**, and all connections in a solution are effectively removed. You just need to reset **tos**, which effectively clears the backtrack stack, before finding the next solution.

The path-removal method finds the following solutions:

```
New York to Chicago to Denver to Los Angeles
Distance is 3000.
New York to Toronto to Los Angeles
Distance is 2600.
New York to Denver to Los Angeles
Distance is 2900.
```

The search found the three best solutions. However, this result cannot be generalized because it is based upon how the data is placed in the database and the actual situation under study.

Node Removal

The second way to force the generation of additional solutions, *node removal*, simply removes the last node in the current solution path and tries again. To do this, the function **main( )** must pop the last node off the backtrack stack and remove it from the database by using a new function called **retract( )**. Also, all the **skip** fields must be reset by using **clearmarkers( )**, and the backtrack stack must be cleared. The functions **main( )**, **clearmarkers( )**, and **retract( )** are shown here:

```c
int main(void)
{
  char from[20], to[20], c1[20], c2[20];
  int d;

  setup();

  printf("From? ");
  gets(from);
  printf("To? ");
  gets(to);
  do {
    isflight(from, to);
    route(to);
    clearmarkers();  /* reset the database */
    if(tos > 0) pop(c1, c2, &d);
    retract(c1, c2);  /* remove last node from database */
    tos = 0;  /* reset the backtrack stack */
  } while(getchar() != 'q');
```

```
    return 0;
}

/* Reset the "skip" field - i.e., re-activate all nodes, */
void clearmarkers()
{
  int t;

  for(t=0; t < f_pos; ++t) flight[t].skip = 0;
}

/* Remove an entry from the database. */
void retract(char *from, char *to)

{
  int t;

  for(t=0; t < f_pos; t++)
    if(!strcmp(flight[t].from, from) &&
      !strcmp(flight[t].to, to)) {
        strcpy(flight[t].from, "");
        return;
    }
}
```

As you can see, retracting an entry is accomplished by using zero-length strings for the names of the cities. For your convenience, the entire node-removal program is shown here:

```
/* Depth-first with multiple solutions
   using node removal */
#include <stdio.h>
#include <string.h>

#define MAX 100

/* structure of the flight database */
struct FL {
  char from[20];
  char to[20];
  int distance;
```

```
    char skip;    /* used in backtracking */
};

struct FL flight[MAX];

int f_pos = 0;    /* number of entries in flight db */
int find_pos = 0; /* index for searching flight db */

int tos = 0;      /* top of stack */
struct stack {
  char from[20];
  char to[20];
  int dist;
} ;
struct stack bt_stack[MAX]; /* backtrack stack */

void retract(char *from, char *to);
void clearmarkers(void);
void setup(void), route(char *to);
void assert_flight(char *from, char *to, int dist);
void push(char *from, char *to, int dist);
void pop(char *from, char *to, int *dist);
void isflight(char *from, char *to);
int find(char *from, char *anywhere);
int match(char *from, char *to);

int main(void)
{
  char from[20],to[20], c1[20], c2[20];
  int d;

  setup();

  printf("From? ");
  gets(from);
  printf("To? ");
  gets(to);
  do {
    isflight(from,to);
    route(to);
    clearmarkers(); /* reset the database */
    if(tos > 0) pop(c1,c2,&d);
```

```
    retract(c1,c2);  /* remove last node from database */
    tos = 0;  /* reset the backtrack stack */
  } while(getchar() != 'q');

  return 0;
}

/* Initialize the flight database. */
void setup(void)
{
  assert_flight("New York", "Chicago", 1000);
  assert_flight("Chicago", "Denver", 1000);
  assert_flight("New York", "Toronto", 800);
  assert_flight("New York", "Denver", 1900);
  assert_flight("Toronto", "Calgary", 1500);
  assert_flight("Toronto", "Los Angeles", 1800);
  assert_flight("Toronto", "Chicago", 500);
  assert_flight("Denver", "Urbana", 1000);
  assert_flight("Denver", "Houston", 1500);
  assert_flight("Houston", "Los Angeles", 1500);
  assert_flight("Denver", "Los Angeles", 1000);
}

/* Put facts into the database. */
void assert_flight(char *from, char *to, int dist)
{
  if(f_pos < MAX) {
    strcpy(flight[f_pos].from, from);
    strcpy(flight[f_pos].to, to);
    flight[f_pos].distance = dist;
    flight[f_pos].skip = 0;
    f_pos++;
  }
  else printf("Flight database full.\n");
}
/* Reset the "skip" field - i.e., re-activate all nodes. */
void clearmarkers()
{
  int t;

  for(t=0; t < f_pos; ++t) flight[t].skip = 0;
}
```

```
/* Remove an entry from the database. */
void retract(char *from, char *to)
{
  int t;

  for(t=0; t < f_pos; t++)
    if(!strcmp(flight[t].from, from) &&
      !strcmp(flight[t].to, to)) {
        strcpy(flight[t].from,"");
        return;


    }
}

/* Show the route and the total distance. */
void route(char *to)
{
  int dist, t;

  dist = 0;
  t = 0;
  while(t < tos) {
    printf("%s to ", bt_stack[t].from);
    dist += bt_stack[t].dist;
    t++;
  }
  printf("%s\n",to);
  printf("Distance is %d.\n", dist);
}

/* Given from, find anywhere. */
int find(char *from, char *anywhere)
{
  find_pos = 0;
  while(find_pos < f_pos) {
    if(!strcmp(flight[find_pos].from, from) &&
      !flight[find_pos].skip) {
        strcpy(anywhere, flight[find_pos].to);
        flight[find_pos].skip = 1;
        return flight[find_pos].distance;
      }
    find_pos++;
  }
```

```
    return 0;
}

/* If flight between from and to, then return
   the distance of flight; otherwise, return 0. */
int match(char *from, char *to)
{
  register int t;

  for(t=f_pos-1; t > -1; t--)
    if(!strcmp(flight[t].from, from) &&
       !strcmp(flight[t].to, to)) return flight[t].distance;

  return 0;  /* not found */
}

/* Determine if there is a route between from and to. */
void isflight(char *from, char *to)
{
  int d, dist;
  char anywhere[20];

  if(d=match(from, to)) {
    push(from, to, d); /* distance */
    return;
  }

  if(dist=find(from, anywhere)) {
    push(from, to, dist);
    isflight(anywhere, to);
  }
  else if(tos > 0) {
    pop(from, to, &dist);
    isflight(from, to);
  }
}

/* Stack Routines */
void push(char *from, char *to, int dist)
{
  if(tos < MAX) {
    strcpy(bt_stack[tos].from, from);
```

```
      strcpy(bt_stack[tos].to, to);
      bt_stack[tos].dist = dist;
      tos++;
  }
  else printf("Stack full.\n");
}

void pop(char *from, char *to, int *dist)
{
  if(tos > 0) {
  tos--;
    strcpy(from, bt_stack[tos].from);
    strcpy(to, bt_stack[tos].to);
    *dist = bt_stack[tos].dist;
  }
  else printf("Stack underflow.\n");
}
```

Using this method produces the following solutions:

```
New York to Chicago to Denver to Los Angeles
Distance is 3000.
New York to Chicago to Denver to Houston to Los Angeles
Distance is 5000.
New York to Toronto to Los Angeles
Distance is 2600.
```

In this case, the second solution is the worst possible route, but the optimal solution is still found. However, remember that you cannot generalize these results because they are based upon both the physical organization of data in the database and the specific situation under study.

Finding the "Optimal" Solution

All of the previous search techniques were concerned, first and foremost, with finding a solution—any solution. As you saw with the heuristic searches, efforts can be made to improve the likelihood of finding a good solution. But no attempt was made to ensure that an optimal solution was found. However, at times you may want *only* the optimal solution. Keep in mind, however, that optimal, as it is used here, simply means the best route that can be found by using one of the various multiple-solution generation techniques—it may not actually be the best solution. (Finding the true optimal solution would, of course, require the prohibitively time-consuming exhaustive search.)

Before leaving the well-worked scheduling example, consider a program that finds the optimal flight schedule given the constraint that distance is to be minimized. To do this, the program employs the path-removal method of generating multiple solutions and uses a least-cost search to minimize distance. The key to finding the shortest path is to keep a solution that is shorter than the previously generated solution. When there are no more solutions to generate, the optimal solution remains.

To accomplish this, you must make a major change to the function **route( )** and create an additional stack. The new stack holds the current solution and, upon completion, the optimal solution. The new stack is called **solution**, and the modified **route( )** is shown here:

```c
/* Find the shortest distance. */
int route(void)
{
  int dist, t;
  static int old_dist = 32000;

  if(!tos) return 0;   /* all done */
  t = 0;
  dist = 0;
  while(t < tos) {
    dist += bt_stack[t].dist;
    t++;
  }

  /* if shorter, then make new solution */
  if(dist<old_dist && dist) {
    t = 0;
    old_dist = dist;
    stos = 0; /* clear old route from location stack */
    while(t < tos) {
      spush(bt_stack[t].from, bt_stack[t].to, bt_stack[t].dist);
      t++;
    }
  }
  return dist;
}
```

The entire program follows. Notice the changes in **main( )** and the addition of **spush( )**, which places the new solution nodes onto the solution stack.

```c
/* Optimal solution using least-cost with
   route removal.
*/
#include <stdio.h>
#include <string.h>

#define MAX 100

/* structure of the flight database */
struct FL {
  char from[20];
  char to[20];
  int distance;
  char skip;  /* used for backtracking */
};

struct FL flight[MAX];  /* array of db structures */

int f_pos = 0;    /* number of entries in flight db */
int find_pos = 0; /* index for searching flight db */

int tos = 0;      /* top of stack */
int stos = 0;     /* top of solution stack */

struct stack {
  char from[20];
  char to[20];
  int dist;
} ;

struct stack bt_stack[MAX]; /* backtrack stack */
struct stack solution[MAX]; /* hold temporary solutions */

void setup(void);
int route(void);
void assert_flight(char *from, char *to, int dist);
void push(char *from, char *to, int dist);
void pop(char *from, char *to, int *dist);
void isflight(char *from, char *to);
void spush(char *from, char *to, int dist);
int find(char *from, char *anywhere);
int match(char *from, char *to);
```

ALGORITHMS AND
APPLICATIONS

```
int main(void)
{
  char from[20], to[20];
  int t, d;

  setup();

  printf("From? ");
  gets(from);
  printf("To? ");
  gets(to);
  do {
    isflight(from, to);
    d = route();
    tos = 0;  /* reset the backtrack stack */
  } while(d != 0);  /* while still finding solutions */

  t = 0;
  printf("Optimal solution is:\n");
  while(t < stos) {
    printf("%s to ", solution[t].from);
    d += solution[t].dist;
    t++;
  }
  printf("%s\n", to);
  printf("Distance is %d.\n", d);

  return 0;
}

/* Initialize the flight database. */
void setup(void)
{
  assert_flight("New York", "Chicago", 1000);
  assert_flight("Chicago", "Denver", 1000);
  assert_flight("New York", "Toronto", 800);
  assert_flight("New York", "Denver", 1900);
  assert_flight("Toronto", "Calgary", 1500);
  assert_flight("Toronto", "Los Angeles", 1800);
  assert_flight("Toronto", "Chicago", 500);
  assert_flight("Denver", "Urbana", 1000);
  assert_flight("Denver", "Houston", 1500);
```

```
  assert_flight("Houston", "Los Angeles", 1500);
  assert_flight("Denver", "Los Angeles", 1000);
}

/* Put facts into the database. */
void assert_flight(char *from, char *to, int dist)
{
  if(f_pos < MAX) {
    strcpy(flight[f_pos].from, from);
    strcpy(flight[f_pos].to, to);
    flight[f_pos].distance = dist;
    flight[f_pos].skip = 0;
    f_pos++;
  }
  else printf("Flight database full.\n");
}

/* Find the shortest distance. */
int route(void)
{
  int dist, t;
  static int old_dist=32000;

  if(!tos) return 0;  /* all done */
  t = 0;
  dist = 0;
  while(t < tos) {
    dist += bt_stack[t].dist;
    t++;
  }

  /* if shorter then make new solution */
  if(dist<old_dist && dist) {
    t = 0;
    old_dist = dist;
    stos = 0; /* clear old route from location stack */
    while(t < tos)  {
      spush(bt_stack[t].from, bt_stack[t].to, bt_stack[t].dist);
      t++;
    }
  }
  return dist;
```

```
}

/* If flight between from and to, then return
   the distance of flight; otherwise, return 0. */
int match(char *from, char *to)
{
  register int t;

  for(t=f_pos-1; t > -1; t--)
    if(!strcmp(flight[t].from, from) &&
       !strcmp(flight[t].to, to)) return flight[t].distance;

  return 0;   /* not found */
}

/* Given from, find anywhere. */
int find(char *from, char *anywhere)
{
  find_pos = 0;
  while(find_pos < f_pos) {
    if(!strcmp(flight[find_pos].from, from) &&
       !flight[find_pos].skip) {
         strcpy(anywhere, flight[find_pos].to);
         flight[find_pos].skip = 1;
         return flight[find_pos].distance;
    }
    find_pos++;
  }
  return 0;
}

/* Determine if there is a route between from and to. */
void isflight(char *from, char *to)
{
  int d, dist;
  char anywhere[20];

  if(d=match(from, to)) {
    push(from, to, d); /* distance */
    return;
  }
```

```
  if(dist=find(from, anywhere)) {

    push(from, to, dist);
    isflight(anywhere, to);
  }
  else if(tos > 0) {
    pop(from, to, &dist);
    isflight(from, to);
  }
}

/* Stack Routines */
void push(char *from, char *to, int dist)
{
  if(tos < MAX) {
    strcpy(bt_stack[tos].from, from);
    strcpy(bt_stack[tos].to, to);
    bt_stack[tos].dist = dist;
    tos++;
  }
  else printf("Stack full.\n");
}

void pop(char *from, char *to, int *dist)
{
  if(tos > 0) {
    tos--;
    strcpy(from, bt_stack[tos].from);
    strcpy(to, bt_stack[tos].to);
    *dist = bt_stack[tos].dist;
  }
  else printf("Stack underflow.\n");
}

/* Solution Stack */
void spush(char *from, char *to, int dist)
{
  if(stos < MAX) {
    strcpy(solution[stos].from, from);
    strcpy(solution[stos].to, to);
    solution[stos].dist = dist;
    stos++;
```

```
     }
  else printf("Shortest distance stack full.\n");
}
```

The one inefficiency in the preceding method is that all paths are followed to their conclusion. An improved method would stop following a path as soon as the length equaled or exceeded the current minimum. You might want to modify this program to accommodate such an enhancement.

Back to the Lost Keys

To conclude this chapter on problem solving, it seems only fitting to provide a C program that finds the lost car keys described in the first example. The accompanying code employs the same techniques used in the problem of finding a route between two cities. By now, you should have a fairly good understanding of how to use C to solve problems, so the program is presented without further explanation.

```
/* Find the keys using a depth-first search. */
#include <stdio.h>
#include <string.h>

#define MAX 100

/* structure of the keys database */
struct FL {
  char from[20];
  char to[20];
  char skip;
};

struct FL keys[MAX];   /* array of db structures */

int f_pos = 0;     /* number of rooms in house */
int find_pos = 0; /* index for searching keys db */

int tos = 0;       /* top of stack */
struct stack {
  char from[20];
  char to[20];
} ;
```

```
struct stack bt_stack[MAX]; /* backtrack stack */

void setup(void), route(void);
void assert_keys(char *from, char *to);
void push(char *from, char *to);
void pop(char *from, char *to);
void iskeys(char *from, char *to);
int find(char *from, char *anywhere);
int match(char *from, char *to);

int main(void)
{
  char from[20] = "front_door";
  char to[20] = "keys";

  setup();
  iskeys(from, to);
  route();

  return 0;
}

/* Initialize the database. */
void setup(void)
{
  assert_keys("front_door", "lr");
  assert_keys("lr", "bath");
  assert_keys("lr", "hall");
  assert_keys("hall", "bd1");
  assert_keys("hall", "bd2");
  assert_keys("hall", "mb");
  assert_keys("lr", "kitchen");
  assert_keys("kitchen", "keys");
}

/* Put facts into the database. */
void assert_keys(char *from, char *to)
{
  if(f_pos < MAX) {
    strcpy(keys[f_pos].from, from);
    strcpy(keys[f_pos].to, to);
    keys[f_pos].skip = 0;
```

```
      f_pos++;
    }
    else printf("Keys database full.\n");
}

/* Show the route to the keys. */
void route(void)
{
  int t;

  t = 0;
  while(t < tos) {
    printf("%s", bt_stack[t].from);
    t++;
    if(t < tos) printf(" to ");
  }
  printf("\n");
}

/* See if there is a match. */
int match(char *from, char *to)
{
  register int t;

  for(t=f_pos-1; t > -1; t--)
    if(!strcmp(keys[t].from, from) &&
      !strcmp(keys[t].to, to)) return 1;

  return 0;  /* not found */
}

/* Given from, find anywhere. */
int find(char *from, char *anywhere)
{
  find_pos = 0;

  while(find_pos < f_pos) {
    if(!strcmp(keys[find_pos].from, from) &&
      !keys[find_pos].skip) {
        strcpy(anywhere, keys[find_pos].to);
```

```
          keys[find_pos].skip = 1;
          return 1;
      }
      find_pos++;
   }
   return 0;
}

/* Determine if there is a route between from and to. */
void iskeys(char *from, char *to)
{
   char anywhere[20];

   if(match(from, to)) {
     push(from, to); /* distance */
     return;
   }

   if(find(from, anywhere)) {
     push(from, to);
     iskeys(anywhere, to);
   }
   else if(tos > 0) {
     pop(from, to);
     iskeys(from, to);
   }
}

/* Stack Routines */
void push(char *from, char *to)
{
   if(tos < MAX) {
     strcpy(bt_stack[tos].from, from);
     strcpy(bt_stack[tos].to, to);
     tos++;
   }
   else printf("Stack full.\n");
}

void pop(char *from, char *to)
```

```
{
  if(tos > 0) {
    tos--;
    strcpy(from, bt_stack[tos].from);
    strcpy(to, bt_stack[tos].to);
  }
  else printf("Stack underflow.\n");
}
```

The Complete Reference

Part V

Software Development Using C

This part of the book examines various aspects of the software development process as they relate to the C programming environment. Chapter 26 shows how to use C to create a skeletal application for the Windows 2000 environment. Chapter 27 presents an overview of the design process using C. Chapter 28 looks at porting, efficiency, and debugging.

Chapter 26

Building a Windows 2000 Skeleton

C is one of the primary languages used for Windows programming. As such, it seems only fitting to include an example of Windows programming in this book. However, Windows is a large and complex programming environment, and it is, of course, not possible to describe all the details necessary to write a Windows application in one chapter. It *is* possible, though, to introduce the basic elements common to all applications. Further, these elements can be combined into a minimal Windows application skeleton that forms the foundation for your own Windows applications.

Windows has gone through several incarnations since it was first introduced. At the time of this writing, the current version is Windows 2000. The material in this chapter is specifically tailored to this version of Windows. However, if you have a newer or older version of Windows, most of the discussion will still be applicable.

 This chapter is adapted from my book Windows 2000 Programming from the Ground Up *(Berkeley, CA: Osborne/McGraw-Hill, 2000). If you are interested in learning more about Windows 2000 programming, you will find this book especially useful.*

Windows 2000 Programming Perspective

At its most fundamental level, the goal of Windows 2000 (and Windows in general) is to enable a person who has basic familiarity with the system to sit down and run virtually any application without prior training. Toward this end, Windows provides a consistent interface to the user. In theory, if you can run one Windows-based program, you can run them all. Of course, in actuality, most useful programs will still require some sort of training in order to be used effectively, but at least this training can be restricted to *what* the program *does*, not *how* the user must *interact* with it. In fact, much of the code in a Windows application is there just to support the user interface.

It is important to understand that not every program that runs under Windows 2000 will automatically present the user with a Windows-style interface. Windows defines an environment that encourages consistency, but does not enforce it. For example, it is possible to write Windows programs that do not take advantage of the standard Windows interface elements. To create a Windows-style program, you must purposely do so. Only those programs written to take advantage of Windows will look and feel like Windows programs. Although you can override the basic Windows design philosophy, you had better have a good reason to do so, because your program will be violating the most fundamental goal of Windows: a consistent user interface. In general, if you are writing application programs for Windows 2000, they should conform to the standard Windows style guidelines and design practices.

Let's look at some of the essential elements that define the Windows 2000 application environment.

The Desktop Model

With few exceptions, the point of a window-based user interface is to provide on the screen the equivalent of a desktop. On a desk may be found several different pieces of paper, one on top of another, often with fragments of different pages visible beneath the top page. The equivalent of the desktop in Windows 2000 is the screen. The equivalents of pieces of paper are windows on the screen. On a desk you may move pieces of paper about, maybe switching which piece of paper is on top or how much of another is exposed to view. Windows 2000 allows the same type of operations on its windows. By selecting a window, you can make it current, which means putting it on top of all other windows. You can enlarge or shrink a window, or move it about on the screen. In short, Windows lets you control the surface of the screen the way you control the surface of your desk. All conforming programs must allow these types of user interactions.

The Mouse

Like all preceding versions of Windows, Windows 2000 uses the mouse for almost all control, selection, and drawing operations. Of course, the keyboard may also be used, but Windows is optimized for the mouse. Thus, your programs must support the mouse as an input device wherever possible. Fortunately, most of the common tasks, such as menu selection, scroll bars, and the like, automatically utilize the mouse.

Icons, Bitmaps, and Graphics

Windows 2000 encourages the use of icons, bitmaps, and other types of graphics. The theory behind the use of these items is found in the old adage: A picture is worth a thousand words. An icon is a small symbol that is used to represent some operation, resource, or program. A bitmap is a rectangular graphics image often used to convey information quickly to the user. However, bitmaps can also be used as menu elements. Windows 2000 supports a full range of graphics capabilities, including the ability to draw lines, rectangles, and circles. The proper use of these graphical elements is an important part of successful Windows programming.

Menus, Controls, and Dialog Boxes

Windows provides several standard items that allow user input. These include the menu, various types of controls, and the dialog box. Briefly, a menu displays options from which the user makes a selection. Since menus are standard elements in Windows programming, built-in menu-selection functions are provided in Windows. This means your program does not need to handle all of the clerical overhead associated with menus, itself.

A *control* is a special type of window that allows a specific type of user interaction. Examples are push buttons, scroll bars, edit windows, and check boxes. Like menus, the controls defined by Windows are nearly completely automated. Your program can use one without having to handle the details.

A dialog box is a special window that enables more complex interaction with the application than that allowed by a menu. For example, your application might use a dialog box that allows users to enter a filename. Dialog boxes are typically used to house controls. With few exceptions, nonmenu input is accomplished via a dialog box.

The Win32 Application Programming Interface

From the programmer's point of view, Windows 2000 is defined by the way a program interacts with it. All application programs communicate with Windows 2000 through a *call-based interface.* The Windows 2000 call-based interface is an extensive set of system-defined functions that provides access to operating system features. Collectively, these functions are termed the *Application Programming Interface*, or API for short. The API contains several hundred functions that your application program uses to perform all necessary operating system–related activities, such as allocating memory, outputting to the screen, creating windows, and the like. A subset to the API called the GDI (Graphics Device Interface) is the part of Windows that provides device-independent graphics support.

There are two basic flavors of the API in common use: Win16 and Win32. Win16 is the older, 16-bit version of the API. Win32 is the modern, 32-bit version. Win16 is used by Windows 3.1. Windows 2000 programs use Win32. (Win32 is also used by Windows 95 and Windows 98.) In general, Win32 is a superset of Win16. Indeed, for the most part, the functions are called by the same name and are used in the same way. However, even though similar in spirit and purpose, the two APIs differ in two fundamental ways. First, Win32 supports 32-bit, flat addressing while Win16 supports only the 16-bit, segmented memory model. This difference means that Win32 often uses 32-bit arguments and return values in places where Win16 uses 16-bit values. Second, Win32 includes API functions that support thread-based multitasking, security, and the other enhanced features that are not available in Win16. If you are new to Windows programming in general, these changes will not affect you significantly. However, if you will be porting 16-bit code to Windows 2000, you will need to carefully examine the arguments you pass to each API function.

Components of a Window

Before moving on to specific aspects of Windows 2000 programming, a few important terms need to be defined. Figure 26-1 shows a standard window with each of its elements pointed out.

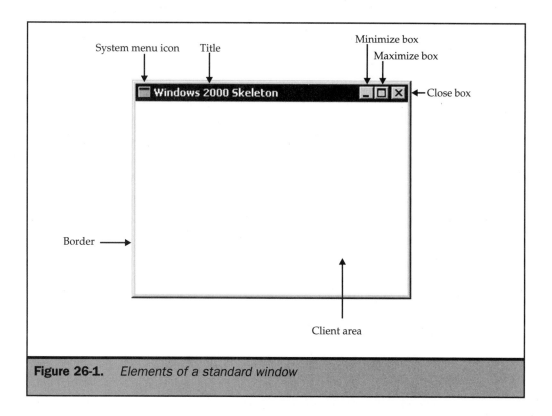

Figure 26-1.   *Elements of a standard window*

All windows have a border that defines the limits of the window and is used to resize the window. At the top of the window are several items. On the far left is the system menu icon (also called the title bar icon). Clicking on this box causes the system menu to be displayed. To the right of the system menu box is the window's title. At the far right are the minimize, maximize, and close boxes. The client area is the part of the window in which your program activity takes place. Most windows also have horizontal and vertical scroll bars that are used to move text through the window.

How Windows and Your Program Interact

When you write a program for many operating systems, it is your program that initiates interaction with the operating system. For example, in a DOS program, it is the program that requests such things as input and output. Put differently, programs written in the "traditional" way call the operating system; the operating system does not call your program. In a large measure, Windows works in the opposite way. It is Windows that calls your program. The process works like this: A program waits until it is sent a *message* by Windows. The message is passed to your program through a special function that is called by Windows. Once a message is received, your program is expected to take an appropriate action. Although your program may call one or more API functions when responding to a message, it is still Windows that initiates the activity. More than anything else, it is the message-based interaction with Windows that dictates the general form of all Windows programs.

There are many different types of messages that Windows 2000 may send your program. For example, each time the mouse is clicked on a window belonging to your program, a mouse-clicked message will be sent. Another type of message is sent each time a window belonging to your program must be redrawn. Still another message is sent each time the user presses a key when your program is the focus of input. Keep one fact firmly in mind: As far as your program is concerned, messages arrive randomly. This is why Windows programs resemble interrupt-driven programs. You can't know what message will be next.

Some Windows 2000 Application Basics

Before developing the Windows 2000 application skeleton, some basic concepts common to all Windows programs need to be discussed.

WinMain( )

All Windows 2000 programs begin execution with a call to **WinMain( )**. (Windows programs do not have a **main( )** function.) **WinMain( )** has some special properties that differentiate it from other functions in your application. First, it must be compiled using the **WINAPI** calling convention. By default, functions use the C calling convention, but it is possible to compile a function so that it uses a different calling convention. For example, a common alternative is to use the Pascal calling convention. For various technical reasons, the calling convention used by Windows 2000 to call **WinMain( )** is **WINAPI**. The return type of **WinMain( )** must be **int**.

The Window Procedure

All Windows programs must contain a special function that is *not* called by your program, but is called by Windows. This function is generally called the *window procedure* or *window function*. It is through this function that Windows 2000 communicates with your program. The window function is called by Windows 2000 when it needs to pass a message to your program. The window function receives the message in its parameters. All window functions must be declared as returning type **LRESULT CALLBACK**. The type **LRESULT** is a 32-bit integer. The **CALLBACK** calling convention is used with those functions that will be called by Windows. In Windows terminology, any function that is called by Windows is referred to as a *callback* function.

In addition to receiving the messages sent by Windows 2000, the window function must initiate any actions indicated by a message. Typically, a window function's body consists of a **switch** statement that links a specific response to each message that the program will respond to. Your program need not respond to every message that it is sent. For messages that your program doesn't care about, you can let Windows 2000 provide default processing. Since Windows can generate hundreds of different messages, it is common for most messages to be processed by Windows and not your program.

All messages are 32-bit integer values. Further, all messages are accompanied by any additional information that the message requires.

Window Classes

When your Windows 2000 program begins execution, it will need to define and register a *window class*, which means the *style* or *type* of the window. When you register a window class, you are telling Windows about the form and function of the window. However, registering the window class does not cause a window to come into existence. To actually create a window requires additional steps.

The Message Loop

As explained earlier, Windows 2000 communicates with your program by sending it messages. All Windows applications must establish a *message loop* inside the **WinMain( )** function. This loop reads any pending message from the application's message queue and then dispatches that message back to Windows, which then calls your program's window function with that message as a parameter. This may seem to be an overly complex way of passing messages, but it is, nevertheless, the way that all Windows programs must function. (Part of the reason for this is to return control to Windows so that the scheduler can allocate CPU time as it sees fit rather than waiting for your application's time slice to end.)

Windows Data Types

The Windows API functions do not make extensive use of standard C data types, such as **int** or **char ***. Instead, many data types used by Windows have been **typdef**ed within the WINDOWS.H file and/or its related files. This file is supplied by Microsoft (and any other company that makes a Windows-based C compiler) and must be included in all Windows programs. Some of the most common types are **HANDLE, HWND, UINT, BYTE, WORD, DWORD, LONG, BOOL, LPSTR**, and **LPCSTR**. **HANDLE** is a 32-bit integer that is used as a handle. There are a number of handle types, but they are all the same size as **HANDLE**. A *handle* is simply a value that identifies some resource. For example, **HWND** is a 32-bit integer that is used as a window handle. Also, all handle types begin with an H. **BYTE** is an 8-bit unsigned character. **WORD** is a 16-bit unsigned short integer. **DWORD** is an unsigned 32-bit integer. **UINT** is an unsigned

32-bit integer. **LONG** is a signed 32-bit integer. **BOOL** is an integer type used to indicate values that are either true or false. **LPSTR** is a pointer to a string, and **LPCSTR** is a **const** pointer to a string.

In addition to the basic types described above, Windows 2000 defines several structures. The two that are needed by the skeleton program are **MSG** and **WNDCLASSEX**. The **MSG** structure holds a Windows 2000 message, and **WNDCLASSEX** is a structure that defines a window class. These structures will be discussed later in this chapter.

A Windows 2000 Skeleton

Now that the necessary background information has been covered, we can develop a minimal Windows 2000 application. As stated, all Windows 2000 programs have certain things in common. The Windows 2000 skeleton developed here provides these necessary features. In the world of Windows programming, application skeletons are commonly used because there is a substantial "price of admission" when creating a Windows program. Unlike DOS programs, for example, in which a minimal program is about 5 lines long, a minimal Windows program is approximately 50 lines long.

A minimal Windows 2000 program contains two functions: **WinMain( )** and the window function. The **WinMain( )** function must perform the following general steps:

1. Define a window class.
2. Register that class with Windows 2000.
3. Create a window of that class.
4. Display the window.
5. Begin running the message loop.

The window function must respond to all relevant messages. Since the skeleton program does nothing but display its window, the only message to which it must respond is the one that tells the application that the user has terminated the program.

Before we get into the specifics, examine the following program, which is a minimal Windows 2000 skeleton. It creates a standard window that includes a title, a system menu, and the standard minimize, maximize and close boxes. The window is, therefore, capable of being minimized, maximized, moved, resized, and closed.

```
/* A minimal Windows 2000 skeleton. */

#include <windows.h>

LRESULT CALLBACK WindowFunc(HWND, UINT, WPARAM, LPARAM);
```

```
char szWinName[] = "MyWin"; /* name of window class */

int WINAPI WinMain(HINSTANCE hThisInst, HINSTANCE hPrevInst,
                   LPSTR lpszArgs, int nWinMode)
{
  HWND hwnd;
  MSG msg;
  WNDCLASSEX wcl;

  /* Define a window class. */
  wcl.cbSize = sizeof(WNDCLASSEX);

  wcl.hInstance = hThisInst;     /* handle to this instance */
  wcl.lpszClassName = szWinName; /* window class name */
  wcl.lpfnWndProc = WindowFunc;  /* window function */
  wcl.style = 0;                 /* default style */

  wcl.hIcon = LoadIcon(NULL, IDI_APPLICATION); /* large icon */
  wcl.hIconSm = NULL; /* use small version of large icon */
  wcl.hCursor = LoadCursor(NULL, IDC_ARROW);  /* cursor style */

  wcl.lpszMenuName = NULL; /* no class menu */
  wcl.cbClsExtra = 0;      /* no extra memory needed */
  wcl.cbWndExtra = 0;

  /* Make the window background white. */
  wcl.hbrBackground = (HBRUSH) GetStockObject(WHITE_BRUSH);

  /* Register the window class. */
  if(!RegisterClassEx(&wcl)) return 0;

  /* Now that a window class has been registered, a window
     can be created. */
  hwnd = CreateWindow(
    szWinName, /* name of window class */
    "Windows 2000 Skeleton", /* title */
    WS_OVERLAPPEDWINDOW, /* window style - normal */
    CW_USEDEFAULT, /* X coordinate - let Windows decide */
    CW_USEDEFAULT, /* Y coordinate - let Windows decide */
    CW_USEDEFAULT, /* width - let Windows decide */
    CW_USEDEFAULT, /* height - let Windows decide */
    NULL,          /* no parent window */
```

```
      NULL,           /* no menu */
      hThisInst,      /* instance handle */
      NULL            /* no additional arguments */
   );

   /* Display the window. */
   ShowWindow(hwnd, nWinMode);
   UpdateWindow(hwnd);

   /* Create the message loop. */
   while(GetMessage(&msg, NULL, 0, 0))
   {
     TranslateMessage(&msg); /* translate keyboard messages */
     DispatchMessage(&msg);   /* return control to Windows 2000 */
   }
   return msg.wParam;
}


/* This function is called by Windows 2000 and is passed
   messages from the message queue.
*/
LRESULT CALLBACK WindowFunc(HWND hwnd, UINT message,
                            WPARAM wParam, LPARAM lParam)
{
  switch(message) {
    case WM_DESTROY: /* terminate the program */
      PostQuitMessage(0);
      break;
    default:
      /* Let Windows 2000 process any messages not specified in
         the preceding switch statement. */
      return DefWindowProc(hwnd, message, wParam, lParam);
  }
  return 0;
}
```

Let's go through this program step by step. First, all Windows programs must include the header file WINDOWS.H. As stated, this file (along with its support files) contains the API function prototypes and various types, macros, and definitions used by Windows. For example, the data types **HWND** and **WNDCLASSEX** are defined in WINDOWS.H (or its subordinate files).

The window function used by the program is called **WindowFunc( )**. It is declared as a callback function because this is the function that Windows calls to communicate with the program.

As stated, program execution begins with **WinMain( )**. **WinMain( )** is passed four parameters. **hThisInst** and **hPrevInst** are handles. **hThisInst** refers to the current instance of the program. Remember, Windows 2000 is a multitasking system, so more than one instance of your program may be running at the same time. For Windows 2000, **hPrevInst** will always be **NULL**. The **lpszArgs** parameter is a pointer to a string that holds any command line arguments specified when the application was begun. In Windows 2000, the string contains the entire command line, including the name of the program itself. The **nWinMode** parameter contains a value that determines how the window will be displayed when your program begins execution.

Inside the function, three variables are created. The **hwnd** variable will hold the handle to the program's window. The **msg** structure variable will hold window messages, and the **wcl** structure variable will be used to define the window class.

Defining the Window Class

The first two actions that **WinMain( )** takes is to define a window class and then register it. A window class is defined by filling in the fields defined by the **WNDCLASSEX** structure. Its fields are shown here:

```
UINT cbSize;            /* size of the WNDCLASSEX structure */
UINT style;             /* type of window */
WNDPROC lpfnWndProc;    /* address to window func */
int cbClsExtra;         /* extra class memory */
int cbWndExtra;         /* extra window memory */
HINSTANCE hInstance;    /* handle of this instance */
HICON hIcon;            /* handle of large icon */
HICON hIconSm;          /* handle of small icon */
HCURSOR hCursor;        /* handle of mouse cursor */
HBRUSH hbrBackground;   /* background color */
LPCSTR lpszMenuName;    /* name of main menu */
LPCSTR lpszClassName;   /* name of window class */
```

As you can see by looking at the program, **cbSize** is assigned the size of the **WNDCLASSEX** structure. The **hInstance** member is assigned the current instance handle as specified by **hThisInst**. The name of the window class is pointed to by **lpszClassName**, which points to the string "MyWin" in this case. The address of the window function is assigned to **lpfnWndProc**. In the program, no default style is specified, no extra information is needed, and no main menu is specified. Although most programs will contain a main menu, the skeleton does not require one.

All Windows applications need to define a default shape for the mouse cursor and for the application's icons. An application can define its own custom version of these resources, or it may use one of the built-in styles, as the skeleton does. In either case, handles to these resources must be assigned to the appropriate members of the **WNDCLASSEX** structure. To see how this is done, let's begin with icons.

A Windows 2000 application has two icons associated with it: one large and one small. The small icon is used when the application is minimized, and it is also the icon that is used for the system menu. The large icon is displayed when you move or copy an application to the desktop. Typically, large icons are 32-by-32 bitmaps, and small icons are 16-by-16 bitmaps. The large icon is loaded by the API function **LoadIcon( )**, whose prototype is shown here:

HICON LoadIcon(HINSTANCE *hInst*, LPCSTR *lpszName*);

This function returns a handle to an icon, or **NULL** on failure. Here, *hInst* specifies the handle of the module that contains the icon, and its name is specified in *lpszName*. However, to use one of the built-in icons, you must use **NULL** for the first parameter and specify one of the following macros for the second:

Icon Macro	Shape
IDI_APPLICATION	Default icon
IDI_ERROR	Error symbol
IDI_INFORMATION	Information
IDI_QUESTION	Question mark
IDI_WARNING	Exclamation point
IDI_WINLOGO	Windows logo

Here are two important points about loading icons: First, if your application does not specify a small icon, the large icon's resource file is examined. If it contains a small icon, then this icon is used. Otherwise, the large icon is simply shrunk when the small icon is needed. If you don't want to specify a small icon, assign the value **NULL** to **hIconSm**, as the skeleton does. Second, in general, **LoadIcon( )** can only be used to load the large icon. You can use **LoadImage( )** to load icons of differing sizes.

To load the mouse cursor, use the API **LoadCursor( )** function. This function has the following prototype:

HCURSOR LoadCursor(HINSTANCE *hInst*, LPCSTR *lpszName*);

This function returns a handle to a cursor resource, or **NULL** on failure. Here, *hInst* specifies the handle of the module that contains the mouse cursor, and its name is specified in *lpszName*. To use one of the built-in cursors, you must use **NULL** for the first parameter and specify one of the built-in cursors using its macros for the second parameter. Here are a few of the built-in cursors:

Cursor Macro	Shape
IDC_ARROW	Default arrow pointer
IDC_CROSS	Cross hairs
IDC_HAND	Hand
IDC_IBEAM	Vertical I-beam
IDC_WAIT	Hourglass

The background color of the window created by the skeleton is specified as white, and a handle to this *brush* is obtained using the API function **GetStockObject( )**. A brush is a resource that paints the screen using a predetermined size, color, and pattern. The function **GetStockObject( )** is used to obtain a handle to a number of standard display objects, including brushes, pens (which draw lines), and character fonts. It has this prototype:

HGDIOBJ GetStockObject(int *object*);

The function returns a handle to the object specified by *object*. **NULL** is returned on failure. (The type **HGDIOBJ** is a GDI handle.) Here are some of the built-in brushes available to your program:

Macro Name	Background Type
BLACK_BRUSH	Black
DKGRAY_BRUSH	Dark gray
HOLLOW_BRUSH	See-through window
LTGRAY_BRUSH	Light gray
WHITE_BRUSH	White

You may use these macros as parameters to **GetStockObject( )** to obtain a brush.

Once the window class has been fully specified, it is registered with Windows 2000 using the API function **RegisterClassEx( )**, whose prototype is shown here:

ATOM RegisterClassEx(CONST WNDCLASSEX *lpWClass*);

The function returns a value that identifies the window class. **ATOM** is a **typedef** that means **WORD**. Each window class is given a unique value. *lpWClass* must be the address of a **WNDCLASSEX** structure.

Creating a Window

Once a window class has been defined and registered, your application can actually create a window of that class using the API function **CreateWindow( )**, whose prototype is shown here:

```
HWND CreateWindow(
            LPCSTR lpszClassName,    /* name of window class */
            LPCSTR lpszWinName,      /* title of window */
            DWORD dwStyle,           /* type of window */
            int X, int Y,            /* upper-left coordinates */
            int Width, int Height,   /* dimensions of window */
            HWND hParent,            /* handle of parent window */
            HMENU hMenu,             /* handle of main menu */
            HINSTANCE hThisInst,     /* handle of creator */
            LPVOID lpszAdditional    /* pointer to additional info */
);
```

As you can see by looking at the skeleton program, many of the parameters to **CreateWindow( )** may be defaulted or specified as **NULL**. In fact, most often the *X, Y, Width*, and *Height* parameters will simply use the macro **CW_USEDEFAULT**, which tells Windows 2000 to select an appropriate size and location for the window. If the window has no parent, which is the case in the skeleton, then *hParent* can be specified as **NULL**. (You can also use **HWND_DESKTOP** for this parameter.) If the window does not contain a main menu or uses the main menu defined by the window class, then *hMenu* must be **NULL**. (The *hMenu* parameter has other uses, too.) Also, if no additional information is required, as is most often the case, then *lpszAdditional* is **NULL**. (The type **LPVOID** is **typedef**ed as **void ***. Historically, **LPVOID** stands for long pointer to **void**.)

The remaining four parameters must be explicitly set by your program. First, *lpszClassName* must point to the name of the window class. (This is the name you gave it when it was registered.) The title of the window is a string pointed to by *lpszWinName*. This can be a null string, but usually a window will be given a title. The style (or type) of window actually created is determined by the value of *dwStyle*. The macro **WS_OVERLAPPEDWINDOW** specifies a standard window that has a system menu, a border, and minimize, maximize, and close boxes. Although this style of window is the most common, you can construct one to your own specifications. To accomplish this, simply OR together the various style macros that you want. Some other common styles are shown here:

Style Macro	Window Feature
WS_OVERLAPPED	Overlapped window with border
WS_MAXIMIZEBOX	Maximize box
WS_MINIMIZEBOX	Minimize box
WS_SYSMENU	System menu
WS_HSCROLL	Horizontal scroll bar
WS_VSCROLL	Vertical scroll bar

The *hThisInst* parameter is ignored by Windows 2000, but for Windows 95/98 it must contain the current instance handle of the application. Thus, to ensure portability to those environments—and to prevent future problems—*hThisInst* should be assigned the current instance handle, as in the skeleton.

The **CreateWindow( )** function returns the handle of the window it creates or **NULL** if the window cannot be created.

Once the window has been created, it is still not displayed on the screen. To cause the window to be displayed, call the **ShowWindow( )** API function. This function has the following prototype:

BOOL ShowWindow(HWND *hwnd*, int *nHow*);

The handle of the window to display is specified in *hwnd*. The display mode is specified in *nHow*. The first time the window is displayed, you will want to pass **WinMain( )**'s **nWinMode** as the *nHow* parameter. Remember, the value of **nWinMode** determines how the window will be displayed when the program begins execution. Subsequent calls can display (or remove) the window as necessary. Some common values for *nHow* are shown here:

Display Macro	Effect
SW_HIDE	Removes the window
SW_MINIMIZE	Minimizes the window into an icon
SW_MAXIMIZE	Maximizes the window
SW_RESTORE	Returns a window to normal size

The **ShowWindow( )** function returns the previous display status of the window. If the window was displayed, nonzero is returned. If the window was not displayed, zero is returned.

Although not technically necessary for the skeleton, a call to **UpdateWindow( )** is included because it is needed by virtually every Windows 2000 application that you will create. It essentially tells Windows 2000 to send a message to your application that the main window needs to be updated.

The Message Loop

The final part of the skeletal **WinMain( )** is the *message loop*. The message loop is a part of all Windows applications. Its purpose is to receive and process messages sent by Windows 2000. When an application is running, it is continually being sent messages. These messages are stored in the application's message queue until they can be read and processed. Each time your application is ready to read another message, it must call the API function **GetMessage( )**, which has this prototype:

BOOL GetMessage(LPMSG *msg*, HWND *hwnd*, UINT *min*, UINT *max*);

The message will be received by the structure pointed to by *msg*. All Windows messages are of structure type **MSG**, shown here:

```
/* Message structure
typedef struct tagMSG
{
  HWND hwnd;       /* window that message is for */
  UINT message;    /* message */
  WPARAM wParam;   /* message-dependent info */
  LPARAM lParam;   /* more message-dependent info */
  DWORD time;      /* time message posted */
  POINT pt;        /* X,Y location of mouse */
} MSG;
```

In **MSG**, the handle of the window for which the message is intended is contained in **hwnd**. All Windows 2000 messages are 32-bit integers, and the message is contained in **message**. Additional information relating to each message is passed in **wParam** and **lParam**. The types **WPARAM** and **LPARAM** are both 32-bit quantities.

The time the message was sent (posted) is specified in milliseconds in the **time** field.

The **pt** member will contain the coordinates of the mouse when the message was sent. The coordinates are held in a **POINT** structure, which is defined like this:

```
typedef struct tagPOINT {
  LONG x, y;
} POINT;
```

If there are no messages in the application's message queue, a call to **GetMessage( )** will pass control back to Windows 2000.

The *hwnd* parameter to **GetMessage( )** specifies for which window messages will be obtained. It is possible (even likely) that an application will contain several windows, and you may only want to receive messages for a specific window. If you want to receive all messages directed at your application, this parameter must be **NULL**.

The remaining two parameters to **GetMessage( )** specify a range of messages that will be received. Generally, you want your application to receive all messages. To accomplish this, specify both *min* and *max* as 0, as the skeleton does.

GetMessage( ) returns zero when the user terminates the program, causing the message loop to terminate. Otherwise it returns nonzero. It will return –1 if an error occurs. Errors can occur only under unusual circumstances that do not apply to most programs.

Inside the message loop two functions are called. The first is the API function **TranslateMessage( )**. This function translates the virtual key codes generated by Windows 2000 into character messages. Although not necessary for all applications, most call **TranslateMessage( )** because it is needed to allow full integration of the keyboard into your application program.

Once the message has been read and translated, it is dispatched back to Windows 2000 using the **DispatchMessage( )** API function. Windows 2000 then holds this message until it can pass it to the program's window function.

Once the message loop terminates, the **WinMain( )** function ends by returning the value of **msg.wParam** to Windows 2000. This value contains the return code generated when your program terminates.

The Window Function

The second function in the application skeleton is its window function. In this case the function is called **WindowFunc( )**, but it could have any name you like. The window function is passed messages by Windows 2000. The first four members of the **MSG** structure are its parameters. For the skeleton, the only parameter that is used is the message itself.

The skeleton's window function responds to only one message explicitly: **WM_DESTROY**. This message is sent when the user terminates the program. When this message is received, your program must execute a call to the API function **PostQuitMessage( )**. The argument to this function is an exit code that is returned in **msg.wParam** inside **WinMain( )**. Calling **PostQuitMessage( )** causes a **WM_QUIT** message to be sent to your application, which causes **GetMessage( )** to return false and thus stops your program.

Any other messages received by **WindowFunc( )** are passed along to Windows 2000, via a call to **DefWindowProc( )**, for default processing. This step is necessary because all messages must be dealt with in one way or another.

Each message specifies the value that must be returned by the window function after the message has been processed. Most of the commonly handled messages require that you return zero. But a few require a different return value.

Definition File No Longer Needed

If you are familiar with 16-bit Windows programming, you have used *definition files*. For 16-bit versions of Windows, all programs need to have a definition file associated with them. A definition file is simply a text file that specifies certain information and settings needed by the 16-bit environment. Because of the 32-bit architecture of Windows 2000 (and other improvements), definition files are not usually needed for Windows 2000 programs. If you are new to Windows programming in general and you don't know what a definition file is, the following discussion will give you a brief overview.

All definition files use the extension .DEF. For example, the definition file for the skeleton program could be called SKEL.DEF. Here is a definition file that you can use to provide downward compatibility to Windows 3.1:

```
DESCRIPTION 'Skeleton Program'
EXETYPE WINDOWS
CODE PRELOAD MOVEABLE DISCARDABLE
DATA PRELOAD MOVEABLE MULTIPLE
HEAPSIZE 8192
STACKSIZE 8192
EXPORTS WindowFunc
```

This file specifies the name of the program and its description, both of which are optional. It also states that the executable file will be compatible with Windows (rather than DOS, for example). The **CODE** statement tells Windows 2000 to load all of the program at startup (PRELOAD), that the code may be moved in memory (MOVEABLE), and that the code may be removed from memory and reloaded if (and when) necessary (DISCARDABLE). The file also states that your program's data must be loaded upon execution and may be moved about in memory. It also specifies that each instance of the program has its own data (MULTIPLE). Next, the size of the heap and stack allocated to the program are specified. Finally, the name of the window function is exported. Exporting allows Windows 3.1 to call the function.

Remember: Definition files are seldom used when programming for 32-bit versions of Windows.

Naming Conventions

Before finishing this chapter, a brief comment on naming functions and variables needs to be made. If you are new to Windows programming, several of the variable and parameter names in the skeleton program and its description probably seem rather unusual. The reason for this is that they follow a set of naming conventions that was invented by Microsoft for Windows programming. For functions, the name consists of a verb followed by a noun. The first character of the verb and noun is capitalized.

For variable names, Microsoft chose to use a rather complex system of imbedding the data type into a variable's name. To accomplish this, a lowercase type prefix is added to the start of the variable's name. The name itself begins with a capital letter. The type prefixes are shown in Table 26-1. The use of type prefixes is controversial and is not universally accepted. Many Windows programmers use this method; many do not. You are, of course, free to use any naming convention you like.

Prefix	Data Type
b	boolean (1 byte)
c	character (1 byte)
dw	long unsigned integer
f	16-bit bit-field (flags)
fn	function
h	handle
l	long integer
lp	long pointer
n	short integer
p	pointer
pt	long integer holding screen coordinates
w	short unsigned integer
sz	pointer to null-terminated string
lpsz	long pointer to null-terminated string
rgb	long integer holding RGB color values

Table 26-1.   *Variable Type Prefix Characters*

The
Complete
Reference

Chapter 27

Software Engineering Using C

Creating a large computer program is a little like designing a large building. In fact, the term "architect" is commonly applied to software designers these days. Of course, what makes the creation of a large building possible is the same thing that makes the creation of a large program possible: the application of the proper engineering methods. In this chapter, several techniques that relate specifically to the C programming environment and that make the creation and maintenance of a program much easier will be examined.

This chapter is written mostly for the benefit of those readers who are newcomers to programming. If you're an experienced pro, you will be familiar with much of the material in this chapter.

Top-Down Design

Without a doubt, the single most important thing that you can do to simplify the creation of a large program is to apply a solid approach. There are three general ways to write a program: top-down, bottom-up, and ad hoc. In the *top-down approach*, you start with the top-level routines and move downward to the low-level routines. The *bottom-up approach* works in the opposite direction: You begin with specific routines and build them progressively into more complex structures, ending at the top. The *ad hoc approach* has no predetermined method.

As a structured language, C lends itself to a top-down approach. The top-down method can produce clean, readable code that you can easily maintain. This approach also helps you clarify the overall structure of the program before you code low-level functions, reducing time wasted by false starts.

Outlining Your Program

Like an outline, the top-down method starts with a general description and works toward specifics. In fact, a good way to design a program is to first define exactly what the program will do at its top level and then fill in the details relating to each action. For example, assume that you have to write a mailing list program. First you should make a list of the operations that the program will perform. Each entry in the list should contain only one functional unit. (You can think of a functional unit as a black box that performs a single task.) For example, your list might look like this:

- Enter a new address.
- Delete an address.
- Print the list.
- Search for a name.
- Save the list.

- Load the list.
- Quit the program.

After you have defined the overall functionality of the program, you can sketch in the details of each functional unit, beginning with the main loop. One way to write the main loop of the mailing list program is like this:

```
main loop
{
  do {
    display menu
    get user selection
    process the selection
  } while selection does not equal quit
}
```

This type of algorithmic notation (sometimes called *pseudocode*) can help you clarify the general structure of your program before you sit down at the computer. C-like syntax has been used because it is familiar, but you can use any type of syntax that you like.

You should give a similar definition to each functional area. For example, you can define the function that writes the mailing list to a disk file like this:

```
save to disk {
  open disk file
  while data left to write {
    write data to disk
  }
  close disk file
}
```

At this point, the save-to-disk function has created new, more specific functional units. These units open a disk file, write data to disk, and close the disk file. You must define each of these. If, in the course of their definition, new functional units are created, they must also be defined, and so on. This process stops when no new functional units are created and all that is left to do is to actually write the C code that implements an action. For example, the unit that closes a disk file will probably translate into a call to **fclose( )**.

Notice that the definition does not mention data structure or variables. This is intentional. So far, you only want to define what your program will do, not how it will actually do it. This definition process will help you decide on the actual structure of the data. (Of course, you need to determine the data structure before you can code the functional units.)

Choosing a Data Structure

After you have determined your program's general outline, you must decide how the data will be structured. The selection of a data structure and its implementation are critical because they help determine the design limits of your program.

A mailing list deals with collections of information: names, street addresses, cities, states, and postal codes. Using a top-down approach, this immediately suggests the use of a structure to hold the information. However, how will these structures be stored and manipulated? For a mailing list program, you could use a fixed-size array of structures. But a fixed-size array has a serious drawback: The size of the array arbitrarily limits the length of the mailing list. A better solution is to allocate memory for each address dynamically, storing each address in some form of dynamic data structure (such as a linked list), which can grow or shrink as needed. In this way the list can be as large or small as needed.

Although dynamic storage allocation has been chosen over a fixed-size array, the exact form of the data still has not been decided. There are several possibilities: You could use a singly linked list, a doubly linked list, a binary tree, or even a hashing method. Each method has its merits and drawbacks. For the sake of discussion, assume that your particular mail list application requires especially fast search times, so you choose a binary tree. Now you can define the structure that holds each name and address in the list, as shown here:

```
struct addr {
  char name[30];
  char street[40];
  char city[20];
  char state[3];
  char zip[11];
  struct addr *left;   /* pointer to left subtree */
  struct addr *right;  /* pointer to right subtree */
};
```

Once the data structure has been defined, you are ready to code your program. To do so, simply fill in the details described in the pseudocode outline you created earlier. If you follow the top-down approach, your programs will not only be much easier to read, but will also take less time to develop and less effort to maintain.

Bulletproof Functions

In large programs, especially those that control potentially life-threatening devices, the potential for error has to be very slight. Although small programs can be verified as correct, this is not the case for large ones. (A verified program is proved to be free of errors and will never malfunction—in theory at least.) For example, consider a program that controls the wing flaps of a modern jet airplane. You cannot test all possible interactions of the numerous forces that will be exerted on the plane. This means that you cannot test the program exhaustively. At best, all you can say is that it performed correctly in such and such situations. In a program of this type, the last thing that you (as a passenger or programmer) want is a crash (of the program or the plane)!

After you have programmed for a few years, you learn that most program failures can be attributed to one of a relatively few types of programmer errors. For example, many catastrophic program errors are caused by one of these relatively common mistakes:

- Some condition causes an unintended infinite loop to be entered.

- An array boundary has been violated, causing damage to adjacent code or data.

- A data type unexpectedly overflows.

In theory, these types of errors can be avoided by careful and thoughtful design and programming practices. (Indeed, professionally written programs should be reasonably free of these types of errors.)

However, another type of error often appears after the initial development stage of a program, occurring either during final "fine tuning" or during the maintenance phase of the program. This error is caused by one function inadvertently interfering with another function's code or data. This type of error is especially hard to find because the code in both functions may appear to be correct. Instead, it is the interaction of the functions that causes the error. Therefore, to reduce the chance of a catastrophic failure, you will want your functions and their data to be as "bulletproof" as possible. The best way to achieve this is to keep the code and data related to each function hidden from the rest of the program.

Hiding code and data is similar to telling a secret only to those who need to know. Simply put, if a function does not need to know about another function or variable, don't let the function have access to it. You must follow four rules to accomplish this:

1. Each functional unit must have one entry point and one exit point.

2. Wherever possible, pass information to functions instead of using global variables.

3. Where global variables are required by a few related functions, you should place both the variables and the functions in a separate file. Also, the global variables must be declared as **static**.

4. Each function must be able to report the success or failure of its intended operation to the caller. That is, the code that calls a function must be able to know if that function succeeded or failed.

Rule 1 states that each functional area has one entry point and one exit point. This means that although a functional unit may contain several functions, the rest of the program communicates through only one of them. Think about the mailing list program discussed earlier. There are seven functional areas. You could put all of the functions needed by each functional area in their own files and compile them separately. If done correctly, the only way in or out of each functional unit is through its top-level function. And, in the mailing list program, these top-level functions are called only by **main( )**, thereby preventing one functional unit from accidentally damaging another. This situation is depicted in Figure 27-1.

Although it decreases performance in some cases, the best way to reduce the possibility of side effects is to always pass all information needed by a function to that function. Avoid the use of global data. This is rule 2, and if you have ever written a large program in standard BASIC—where every variable is global—you already understand its importance.

Rule 3 states that when global data must be used, the global data and the functions that need to access it should be put in one file and compiled separately. The key is to declare the global data as **static**, thereby keeping knowledge of it from the other files. Also, the functions that access the **static** data can, themselves, be declared as **static**, preventing them from being called by other functions not declared within the same file.

Put simply, rule 4 ensures that programs get a second chance by allowing the caller of a function to respond in a reasonable manner to an error condition. For example, if the function that controls the flaps on the airplane experiences an out-of-range condition, you do not want the entire program to fail (and the plane to crash). Rather, you want the program to know that an error occurred within the function. Since an out-of-range condition may be a temporary situation for a program that operates on real-time data, the program could respond to such an error by simply waiting a few clock ticks and trying again.

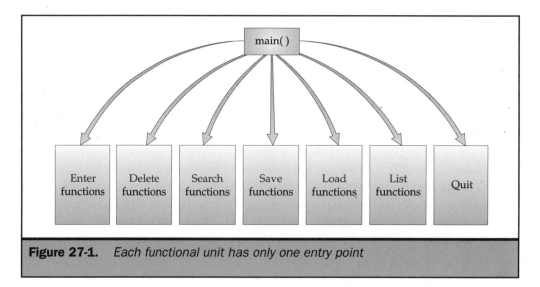

Figure 27-1.   *Each functional unit has only one entry point*

Keep in mind that strict adherence to these rules will not be applicable in every situation, but you should follow the rules whenever possible. The goal of this approach is to create a program that has the highest likelihood of recovering unharmed from an error condition.

 If you are especially interested in the concepts supporting bulletproof functions, you will want to explore C++. C++ provides an even stronger protection mechanism called encapsulation, *which further decreases the chance of one function damaging another.*

Using MAKE

Another type of error that tends to affect the creation of large programs occurs mostly during the development stage and can bring a project to a near standstill. This error occurs when one or more source files are out-of-date with their respective object files when the program is compiled and linked. When this happens, the executable form of the program will not act in accordance with the current state of the source code. Anyone who has ever been involved with the creation or maintenance of a large software project has probably experienced this problem. To help eliminate this type of frustrating error, most C compilers include a utility called MAKE that helps synchronize source and object files. (The exact name of the MAKE utility for your compiler may differ slightly from MAKE, so be sure to check your compiler's documentation.)

MAKE automates the recompilation process for large programs comprised of several files. Often, many small changes will be made to many files in the course of program development. After the changes have been made, the program is recompiled and tested. Unfortunately, it is easy to forget which of the files need to be recompiled. In this situation, you can either recompile all the files—a waste of time—or accidentally miss a file that should be recompiled, potentially adding several hours of frustrating debugging. The MAKE program solves this problem by automatically recompiling only those files that have been altered.

The examples presented in this section are compatible with the MAKE programs supplied with Microsoft C/C++. Currently, Microsoft's version of MAKE is called NMAKE. The examples will also work with most other mainstream MAKE utilities, and the general concepts described are applicable to all MAKE programs.

 In recent years, MAKE programs have become very sophisticated. The examples presented here illustrate the essence of MAKE. You will want to explore the MAKE utility supported by your compiler. It may contain features that are especially useful to your development environment.

MAKE is driven by a *make file*, which contains a list of target files, dependent files, and commands. A *target file* requires its *dependent files* to produce it. For example, T.C would be a dependent file of T.OBJ because T.C is required to make T.OBJ. MAKE works by comparing the dates between a dependent file and its target file. (As used here, the term "date" includes both the calendar date and the time.) If the target file has a date that is older than its dependent file (or if the target does not exist), the specified command sequence is executed. If that command sequence contains target files defined by other dependencies, then those dependencies are also updated, as needed. When the MAKE process is over, all target files have been updated. Therefore, in a correctly constructed make file, all source files that require compilation are automatically compiled and linked, forming the new executable file. In this way, source files are kept in synchronization with object files.

The general form of the make file is

target_file1 : dependent_file list
  command_sequence

target_file2 : dependent_file list
  command_sequence

target_file3 : dependent_file list
  command_sequence

.
.
.

target_fileN : dependent_file list
  command_sequence

The target filename must start in the leftmost column and be followed by a colon and its list of dependent files. The command sequence associated with each target must be preceded by at least one space or a tab. Comments are preceded by a # and may follow the dependent file list and/or the command sequence. They can also appear on a line of their own. Each target-file specification must be separated from the next by at least one blank line.

The most important thing that you need to understand about a make file is this: Execution of a make file stops as soon as the first dependency succeeds. This means that you must design your make files in such a way that the dependencies are hierarchical. Remember that no dependency can succeed until all subordinate dependencies relating to it are also resolved.

To see how MAKE works, consider a very simple program. The program is divided into four files called TEST.H, TEST.C, TEST2.C, and TEST3.C. This situation is illustrated in Figure 27-2. (To follow along, enter each part of the program into the indicated files.)

TEST.H:

```
extern int count;
```

TEST.C:

```
#include <stdio.h>
void test2(void), test3(void);

int count = 0;

int main(void)
{
  printf("count = %d\n", count);
  test2();
  printf("count = %d\n", count);
  test3();
  printf("count = %d\n", count);

  return 0;
}
```

TEST2.C:

```
#include <stdio.h>
#include "test.h"

void test2(void)
{
  count = 30;
}
```

TEST3.C:

```
#include <stdio.h>
#include "test.h"

void test3(void)
{
  count = -100;
}
```

Figure 27-2.   *A simple four-file program*

If you are using Visual C++, the following make file will recompile the program when you make changes:

```
test.exe:  test.h test.obj test2.obj test3.obj
        cl test.obj test2.obj test3.obj

test.obj: test.c test.h
        cl -c test.c

test2.obj: test2.c test.h
        cl -c test2.c

test3.obj: test3.c test.h
        cl -c test3.c
```

By default, a MAKE program will use the directives contained in a file called MAKEFILE. However, you will usually want to use another name for your make file. When using another name for the make file, you must use the **–f** option on the command line. For example, if the name of the preceding make file is TEST, for Microsoft's NMAKE program, you would type something like

nmake –f test

at the command prompt to compile the necessary modules and create an executable program. (This applies to Microsoft's NMAKE. A different option may be needed if you use a different MAKE utility.)

Order is very important in the make file because, as stated earlier, MAKE stops processing the directives contained in the file as soon as the first dependency is satisfied. For example, if the preceding make file were changed to look like this:

```
# This is an incorrect make file.
test.obj: test.c test.h
        cl -c test.c

test2.obj: test2.c test.h
        cl -c test2.c

test3.obj: test3.c test.h
        cl -c test3.c

test.exe: test.h test.obj test2.obj test3.obj
        cl test.obj test2.obj test3.obj
```

it would no longer work correctly when the file TEST.H (or any other source file) was changed. This is because the final directive (which creates a new TEST.EXE) will no longer be executed.

Using Macros in MAKE

MAKE allows macros to be defined in the make file. These macro names are simply placeholders for the information that will actually be determined either by a command line specification or by the macro's definition in the make file. Macros are defined according to this general form:

macro_name = definition

If there is to be any white space in the macro definition, you must enclose the definition within double quotation marks.

Once a macro has been defined, it is used in the make file like this:

$(*macro_name*)

Each time this statement is encountered, the definition linked to the macro is substituted. For example, this make file uses the macro **LIBFIL** to determine which library is used by the linker:

```
LIBFIL = graphics.lib

prog.exe: prog.obj prog2.obj prog3.obj
        cl prog.obj prog2.obj prog3.obj $(LIBFIL)
```

Many MAKE programs have additional features, so it is very important to consult your compiler's documentation.

Using an Integrated Development Environment

Most modern compilers are supplied in two different forms. The first form is the stand-alone, command line compiler. Using this form, you use a separate editor to create your program, then you compile your program, and, finally, you execute your program. These events all occur as separate commands given by you on the command line. Any debugging or source file control (such as using MAKE) also occurs separately. The command line compiler is the traditional way compilers were implemented.

The second form of a compiler is found in an integrated development environment (IDE), such as the Visual C++ IDE. In this form, the compiler is integrated with an editor, a debugger, a project manager (that takes the place of a separate MAKE utility), and a run-time support system. Using an IDE, you edit, compile, and run your program without ever leaving the IDE. When IDEs were first invented, they were somewhat cumbersome to use and tedious to work with. However, today the IDEs provided by the major compiler manufacturers have much to offer the programmer. If you take the time to set the IDE's options so that it is optimized for your needs, you will find that using the IDE streamlines the development process.

Of course, whether you use an IDE or the traditional command line approach is also a matter of taste. If you like using the command line, then by all means, use it. Also, one point that is still in favor of the traditional approach is that you can personally select every tool you use, rather than taking what the IDE has to offer.

Chapter 28

Efficiency, Porting, and Debugging

The ability to write programs that make efficient use of system resources, are bug free, and can be ported to new environments is the mark of a professional programmer. It is also in these areas that computer science becomes the "art of computer science." In this chapter we will explore some of the methods that help achieve these goals.

Efficiency

This section explores several techniques that can improve the efficiency of your programs. In programming, the term "efficiency" can refer to the speed of execution, the use of system resources, or both. System resources include such things as memory, disk space, CPU time, and the like—basically anything that you can allocate and use up. Whether a program is efficient or not is sometimes a subjective judgment that can change from situation to situation. For example, the same programming techniques used to create a user-oriented program, such as a word processor, may not be appropriate for a piece of system code, such as a network router.

Efficiency often involves trade-offs. For example, making a program execute faster often means making it bigger when you use in-line code to eliminate the overhead of a function call. By the same token, making a program smaller by replacing in-line code with function calls sometimes makes the program run slower. In the same vein, making more efficient use of disk space might mean compacting the data, which might make accessing that data slower because of the extra processing overhead. These and other types of efficiency trade-offs can be very frustrating—especially to nonprogrammers and end users who cannot see why one thing should affect the other. Fortunately, there are a few techniques that can increase speed and reduce size at the same time.

Whether you are optimizing for speed or size, C is a language that lets you effectively implement your optimizations. The following sections present several of the most commonly used techniques, but the enterprising programmer is certain to discover more.

The Increment and Decrement Operators

Discussions of the efficient use of C almost always start with the increment and decrement operators. In some situations, the use of these operators may allow the compiler to create more efficient object code. For example, consider the following statement sequences:

```
/* first way */
a = a + b;
b = b + 1;

/* second way */
a = a + b++;
```

Both statements assign to **a** the value of **a + b** and then increase the value of **b** by 1. However, using the second way is often more efficient because the compiler may be able to avoid using redundant load and store instructions when accessing **b**. That is, **b** won't have to be loaded into a register twice—once to add it to **a** and once to increment it. Although some compilers will automatically optimize both ways into the same object code, this cannot be taken for granted. In general, the careful use of the **++** and **−−** operators can improve the execution speed of your program and at the same time reduce its size. You should look for ways to employ them.

Using Register Variables

One of the most effective ways to speed up your code is through the use of **register** variables. Although **register** variables are effective in other uses, they are particularly well suited for loop control. Recall that any variable specified as **register** is stored in a manner that produces the shortest access time. For integer types, this usually means a register of the CPU. This is important because the speed with which the critical loops of a program execute sets the pace for the overall program speed. For example:

```
for(i=0; i < MAX; i++) {
   /* do something */
}
```

Here, **i** is being repeatedly tested and set. That is, each time the loop iterates, the value of **i** is tested, and if it has not yet reached the target value, it is incremented. Since this happens over and over again, the speed with which **i** can be accessed governs the speed of the entire loop.

In addition to loop control variables, any variables used inside the body of a loop are also good candidates for the **register** modifier. For example:

```
for(i=0; i < MAX; i++) {
   sum = a + b;
   /* ... */
}
```

Here, the variables **sum**, **a**, and **b** are accessed each time the loop repeats. Also, **sum** is assigned a value with each iteration. Thus, the speed with which these variables can be accessed affects the overall performance of the loop.

Although you can declare as many variables as you like using **register**, in reality, within any single function, most compilers can optimize the access time of only a few. In general, you can expect that at least two integer variables can be held in registers of the CPU at any one time. Other types of fast storage, such as cache memory, may also be used, but it too is limited. Since it may not be possible to optimize every variable that you modify with **register**, C allows the compiler to disregard the **register** specifier and simply handle the variable normally. This provision also enables code created for one environment to be compiled in another environment in which there are fewer fast-access storage locations. Since fast-access storage is always limited, it is best to choose carefully those variables that you want to be optimized for fast access.

Pointers vs. Array Indexing

In some cases you can substitute pointer arithmetic for array indexing. Doing so might produce smaller and faster code. For example, the following two code fragments do the same thing:

```
Array Indexing                Pointer Arithmetic

                              p = array;
for(;;) {                     for(;;) {
  a = array[t++];               a = *(p++);
  .                              .
  .                              .
  .                              .
}                             }
```

The advantage of the pointer method is that once **p** has been loaded with the address of **array**, only an increment must be performed each time the loop repeats. However, the array index version must always compute the array index based on the value of **t**—a more complex task.

Be careful. You should use array indexes when the index is derived through a complex formula and pointer arithmetic would obscure the meaning of the program. It is usually better to degrade performance slightly than to sacrifice clarity. Also, the disparity between array indexing and pointer arithmetic may not be significant for highly optimizing compilers or on all processor types or in all environments.

Use of Functions

Remember at all times that the use of stand-alone functions with local variables helps form the basis of structured programming. Functions are the building blocks of C programs and are one of C's strongest assets. Do not let anything that is discussed in this section be construed otherwise. Having been warned, there are a few things about C functions and their ramifications on the size and speed of your code that are worthy of consideration when optimizing your programs.

When a C compiler compiles a function, it uses the stack to hold the parameters (if any) to the function and any local variables used by the function. When a function is called, the return address of the calling routine is placed on the stack as well. (This enables the subroutine to return to the location from which it was called.) When a function returns, this address and all local variables and parameters have to be removed from the stack. The process of pushing this information is generally referred to as the *calling sequence*, and the popping process is called the *returning sequence*. These sequences take time—sometimes quite a bit of time.

To understand how a function call can slow down your program, look at these two code fragments:

```
Version 1                          Version 2
for(x=1; x < 100; ++x) {           for(x=1; x < 100; ++x) {
  t = compute(x);                    t = fabs(sin(x)/100/3.1416);
}                                  }


double compute(int q)
{
  return fabs(sin(q)/100/3.1416);
}
```

Although each loop performs the same operation, Version 2 is faster because the overhead of the calling and returning sequence has been eliminated through the use of in-line code. (That is, the code for **compute( )** is simply replicated inside the loop, rather than called.)

To fully understand the overhead associated with a function call, we will look at the assembly code instructions required to call and return from a function. As you may know, many C compilers provide an option that causes the compiler to create an assembly code file rather than an object code file. Using this option allows us to examine the code produced by the compiler. For the example that follows, we will use the assembly code file created by Visual C++ when the **-Fa** option is specified. We can examine this file to see precisely what code is generated for the calling and returning sequence. Given this program,

```
int max(int a, int b);

int main(void)
{
    int x;

    x = max(10, 20);

    return 0;
}

int max(int a, int b)
{
  return a>b ? a : b;
}
```

the following assembly code file is produced. The calling and returning sequences are indicated by comments beginning with asterisks added by the author. As you can see, the calling and returning sequences amount to a sizable part of the program code.

```
        TITLE   test.c
        .386P
include listing.inc
if @Version gt 510
.model FLAT
else
_TEXT   SEGMENT PARA USE32 PUBLIC 'CODE'
_TEXT   ENDS
_DATA   SEGMENT DWORD USE32 PUBLIC 'DATA'
_DATA   ENDS
CONST   SEGMENT DWORD USE32 PUBLIC 'CONST'
CONST   ENDS
_BSS    SEGMENT DWORD USE32 PUBLIC 'BSS'
_BSS    ENDS
_TLS    SEGMENT DWORD USE32 PUBLIC 'TLS'
_TLS    ENDS
FLAT    GROUP _DATA, CONST, _BSS
        ASSUME  CS: FLAT, DS: FLAT, SS: FLAT
endif
PUBLIC  _max
PUBLIC  _main
_TEXT   SEGMENT
_x$ = -4
_main   PROC NEAR
; File ex2.c
; Line 4
        push    ebp
        mov     ebp, esp
        push    ecx
; Line 7
; *******************************************************
; This is the start of the calling sequence.
; *******************************************************
        push    20                                      ; 00000014H
        push    10                                      ; 0000000aH
        call    _max
; *******************************************************
;
; *******************************************************
; The next line is part of the returning sequence.
; *******************************************************
        add     esp, 8
```

```
        mov      DWORD PTR _x$[ebp], eax
; Line 9
        xor      eax, eax
; Line 10
        mov      esp, ebp
        pop      ebp
        ret      0
_main   ENDP
_a$ = 8
_b$ = 12
_max    PROC NEAR
; Line 13
; ******************************************************
; More of the calling sequence.
; ******************************************************
        push     ebp
        mov      ebp, esp
        push     ecx
; ******************************************************
; Line 14
        mov      eax, DWORD PTR _a$[ebp]
        cmp      eax, DWORD PTR _b$[ebp]
        jle      SHORT $L48
        mov      ecx, DWORD PTR _a$[ebp]
        mov      DWORD PTR -4+[ebp], ecx
        jmp      SHORT $L49
$L48:
        mov      edx, DWORD PTR _b$[ebp]
        mov      DWORD PTR -4+[ebp], edx
$L49:
; ******************************************************
; The returning sequence.
; ******************************************************
        mov      eax, DWORD PTR -4+[ebp]
; Line 15
        mov      esp, ebp
        pop      ebp
        ret      0
_max    ENDP
_TEXT   ENDS
END
```

The actual code produced depends on how the compiler is implemented and what processor is being used, but it will generally be similar to this.

The preceding discussion is not to suggest that you should write programs with only a few very large functions so that they run quickly. Doing so would be bad practice. First, in the vast majority of cases the slight time differential gained by avoiding function calls is not meaningful and the loss of structure is acute. But there is another problem. Replacing functions that are used by several routines with in-line code causes your program to become larger because the same code is duplicated several times. Keep in mind that subroutines were invented in part as a way to make efficient use of memory. In fact, this is why, as a rule of thumb, making a program faster means making it bigger, while making it smaller means making it slower.

If you are going to use in-line code as a means of improving the run-time performance of a program, and if you are using a C99-compatible compiler, then you should use the **inline** keyword to create in-line functions, rather than actually copying the source code by hand. If you are not using a C99-compatible compiler, then you should use function-like macros to achieve a similar result, where possible. Of course, function-like macros do not provide the flexibility of **inline** functions.

Porting Programs

It is common for a program written on one machine to be ported to another computer with a different processor, operating system, or both. This process is called *porting*, and it can be very easy or extremely hard, depending upon how the program was originally written. A program that can be easily ported is called *portable*. When a program is not portable, this is usually because it contains numerous *machine dependencies*—that is, it has code fragments that work only with one specific operating system or processor. C allows you to create portable code, but achieving this goal requires care and attention to detail. This section examines a few specific problem areas and offers some solutions.

Using #define

Perhaps the single most effective way to make programs portable is to make every system- or processor-dependent "magic number" a **#define** macro. These magic numbers include things like buffer sizes for disk accesses, special screen and keyboard commands, memory allocation information—anything that has the possibility of changing when the program is ported. These **#define**s not only make all magic numbers obvious to the person doing the porting, but also simplify the job because their values have to be changed only once instead of throughout the program.

For example, here is an **fread( )** statement that is inherently nonportable:

```
fread(buf, 128, 1, fp);
```

The problem is that the buffer size, 128, is hard-coded into **fread( )**. This might work for one operating system but be less than optimal for another. Here is a better way to code this function:

```
#define BUF_SIZE 128

fread(buf, BUF_SIZE, 1, fp);
```

In this case, when moving to a different system, only the **#define** has to change and all references to **BUF_SIZE** are automatically corrected. This not only makes it easier to change, but also avoids many editing errors. Remember that there will probably be many references to **BUF_SIZE** in a real program, so the gain in portability is often great.

Operating-System Dependencies

Virtually all commercial programs contain code specific to the operating system that they are designed to run under. For example, a program written for Windows 2000 can use multithreaded multitasking, but a program written for 16-bit Windows 3.1 can't. The point is that some operating-system dependencies are necessary for truly good, fast, and commercially viable programs. However, operating-system dependencies also make your programs harder to port.

Although there is no hard-and-fast rule that you can follow to minimize your operating-system dependencies, let me offer one piece of advice: Separate the parts of your program that relate directly to your application from those parts that interface with the operating system. In this way, if you port your program to a new environment, only the interfacing modules will need to be changed.

Differences in Data Sizes

If you want to write portable code, you must never make assumptions about the size of a data type. For example, consider the difference between 16- and 32-bit environments. The size of a word for a 16-bit processor is 16 bits; for a 32-bit processor it is 32 bits. Because the size of a word tends to be the size of the **int** data type, code that assumes that **int**s are 16 bits, for example, will not work when ported to a 32-bit environment. To avoid size dependencies, use **sizeof** whenever your program needs to know how many bytes long something is. For example, this statement writes an **int** to a disk file and works in any environment:

```
fwrite(&i, sizeof(int), 1, stream);
```

Debugging

To paraphrase Thomas Edison, programming is 10 percent inspiration and 90 percent debugging. All really good programmers are good debuggers. To help avoid bugs, it is useful to review some the common ways in which bugs can occur.

Order-of-Evaluation Errors

The increment and decrement operators are used in most C programs, and the order in which the operations take place is affected by whether these operators precede or follow the variable. Consider the following:

```
y = 10;                     y = 10;
x = y++;                    x = ++y;
```

These two sequences are not the same. The one on the left assigns the value of **10** to **x** and then increments **y**. The one on the right increments **y** to **11** and then assigns the value **11** to **x**. Therefore, in the first case **x** contains **10**; in the second, **x** contains **11**. In the general case, a prefix increment (or decrement) operation occurs before the value of the operand is obtained for use in the larger expression. A postfix increment (or decrement) occurs after the value of the operand is obtained for use in the larger expression. If you forget these rules, problems will result.

The way an order-of-evaluation error usually occurs is through changes to an existing statement sequence. For example, when optimizing a piece of code, you might change this sequence

```
/* original code */
x = a + b;
a = a + 1;
```

into the following:

```
/* "improved" code -- wrong! */
x = ++a + b;
```

The trouble is that the two code fragments do not produce the same results. The reason is that the second way increments **a** before it is added to **b**. This was not the case in the original code!

Errors like this can be very hard to find. There may be clues such as loops that don't run right or routines that are off by one. If you have any doubt about a statement, recode it in a way that you are sure about.

Pointer Problems

A very common error in C programs is the misuse of pointers. Pointer problems fall into two general categories: misunderstanding indirection and the pointer operators, and accidentally using invalid or uninitialized pointers. The solution to the first problem is easy: Simply be clear on what the * and & operators mean! The second type of pointer problems is a bit trickier.

Here is a program that illustrates both types of pointer errors:

```c
/* This program has an error. */
#include <stdlib.h>
#include <stdio.h>

int main(void)
{
  char *p;

  *p = (char *) malloc(100); /* this line is wrong */
  gets(p);
  printf(p);

  return 0;
}
```

This program will most likely crash. The reason is that the address returned by **malloc( )** was not assigned to **p** but rather to the memory location pointed to by **p**, which in this case is completely unknown. This type of error represents a fundamental misunderstanding of the * pointer operator. It is usually created by novice C programmers—and sometimes by experienced pros who just make a silly mistake! To correct this program, substitute

```c
p = (char *) malloc(100); /* this is correct */
```

for the wrong line.

The program also contains a second and more insidious error. There is no run-time check on the address returned by **malloc( )**. Remember, if memory is exhausted, **malloc( )** returns **NULL**, and the pointer should not be used. Using a **NULL** pointer is invalid and nearly always leads to a program crash. Here is a corrected version of the program, which includes a check for pointer validity:

```c
/* This program is now correct. */
```

```
#include <stdio.h>
#include <stdlib.h>

int main(void)
{
  char *p;

  p = (char *) malloc(100); /* this is correct */

  if(!p) {
    printf("Out of memory.\n");
    exit(1);
  }

  gets(p);
  printf(p);

  return 0;
}
```

Another common error is forgetting to initialize a pointer before using it. Consider the following code fragment:

```
int *x;
*x = 100;
```

This will cause trouble because x has not been initialized to point to anything. Thus, you don't know where x is pointing. Assigning a value to that unknown location may destroy something of value, such as other code or data.

The troublesome thing about wild pointers is that they are so hard to track down. If you are making assignments through a pointer that does not contain a valid address, your program may appear to function correctly some of the time and crash at other times. The smaller your program, the more likely it will run correctly, even with a stray pointer. This is because very little memory is in use, and the odds are that the offending pointer is pointing to memory that is not being used. As your program grows, failures will become more common, but you will be thinking about current additions or changes to your program, not about pointer errors. Hence, you will tend to look in the wrong spot for the bug.

The way to recognize a pointer problem is that errors are often erratic. Your program will work correctly one time, wrong another. Sometimes other variables will contain garbage for no apparent reason. If these problems begin to occur, check your pointers. As a matter of procedure, you should always check all pointers when bugs begin to occur.

As a consolation, remember that although pointers can be troublesome, they are also one of the most powerful aspects of the C language and are worth whatever trouble they may cause you. Make the effort early on to learn to use them correctly.

Interpreting Syntax Errors

Once in a while you will see a syntax error that does not make sense. Either the error message is cryptic, or the error being reported doesn't seem like an error at all. However, in most cases the compiler is right about detecting an error; it is just that the error message is less than perfect! Finding the cause of unusual syntax errors usually requires some backtracking on your part. If you encounter an error message that doesn't seem to make sense, try looking for a syntax error one or two lines earlier in your program.

One particularly unsettling error occurs when you try to compile the following code:

```
char *myfunc(void);

int main(void)
{
  /* ... */
}

int myfunc(void) /* error reported here */
{
  /* ... */
}
```

Your compiler will issue an error message along the lines of that shown here,

```
Type mismatch in redeclaration of myfunc(void)
```

in reference to the line indicated in the listing. How can this be? There are not two **myfunc( )**s. The answer is that the prototype at the top of the program shows **myfunc( )** having a character pointer return type. This caused a symbol table entry to be made with that information. When the compiler encountered **myfunc( )** later in the program, the return type was specified as **int**. Therefore, you were "redeclaring" or "redefining" the function.

Another syntax error that is difficult to understand is generated with the following code:

```
/* This program has a syntax error in it. */
#include <stdio.h>
```

```
void func1(void);

int main(void)
{
  func1();

  return 0;
}

void func1(void);
{
  printf("This is in func1.\n");
}
```

The error here is the semicolon after the definition of **func1( )**. The compiler will see this as a statement outside of any function, which is an error. However, the way that various compilers report this error differs. Some compilers issue an error message like **bad declaration syntax** while pointing at the first open brace after **func1( )**. Because you are used to seeing semicolons after statements, it can be very hard to see the source of this error.

One-Off Errors

As you know, in C all array indexes start at 0. However, even experienced pros have been known to forget this well-known fact while in the heat of programming! Consider the following program, which is supposed to initialize an array of 100 integers:

```
/* This program will not work. */

int main(void)
{
  int x, num[100];

  for(x=1; x <= 100; ++x) num[x] = x;

  return 0;
}
```

The **for** loop in this program is wrong in two ways. First, it does not initialize **num[0]**, the first element of array **num**. Second, it goes one past the end of the array because **num[99]** is the last element and the loop runs to 100. The correct way to write this program is

```
/* This is right. */

int main(void)
{
  int x, num[100];

  for(x=0; x < 100; ++x) num[x] = x;

  return 0;
}
```

Remember, an array of 100 has elements 0 through 99.

Boundary Errors

Both the C run-time environment and many standard library functions have very little or no run-time bounds checking. For example, you can easily overrun arrays. Consider the following program, which is supposed to read a string from the keyboard and display it on the screen:

```
#include <stdio.h>

int main(void)
{
  int var1;
  char s[10];
  int var2;

  var1 = 10;  var2 = 10;
  gets(s);
  printf("%s %d %d", s, var1, var2);

  return 0;
}
```

Here, there are no direct coding errors. Indirectly, however, calling **gets( )** with **s** may cause a bug. In the program, **s** is declared to be 10 characters long, but what if the user enters more than 10 characters? This causes **s** to be overrun, and the value of **var1**, **var2**, or both will be overwritten. Thus, **var1** and/or **var2** will not contain the correct value. This is because all C compilers use the stack to store local variables. The variables **var1**, **var2**, and **s** might be located in memory as shown in Figure 28-1. (Your C compiler may exchange the order of **var1**, **var2**, and **s**.)

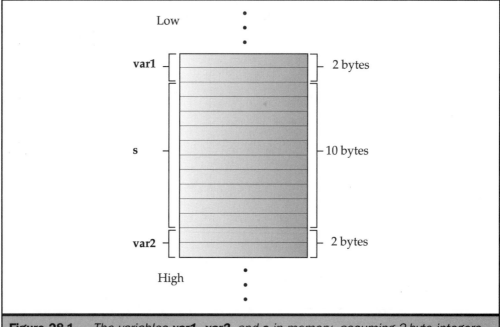

Figure 28-1.   *The variables **var1**, **var2**, and **s** in memory, assuming 2-byte integers*

Assuming the order shown in Figure 28-1, when **s** is overrun, the additional information is placed into the area that is supposed to be **var2**, destroying any previous contents. Therefore, instead of printing the number **10** for both integer variables, the variable destroyed by the overrun of **s** displays something else. This makes you look for the problem in the wrong place.

In the case of the preceding program, the potential boundary error can be eliminated by using the **fgets( )** function rather than **gets( )**. The **fgets( )** function lets you specify the maximum number of characters to read. The only trouble is that **fgets( )** also reads and stores the newline character, so you will need to strip that off in most applications.

Function Prototype Omissions

In today's programming environment, failure to use full function prototyping is an inexcusable lapse of judgment. To understand why, consider the following program, which multiplies two floating-point numbers:

```
/* This program is wrong. */
#include <stdio.h>
```

```
int main(void)
{
  float x, y;

  scanf("%f%f", &x, &y);
  printf("%f", mul(x, y));

  return 0;
}

double mul(float a, float b)
{
  return a*b;
}
```

Here, since no prototype for **mul( )** is used, **main( )** expects an integer value to be returned from **mul( )**. But in reality, **mul( )** returns a floating-point number. Assuming 4-byte integers and 8-byte **double**s, this means that only 4 bytes out of the 8 needed for a **double** are actually used by the **printf( )** statement within **main( )**. This causes the wrong answer to be displayed.

The way to correct this program is to prototype **mul( )**. The corrected version follows.

```
/* This program is correct. */
#include <stdio.h>

double mul(float a, float b);

int main(void)
{
  float x, y;

  scanf("%f%f", &x, &y);
  printf("%f", mul(x, y));

  return 0;
}

double mul(float a, float b)
{
  return a*b;
}
```

Here, the prototype tells **main( )** to expect **mul( )** to return a double value.

Argument Errors

You must be sure to match whatever type of argument a function expects with the type you give it. While function prototypes catch many argument/parameter type mismatches, they can't catch all. Furthermore, when a function takes a variable number of arguments, it is not possible for the compiler to catch argument/parameter type mismatches. For example, consider **scanf( )**, which takes a variable number of arguments. Remember that **scanf( )** expects to receive the *addresses* of its arguments, not their values. However, there is nothing that enforces this. For example,

```
int x;
scanf("%d", x);
```

is wrong because the value (not the address) of **x** is being passed. However, this call to **scanf( )** will be compiled without error, and executing this statement will cause a run-time error. The corrected call to **scanf( )** is shown here:

```
scanf("%d", &x);
```

Stack Overruns

All C compilers use the stack to store local variables, return addresses, and parameters passed to functions. However, the stack is not infinite and it can be exhausted. This results in a stack overrun. When this happens, the program either dies completely or continues executing in a bizarre fashion. The worst thing about stack overruns is that they generally occur without any warning and affect the program so profoundly that determining what went wrong is sometimes difficult. The only advice that can be offered is that some stack overruns are caused by runaway recursive functions. If your program uses recursion and you experience unexplainable failures, check the terminating conditions in your recursive functions.

One other point: With some compilers you can increase the amount of memory set aside for the stack. If your program is otherwise correct, but runs out of stack space (possibly due to deeply nested, recursive functions), then you will need to increase the stack size.

Using a Debugger

Many compilers provide a debugger, which is a program that helps you debug your code. In general, debuggers work by allowing you to execute your code step by step, set breakpoints, and inspect the contents of variables. Modern debuggers, such as that provided by Visual C++, are truly wonderful tools that can help find problems in your code. A good debugger is worth the time and effort it takes to learn to use it effectively. However, a good programmer *never* substitutes a debugger for solid design and craftsmanship.

Debugging Theory in General

Everyone has a different approach to programming and debugging. However, certain techniques have, over time, proven to be better than others. In the case of debugging, incremental testing is considered to be the most cost- and time-effective method, even though it can appear to slow the development process at first. *Incremental testing* is the process of always having a working program. That is, very early in the development process, an operational unit is established. An *operational unit* is simply a piece of working code. As new code is added to this unit, it is tested and debugged. In this way, the programmer can easily find errors because the errors probably occur in the newly added code or in the way that it interacts with the operational unit.

Debugging time is proportional to the total number of lines of code in which a bug could reside. With incremental testing, you can often restrict the number of lines of code that may contain a bug to only those that are newly added—that is, those not part of the operational unit. This situation is shown in Figure 28-2. As a programmer, you want to deal with the smallest possible area while debugging. Through incremental testing, you can subtract the area already tested from the total area, thereby reducing the region in which a bug is most likely to occur.

In large projects, there are often several modules that have little interaction. In these cases, you can establish several operational units to allow concurrent development.

Incremental testing is simply the process of always having working code. As soon as it is possible to run a piece of your program, you should do so, testing that section completely. As you add to the program, continue to test the new sections as well as the way they connect to the known operational code. In this way, you concentrate most bugs in a small area of code. Of course, you must always be alert to the possibility that a bug may have been overlooked in the operational unit, but you have reduced the likelihood of this being the case.

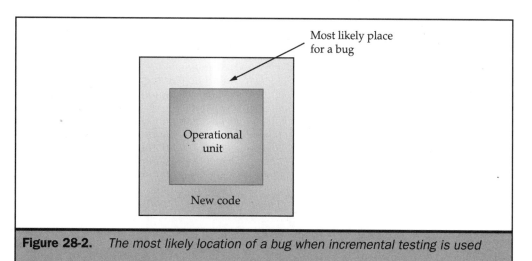

Figure 28-2. *The most likely location of a bug when incremental testing is used*

The Complete Reference

Part VI

A C Interpreter

Part Six concludes this book by developing an interpreter for C. This accomplishes two important things. First, it illustrates several aspects of C programming that are common to most larger projects. Second, it gives insight into the nature and design of the C language.

Chapter 29

A C Interpreter

L anguage interpreters are fun! And what could be more fun for a C programmer than a C interpreter?

To end this book I wanted a topic that would be of interest to virtually all C programmers and, at the same time, illustrate several features of the C language. I also wanted the topic to be fresh, exciting, and useful. After rejecting many ideas, I finally decided upon the creation of the Little C interpreter. Here's why.

As valuable and important as compilers are, the creation of a compiler can be a difficult and lengthy process. In fact, just the creation of a compiler's run-time library is a large job in itself. By contrast, the creation of a language interpreter is an easier, more manageable task. Also, if it is correctly designed, the operation of an interpreter can be easier to understand than that of a comparable compiler. Beyond ease of development, language interpreters offer an interesting feature not found in compilers—an engine that actually executes the program. Remember, a *compiler* only *translates* your program's source code into a form that the computer can execute. An *interpreter* actually *executes* the program. It is this distinction that makes interpreters interesting.

If you are like most C programmers, you use C not only for its power and flexibility but also because the language itself represents an almost intangible, formal beauty that can be appreciated for its own sake. In fact, C is often referred to as "elegant" because of its consistency and purity. Much has been written about the C language from the "outside looking in," but seldom has it been explored from the "inside." Therefore, what better way to end this book than to create a C program that interprets a subset of the C language?

In the course of this chapter an interpreter is developed that can execute a subset of the C language. Not only is the interpreter functional, but it is also designed so that you can easily enhance it, extend it, and even add features not found in C. If you haven't thought about how C really works, you will be pleasantly surprised to see how straightforward it is. The C language is one of the most theoretically consistent computer languages ever developed. By the time you finish this chapter, you will not only have a C interpreter that you can use and enlarge, but you will also have gained considerable insight into the structure of the C language itself. Of course, if you're like me, you'll find the C interpreter presented here just plain fun to play with!

The source code to the C interpreter presented in this chapter is fairly long, but don't be intimidated by it. If you read through the discussion, you will have no trouble understanding it and following its execution.

The Practical Importance of Interpreters

Although the Little C interpreter is interesting in and of itself, language interpreters do have some practical importance in computing.

As you know, C programs are usually compiled. The main reason for this is that C is a language used to produce commercially salable programs. Compiled code is desirable for commercial software products because it protects the privacy of the source code, prevents the user from changing the source code, and allows the programs to make the most efficient use of the host computer, to name a few reasons. Frankly, compilers will always dominate C-based software development, as they should; however, any computer language can be compiled or interpreted. In fact, in recent years a few C interpreters have appeared on the market.

There are two traditional reasons that interpreters have been used: They can be easily made interactive, and they can support substantial debugging aids. However, in recent years, compiler developers have created Integrated Development Environments (IDEs) that provide as much interactivity and debugging capability as any interpreter. Therefore, these two traditional reasons for using an interpreter no longer apply in any real sense. However, interpreters have their uses. For example, most database query languages are interpreted. Also, many industrial robotic control languages are interpreted.

In recent years, another benefit of interpretation has emerged: cross-platform portability. The quintessential example of this is Java. Java was designed as an interpreted language because it allowed the same Java program to run on any environment that provided a Java interpreter. Such a capability is valuable when you want to run the same program on many different types of computers, such as in a networked environment like the Internet. The creation of Java and the success of the Internet have sparked new interest in interpreters in general.

There is another reason why language interpreters are interesting: They are easy to modify, alter, or enhance. This means that if you want to create, experiment with, and control your own language, it is easier to do so with an interpreter than with a compiler. Interpreters make great language prototyping environments because you can change the way the language works and see the effects very quickly.

Interpreters are (relatively) easy to create, easy to modify, easy to understand, and, perhaps most important, fun to play with. For example, you can rework the interpreter presented in this chapter to execute your program backward—that is, executing from the closing brace of **main( )** and terminating when the opening brace is encountered! Or, you can add a special feature to C that you have always wanted. The point is that while compilers are needed for commercial software development, interpreters let you really have fun with the C language. It is in this spirit that this chapter was written. I hope you will enjoy reading it as much as I enjoyed writing it!

The Little C Specifications

Despite the fact that C has only a few keywords, C is a very rich and powerful language. It would take far more than a single chapter to fully describe and implement an interpreter for the entire C language. Instead, the Little C interpreter understands a fairly narrow subset of the language. However, this particular subset includes many of C's most important aspects. What to include in the subset was decided mostly by whether it fit one (or both) of these two criteria:

■ Is the feature fundamentally inseparable from the C language?

■ Is the feature necessary to demonstrate an important aspect of the language?

For example, features such as recursive functions and global and local variables meet both criteria. The Little C interpreter supports all three loop constructs (not because of the first criterion, but because of the second criterion). However, the **switch** statement is not implemented because it is neither necessary (nice, but not necessary) nor does it demonstrate anything that the **if** statement (which is implemented) does not. (Implementation of **switch** is left to you for entertainment!)

For these reasons, I implemented the following features in the Little C interpreter:

■ Parameterized functions with local variables

■ Recursion

■ The **if** statement

■ The **do-while**, **while**, and **for** loops

■ Local and global variables of type **int** and **char**

■ Function parameters of type **int** and **char**

■ Integer and character constants

■ String constants (limited implementation)

■ The **return** statement, both with and without a value

■ A limited number of standard library functions

■ These operators: +, –, *, /, %, <, >, <=, >=, ==, !=, unary –, and unary +

■ Functions returning integers

■ /* ... */-style comments

Even though this list may seem short, it takes a relatively large amount of code to implement it. One reason for this is that a substantial "price of admission" must be paid when interpreting a structured language such as C.

Some Little C Restrictions

The source code for the Little C interpreter is quite long—longer, in fact, than I would normally put in a book. In order to simplify and shorten the source code for Little C, I have imposed a few small restrictions on the C grammar. The first is that the targets of **if**, **while**, **do**, and **for** must be blocks of code surrounded by beginning and ending curly braces. You cannot use a single statement. For example, Little C will not correctly interpret code such as this:

```
for(a=0; a < 10; a=a+1)
  for(b=0; b < 10; b=b+1)
    for(c=0; c < 10; c=c+1)
      puts("hi");

if(...)
   if(...) x = 10;
```

Instead, you must write the code like this:

```
for(a=0; a < 10; a=a+1) {
  for(b=0; b < 10; b=b+1) {
    for(c=0; c < 10; c=c+1) {
      puts("hi");
    }
  }
}

if(...) {
  if(...) {
    x = 10;;
  }
}
```

This restriction makes it easier for the interpreter to find the end of the code that forms the target of one of these program control statements. However, since the objects of the program control statements are often blocks of code anyway, this restriction does not seem too harsh. (With a little effort, you can remove this restriction, if you like.)

Another restriction is that prototypes are not supported. All functions are assumed to return an integer type (**char** return types are allowed, but elevated to **int**), and no parameter type checking is performed.

All local variables must be declared at the start of a function, immediately after the opening brace. Local variables cannot be declared within any other block. Thus, the following function is invalid:

```
int myfunc()
{
  int i; /* this is valid */
```

```
    if(1) {
       int i; /* not allowed in Little C */
       /* ... */
    }
}
```

Here, the declaration of **i** within the **if** block is invalid for Little C. The requirement that local variables be declared at the start of the function block makes it a bit easier to implement the interpreter. This is a restriction that you can remove with a little effort.

Finally, all functions must be preceded by either an **int** or **char** type specifier. Therefore, the Little C interpreter does not support the old "default-to-**int**" (or "implicit **int**") rule. Thus, this declaration is valid:

```
int main()
{
   /* ... */
}
```

But this one isn't:

```
main()
{
   /* ... */
}
```

Dropping default-to-**int** for function declarations brings Little C in line with the C99/C++ approach.

Interpreting a Structured Language

As you know, C is structured: It allows stand-alone subroutines with local variables. It also supports recursion. What you might find interesting is that, in some areas, it is easier to write a compiler for a structured language than it is to write an interpreter for it. For example, when a compiler generates code to call a function, it simply pushes the calling arguments onto the system stack and executes a machine language CALL to the function. To return, the function puts the return value in a register of the CPU, clears the stack, and executes a machine language RET. However, when an interpreter must "call" a function, it has to stop what it is doing, save its current state, find the location of the function, execute the function, save the return value, and return to the original point, restoring the old environment. (You will see an example of this in the interpreter that follows.) In essence, the interpreter must emulate the equivalent of a machine language CALL and RET. Also, while support for recursion is easy in a compiled language, it requires some effort in an interpreted one.

Several years ago, in my book *The Art of C* (Berkeley, CA: Osborne/McGraw-Hill, 1991), I introduced the subject of language interpreters by developing a small BASIC interpreter. In that book, I stated that it is easier to interpret a language such as traditional BASIC than C because BASIC was designed to be interpreted. What makes traditional BASIC easy to interpret is that it is not structured. All variables are global, and there are no stand-alone subroutines. I still stand by this statement; however, once you have created the support for functions, local variables, and recursion, the C language is actually easier to interpret than BASIC. This is because a language such as BASIC is full of exceptions at the theoretical level. For example, in BASIC the equal sign is an assignment operator in an assignment statement, but an equality operator in a relational statement. C has few of these inconsistencies.

Note *Readers interested in interpreters will find my implementation of a small BASIC interpreter useful. The current version of the small BASIC interpreter is found in* The C/C++ Annotated Archives *(Berkeley, CA: Osborne/McGraw-Hill, 1999).*

An Informal Theory of C

Before we can begin to develop the C interpreter, it is necessary to understand how the C language is structured. If you have ever seen a formal specification for the C language (such as that found in the ANSI/ISO C standard), you know that it is quite long and filled with rather cryptic statements. Don't worry—we won't need to deal this formally with the C language to design our interpreter, because most of the C language is so straightforward. Although the formal specification of a language is necessary for the creation of a commercial compiler, it is not needed for the creation of the Little C interpreter. (Frankly, there isn't space in this chapter to explain how to understand the C formal syntax definition; it could fill a book!)

This chapter is designed to be understood by the widest variety of readers. It is not intended to be a formal introduction to the theory of structured languages in general or C in particular. As such, it intentionally simplifies a few concepts. As you will see, the creation of an interpreter for a subset of C does not require formal training in language theory.

Although you do not need to be a language expert to implement and understand the Little C interpreter, you will still need a basic understanding of how the C language is defined. For our purposes, the discussion that follows is sufficient. Those of you who want a more formal discussion should refer to the ANSI/ISO standard for C.

To begin, all C programs consist of a collection of one or more functions, plus global variables (if any exist). A *function* is composed of a function name, its parameter list, and the block of code associated with the function. A *block* begins with a { , is followed by one or more statements, and ends with a }. In C, a statement either begins with a C keyword, such as **if**, or it is an expression. (We will see what constitutes an expression in the next section.) Summarizing, we can write the following *transformations* (sometimes called *production rules*):

program ⟶ collection of functions (plus global variables)

function ⟶ function-specifier parameter-list code-block

code-block ⟶ { statement sequence }

statement ⟶ keyword, expression, or code-block

All C programs begin with a call to **main( )** and end when either the last } or a **return** has been encountered in **main( )**—assuming that **exit( )** or **abort( )** has not been called elsewhere. Any other functions contained in the program must be either directly or indirectly called by **main( )**; thus, to execute a C program, simply begin at the start of the **main( )** function and stop when **main( )** ends. This is precisely what Little C does.

C Expressions

C expands the role of expressions relative to many other computer languages. In general terms, a statement is either a C keyword statement, such as **while** or **switch**, or it is an expression. For the sake of discussion, let's categorize all statements that begin with C keywords as *keyword statements.* Any statement in C that is not a keyword statement is, by definition, an *expression statement.* Therefore, in C the following statements are all expressions:

```
count = 100;                       /* line 1 */
sample = i / 22 * (c-10);          /* line 2 */
printf("This is an expression.");  /* line 3 */
```

Let's look more closely at each of these expression statements. In C, the equal sign is an *assignment operator.* C does not treat the assignment operation the way a language such as BASIC would, for example. In BASIC, the value produced by the right side of the equal sign is assigned to the variable on the left. But, and this is important, in BASIC, the entire statement does not have a value. In C, the equal sign is an assignment operator, and the value produced by the assignment operation is equal to that produced by the right side of the expression. Therefore, an assignment statement is actually an *assignment expression* in C; because it is an expression, it has a value. This is why it is legal to write expressions such as the following:

```
a = b = c = 100;
printf("%d", a=4+5);
```

The reason these work in C is that an assignment is an operation that produces a value.

Line 2 of the sample expressions shows a more complex assignment. In line 3, **printf( )** is called to output a string. In C, all non-**void** functions return values, whether explicitly specified or not. Thus, a non-**void** function call is an expression that returns a value—whether the value is actually assigned to something or not. Calling a **void** function also constitutes an expression. It is just that the outcome of the expression is **void**.

Evaluating Expressions

Before we can develop code that will correctly evaluate C expressions, you need to understand in more formal terms how expressions are defined. In virtually all computer languages, expressions are defined recursively using a set of production rules. The Little C interpreter supports the following operations: +, −, *, /, %, =, the relational operators (<, ==, >, and so forth), and parentheses. Therefore, we can use these production rules to define Little C expressions:

expression ⟶ [assignment] [rvalue]

assignment ⟶ lvalue = rvalue

lvalue ⟶ variable

rvalue ⟶ part [rel-op part]

part ⟶ term [+term] [−term]

term ⟶ factor [*factor] [/factor] [%factor]

factor ⟶ [+ or −] atom

atom ⟶ variable, constant, function, or (expression)

Here, *rel-op* refers to any of C's relational operators. The terms *lvalue* and *rvalue* refer to objects that can occur on the left side and right side of an assignment statement, respectively. One thing that you should be aware of is that the precedence of the operators is built into the production rules. The higher the precedence, the farther down the list the operator will be.

To see how these rules work, let's evaluate this C expression:

```
count = 10 - 5 * 3;
```

First, we apply rule 1, which dissects the expression into these three parts:

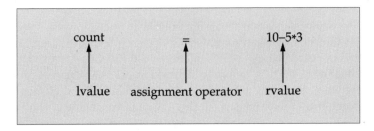

Since there are no relational operators in the "rvalue" part of the subexpression, the "term" production rule is invoked:

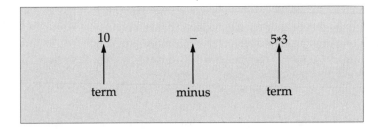

Of course, the second term is composed of the following two factors: 5 and 3. These two factors are constants and represent the lowest level of the production rules.

Next, we must begin moving back up the rules to compute the value of the expression. First, we multiply 5*3, which yields 15. Next, we subtract that value from 10, yielding –5. Finally, this value is assigned to **count** and is also the value of the entire expression.

The first thing we need to do to create the Little C interpreter is to construct the computerized equivalent of the expression evaluation we just performed in our minds.

The Expression Parser

The piece of code that reads and analyzes expressions is called an *expression parser*. Without a doubt, the expression parser is the single most important subsystem needed by the Little C interpreter. Because C defines expressions more broadly than do many other languages, a substantial amount of the code that constitutes a C program is actually executed by the expression parser.

There are several different ways to design an expression parser for C. Many commercial compilers use a *table-driven parser*, which is usually created by a parser-generator program. Although table-driven parsers are generally faster than other methods, they are very hard to create by hand. For the Little C interpreter developed here, we will use a *recursive-descent parser*, which implements in logic the production rules discussed in the previous section.

A recursive-descent parser is essentially a collection of mutually recursive functions that process an expression. If the parser is used in a compiler, it generates the proper object code that corresponds to the source code. However, in an interpreter, the object of the parser is to evaluate a given expression. In this section, the Little C parser is developed.

     Expression parsing is introduced in Chapter 24. The parser used in this chapter expands upon that simple foundation.

Reducing the Source Code to Its Components

Fundamental to all interpreters (and compilers, for that matter) is a special function that reads the source code and returns the next logical symbol from it. For historical reasons, these logical symbols are generally referred to as *tokens*. Computer languages in general, and C in particular, define programs in terms of tokens. You can think of a token as an indivisible program unit. For example, the equality operator == is a token. The two equal signs cannot be separated without changing the meaning. In the same vein, **if** is a token. Neither "i" nor "f" by itself has any meaning to C.

In C, tokens are defined as belonging to one of these groups:

keywords	identifiers	constants
strings	operators	punctuation

The *keywords* are those tokens that make up the C language, such as **while**. *Identifiers* are the names of variables, functions, and user-types (not implemented by Little C). Constants and strings are self-explanatory, as are operators. Punctuation includes several items, such as semicolons, commas, braces, and parentheses. (Some of these are also operators, depending upon their use.) Given the statement

```
for(x=0; x<10; x=x+1) printf("hello %d", x);
```

the following tokens are produced, reading left to right:

Token	Category
for	keyword
(	punctuation
x	identifier
=	operator

Token	Category
0	constant
;	punctuation
x	identifier
<	operator
10	constant
;	punctuation
x	identifier
=	operator
x	identifier
+	operator
1	constant
)	punctuation
printf	identifier
(	punctuation
"hello %d"	string
,	punctuation
x	identifier
)	punctuation
;	punctuation

However, in order to make the interpretation of C easier, Little C categorizes tokens as shown here:

Token Type	Includes
delimiter	punctuation and operators
keyword	keywords
string	quoted strings
identifier	variable and function names
number	numeric constant
block	{ or }

The function that returns tokens from the source code for the Little C interpreter is called **get_token( )**, and it is shown here:

```
/* Get a token. */
int get_token(void)
{

  register char *temp;

  token_type = 0; tok = 0;

  temp = token;
  *temp = '\0';

  /* skip over white space */
  while(iswhite(*prog) && *prog) ++prog;

  if(*prog == '\r') {
    ++prog;
    ++prog;
    /* skip over white space */
    while(iswhite(*prog) && *prog) ++prog;
  }

  if(*prog == '\0') { /* end of file */
    *token = '\0';
    tok = FINISHED;
    return (token_type = DELIMITER);
  }

  if(strchr("{}", *prog)) { /* block delimiters */
    *temp = *prog;
    temp++;
    *temp = '\0';
    prog++;
    return (token_type = BLOCK);
  }

  /* look for comments */
  if(*prog == '/')
    if(*(prog+1) == '*') { /* is a comment */
      prog += 2;
      do { /* find end of comment */
```

```c
      while(*prog != '*') prog++;
      prog++;
    } while (*prog != '/');
    prog++;
  }


if(strchr("!<>=", *prog)) { /* is or might be
                               a relational operator */
  switch(*prog) {
    case '=': if(*(prog+1) == '=') {
        prog++; prog++;
        *temp = EQ;
        temp++; *temp = EQ; temp++;
        *temp = '\0';
      }
      break;
    case '!': if(*(prog+1) == '=') {
        prog++; prog++;
        *temp = NE;
        temp++; *temp = NE; temp++;
        *temp = '\0';
      }
      break;
    case '<': if(*(prog+1) == '=') {
        prog++; prog++;
        *temp = LE; temp++; *temp = LE;
      }
      else {
        prog++;
        *temp = LT;
      }
      temp++;
      *temp = '\0';
      break;
    case '>': if(*(prog+1) == '=') {
        prog++; prog++;
        *temp = GE; temp++; *temp = GE;
      }
      else {
        prog++;
        *temp = GT;
      }
      temp++;
```

```
      *temp = '\0';
      break;
    }
    if(*token) return (token_type = DELIMITER);
  }

  if(strchr("+-*^/%=;(),'", *prog)){ /* delimiter */
    *temp = *prog;
    prog++; /* advance to next position */
    temp++;
    *temp = '\0';
    return (token_type = DELIMITER);
  }

  if(*prog=='"') { /* quoted string */
    prog++;
    while(*prog != '"'&& *prog != '\r') *temp++ = *prog++;
    if(*prog == '\r') sntx_err(SYNTAX);
    prog++; *temp = '\0';
    return (token_type = STRING);
  }

  if(isdigit(*prog)) { /* number */
    while(!isdelim(*prog)) *temp++ = *prog++;
    *temp = '\0';
    return (token_type = NUMBER);
  }

  if(isalpha(*prog)) { /* var or command */
    while(!isdelim(*prog)) *temp++ = *prog++;
    token_type = TEMP;
  }

  *temp = '\0';

  /* see if a string is a command or a variable */
  if(token_type==TEMP) {
    tok = look_up(token); /* convert to internal rep */
    if(tok) token_type = KEYWORD; /* is a keyword */
    else token_type = IDENTIFIER;
  }
  return token_type;
}
```

The **get_token( )** function uses the following global data and enumeration types:

```
extern char *prog;  /* current location in source code */
extern char *p_buf;  /* points to start of program buffer */

extern char token[80]; /* string representation of token */
extern char token_type; /* contains type of token */
extern char tok; /* internal representation of token */

enum tok_types {DELIMITER, IDENTIFIER, NUMBER, KEYWORD,
                TEMP, STRING, BLOCK};

enum double_ops {LT=1, LE, GT, GE, EQ, NE};

/* These are the constants used to call sntx_err() when
   a syntax error occurs. Add more if you like.
   NOTE: SYNTAX is a generic error message used when
   nothing else seems appropriate.
*/
enum error_msg
     {SYNTAX, UNBAL_PARENS, NO_EXP, EQUALS_EXPECTED,
      NOT_VAR, PARAM_ERR, SEMI_EXPECTED,
      UNBAL_BRACES, FUNC_UNDEF, TYPE_EXPECTED,
      NEST_FUNC, RET_NOCALL, PAREN_EXPECTED,
      WHILE_EXPECTED, QUOTE_EXPECTED, NOT_TEMP,
      TOO_MANY_LVARS, DIV_BY_ZERO};
```

The current location in the source code is pointed to by **prog**. The **p_buf** pointer is unchanged by the interpreter and always points to the start of the program being interpreted. The **get_token( )** function begins by skipping over all white space, including carriage returns and linefeeds. Since no C token (except for a quoted string or character constant) contains a space, spaces must be bypassed. The **get_token( )** function also skips over comments. (Remember, only /* */ comments are accepted.) Next, the string representation of each token is placed into **token**; its type (as defined by the **tok_types** enumeration) is put into **token_type**; and, if the token is a keyword, its internal representation is assigned to **tok** via the **look_up( )** function (shown in the full parser listing that follows). The reason for the internal representation of keywords will be discussed later. As you can see by looking at **get_token( )**, it converts C's two-character relational operators into their corresponding enumeration value. Although not technically necessary, this step makes the parser easier to implement. Finally, if the parser encounters a syntax error, it calls the function **sntx_err( )** with an enumerated value that corresponds to the type of error found. The **sntx_err( )** function

is also called by other routines in the interpreter whenever an error occurs. The
sntx_err( ) function is shown here:

```c
/* Display an error message. */
void sntx_err(int error)
{
  char *p, *temp;
  int linecount = 0;
  register int i;

  static char *e[]= {
    "syntax error",
    "unbalanced parentheses",
    "no expression present",
    "equals sign expected",
    "not a variable",
    "parameter error",
    "semicolon expected",
    "unbalanced braces",
    "function undefined",
    "type specifier expected",
    "too many nested function calls",
    "return without call",
    "parentheses expected",
    "while expected",
    "closing quote expected",
    "not a string",
    "too many local variables",
    "division by zero"
  };
  printf("\n%s", e[error]);
  p = p_buf;
  while(p != prog) {  /* find line number of error */
    p++;
    if(*p == '\r') {
      linecount++;
    }
  }
  printf(" in line %d\n", linecount);

  temp = p;
  for(i=0; i < 20 && p > p_buf && *p != '\n'; i++, p--);
```

```
   for(i=0; i < 30 && p <= temp; i++, p++) printf("%c", *p);

   longjmp(e_buf, 1); /* return to safe point */
}
```

Notice that **sntx_err( )** also displays the line number in which the error was detected (which may be one line after the error actually occurred) and displays the line in which it occurred. Further, notice that **sntx_err( )** ends with a call to **longjmp( )**. Because syntax errors are frequently encountered in deeply nested or recursive routines, the easiest way to handle an error is simply to jump to a safe place. Although it is possible to set a global error flag and interrogate the flag at various points in each routine, this adds unnecessary overhead.

The Little C Recursive-Descent Parser

The entire code for the Little C recursive-descent parser is shown here, along with some necessary support functions, global data, and data types. This code, as shown, is designed to go into its own file. For the sake of discussion, call this file PARSER.C. (Because of its size, the Little C interpreter is spread among three separate files.)

```
/* Recursive descent parser for integer expressions
   which may include variables and function calls.
*/
#include <setjmp.h>
#include <math.h>
#include <ctype.h>
#include <stdlib.h>
#include <string.h>
#include <stdio.h>

#define NUM_FUNC        100
#define NUM_GLOBAL_VARS 100
#define NUM_LOCAL_VARS  200
#define ID_LEN          31
#define FUNC_CALLS      31
#define PROG_SIZE       10000
#define FOR_NEST        31

enum tok_types {DELIMITER, IDENTIFIER, NUMBER, KEYWORD,
                TEMP, STRING, BLOCK};

enum tokens {ARG, CHAR, INT, IF, ELSE, FOR, DO, WHILE,
```

```
                 SWITCH, RETURN, EOL, FINISHED, END};

enum double_ops {LT=1, LE, GT, GE, EQ, NE};

/* These are the constants used to call sntx_err() when
   a syntax error occurs. Add more if you like.
   NOTE: SYNTAX is a generic error message used when
   nothing else seems appropriate.
*/
enum error_msg
     {SYNTAX, UNBAL_PARENS, NO_EXP, EQUALS_EXPECTED,
      NOT_VAR, PARAM_ERR, SEMI_EXPECTED,
      UNBAL_BRACES, FUNC_UNDEF, TYPE_EXPECTED,
      NEST_FUNC, RET_NOCALL, PAREN_EXPECTED,
      WHILE_EXPECTED, QUOTE_EXPECTED, NOT_TEMP,
      TOO_MANY_LVARS, DIV_BY_ZERO};

extern char *prog;  /* current location in source code */
extern char *p_buf;  /* points to start of program buffer */
extern jmp_buf e_buf; /* hold environment for longjmp() */

/* An array of these structures will hold the info
   associated with global variables.
*/
extern struct var_type {
  char var_name[32];
  int v_type;
  int value;
}  global_vars[NUM_GLOBAL_VARS];

/*  This is the function call stack. */
extern struct func_type {
  char func_name[32];
  int ret_type;
  char *loc;  /* location of function entry point in file */
} func_stack[NUM_FUNC];

/* Keyword table */
extern struct commands {
  char command[20];
  char tok;
} table[];
```

```
/* "Standard library" functions are declared here so
   they can be put into the internal function table that
   follows.
 */
int call_getche(void), call_putch(void);
int call_puts(void), print(void), getnum(void);

struct intern_func_type {
  char *f_name; /* function name */
  int (*p)();   /* pointer to the function */
} intern_func[] = {
  "getche", call_getche,
  "putch", call_putch,
  "puts", call_puts,
  "print", print,
  "getnum", getnum,
  "", 0  /* null terminate the list */
};

extern char token[80]; /* string representation of token */
extern char token_type; /* contains type of token */
extern char tok; /* internal representation of token */

extern int ret_value; /* function return value */

void eval_exp0(int *value);
void eval_exp(int *value);
void eval_exp1(int *value);
void eval_exp2(int *value);
void eval_exp3(int *value);
void eval_exp4(int *value);
void eval_exp5(int *value);
void atom(int *value);
void sntx_err(int error), putback(void);
void assign_var(char *var_name, int value);
int isdelim(char c), look_up(char *s), iswhite(char c);
int find_var(char *s), get_token(void);
int internal_func(char *s);
int is_var(char *s);
char *find_func(char *name);
void call(void);
```

```
/* Entry point into parser. */
void eval_exp(int *value)
{
  get_token();
  if(!*token) {
    sntx_err(NO_EXP);
    return;
  }
  if(*token == ';') {
    *value = 0; /* empty expression */
    return;
  }
  eval_exp0(value);
  putback(); /* return last token read to input stream */
}

/* Process an assignment expression */
void eval_exp0(int *value)
{
  char temp[ID_LEN];  /* holds name of var receiving
                         the assignment */
  register int temp_tok;

  if(token_type == IDENTIFIER) {
    if(is_var(token)) {  /* if a var, see if assignment */
      strcpy(temp, token);
      temp_tok = token_type;
      get_token();
      if(*token == '=') {  /* is an assignment */
        get_token();
        eval_exp0(value);  /* get value to assign */
        assign_var(temp, *value);  /* assign the value */
        return;
      }
      else {  /* not an assignment */
        putback();  /* restore original token */
        strcpy(token, temp);
        token_type = temp_tok;
      }
    }
  }
  eval_exp1(value);
```

```c
}

/* Process relational operators. */
void eval_exp1(int *value)
{
  int partial_value;
  register char op;
  char relops[7] = {
    LT, LE, GT, GE, EQ, NE, 0
  };

  eval_exp2(value);
  op = *token;
  if(strchr(relops, op)) {
    get_token();
    eval_exp2(&partial_value);
    switch(op) {   /* perform the relational operation */
      case LT:
        *value = *value < partial_value;
        break;
      case LE:
        *value = *value <= partial_value;
        break;
      case GT:
        *value = *value > partial_value;
        break;
      case GE:
        *value = *value >= partial_value;
        break;
      case EQ:
        *value = *value == partial_value;
        break;
      case NE:
        *value = *value != partial_value;
        break;
    }
  }
}

/*  Add or subtract two terms. */
void eval_exp2(int *value)
{
```

```
  register char  op;
  int partial_value;

  eval_exp3(value);
  while((op = *token) == '+' || op == '-') {
    get_token();
    eval_exp3(&partial_value);
    switch(op) { /* add or subtract */
      case '-':
        *value = *value - partial_value;
        break;
      case '+':
        *value = *value + partial_value;
        break;
    }
  }
}

/* Multiply or divide two factors. */
void eval_exp3(int *value)
{
  register char  op;
  int partial_value, t;

  eval_exp4(value);
  while((op = *token) == '*' || op == '/' || op == '%') {
    get_token();
    eval_exp4(&partial_value);
    switch(op) { /* mul, div, or modulus */
      case '*':
        *value = *value * partial_value;
        break;
      case '/':
        if(partial_value == 0) sntx_err(DIV_BY_ZERO);
        *value = (*value) / partial_value;
        break;
      case '%':
        t = (*value) / partial_value;
        *value = *value-(t * partial_value);
        break;
    }
  }
}
```

```
}

/* Is a unary + or -. */
void eval_exp4(int *value)
{
  register char  op;

  op = '\0';
  if(*token == '+' || *token == '-') {
    op = *token;
    get_token();
  }
  eval_exp5(value);
  if(op)
    if(op == '-') *value = -(*value);
}

/* Process parenthesized expression. */
void eval_exp5(int *value)
{
  if((*token == '(')) {
    get_token();
    eval_exp0(value);    /* get subexpression */
    if(*token != ')') sntx_err(PAREN_EXPECTED);
    get_token();
  }
  else
    atom(value);
}

/* Find value of number, variable, or function. */
void atom(int *value)
{
  int i;

  switch(token_type) {
  case IDENTIFIER:
    i = internal_func(token);
    if(i!= -1) {  /* call "standard library" function */
      *value = (*intern_func[i].p)();
    }
    else
```

```
      if(find_func(token)) { /* call user-defined function */
        call();
        *value = ret_value;
      }
      else *value = find_var(token); /* get var's value */
      get_token();
      return;
    case NUMBER: /* is numeric constant */
      *value = atoi(token);
      get_token();
      return;
    case DELIMITER: /* see if character constant */
      if(*token == '\'') {
        *value = *prog;
        prog++;
        if(*prog!='\'') sntx_err(QUOTE_EXPECTED);
        prog++;
        get_token();
        return ;
      }
      if(*token==')') return; /* process empty expression */
      else sntx_err(SYNTAX); /* syntax error */
    default:
      sntx_err(SYNTAX); /* syntax error */
  }
}

/* Display an error message. */
void sntx_err(int error)
{
  char *p, *temp;
  int linecount = 0;
  register int i;

  static char *e[]= {
    "syntax error",
    "unbalanced parentheses",
    "no expression present",
    "equals sign expected",
    "not a variable",
    "parameter error",
    "semicolon expected",
```

```
    "unbalanced braces",
    "function undefined",
    "type specifier expected",
    "too many nested function calls",
    "return without call",
    "parentheses expected",
    "while expected",
    "closing quote expected",
    "not a string",
    "too many local variables",
    "division by zero"
  };
  printf("\n%s", e[error]);
  p = p_buf;
  while(p != prog) {   /* find line number of error */
    p++;
    if(*p == '\r') {
      linecount++;
    }
  }
  printf(" in line %d\n", linecount);

  temp = p;
  for(i=0; i < 20 && p > p_buf && *p != '\n'; i++, p--);
  for(i=0; i < 30 && p <= temp; i++, p++) printf("%c", *p);

  longjmp(e_buf, 1); /* return to safe point */
}

/* Get a token. */
int get_token(void)
{

  register char *temp;

  token_type = 0; tok = 0;

  temp = token;
  *temp = '\0';

  /* skip over white space */
  while(iswhite(*prog) && *prog) ++prog;
```

```
if(*prog == '\r') {
  ++prog;
  ++prog;
  /* skip over white space */
  while(iswhite(*prog) && *prog) ++prog;
}

if(*prog == '\0') { /* end of file */
  *token = '\0';
  tok = FINISHED;
  return (token_type = DELIMITER);
}

if(strchr("{}", *prog)) { /* block delimiters */
  *temp = *prog;
  temp++;
  *temp = '\0';
  prog++;
  return (token_type = BLOCK);
}

/* look for comments */
if(*prog == '/')
  if(*(prog+1) == '*') { /* is a comment */
    prog += 2;
    do { /* find end of comment */
      while(*prog != '*') prog++;
      prog++;
    } while (*prog != '/');
    prog++;
  }

if(strchr("!<>=", *prog)) { /* is or might be
                               a relational operator */
  switch(*prog) {
    case '=': if(*(prog+1) == '=') {
        prog++; prog++;
        *temp = EQ;
        temp++; *temp = EQ; temp++;
        *temp = '\0';
      }
      break;
```

```
     case '!': if(*(prog+1) == '=') {
         prog++; prog++;
         *temp = NE;
         temp++; *temp = NE; temp++;
         *temp = '\0';
      }
      break;
     case '<': if(*(prog+1) == '=') {
         prog++; prog++;
         *temp = LE; temp++; *temp = LE;
      }
      else {
         prog++;
         *temp = LT;
      }
      temp++;
      *temp = '\0';
      break;
     case '>': if(*(prog+1) == '=') {
         prog++; prog++;
         *temp = GE; temp++; *temp = GE;
      }
      else {
        prog++;
        *temp = GT;
      }
      temp++;
      *temp = '\0';
      break;
   }
   if(*token) return(token_type = DELIMITER);
 }

 if(strchr("+-*^/%=;(),'", *prog)){ /* delimiter */
   *temp = *prog;
   prog++; /* advance to next position */
   temp++;
   *temp = '\0';
   return (token_type = DELIMITER);
 }

 if(*prog=='"') { /* quoted string */
```

```
    prog++;
    while(*prog != '"'&& *prog != '\r') *temp++ = *prog++;
    if(*prog == '\r') sntx_err(SYNTAX);
    prog++; *temp = '\0';
    return (token_type = STRING);
  }

  if(isdigit(*prog)) { /* number */
    while(!isdelim(*prog)) *temp++ = *prog++;
    *temp = '\0';
    return (token_type = NUMBER);
  }

  if(isalpha(*prog)) { /* var or command */
    while(!isdelim(*prog)) *temp++ = *prog++;
    token_type = TEMP;
  }

  *temp = '\0';

  /* see if a string is a command or a variable */
  if(token_type==TEMP) {
    tok = look_up(token); /* convert to internal rep */
    if(tok) token_type = KEYWORD; /* is a keyword */
    else token_type = IDENTIFIER;
  }
  return token_type;
}

/* Return a token to input stream. */
void putback(void)
{
  char *t;

  t = token;
  for(; *t; t++) prog--;
}

/* Look up a token's internal representation in the
   token table.
*/
int look_up(char *s)
```

```
{
  register int i;
  char *p;

  /* convert to lowercase */
  p = s;
  while(*p) { *p = tolower(*p); p++; }

  /* see if token is in table */
  for(i=0; *table[i].command; i++) {
    if(!strcmp(table[i].command, s)) return table[i].tok;
  }
  return 0; /* unknown command */
}

/* Return index of internal library function or -1 if
   not found.
*/
int internal_func(char *s)
{
  int i;

  for(i=0; intern_func[i].f_name[0]; i++) {
    if(!strcmp(intern_func[i].f_name, s))  return i;
  }
  return -1;
}

/* Return true if c is a delimiter. */
int isdelim(char c)
{
  if(strchr(" !;,+-<>'/*%^=()", c) || c == 9 ||
    c == '\r' || c == 0) return 1;
  return 0;
}

/* Return 1 if c is space or tab. */
int iswhite(char c)
{
  if(c == ' ' || c == '\t') return 1;
  else return 0;
}
```

The functions that begin with **eval_exp** and the **atom( )** function implement the production rules for Little C expressions. To verify this, you might want to execute the parser mentally, using a simple expression.

The **atom( )** function finds the value of an integer constant or variable, a function, or a character constant. There are two kinds of functions that may be present in the source code: user defined or library. If a user-defined function is encountered, its code is executed by the interpreter in order to determine its return value. (The calling of a function will be discussed in the next section.) However, if the function is a library function, first its address is looked up by the **internal_func( )** function, and then it is accessed via its interface function. The library functions and the addresses of their interface functions are held in the **intern_func** array shown here:

```
/* "Standard library" functions are declared here so
   they can be put into the internal function table that
   follows.
 */
int call_getche(void), call_putch(void);
int call_puts(void), print(void), getnum(void);

struct intern_func_type {
  char *f_name; /* function name */
  int (*p)();   /* pointer to the function */
} intern_func[] = {
  "getche", call_getche,
  "putch", call_putch,
  "puts", call_puts,
  "print", print,
  "getnum", getnum,
  "", 0  /* null terminate the list */
};
```

As you can see, Little C knows only a few library functions, but you will soon see how easy it is to add any others that you might need. (The actual interface functions are contained in a separate file, which is discussed in the section "The Little C Library Functions.")

One final point about the routines in the expression parser file: To correctly parse the C language occasionally requires what is called *one-token lookahead*. For example, given

```
alpha = count();
```

in order for Little C to know that **count** is a function and not a variable, it must read both **count** and the next token, which in this case is a parenthesis. However, if the statement had read

```
alpha = count * 10;
```

then the next token after **count** is an *****, which would need to be returned to the input stream for later use. For this reason, the expression parser file includes the **putback( )** function, which returns the last token read to the input stream.

There may be functions in the expression parser file that you don't fully understand at this time, but their operation will become clear as you learn more about Little C.

The Little C Interpreter

In this section, the heart of the Little C interpreter is developed. Before jumping right into the actual code of the interpreter, it will help if you understand how an interpreter operates. In many ways, the code of the interpreter is easier to understand than the expression parser because, conceptually, the act of interpreting a C program can be summed up by the following algorithm:

```
while(tokens_present) {
   get next token;
   take appropriate action;
}
```

This algorithm may seem unbelievably simple when compared to the expression parser, but this really is exactly what all interpreters do! One thing to keep in mind is that the "take appropriate action" step may also involve reading additional tokens from the input stream. To understand how the algorithm actually works, let's manually interpret the following C code fragment:

```
int a;

a = 10;

if(a < 100)  printf("%d", a);
```

Following the algorithm, read the first token, which is **int**. The appropriate action given this token is to read the next token in order to find out what the variable being declared is called (in this case **a**) and then to store it. The next token is the semicolon that ends the line. The appropriate action here is to ignore it. Next, go back and get another token. This token is **a**. Since this line does not begin with a keyword, it must begin a C expression. Thus, the appropriate action is to evaluate the expression using the parser. This process eats up all the tokens in that line. Finally, we read the **if** token. This signals the beginning of an **if** statement. The appropriate action is to process the **if**. The sort of process described here takes place for any C program until the last token has been read. With this basic algorithm in mind, let's begin building the interpreter.

The Interpreter Prescan

Before the interpreter can actually start executing a program, a few clerical tasks must be performed. One characteristic of languages that were designed with interpretation rather than compilation in mind is that they begin execution at the top of the source code and end when the end of the source code is reached. This is the way traditional BASIC works. However, C (or any other structured language) does not lend itself to this approach for three main reasons. First, all C programs begin execution at the **main( )** function. There is no requirement that **main( )** be the first function in the program; therefore, it is necessary that the location of the **main( )** function within the program's source code be known so that execution can begin at that point. (Remember also that global variables may precede **main( )**, so even if it is the first function, it is not necessarily the first line of code.) Some method must be devised to allow execution to begin at the right spot.

Another problem that must be overcome is that all global variables must be known and accounted for before **main( )** begins executing. Global variable declaration statements are never executed by the interpreter, because they exist outside of all functions. (Remember: In C all executable code exists *inside* functions, so there is no reason for the Little C interpreter to go outside a function once execution has begun.)

Finally, in the interest of speed of execution, it is important (although not technically necessary) that the location of each function defined in the program be known so that a call to a function can be as fast as possible. If this step is not performed, a lengthy sequential search of the source code will be needed to find the entry point to a function each time it is called.

The solution to these problems is the *interpreter prescan.* Prescanners (or preprocessors, as they are sometimes called, although they have little resemblance to a C compiler's preprocessor) are used by all commercial interpreters regardless of what language they are interpreting. A prescanner reads the source code to the program before it is executed and performs whatever tasks can be done prior to execution. In our Little C interpreter, it performs two important jobs: First, it finds and records the location of all user-defined functions, including **main( )**; second, it finds and allocates space for all global variables. In the Little C interpreter, the function that performs the prescan is called **prescan( )**. It is shown here:

```
/* Find the location of all functions in the program
   and store global variables. */
void prescan(void)
{
  char *p, *tp;
  char temp[32];
  int datatype;
  int brace = 0;  /* When 0, this var tells us that
                     current source position is outside
```

```
                     of any function. */

  p = prog;
  func_index = 0;
  do {
    while(brace) {   /* bypass code inside functions */
      get_token();
      if(*token == '{') brace++;
      if(*token == '}') brace--;
    }

    tp = prog; /* save current position */
    get_token();
    /* global var type or function return type */
    if(tok==CHAR || tok==INT) {
      datatype = tok; /* save data type */
      get_token();
      if(token_type == IDENTIFIER) {
        strcpy(temp, token);
        get_token();
        if(*token != '(') { /* must be global var */
          prog = tp; /* return to start of declaration */
          decl_global();
        }
        else if(*token == '(') {  /* must be a function */
          func_table[func_index].loc = prog;
          func_table[func_index].ret_type = datatype;
          strcpy(func_table[func_index].func_name, temp);
          func_index++;
          while(*prog != ')') prog++;
          prog++;
          /* now prog points to opening curly
             brace of function */
        }
        else putback();
      }
    }
    else if(*token == '{') brace++;
  } while(tok != FINISHED);
  prog = p;
}
```

The **prescan( )** function works like this: Each time an opening curly brace is encountered, **brace** is incremented. Whenever a closing curly brace is read, **brace** is decremented. Therefore, whenever **brace** is greater than zero, the current token is being read from within a function. However, if **brace** equals zero when a variable is found, the prescanner knows that it must be a global variable. By the same method, if a function name is encountered when **brace** equals zero, it must be that function's definition. (Remember, Little C does not support function prototypes.)

Global variables are stored in a global variable table called **global_vars** by **decl_global( )**, shown here:

```
/* An array of these structures will hold the info
   associated with global variables.
*/
struct var_type {
  char var_name[ID_LEN];
  int v_type;
  int value;
} global_vars[NUM_GLOBAL_VARS];

int gvar_index; /* index into global variable table */

/* Declare a global variable. */
void decl_global(void)
{
  int vartype;

  get_token();  /* get type */

  vartype = tok; /* save var type */

  do { /* process comma-separated list */
    global_vars[gvar_index].v_type = vartype;
    global_vars[gvar_index].value = 0;  /* init to 0 */
    get_token();  /* get name */
    strcpy(global_vars[gvar_index].var_name, token);
    get_token();
    gvar_index++;
  } while(*token == ',');
  if(*token != ';') sntx_err(SEMI_EXPECTED);
}
```

The integer **gvar_index** holds the location of the next free element in the array.

The location of each user-defined function is put into the **func_table** array, shown here:

```
struct func_type {
  char func_name[ID_LEN];
  int ret_type;
  char *loc;  /* location of entry point in file */
} func_table[NUM_FUNC];

int func_index; /* index into function table */
```

The **func_index** variable holds the index of the next free location in the table.

The main( ) Function

The **main( )** function to the Little C interpreter, shown here, loads the source code, initializes the global variables, calls **prescan( )**, "primes" the interpreter for the call to **main( )**, and then executes **call( )**, which begins execution of the program. The operation of the **call( )** function will be discussed shortly.

```
int main(int argc, char *argv[])
{
  if(argc != 2) {
    printf("Usage: littlec <filename>\n");
    exit(1);
  }

  /* allocate memory for the program */
  if((p_buf = (char *) malloc(PROG_SIZE))==NULL) {
    printf("Allocation Failure");
    exit(1);
  }

  /* load the program to execute */
  if(!load_program(p_buf, argv[1])) exit(1);
  if(setjmp(e_buf)) exit(1); /* initialize long jump buffer */

  gvar_index = 0;  /* initialize global variable index */

  /* set program pointer to start of program buffer */
  prog = p_buf;
  prescan(); /* find the location of all functions
```

```
                   and global variables in the program */

  lvartos = 0;      /* initialize local variable stack index */
  functos = 0;      /* initialize the CALL stack index */

  /* setup call to main() */
  prog = find_func("main"); /* find program starting point */

  if(!prog) { /* incorrect or missing main() function in program */
    printf("main() not found.\n");
    exit(1);
  }

  prog--; /* back up to opening ( */
  strcpy(token, "main");
  call(); /* call main() to start interpreting */

  return 0;
}
```

The interp_block( ) Function

The **interp_block( )** function is the heart of the interpreter. It is the function that decides what action to take based upon the next token in the input stream. The function is designed to interpret one block of code and then return. If the "block" consists of a single statement, that statement is interpreted and the function returns. By default, **interp_block( )** interprets one statement and returns. However, if an opening curly brace is read, the flag **block** is set to 1 and the function continues to interpret statements until a closing curly brace is read. The **interp_block( )** function is shown here:

```
/* Interpret a single statement or block of code. When
   interp_block() returns from its initial call, the final
   brace (or a return) in main() has been encountered.
*/
void interp_block(void)
{
  int value;
  char block = 0;

  do {
```

```
    token_type = get_token();

    /* If interpreting single statement, return on
       first semicolon.
    */

    /* see what kind of token is up */
    if(token_type == IDENTIFIER) {
      /* Not a keyword, so process expression. */
      putback();  /* restore token to input stream for
                     further processing by eval_exp() */
      eval_exp(&value);  /* process the expression */
      if(*token!=';') sntx_err(SEMI_EXPECTED);
    }
    else if(token_type==BLOCK) { /* if block delimiter */
      if(*token == '{') /* is a block */
        block = 1; /* interpreting block, not statement */
      else return; /* is a }, so return */
    }
    else /* is keyword */
      switch(tok) {
        case CHAR:
        case INT:      /* declare local variables */
          putback();
          decl_local();
          break;
        case RETURN:  /* return from function call */
          func_ret();
          return;
        case IF:       /* process an if statement */
          exec_if();
          break;
        case ELSE:    /* process an else statement */
          find_eob(); /* find end of else block
                         and continue execution */
          break;
        case WHILE:   /* process a while loop */
          exec_while();
          break;
        case DO:       /* process a do-while loop */
          exec_do();
          break;
```

```
      case FOR:      /* process a for loop */
        exec_for();
        break;
      case END:
        exit(0);
    }
  } while (tok != FINISHED && block);
}
```

Calls to functions like **exit( )** excepted, a C program ends when the last curly brace (or a **return**) in **main( )** is encountered—not necessarily at the last line of source code. This is one reason that **interp_block( )** executes only a statement or a block of code, and not the entire program. Also, conceptually, C consists of blocks of code. Therefore, **interp_block( )** is called each time a new block of code is encountered. This includes both function blocks as well as blocks begun by various C statements, such as **if**. This means that in the process of executing a program, the Little C interpreter may call **interp_block( )** recursively.

The **interp_block( )** function works like this: First, it reads the next token from the program. If the token is a semicolon and only a single statement is being interpreted, the function returns. Otherwise, it checks to see if the token is an identifier; if so, the statement must be an expression, so the expression parser is called. Since the expression parser expects to read the first token in the expression itself, the token is returned to the input stream via a call to **putback( )**. When **eval_exp( )** returns, **token** will hold the last token read by the expression parser, which must be a semicolon if the statement is syntactically correct. If **token** does not contain a semicolon, an error is reported.

If the next token from the program is a curly brace, then either **block** is set to 1 in the case of an opening brace, or, if it is a closing brace, the function returns.

Finally, if the token is a keyword, the **switch** statement is executed, calling the appropriate routine to handle the statement. The reason that keywords are given integer equivalents by **get_token( )** is to allow the use of the **switch** statement instead of requiring a sequence of **if** statements involving string comparisons (which are quite slow).

The interpreter file is shown here. You should call this file LITTLEC.C. In the sections that follow, we will examine the functions that actually execute C keyword statements.

```
/* A Little C interpreter. */

#include <stdio.h>
#include <setjmp.h>
```

```
#include <math.h>
#include <ctype.h>
#include <stdlib.h>
#include <string.h>

#define NUM_FUNC         100
#define NUM_GLOBAL_VARS  100
#define NUM_LOCAL_VARS   200
#define NUM_BLOCK        100
#define ID_LEN            31
#define FUNC_CALLS        31
#define NUM_PARAMS        31
#define PROG_SIZE       10000
#define LOOP_NEST         31

enum tok_types {DELIMITER, IDENTIFIER, NUMBER, KEYWORD,
                TEMP, STRING, BLOCK};

/* add additional C keyword tokens here */
enum tokens {ARG, CHAR, INT, IF, ELSE, FOR, DO, WHILE,
             SWITCH, RETURN, EOL, FINISHED, END};

/* add additional double operators here (such as ->) */
enum double_ops {LT=1, LE, GT, GE, EQ, NE};

/* These are the constants used to call sntx_err() when
   a syntax error occurs. Add more if you like.
   NOTE: SYNTAX is a generic error message used when
   nothing else seems appropriate.
*/
enum error_msg
     {SYNTAX, UNBAL_PARENS, NO_EXP, EQUALS_EXPECTED,
      NOT_VAR, PARAM_ERR, SEMI_EXPECTED,
      UNBAL_BRACES, FUNC_UNDEF, TYPE_EXPECTED,
      NEST_FUNC, RET_NOCALL, PAREN_EXPECTED,
      WHILE_EXPECTED, QUOTE_EXPECTED, NOT_TEMP,
      TOO_MANY_LVARS, DIV_BY_ZERO};

char *prog;    /* current location in source code */
char *p_buf;   /* points to start of program buffer */
jmp_buf e_buf; /* hold environment for longjmp() */
```

```c
/* An array of these structures will hold the info
   associated with global variables.
*/
struct var_type {
  char var_name[ID_LEN];
  int v_type;
  int value;
}  global_vars[NUM_GLOBAL_VARS];

struct var_type local_var_stack[NUM_LOCAL_VARS];

struct func_type {
  char func_name[ID_LEN];
  int ret_type;
  char *loc;  /* location of entry point in file */
} func_table[NUM_FUNC];

int call_stack[NUM_FUNC];

struct commands { /* keyword lookup table */
  char command[20];
  char tok;
} table[] = { /* Commands must be entered lowercase */
  "if", IF, /* in this table. */
  "else", ELSE,
  "for", FOR,
  "do", DO,
  "while", WHILE,
  "char", CHAR,
  "int", INT,
  "return", RETURN,
  "end", END,
  "", END  /* mark end of table */
};

char token[80];
char token_type, tok;

int functos;  /* index to top of function call stack */
int func_index; /* index into function table */
int gvar_index; /* index into global variable table */
int lvartos; /* index into local variable stack */
```

```
int ret_value; /* function return value */

void print(void), prescan(void);
void decl_global(void), call(void), putback(void);
void decl_local(void), local_push(struct var_type i);
void eval_exp(int *value), sntx_err(int error);
void exec_if(void), find_eob(void), exec_for(void);
void get_params(void), get_args(void);
void exec_while(void), func_push(int i), exec_do(void);
void assign_var(char *var_name, int value);
int load_program(char *p, char *fname), find_var(char *s);
void interp_block(void), func_ret(void);
int func_pop(void), is_var(char *s), get_token(void);
char *find_func(char *name);

int main(int argc, char *argv[])
{
  if(argc != 2) {
    printf("Usage: littlec <filename>\n");
    exit(1);
  }

  /* allocate memory for the program */
  if((p_buf = (char *) malloc(PROG_SIZE))==NULL) {
    printf("Allocation Failure");
    exit(1);
  }

  /* load the program to execute */
  if(!load_program(p_buf, argv[1])) exit(1);
  if(setjmp(e_buf)) exit(1); /* initialize long jump buffer */

  gvar_index = 0;  /* initialize global variable index */

  /* set program pointer to start of program buffer */
  prog = p_buf;
  prescan(); /* find the location of all functions
               and global variables in the program */

  lvartos = 0;    /* initialize local variable stack index */
  functos = 0;    /* initialize the CALL stack index */
```

```
  /* setup call to main() */
  prog = find_func("main"); /* find program starting point */

  if(!prog) { /* incorrect or missing main() function in program */
    printf("main() not found.\n");
    exit(1);
  }

  prog--; /* back up to opening ( */
  strcpy(token, "main");
  call(); /* call main() to start interpreting */

  return 0;
}

/* Interpret a single statement or block of code. When
   interp_block() returns from its initial call, the final
   brace (or a return) in main() has been encountered.
*/
void interp_block(void)
{
  int value;
  char block = 0;

  do {
    token_type = get_token();

    /* If interpreting single statement, return on
       first semicolon.
    */

    /* see what kind of token is up */
    if(token_type == IDENTIFIER) {
      /* Not a keyword, so process expression. */
      putback();  /* restore token to input stream for
                     further processing by eval_exp() */
      eval_exp(&value);  /* process the expression */
      if(*token!=';') sntx_err(SEMI_EXPECTED);
    }
    else if(token_type==BLOCK) { /* if block delimiter */
      if(*token == '{') /* is a block */
        block = 1; /* interpreting block, not statement */
```

```
      else return; /* is a }, so return */
    }
    else /* is keyword */
      switch(tok) {
        case CHAR:
        case INT:      /* declare local variables */
          putback();
          decl_local();
          break;
        case RETURN:  /* return from function call */
          func_ret();
          return;
        case IF:       /* process an if statement */
          exec_if();
          break;
        case ELSE:     /* process an else statement */
          find_eob(); /* find end of else block
                          and continue execution */
          break;
        case WHILE:   /* process a while loop */
          exec_while();
          break;
        case DO:       /* process a do-while loop */
          exec_do();
          break;
        case FOR:      /* process a for loop */
          exec_for();
          break;
        case END:
          exit(0);
      }
  } while (tok != FINISHED && block);
}

/* Load a program. */
int load_program(char *p, char *fname)
{
  FILE *fp;
  int i=0;

  if((fp=fopen(fname, "rb"))==NULL) return 0;
```

```
    i = 0;
    do {
      *p = getc(fp);
      p++; i++;
    } while(!feof(fp) && i<PROG_SIZE);

    if(*(p-2) == 0x1a) *(p-2) = '\0'; /* null terminate the program */
    else *(p-1) = '\0';
    fclose(fp);
    return 1;
}

/* Find the location of all functions in the program
   and store global variables. */
void prescan(void)
{
  char *p, *tp;
  char temp[32];
  int datatype;
  int brace = 0;   /* When 0, this var tells us that
                      current source position is outside
                      of any function. */

  p = prog;
  func_index = 0;
  do {
    while(brace) {  /* bypass code inside functions */
      get_token();
      if(*token == '{') brace++;
      if(*token == '}') brace--;
    }

    tp = prog; /* save current position */
    get_token();
    /* global var type or function return type */
    if(tok==CHAR || tok==INT) {
      datatype = tok; /* save data type */
      get_token();
      if(token_type == IDENTIFIER) {
        strcpy(temp, token);
        get_token();
```

```
        if(*token != '(') { /* must be global var */
          prog = tp; /* return to start of declaration */
          decl_global();
        }
        else if(*token == '(') {   /* must be a function */
          func_table[func_index].loc = prog;
          func_table[func_index].ret_type = datatype;
          strcpy(func_table[func_index].func_name, temp);
          func_index++;
          while(*prog != ')') prog++;
          prog++;
          /* now prog points to opening curly
             brace of function */
        }
        else putback();
      }
    }
    else if(*token == '{') brace++;
  } while(tok != FINISHED);
  prog = p;
}

/* Return the entry point of the specified function.
   Return NULL if not found.
*/
char *find_func(char *name)
{
  register int i;

  for(i=0; i < func_index; i++)
    if(!strcmp(name, func_table[i].func_name))
      return func_table[i].loc;

  return NULL;
}

/* Declare a global variable. */
void decl_global(void)
{
  int vartype;

  get_token();   /* get type */
```

```
    vartype = tok; /* save var type */

    do { /* process comma-separated list */
      global_vars[gvar_index].v_type = vartype;
      global_vars[gvar_index].value = 0;  /* init to 0 */
      get_token();  /* get name */
      strcpy(global_vars[gvar_index].var_name, token);
      get_token();
      gvar_index++;
    } while(*token == ',');
    if(*token != ';') sntx_err(SEMI_EXPECTED);
  }

  /* Declare a local variable. */
  void decl_local(void)
  {
    struct var_type i;

    get_token();  /* get type */

    i.v_type = tok;
    i.value = 0;  /* init to 0 */

    do { /* process comma-separated list */
      get_token(); /* get var name */
      strcpy(i.var_name, token);
      local_push(i);
      get_token();
    } while(*token == ',');
    if(*token != ';') sntx_err(SEMI_EXPECTED);
  }

  /* Call a function. */
  void call(void)
  {
    char *loc, *temp;
    int lvartemp;

    loc = find_func(token); /* find entry point of function */
    if(loc == NULL)
      sntx_err(FUNC_UNDEF); /* function not defined */
    else {
```

```
      lvartemp = lvartos;  /* save local var stack index */
      get_args();  /* get function arguments */
      temp = prog; /* save return location */
      func_push(lvartemp);  /* save local var stack index */
      prog = loc;  /* reset prog to start of function */
      get_params(); /* load the function's parameters with
                        the values of the arguments */
      interp_block(); /* interpret the function */
      prog = temp; /* reset the program pointer */
      lvartos = func_pop(); /* reset the local var stack */
  }
}

/* Push the arguments to a function onto the local
   variable stack. */
void get_args(void)
{
  int value, count, temp[NUM_PARAMS];
  struct var_type i;

  count = 0;
  get_token();
  if(*token != '(') sntx_err(PAREN_EXPECTED);

  /* process a comma-separated list of values */
  do {
    eval_exp(&value);
    temp[count] = value;  /* save temporarily */
    get_token();
    count++;
  }while(*token == ',');
  count--;
  /* now, push on local_var_stack in reverse order */
  for(; count>=0; count--) {
    i.value = temp[count];
    i.v_type = ARG;
    local_push(i);
  }
}

/* Get function parameters. */
void get_params(void)
```

```
{
  struct var_type *p;
  int i;

  i = lvartos-1;
  do { /* process comma-separated list of parameters */
    get_token();
    p = &local_var_stack[i];
    if(*token != ')' ) {
      if(tok != INT && tok != CHAR)
        sntx_err(TYPE_EXPECTED);

      p->v_type = token_type;
      get_token();

      /* link parameter name with argument already on
         local var stack */
      strcpy(p->var_name, token);
      get_token();
      i--;
    }
    else break;
  } while(*token == ',');
  if(*token != ')') sntx_err(PAREN_EXPECTED);
}

/* Return from a function. */
void func_ret(void)
{
  int value;

  value = 0;
  /* get return value, if any */
  eval_exp(&value);

  ret_value = value;
}

/* Push a local variable. */
void local_push(struct var_type i)
{
  if(lvartos > NUM_LOCAL_VARS)
```

```
      sntx_err(TOO_MANY_LVARS);

  local_var_stack[lvartos] = i;
  lvartos++;
}

/* Pop index into local variable stack. */
int func_pop(void)
{
  functos--;
  if(functos < 0) sntx_err(RET_NOCALL);
  return call_stack[functos];
}

/* Push index of local variable stack. */
void func_push(int i)
{
  if(functos>NUM_FUNC)
   sntx_err(NEST_FUNC);
  call_stack[functos] = i;
  functos++;
}

/* Assign a value to a variable. */
void assign_var(char *var_name, int value)
{
  register int i;

  /* first, see if it's a local variable */
  for(i=lvartos-1; i >= call_stack[functos-1]; i--)  {
    if(!strcmp(local_var_stack[i].var_name, var_name)) {
      local_var_stack[i].value = value;
      return;
    }
  }
  if(i < call_stack[functos-1])
  /* if not local, try global var table */
    for(i=0; i < NUM_GLOBAL_VARS; i++)
      if(!strcmp(global_vars[i].var_name, var_name)) {
        global_vars[i].value = value;
        return;
      }
```

```
    sntx_err(NOT_VAR); /* variable not found */
}

/* Find the value of a variable. */
int find_var(char *s)
{
  register int i;

  /* first, see if it's a local variable */
  for(i=lvartos-1; i >= call_stack[functos-1]; i--)
    if(!strcmp(local_var_stack[i].var_name, token))
      return local_var_stack[i].value;

  /* otherwise, try global vars */
  for(i=0; i < NUM_GLOBAL_VARS; i++)
    if(!strcmp(global_vars[i].var_name, s))
      return global_vars[i].value;

  sntx_err(NOT_VAR); /* variable not found */
  return -1;
}

/* Determine if an identifier is a variable. Return
   1 if variable is found; 0 otherwise.
*/
int is_var(char *s)
{
  register int i;

  /* first, see if it's a local variable */
  for(i=lvartos-1; i >= call_stack[functos-1]; i--)
    if(!strcmp(local_var_stack[i].var_name, token))
      return 1;

  /* otherwise, try global vars */
  for(i=0; i < NUM_GLOBAL_VARS; i++)
    if(!strcmp(global_vars[i].var_name, s))
      return 1;

  return 0;
}
```

```c
/* Execute an if statement. */
void exec_if(void)
{
  int cond;

  eval_exp(&cond); /* get if expression */

  if(cond) { /* is true so process target of IF */
    interp_block();
  }
  else { /* otherwise skip around IF block and
            process the ELSE, if present */
    find_eob(); /* find start of next line */
    get_token();

    if(tok != ELSE) {
      putback();  /* restore token if
                     no ELSE is present */
      return;
    }
    interp_block();
  }
}

/* Execute a while loop. */
void exec_while(void)
{
  int cond;
  char *temp;

  putback();
  temp = prog;  /* save location of top of while loop */
  get_token();
  eval_exp(&cond);  /* check the conditional expression */
  if(cond) interp_block();  /* if true, interpret */
  else {  /* otherwise, skip around loop */
    find_eob();
    return;
  }
  prog = temp;  /* loop back to top */
}
```

```
/* Execute a do loop. */
void exec_do(void)
{
  int cond;
  char *temp;

  putback();
  temp = prog;  /* save location of top of do loop */

  get_token(); /* get start of loop */
  interp_block(); /* interpret loop */
  get_token();
  if(tok != WHILE) sntx_err(WHILE_EXPECTED);
  eval_exp(&cond); /* check the loop condition */
  if(cond) prog = temp; /* if true loop; otherwise,
                          continue on */
}

/* Find the end of a block. */
void find_eob(void)
{
  int brace;

  get_token();
  brace = 1;
  do {
    get_token();
    if(*token == '{') brace++;
    else if(*token == '}') brace--;
  } while(brace);
}

/* Execute a for loop. */
void exec_for(void)
{
  int cond;
  char *temp, *temp2;
  int brace ;

  get_token();
  eval_exp(&cond);  /* initialization expression */
  if(*token != ';') sntx_err(SEMI_EXPECTED);
```

```
    prog++; /* get past the ; */
    temp = prog;
    for(;;) {
      eval_exp(&cond);   /* check the condition */
      if(*token != ';') sntx_err(SEMI_EXPECTED);
      prog++; /* get past the ; */
      temp2 = prog;

      /* find the start of the for block */
      brace = 1;
      while(brace) {
        get_token();
        if(*token == '(') brace++;
        if(*token == ')') brace--;
      }

      if(cond) interp_block();  /* if true, interpret */
      else {  /* otherwise, skip around loop */
        find_eob();
        return;
      }
      prog = temp2;
      eval_exp(&cond); /* do the increment */
      prog = temp;  /* loop back to top */
    }
  }
```

Handling Local Variables

When the interpreter encounters an **int** or **char** keyword, it calls **decl_local( )** to create storage for a local variable. As stated earlier, no global variable declaration statement will be encountered by the interpreter once the program is executing, because only code within a function is executed. Therefore, if a variable declaration statement is found, it must be for a local variable (or a parameter, which will be discussed in the next section). In structured languages, local variables are stored on a stack. If the language is compiled, the system stack is generally used; however, in an interpreted mode, the stack for local variables must be maintained by the interpreter. The stack for local variables is held by the array **local_var_stack**. Each time a local variable is encountered, its name, type, and value (initially zero) are pushed onto the stack using **local_push( )**. The global variable **lvartos** indexes the stack. (For reasons that will become clear, there is no corresponding "pop" function. Instead, the local variable stack is reset each time a function returns.) The **decl_local** and **local_push( )** functions are shown here:

```
/* Declare a local variable. */
void decl_local(void)
{
  struct var_type i;

  get_token();  /* get type */

  i.v_type = tok;
  i.value = 0;  /* init to 0 */

  do { /* process comma-separated list */
    get_token(); /* get var name */
    strcpy(i.var_name, token);
    local_push(i);
    get_token();
  } while(*token == ',');
  if(*token != ';') sntx_err(SEMI_EXPECTED);
}

/* Push a local variable. */
void local_push(struct var_type i)
{
  if(lvartos > NUM_LOCAL_VARS)
    sntx_err(TOO_MANY_LVARS);

  local_var_stack[lvartos] = i;
  lvartos++;
}
```

The **decl_local( )** function first reads the type of the variable or variables being declared and sets the initial value to zero. Next, it enters a loop, which reads a comma-separated list of identifiers. Each time through the loop, the information about each variable is pushed onto the local variable stack. At the end, the final token is checked to make sure that it contains a semicolon.

Calling User-Defined Functions

Probably the most difficult part of implementing an interpreter for C is the execution of user-defined functions. Not only does the interpreter need to begin reading the source code at a new location and then return to the calling routine after the function terminates, but it must also deal with these three tasks: the passing of arguments, the allocation of parameters, and the return value of the function.

All function calls (except the initial call to **main( )**) take place through the expression parser from the **atom( )** function by a call to **call( )**. It is the **call( )** function that actually handles the details of calling a function. The **call( )** function is shown here, along with two support functions. Let's examine these functions closely.

```c
/* Call a function. */
void call(void)
{
  char *loc, *temp;
  int lvartemp;

  loc = find_func(token); /* find entry point of function */
  if(loc == NULL)
    sntx_err(FUNC_UNDEF); /* function not defined */
  else {
    lvartemp = lvartos;  /* save local var stack index */
    get_args();  /* get function arguments */
    temp = prog; /* save return location */
    func_push(lvartemp);  /* save local var stack index */
    prog = loc;  /* reset prog to start of function */
    get_params(); /* load the function's parameters with
                     the values of the arguments */
    interp_block(); /* interpret the function */
    prog = temp; /* reset the program pointer */
    lvartos = func_pop(); /* reset the local var stack */
  }
}

/* Push the arguments to a function onto the local
   variable stack. */
void get_args(void)
{
  int value, count, temp[NUM_PARAMS];
  struct var_type i;

  count = 0;
  get_token();
  if(*token != '(') sntx_err(PAREN_EXPECTED);

  /* process a comma-separated list of values */
  do {
    eval_exp(&value);
    temp[count] = value;  /* save temporarily */
    get_token();
```

```
      count++;
    } while(*token == ',');
    count--;
    /* now, push on local_var_stack in reverse order */
    for(; count>=0; count--) {
      i.value = temp[count];
      i.v_type = ARG;
      local_push(i);
    }
  }
}

/* Get function parameters. */
void get_params(void)
{
  struct var_type *p;
  int i;

  i = lvartos-1;
  do { /* process comma-separated list of parameters */
    get_token();
    p = &local_var_stack[i];
    if(*token != ')' ) {
      if(tok != INT && tok != CHAR)
        sntx_err(TYPE_EXPECTED);

      p->v_type = token_type;
      get_token();

      /* link parameter name with argument already on
         local var stack */
      strcpy(p->var_name, token);
      get_token();
      i--;
    }
    else break;
  } while(*token == ',');
  if(*token != ')') sntx_err(PAREN_EXPECTED);
}
```

The first thing that **call( )** does is find the location of the entry point in the source code to the specified function by calling **find_func( )**. Next, it saves the current value of the local variable stack index, **lvartos**, into **lvartemp**; then it calls **get_args( )** to process any function arguments. The **get_args( )** function reads a comma-separated list of expressions and pushes them onto the local variable stack in reverse order. (The expressions are pushed in reverse order so that they can be more easily matched with their corresponding parameters.) When the values are pushed, they are not given names. The names of the parameters are given to them by the **get_params( )** function, which will be discussed in a moment.

Once the function arguments have been processed, the current value of **prog** is saved in **temp**. This location is the return point of the function. Next, the value of **lvartemp** is pushed onto the function call stack. The routines **func_push( )** and **func_pop( )** maintain this stack. Its purpose is to store the value of **lvartos** each time a function is called. This value represents the starting point on the local variable stack for variables (and parameters) relative to the function being called. The value on the top of the function call stack is used to prevent a function from accessing any local variables other than those it declares.

The next two lines of code set the program pointer to the start of the function and link the name of its formal parameters with the values of the arguments already on the local variable stack with a call to **get_params( )**. The actual execution of the function is performed through a call to **interp_block( )**. When **interp_block( )** returns, the program pointer (**prog**) is reset to its return point, and the local variable stack index is reset to its value before the function call. This final step effectively removes all of the function's local variables from the stack.

If the function being called contains a **return** statement, then **interp_block( )** calls **func_ret( )** prior to returning to **call( )**. This function processes any return value. It is shown here:

```
/* Return from a function. */
void func_ret(void)
{
  int value;

  value = 0;
  /* get return value, if any */
  eval_exp(&value);

  ret_value = value;
}
```

The variable **ret_value** is a global integer that holds the return value of a function. At first glance, you might wonder why the local variable **value** is first assigned the return value of the function and then is assigned to **ret_value**. The reason is that functions can be recursive and **eval_exp( )** may need to call the same function in order to obtain its value.

Assigning Values to Variables

Let's return briefly to the expression parser. When an assignment statement is encountered, the value of the right side of the expression is computed, and this value is assigned to the variable on the left using a call to **assign_var( )**. However, as you know, the C language is structured and supports global and local variables. Thus, given a program such as this

```
int count;

int main()
{
  int count, i;

  count = 100;

  i = f();

  return 0;
}

int f()
{
  int count;
  count = 99;
  return count;
}
```

how does the **assign_var( )** function know which variable is being assigned a value in each assignment? The answer is simple: First, in C, local variables take priority over global variables of the same name; second, local variables are not known outside their own function. To see how we can use these rules to resolve the above assignments, examine the **assign_var( )** function, shown here:

```
/* Assign a value to a variable. */
void assign_var(char *var_name, int value)
{
  register int i;

  /* first, see if it's a local variable */
  for(i=lvartos-1; i >= call_stack[functos-1]; i--)  {
    if(!strcmp(local_var_stack[i].var_name, var_name)) {
```

```
        local_var_stack[i].value = value;
        return;
      }
    }
    if(i < call_stack[functos-1])
    /* if not local, try global var table */
      for(i=0; i < NUM_GLOBAL_VARS; i++)
        if(!strcmp(global_vars[i].var_name, var_name)) {
          global_vars[i].value = value;
          return;
        }
    sntx_err(NOT_VAR); /* variable not found */
}
```

As explained in the previous section, each time a function is called, the current value of the local variable stack index (**lvartos**) is pushed onto the function call stack. This means that any local variables (or parameters) defined by the function will be pushed onto the stack above that point. Therefore, the **assign_var( )** function first searches **local_var_stack**, beginning with the current top-of-stack value and stopping when the index reaches that value saved by the latest function call. This mechanism ensures that only those variables local to the function are examined. (It also helps support recursive functions because the current value of **lvartos** is saved each time a function is invoked.) Therefore, the line "count = 100;" in **main( )** causes **assign_var( )** to find the local variable **count** inside **main( )**. In **f( )**, **assign_var( )** finds its own **count** and does not find the one in **main( )**.

If no local variable matches the name of a variable, the global variable list is searched.

Executing an if Statement

Now that the basic structure of the Little C interpreter is in place, it is time to add some control statements. Each time a keyword statement is encountered inside **interp_block( )**, an appropriate function is called, which processes that statement. One of the easiest is the **if**. The **if** statement is processed by **exec_if( )**, shown here:

```
/* Execute an if statement. */
void exec_if(void)
{
  int cond;

  eval_exp(&cond); /* get if expression */
```

```
  if(cond) { /* is true so process target of IF */
    interp_block();
  }
  else { /* otherwise skip around IF block and
            process the ELSE, if present */
    find_eob(); /* find start of next line */
    get_token();

    if(tok != ELSE) {
      putback();   /* restore token if
                      no ELSE is present */
      return;
    }
    interp_block();
  }
}
```

Let's look closely at this function. The first thing the function does is to compute the value of the conditional expression by calling **eval_exp( )**. If the condition (**cond**) is true (nonzero), the function calls **interp_block( )** recursively, allowing the **if** block to execute. If **cond** is false, the function **find_eob( )** is called, which advances the program pointer to the location immediately after the end of the **if** block. If an **else** is present, the **else** is processed by **exec_if( )**, and the **else** block is executed. Otherwise, execution simply begins with the next line of code.

If the **if** block executes and there is an **else** block present, there must be some way for the **else** block to be bypassed. This is accomplished in **interp_block( )** by simply calling **find_eob( )** to bypass the block when an **else** is encountered. Remember, the only time an **else** will be processed by **interp_block( )** (in a syntactically correct program) is after an **if** block has been executed. When an **else** block executes, the **else** is processed by **exec_if( )**.

Processing a while Loop

A **while** loop, like the **if**, is quite easy to interpret. The function that actually performs this task, **exec_while( )**, is shown here:

```
/* Execute a while loop. */
void exec_while(void)
{
  int cond;
  char *temp;
```

```
    putback();
    temp = prog;  /* save location of top of while loop */
    get_token();
    eval_exp(&cond);  /* check the conditional expression */
    if(cond) interp_block();  /* if true, interpret */
    else {  /* otherwise, skip around loop */
      find_eob();
      return;
    }
    prog = temp;  /* loop back to top */
}
```

The **exec_while( )** works like this: First, the **while** token is put back into the
input stream, and the location of the **while** is saved into **temp**. This address
will be used to allow the interpreter to loop back to the top of the **while**. Next, the
while is reread to remove it from the input stream, and **eval_exp( )** is called to
compute the value of the **while**'s conditional expression. If the conditional expression
is true, then **interp_block( )** is called recursively to interpret the **while** block. When
interp_block( ) returns, **prog** (the program pointer) is loaded with the location of the
start of the **while** loop, and control returns to **interp_block( )**, where the entire process
repeats. If the conditional expression is false, the end of the **while** block is found,
and the function returns.

Processing a do-while Loop

A **do-while** loop is processed much like the **while**. When **interp_block( )** encounters a
do statement, it calls **exec_do( )**, shown here:

```
/* Execute a do loop. */
void exec_do(void)
{
  int cond;
  char *temp;

  putback();
  temp = prog;  /* save location of top of do loop */

  get_token(); /* get start of loop */
  interp_block(); /* interpret loop */
  get_token();
  if(tok != WHILE) sntx_err(WHILE_EXPECTED);
```

```
eval_exp(&cond); /* check the loop condition */
if(cond) prog = temp; /* if true loop; otherwise,
                          continue on */
}
```

The main difference between the **do-while** and the **while** loops is that the **do-while** always executes its block of code at least once because the conditional expression is at the bottom of the loop. Therefore, **exec_do( )** first saves the location of the top of the loop into **temp** and then calls **interp_block( )** recursively to interpret the block of code associated with the loop. When **interp_block( )** returns, the corresponding **while** is retrieved, and the conditional expression is evaluated. If the condition is true, **prog** is reset to the top of the loop; otherwise, execution will continue on.

The for Loop

The interpretation of the **for** loop poses a more difficult challenge than the other constructs. Part of the reason for this is that the structure of the C **for** is definitely designed with compilation in mind. The main trouble is that the conditional expression of the **for** must be checked at the top of the loop, but the increment portion occurs at the bottom of the loop. Therefore, even though these two pieces of the **for** loop occur next to each other in the source code, their interpretation is separated by the block of code being iterated. However, with a little work, the **for** can be correctly interpreted.

When **interp_block( )** encounters a **for** statement, **exec_for( )** is called. This function is shown here:

```
/* Execute a for loop. */
void exec_for(void)
{
  int cond;
  char *temp, *temp2;
  int brace ;

  get_token();
  eval_exp(&cond);  /* initialization expression */
  if(*token != ';') sntx_err(SEMI_EXPECTED);
  prog++; /* get past the ; */
  temp = prog;
  for(;;) {
    eval_exp(&cond);  /* check the condition */
    if(*token != ';') sntx_err(SEMI_EXPECTED);
    prog++; /* get past the ; */
```

```
  temp2 = prog;

  /* find the start of the for block */
  brace = 1;
  while(brace) {
    get_token();
    if(*token == '(') brace++;
    if(*token == ')') brace--;
  }

  if(cond) interp_block();  /* if true, interpret */
  else {  /* otherwise, skip around loop */
    find_eob();
    return;
  }
  prog = temp2;
  eval_exp(&cond); /* do the increment */
  prog = temp;  /* loop back to top */
 }
}
```

This function begins by processing the initialization expression in the **for**. The initialization portion of the **for** is executed only once and does not form part of the loop. Next, the program pointer is advanced to a point immediately after the semicolon that ends the initialization statement, and its value is assigned to **temp**. A loop is then established, which checks the conditional portion of the **for** loop and assigns **temp2** a pointer to the start of the increment portion. The beginning of the loop code is found, and, finally, if the conditional expression is true, the loop block is interpreted. (Otherwise, the end of the block is found, and execution continues on after the **for** loop.) When the recursive call to **interp_block( )** returns, the increment portion of the loop is executed, and the process repeats.

The Little C Library Functions

Because the C programs executed by Little C are never compiled and linked, any library routines they use must be handled directly by Little C. The best way to do this is to create an interface function that Little C calls when a library function is encountered. This interface function sets up the call to the library function and handles any return values.

Because of space limitations, Little C contains only five "library" functions: **getche( )**, **putch( )**, **puts( )**, **print( )**, and **getnum( )**. Of these, only **puts( )**, which outputs a string to the screen, is part of Standard C. The **getche( )** function is a common extension to C for interactive environments. It waits for and returns a key struck at the keyboard. This function is found in many compilers. **putch( )** is also defined by many compilers that are designed for use in an interactive environment. It outputs a single character argument to the console. It does not buffer output. The functions **getnum( )** and **print( )** are my own creations. The **getnum( )** function returns the integer equivalent of a number entered at the keyboard. The **print( )** function is a very handy function that can output either a string or an integer argument to the screen. The five library functions are shown here in their prototype forms:

```
int getche(void);    /* read a character from keyboard and
                            return its value */
int putch(char ch);  /* write a character to the screen */
int puts(char *s);   /* write a string to the screen */
int getnum(void);    /* read an integer from the keyboard and
                            return its value */
int print(char *s);  /* write a string to the screen */
or
int print(int i);    /* write an integer to the screen */
```

The Little C library routines are shown here. You should call the file LCLIB.C.

```
/****** Internal Library Functions *******/

/* Add more of your own, here. */

#include <conio.h>  /* if your compiler does not
                        support this header file,
                        remove it */
#include <stdio.h>
#include <stdlib.h>

extern char *prog; /* points to current location in program */
extern char token[80]; /* holds string representation of token */
extern char token_type; /* contains type of token */
extern char tok; /* holds the internal representation of token */

enum tok_types {DELIMITER, IDENTIFIER, NUMBER, KEYWORD,
                TEMP, STRING, BLOCK};

/* These are the constants used to call sntx_err() when
   a syntax error occurs. Add more if you like.
```

```
     NOTE: SYNTAX is a generic error message used when
     nothing else seems appropriate.
*/
enum error_msg
        {SYNTAX, UNBAL_PARENS, NO_EXP, EQUALS_EXPECTED,
         NOT_VAR, PARAM_ERR, SEMI_EXPECTED,
         UNBAL_BRACES, FUNC_UNDEF, TYPE_EXPECTED,
         NEST_FUNC, RET_NOCALL, PAREN_EXPECTED,
         WHILE_EXPECTED, QUOTE_EXPECTED, NOT_STRING,
         TOO_MANY_LVARS, DIV_BY_ZERO};

int get_token(void);
void sntx_err(int error), eval_exp(int *result);
void putback(void);

/* Get a character from console. (Use getchar() if
   your compiler does not support _getche().) */
int call_getche()
{
  char ch;
  ch = _getche();
  while(*prog!=')') prog++;
  prog++;   /* advance to end of line */
  return ch;
}

/* Put a character to the display. */
int call_putch()
{
  int value;

  eval_exp(&value);
  printf("%c", value);
  return value;
}

/* Call puts(). */
int call_puts(void)
{
  get_token();
  if(*token!='(') sntx_err(PAREN_EXPECTED);
  get_token();
```

```c
  if(token_type!=STRING) sntx_err(QUOTE_EXPECTED);
  puts(token);
  get_token();
  if(*token!=')') sntx_err(PAREN_EXPECTED);

  get_token();
  if(*token!=';') sntx_err(SEMI_EXPECTED);
  putback();
  return 0;
}

/* A built-in console output function. */
int print(void)
{
  int i;

  get_token();
  if(*token!='(') sntx_err(PAREN_EXPECTED);

  get_token();
  if(token_type==STRING) { /* output a string */
    printf("%s ", token);
  }
  else {  /* output a number */
   putback();
   eval_exp(&i);
   printf("%d ", i);
  }

  get_token();

  if(*token!=')') sntx_err(PAREN_EXPECTED);

  get_token();
  if(*token!=';') sntx_err(SEMI_EXPECTED);
  putback();
  return 0;
}

/* Read an integer from the keyboard. */
int getnum(void)
{
```

```
    char s[80];

    gets(s);
    while(*prog != ')') prog++;
    prog++;  /* advance to end of line */
    return atoi(s);
}
```

To add library functions, first enter their names and the addresses of their interface functions into the **intern_func** array. Next, following the lead of the functions shown previously, create appropriate interface functions.

Compiling and Linking the Little C Interpreter

Once you have entered all three files that make up Little C, compile and link them together. You can use just about any modern C compiler, including Visual C++. If you use Visual C++, you can use a sequence such as the following:

```
cl -c parser.c
cl -c lclib.c
cl littlec.c parser.obj lclib.obj
```

For some versions of Visual C++, Little C may not be given sufficient stack space. You can use the /F option to increase the stack. Specifying /F 6000 will be sufficient for most uses. However, you might need to increase the size of the stack even more when interpreting highly recursive programs.

If you use a different C compiler, simply follow the instructions that come with it.

Demonstrating Little C

The following C programs demonstrate Little C. The first demonstrates all features supported by Little C.

```
/* Little C Demonstration Program #1.

   This program demonstrates all features
   of C that are recognized by Little C.
*/
```

```
int i, j;    /* global vars */
char ch;

int main()
{
  int i, j;   /* local vars */

  puts("Little C Demo Program.");

  print_alpha();

  do {
    puts("enter a number (0 to quit): ");
    i = getnum();
    if(i < 0 ) {
      puts("numbers must be positive, try again");
    }
    else {
      for(j = 0; j < i; j=j+1) {
        print(j);
        print("summed is");
        print(sum(j));
        puts("");
      }
    }
  } while(i!=0);

  return 0;
}

/* Sum the values between 0 and num. */
int sum(int num)
{
  int running_sum;

  running_sum = 0;

  while(num) {
    running_sum = running_sum + num;
    num = num - 1;
  }
  return running_sum;
```

```
}

/* Print the alphabet. */
int print_alpha()
{
  for(ch = 'A'; ch<='Z'; ch = ch + 1) {
    putch(ch);
  }
  puts("");

  return 0;
}
```

The next example demonstrates nested loops.

```
/* Nested loop example. */
int main()
{
  int i, j, k;

  for(i = 0; i < 5; i = i + 1) {
    for(j = 0; j < 3; j = j + 1) {
      for(k = 3; k ; k = k - 1) {
        print(i);
        print(j);
        print(k);
        puts("");
      }
    }
  }
  puts("done");

  return 0;
}
```

The next program demonstrates the assignment operator.

```
/* Assignments as operations. */    .
int main()
{
  int a, b;
```

```
  a = b = 10;

  print(a); print(b);

  while(a=a-1) {
    print(a);
    do {
       print(b);
    } while((b=b-1) > -10);
  }

  return 0;
}
```

Recursive functions are demonstrated by the next program. In it, the function **factr( )** computes the factorial of a number.

```
/* This program demonstrates recursive functions. */

/* return the factorial of i */
int factr(int i)
{
  if(i<2) {
    return 1;
  }
  else {
     return i * factr(i-1);
  }
}

int main()
{
  print("Factorial of 4 is: ");
  print(factr(4));

  return 0;
}
```

The next program fully demonstrates function arguments.

```
/* A more rigorous example of function arguments. */

int f1(int a, int b)
```

```
{
  int count;

  print("in f1");

  count = a;
  do {
    print(count);
  } while(count=count-1);

  print(a); print(b);
  print(a*b);
  return a*b;
}

int f2(int a, int x, int y)
{
  print(a); print(x);
  print(x / a);
  print(y*x);

  return 0;
}

int main()
{
  f2(10, f1(10, 20), 99);

  return 0;
}
```

The final program exercises the loop statements.

```
/* The loop statements. */
int main()
{
  int a;
  char ch;

  /* the while */
  puts("Enter a number: ");
  a = getnum();
  while(a) {
```

```
      print(a);
      print(a*a);
      puts("");
      a = a - 1;
   }

   /* the do-while */
   puts("enter characters, 'q' to quit");
   do {
      ch = getche();
   } while(ch !='q');

   /* the for */
   for(a=0; a<10; a = a + 1) {
      print(a);
   }

   return 0;
}
```

Improving Little C

The Little C interpreter presented in this chapter was designed with transparency of operation in mind. The goal was to develop an interpreter that could be easily understood with the least amount of effort. It was also designed in such a way that it could be easily expanded. As such, Little C is not particularly fast or efficient; however, the basic structure of the interpreter is correct, and you can increase its speed of execution by following the steps described in this section.

Virtually all commercial interpreters expand the role of the prescanner. The entire source program being interpreted is converted from its ASCII human-readable form into an internal form. In this internal form, all but quoted strings and constants are transformed into single-integer tokens, much the way that Little C converts the C keywords into single-integer tokens. It may have occurred to you that Little C performs a number of string comparisons. For example, each time a variable or function is searched for, several string comparisons take place. String comparisons are very costly in terms of time; however, if each token in the source program is converted into an integer, much faster integer comparisons can be used. The conversion of the source program into an internal form is the *single most important change* you can make to Little C in order to improve its efficiency. Frankly, the increase in speed will be dramatic.

Another area of improvement, meaningful mostly for large programs, is the lookup routines for variables and functions. Even if you convert these items into integer tokens, the current approach to searching for them relies upon a sequential search. You could, however, substitute some other, faster method, such as a binary tree or some sort of hashing method.

As stated earlier, one restriction that Little C has relative to the full C grammar is that the objects of statements such as **if**—even if single statements—must be blocks of code enclosed between curly braces. The reason for this is that it greatly simplifies the **find_eob( )** function, which is used to find the end of a block of code after one of the control statements executes. The **find_eob( )** function simply looks for a closing curly brace to match the one that starts the block. You might find it an interesting exercise to remove this restriction. One approach to this is to redesign **find_eob( )** so that it finds the end of a statement, expression, or block. Keep in mind, however, that you will need to use a different approach to finding the end of the **if, while, do-while,** and **for** statements when they are used as single statements.

Expanding Little C

There are two general areas in which you can expand and enhance the Little C interpreter: C features and ancillary features. Some of these are discussed briefly in the following sections.

Adding New C Features

There are two basic categories of C statements you can add to Little C. The first is additional action statements, such as the **switch,** the **goto,** and the **break** and **continue** statements. You should have little trouble adding any of these if you study closely the construction of the statements that Little C does interpret.

The second category of C statement you can add is support for new data types. Little C already contains the basic "hooks" for additional data types. For example, the **var_type** structure already contains a field for the type of variable. To add other elementary types (for example, **float, double,** and **long**), simply increase the size of the value field to the size of the largest element you wish to hold.

Supporting pointers is no more difficult than supporting any other data type. However, you will need to add support for the pointer operators to the expression parser.

Once you have implemented pointers, arrays will be easy. Space for an array should be allocated dynamically using **malloc( ),** and a pointer to the array should be stored in the **value** field of **var_type.**

The addition of structures and unions poses a slightly more difficult problem. The easiest way to handle them is to use **malloc( )** to allocate space for an object and then store a pointer to the object in the **value** field of the **var_type** structure. (You will also need special code to handle the passing of structures and unions as parameters.)

To handle different return types for functions, you will need to make use of the **ret_type** field in the **func_type** structure. This field defines what type of data a function returns. It is currently set, but otherwise unused.

You might also want to try allowing Little C to accept //-style comments. This change takes place within **get_token( )** and is easy to implement.

One final thought—if you like to experiment with language constructs, don't be afraid to add a non-C extension. By far the most fun I've had with language interpreters is making them do things not specified by the language. If you want to add a Pascal-like **REPEAT-UNTIL** construct, for example, go ahead and do it! If something doesn't work the first time, try finding the problem by printing out each token as it is processed.

Adding Ancillary Features

Interpreters give you the opportunity to add several interesting and useful features. For example, you can add a trace facility that displays each token as it is executed. You can also add the ability to display the contents of each variable as the program executes. Another feature you might want to add is an integrated editor so that you can "edit and go" instead of having to use a separate editor to create your C programs.

Index

X